DISCOVERING SPAIN

THE BEST OF SPAIN

Mar Cantábric

Rías Altas

Garita de Herbeira

COSTA VERDE

Cuevas de Altamir
Santillana del
SANTAN

LA CORUÑA

Caaveiro

Taramundi

OVIEDO
Picos de
Europa

ASTURIAS

CANTABRIA

Bárcena
Mayor

Finisterre

Santa Eulalia
de Bóveda

Santiago de
Compostela

LUGO

CANTABRI

Cebreiro

CORDILLERA

Tres
Mares

R. Ebr

La Curota

GALICIA

Foncebadón

Santo Dom
de la Cal

Combarro

PONTEVEDRA

San Esteban de
Ribas de Sil

Compludo

LEÓN

Olleros

Hío

Peñalba de
Santiago

BURG

ORENSE

Frómista

Quintanilla
de las Viñas

PALENCIA

CASTILLA-LEÓN

Santo Don
de Silo
Peñaran
de Duer

Simancas

VALLADOLID

ZAMORA

Peñafiel

Toro

Tordesillas

Coca

San Frutos

R. Duero

SALAMANCA

SEGOVIA

Pedraza

La Granja

CENTR

ÁVILA

El
Pau

La Peña
de Francia

GUADALAJAR

La Alberca

Toros de
Guisando

El Escorl

MADR

PORTUGAL

Yuste

GREDOS

MADRI

La Vera

Aranjuez

R. Tajo

R. Tajo

San Pedro de
Alcántara

CORDILLERA

TOLEDO

Tembleque

Consuegra

CÁCERES

Guadalupe

CASTILLA
LA MANC

Trujillo

Campo de
Criptana

EXTREMADURA

CIUDAD

BADAJOZ

Mérida

Almagro

SIERRA MOREN

SIERRA
DE ARACENA

Medina
Azahara

Baeza Úb

R. Guadalquivir

CÓRDOBA

JAÉN

ANDALUCÍA

SIERR

HUELVA

SEVILLA

Guad

La Rábida

Coto Doñana

GRANADA

Jerez de la
Frontera

SIERRA NEVAD

Sanlúcar de
Barrameda

Setenil

MÁLAGA

COSTA DE LA LUZ

Arcos de la
Frontera

Ronda

Ojén

Nerja

CADIZ

Vejer de
la Frontera

COSTA DEL

Atlantic Ocean

Castellar de la Frontera

Gibraltar

Tarifa

Atlantic Ocean

| 0 | 100 | 200 | 300 Miles |

| 0 | 100 | 200 | 300 | 400 | 500 |

Kilomet

FRANCE

Juan de
telugache
Izkibel Fuenterrabia
SAN SEBASTIÀN
PYRENEES ANDORRA
AÍS Roncesvalles
SCO
kadi)
A Estella PAMPLONA Sos del Vall de Aran
rdla Leyre Rey Ordesa
NAVARRA Católico Algües Cadaqués COSTA BRAVA
LOGROÑO San Juan Tortes Sant Joan de
Clavijo de la Peña les Abadesses Besalú
RIOJA Loarre Ripoll Alguablava
illán de HUESCA GIRONA
olla CATALUNYA
aguna R. Ebro
egra
SORIA LLEIDA Montserrat
ZARAGOZA BARCELONA
Belchite Poblet
ARAGÓN R. Ebro TARRAGONA
nacell COSTA DORADA
Alcañiz
enza
Molina de Morella
Aragón Mirambel
Tajo TERUEL Peñíscola COSTA DEL AZAHAR
Albarracin MAESTRAZGO
CUENCA CASTELLÓN DE Mediterranean Sea
LA PLANA
Alarcón Sagunto
monte LEVANTE VALENCIA
Alcalá del La Albufera
Júcar
ALBACETE
MENORCA
Alcaraz Guadalest
PALMA DE
Elche MALLORCA
ALICANTE MALLORCA
MURCIA IBIZA
Alcantarilla BALEARES
COSTA
BLANCA FORMENTERA
ARRAS LANZAROTE
Mojácar CANARIAS
ALMERÍA LA PALMA
Cabo de TENERIFE
Gata SANTA CRUZ
DE TENERIFE
LA GOMERA LAS PALMAS
DE GRAN FUERTEVENTURA
EL HIERRO CANARIA
GRAN CANARIA

DISCOVERING

SPAIN

THE COMPLETE GUIDE

PENELOPE CASAS

PAVILION

First published in Great Britain in 1992 by
PAVILION BOOKS LIMITED
196 Shaftesbury Avenue, London WC2H 8JL

A CIP record for this book is available from the British Library.

ISBN 1 85145 871 9
10 9 8 7 6 5 4 3 2 1

Printed and bound in the United States of America by R. R. Donnelley & Sons

TO LUIS—

YOUR PASSION FOR SPAIN

AND THIRST FOR DISCOVERY

HAVE BEEN MY INSPIRATION.

CONTENTS

ACKNOWLEDGMENTS

MANY THANKS to my parents—you were always standing by to offer love and encouragement, and your considerable editorial skills helped me in my struggles with wayward conjunctions and prepositions; to my daughter Elisa—I appreciate your enthusiasm and solid support for this project . . . and your care for Happi and Houdini while we were off in Spain; to my special friend Marsha Stanton—I could always turn to you for guidance, to raise flagging spirits, and for extraordinarily on-target personal and professional advice. Thank you, Pilar Vico—your cooperation and friendship have been invaluable; and *muchísimas gracias* to all my wonderful friends in Spain for your generosity and warmth and all the good times we have shared together.

My editor, Judith Jones, with whom I have worked since I began my writing career, once more displayed remarkable perceptiveness, patience, and understanding, and her dazzling editorial abilities kept me on course throughout this endeavor.

DISCOVERING
SPAIN

SPAIN'S EXTRAORDINARY YEAR: 1992

1992 promises to be a momentous year for Spain and cause for great celebration. It marks the quincentennial of the first voyage of Columbus to America, under the auspices of Spain; the year in which Barcelona hosts the summer Olympic games, Sevilla welcomes millions of visitors to Expo '92, and Madrid is designated Cultural Capital of Europe. During this same year Spain becomes a full member of the European Economic Community and once more takes its place among the great nations of the world.

The summer Olympics in Barcelona begin July 25 and close August 9. For ticket information contact Olson Travelworld, El Segundo, California 90247, tel: 1-800-US-4-1992. Be advised that most hotel rooms in central Barcelona have been booked by the Olympic Committee and whatever accommodations may be available could be several hours away from the city. In conjunction with the Olympics, Barcelona plans other special events, such as art exhibits and music festivals.

Expo '92 commences April 20 in Sevilla and comes to an end on Columbus Day, October 12, a day which of course will be honored with great ceremony. Some one hundred countries and all of Spain's regional autonomies will participate in Expo '92. Activities include cultural, sports, and musical events, exhibits at each nation's pavilion plus special exhibits at monographic pavilions, centering on the general theme: The Age of Discovery, past, present and future. Expo '92 takes place on the island of La Cartuja, located on the Guadalquivir river. Tickets are available at the gate or through your travel agency. Hotel space is at a premium, and you may have to stay a considerable distance from the city. If you are interested in visiting the monastery where Columbus lived for a time, the village where he recruited his men, and the place from which he set sail on his first voyage, turn to the chapter on the province of Huelva.

As Cultural Capital of Europe, Madrid will naturally concentrate on cultural affairs for its special activities in 1992. There will be concerts, dance, film, theater, art exhibits, and lectures. Contact the Tourist Office of Spain for additional information on all of Spain's 1992 events.

Expect Barcelona and Sevilla to be overflowing with visitors; if you find the crowds and the heightened activity invigorating, by all means head for those cities. If, on the other hand, you would like to experience a more peaceful, timeless Spain, I suggest saving the regions of Catalunya and Andalucía for a future visit and concentrating for 1992 on areas well away from the tumult, such as Galicia, Asturias, Aragón, and Castilla-León.

AN INTRODUCTION TO SPAIN

THIS IS AN unabashedly personal guidebook. It's for the traveler who wants something more—adventure, the discovery of out-of-the-way places, immersion in the culture, connection with the Spanish people. In other words, I am writing for the tourist who is not content to be simply an onlooker, but who wants to participate in Spanish life and return home with an understanding of Spain that goes beyond monuments and scenic wonders.

The physical and cultural diversity of Spain is indeed astonishing. Few people realize that Spain can be so green, so mountainous, so scenically spectacular, so gastronomically exciting. Packed into an area smaller than Texas you will find contrasts more often found in an entire continent. Spain has dense tropical vegetation, thick forests, vast marshlands, endless plains, desert-like environments, extreme heat and intense cold. It has Europe's longest coastline, with shores along the Mediterranean and Atlantic, and it is almost as mountainous as Switzerland. It can be barren or it can be lush, and it is crossed by four mighty rivers.

Each region of Spain has a look of its own and a unique cuisine; in Spain foods still have their place and do not "travel well," and for me, varying my diet according to the region I am in is part of the excitement. Local customs, history, and sometimes even the language, all discussed in detail in each chapter, are distinct. There are times when you wonder if you are still in Spain. For example, in Galicia, because of its Celtic heritage, bagpipes are played, and the men wear cropped pants resembling kilts on festive occasions. In the Basque Country, Basques speak a language unrelated to any other known tongue in the world, and in the Levante, endless rice paddies bring to mind some Far Eastern land.

From the ancient Romans, who built great cities and monuments, to the Arab invaders, who brought refined artistic sensibility and occupied the country for almost eight hundred years, to the Christian reconquerors, who took Spanish society to great heights, Spain's history is an intricately woven tapestry that blends elements from the many cultures that have passed through, creating a nation of uncommon character. It is a history that lends itself to endless legends and tales of miraculous happenings; fact and fiction effortlessly overlap. So you will find sprinkled throughout *Discovering Spain* dozens of the charming, sometimes apocryphal tales that bring Spain's past to life. Some of the important events that shaped Spain are highlighted in the boxes on pages 9–11 for quick reference, but I refer you to individual chapters for more detailed history peculiar to each region. Similarly, the country's artistic style, also a product of many cultures, is summarized in another box, but a fuller discussion of the culture that is unique to a region is reserved for the appropriate chapters.

Visiting Spain is a chance to get to know a way of life different from ours. Of course you'll want to take in the sights, but just as important, you'll want to get to know Spain's people. One way to do this is through food. Food tells us a lot about a country, and the food of Spain, filled with robust Mediterranean flavors—garlic, olive oil, tomatoes, peppers—has a personality of its own. Arabs brought a Mideastern flair to Spanish cooking; rice, coriander, cumin, and saffron are all inherited from those times. Contrary to what many Americans think when they hear the word *Spanish*, the food of Spain is not related to Mexican cooking; it is not hot and highly spiced.

Spaniards are passionate on the subject of food. City dwellers will plan a whole weekend around a particular eating experience, traveling several hours to a country inn to eat such delicacies as tender baby lamb slowly cooked to a turn in a brick-vaulted wood-burning oven, or to a seaside restaurant for fish of insuperable freshness. Whatever the food, country folk are tremendously proud of their local specialties. But most important for the traveler, a meal provides relaxation, a time to observe, to exchange, to share in the pleasures that Spain has to offer. Eating fine food is high on Spain's list of life's priorities and occupies an inordinate portion of each day. It's a habit visitors can easily slip into. I put considerable emphasis on food and drink in the hope that by helping you to know what to look for, and where to look for it, you'll be able to enjoy Spain that much more.

To really share the Spanish way of life, you have to take on the country's rhythm. Eat lunch at 2:00, never go to dinner until 9:30 or 10:00 (unless you want to dine with only a few fellow tourists). To ward off hunger, there are always tapas, the wonderful little appetizers that are a firmly established part of Spain's being; indulge in them as a pause in the late morning, or as relaxation as the day comes to a close. Once you have adjusted to the cadence of life in Spain, bar stops will be sprinkled throughout your day. You may want to order only a bottle of water—these stops are not necessarily meant to satisfy hunger and thirst, but to provide a wonderful opportunity to savor life in the slow lane. The atmosphere is casual and unstructured, and it is easy to strike up a conversation (despite any language limitations) and make a new

PUTTING TOGETHER A SPANISH PICNIC

The easiest way, of course, to assemble a picnic is to ask the help of your hotel the night before; I have always found hotels to be very accommodating. Spaniards would most likely request *ternera empanada* (breaded beef), *tortilla de patata* (potato omelet), *pan* (bread), *queso* (cheese) and *fruta* (fruit).

Or you can go to a *supermercado*, where you will find everything you need under one roof. But to shop the way a Spanish housewife would, go to specialized stores—the *frutería*, *panadería*, and *tienda de ultramarinos*—a delicatessen that has cold cuts, cheese, canned goods, and a few fruits and vegetables.

friend. It happens all the time. Tapas can be so satisfying that you may choose to make them your meal. Especially at midday, when Spaniards break for their main meal of the day, tapas are a welcome alternative to lunch in a restaurant.

Variously called *tabernas*, *bares*, *tascas*, *mesones*, or *bodegas*, tapas bars can be noisy and chaotic; no matter, plunge right in and become part of the fun. Most tapas dishes are on display, so you need only point (other choices are sometimes listed on a chalkboard). Tapas can be as simple as slices of *chorizo* sausage and *serrano* ham and chunks of cheese, but they multiply into an astonishing array of dishes; almost anything served in a small portion is transformed into a tapa. If you don't know what to order, see what everyone else is having—usually the tapas that the bar is best known for. Eating tapas is a communal event, and although forks are provided, you and those with you are expected to take tapas from a common plate. It is a grave faux pas and an unsociable act to ask for separate plates and divvy up the food.

In small towns during evening tapas hours, everyone gets dressed up and takes to the streets for the ritual stroll, or *paseo*, that has no particular destination in mind. The local people will stop to chat with neighbors and to sit down in bars and cafés for drinks and tapas before heading home for dinner—one more example of how food and drink are inseparably intertwined with the social fiber of the country. It's a lovely time of day for you to sit at an outdoor café and observe the life that swirls around you.

After a late dinner you may be ready for bed, but you can always make the rounds of the busy bars, pubs, and discotheques, and if you like, dance the night away.

I myself fell in love with Spain as a student thirty years ago—and with the Spaniard who became my husband. Together we have gone back to Spain year after year, traveling the length and breadth of the country; during those first years we discovered the tiny fishing villages along the rugged Basque coastline and the undisturbed gentle beauty of Galicia, and we developed a strong attachment to vivacious Andalucía.

There were times when we traveled to Spain specifically for a fiesta, such as our trips to see the Running of the Bulls in Pamplona, Holy Week in Sevilla, and Las Fallas in Valencia. But mostly we went to explore. Finally we had exhausted the possibilities in the guidebooks, and greedy for more, we pumped Spanish friends and casual acquaintances, and their tips led us to lesser-known places. Then the fun really began.

I remember a bartender at the Hotel Villamagna in Madrid who drew a crude map on a cocktail coaster which we followed to the breathtaking site of the San Frutos hermitage; a friend of the Spanish consul in New York who sent us on the Route of the Oases in desert-like Almería; a photograph that beguiled us into visiting the isolated medieval village of Peñalba de Santiago; a passing reference to El Palancar, which took us to the world's smallest monastery. "How do you *find* these places?" a friend once asked. Whenever possible we try to reach our destination on a new road; this began as a game, but turned into a lifelong quest that has led us to the most unexpected sights.

So when New York University's School of Continuing Education offered me the chance to lead tours to Spain and to show others what we had spent three decades amassing, we jumped at the chance. For the past seven years we have shared our discoveries with those who joined us, and I now know that we are not alone in our enthusiasm for Spain. We've learned what Americans seem to like the most, and with us our travelers have enjoyed the marvelous scenery of the Pyrenees and the Picos de Europa, the beauty of the Galician coast and of the marshlands of Huelva. They have seen glittering cathedrals, solitary castles rising from the Castilian plains, and museums filled with treasures from Spain's past. But we have also introduced them to some of our Spanish friends, and on several occasions chance

THE FUN OF SPANISH FIESTAS

You are likely to run into some kind of celebration no matter where or when you travel ("those innumerable holidays which are rather more numerous to Spain than the days of the week," as Washington Irving put it). Many are related to religious observances and may include processions, bullfights, song and dance. Although sometimes solemn affairs, they are often joyful events. Here are some that are so colorful or inspiring that you might consider planning your trip around them (all are further described in the chapter on the region in which they are celebrated):

February or March (depending on when Easter falls) Carnaval (Cádiz and Santa Cruz de Tenerife)

March 12–19 Las Fallas (Valencia)

Easter week (Semana Santa) (Sevilla, Málaga, Zamora, Valladolid, Cuenca)

April Feria de Abril (April Fair) (Sevilla)

May Feria de Caballos (Horse Fair) (Jerez de la Frontera)

June and July International Festival of Dance and Music (Granada)

July 7–14 San Fermín (Running of the Bulls) (Pamplona)

July and August International Music Festival (Santander)

July, August, and September International Music Festival (Pollença, Mallorca)

September La Vendimia (Grape Harvest) (Jerez de la Frontera and La Rioja)

Note: Consult the Tourist Office of Spain for events with unspecified dates.

encounters with local people turned into lusty song fests. Those are memories that I know will be cherished as well as the remembrance of an outdoor lunch in the tiny unpaved village of Compludo, accompanied by the clucking of hens. Grilled lamb chops and sausage, garden-fresh salad, tortilla, crusty bread, and plenty of jug wine were all served by a young couple whose pride in having us there knew no bounds. The people of Spain and their fun-loving spirit and innate dignity have endeared everyone—so much so that dozens from our groups have returned with us time and time again, even when we go back to places they have been before; they are always eager to be a part of Spain once more.

Spain is a country with a strong collective personality. Most Spaniards share a touch of Gypsy fire, the pride of an hidalgo, the romance of Don Juan, the idealism of Don Quijote. But Spanish character is regionally defined as well, a product of climate and of diverging histories. In a broad sense you might say that the gentle lands of Galicia produce a placid people; the stormy weather and rocky shores of the north shape Spaniards of strong character, willing to take risks. Cataluña instills a business-like approach to life and a solid sense of regional pride. The some-

what bleak lands of Ca-
stilla and Extremadura
breed austerity; and the
warm weather of Anda-
lucía produces a sunny,
carefree temperament,
albeit tinged with a tragic
underside, typified by the
Andalusian fascination
with bullfighting. In all
regions, however, the
Spanish people have
reached the late twentieth
century jealously guarding
their past. Spaniards can
be more avant-garde than
anyone else, but at the
same time tradition is invi-
olable. During Holy Week
processions in Sevilla or
Zamora, or El Rocío pil-
grimage in Huelva, the
younger   generation
embraces the events with a
fervor matching that of
their parents and grandpar-
ents. And love for the land

ᗺULLFIGHTS

Bullfighting is considered an art, not a sport,
and has a long Spanish tradition. It can be a
thrilling experience, so closely tied to Spain's
"tragic sense of life," as writer Miguel de
Unamuno described the Spanish preoccupation with death. But you must be prepared to
appreciate the bullfight in the context of
Spanish tradition and culture, to attempt to
understand what is happening and why it is
happening, and to suspend preconceived
notions. You may find the pageantry exciting,
but that is not enough; it is necessary to comprehend the entire life-and-death struggle that
is taking place and the purpose served by each
part of the ritual. Otherwise the bullfight can
be an unpleasant experience, and it is point-
less to go. For a lively and most informative
account of bullfighting, read *Death in the
Afternoon* by Ernest Hemingway.

means as much to city residents, who often maintain ancestral homes in
the country, as to those who till the soil.

This country of free spirited individualists likes to live in the present
(yes, the *mañana* philosophy endures) and confronts the future only when it
has arrived. In the past such lack of planning and togetherness was one element in Spain's fall from grace.

> Spain is essentially the nation of gentlemen, which for three
> centuries has lived by doing nothing at the expense of the Indies
> and America. . . . In Spain they used to await the galleon as, in
> France, they vote the budget.   *Victor Hugo*

Although politically Spain's democratic tradition in the past was weak, its
people are innately egalitarian and independent—one reason why this has
always been a difficult country to govern. Spaniards maintain their dignity
no matter what their social class.

> . . . in Spain the duke or the marquis can scarcely entertain a
> very over-weening opinion of his own consequence, as he finds
> no one, with perhaps the exception of his French valet, to fawn
> upon or flatter him.   *George Borrow*

It's this "*Viva Yo*" (Long Live Me) mentality that sends each Spaniard off in his own direction. You will surely notice in Spain how exquisitely young children are dressed, no matter how little money the family may have; within their families they are little princes and princesses, admired and catered to. By the time they are adults the "*Viva Yo*" mentality is firmly entrenched and manifests itself in various ways: Spaniards hate to form lines, are short on patience, and love spontaneity. There's no need to call friends weeks in advance to make dinner arrangements. Spaniards keep their calendars open and make dates only when the mood strikes them. It is this spirit that makes Spain so much livelier and more fun than nations in which conformity is a virtue.

Nevertheless, Spaniards are very anxious to please; they warmly embrace visitors and are totally approachable. They want you to love their country as they do, and they will bend over backwards to be helpful. Language is never a barrier. Friends that we have sent to Spain come back with glowing accounts of the kindness and warmth they encountered, sometimes under the most trying circumstances. Alvin and Rita Greenberg enjoy telling the story of the time their car broke down on a mountain road in León. An entire village turned out to help and to send them on their way (this with just a few Spanish words to their credit). Charlie Millevoi and Lee Levy often reminisce about the evening they arrived in El Grove in Galicia and were unable to find hotel rooms. They inquired at a small restaurant; immediately the proprietor took charge and they were escorted to his home above the restaurant. The wine began to flow; toddlers ran about. That taste of everyday life was a highlight of their trip.

It's hard to explain why, but one visit to Spain just whets your appetite for more. Certainly Spain has cast its spell on generations of foreign writers, who found a sometimes exasperating country, but one that bewitched them. Victor Hugo observed:

> Everything here is capricious, contradictory, strange. . . . It is old, yet it is being born; it is rancid and yet fresh. It is indescribable.

And Washington Irving wrote:

> Let others repine at the lack of turnpike-roads and sumptuous hotels, and all the elaborate comforts of a country cultivated into tameness and the commonplace, but give me the rude mountain scramble, the roving, haphazard wayfaring, the frank, hospitable, though half wild manners that give such a true game flavour to romantic Spain!

Naturally, times have changed, but the exoticism and Moorish mystery that these writers experienced in Spain simmers close to the surface, still making Spain different from any other country. Just a few short miles from major cities and from busy tourist enclaves, Spain keeps its timeless aura.

KEY PERIODS AND EVENTS IN SPANISH HISTORY

20,000– 10,000 B.C.	Evidence of advanced **cave cultures** in cave drawings found princi-pally along the northern coast of Spain.
13,000– 200 B.C.	Many European and Middle Eastern cultures intermingle and periodi-cally engage in warfare for control of Spain. Early settlers were **Iberians,** followed by **Greeks, Phoenicians, Celts,** and **Carthaginians,** attracted to Spain because of its strategic importance at the mouth of the Mediterranean and because of its mineral wealth.
206 B.C.	**Roman** domination of Spain begins, bringing culture, stupendous architectural works, networks of roads, great cities, a formal lan-guage, and great literary achievement.
500– 600	Waves of barbarian invasions. **Visigoths** overrun Spain; they bring Christianity, but never create a cohesive society and leave behind few reminders of their rule.
711	**Arabs** cross the Strait of Gibraltar into Spain, conquering most of the country within seven or eight years. The **Moors,** as Arabs in Spain were called, imposed the Moslem religion while tolerating Jewish and Christian beliefs. They brought cultural splendor to Spain.
722	The **Christian Reconquest,** which will last almost 800 years, begins in Asturias. It proceeds to Catalunya and to Aragón under **Jaime El Conquistador. El Cid** in the eleventh century leads the Christians to victory in Castile and León. These reconquered lands become powerful kingdoms and melting pots of cultures, making Spain a country of astonishing intellectual achievements. Through the darkest ages of the continent, Spain preserves European and orien-tal cultures, principally in Christian-controlled Toledo and Moorish-occupied Córdoba, where knowledge is compiled and translated from one language to another. By the eleventh century religious pilgrimages to Santiago de Compostela have become occurrences of extraordinary cultural importance.
1212	**Battle of Las Navas de Tolosa** takes place at the border between Christian and Moslem Spain in the province of Jaén and is a key event in Spanish history. The Christian victory marks the begin-ning of the end of Moorish domination in Spain.
1469	Marriage of **Isabel** of Castile to **Fernando** of Aragón. In 1474 Isabel becomes Queen of Castile. Five years later Fernando inherits the throne of Aragón, opening the way for the union of Spain's king-doms into a nation under the **Catholic Kings.**
1492	An extraordinarily eventful year in which **Columbus** sails to America; Granada, the last Moorish stronghold in Spain, is won by the Catholic Kings; and religious fervor leads to the conversion or expulsion of Spanish Jews.
1516	**Charles,** son of Juana la Loca (daughter of the Catholic Kings) and Philip the Fair of Austria, takes the throne as Carlos I of Spain, and in 1519 becomes **Charles V, Holy Roman Emperor,** ruling a vast domain, the first empire on which the sun never set. It included Germany, Austria, the Low Countries, the Philippines, and about half of the New World. Gold and silver poured into the coffers from

America; Spain was supreme on land and at sea, and in typical Spanish style, the country enjoyed those years with little thought of the future.

1556   **Charles V** abdicates, and his son **Philip II** takes command. During the 42-year reign of Phillip II, Spanish wealth and prosperity is tempered by political and economic problems. These are times of cultural splendor—a Golden Age for Spanish literature and sculpture and a period during which grand architectural works arise.

1571   The **Battle of Lepanto,** resulting in a decisive victory over the Turks, gives Spain supremacy in the Mediterranean. The defeat of the **Spanish Armada** in 1588, however, crushes Spain's sea power.

1598–1700   Under **Philip III, Philip IV,** and **Charles II,** Spain begins its long decline, although during the reign of Philip IV one of Spain's greatest artistic flowerings takes place, particularly in painting. These are times of revolt throughout the Spanish empire.

1701   The **War of Spanish Succession** begins on the death of Hapsburg king Charles II, who leaves no heir. In 1714 the war ends, and **Philip V** becomes the first Spanish king of French Bourbon lineage.

1759   **Charles III** (1759–1788) brings peace, sophistication, and cultural distinction to Spain.

1808   Napoleon overruns Spain, and the revolt of the Spanish people in Madrid on May 2 (**Dos de Mayo**) marks the beginning of the **War of Independence,** during which Napoleon's brother Joseph takes the Spanish throne. Under king-in-exile Fernando VII, the **Constitution of Cádiz** is promulgated in 1812 and is one of the first liberal documents of its kind.

1813   Spain's American colonies begin revolts that eventually lead to their independence.

1833   The **First Carlist War** begins. **Don Carlos,** brother of Fernando VII, contests the throne with Fernando's daughter Isabel (future Isabel II). During this time Prime Minister Mendizábal orders the confiscation of all church property (**disamortization**). Although Isabel II takes the throne, the conflict over succession remains unresolved and leads to the **Second Carlist War** (1847). In 1868 Isabel II goes into exile, and during the **Third Carlist War** (1872) the first **Spanish Republic** is declared (1873), but is short-lived.

1874   **Alfonso XII,** son of Isabel II, is proclaimed king and rules until his death in 1885. His wife María Cristina becomes regent for their young son, the future Alfonso XIII.

1898   Spain's colonial power in America and the Philippines comes to an end after the **Spanish-American War.**

1902   **Alfonso XIII,** son of Alfonso XII, is declared king.

1923   With the king still on the throne, **General Primo de Rivera** becomes dictator of Spain in an attempt to restore order to a country on the verge of chaos.

1931   A liberal **Republican Government** comes to power and gives equality to women and attempts to turn the land over to the people. Alfonso XIII goes into exile.

1936   The **Spanish Civil War** begins, one of the most horrifying civil wars in world history; it pits brother against brother, liberals against conservatives, the church against communism, free thinking against traditional values.

1939	The Spanish Civil War ends with the victory of the Nationalists. **Francisco Franco** becomes head of state (1939–1975), ruling over a poor country in chaos. In the latter years of his rule, Spain enters a period of growing prosperity, aided by a boom in tourism, and gains world acceptance. Within the framework of a dictatorship, a strong middle class emerges.
1975	Franco dies and **Juan Carlos,** Bourbon successor to the long-vacant Spanish throne, becomes king. The infrastructure is already in place to support a stable democracy, wisely conceived under the symbolic authority of the king.
1985	Spain, now a modern, dynamic, and democratic nation, enters the European Economic Community, achieving new status in the world order and a prosperity unlike anything it has known before.

ARTISTIC STYLE IN SPAIN

EARLY PREHISTORIC
Technically and artistically advanced cave drawings and paintings, the best examples of which are in **Asturias** and **Cantabria.** Stone monoliths and stone funerary chambers, found in **Antequera** and on the island of **Menorca.**

IBERIAN   (first millennium B.C.)
Stone sculpture of an indigenous civilization, surprisingly sophisticated and artistically skilled. The **Toros de Guisando** in Ávila are thought to be from this period, as well as such sculpture as **La Dama de Elche** and **La Dama de Baza** in Madrid's Museo Arqueológico.

ROMAN   (third century b.c. to fifth century A.D.)
Monumental architecture; carefully planned cities and towns; roads, bridges, aqueducts, triumphal arches, theaters, and temples, examples of which can be found in **Mérida, Tarragona,** and **Segovia.**

VISIGOTHIC   (fifth to seventh century)
Architecture in the Roman tradition, but with Germanic, Byzantine, and oriental decorative details. Small stone churches, often with horseshoe-shaped arches, friezes in geometric shapes, carved foliage motifs, and Christian symbols, such as those of **Quintanilla de las Viñas** in the province of Burgos, **San Pedro de la Nave** in the province of Zamora, and **Baños de Cerrato** near Palencia. Magnificent jewelry, such as the **Tesoro de Guarrazar,** on display in the Museo Arqueológico of Madrid.

ASTURIAN   (eighth to tenth century)
Pre-Romanesque Christian style of Byzantine influence, seen in palaces and churches and localized in Asturias. Ribbed vaulted ceilings, decorative (nonsupporting) columns, stone-carved ornamentation in geometric and plant motifs, and wall frescoes. Most surviving examples are not far from Oviedo: **Santa María de Naranco, San Miguel de Lillo,** and **San Salvador de Valdediós.**

SAN MIGUEL DE LILLO

MOORISH   (eighth to fifteenth century)
Architecture and design elements brought by Moslem invaders that evolved into a uniquely Spanish style. Brick construction with horseshoe-shaped arches; ceramic ornamentation, delicate designs in stucco; strong emphasis on decorative work (calligraphy; geometric and plant designs), but rarely representing humans or animals. Fountains and lush gardens. The finest examples are concentrated in southern Spain: **La Alhambra** in Granada; the **Mosque** (Mezquita) of Córdoba and the palace of **Medina Azahara** just outside Córdoba; and in Sevilla, **La Giralda** and parts of **El Alcázar** (the rest of the structure is Mudéjar).

MOZARABIC   (ninth to tenth century)
Churches designed by Christians who had lived in Arab-controlled Spain but fled north to Christian-reconquered territories. Strong Moorish influence (brickwork, horseshoe arches, carved capitals) applied to churches of otherwise

Visigothic style. Few of these churches remain; the best are **San Miguel de la Escalada** in the province of León, **San Cebrián de Mazote** (Valladolid), and **San Baudelio de Berlanga** in Soria.

ROMANESQUE (eleventh to thirteenth century)

Austere, simple structures built on a small scale and lacking ostentation. Latin cross shape replaces long rectangular or square shaped basilica from Roman times; heavy walls support rounded arches; interior ornamentation is spare, except for naif frescoes in which human figures appear stiff, emotionless, and remote. In later Romanesque there is abundant sculpture on portals and capitals and an increased Moorish influence. Polychrome statues and altar fronts are popular. In the province of Lleida, **Sant Clemint de Taüll** and the monastery of **Ripoll** are fine examples, as are the **Pórtico de la Gloria** of the cathedral of Santiago de Compostela and the **San Juan de la Peña** monastery in Huesca.

MUDÉJAR (eleventh to fifteenth century)

Moorish brick, ceramic, and stucco work created by Moslems living under Christian rule and adapted to Christian themes and building styles. *Artesonado* wood ceilings—intricately dovetailed, inlaid, and sometimes painted in geometric and floral patterns—remained popular in Spain for centuries. In Castilla y León and Aragón there are many fine examples: **El Tránsito** and **Santa María La Blanca** synagogues in Toledo, the **Towers** of Teruel, **Coca** castle in Segovia province, and the **Convento de Santa Clara** in Tordesillas (Valladolid).

COCA CASTLE

GOTHIC (thirteenth to sixteenth century)

Airy construction, more open space, more delicacy; soaring spires and pinnacles, pointed arches. Pillars and flying buttresses replace heavy Romanesque walls, no longer needed for principal support. Walls become frames for large stained-glass windows, which replace frescoes. Later Flamboyant Gothic style gives more emphasis to ornamentation. In painting a pronounced Flemish influence, especially when applied to large painted altarpieces. A more humanized portrayal of man in painting and sculpture. The **Burgos** and **León cathedrals** are supreme religious interpretations of the style; **La Lonja** in Valencia is an example of Gothic applied to civilian architecture.

ISABELLINE (fifteenth to sixteenth century)

A Flamboyant Gothic style under Moorish influence, associated with the rule of Queen Isabel. She commissioned many of the outstanding examples of this free-flowing, exceptionally detailed stone carving, usually imposed over the facades of Gothic structures. **La Cartuja de Miraflores** outside Burgos, the **Colegio de San Gregorio** in Valladolid, and **San Juan de los Reyes** monastery in Toledo were all built during the reign of the Catholic Kings.

SAN PABLO, VALLADOLID

PLATERESQUE   (sixteenth century)
The word derives from *plata*, or silver, because the intricate stone carving resembles the work of silversmiths. Highly complex ornamentation, but applied in structured, orderly patterns, often covering the facades of Renaissance buildings. Some of the best works are the **Old University** of Salamanca, the **Hostal de los Reyes Católicos** in Santiago de Compostela, the **Hostal de San Marcos** in León, and the **Colegio de San Ildefonso** in Alcalá de Henares.

SAN PABLO, VALLADOLID

RENAISSANCE   (sixteenth to seventeenth century)
Return to ancient, "classic" architecture in the Roman style. Less ornate, but in any case, never a highly developed style in Spain. Generally nonreligious application; landscaping becomes important and the decorative arts flourish. Among the best examples are the **palaces** in **Úbeda,** the palace of **Charles V** (Granada), and the palace and monastery of **El Escorial** in Madrid province.

BAROQUE   (seventeenth to eighteenth century)
Structurally related to Renaissance, but extravagantly ornate. The great churches and cathedrals of Spain "updated" their interiors with Baroque chapels and dramatic wood polychrome statuary, designed to impress and evoke admiration and awe. **La Cartuja** in Granada and the **Murcia cathedral** represent the style. This was also the Golden Age of Spanish painting, when Velázquez, Murillo, Zurbarán, and José Ribera were favored artists.

CHURRIGUERESQUE   (eighteenth century)
Baroque ornamentation in flowing designs, under Moorish and Plateresque influence, but carried to an extreme. Initiated by the Churriguera brothers, the style takes their name. The most striking examples are the **Palacio del Marqués de Dos Aguas** in Valencia, the **Transparente** chapel of the Toledo cathedral, and the **Cristo de las Batallas** chapel and the **choir** in the New Cathedral of Salamanca.

NEOCLASSIC
(eighteenth to nineteenth century)
A return to Greek and Roman elegance and classic style, especially in Madrid under the influence of the Bourbon kings. Fine examples are the **Palacio Real** and the **Museo del Prado** in the city of Madrid, and the **Aranjuez** palace in Madrid province. This stately, serene architecture is in surprising contrast to the turbulent works of Goya painted in Madrid during the same period.

PALACIO DEL MARQUÉS DE DOS AQUAS

SPANISH FOOD GLOSSARY

The glossary that follows includes foods commonly found in many parts of Spain. Dishes and foods associated with just one region are described in each chapter. (See page 25 for Spanish pronunciation.)

Shellfish is generally ordered by weight: 100 to 150 grams of shrimp or *percebes* serves two as an appetizer; 2 medium-size crabs weigh about 250 grams; 1 kilo of lobster will generally make a meal for two.

Tipping: gratuities are included in your restaurant bill, but it is customary to leave a little more. Ten percent is considered generous.

A Spanish menu tends to be lengthy and divided into many categories, such as appetizers, soups, vegetables, eggs, shellfish, fish, meat, and desserts. Feel free to select from whatever category and in whatever order you wish. Restaurants are required to have a prix fixe special menu called the *menú del día,* but it is usually uninspired and often does not include house specialties.

PREPARATIONS

al ajillo in garlic sauce

a la parrilla, a la plancha barbecued, on the griddle

a la romana egg- and flour-coated and fried

asado roasted

cocido boiled

en salsa verde, a la vasca in green sauce

en su punto, muy hecho, poco hecho medium rare, well done, rare

estofado stewed

frito fried

salpicón de, en escabeche marinated

salteado sautéed

TAPAS

aceitunas olives

albóndigas meatballs

almendras almonds

caracoles snails

chorizo garlic, herb, and paprika cured sausage

croquetas croquettes

empanadillas savory turnovers

Ensaladilla Rusa potato and vegetable salad

jamón serrano cured ham

morcilla black sausage

Pincho Moruno small shish kabob

queso cheese

HUEVOS Y TORTILLAS
(Egg Dishes)

Huevos a la Flamenca baked eggs with chorizo and vegetables

Tortilla Española, tortilla de patata potato omelet

revuelto lightly scrambled eggs, usually mixed with additional ingredients like vegetables or shellfish

Huevos con migas fried eggs with crisp bread bits

ARROZ, ARROCES
(Rice, Rice Dishes)

Paella a la Valenciana/mixta chicken and seafood rice

Paella a la Marinera seafood rice

PESCADOS Y MARISCOS
(Fish and Shellfish)

almejas clams

ancas de rana frog's legs

angulas baby eels

atún tuna

bacalao salt cod

besugo sea bream, porgy

boquerón white anchovy

calamares squid

cigala langoustine

gambas shrimp

langosta, bogavante spiny lobster, lobster

langostinos prawns

lenguado sole

lubina bass

mejillones mussels

merluza hake

mero grouper

percebes goose barnacles

pulpo octopus

rape monkfish

rodaballo turbot

salmón salmon

salmonete red mullet

sardina sardine

trucha trout

vieiras scallops

AVES Y CAZA
(Poultry and Game)

codorniz quail

conejo rabbit

faisán pheasant

pato duck

perdiz partridge

pollo chicken

venado venison

CARNES
(Meats)

cabrito kid

callos tripe

carne de res beef

cerdo pork

cochinillo suckling pig

cordero, chuletas de cordero lamb, lamb chops

criadillas Rocky Mountain oysters

hígado liver

riñones kidneys

sesos brains

ternera young beef

FRUTAS Y VERDURAS
(Fruit and Vegetables)

berengena eggplant

cerezas cherries

champiñones mushrooms

ciruelas plums

ensalada, ensalada mixta lettuce and tomato salad, salad with more additions

espinacas spinach

fresas, fresones small, large strawberries

guisantes peas

habas fresh fava beans

lechuga lettuce

limón lemon

manzana apple

melocotón peach

melón melon

menestra vegetable medley

naranja orange

patatas potatoes

pera pear

pimientos (morrones, verdes) peppers (red, green)

plátano banana

sandía watermelon

setas wild mushrooms

tomate tomato

POSTRES
(Desserts)

arroz con leche rice pudding

buñuelos fritters, doughnuts

Brazo de Gitano custard cake roll

cuajada rennet pudding

flan custard

helado (de vainilla, chocolate) ice cream (vanilla, chocolate)

membrillo con queso quince paste with cheese

natillas soft custard

pasteles pastries

sorbete sherbet

tarta tart, cake

Tocino de Cielo rich flan

turrón almond candy

BEBIDAS
(Beverages)

agua (con gas) water (carbonated)

café (solo, cortado, con leche)
  coffee (black, a little milk,
  with milk)

chocolate thick hot chocolate

horchata tiger nut (chufa) soft drink

leche milk

té tea

cerveza beer

vino tinto red wine

vino blanco white wine

VARIOUS

azúcar sugar

bollos, suizos sweet rolls

churros breakfast fritters

miel honey

pan, pan de molde bread, sandwich
  bread

pepito sautéed beef or pork on roll

WAS IT A GOOD YEAR
FOR WINE?
THE BEST
SPANISH VINTAGES

Note: Regional wines are discussed in appropriate chapters. Restaurant house wines are generally good choices; they will be wines of the region or, in the case of a very fine restaurant, a carefully chosen personal selection.

RIOJA		RIBERA DEL DUERO		PENEDÉS	
1952	Excellent	1972	Very good	1972	Excellent
1964	Excellent	1976	Very good	1973	Very good
1970	Excellent	1981	Excellent	1975	Very good
1981	Very good	1982	Very good	1976	Excellent
1982	Excellent	1983	Very good	1978	Excellent
1987	Very good	1985	Very good	1980	Very good
		1986	Very good	1981	Very good
				1982	Very good
				1984	Very good
				1985	Very good
				1988	Very good

PRACTICAL TIPS ON TRAVELING IN SPAIN

PLANNING A TRIP
TO SPAIN

Don't be overambitious. Spain is a big country; you can't see it all on a ten-day trip, and whirlwind tours do not give you the opportunity to explore the countryside. See Appendix 1 (p. 535) for trips that are varied but not overwhelming. Keep in mind that Spain has *two* hours of daylight savings time in the summer (one in the winter), and in summer it does not get dark until ten—a real bonus for travelers.

When to Go

May, June, July, September, and the beginning of October are the best months to find warm temperatures and clear skies (July, however, can get very hot in central and southern Spain, and there's always a chance of showers in the north). March and April are fickle months; you may find snow, glorious spring weather, or rain. But I have nevertheless often gone at those times for the many fiestas that are celebrated during those months and enjoyed myself no less because of changeable conditions. In the Canary Islands the weather is good all year round. Try to avoid August all over Spain; cities become ghost towns, vacation areas are very crowded, and it is usually very hot.

Getting to Spain

Several airlines fly to Spain, but I have found that Iberia Airlines, the airline of Spain, provides fine service and an up-to-date fleet of airplanes. Consult your travel agent for fly-and-drive or flight-and-hotel packages that can lower the cost of your trip considerably.

Renting a Car

A car is the best way to get around Spain; you travel at your own pace and can reach out-of-the-way destinations. If you book from home (through a travel agency), the cost is much lower than reserving within Spain. Remember that clutch cars are standard; if you must have automatic, the price is much higher, as it is if you want air conditioning.

I highly recommend purchasing a complete road map, such as the one by Michelin, for general orientation. Once you are in Spain, buy Firestone maps, which divide the country into nine separate areas and are more detailed and easier to follow. They are available in bookstores.

Other Means of Transportation

Spain has an extensive network of railroads that provides excellent service. Use express trains like the TALGO whenever possible, and for a real treat, look into the vintage trains like Al Andalus (see box, p. 397). I would not recommend regular bus lines; travel is much too slow and uncomfortable.

Staying There

Hotels in Spain are not always what they should be, although in recent years improvement has been noticeable. Paradors, the government-sponsored hotels, are unfailingly in prime locations and often in historic buildings, and they are always reliable. It is, in fact, worthwhile to plan your entire trip, if possible, around nights in the paradors. Major cities do not have paradors, but here the hostelry tradition is stronger and more options are available.

HOURS AND CLOSINGS

Restaurants:

1:00–3:30 P.M. for lunch, 8:30–11:00 P.M. for dinner. In large cities many restaurants close on Sundays and holidays and during the month of August. If you are looking for a bite at other hours, bars and cafeterias are open all day.

Stores:

9:30 A.M.–1:30 P.M. and 5:00–8:00 P.M. Department stores usually stay open all day.

Museums:

9:30 A.M.–1:30 P.M. and 5:00–7:00 P.M.; as a rule, closed on Mondays. Check individual listings for exceptions.

NATIONAL HOLIDAYS

January 1 (New Year's Day)
January 6 (Epiphany)
March 19 (San José)
Holy Thursday
Good Friday
May 1 (Labor Day)
Corpus Christi
August 15 (Assumption)

October 12 (Día de la Hispanidad, or Columbus Day)
November 1 (All Saints Day)
December 6 (Constitution)
December 8 (Immaculate Conception)
December 25 (Christmas)

Note: There are some regionally celebrated holidays as well.

SHOPPING

The rule is to buy what you like when you see it without prolonged deliberation; you are not likely to see the same item twice. If a shop is a small family operation, you might try bargaining.

Recommended purchases include ceramics and pottery, embroidery, lace, metalwork, fine jewelry (be sure to purchase it only at a *joyería*), wood inlay (*taracea*), Spanish soaps, antiques, leather, children's clothes, and food items (jams, marmalades, olive oil, Spanish rice, cheese, saffron). See each chapter for regional crafts.

THINGS TO BRING WITH YOU

Kleenex, 220-volt appliances (or those with adapters for 220 volts) with rounded two-prong plugs, a pocket flashlight, a can/bottle opener, a small knife, and pocket binoculars.

WHAT TO WEAR

Times have changed, and dress is much more casual than it once was. There are no longer dress requirements to enter a church or cathedral. Restaurants are usually casual—jackets are optional for men. But Spanish women still like to dress up and will rarely wear pants in the evening.

FISHING AND HUNTING IN SPAIN

Spain is considered a fishing and hunting paradise and attracts sportsmen from all over the world, interested in trout and salmon fishing and in hunting partridge, quail, pheasant, wild boar, and deer. Consult the Tourist Office of Spain regarding permits.

EQUIVALENTS

10 miles = 16 kilometers (16,000 meters)

32° Fahrenheit = 0° centigrade (use formula ⅘ × (centigrade) + 32 to convert centigrade to Fahrenheit)

3½ ounces = 100 grams

2 pounds plus 3¼ ounces = 1 kilogram (1,000 grams)

1 quart plus 3 tablespoons = 1 liter

3 feet (1 yard) plus 3⅜ inches = 1 meter

MONEY EXCHANGE

Most hotels give approximately the same exchange rate as banks (which are open only from 8:30 A.M. to 2:00 P.M.) and will save you considerable time. The Spanish monetary unit is the *peseta*.

HOTEL AND RESTAURANT PRICE EQUIVALENTS

Note: Hotels and restaurants are listed in each chapter in the general order of my personal preferences.

HOTELS   (price per double room)

inexpensive   up to $50

moderate $50–$90

moderate–expensive
   $90–$150

expensive $150–$220

very expensive $220–$300

deluxe $300–$400

ultra-deluxe   over $400

RESTAURANTS
(price per person with
house wine)

inexpensive   up to $20

inexpensive–moderate
   $20–$30

moderate $30–$40

moderate–expensive $40–$50

expensive $50–$70

very expensive   over $70

TIPPING

When in doubt, give a tip, even for the smallest favor. A hundred pesetas will suffice when luggage is brought to your room. For taxis and in restaurants, give 5 to 10 percent. Theater ushers and gas station attendants also expect a small tip.

FORK AND STAR RATINGS FOR RESTAURANTS AND HOTELS

Two decades ago the Spanish government devised a system of symbols—forks for restaurants, stars for hotels—to give the consumer an indication of the prices charged by these establishments and of the services they provide. Five forks is the maximum for a restaurant, five stars GL (*Gran Lujo,* or Deluxe) for hotels. Restaurant ratings are based on décor, menu, and service; for hotels, on such things as public rooms, banquet facilities, and room amenities.

Although well intentioned, these ratings today have largely lost their significance, and I set little store by them. A five-fork restaurant may be very elegant, but its cooking can be ordinary. A small luxury hotel that lacks dining facilities may receive only four stars, and yet its prices may be super-deluxe. A restaurant of simple décor can fall low in the hierarchy yet serve, for example, superb—and very expensive—seafood. A five-star hotel that has not been renovated in twenty years and is drab, musty, and outdated may retain its original rating.

You can, however, trust those hotels (there are very few of them) designated *Gran Lujo.* They take great care with every detail, and are often decorated with antiques or costly furnishings, and like to pamper their clients. Generally they are very expensive—but not all of them are.

SAFETY

Exercise the same precautions in Spain as you do elsewhere in the world. Always keep your handbag in front of you and never leave luggage unattended on a train or in a car, even if it is in the trunk of the car (a license plate from a different province and items in the car, such as maps and guidebooks, identify you as a traveler and therefore likely to have luggage). Carry your passport separately from your wallet. Replacements can be obtained only in Madrid or Barcelona. Be especially on guard for pickpockets in Sevilla, Córdoba, Valencia, Madrid, and Barcelona.

NIGHTLIFE

Dinner is so late in Spain that there is little need for additional evening activities unless you are prepared to stay up very late. Discotheques are everywhere, but aside from some in major cities, they are generally not very good. First-rate flamenco is hard to find; your best bets are in Madrid and Sevilla, or as part of an Andalusian fiesta (flamenco, after all, comes from Andalucía). There are always plenty of bars, cafés, and pubs for a nightcap.

CALLING TO AND
FROM SPAIN

To call Spain from the United States, dial the international code, 011 (from the United Kingdom the code is 010), 34 (code for Spain), the Spanish province code (leave out the 9 that you will find at the beginning of all province codes in this book; the 9 is used only for calls within Spain), and then the number.

If you are calling the United States from Spain, consider that the time in Spain is six or seven hours later than Eastern Standard Time, depending on the time of year. To call direct, dial 07 (international line), wait for the tone, then dial 1 (code for the United States), the area code, and the number. To call the United Kingdom, dial 07, wait for the dial tone, and follow with 44 (country code), the local area code, and the number. If you choose to call with the help of a Spanish operator, service is sometimes slow. Inquire about telephone surcharges in hotels; some are unreasonable. AT&T now provides direct access to United States operators from any telephone in Spain; dial 900 99 00 11 and give the operator your AT&T calling card number or the number to which your call will be charged.

HELPFUL CONTACTS

NATIONAL TOURIST OFFICE OF SPAIN

United States

665 Fifth Avenue
New York, NY 10022
(212) 759-8822

San Vicente Plaza Building
8383 Wilshire Boulevard, Suite 960
Beverly Hills, CA 90211
(213) 658-7188

845 North Michigan Avenue
Chicago, IL 60611
(312) 642-1992

1221 Brickell Avenue, Suite 1850
Miami, FL 33131
(305) 358-1992

United Kingdom

57 St. James's Street
London, SW1A 1LD
(071) 499 0901

Canada

102 Bloor Street West, 14th floor
Toronto, Ontario M5S 1M8
(416) 961-3131

IBERIA AIRLINES

Consult your telephone directory for ticket offices, or in the United States
dial (800) 722-4642

INTRODUCING YOU TO THE SPANISH LANGUAGE

Many Spaniards speak English, and there is almost always someone who
knows English in hotels (French is also easily understood). In other situa-
tions when an interpreter may not be at hand, there's no need to worry,
even if you travel in the most out-of-the-way places; Spaniards will always
find a way to help you. Nevertheless, you will enjoy yourself more, get
around more easily, and have more contact with the Spanish people if you
have a little knowledge of the language and make some attempt to speak it;
Spaniards really appreciate your efforts.

In the Basque Country and Catalunya the Basque and Catalan languages are spoken, but Spanish is always understood. See p. 328 for Catalan
vocabulary.

PRONUNCIATION

a	ah
e	ey
i	ee
o	oh
u	oo
ca, co, cu	cah, coh, coo
ce, ci	thay, thee
ge, gi	hey, hee
j	pronounced like English *h*
h	silent

ll like *lli* in English *million* or English y
ñ like *ni* in English *onion*
que, qui kay, key
rr rolled *r*
z pronounced *th*
Note: Remaining letters of the alphabet have pronunciations. similar to English.

DAYS

Monday	*lunes*	Friday	*viernes*
Tuesday	*martes*	Saturday	*sábado*
Wednesday	*miércoles*	Sunday	*domingo*
Thursday	*jueves*		

MONTHS

January	*enero*	July	*julio*
February	*febrero*	August	*agosto*
March	*marzo*	September	*septiembre*
April	*abril*	October	*octubre*
May	*mayo*	November	*noviembre*
June	*junio*	December	*diciembre*

NUMBERS

one	*uno*	sixteen	*dieciséis*
two	*dos*	seventeen	*diecisiete*
three	*tres*	eighteen	*dieciocho*
four	*cuatro*	nineteen	*diecinueve*
five	*cinco*	twenty	*veinte* (*veintiuno,* etc.)
six	*seis*		
seven	*siete*	thirty	*treinta* (*treinta y uno,* etc.)
eight	*ocho*		
nine	*nueve*	forty	*cuarenta* (*cuarenta y uno,* etc.)
ten	*diez*		
eleven	*once*	fifty	*cincuenta* (*cincuenta y uno,* etc.)
twelve	*doce*		
thirteen	*trece*	sixty	*sesenta* (*sesenta y uno,* etc.)
fourteen	*catorce*		
fifteen	*quince*	seventy	*setenta* (*setenta y uno,* etc.)

eighty   *ochenta*
(*ochenta y uno*, etc.)

ninety   *noventa*
(*noventa y uno*, etc.)

one hundred   *cien, ciento*

two hundred   *doscientos*

three hundred   *trescientos*

four hundred   *cuatrocientos*

five hundred   *quinientos*

six hundred   *seiscientos*

seven hundred   *setecientos*

eight hundred   *ochocientos*

nine hundred   *novecientos*

one thousand   *mil*
(*dos mil, tres mil*, etc.)

TIME

It is one o'clock (at one o'clock)
Es la una (a la una)

It is two o'clock (at two o'clock)
Son las dos (a las dos)

Note: The remaining hours follow
the form for two o'clock.

VOCABULARY

today   *hoy*
yesterday   *ayer*
tomorrow   *mañana*
now   *ahora*

here   *aquí*
there   *allí*

big   *grande*
small   *pequeño*

much   *mucho*
little   *poco*
very   *muy*

hot   *caliente*
cold (it is cold)   *frío (hace frío)*
heat (it is hot)   *calor (hace calor)*

good   *bueno*
bad   *malo*
well, very well   *bien (muy bien)*

pretty   *bonito (bonita)*
handsome (pretty)   *guapo (guapa)*
ugly   *feo (fea)*

open   *abierto*
closed   *cerrado*

near   *cerca*
far   *lejos*

morning   *mañana*
afternoon   *tarde*
evening   *noche*

exit   *salida*
entrance   *entrada*

week   *semana*
month   *mes*
year   *año*

waiter (waitress)
camarero (camarera)

menu   *carta*
bill   *cuenta*

store   *tienda*
house   *casa*

breakfast   *desayuno*
early (late) lunch   *almuerzo*
(*comida*)
dinner *cena*

man   *hombre*
woman   *mujer*
boy (girl)   *chico (chica)*
child, baby   *niño (niña)*
mister   *señor*

married woman   *señora*
single woman   *señorita*
father   *padre*
mother   *madre*
son (daughter)   *hijo (hija)*
brother (sister)   *hermano (hermana)*
friend   *amigo (amiga)*

COMMON PHRASES

What time is it?   *¿Qué hora es?*

How much is it?   *¿Cuánto cuesta?, ¿Cuánto vale?*

How are you?   *¿Cómo está usted?, ¿Cómo estás?* (formal and familiar forms)

Where is?   *Dónde está?*

What is your name?   *¿Cómo se llama?, ¿Cómo te llamas?* (formal and
  familiar forms)

please   *por favor*

the check, please   *la cuenta, por favor*

excuse me   *perdone, perdona* (formal and familiar forms)

thank you (thank you very much)   *gracias (muchas gracias)*

you're welcome   *de nada*

hi   *hola*

good morning   *buenos días*

good afternoon (used after lunch)   *buenas tardes*

good evening (used after dinner)   *buenas noches*

goodbye   *adiós*

a pleasure to meet you   *mucho gusto (encantado)*

to the left   *a la izquierda*

to the right   *a la derecha*

I don't understand   *no entiendo*

I speak (do not speak) Spanish, English   *hablo (no hablo) español, inglés*

THE IRREPRESSIBLE CITY
AND STERN CASTILIAN
COUNTRYSIDE OF MADRID

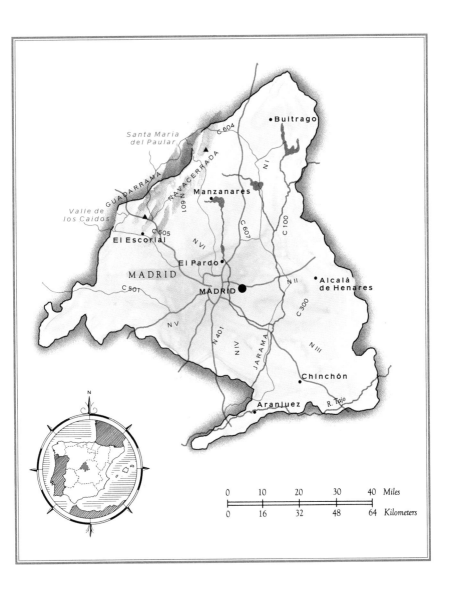

THE PROVINCE AND REGION OF MADRID

WHAT BETTER PLACE to begin a trip to Spain than right here in the spiritual, political, and economic heart of the country. Madrid (mah-*dreed*) is a world unto itself, and although I love to escape to tiny villages and immerse myself in the Spain of the past, I always feel the city of Madrid must be visited. If you haven't seen Madrid, you haven't seen Spain.

Madrid province was traditionally a part of Castilla–La Mancha, but since in this case the capital of the province is also the capital of the country, the province was given regional status and today is designated an autonomous region. It is a region, however, artificially conceived in the nineteenth century, when the city acquired bits and pieces of other provinces to form its own geographic entity. Even the choice of Madrid as capital was an arbitrary decision made by Philip II in the sixteenth century, but once established, Madrid thrived and took on a life of its own. It soon spawned monumental works built in the province by the whims of subsequent kings: the vast El Escorial palace and monastery, and the regal summer palaces of Aranjuez and El Pardo. The only city in the province that was important before Madrid gave its stamp to the region was Alcalá de Henares.

Obviously a city of more than three million residents is light-years away from the slow pace and age-old ways of the wheatfields and whitewashed villages of La Mancha. But just outside the metropolis the look of the land and the traditions of Madrid province are pure Castilian. How quickly the high-rise buildings of Madrid give way to the austere, arid mountains to the north, where Madrileños—who still have strong bonds to the land—escape to weekend retreats, and where the air is

FOODS AND WINES OF MADRID

GENERAL
Lamb, *serrano* ham, seafood, beans, tapas

SPECIALTIES
Soldaditos de Pavía—batter-fried cod
Caracoles a la Madrileña—snails and *chorizo* in paprika sauce
Sopa de Ajo—garlic soup
Callos a la Madrileña—tripe and *chorizo* stew
Cocido Madrileño—chickpea stew
Besugo a la Madrileña—porgy in tomato and wine sauce
Cordero asado—roast baby lamb
Churros—breakfast fritters
Buñuelos de Viento—doughnuts
Almendras de Alcalá—sugar-coated almonds
Leche Merengada—cinnamon-scented iced milk
Torrijas—batter-fried toast

WINES AND SPIRITS
Valdecepa from Navalcarnero
Orusco from Arganda
Anís de Chinchón—anise liqueur, dry or sweet

fresh and cool and life is much simpler. Madrid province becomes more gentrified every day, but the landscape is no less majestic.

Some of Spain's greatest sights are in this province. You can easily keep on your toes for more than a week just visiting the capital, Alcalá de Henares, Aranjuez, Chinchón, and El Escorial, all within the provincial borders, and perhaps you might extend your activities to skiing in winter and visiting the lakes in summer. Just beyond Madrid province, but still within two hours of the capital, there are rewarding excursions to several of the country's most historically significant cities, like Toledo, Segovia, Ávila, and Valladolid. If time permits, of course, it is far better to spend at least one night in each of these cities (see Itineraries, Appendix).

Located in the geographic center of the country, Madrid province has ties to all five provinces that surround it, but its character, history, and geography are more closely bound to northern Castilla than to Castilla–La Mancha, to which it was officially joined. Its gastronomy also parallels the north's: roasts of baby lamb and suckling pig, tiny lamb chops, and wonderful stews of chickpeas, tripe, or beans. *Chorizo* sausage and *serrano* ham enter into a variety of traditional dishes. Of course, as the capital of the country, the city of Madrid is unique in that it offers foods from all regions of Spain as well as international and nouvelle cuisines.

THE SPIRIT OF MADRID

I have always had a special affection for the city of Madrid and its vivacious people, because thirty years ago Madrid was my very first introduction to Spain. I came as an impressionable college freshman and met in Madrid my future husband, Luis (I was assigned to his mother's house as part of a student exchange program). From then on, my summers were spent in Madrid, until we were married in Madrid three years later and then lived there for several years. Now I return regularly, at the beginning or on the last lap of my travels through Spain. It's like going home.

When I arrived that summer of '62, I immediately plunged into the carefree world of Old Madrid. Evenings I would visit the Plaza Mayor, where outdoor cafés and *tabernas* spilled over with high-spirited Madrileños, and from there I would descend to the gently curved Cava Baja, where I'd spend hours at cavelike taverns called *mesones*. There was no need to purchase theater or movie tickets or have a specific place to go; singing, music, and dance filled the streets, and one could join in; lively conversation was to be found everywhere.

Despite having to attend morning classes at the university, I found every day a party, a new experience, an adventure. I frequented tapas bars, taverns, occasionally an elegant restaurant (in those days even that was within my student budget). I took weekend excursions to the mountains and lakes, was thrilled by spontaneous flamenco fests at bars and taverns, and reveled in the nighttime ambiance of Old Madrid. This was a way to live that I had never known before. Could anyone resist falling in love with a city so enchanting and full of life?

Madrileños, I thought then, and continue to believe, are unique: warm, friendly, and exuberant, proud and innately elegant. They live for the day, and in many ways seem more closely related to the devil-may-care Andalusians than to sober Castellanos. They are perhaps the foremost exponents of the "*Viva Yo*" mentality—believing, in a lighthearted way, that the world revolves exclusively around them.

The Madrid I knew so long ago was much smaller, more personal, and slower paced. Everyone seemed to know everyone else, friends lived near to one another and gathered regularly at one another's homes, in nearby tapas bars, and in restaurants. *Tertulias*—leisurely afternoon reunions of friends and fellow professionals—were daily occurrences (and continue to be today) and provided an opportunity to exchange views, talk business, discuss politics, and catch up on the latest jokes.

Madrid even then had undeniable polish and a fun-loving spirit, but it is of course a much larger city now and a whirlwind of activity. It dominates the international spotlight and seems to be hurtling breathlessly toward the twenty-first century with hardly a pause for the twentieth. Nevertheless, street life continues to be Madrid's trademark, and my old haunts are still there: the cobbled streets of Old Madrid conjure up images of stagecoaches, mysterious inns, and a world of court intrigue and legend. The "bandit" who stands guard with a blunderbuss at the door of Cuevas de Luis Candelas reminds me of the famous outlaw Luis Candelas, who from this ancient tavern, under the steps of the Plaza Mayor, peered through a grating to watch for the law. Bola street, they say, is so named because the son of King Philip II rolled snowballs (*bolas de nieve*) down its hill. Cloaked royalty used to prowl the streets of Old Madrid, seeking anonymity for their peccadilloes in the teeming streets; and in front of one timeworn tavern the painter and bon vivant Francisco de Goya was stabbed by a jealous husband.

There are other pockets of the past amid Madrid's rush to the future. Neighborhood fiestas, called *verbenas*, are popular events: Everyone joins in the street dancing, doing a slow and stately three-step typical of Madrid, called the *chotis*. *Zarzuela*—Spanish light opera (see box, p. 50) that dates back to the fifteenth century—has its loyal fans and an ever-increasing following. And most especially on Sundays a whiff of bygone Madrid floats through the city when the Rastro flea market functions as it has for five centuries; around the Plaza Mayor you may see organ grinders and vendors (they dress in black-and-white-checkered jackets with matching caps) selling crisp rolled wafers (*barquillos*)—a typical Sunday treat; in the meadows along the banks of the Río Manzanares under luminous blue skies, one can picture the languid, voluptuous damsels painted by Goya, enjoying warm summer Sunday afternoons.

Despite these enticing tidbits from the past, the Madrid I know in the 1990s is simply in another league from anyplace else in Spain. While some cities of the world are dying, Madrid is aglow, revitalized, livelier than ever, with signs of prosperity and refurbishing everywhere. By night its freshly painted, creamy white buildings, bathed in silver and gold floodlights, gleam like jewels. Elegant new restaurants seem to appear overnight, nightclubs are scenes of frantic energy until the small hours of the morning, and outdoor café terraces have become places to party (see box, p. 49).

When I visit Madrid today I always sense the heightened excitement, the optimism, and the pride of at last being a European Community member of equal standing. If you sit in the Palace Hotel lobby in the evening and watch the high society of Madrid parade by, dressed with an elegance and style seldom seen at the poshest affairs in New York City, you will feel magic in the air. The electricity, the vibrancy, and unending activity of Madrid—collectively known as "*La Movida*"—is simply without equal. Madrileños today wholeheartedly endorse the traditional expression of self-praise, "*De Madrid al Cielo*" (from Madrid to Heaven).

Of course, this rush into a new era comes at a price. Madrid has lost some of its Castilian character, its cherished traditional ways, and the small-town qualities that were part of the city's charm. Madrileños mourn the loss of several grand boulevards with their mansions and shady promenades. Growth has been anarchic, yet not unexpectedly so. Madrid from its inception was a city on the verge of chaos, wantonly tearing down and rebuilding, designing and redesigning, always impatient to progress to the next project, to the next fashion. It's a capricious city, taking on styles overnight, carrying them to extremes, and discarding them just as rapidly. There is a scramble to catch up, to be more "in" than anyone else in the world. In the past Madrid emulated France and then America, but through it all Madrid has remained Madrid, saving bits and pieces from the past and rearranging them to conform to the present.

Madrid's Past

Known to the Moors as Mayrit, or Magerit, Madrid sits on a hill above the Castilian meseta, on the banks of the Río Manzanares, ringed by mountains. Madrid began its life as a small and undistinguished town of humble white-washed homes, where lambs, pigs, and cows circulated through its streets (well into this century herdsmen retained the right to pass their animals through downtown Madrid on their annual migrations; see box, p. 63). Then Philip II in 1561 made Madrid the nation's capital (before him, monarchs traveled from one residence to another, never establishing a home base). It was a surprising and much-criticized selection, considering the many well-established cities rich in history from which to choose. But Madrid's symbolically unifying location at the geographic center of Spain and its distance from political rivalries and intrigues may have played an important part in Philip's decision.

Once Madrid became the capital, it blossomed, acquiring the elegant veneer and high style of a royal court and becoming a center of wealth and power. Artistically it also gained dominance, attracting some of the finest writers and artists of the seventeenth and eighteenth centuries. Madrid developed, however, at a time when the building boom brought on by the Reconquest of Spain from the Arabs had peaked, and the city was left with

ᴛRADITIONAL MADRID FARE: LONG-SIMMERING COCIDO

If you hear a Madrileño wax rhapsodic over his little "*coci,*" or "*cocidito,*" you might think he speaks of a dear grandchild or a pet poodle. But he is talking about *Cocido Madrileño*, an elaborate boiled meal served in three courses, beginning with soup, progressing to chickpeas (a key ingredient) and other vegetables, and then to a platter of meats, sausages, and quenelle-like meatballs called *pelotas*. It is a dish so popular that it has been praised in poetry and lauded in song and is eaten by aristocrats and common folk alike.

A descendant of the *Olla Podrida*, literally the "rotten pot," which never left the stove and was replenished by anything at hand, *cocido* developed from the Jewish *Adafina*—a similar stew but without pork products. When the Jews were expelled, some stayed behind and converted to Christianity, adding pork, it is said, to their stewpots, either to prove the sincerity of their conversion or to mask their continuing practice of Judaism.

Why, you might wonder, should a dish this down-to-earth continue to stir such fervor in the hearts of sophisticated city dwellers? Simply, it represents tradition and is a comfort food without equal. As the saying goes, there are only two kinds of *cocido:* the good ones and the better ones.

no distinguished cathedral and without grand churches. Instead, Madrid became a city of fine civilian architecture and lavish interiors.

Little is left of Madrid's more distant past. Of the Moorish quarter, the squares of Puerta de Moros, Los Carros, Cruz Verde, and Alamillo remain; its Mudéjar architecture has disappeared (except for San Nicolás church, San Francisco convent, and the tower of Pedro el Viejo); and from the times of the Catholic Kings the Lujanes tower stands. What makes the city handsome and distinguished are works from later periods, like the Royal Palace, the city's many monumental fountains, its gracious grand squares, and its stately eighteenth century neoclassic architecture. To compensate for its lack of older monuments, Madrid instead became a compilation of Spain's history and artistic wealth through its impressive museum collections, some gathered by the kings of Spain.

ᴠISITING MADRID

Because of Madrid's relative "newness," its neighborhoods are well defined. A route through the city that begins at the Plaza Mayor and ends on the modern extension of Paseo de la Castellana is a march through time. From the city's oldest streets, narrow and winding, that developed around Madrid's first important street, Calle de Segovia, you pass to a distinguished seventeenth century historic district in the style of the Hapsburg dynasty, known as "Madrid of the Austrias." This was a Madrid known to classic writers like Cervantes, Calderón de la Barca, and Lope de Vega, and the city that Velázquez called home. It centers on the splendid Plaza Mayor and includes a collection of fine Renaissance buildings such as the monastery of the Descalzas Reales.

In the eighteenth century the Bourbons came to power, and Charles III gave Madrid the neoclassic look it has today: the "Madrid of the Bourbons" centered on the grand boulevard of the Paseo del Prado. Charles III was Madrid's great builder and urban reformer who paved the streets and installed sewer systems. He was responsible for the reconstruction of the Royal Palace (it had been destroyed by fire), for the Prado Museum, for the Botanical Gardens, for the city's monumental gateways and fountains, broad boulevards, and networks of roads leading from Madrid to Spain's other major cities. Eighteenth century Madrid was haunted by Goya, and court musicians—Scarlatti and Boccherini—lived here. Extending beyond the city of the Bourbons, the fashionable residential neighborhood, Barrio de Salamanca, arose in the nineteenth century, and farther north, in this century, the newest expansion of the city was built.

Since Madrid's districts are clearly defined and main arteries are few, it is easy to grasp the layout of the city. Most of the areas where I spend my time, and where you will want to be, spring like tree branches from one central trunk, the wide and lushly shaded boulevard that takes three different names as it passes through the city: Paseo del Prado in its trajectory past the Prado Museum, Paseo de Recoletos as it continues north, and Paseo de la Castellana as it approaches the newer quarters of the city. Madrid's principal plazas and museums fall along the same course. Its shopping streets and restaurants spring from the branches of this boulevard.

As capital and center of business, Madrid is also the focus of the country's restaurants. Twenty years ago you could count the city's fine eating establishments on one hand (Jockey, Horcher, Club 31, the Ritz—all still thriving). But today gastronomy plays a lively role in city life and is infinitely varied, from down-to-earth and traditional to elegant and creative. Madrid also features an ever-growing number of foreign cuisines and is a melting pot of regional Spanish cooking;

MUNCHING ON CHURROS

Undoubtedly the nutritional worth of *churros*, made from a batter of flour, salt, and water, then looped into circles and fried, is nil. And yet when freshly fried, then dipped in sugar or dunked in thick hot chocolate, they are irresistible.

You can find *churros* all over Spain at the breakfast hour, and at local festivals they are usually fried outdoors in huge vats. But in Madrid, especially at the classic Churrería de San Ginés, which has been serving *churros* since the last century, eating *churros* is a ritual. When its doors open at 4:00 a.m. a long line of bleary-eyed Madrileños has already formed. Some who patiently wait are the last remnants of the party crowd from nightclubs and discotheques, here for a last bite before bed. They mix with laborers who come to fortify themselves for the workday ahead.

The *churrería* has a loyal staff that doesn't seem to mind the odd working day, from pre-dawn until 10:00 a.m. and then from 5:00 p.m. to 10:00 p.m. (to serve those in need of a pre-dinner snack). La Churrería de San Ginés is an enduring link between modern Madrid and its picturesque past.

although Madrileños generally favor Castilian and Basque cuisine, you can take a complete gastronomic tour of Spain without ever leaving the confines of the city.

Despite Madrid's inland location, Madrileños are fish fanatics; they demand the freshest and best-quality fish and shellfish, and they get it. Caravans of trucks, even fleets of private planes, rush seafood in from all coasts of Spain (a traditional Christmas dish, *Besugo a la Madrileña*—porgy Madrid style—is also called "*mata mulo*"—mule killer—because of the speed with which the fish was transported to the capital). Fish that is auctioned in the ports in the afternoon is on exhibit, glistening fresh, the next morning in Madrid markets and in restaurant showcases. Such displays, appetizing and artfully arranged, are called *joyerías* (jeweler's showcases), and from a gastronome's viewpoint certainly rival Tiffany's. Lobster, langoustine, spider crabs, shrimp, prawn, barnacles (see box, p. 230), clams and oysters, *angulas* (see box, p. 267), hake, halibut, red snapper, striped bass, tuna, salmon, trout, and turbot are part of what seems like an infinite array.

Creative cooking is the fashion, and in Madrid there are world-class restaurants practicing the art. Gone is tired French fare, once the standard by which elegant dining was measured. A new generation of innovative chefs is blending the best of Spain's incredibly good native produce into exciting variations on traditional dishes, and into completely new creations of *la nueva cocina española*. The first restaurant in Spain to receive Michelin's coveted three stars was Zalacaín in Madrid.

But the traditional foods of Madrid and Castilla are still the sentimental favorites. You may have a yen for an elegant dining experience, but for local flavor, distinctive to Madrid, seek out simpler restaurants. Madrileños love suckling pig and have a passion for roast baby lamb (see "The Province of Segovia"), both cooked in aromatic-wood-burning ovens; they have been served for centuries in the inns of Old Madrid. *Cocido Madrileño*, or chickpea stew (see box, p. 34), and *Sopa de Ajo*, garlic soup, are also foods that bring back warm childhood memories for most Madrileños.

Madrid's customary desserts are simple and appealing: *Buñuelos de Viento* ("puffs of wind")—light doughnuts sometimes filled with custard—and *torrijas* (sugar-coated batter-fried bread). And although breakfast fritters—*churros*—may be associated with many parts of Spain, nowhere are they as important as in Madrid, where sampling them after a long night of partying is a standing tradition (see box, p. 35). Summer is heralded by the appearance of *Leche Merengada*—a wonderfully refreshing cinnamon- and lemon-scented iced milk, sometimes added to cold coffee and called *Blanco y Negro*.

My first introduction to the foods of Spain were the tapas I ate every evening during that first summer in Madrid. And despite all the exciting restaurants in Madrid today, tapas are still my first love. Many of the foods most closely associated with the city are served as tapas, in countless bars and taverns (I doubt there is another European city with so many). Madrid is second only to Sevilla in the variety of tapas served and in the verve with which they are eaten.

Callos a la Madrileña (tripe with *chorizo* in a paprika sauce), *Caracoles a la Madrileña* (snails similarly prepared), and *Soldaditos de Pavía* (batter-fried salt cod) are three tapas most closely associated with the city, but you can also find bars serving popular tapas of other Spanish regions. I have never seen so much *serrano* ham—the best ones from Huelva and Salamanca—consumed anywhere in Spain, despite its extraordinarily high price. In recent years Madrid's addiction to cured ham has spawned "ham palaces," serving exclusively cured hams from all the ham-producing regions of the country.

When I first came to Madrid I was surprised at the long hours Madrileños would spend at cafés, tapas bars, and over meals and coffee. I still love to begin the day with *churros*, progress to before-lunch tapas, and continue with a midday meal with friends or family that ends at perhaps five o'clock with coffee. In the evening we will have more tapas, a late dinner, go bar hopping, and perhaps visit one club for a flamenco spectacle and another to watch the public dance Sevillanas, then pause afterward at Las Terrazas (see box, p. 49).

Perhaps the words of Madrid's famous bandit, folk hero, and ladies' man, Luis Candelas, best sum up Madrid's philosophy of life. Captured by the law and condemned to a public hanging, his last words reportedly were: "Be happy, my beloved city."

SEEING MADRID

It is simple to reach most of the city's major sights on foot. If you have been traveling in a rented car that you will continue to use after your visit to Madrid, stash it away in a garage for the duration of your stay. Traffic is chaotic, and parking is almost impossible. Aside from rush hours (mornings and at about 1:00 p.m. and 7:00 p.m.), I find taxis a quick and relatively inexpensive way to get around. Madrid's bus and subway systems are extensive and reliable.

♦ Avoid August in Madrid; Madrileños abandon the city, and many shops are closed, as are most of the fine restaurants.

♦ Avoid travel to and from Madrid on weekends and at the beginning and end of holidays; delays can be lengthy.

THE MUSEUMS

♦ El Museo del Prado is of course a must in Madrid, but I highly recommend also exploring some of the lesser-known museums suggested below.

♦ All museums are closed Mondays and at lunch hour unless otherwise noted.

MUSEO DEL PRADO   Begun as a place to display the immense art collection of the Spanish kings, the Prado is today one of the world's foremost art museums. Of particular interest is the extraordinary representation of Spanish masters: El Greco (including *Christ Bearing the Cross, The Resurrection, Descent of the Holy Ghost*); hundreds of Goyas (Clothed Maja,

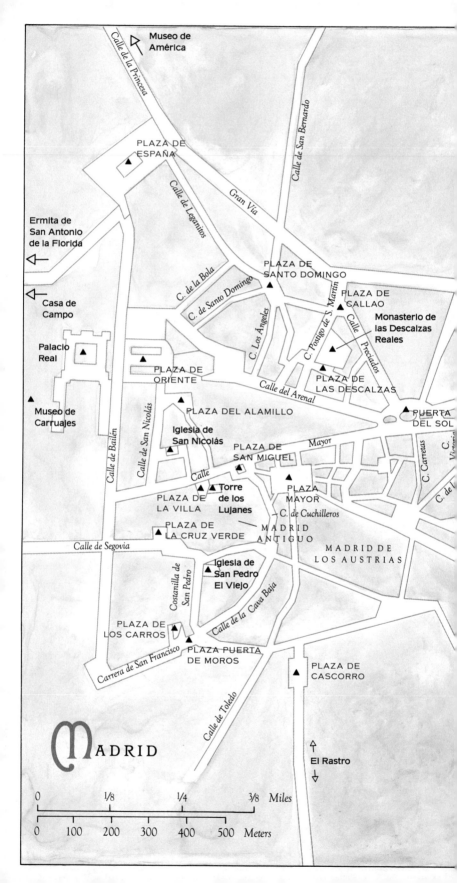

Nude Maja, *Dos de Mayo, Tres de Mayo*, bullfight engravings, and paintings from his "black" period); masterpieces of Velázquez (*Las Meninas, The Spinners, Surrender of Breda*); still lifes and religious portraits by Zurbarán; and many works by Murillo and Ribera. There are also paintings by Titian, Tintoretto, Bosch (his amazingly detailed *Garden of Earthly Delights*), Raphael, Dürer, Rubens, and Van Dyck. One visit will hardly cover the highlights. (No lunch hour closing.)

♦ In the **CASÓN DEL BUEN RETIRO** behind the Prado hangs Picasso's masterly **GUERNICA,** formerly at the Museum of Modern Art in New York. Enclosed by bullet-proof glass and in a huge, dark stone hall, it loses, I think, some of its immediacy, but its emotional impact remains powerful. (See box, p. 275.)

PALACIO REAL   Built at Madrid's highest point, where once the Arab Alcázar stood, then an earlier royal palace that burned to the ground in 1734, the Palacio Real is a fine example of eighteenth century neoclassic architecture of Italian and French influence. It is impressively opulent and quite dazzling, with a wealth of frescoes, tapestries, an extensive royal antique clock collection, finest cut-crystal chandeliers, and gold-leaf furnishings. Not an inch of wall, ceiling, or floor goes unadorned: there are inlaid marble floors, frescoed ceilings, raised ceramic work on walls and ceilings, silk and velvet wall coverings. (Open Mondays.)

The **MUSEO DE CARRUAJES** has a fabulous exhibit of royal horse-drawn carriages, many from the eighteenth century.

In the **REAL ARMERÍA** is an outstanding collection of Hapsburg arms and armor.

MONASTERIO DE LAS DESCALZAS REALES   The daughter of Charles V, Juana de Austria, resided in this exceptional sixteenth century Renaissance palace, founded a convent here, and became a cloistered nun. Royal families retired their illegitimate daughters to this convent when they reached six or seven years of age—thus the collection of dolls and dollhouses. Extravagant chapels, a grand stairway, and a magnificent seventeenth century tapestry collection.

♦ Thirty cloistered nuns still reside here, so visiting hours are short, 10:30 a.m.–12:30 p.m., 4:00–5:15 p.m. (Friday and Sunday mornings only.)

MUSEO ARQUEOLÓGICO   This is an admirable assemblage of artifacts and objects from Spain's rich prehistory and ancient history. Among my favorite pieces are the unique statues made by pre-Roman indigenous Iberians, surprisingly sophisticated in artistic detail and uncommonly expressive—note especially the *Dama de Elche* (see box, p. 387) and the *Dama de Baza*; the striking royal crowns and jewelry of the seventh century Visigothic *Tesoro de Guarrazar*; and outstanding examples of Moorish decorative arts, such as the splendid tenth century ivory jar from Zamora. (Mornings only.)

♦ If you haven't seen the extraordinary Cuevas de Altamira (Altamira Caves) in Santander province, see the reproduction, below ground, just in front of the museum entrance.

REAL ACADEMIA DE BELLAS ARTES DE SAN FERNANDO   The academy, established in the eighteenth century by Philip V, was moved by Charles III to its present location in this Baroque palace. There are several paintings by Goya, Murillo, and Zurbarán, and a fine collection of early twentieth century Spanish art. (Open Mondays.)

✦ Available for sale are quality engravings from original plates, many of them by Goya.

REAL FÁBRICA DE TAPICES   Exquisite tapestries and rugs are exhibited here and continue to be woven as they were in the eighteenth century. This Royal Factory supplies the Royal House, and its works are in demand by many elegant hotels and private establishments. (Mornings only; open Mondays, closed Saturdays and Sundays.)

ERMITA DE SAN ANTONIO DE LA FLORIDA   This hermitage has an extraordinary cupola, painted in oil and watercolor by Goya. It shows a scene of elegant women (he used real people of the period as models) witnessing a miracle, and is painted in the somewhat impressionistic style of late Goya: unstudied, natural, and vibrant (be sure to bring binoculars). The artist's mausoleum is also here. (Closed Wednesdays.)

MUSEO DE AMÉRICA   A fine collection of Inca and other American treasures and documents. (No lunch hour closing.)

MUSEO LÁZARO GALDIANO   The eclectic personal art collection of José Lázaro Galdiano is displayed in what was his private mansion. Spectacular antique ivory carvings; enamels of amazing detail and intricacy; Renaissance jewelry of fascinating design; cloisonné boxes and paintings by Spanish, English, and Italian masters. (Mornings only.)

MUSEO DE ARTES DECORATIVAS   In this stately town house with *artesonado* ceilings are six floors of mostly Spanish decorative arts, from crystal, ladies' fans, crèches, and dollhouses to wood-inlay boxes, ceramics, jewelry, embroidery, wrought-iron and antique furniture. On the top floor there is a beautifully reproduced Valencian kitchen. (Mornings only.)

CENTRO CULTURAL REINA SOFÍA   In an eighteenth century neoclassic building, to which exterior glass enclosed elevators have been added, this museum has an excellent collection of works by Miró, Dalí, and Picasso and stages important art exhibits. (Closed Tuesdays; no lunch hour closing.)

OTHER VISITS IN THE CITY

EL RETIRO   This is one of Europe's great parks, once the gardens of a nearby palace that was a royal retreat. There is a grand promenade lined with distinguished statuary of Spanish monarchs, as well as a large lake (rowboats to rent), lush greenery, and well-tended gardens. It is a cool respite from the rigors of sightseeing.

EL RASTRO   Go to Madrid's famous flea market Sunday mornings for the lively ambiance (beware of pickpockets). Unfortunately, most of the outdoor stalls no longer sell antiques, just trinkets from Hong Kong. For quality items (but no bargains) go to El Rastro's permanent antique shops, which are also open during the week.

CASA DE CAMPO   Near the banks of the Río Manzanares, this wooded parkland was acquired by Philip II to be part of the palace grounds. Madrileños like to spend relaxing Sunday afternoons here.

PLAZA DE TOROS   The "cathedral" of bullfighting, on a par with the Maestranza of Sevilla. The best bullfighters and most knowledgeable fans come here.

PUERTA DEL SOL   This once-important gateway to the city is today restored to its harmonious nineteenth century design. Puerta del Sol is "kilometer 0"; from here all major Spanish roads mark distances. Madrileños ring in the New Year in the Puerta del Sol by eating twelve grapes, one for each chime struck before midnight.

A plaque on an eighteenth century government building (now police headquarters) commemorates the spontaneous uprising of the citizens of Madrid on May 2, 1808, against the troops of Napoleon, marking the beginning of the War of Independence. Losses were appalling, but the blind courage of the people was never forgotten; Goya's masterpiece *Dos de Mayo* that hangs in the Prado museum graphically records the event.

◆ **CALLE VICTORIA** extends from the Puerta del Sol and is filled with tapas bars and bullfight fans who congregate to discuss *las corridas* and buy tickets.

PLAZA MAYOR   A masterpiece of Renaissance architecture, this square was built in the seventeenth century and recently restored to its original beauty. A statue on horseback of Philip III, responsible for construction of the plaza, is at its center. The plaza is a large, perfect rectangle, in contrast to the narrow twisting streets that emerge from it. Once the commercial hub of Madrid, guild artisans set up shop under its porticoes, bullfights, fiestas, and autos-da-fé were held, and kings were crowned. This is a popular nighttime place for tapas bars, outdoor cafés, and alfresco dining. In summer there are festivals of music and dance.

◆ On Sunday mornings an important philatelic market takes place under the porticoes of the plaza.

◆ The streets of Old Madrid radiate from the Plaza Mayor. See especially the Calle Cuchilleros and Cava Baja, both filled with tapas bars and *mesones*. There are still some centuries-old posadas there and old-fashioned shops selling wood and ceramic utensils.

THE MONUMENTAL FOUNTAINS AND PLAZAS

Beautiful plazas and squares, many from the eighteenth and nineteenth century expansion of the city, are a feature of Madrid. Some of the more famous ones include: **PLAZA DE LA INDEPENDENCIA,** incorporating the old

Puerta de Alcalá gateway to the city; **PLAZA DE CIBELES,** centering on one of Madrid's most recognizable landmarks, the goddess of fertility in a lion-drawn carriage; **PLAZA DE NEPTUNO** or **PLAZA CÁNOVAS DEL CASTILLO,** and its famous Neptune fountain, bordered by a magnificent assemblage of great buildings (the Ritz and Palace hotels and the Prado Museum); **PLAZA DE SANTA ANA,** one of the city's most charming and traditional squares, bustling in the evenings with tapas-bar activity; **PLAZA DE ESPAÑA,** in downtown Madrid, in size more like a park than a plaza and dominated by the figures of Don Quijote and Sancho Panza; **PLAZA DE ORIENTE,** built during the brief French domination of Spain as the beginning of a monumental boulevard to cut across Madrid. The plaza today has gardens, statuary, and the Royal Theater; **PLAZA DE LA VILLA,** near the Royal Palace, framed by lovely historic buildings.

FIESTAS

SAN ISIDRO   A week of festivities, May 8–15, in honor of Madrid's patron saint. Bullfights every day featuring the country's top toreros.

LAS VERBENAS   Neighborhood festivals in traditional Madrid style. (Second week in June for San Antonio; second week in August for La Paloma; and San Isidro—see above.)

STAYING IN MADRID

PALACE   Plaza de las Cortes 7   tel. (91) 429 75 51   Every night is a show as Madrid's upper crust saunters through the hotel's elegant lobby on the way to the hotel ballrooms for weddings and other society-page affairs. This stately turn-of-the-century hotel is my hands-down favorite for style, ambiance, and location. (Deluxe.)
◆ The restaurant is topnotch, with faultless service to match the outstanding food. (Very expensive.)

RITZ   Plaza de la Lealtad 5   tel. (91) 521 28 57   The grande dame of Madrid hotels, the Ritz is impeccably elegant and deluxe in every detail, with a price to match. Its formality, however, is not to all tastes—for example, jackets and ties are required in the bar. (Ultra Deluxe.)
◆ The Ritz has always been known for fine dining in its opulent dining room. In the hotel's delightful gardens, lunch, dinner, and a popular Sunday brunch are served.

WELLINGTON   Velázquez 8   tel. (91) 575 44 00   A sleeper, but highly praised by those who appreciate its peaceful location in the Barrio de Salamanca near the Retiro park, convenient to sights and shopping. (Very expensive; pool.)

VILLA REAL   Plaza de las Cortes 10   tel. (91) 420 37 67   A new hotel in a beautifully restored building right next to the Palace Hotel. Villa Real is stylish but relatively small and lacking some of the excitement of a big-city hotel. (Very expensive.)

SOL LOS GALGOS   Claudio Coello 139   tel. (91) 262 66 00   A short distance from major sights, but right next to good shopping on Calle de Serrano. (Expensive.)

SUECIA   Marqués de Casa Riera 4   tel. (91) 531 69 00   The rooms are small, but the location could not be better. Make sure to ask for an exterior room that has been renovated. (Moderate–expensive.)

ALCALÁ   Alcalá 66   tel. (91) 435 10 60   Small, peaceful and well located. Rooms face either an interior patio (quiet) or the Calle de Alcalá (noisy). (Moderate–expensive.)

VICTORIA   Plaza del Ángel 7   tel. (91) 531 60 00   It once had old-fashioned charm, but since its renovation, it has only glitz and a good location. (Moderate–expensive.)

HOSTAL RESIDENCIA GALIANO   Alcalá Galiano 6   tel. (91) 319 20 00   A small, simple hotel with a pleasant salon furnished with antiques. Be sure to request a room facing the street. (Moderate–expensive.)

MADRID'S DIVERSITY OF DINING EXPERIENCES

In the city's elegant restaurants, you will see the beautiful people of Madrid and find excellent food that is international and nouvelle in style. For an experience more typical of Madrid, I suggest trying a *mesón* or a restaurant specializing in roasts or seafood. At least one afternoon or evening should be spent sampling tapas.

ELEGANT AND HAUTE

ZALACAÍN   Álvarez de Baena 4   tel. (91) 261 48 40   A three-star Michelin-rated restaurant. Sumptuous table settings and first-rate *alta cocina*. Reserve several days in advance. (Very expensive.)

EL CENADOR DEL PRADO   Prado 4   tel. (91) 429 15 61   Chef Tomás Herranz is the rising young star on the Madrid restaurant scene. An elegant restaurant serving the inspired creations of this talented chef. (Expensive.)

EL AMPARO   Callejón de Puigcerdá 8 (corner of Jorge Juan)   tel. (91) 431 64 56   The chef creates innovative food with a sure hand in this tasteful restaurant on a charming vine-covered alleyway. Praiseworthy desserts. (Expensive.)

JOCKEY   Amador de los Ríos 6   tel. (91) 419 10 03   A bit staid these days, but still serving some of the capital's finest food, both traditional and creative. (Very expensive.)

SEÑORÍO DE BERTIZ   Comandante Zorita 4   tel. (91) 533 27 57   An ever-popular, dependable restaurant serving fine-quality Basque food. Extraordinary hake *al pil pil*. (Expensive.)

PRÍNCIPE DE VIANA   Manuel de Falla 5   tel. (91) 259 14 48   Basque cuisine at its best, very popular among Madrileños. (Expensive.)

CLUB 31   Alcalá 58   tel. (91) 531 00 92   An old-timer, but as stylish as ever. International menu with some Spanish specialties. (Very expensive.)

EL BODEGÓN   Pinar 15   tel. (91) 262 31 37   A framed "still life" of perfectly fresh foods at the entrance and classic décor set the mood for the fine cooking of this always reliable restaurant. (Expensive.)

FORTUNY   Fortuny 34   tel. (91) 308 32 67   A nineteenth century palatial home, now a luxurious restaurant serving sophisticated but somewhat over-priced food. Lovely outdoor terrace for summer dining. (Very expensive.)

HORCHER   Alfonso XII 6   tel. (91) 532 35 96   Of German origins, this Madrid fixture stakes its reputation on outstanding game dishes along with other foods in the grand European style. (Very expensive.)

PARADÍS MADRID   Marqués de Cubas 14   tel. (91) 429 73 03   A newcomer to Madrid but already popular for its Catalan specialties, not normally found in Madrid, like *pulpitos* (tiny octopus), *espardenyes* (sea cucumbers), and a variety of wild mushrooms and codfish preparations. (Expensive.)

STRICTLY SEAFOOD

LA TRAINERA   Lagasca 60   tel. (91) 576 80 35   Simply prepared fish of freshness beyond compare. The sole and hake are unbeatable. (Expensive.)

LA DORADA   Orense 64–66   tel. (91) 570 20 04   Seafood that transports you to Andalucía. Every bit as good as its parent restaurant of the same name in Sevilla (for specialties, see p. 429). (Moderate–expensive.)

COMBARRO   Reina Mercedes 12   tel. (91) 554 77 84   Only the best fish and shellfish from Galicia. The *Merluza Rebozada* (fried hake) is incredibly good. (Expensive.)

EL PESCADOR   Ortega y Gasset 75   tel. (91) 402 12 90   Checkered table-cloths create a casual fishermen's ambiance for Galician seafood. (Moderate–expensive.)

O'PAZO   Reina Mercedes 20   tel. (91) 553 23 33   The same owner and basically the same food as the above, but in a more upscale setting. (Expensive.)

CABO MAYOR   Juan Ramón Jiménez 37   tel. (91) 250 87 76   Although begun as an offshoot of El Molino in Santander, Cabo Mayor has a firmly established reputation in Madrid as a leader in innovative fish cookery using irreproachable ingredients. (Expensive.)

CASTILIAN ROASTS

ASADOR REAL   Panamá 3 (corner Dr. Fleming)   tel. (91) 250 84 60   In a newer neighborhood of Madrid, this pleasant restaurant of soothing décor serves simple but memorable food. My ideal meal: roast red peppers; fried eggs and potatoes (cut up and mixed together—try it!); salad; and roast baby lamb. (Moderate.)

POSADA DE LA VILLA   Cava Baja 9   tel. (91) 266 18 60   A stunning, spacious inn of the seventeenth century in Old Madrid for roast lamb and for *Cocido Madrileño*, served only at lunchtime (see box, p. 34). Excellent *serrano* ham and cured pork loin. (Moderate.)

CASA BOTÍN   Cuchilleros 17   tel. (91) 266 42 17   A required stop for all tourists to Madrid (you will find few Madrileños here), this charming eighteenth century inn in Old Madrid continues to serve fine roast suckling pig and baby lamb, cooked in an inlaid ceramic wood-burning oven as old as the restaurant. (Moderate.)

MESONES AND TASCAS

These are rustic restaurants, typically Madrileño, and most are located in Old Madrid.

CASA LUCIO   Cava Baja 35   tel. (91) 265 32 52   Despite being an earthy seventeenth century *mesón* serving simple foods, our old friend Lucio has achieved star status, packing in the rich and famous every day for lunch and dinner. His clientele dresses to kill. The king likes to come here, as do other government leaders, movie stars, and all important visitors to the city. I like the soft-set eggs with shrimp as a first course, then garlic chicken that no one makes like Lucio does. (Moderate.)

ESTEBAN   Cava Baja 36   tel. (91) 265 90 91   A cozy rustic setting where owner Esteban warmly attends to his loyal clientele. The specialty is roast shoulder of baby lamb. (Moderate.)

LA BOLA   Bola 5   tel. (91) 247 69 30   Centuries old and still serving its celebrated *Cocido Madrileño* (see box, p. 34), simmered slowly in individual earthenware crocks over a wood-burning stove. (Moderate.)

CASA PACO   Puerta Cerrada 11   tel. (91) 266 31 66   A tradition in Old Madrid for steaks, served on sizzling platters and accompanied by Valdepeñas wine. (Moderate.)

LA CORRALADA   Villanueva 21   tel. (91) 576 41 09   Always busy with those who know they will eat well at a reasonable price in this antique-laden country-style restaurant. (Moderate.)

BUEY II   Plaza Marina Española 1 (near Plaza de Oriente)   tel. (91) 541 30 31   Extremely busy, and almost everyone orders the same item: sliced steak cooked right on the fiery dinner plate and accompanied by a mustard sauce. (Moderate.)

MAKING THE ROUNDS
OF MADRID'S TAPAS BARS

DOWNTOWN AND OLD MADRID

Tapas bars in this area cluster around the Puerta del Sol, Plaza Mayor, Plaza de Santa Ana, and along Cava Baja and Victoria streets. I have put them in a rough order so that you can plot a course to cover several of them. The tour begins on Calle Libertad, not far from the Plaza de Cibeles, then continues into Old Madrid.

BOCAÍTO   Libertad 6   Of cheerful Andalusian inspiration, with overwhelming variety and ensured freshness. You can also order a full meal from the restaurant menu and eat it inexpensively at the bar. There are many more tapas bars along this same street and nearby, like **CASA POLI**   (Infantas 23), an old-timer known for its tapa of cured ham and mackerel.

LERRANZ   Echegaray 26   In a high-tech setting, tapas as only Tomás Herranz of El Cenador del Prado restaurant (see p. 44) can make them. Unbeatable quality and taste—they make an outstanding dinner. Delicious desserts.

LA TRUCHA   Núñez de Arce 6 (also at Manuel Fernández y González 3)   A huge variety of tapas, but specializing in trout, as the bar's name suggests. You can sit down and make a meal of the tapas.

CERVECERÍA ALEMANA   Plaza de Santa Ana   A Hemingway haunt, serving fine *serrano* ham, *Ensaladilla Rusa* (potato and vegetable salad), and a selection of national and international beers.

LA CASA DEL ABUELO   Victoria 12   For generations, it has served nothing but grilled shrimp and a slightly sweet red house wine.

SOL Y SOMBRA   Victoria 1   Great mushrooms simply grilled with garlic and parsley.

VISTA ALEGRE   Pozo 2   *Albóndigas* (meatballs), grilled pimientos, and mushrooms in a bar with a decidedly bullfight ambience.

MUSEO DEL JAMÓN   Victoria 1   Cured hams by the hundreds from various regions of Spain.

LHARDY   San Jerónimo 8   An elegant Madrid classic from the nineteenth century. Serve yourself sherried consommé from a silver tureen, a glass of sherry, and tapas such as chicken and ham croquettes and tea sandwiches. Pay as you leave, on the honor system. Before lunch is the time to come.

LAS BRAVAS   Álvarez Gato   Where a famous and now traditional tapa, *Patatas a la Brava* (fried potatoes with a spicy tomato sauce), was created.

CASA LABRA   Tetuán 12   Dating back to the last century, and famous for its *Soldaditos de Pavía*—batter-fried salt cod.

LAS CUEVAS DE LUIS CANDELAS   Calle de Cuchilleros   An old inn once frequented by legendary Luis Candelas. Bullfight décor, excellent sangría, gazpacho, *serrano* ham, garlic shrimp.

CASA PALACIOS   Cava Baja   Large selection of tapas: snails, chicken wings, and grilled mushrooms.

LOS CARACOLES   Plaza Cascorro 18   In El Rastro, specializing in Madrid's own *Caracoles a la Madrileña* (snails and *chorizo* in paprika sauce).

TABERNA DE ANTONIO SÁNCHEZ   Mesón de Paredes 13   A two-hundred-year-old tavern once owned by famous bullfighter and artist Antonio Sánchez. Madrid's intelligentsia used to gather here.

BARRIO DE SALAMANCA

Most of these tapas bars (and many others) are on and around Calle de Serrano.

JOSÉ LUIS   Serrano 91   Elegant tapas served by tuxedoed waiters: canapés of smoked fish, caviar, and prawns, and one of Madrid's best tortillas (potato omelet).

BAR HEVIA   Serrano 118   The same upscale crowd as at José Luis. Excellent are the smoked fish salad on garlic toast and crabmeat salad.

CASA RAFA   Narváez 68   Madrid's men on the move come here for outstanding *serrano* ham and the best in shellfish tapas (both expensive).

MALLORCA   The tapas bars in these gourmet shops feature mini-sandwiches, tartlets, *empanadillas,* and puff-pastry tidbits (see below for more information).

EL AGUILUCHO   Hermosilla 18   Excellent shellfish tapas.

ASSORTED AND SUNDRY FOOD SUGGESTIONS

CAFE GIJÓN   Paseo de Recoletos 19   Artists, writers, and actors traditionally gather here. Simple foods are available, but I prefer to come in summer for a late-night *Blanco y Negro* (iced coffee with *Leche Merengada*, p. 36), either inside the café or on its lively terrace.

CALIFORNIA   cafeterias   On Gran Vía 39 and 49 and on Calle de Goya 21 and 47, these are always dependable for quick meals, snacks, and good desserts.

RODILLA   On the Plaza Callao near Galerías Preciados, excellent sandwiches, sold in halves with a variety of tasty fillings. Great for picnics.

VIPS   Gran Vía 43 (among other locations)   Open twenty-four hours, VIPS has a little of everything (some groceries, drug items, magazines, etc.) plus a cafeteria popular with young Madrileños.

CHURRERÍA DE SAN GINÉS   Pasadizo de San Ginés   Serves freshly made *churros* (see box, p. 35) for breakfast or as an afternoon snack, with thick hot chocolate.

ANTIGUA PASTELERÍA DEL POZO   Pozo 8   Madrid's oldest pastry shop, famed and unchanged since 1830. *Empanadas* with meat and fish fillings, pastries, and cookies.

MALLORCA   Velázquez 59 and Serrano 6   Each store has an outstanding tapas bar, great takeout foods, and select food items to carry home, like artisan cheeses, fruit compotes, jams, marmalades, *marrons glacés,* and unfiltered olive oil.

GOURMET DEL PRADO   In the Galería del Prado (see Shopping), this is a beautiful store with appetizing gourmet foods, wines, liqueurs, and a small eat-in menu.

EL CORTE INGLÉS SUPERMARKET Calle Preciados You wouldn't expect such an elaborate setup in a major department store, but this is one of the most popular places in town to shop for food. Great selection of liquor and wine, cheese, canned goods, etc.

NIGHTLIFE

CLUBS

CORRAL DE LA MORERÍA Morería 7 tel. (91) 266 84 46, and **CAFÉ DE CHINITAS** Torija 7 tel. (91) 248 51 35, are the best places to hear authentic flamenco. Reserve well in advance.

✦ At **EL PORTÓN** López de Hoyos 25, a form of flamenco called Sevillanas, all the rage in Madrid, is danced by the clientele.

ARCHY Marqués de Riscal 11, and **JOY ESLAVA** Arenal 11, are among the most trendy discotheques. It is the custom to go for *churros* when they close at 5:00 a.m.

WHISKEY JAZZ CLUB Diego de León 7 In the past and still today the best for American jazz in a cozy setting.

OTHER NIGHTTIME SUGGESTIONS

"LAS TERRAZAS" See box. Some of the most popular terraces are on the broad boulevards: **EL HISPANO** and **LA PANOLETA** on the Castellana, **CAFÉ GIJÓN** and **EL ESPEJO** on Recoletos, and **NEPTUNO** on the Paseo del Prado.

BAR HOPPING You can spend the night, as many Spaniards do, just moving from one bar to another. Especially popular are the areas around Paseo de la Castellana, Plaza de Santa Ana, Calle de Echegaray (at one-hundred-year-old **LOS GABRIELES,** Andalusian scenes in tile cover the walls and the bar), and Paseo de la Habana (currently popular is **BORAK** Victor Andrés Belaunde 25, designed to look like a posh living room).

ZARZUELA Typical theater of Madrid (see box, p. 50).

LAS TERRAZAS: EXUBERANT NIGHTLIFE OF THE CASTELLANA

The once-sedate and peaceful outdoor cafés along the broad boulevards of the city have exploded into high fashion, and in summer are crowded and lively, to say the least, until all hours of the morning. Some feature old-fashioned bands, others flamenco music, others nightclub spectacles. But most have nothing more than drinks, tapas, and lots of free-spirited Madrileños.

Las Terrazas, as they are collectively called, are *the* way to spend hot summer evenings in the city. The most popular strip—from the Paseo del Prado and continuing the length of the Castellana—is sometimes called "Madrid's beach," a warm-weather substitute for a trip to the shore. Las Terrazas are certainly the least expensive and one of the most diverting ways to sample Madrid's much-touted nightlife.

ZARZUELA: THE TRADITIONAL MUSICAL OF MADRID

It is the Spanish equivalent of the English musical comedy, Italian operetta, and French *opéra comique*, and yet it is a genre all its own, closely tied to Spanish literary history and to Spain's special musical style. In the past some considered the *zarzuela* vulgar, but Spaniards reveled in its rapid action, variety, lightness, simple folk-oriented themes, and eminently likable tunes.

Zarzuela began in the fifteenth century in the times of the Catholic Kings and was popularized in the seventeenth century when a work by Golden Age writer Lope de Vega, for which he also wrote the music, was performed at the Royal Palace in Madrid. When a play by Calderón de la Barca was set to music and performed for King Philip IV at a hunting lodge outside Madrid, called La Zarzuela (the name, some say, relates to the *zarzas*—bramble bushes—around the palace), *zarzuela* was born and began its climb to mass popularity.

Zarzuela is today making a comeback, in part because of Plácido Domingo's efforts to gain recognition for the music of his homeland. You will always find a production in progress in Madrid, and be it good or mediocre, *zarzuela* never fails to entertain.

La Gran Vía is Madrid's famous shopping street, and the pedestrian mall on Calle Preciados between Plaza de Callao and Puerta del Sol is always busy (the city's two major department stores are there). Luxury boutiques are concentrated on Calle de Serrano and other streets around it in the elegant Barrio de Salamanca. Calle del Almirante, not far from Serrano, features fashions from the hottest designers.

GALERÍAS PRECIADOS and **EL CORTE INGLÉS** Calle Preciados and branch locations The merchandise at these all-purpose department stores ranges from drugstore items to designer fashions and accessories. If food purchases interest you, be sure to visit the supermarket of this downtown El Corte Inglés.

LOEWE Four shops, one on the Gran Vía, two on Calle de Serrano, and another in the Hotel Palace, have leather products of high style and exquisite quality. (Very expensive.)

LA GALERÍA DEL PRADO A stylishly designed two-level shopping center attached to the Hotel Palace, with boutiques, a gourmet shop, café, and an elegant self-service restaurant.

LA VAGUADA A huge shopping mall in a newer neighborhood of Madrid with several movie theaters, and a multitude of restaurants, bars, and boutiques.

MERCADO PUERTA DE TOLEDO This was once the central fish market, but is now a magnet for antique stores, boutiques, and restaurants.

ARTESPAÑA   Don Ramón de la Cruz 33 and Hermosilla 14, both off Serrano street   Government-sponsored shops, with the very finest in Spanish handcrafts from all parts of the country, from rustic to refined, from pottery to furniture.

GAITÁN   Jorge Juan 13   The finest boots and shoes made to order, and as comfortable as slippers. Shoes are expensive, but boots are similar in price to ready-made. Once Gaitán has your mold, you can order anytime by mail or phone.

SESEÑA   Cruz 23   Authentic, fine-quality Spanish wool capes, embroidered or plain, with silver fittings. Traditionally a man's garb and for centuries standard dress in cool weather, these capes are now popular with women as well.

EIGHTH WONDER OF THE WORLD: THE SOMBER EL ESCORIAL OF PHILIP II

IT WAS KNOWN as the Eighth Wonder of the World—no one had seen anything this massive and ambitious before: a monastery, church, palace, and royal pantheon all wrapped into one, the long, low line relieved only by four corner towers and the height of the basilica. Enclosed by a 3,000-foot perimeter of gray granite walls, El Escorial stretched more than the length of two football fields and covered 340,000 square feet. Some considered El Escorial unbearably depressing, gloomy, and unexciting, and many today think the same. But El Escorial was certainly an awesome undertaking and an architectural marvel.

El Escorial was a project that gradually took shape in the mind of Philip (or Felipe) II, the most powerful monarch of sixteenth century Europe, whose empire embraced Spain, Portugal, the Low Countries, a substantial part of Europe and America, the Philippines (named after him) and other South Sea Islands, as well as possessions in Africa and Asia.

Philip had several reasons to build El Escorial. Most immediately, he wished to commemorate Spain's victory over the French at Saint Quentin (the French had supported the pope in an attempt to strip Spain of its Italian possessions). The event took place on the day of Saint Lawrence (San Lorenzo), and the monastery—Real Monasterio de San Lorenzo de El Escorial—is named for the saint. Also weighing on Philip's mind was his father's wish to establish a formal burial site for the Spanish Hapsburg rulers and their families. And third, Philip, an ardent Catholic, pictured a grand monument to his faith as a symbolic repudiation of the Reformation, then sweeping Europe. Perhaps also in Philip's thoughts was the palace his father built in Yuste—also adjoining a monastery—and Charles's austere life in the company of the monks. El Escorial would be much grander, of course, but Philip idolized his father and always sought to emulate his deeds.

Once Philip chose Madrid as the nation's capital, he began his search for a place nearby to make his grand plan a reality. He decided on El Escorial because it was just 56 kilometers from Madrid in the Guadarrama mountains, had an ample supply of pure mountain water and plentiful food sources, especially game, and was cool in summer. Besides, there were quarries in the vicinity that could provide the mammoth quantities of top-quality granite that would be needed for construction. When you travel to El Escorial today you will see mountains everywhere strewn with granite boulders.

The cost ran to many millions of pesetas, or about $45 million, a vast sum at the time, and Spaniards criticized the extravagance. But New World wealth was pouring into the coffers, and Philip believed the worthiness of the project justified its high price.

Despite mounting problems with his rebellious empire, El Escorial was Philip's obsession, and he devoted an inordinate amount of time to the most minute details of its planning and construction. A learned man himself, skilled in mathematics and with clear ideas for the project, Philip evolved a design that was as much his own as it was that of his renowned architects, Juan Bautista de Toledo and Juan de Herrera.

El Escorial takes the form of a gridiron, symbolizing San Lorenzo, who supposedly was roasted to death on such a grill. The basilica is at the center of the complex; the palace, a college, the library, monastery dependencies, and more than a dozen courtyards are in the four quadrants (including the severe and majestic Patio of the Kings). In the "handle" of the gridiron, overlooking the altar of the basilica, were the king's private quarters.

Although Philip was certainly devout and reputed to be unsmiling, cold, and distant, he, like his father, appreciated the finer things of life. Everything had to be the best—expensive and of highest quality, but never showy or ostentatious. There are reams of documents detailing his involvement in El Escorial. He hired craftsmen and artists and rejected any of their works that did not conform to his traditional and straightforward tastes.

Totally out of character was his attachment to the somewhat risqué *Garden of Earthly Delights,* by Bosch (now in the Prado), which hung in his bedroom. He ordered sculpture from Milan, bronzes from Zaragoza, silver from Toledo, wood from Cuenca, jasper from Burgo de Osma, and marble from various parts of Spain. Although he solicited the participation of Michelangelo and Titian, both were already more than eighty years old, and unwilling or unable to travel to Spain. He even took care of his workmen by providing a hospital, housing, and bars for their well being and pleasure, and compensation in case of injury.

Philip took great pleasure in spending time with his family in El Escorial in the summer and traveled there at other times, particularly to celebrate religious holidays. But like his father, Philip suffered from gout that progressively worsened and eventually incapacitated him. When his death was imminent, he asked to be taken from Madrid to El Escorial, where he stoically endured excruciating pain, died, and was interred in the Royal Pantheon on its completion. In his forty-year rule, he enjoyed El Escorial for the last fourteen.

$\mathcal{V}$ISITING THE MONASTERY

◆ Guided tours are no longer necessary; go at your own pace. What you will see is only a small part of the complex; cloistered monks still reside here.

◆ If expense is not a factor, I recommend hiring one of the private guides available near the entrance (about 5,000 pesetas).

ROYAL PALACE   There are two parts to the palace: the original six-teenth century quarters of Philip II (small and simple, as befit his austere nature) and the more lavish eighteenth century rooms of Charles III. Tapestries are notable, especially one of Neptune with unusual movement and flow; and furnishings are from the times of Charles IV. A fascinating wall fresco runs the length of a long gallery and shows in finest detail a massive battle scene between Christians and Moors.

PANTHEON   Just about all the monarchs and queens that were mothers of kings since Charles V (the Catholic Kings and daughter Juana La Loca are in the Granada cathedral; Philip V and Ferdinand VI did not choose to be buried here) are interred in this grandiose yet severe Baroque pantheon below the basilica. Niches are reserved for the present king and queen, and the head of the coffin of Charles V is placed directly under the feet of the priest reciting mass. More cheerful is the pantheon of Los Infantes, for children of royal birth, arranged in circular tiers of white marble and looking somewhat like a wedding cake. Another room is set aside for illegitimate royal children recognized by their fathers. Don Juan de Austria (see box, p. 189) has a place of honor.

BASILICA   As vast as this church is, it was designed for Philip's personal use. The grand frescoed dome is somewhat like that of Saint Peter's but less embellished. The altar is three hundred feet high and made of jasper and marble with gilded figures of Charles V and his wife, and of Philip II and three of his four wives (the other was "Bloody Mary" of England). Doors on one side open to the king's private quarters, on the other to his daughter's. Showcased at the rear of the basilica is a remarkable life-size marble Christ by Cellini.

SALA CAPITULAR   Here hangs El Greco's masterpiece, *Martyrdom of San Mauricio*, which so displeased Philip (see p. 176), as well as other El Greco paintings and works by Bosch, Titian, Tintoretto, Ribera, and Velázquez, all part of Philip's noteworthy collection.

LIBRARY   A treasure of inestimable value. Besides collecting hundreds of prayer books painted with exquisitely detailed miniatures, Philip's goal was to amass every book ever published in Spain. He also had a considerable collection of works in Arabic, Greek, Latin, and Hebrew. The oldest work is from the fifth century, written by Saint Augustine; another is written with fourteen pounds of gold. There are original works by Santa Teresa, an extraordinary sixteenth century Koran, and a fifteenth century Hebrew Bible.

PATIO DE LOS REYES   Six kings from the Old Testament preside here, each carved from a single piece of granite and wearing golden crowns. The basilica dome, seen from here, has a single gold brick, supposedly the last put in place on the completion of El Escorial.

SILLA DE FELIPE II   In the hills above El Escorial are boulders in the shape of seats, where tradition holds that Philip II often came to watch the progress of his project (the views are exceptional from here).

CASITA DEL PRÍNCIPE   A very luxurious but charmingly small palace built in the eighteenth century for the future Charles IV. The walk from town is most pleasant.

THE TOWN OF EL ESCORIAL

El Escorial is a summer retreat for Madrileños, just as it was for the king. It has a charming provincial air, with turn-of-the-century cafés and an ornate but intimate theater from the times of Charles III. I highly recommend an overnight stay in El Escorial.

STAYING IN EL ESCORIAL

VICTORIA PALACE   Juan de Toledo 4   tel. (91) 890 15 11   In Victorian style, Old World but not stuffy. Request rooms facing the rear gardens. (Moderate–expensive; pool.)

PARRILLA PRÍNCIPE   Floridablanca 6   tel. (91) 890 16 11   Spare but adequate accommodations, most reasonably priced. (Inexpensive.) The restaurant is stylish and pleasant, serving well-prepared national and international foods. (Moderate–expensive.)

EATING IN EL ESCORIAL

LA CUEVA   San Antón 4   tel. (91) 890 15 16   Down-to-earth Castilian fare in an eighteenth century inn. Tapas at the bar. (Moderate.)

CHAROLES   Floridablanca 24   tel. (91) 890 59 75   An elegant setting for nouvelle cooking. (Expensive.)

VISITING THE PROVINCE OF MADRID

ARANJUEZ   A town in a valley in which the Río Tajo flows and where there has been a palace since medieval times. Aranjuez was called a "royal place," because kings came here to rest. No wonder. This is a cool, wooded, and lushly green oasis in the arid lands of Castilla and a haven of peace and refinement not far from Madrid. The famous musical composition *Concierto* *de Aranjuez* by Joaquín Rodrigo perfectly captures the elegance and coolness of the place.

In the eighteenth century Philip V took a particular liking to Aranjuez and embarked on an ambitious building project to expand the Royal Palace there. Later kings made more additions, including extravagant formal gardens and ornamental fountains. In the eighteenth century Charles IV built the charming Casita del Labrador (Laborer's Cottage)—an odd name for a luxurious palace in miniature. Visit the palace and the Casita del Labrador, both graced with rich fabrics, Brussels tapestries, frescoes, porcelain walls, and regal furnishings.

The stately town that grew up around the palace of Aranjuez has wide, lineal streets—at the time, in the eighteenth century, a model of urban planning.

♦ You can rent a rowboat in summer and take a leisurely tour along the river, through the "floating" gardens.

♦ Along one of the oldest railroad lines, which rushed the prized strawberries of Aranjuez to Madrid, runs the steam-powered Strawberry Train, which carries tourists on excursions to Aranjuez.

♦ Aranjuez is also known for its green asparagus. You can buy it and the above-mentioned strawberries, in season, at local stands.

At **LA RANA VERDE**   Reina 1   tel. (91) 891 32 38, sample the asparagus and strawberries of Aranjuez plus frog's legs. The Río Tagus flows past the restaurant. (Moderate.) Or try **CASA PABLO**   Almíbar 42   tel. (91) 891 14 51, a well-regarded long-time restaurant that serves Aranjuez specialties. (Moderate.)

CHINCHÓN   A white town that I especially like, unspoiled despite its proximity to Madrid. Steep cobbled streets lead down to the main attraction, an exceptional Plaza Mayor. Large and unpaved, and roughly circular, the plaza is faced by three-story green-trimmed houses with wood balconies from which to observe the bullfights, held here since the sixteenth century. Quinine is named after the Countess of Chinchón. (See box, p. 56.)

♦ The old-fashioned bread bakery off the plaza sells elaborately braided breads.

PARADOR DE CHINCHÓN   Generalísimo 1   tel. (91) 894 08 36, was a seventeenth century Augustine monastery, beautifully rebuilt and restored. (Expensive; pool.)

MESÓN CUEVAS DEL VINO   Benito Hortelano 13   tel. (91) 894 02 06, is a large country restaurant with a hearth as its centerpiece, and huge wine jugs (*tinajas*), wine presses, and grain mills are on display. Castilian fare—I like the lamb chops, grilled *chorizo*, roasted red-pepper salad, and the hearty jug wine of Chinchón. Very good *hojuelas* (fried pastries) for dessert or packaged to take home. Finish with a glass of local anise-scented Chinchón liqueur. (Moderate.)

♦ The town's fiesta is July 25, when the plaza is closed off and once more becomes a bullring.

JARAMA VALLEY   Scene of a bloody Civil War battle between the Nationalists and the Republicans, aided by the American Abraham Lincoln Brigade, in which there were more than three hundred American casualties. The peaceful green valley belies the wartime tragedy.

QUININE: THE MIRACULOUS CURE OF THE COUNTESS OF CHINCHÓN

Don Luis Jerónimo, seventeenth century Count of Chinchón, and Viceroy of Peru by order of the Spanish king, set off on his assignment to the Spanish colony of Peru with his wife, Doña Ana de Osorio. Once there, however, she fell ill, overcome with a mysterious fever for which European medicine knew no remedy. In desperation, the countess resorted to an Indian potion and miraculously recovered from what would later be known as malaria.

In 1632 she brought this magic medicine, made from tree bark, to Spain and gave it to Cardinal Lugo, who in turn took it to Rome. The Jesuits promoted the remedy under the name "Powders of the Countess" or alternately, "Powders of the Jesuits."

Swedish botanist Carolus Linnaeus christened the native tree from which the medicine came cinchona, and the medicine acquired the same name, both in honor of the countess (the medicine's name was corrupted to quinine). And although some dispute the connection between the countess and the first use of quinine, her name remains firmly attached to this famous medication—the first chemical ever used to cure an illness.

ALCALÁ DE HENARES

A city of noble history, birthplace of Miguel de Cervantes, and site of a famous fifteenth century university founded by the great educator Cardenal Cisneros. Writers Cervantes, Lope de Vega, Calderón de la Barca, Tirso de Molina, and Quevedo and missionary Saint Ignacio de Loyola all studied here. See the striking Plateresque facade and lovely patios of the university and the elaborately carved marble sepulcher of Cardinal Cisneros in the Capilla de San Ildefonso, next to the university. Visit also the Casa de Cervantes, a reproduction of a house of the writer's times with a modest Cervantes museum.

HOSTERÍA DEL ESTUDIANTE Los Colegios 3 tel. (91) 888 03 30, was once the Colegio de San Jerónimo, founded in 1510 by Cardinal Cisneros for the study of languages. It is now a delightful restaurant in rustic Castilian style. (Moderate.)

♦ In any of the pastry shops around the main square, buy the town's celebrated caramelized sugar-coated almonds, *Almendras de Alcalá.*

EL PARDO Once a royal hunting preserve, then for many years the residence of Francisco Franco, the town of El Pardo has a royal palace, originally built by Philip II but refurbished in the eighteenth century style of Charles III, and a royal retreat called the Casita del Príncipe, both sumptuously decorated with antique furniture, silks, a royal clock collection, porcelains, fine tapestries, and artwork. The nearby **PALACIO DE LA ZARZUELA,** which gave rise to the *zarzuela* musical genre (see box, p. 50), is where King Juan Carlos and his family live.

VALLE DE LOS CAÍDOS This basilica, excavated from a rocky mound in the Cuelgamuros valley, has a 750-foot cross that stands above the mountain and can be seen from many miles away. Built by Franco in tribute to his victory, many consider its combination of religious and military themes and its associations with the Spanish Civil War distasteful. But it is nonetheless a prodigious feat of engineering and among the most impressive and mammoth monuments of the twentieth century.

NAVACERRADA   In the high Guadarrama mountains north of Madrid, this is a popular ski area.

MANZANARES EL REAL   A fifteenth century castle with four turreted towers and outer walls all around that follow the curves of the towers. It has been restored to its former splendor. A beautiful carved stone frieze in Plateresque style runs around the top of the castle.

BUITRAGO   A Roman town founded in 190 B.C. with well-preserved Arab walls and a curious Picasso museum in the town hall set up by the artist's barber, a native of Buitrago, who received paintings as gifts from his friend Picasso when they lived in exile in France. It is a modest collection of autographed books, ceramics, and simple paintings, tastefully displayed.

SANTA MARÍA DEL PAULAR   Carretera de Cotos, near Rascafría   Just over an hour from Madrid, a fourteenth century Carthusian monastery, part of which has been turned into a magnificent hotel, arranged around the monastery's seventeenth century patio. A wonderfully peaceful—monastic, if you will—retreat, where the rustling of leaves, the chatter of birds, and fountains spouting mountain water are about the only sounds you will hear. The monks (today Benedictine) still farm the land and make a semisoft cow's-and-sheep's-milk cheese, in the artisan manner (for sale in the gift shop). In the sixteenth century church of the monastery is one of Spain's most beautifully worked wrought-iron grilles and an alabaster altarpiece of great artistic worth.
HOTEL SANTA MARÍA DEL PAULAR   Carretera de Cotos, Rascafría   tel. (91) 869 10 11   Reserve well in advance (best rooms face the patio). (Expensive; pool.)

2

THE AUSTERE GRANDEUR OF CASTILLA-LEÓN AND THE FERTILE VALLEYS OF LA RIOJA

NTÁBRICA

Puenteday
Villarcayo
San Pantaleón
de Losa
Aguilar de Campo
yes
Olleros
de Pisuerga
Oña
Santa Gadea
del Cid
Frias
BURGOS
Briviesca
Haro
Santo Domingo
de la Calzada
LOGROÑO
BURGOS
Castrojeriz
San Juan
de Ortega
San Millán
de la Cogolla
Nájera
Clavijo
Quintanilla
de las Viñas
LA RIOJA
Covarrubias
Lerma
Viniegra de Abajo
Santo Domingo
de Silos
Salas de los
Infantes
R. Duero
Aranda
de Duero
Peñaranda
de Duero
SORIA
Numancia
Ágreda
Refugio
de Rapaces
Calatañazor
El Burgo
de Osma
SORIA
Fuentidueña
Gormaz
Almazán
llar
San Frutos
Maderuelo
Aylión
Berlanga
de Duero
Morón de Almazán
GOVIA
Sepúlveda
Riaza
Santa Maria
de Huerta
egano
Pedraza
de la Sierra
Cantimpalos
Sotosalbos
Medinaceli
Torrecaballeros
SEGOVIA
La Granja
de San Ildefonso
eal Sitio de Riofrio
DARRAMA

| 0 | 10 | 20 | 30 | 40 | Miles |
| 0 | 16 | 32 | 48 | 64 | Kilometers |

N

INTRODUCTION

CASTILLA-LEÓN occupies the northern portion of Spain's central meseta and is Spain's largest region. It covers more than a fifth of the country and comprises nine provinces. (La Rioja, now an independent region, was once the tenth province, and has also been included in this chapter.)

One might imagine Castilla-León as a vast dry plain, monotonous and austere. But in reality it is surprisingly mountainous, dotted with lakes and reservoirs, and in some areas covered with pine forests or chestnut, beech, and walnut trees. Mountains, often snow-covered, outline the region and rise like walls, virtually isolating Castilla-León from the rest of the country. To the north and west the Cordillera Cantábrica, of which the mighty Picos de Europa are a part, cut off access to the sea; to the south the Cordillera Central, including the Gredos mountains and the Guadarrama range, impede communication with Castilla–La Mancha and Madrid (a tunnel built some years ago through the Guadarrama mountains has considerably eased the problem).

The Duero, one of Spain's largest and most important rivers, forms a wide basin of fertile land and bisects Castilla-León east to west. Historically a life-giving force, the Duero is often referred to as Padre Duero (Father Duero), and in fact many of Spain's great cities are on its banks or on those of its tributaries, the Tormes, Pisuerga, and Esla rivers. Another major river, the Ebro, skirts the northeast limits of the region and is important to agriculture in La Rioja.

Still, what impresses you most in Castilla-León is the immensity of the parched plains and the endless acres of wheatfields. This is the breadbasket of Spain, and the bread here can be uncommonly good. Aromatic bushes like rosemary and

---

FOODS AND WINES OF CASTILLA-LEÓN AND LA RIOJA

GENERAL
Lamb, pork, *chorizo*, black sausage (*morcilla*), game, beans, trout, river crabs, breads

SPECIALTIES
Cordero (lechón) asado—roast baby lamb
Cochinillo (tostón) asado—roast suckling pig
Chuletitas de cordero—baby lamb chops
Cocido—chickpea stew
Judías con Chorizo—bean stew with *chorizo*
Sopa Castellana—garlic soup
Yemas—egg-yolk candies
Queso de Burgos—fresh sheep's milk cheese

WINES
Artadi, Murmurón, Berberana, Imperial, Viña Ardanza, Viña Monty, Viña Real, Marqués de Arienzo, Viña Tondonia, Orozco from Rioja
Pesquera, Valbuena, Vega Sicilia Único, Yllera, Torremilanos from Ribera del Duero
Marqués de Riscal, Martivilli, Castilla La Vieja (*white wines*) from Rueda
Señorío del Bierzo, Guerra, Fontousal from El Bierzo
Señorío de Toro, Gran Colegiata from Toro

QUINTANILLA DE LAS VIÑAS

thyme grow wild and are ideal feed for grazing flocks of sheep. It is impossible to picture the countryside without the sheep that are so closely associated with Castilla. Traditionally Spanish sheep were prized for their Merino wool (see box, p. 63), but today are much more appreciated gastronomically for their tenderness and subtle flavor (see "The Province of Segovia"). The plains also provide ideal terrain for raising fighting bulls, and although bullfighting is closely associated with Andalucía, the Castilian tradition remains vigorous and has produced exceptional bullfighters, such as El Viti and Andrés Vázquez.

La Rioja does not quite fit into the general description of Castilla-León, for its climate is gentle, its land more fertile and well watered, its crops more varied. Nevertheless, La Rioja's historic ties are principally with the Spanish heartland.

Romans and Arabs may have shaped the earlier history of Spain, but Christian Castilla La Vieja (Old Castile), as it was once called, was the birthplace and the very soul of the modern nation. And yet impressive monuments have survived from past civilizations. The Iberians left the remarkable life-size, stone-carved bulls of Guisando (see box, p. 80); the Romans their roads, a grand aqueduct, and the remains of their cities; the Visigoths their temples; and the Arabs imposing fortresses and a lasting influence on Spanish architecture.

The Spanish nation was forged as the Christians pushed the Moors south from Asturias into Castilla-León, where both sides set up defensive positions along the Duero. Spain's legendary hero, El Cid was instrumental in Christian victories that ultimately brought the expulsion of the Moors from Castilla-León in the eleventh century. Massive castles and fortresses, many of which remain, set on hilltops, gave name to the region and are haunting reminders of an eventful past. They are so common in Castilla-León that unless a castle is unusually large, well designed, or well preserved, you may not give it a second glance.

As Moors fled south from the Christian onslaught, Christians who had been living in Moorish Andalucía and who had become subject to increasing persecution, migrated north. They created a new architecture called Mozarabic that combined Christian themes with Moorish style, and is seen more frequently in Castilla-León than elsewhere in Spain. So too the Mudéjar style, legacy of Moorish artisans in Christian lands, which left its mark here with a peculiar style known as Brick Romanesque (the architecture is Romanesque, the execution in Arab brickwork).

As Christian repopulation gained momentum, a semblance of normality returned to life in the region, and trade became increasingly important.

BEANS WITH CHORIZO

Soak 1 pound large white beans in water overnight. Drain and place in a pot with a peeled onion, a few sprigs of parsley, 2 bay leaves, ground pepper, a peeled garlic clove, 1 teaspoon paprika, 3 tablespoons olive oil, a ¼-pound piece of slab bacon, and ¼-pound of *chorizo*. Cover with water and simmer until the beans are tender, about 2 hours. Season with salt, and add 3 tablespoons chopped tomato. Cook 10 minutes more, then let sit a few minutes before serving. Serves 4–5.

Castles that were built in the fifteenth and sixteenth centuries, set on flat land, no longer served defensive purposes but were there to protect trade routes, to guard the paths of migratory Merino sheep, and to house feudal lords in grand style.

The kingdoms of Castilla and León joined in the fourteenth century, and great cities arose. Their names ring of history: Burgos, León, Salamanca, Segovia, Ávila, and Valladolid, all seats of government, learning, religion, and commerce. Pilgrims on their way to Santiago de Compostela (see box, p. 220) crossed the northern sector of Castilla-León and spurred the construction of noteworthy Romanesque churches, great monasteries, and eventually two sublime works of Gothic art, the cathedrals of Burgos and León. In the sixteenth century spectacular examples of the Plateresque style graced, in particular, the city of Salamanca.

Isabel la Católica spent her childhood in Castilla-León and as monarch made it her center of operations. But once Madrid became the permanent home of government and the wool industry declined, Castilla-León went into a deep sleep, from which it is only now awakening. Antonio Machado described Castilla's plight:

> Oh sad and noble land
> of high barren plains, and rocky ground,
> of fields without plows, rivulets or trees;
> decrepit cities, roads without inns,
> and startled country boors without dances nor songs
> that continue to go, abandoning the dying homeland,
> just like your long rivers, Castilla, towards the sea!
>
> Miserable Castilla, once dominant,
> wrapped in its rags, despises what it can't understand.

The climate, it is true, can be harsh—cold and snowy in winter, hot and rainless in summer, turning the land straw-colored and the wheatfields a sea of gold. Countryfolk are amiable but somber and stoic, just what you might expect from a land that does not easily bear fruits and from people living simple lives of hard work. "There is little that is blithesome and cheerful, but much that is melancholy," observed nineteenth century Bible peddler George Borrow. Certainly we are very distant both physically and spiritually from the gay colorful life of the south and from the brightness of Castilla–La Mancha, influenced by southern ways and by a gentler climate.

Even Castilian fiestas can be solemn affairs. The silent processions and the serious mood of the people during Holy Week seems worlds away from the event's counterpart in Andalucía. But as in Andalucía, the bull plays an important role in local celebrations, either as part of the traditional bullfight or when set loose in village streets or in town plazas to sow excitement.

While some Castilian villages can be dreary, others are among the most enchanting in Spain—not whitewashed, flower-laden, and vivacious, as in Andalucía, but built of stone, wood, and adobe, a monochrome of browns that blend into the ocher landscape. An outstanding feature is the village porticoes; houses are supported on stone or wood columns—sometimes uncarved tree trunks—and the deep, covered walkways provide protection from summer sun, rain, winter snow, and cold and are often used as marketplaces. Many of the large and bare plazas that you see were designed

TRADITIONAL SHEEP MIGRATIONS: LA MESTA

For countless centuries the milk, meat, and wool provided by sheep was a means of survival in Spain. But by the fourteenth century, sheepherding had taken a new turn. Spain developed a new breed that crossed African with Spanish stock. The result was an animal that produced wool of incredibly fine quality. Merino wool, as it was called, became a prized commodity all over Europe and a flourishing industry in Spain.

Merino sheep are not barnyard animals; they need open space and, more important, cool mountain air in summer and a warmer climate in winter. From the northern extreme of León they traveled south (and continue to do so today) to Andalucía, then returned several months later. The logistics of moving what by the sixteenth century was a flock of three million became a daunting task indeed.

In the thirteenth century King Alfonso el Sabio eased the problems by creating La Mesta, a brotherhood of shepherds and sheep owners, whose purpose was to maintain the breed, protect the migratory paths (cañadas), and, not incidentally, to collect taxes (tolls were charged en route). Agricultural workers complained of the encroachment on their livelihood by sheep free to consume everything in their paths, but the cañadas were sacred, and the animals passed through open fields, villages, even cities (until the last few decades they even passed through the main thoroughfares of Madrid).

Markets sprung up along the way; Medina del Campo, a crossroads of paths and commercial routes to the northern ports, became an international banking center. Exports boomed, and many of those who lived along the route of La Mesta grew wealthy from the wool and textile industry; some of the noble houses you see in Castilla-León belonged to well-to-do wool merchants.

Spain's wool industry reached a crescendo in the fifteenth and sixteenth centuries, but in the seventeenth century higher prices and diminishing demand destroyed this profitable business. Castilla had devoted up to two-thirds of its land to grazing and was left without a firm income base.

Few men today are willing to accept the lonely life of a migratory shepherd, but the practice does continue, and the rules and privileges, established so many centuries ago, still give the sheep the right of way.

for use as bullrings and for other local festivities. It is this countryside and these villages that draw us back time and time again to Castilla-León.

As you might expect from a region with no exit to the sea, fish does not play a major role in its gastronomy, although the rivers do yield fine trout and tasty river crabs. There is nevertheless sufficient variety in food, and when you have tender suckling pig, just big enough for four portions, and exquisite baby lamb only weeks old, nothing could be better.

Castilla-León also has some of Spain's best *chorizo;* superb black sausage; exceptional bean dishes and chickpea stews; and simple garlic soup (*Sopa Castellana*), which despite its limited ingredients is thoroughly satisfying. Castilian terrain favors such small game as partridge, dove, woodcock, hare, and rabbit, which are prepared in sauces or in escabeche. All these foods find perfect accompaniment in the wonderfully moist breads, coarse and fine, elongated and round, made from Castilian wheat.

Castilla-León has excellent milk products, made almost exclusively from sheep's milk, like the Burgos and Villalón cheeses and *cuajada,* similar to rennet pudding and, when sprinkled with sugar or drizzled with honey, eaten for dessert.

Complementing the food of Castilla-León are some extraordinary wines. Mellow, sophisticated, and today world-famous Rioja wines are made here from grapes grown in the valley of the Río Ebro. Lesser known but rapidly gaining in popularity and prestige are the crisp wines of Ribera del Duero, Rueda, and Toro, all products of the Duero basin.

Castilla-León is so vast and varied that you could easily spend an entire vacation without going beyond its borders. We certainly have spent considerable time here and take enormous pleasure and inspiration from its austere mood, exciting scenery, and memorable foods. But don't be overambitious; you can't do it all in two weeks. Select what most appeals to you and see, for example, some of Segovia, Ávila, Salamanca, Valladolid, and Zamora; at another time León, Palencia, Burgos, La Rioja, and Soria. Castilla-León also combines well with travel to Madrid and with visits to the coasts of Galicia, Asturias, Cantabria, and the Basque Country.

THE PROVINCE OF SEGOVIA

SEGOVIA is an inviting province that borders Madrid, and Madrileños love to come here for weekend outings and for summer vacations. The pine-covered Sierra de Guadarrama rises in the south of the province and is popular for winter sports and appreciated in summer for the fresh air and cool temperatures it provides. Northern Segovia belongs to the thirsty Castilian plain, broken by occasional oases of thick vegetation that grows around the province's many small rivers.

The Roman Aqueduct in the city of Segovia stands in solemn tribute to Segovia's prominence in the first and second centuries A.D. The Moors were here only briefly, yet their influence on architecture throughout the province was considerable. But it was the Romanesque period in which Segovia excelled, producing a surprising concentration of twelfth century churches in a style peculiar to Segovia: with front galleries or porches; one square, flat-topped tower; and profuse decoration. They were often constructed in brick with blind horseshoe arches, in the Mudéjar style (the province forms part of what is called the "Route of Brick Romanesque"). In medieval times Segovia was frequented by Castilian kings and other royalty, and that is one of the reasons why castles are so common here. Those in Turégano and Coca are among Spain's most distinguished examples.

Once Spain became a nation, royal visits to Segovia were less frequent, limited principally to hunting and to cool summer respites in the mountains. Then in the eighteenth century Bourbon King Philip V fell in love with Segovia and gave the province a new lease on life and a renewed noble presence. The stately palaces at La Granja and Riofrío are products of that later era.

There are beautiful villages throughout Castilla-León, but, to me, Segovia is an anthology of peerless towns in incomparable settings. The village squares, especially those of Sepúlveda, Riaza, Ayllón, and Pedraza de la Sierra, are the epitome of Castilian austerity and distinction. I go to the city of Segovia to see its monuments and other artistic works, but it is the villages that I love best. Most lie along what I like to call the "Route of Roast Lamb." You can plan an appetizing trip of eating and sightseeing, beginning in the city of Segovia and proceeding up the eastern length of the province through the best of the Segovian villages, eating at the many celebrated *asadores*, restaurants featuring wood-burning ovens. Certainly you should not miss Coca castle in the western part of the province, but that could be visited en route to Valladolid.

For centuries lamb was a key ingredient in Segovia's economic wellbeing. Seasonal sheep migrations (see box, p. 63) passed through the province, and textile production based on lamb's wool was for a time a flourishing industry. Not surprisingly, lamb became and continues to be a tantalizing feature of local gastronomy.

Segovia to me means roast lamb and, to a lesser extent, suckling pig, and I have often come here expressly for these two great delicacies of Castilian cooking: to the city of Segovia for suckling pig, but most especially to the villages that specialize in baby lamb. Centuries ago, these succulent meats were the pleasure of the rich and royal, and the objects of boisterous feasts, but today the roads clog on weekends with commoners from Madrid seeking simple foods of the land. In village squares cars park every which way, and country inns are scenes of tumultuous activity. There are fine lamb and suckling pig all over Castilla-León, to be sure, but Segovia provides the ideal by which all the rest are measured.

Baby pig (*cochinillo*) and lamb (*cordero lechal*) are traditionally roasted in vaulted brick baker's ovens (villagers used to, and often still do, take their meats to the local bakery for roasting). So exquisite is their taste that nothing but a sprinkling of salt is added. This special oven (*horno de asar*), however, is essential to give the skin its special crackle and impart the flavors of

WILD MUSHROOMS, SEGOVIA-STYLE

Brush clean wild or cultivated mushrooms, cut in halves or quarters, and place in a shallow greased casserole dish. Sprinkle with minced garlic and parsley, bread crumbs, salt, pepper, and olive oil. Place in a 450°F oven for about 15 minutes, sprinkle with lemon juice, and serve.

the aromatic woods that light the fires.

Suckling pig is only weeks old and so small that typically it feeds just four diners, so tender that it is traditionally cut up with the edge of a dinner plate. It has a skin so crisp that I would be happy to make a meal of it. Properly presenting a suckling pig to table is a ritual going back at least to the times of Castilian King Enrique IV, half brother of Isabel la Católica, who decreed that only nobility could perform pig-cutting ceremonies unless royal permission was otherwise granted.

Cándido López, Master Innkeeper of Castile (so named by King Juan Carlos) and owner of Mesón de Cándido in the city of Segovia, is in possession of just such permission—today, of course, merely symbolic. Although Cándido, as he is universally known, is an octogenarian, he still takes great pleasure in performing his duties. I have seen him take command of the dining room (he only does this for large dinner parties) while his assistants bring in the roast pigs and read the royal edict of Enrique IV. Without further ado Cándido quarters the pigs with the edge of a dish and dramatically tosses the plate to the floor, where it shatters. There is a moment of stunned silence, followed by the cheers of diners. He departs just as suddenly as he had appeared.

Piglets are kept carefully protected in villages and on farms and are not at all in evidence as you travel through Segovia, but you will have no doubts that this is lamb country. Along the vast plains, lone shepherds and their loyal dogs tend to the flocks, which graze on wild herbs like sage, thyme, and rosemary, which grow in bushy clusters. Baby lambs, however, are nurtured solely on mother's milk and do not have a trace of the muttony taste sometimes associated with lamb; the meat is tender enough to cut with a fork.

For Spaniards, discussions about *the* best place to eat lamb, the superiority of the left forequarter (the young lamb rests on its right side, ever so slightly toughening the meat), and remembrances of indulgences past are almost as important as the act of eating. Villages like Cuéllar, Riaza, Turégano, and Pedraza de la Sierra are names that come to mind in connection with roast lamb, but if one place were singled out, it would be Sepúlveda. Even the king of Spain comes to this village when he seeks roast lamb, and more specifically to the humble setting of Figón Zute El Mayor.

Ebullient Martín Antoranz Albarrán, known by all as Tinín, single-handedly takes care of the restaurant. He accompanies the lamb with equally simple foods: salad, a round loaf of Castilian bread, and a jug of hearty local red wine. Dessert is Manchego cheese (made from sheep's milk, naturally) and quince paste. We like to make it a long and sensuous meal, during which each morsel of meat is lovingly savored and the bones picked clean. When our appetites have finally been sated and the table littered with bread crusts, plates piled high with bones, empty earthenware casseroles, and wine jugs, the scene somewhat resembles a spectacle of medieval gluttony.

Although lamb and suckling pig capture the gastronomic spotlight in Segovia, there is much more good eating. It is no wonder that lamb chops, tinier than I'm sure you've ever seen them, are also a treat. *Chorizo* from Cantimpalos receives high praise in Spain and is a part of the tasty Segovian dish *Judiones de la Granja*, a stew of oversize broad white beans from La Granja. Other Segovian specialties are wild mushrooms from the pine forests, in garlic sauce (*Níscalos a la Segoviana*) (p. 66), and Segovia's celebrated dessert, *Ponche Segoviano*, a liqueur-dipped, custard-filled cake frosted with marzipan.

THE CITY OF SEGOVIA

On a cliff rising between deep valleys and gorges and against the backdrop of the Sierra de Guadarrama, Segovia is immediately impressive. A natural fortress, the city is long and narrow, protected by the Eresma and Clamores rivers on either side and reinforced by walls, and is often described as resembling a beached ship. The narrow wedge where the Alcázar castle dramatically stands forms the prow, the cathedral the masts, and the Roman Aqueduct the stern. Within these confines is a tawny-colored city of old churches and mansions, humble houses, and centuries-old inns.

The great Roman Aqueduct stands guard at the entrance to Segovia. The largest and best preserved from the Roman Empire, it is a remarkable engineering achievement, of a scale unmatched by succeeding civilizations. At its greatest height, where its arches are two-tiered, the aqueduct rises to 96 feet; it is more than 2,000 feet long with some 160 arches, and it boggles the mind to think that these gargantuan granite blocks are set in place without mortar and that the arches are supported only by the pressure of their keystones.

Erected between the first and second centuries A.D. under Emperor Augustus, or Emperor Trajan, the aqueduct still brings water to the city from the Río Acebeda in the mountains of Fuenfría sixteen kilometers away. It overwhelms the city and looms over the houses that stand in the shadows of its arches, dwarfing them to the size of toys. Not only is the aqueduct an extraordinarily practical construction, but it is also a work of exceptional beauty whose presence sets Segovia apart from other Castilian cities.

Segovia was founded by the Celts and became a preeminent city of the Roman Empire in Spain. Portions of the Arab walls remain, but Segovia was never a primary city of the Moors. After the Reconquest, however, it once more rose to prominence. Castilian kings Juan II and Enrique IV, father and half brother, respectively, of Isabel la Católica, made Segovia their capital and continued the church building that had begun after the eleventh century Reconquest. The Alcázar became their official residence, and it was in Segovia that Isabel was proclaimed queen.

Segovia can be seen in the space of a day on a walking tour that starts at the aqueduct, which is at the entrance to town. Just beyond the aqueduct is the Plaza Azoguejo, once a marketplace and still a bustling square. Following Cervantes street, which begins at this square, you will quickly come upon several of Segovia's seignorial homes—the fifteenth century Casa de los Picos is particularly striking because of the pointed stones of its facade, and the sixteenth century palace of Count Alpuente shows Moorish-influenced plaster wall decorations, typical of Segovia, called *esgrafiado*, a word from which graffiti is derived. The San Martín church, on a lovely plaza faced by old mansions, is an exceptional example of Segovian Romanesque and the distinctive galleries that characterize it. It is just one of more than a dozen twelfth and thirteenth century churches in the city.

Beyond the Plaza de San Martín the street forks, and taking either Calle Isabel la Católica or Judería Vieja (once the center of the city's Jewish quarter, where a synagogue stood), you come upon the cathedral, sometimes called the Dama de las Catedrales because of its Gothic grace. It stands tall, on a rise of land that accentuates its slender elegance, and faces two of Segovia's lively main squares, the spacious, porticoed Plaza de la Catedral and the Plaza Mayor. Tapas bars are everywhere, and it's a good idea to sit down, lean back, and take a leisurely look at city life. By way of Velarde or Daoiz streets, both in picturesque quarters, you will arrive at the "prow" of the old city and the Alcázar castle.

Segovia is especially impressive after dark, when the cathedral and aqueduct are illuminated, the tour buses have departed, and the city, its bars and restaurants, are returned to Segovianos. Drive down to the Río Eresma to see the Alcázar from below. I always remember the Alcázar as I saw it one moonlit night, silhouetted against the sky while puffy clouds scuttled by.

But what will stay with you forever is the greatness of the Roman Aqueduct:

And beyond any other building, Romanesque or Gothic, [the aqueduct] is that which gives [Segovia] character, and is what we chiefly remember in any mental picture we have of her. . . . Long after we have forgotten the sweet bravura of the cathedral, the profound sadness of those ruined Romanesque churches, the gaiety of the shady summer streets, and even the beauty of the lonely city herself, abandoned there like a ship in full sail stranded among the mountains, those great Roman arches remain with us, symbols of some majesty that was once in the world. . . .

Edward Hutton

SEEING THE CITY OF SEGOVIA

ROMAN AQUEDUCT   A grand achievement and the monument that dominates the city (see text).

THE ROMANESQUE CHURCHES   The most interesting features of Segovia's churches are their exteriors. See especially **SAN MARTÍN** and its splendid porches, beautifully carved portal, and its cloister capitals, **SAN ESTEBAN** for its original tower of a somewhat Byzantine appearance; **SAN MILLÁN,** one of Segovia's earliest churches from the beginning of the twelfth century, and its Moorish-influenced tower (inside the church some portions of thirteenth century frescoes are preserved); **VERA CRUZ,** thought to have been founded by the Templars (see Index), with its unusual twelve-sided exterior and rounded interior; and **SAN JUAN DE LOS CABALLEROS** and its richly carved portal, beautiful portico, and museum of ceramics and paintings by the brothers Daniel and Ignacio Zuloaga (see Index), respectively.

♦ San Millán and Vera Cruz churches are outside the walls. Pick up a city map at the tourist office in the Plaza Mayor for specifics.

CATHEDRAL   Sixteenth century late Gothic of slender and elegant design, this cathedral has an interior that is spacious and well lit by lovely stained-glass windows from the sixteenth and seventeenth centuries. See the fifteenth century cloister and Gothic choir stalls, both brought from a previous cathedral that stood near the Alcázar; in the Baroque Sagrario chapel is a statue, *Christ in Agony*, by José Churriguera, a creator of the turbulent Churrigueresque style (p. 88). The museum has a fine Baroque Brussels tapestry collection and paintings by Pedro Berruguete (see Index).

ALCÁZAR   Built in the thirteenth century, this castle became the residence of the Castilian kings in the fifteenth century. It was updated by Philip II and given the dreamy appearance it has today by Charles III in the eighteenth century. Its original style was Moorish and said to have rivaled the Alhambra in beauty, but today only two rooms and traces of Mudéjar frescoes remain from those times. Isabel la Católica stayed here before her coronation at the San Miguel church, and Philip II married his fourth wife here.

ROMAN WALLS   The remains of the Roman Walls, rebuilt by the Arabs, are on the south side of the city and very well preserved.

♦ The quickest way to reach Segovia from Madrid is through the tunnel that cuts through the Sierra de Guadarrama, but I prefer the scenic route that climbs through the mountains on a wide, well-paved road to Navacerrada. From that height there are beautiful views of Segovia province. The road descends through thick forests.

STAYING IN THE CITY OF SEGOVIA

PARADOR DE SEGOVIA   Carretera de Valladolid s/n   tel. (911) 43 04 62 Just outside of town, the parador offers views of Segovia that are sensational. This parador is sweepingly modern: high ceilings, spacious salons, black slate floors, and decorated with works of contemporary art and oversize dark-brown pottery jugs. (Moderate–expensive; indoor and outdoor pools.) The restaurant is excellent; try the *entremeses*—a tasting of twenty appetizers—the garlic mushrooms (*Setas al Ajillo*), garlic soup, and other traditional and creative dishes.

EATING IN THE CITY OF SEGOVIA

MESÓN DE CÁNDIDO   Azoguejo 5   tel. (911) 42 59 11   In an unbeatable setting on the Plaza de Azoguejo in the shadow of the aqueduct, this inn was founded in the fifteenth century by the royal innkeeper to Enrique IV of Castilla. Divided into several cozy dining rooms, it has a rustic décor and its interesting memorabilia make a visit here a pleasurable experience. Despite the restaurant's busyness (it's a required stop for illustrious guests to Spain, including heads of state), the food is very good. Try to come in the evening when the atmosphere is more peaceful. The specialty is suckling pig, and I have also enjoyed river crabs in clove-scented marinade, liver in rhubarb sauce, beans (*Judiones de la Granja*), frog's legs, and *Níscalos a la Segoviana* (wild mushrooms with garlic and parsley—p. 66). (Moderate.)

MESÓN JOSÉ MARÍA   Cronista Lecea 11   tel. (911) 43 44 84   Known for its tapas bar, the restaurant also attracts a large clientele with dishes similar to those of Mesón de Cándido. The wine cellar is especially well stocked with wines of Ribera del Duero. (Moderate.)

MESÓN DUQUE   Cervantes 12   tel. (911) 43 05 37   Another popular and attractive *mesón* for suckling pig and other Castilian specialties. (Moderate.)

♦ Tapas activity centers around the Plaza Mayor and the Plaza de San Martín. Try **MESÓN JOSÉ MARÍA** (see above), **LA CONCEPCIÓN** in the Plaza Mayor, and **TASCA LA POSADA** on Judería Vieja.

SHOPPING

There are many stores in and around the Plaza Mayor—among them, **EL ALCÁZAR** pastry shop sells *yemas* (egg-yolk candies) and the typical cake of Segovia, *Ponche Segoviano*. Grocery stores all over the city sell beans from La Granja, which you can take home. **MADRES DOMINI-CAS** (Dominican nuns), at Capuchinas Altas 2, offer artisan polychrome works.

$\mathcal{V}$ISITING THE PROVINCE OF SEGOVIA

EL REAL SITIO DE RIOFRÍO   You would do well to avoid the crowds and come to this "Royal Place" on a weekday. The palace, built by the widow of Philip V in the neoclassic style of La Granja (see below), was used as a hunting lodge. Today it houses a museum dedicated to the hunt and includes a painting by Velázquez, a tapestry by Goya, and dioramas of Spanish wildlife. Deer roam the grounds.

LA GRANJA DE SAN ILDEFONSO   King Enrique IV of Castilla used to hunt here, and he founded a hermitage in honor of San Ildefonso. Much later, in the eighteenth century, Philip V fell in love with the site and undertook the building of this elegant palace, a mix of Spanish Baroque and French neoclassic styles. For the next two centuries it was used as a *real sitio*, a place for kings to relax.

Set in a cool green oasis of thick forest around the Eresma River (a good place to picnic), La Granja has all the elegance you might expect from a "Royal Place": fine artwork, extraordinary Flemish and Spanish tapestries, ornate furnishings, antique clocks, and crystal chandeliers. Philip V, of French origin, sought to emulate France's glasswork and established a glass factory that, in its own right, developed an international reputation. Despite all the opulence, however, what has always impressed me about La Granja is the palace's almost homey atmosphere, created by its small scale and country-decorative details like lace curtains.

Complementing the palace are the Versailles-style formal gardens and twenty-six monumental Baroque fountains, some of which, "Las Fuentes Caprichosas," put on elaborate displays of "dancing waters," rising in tall jets to form sprays that trace intricate designs. Twice a year all of them are successively set in motion. Try to catch one of the shows, July 25, and August 24 at 5:30 p.m. On Thursdays, weekends, and holidays, from May to November, there is a partial display, with four fountains functioning.

King Philip V and his wife are buried in La Granja's Colegiata, one of the few kings of Spain not interred in the Royal Pantheon of El Escorial.

TORRECABALLEROS A little village of medieval flavor, noteworthy especially for a roadside restaurant, **LA POSADA DE JAVIER** Carretera Segovia-Soria s/n tel. (911) 40 11 36, where owners Paloma and Javier have created a charming country setting for well-prepared regional dishes, especially lamb, roasted in an igloo-shaped wood-burning oven. (Moderate.)

SOTOSALBOS In this village bordered by forests there is a magnificent example of a Segovian-style porched Romanesque church, the twelfth-century San Miguel. In the church are some fine Romanesque carvings. **LAS CASILLAS** Eras 3 tel. (911) 40 30 68 (open weekends and holidays), is a charming three-hundred-year-old inn that serves excellent local *chorizo* and roast lamb. (Moderate.)

PEDRAZA DE LA SIERRA If I had to pick the perfect Castilian village, this might be it: frozen in the sixteenth century, it has a fine Plaza Mayor, impeccably kept stone mansions in the color of the surrounding crags, cobbled streets, a castle above the town, where works by the painter Zuloaga are exhibited, and just one entrance through a stone-arched gateway in the walls. Some say this is the birthplace of Roman Emperor Trajan. **EL YANTAR DE PEDRAZA**, in the Plaza Mayor, tel. (911) 50 98 42, offers fine roasts in a charming country setting (lunch only, except in summer). (Moderate.) **BODEGÓN MANRIQUE** Procuradores 6 tel. (911) 50 98 10, is excellent for roast lamb, served at communal tables. (Moderate.) **LA TABERNA DE MARIANO**, also in the Plaza Mayor, is a cozy 150-year-old bar for tapas and regional wines. And the **HOSTERÍA PINTOR ZULOAGA** Matadero 1 tel. (911) 50 98 35, although part of the parador network, does not have accommodations but is an attractive place for a drink or tapas (I prefer one of the above-mentioned restaurants for lunch or dinner).

With the opening of the lovely **LA POSADA DE DON MARIANO**
Mayor 14   tel. (911) 50 98 86, in a restored house of Pedraza, each room distinctively decorated, it is now possible to enjoy an evening in this singular
village. (Moderate–expensive.)

DE NATURA on Matadero street is an unexpectedly sophisticated store, set
in a village mansion, that carries everything from all-natural candies to
antique furniture and unusually designed pewterware made in Pedraza,
which I especially like. Next door you can browse in an antique store featuring rustic furnishings and old-fashioned decorative objects collected from
around the area.

TURÉGANO   The village itself is not outstanding, but the view of the castle from the elongated Plaza Mayor certainly is. This is not really a castle but
a twelfth century church disguised behind defensive walls. The walls were
added in the fifteenth century while Isabel la Católica was fighting for her
right to the throne of Castile (see "Toro," p. 106). The bishop, a supporter
of Isabel's, built the protections around the church so that her husband,
Fernando, could safely stay here.

SEPÚLVEDA   One of my favorite Castilian towns, Sepúlveda is poetically set over the gorges of the Duratón and Carlilla rivers, its buildings blending with the earth tones of the countryside. At its highest point is the
fissured twelfth century castle, into which the eighteenth century town hall
was built. Just above and beyond the castle is the Romanesque church, El
Salvador, porticoed in Segovian style (and said to be the precursor of this
architectural style). Along the arcaded streets are noble residences, and
many Romanesque churches, and through the brick arches at the end of
Calle de Santiago a Jewish community once thrived. Around the main
square stores sell earthenware pots and casseroles in unusual sizes and
shapes, and beans by the kilo, displayed in burlap bags. Sepúlveda's roast
lamb is among the best in Castilla, and I come here often to have it at
FIGÓN ZUTE EL MAYOR "TINÍN,"   Lope Tablada 6   tel. (911) 54 01
65 (moderate; lunch only), a local inn of national renown (see text).

SAN FRUTOS is a semi-abandoned twelfth century monastery on the site
of a hermitage where three siblings took refuge from the Moors and were
later buried then canonized (one of them, San Frutos, is the patron saint of
Segovia). The setting is sensational, surrounded on three sides by the mean-
dering green waters of the Río Duratón and by the gorge of the Duratón.
From the windy heights of the church you will see dozens of circling vultures
that nest in the straight-cut, stratified red cliffs across the river. If you come
to Sepúlveda you mustn't miss this. (From Sepúlveda take the road toward
Peñafiel, about six kilometers. Turn left to Castrillo-Villaseca. In Villaseca,
a road to the right leads to San Frutos.)

RIAZA   A lovely Castilian village, with a circular porticoed Plaza Mayor
and balconies with pretty wrought-iron grillwork. In the plaza, **LA TAURI-
NA**   Plaza del Generalísimo 6   tel. (911) 55 01 05, serves traditional Segovian
fare, like beans of La Granja and roast lamb. (Inexpensive.)

AYLLÓN   The beautiful porticoed Plaza Mayor, over which the belfry of
the Santa María church presides, is reached through the golden-stone El

Arco, a gate in the original walls of this medieval village. The Flamboyant Gothic facade of the fifteenth century Palacio de los Contreras, right within the gateway, is particularly attractive.

MADERUELO   This walled village sits over the Linares reservoir and has become popular as a summer retreat without losing the ambiance of its thirteenth century period of splendor. The unusually stylized and free-flowing twelfth century frescoes from the Santa Cruz church near the reservoir are today in the Prado Museum in Madrid.
◆ A nesting ground for vultures, in a beautiful setting, is not far from here (see Aranda de Duero).

FUENTIDUEÑA   The interior of this town's San Martín church was transported to the Cloisters in New York City, but another, similar church, San Miguel, has been restored, and the imposing twelfth century walls still stand.

CUÉLLAR   As you approach this walled town of noble houses, the brick Mudéjar towers of its many Moorish-influenced churches stand out. Above Cuéllar is an odd fifteenth century castle-palace of mixed styles belonging to the Dukes of Alburquerque. Its double-galleried patio is especially beautiful. Since the fifteenth century the Running of the Bulls has taken place in Cuéllar (last Sunday in August) and is said to be the origin of the famous Pamplona event.

COCA   The town's massive but delicate castle, surrounded by a moat, is built in Mudéjar brickwork in two crenelated tiers and is such a perfect example of a castle in Spain that it almost looks like a Disney creation. In reality it is fifteenth century and Spain's supreme example of civilian Mudéjar construction. Built by Moorish artisans for the bishop Fonseca of Sevilla, it blends Moorish horseshoe arches with architecture of Gothic influence.

THE PROVINCE OF ÁVILA

ÁVILA (*ah-vee-la*), at the southern extreme of the Castilla-León meseta, is backed by the wooded Gredos mountains, which separate the province from Castilla–La Mancha. Ávila's pleasant summer temperatures make the towns of Las Navas del Marqués, El Barco de Ávila, and Arenas de San Pedro favorites with summer vacationers. But Ávila also looks like the dry Castilian tableland, even though parched earth alternates with the fertile valleys of the Tormes, Alberche, and Tiétar rivers, where orchards flourish, tobacco grows tall, and pasturelands are green. Some villages, especially along the Tiétar, resemble the quaint towns of La Vera, which is in the same river valley but part of Cáceres province.

The history of Ávila goes back at least to the Iberians, who left us their massive stone zoomorphic sculptures of bulls and boars. They are sometimes on display in town squares; others are left in the forsaken fields where they have stood for millennia (see box, p. 80). It is thought that Ávila's name originated in those times, when the Celts called the area Obila.

The passage of the Romans through Ávila is marked by stretches of the old Roman road that wind through high, rugged mountains. Known as Vía de la Plata, this was a commercial route from the silver mines of Asturias south to Andalucía. In the city of Ávila the famous walls were built over those first put in place by the Romans. Both are impressive reminders of the tenacity and the building skills of these early conquerors.

With the completion of the Reconquest in Castilla-León in the eleventh century, Christians under Don Raimundo de Borgoña repopulated Ávila, and its modern history began. The king granted privileges to noblemen, who in turn built themselves elegant palaces and sponsored church construction, in the Mozarabic and Mudéjar-influenced Romanesque style of the times. Unable to shake their warrior mentality, they enclosed their houses behind the massive walls of the city of Ávila.

Two great women of Spain, who dared to be different and had a profound effect on the course of Spanish history, were Catholic Queen Isabel and mystic saint and church reformer Santa Teresa de Jesús, both born and raised in the province of Ávila. Another admired mystic and a disciple of Santa Teresa's, San Juan de la Cruz, who wrote poetry of exquisite purity and exalted mystic sentiment unequaled in the Castilian language, was born in Ávila in the village of Fontiveros. All were devout Catholics, whose fervor was perhaps 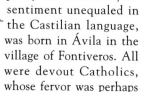 influenced by the long Moslem domination of Spain and by the sense of eternity they found in the unlimited horizons of Ávila.

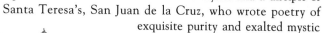

Visits in Ávila, however, are not all centered on the plains, although the city of Ávila and its celebrated walls certainly are. But you should also spend a day or so to the south in the Sierra de Gredos area. Madrigal de las Altas Torres and Arévalo are at the northern tip of the province and are best combined with travel to Salamanca or Valladolid.

There is good eating in Ávila, beginning with the baby lamb and the garlic soups typical of Castilla-León. Particularly characteristic of Ávila, however, are the locally grown beans of El Barco, which when dried and combined with *chorizo* make a delicious stew; roast suckling pig (called *tostón* here); fine young beef from Ávila's pasturelands; trout and frog's legs from the rivers; fruits and vegetables from the orchards. Egg-yolk candies (*yemas*), so closely associated with convent nuns (see box, p. 398), are called in Ávila *Yemas de Santa Teresa* in honor of the province's famous saint. The wines from Cebreros are robust, yet smooth and palatable and well suited to the cuisine.

THE WALLED CITY OF ÁVILA

Before you even enter Ávila, drive to a lookout called Cuatro Postes, across the bridge over the Río Adaja on the road to Salamanca. From there you can see the city's intact walls, and what a splendid sight they are. Encircling the old city, they extend more than 7,500 feet. They are about 36 feet high, 9 feet thick, and punctuated by nine gateways and ninety fortified towers. Look to the far left of the walls, and you will see the cathedral apse built into a portion of the wall.

Ávila was built on a hill—it is the highest capital city in Spain—and its site gave natural protection from enemy attack. But the knights of the Reconquest who settled here in the eleventh century took no chances. Construction of the walls (built over the ruined Roman walls) began immediately, and the palaces and noble houses that followed, embellished with coats of arms, were almost always built close to and sometimes abutting the walls. Such is the case with the sober Núñez Vela palace and the fifteenth century Dávila palace, graced by an unusually elongated coat of arms. Churches were built in the Romanesque style of the times. But once Emperor Charles V decided to move his court from northern Castilla to Toledo, Ávila, along with other great cities of thirteenth and fourteenth century Castilla-León, lost their importance, and further expansion was halted. The population also stopped growing—in fact, went into decline—and that is why the walls of Ávila remain in place and why so many monuments from the Romanesque and early Gothic periods are in evidence.

Ávila is indeed filled with churches, some from the twelfth century, and with palaces built in the solid austere-fortress style appropriate to the warrior mentality of Ávila's inhabitants. I can imagine Santa Teresa, who was born and lived her life in Ávila, growing up in such a house, and I can also understand her feisty spirit and her fascination with novels of knightly deeds. Ávila's decline did not dampen interest in Santa Teresa and her place of birth. Her home, her convent cell, and a convent she founded, albeit excessively embellished and out of character with the saint's earthy nature, became places of pilgrimage, and the old city still keeps the flavor of her times. At the turn of this century, British travel writer Edward Hutton felt the spirit of the saint in Ávila: "And even as Assisi is nothing without the life of St. Francis . . . so Ávila is . . . just a ruin without the life of Santa Teresa which is as it were the soul of this fiery solitary place."

Be sure to walk around the old quarters, and climb the walls for views of the countryside. Also venture beyond the walls, where there are several churches and monasteries. An afternoon in Ávila should suffice, but there is mystery in exploring the city at night, when the streets are dark and the city walls are illuminated. A parador built into the walls makes the prospect that much more enticing.

SEEING THE CITY OF ÁVILA

Within the City Walls

CATHEDRAL   Although it was begun in twelfth century Romanesque style, the cathedral's overall effect is Gothic, and it was the first Gothic cathedral in Castilla. Designed to be as strong and well defended as a fortress, the cathedral apse, called the Cimorrio, forms part of the city walls. One tower is unfinished, giving the building an unbalanced appearance.

The interior, however, is more delicately conceived, and a high Gothic nave gives it a spaciousness not apparent from the outside. Mottled rust-colored stone used for the walls adds a decorative touch, as do colorful Mudéjar frescoes. The cathedral has retained its original simplicity, devoid of ornate Baroque chapels often added to cathedrals in later centuries. Pedro Berruguete created the main altar's wonderful Gothic paintings.

Of prime interest in the cathedral is a sixteenth century masterpiece commonly called El Tostado. It is the alabaster tomb of a fifteenth century bishop of Ávila, famous for his erudition. We see him seated and deeply engrossed in his writing. His robes and bishop's miter (headdress) are carved in extraordinary detail. The work receives the name El Tostado (the toasted one), by some accounts, because of the figure's darkened face.

The *trascoro* (retrochoir) is a beautifully carved Renaissance work; an unusual pulpit is intricately fashioned in wrought iron; and the choir stalls are fine sixteenth century works.

CONVENTO DE SANTA TERESA   Today a Baroque convent, this was the site of the seignorial house where Santa Teresa was born. You can still see the gardens where she played, and her bedroom has been converted into an ornate chapel.

PALACES AND MANSIONS   Besides the Dávila and Núñez Vela palaces already mentioned, there are many more noble houses in the old quarters. One of the finest is the sixteenth century **POLENTINOS** palace, its doorway richly carved in stone, and another the fifteenth century **VALDERRÁBANOS** palace, today a hotel, next to the cathedral.

Outside the City Walls

BASÍLICA DE SAN VICENTE   The twelfth century Romanesque Door of the Apostles of this church shows the masterly touch and unaffected style of the Pórtico de la Gloria in Santiago, although the author is not thought to be the same Master Mateo. Like the Ávila cathedral, San Vicente is incomplete, missing both of its towers. Inside, the tomb of the martyred San Vicente is an extraordinary creation that shows in graphic detail scenes of the martyrdom, carved in limestone; note particularly the beautifully sculpted work depicting the "Repentant Jew." The odd pagoda-like canopy over the tomb is a much later addition.

MONASTERIO DE SANTO TOMÁS   Built by the Catholic Kings in fifteenth century Gothic style, this edifice has decorative elements much like the monastery of San Juan de los Reyes in Toledo, also commissioned by the kings. We see the symbolic yoke and arrows of Isabel and Fernando and the initials of the monarchs carved in stone. When the Inquisition was centralized under the auspices of the feared Tomás de Torquemada, the monastery was its headquarters. Torquemada was interred here until, in the nineteenth century, the tomb and his remains were profaned.

Don Juan, the only son of the Catholic Kings, died at nineteen of tuberculosis and is buried here in a magnificent alabaster tomb sculpted by the Italian Fancelli, who also created the tombs of the Catholic Kings in Granada. The main altarpiece is by Pedro Berruguete (see Index), and is one of his finest works. The choir includes the chairs used by the Catholic Kings when they came to Ávila, decorated with their yoke, arrow, and crown symbols. See the monastery's two cloisters, the Cloister of Silence and the Cloister of the Kings.

MONASTERIO DE LA ENCARNACIÓN   There is a museum in the monastery related to Santa Teresa, who as a nun lived here for twenty-nine years. Her simple cell has been transformed into an ornate chapel. In the museum I especially like a dramatic sketch of *Christ on the Cross* painted by mystic poet San Juan de la Cruz. It apparently inspired Salvador Dalí to paint his celebrated *Crucifixion*, on exhibit at the Metropolitan Museum of Art in New York.

CONVENTO DE SAN JOSÉ   popularly called the Convento de Las Madres, this was the first convent founded by Santa Teresa. There is another museum devoted to Santa Teresa here.

STAYING IN ÁVILA

PARADOR RAIMUNDO DE BORGOÑA   Marqués de Canales y Chozas 16 tel. (918) 21 13 40   Named after the knight who founded the city following the Reconquest, the parador is a reconstructed fifteenth century palace built into the city walls and decorated in Castilian style. (Moderate.)

PALACIO DE VALDERRÁBANOS   Plaza de la Catedral 9   tel. (918) 21 10 23   A fifteenth century palace, set off by a magnificently carved portal, this hotel is well located and tastefully decorated, but a trifle shabby. (Moderate.)

EATING IN ÁVILA

EL MOLINO DE LA LOSA   Bajada de la Losa 12   tel. (918) 21 11 01 Once a fifteenth century water mill on the Adaja river and today the most charming setting for dining in Ávila. Regional cooking—beans from El Barco, suckling pig and exceptional stuffed red peppers. (Moderate.)

PIQUÍO   Estrada 4   tel. (918) 21 14 18   For four decades this simple restaurant has been serving specialties of Ávila, like frog's legs and Ávila beef. (Moderate.)

◆ You can buy *Yemas de Santa Teresa* at La Flor de Castilla, Plaza San Tomé.

ISABEL LA CATÓLICA AND SANTA TERESA DE JESÚS: TWO REMARKABLE WOMEN OF ÁVILA

One was a queen, the other a nun; they were born within fifty years of each other and less than thirty miles apart, and they changed the face of Spain. Born to privileged lives of wealth and nobility, Isabel in Madrigal de las Altas Torres, Teresa (to a father of Jewish descent) in the city of Ávila, they received superior educations and maintained a keen interest in learning throughout their lives. As queen of Spain, Isabel became a leading patron of the arts, amassing an impressive collection of master paintings and commissioning extraordinary sculptural works.

As a child, Teresa was an insatiable reader who could never be without a book. Among her favorites were the popular novels of chivalry in which the knightly deeds of the Reconquest were recounted. "To the distress of my father . . . I spent long hours of the day and night in this vain exercise, although always hiding it from my father," wrote Santa Teresa in her autobiography. She became an indefatigable writer whose works on mystic discovery and convent reform are literary and religious classics. Teresa was a bubbly child, full of fun, fantasy, and mischief. In one famous escapade, she and her brother Rodrigo sneaked out of the house and beyond the walls of Ávila to a place now called Cuatro Postes. They went in search of "martyrdom" in the land of the infidel, or so their young minds imagined this unknown territory. Santa Teresa tells of her materialistic leanings: "I began to dress up and worry about looking pretty, taking great care of my hands and my hair. . . ."

Both women were born, however, into a world dominated by men, and they fully expected to lead subordinate lives. But they both possessed wills of steel that led them in other directions, and in the process they crossed seemingly insurmountable barriers.

While still a teenager, Isabel showed her toughness by defying her half brother, King Enrique IV, and marrying the man of her choice, Fernando of rival Aragón (see box, p. 120). She informed the king only after the wedding had taken place, and in his fury, he disinherited her (on his death, however, political maneuvering gave her the crown). Similarly, Teresa, undeterred by her father's adamant opposition, ran away from home and joined a local convent.

Their destinies decided, Isabel and Teresa fell into conventional feminine life-styles for some twenty years before turning their irrepressible energies to reforming Spain. Isabel neutralized the power of the nobility and took firm control of the country. As a fervent Catholic, she promoted religious unity as well, and she founded churches, monasteries, hospitals, and universities. During the Reconquest of Granada, Isabel went to the battle camps to raise the spirits of the soldiers and personally take charge of the war; she was apparently a brilliant strategist. It was Isabel who from the start enthusiastically supported the proposals of Columbus, and to back up her convictions, she reportedly promised Fernando, "You need not expose the treasury of your Kingdom of Aragón; I will undertake this venture at the expense of my crown of Castilla, and if this is not enough, I will pawn my jewels to pay the cost."

Teresa's mission was to reform the Carmelite Order and create Las Descalzas, the Barefoot Ones—nuns dedicated to a life of utter austerity and to upholding rigorously the founding ideals of the order. She crisscrossed Spain seeking support, in the scorching heat of summer and through the winter snows, overcoming almost insuperable political and monetary obstacles to achieve her goals. The church was against her; some clergy resented her liberated ways, her daring, and her drive. At first she was distrusted, but her perseverance eventually led to the founding of thirty-two reform convents.

Although surprisingly astute businesswomen (Teresa took charge of the convents' finances; Isabel centralized the country's monetary system and fomented industry), they were at the same time unpretentious, humble, and deeply concerned for the poor and for "equal rights." Teresa declared, "God is there in the kitchen, among the pots and pans," and the motto of the Catholic Kings, "*Tanto monta, monta tanto, Isabel como Fernando*" (Isabel is as important as Fernando), was for those times a startling concept indeed.

Their paths never crossed, for Isabel died before Teresa was born. But in the larger context of history they were kindred souls. Reminders of them and of their accomplishments are found all over the province of Ávila.

VISITING THE PROVINCE OF ÁVILA

GREDOS   In these majestic mountains that culminate in Castilla's highest peak, Almanzor (almost eight thousand feet high), the Tormes river is born, and the scenery is ruggedly beautiful. Gredos is a National Reserve, very close to Madrid and popular among Madrileños, yet still unaffected by change. Using the parador as a base, you can hike or drive through the mountains, walk among pine groves down to the densely green-covered banks of the river, spy the protected *Capra Hispanica* (wild goats), and visit nearby villages. In **HOYO DEL ESPINO** and **NAVARREDONDA DE LA SIERRA** explore the back streets, where the village houses are built of unmortared stone covered by tile roofs, and where property boundaries are defined by the same primitive stone construction.

PARADOR DE GREDOS   Carretera Barraco-Béjar, km 4.3   tel. (918) 34 80 48, was the first of the paradors, built by King Alfonso XIII in 1928. At 5,000 feet above the sea in the heart of the sierra, this is a privileged location, and I enjoy sitting on the terrace with a drink in hand watching the late-afternoon light play through the trees. The grander views, unfortunately, are partially obscured by overgrown trees. (Moderate.)

Nearby in San Martín del Pimpollar, **VENTA DE RASQUILLA** was once a stagecoach stop and is now a restaurant serving simple hearty fare like marinated pork fillets, bean stews, and *tortillas* (potato omelets). (Inexpensive.)

CANDELEDA and **GUISANDO** are two precious towns in the rustic style of the villages of La Vera, and not far from Gredos.

ARENAS DE SAN PEDRO   The most austere saint of all, San Pedro de Alcántara (see box, p. 197), lived here for a time, and he is buried here. The town is a center for mountain excursions.

MOMBELTRÁN, a perfectly conserved fourteenth century Castilian castle with cylindrical corner towers, belonged to the Dukes of Alburquerque.

PUERTO DEL PICO   There are wonderful views of mountains and valleys from this mountain pass, and you can also see the huge stone slabs of the old Roman Road **(LA CALZADA ROMANA),** still imposing after almost two thousand years. Take a short walk on the old road and look into the hills for mountain goats.

THE MYSTERIOUS BULLS OF GUISANDO

I have always loved the Toros de Guisando, four life-size bulls carved from granite that watch over a meadow near El Tiemblo. They are pre-Roman, and their purpose remains unclear, although some think they are symbols of fertility and were placed in the open fields

near livestock pastures to encourage reproduction. Their bulk is impressive, but the folds in their massive necks, creases in their "skin," and their gentle eyes are the work of a primitive sculptor with great sensitivity.

An occasional car stops by, but otherwise you will find yourself alone—no guides, no admission fees—free to contemplate these weathered bulls that have been out in this pasture for well over two thousand years.

EL TIEMBLO   Near this town are the remarkable Toros de Guisando (see box), and here too is the historic site where Isabel and her half brother, Enrique IV, signed the Pact of Toros de Guisando. A plaque reads: "At this site Doña Isabel La Católica was sworn princess and legitimate heir to the Kingdoms of Castilla and of León, September 1, 1468.

CEBREROS   A summer vacation town in a wine-producing region. **MESÓN LAS TINAJAS,** at Onésimo Redondo 15, right off the Plaza Mayor, is a typical Castilian tavern with a lively local atmosphere. Excellent tapas, like lamb chops, grilled mushrooms, frog's legs, *chorizo*, and cheese. (Inexpensive.)

EL QUEXIGAL   Finca El Quexigal tel. (91) 899 50 05, was once a farm under the care of Hieronymite monks, who provided foods, wines, oils, and honeys to the palace of El Escorial. Today it makes and sells finest-quality honeys, jams, herbs, and beeswax candles. Their products are also available at many of Madrid's gourmet shops.

♦ The road toward Madrid from Cebreros to Navalperal is especially beautiful, gently winding through a landscape of pine groves, boulders, and vineyards.

MADRIGAL DE LAS ALTAS TORRES   A dusty Castilian town of Mudéjar-style brickwork, surrounded in the eleventh century by 7,000 feet of circular walls (only parts of them remain). Its name—Madrigal of the Lofty Towers—is wonderfully sonorous and refers to the eighty-two towers that the town once had. Queen Isabel was born here in the palace of her father, which is today the Augustinian convent of Santa María La Real. It has a collection of objects related to the queen, and you can see the bedroom where she was born. Her great-granddaughter Doña Ana, daughter of Emperor Charles's bastard son Don Juan de Austria (see box, p. 189), was a nun in this convent. Isabel was baptized at the San Nicolás church, and the famous bishop of Ávila, called El Tostado, was also born here.

ARÉVALO   A typical town on the parched Castilian plains that has conserved its character. In the spacious, cobbled Plaza de la Villa the houses are built in Mudéjar brickwork with porticoes supported on tree trunks. They echo the style of the Mudéjar church that is off to one side of the plaza. Arévalo is partially surrounded by walls, entered through the Mudéjar Alcocer arch and overlooked by its castle, where Queen Isabel spent many childhood years.

Arévalo is known for its excellent bread and baby lamb, especially at **LA PINILLA**   Teniente García Fanjul   tel. (918) 30 00 63 (moderate), in the pretty, porticoed Plaza de Arrabal.
LA LUGAREJA, just outside town, is an unusually designed Mudéjar church from the twelfth century that has narrow brickwork and three apses.

THE PROVINCE OF SALAMANCA

SALAMANCA (sah-lah-*mahn*-cah), a large province in southwestern Castilla, marks a long western border with Portugal and divides into two basic landscapes. To the south and west, unlimited rolling meadows, known as La Charrería (Peasant's Land), are dotted with evergreen oaks and are ideal for raising livestock. The climate and terrain are also perfect for breeding brave bulls, although aficionados declare that they are not nearly as brave or strong as Andalusian bulls. In the northern and eastern areas of the province, despite the presence of the Tormes river, the typically dry meseta of Castilla stretches flat across the horizon, and we are once more in grain country. In contrast, La Sierra de la Peña de Francia is a relatively small but spectacularly beautiful mountain range of high peaks and deep, luxuriant valleys dense with almond, chestnut, olive, and prickly-pear trees.

Some of Castilla's best-preserved villages with unique personalities are in this isolated mountain setting, and you can explore from a base either in Ciudad Rodrigo or the city of Salamanca. In La Alberca, for example, local folklore, dress, and customs survive, and especially on holidays you will find the townsfolk in ancestral costume. For the men, this means cropped black pants, short embroidered jackets, and white stockings; for women, embroidered and ribboned full-skirted long dresses and string upon string of colorful beads in ever-longer lengths until they almost reach the ground.

The bold Carthaginian general Hannibal conquered Salamanca and was soon followed by the Romans, for whom Salamanca was an important colony and a part of the famous Vía de la Plata, which carried silver south from the Asturian mines. We don't hear much about Salamanca in the time of the Arabs; the land was too flat to be defensively important to them. In the mountains of La Peña de Francia, however, many stories are told of venerated figures of the Virgin hidden here for safekeeping. Don Raimundo de Borgoña, the same knight who repopulated Ávila after the Reconquest, took charge of Salamanca. The province's location on the route of La Mesta (see box, p. 63) brought prosperity for a time, and the town of Béjar was, and to a lesser extent continues to be, a textile center (Béjar cloth is traditionally used to make Spanish wool capes).

In the nineteenth century the Duke of Wellington, aiding Spain in its fight against Napoleonic invasion, for a time made Salamanca his headquarters. More specifically, he stayed at the family ranch house of my husband's childhood friend, Fernando Martín Aparicio, and when he departed after his decisive victory over the French at Arapiles, just south of the city of Salamanca, the duke showed his appreciation by giving the family his Wedgwood china, which today is proudly displayed in dining-room vitrines.

Foods of Salamanca are lusty, based on pork, lamb, and kid. Some of the finest hams of native Iberian pigs are from this province and find their way to elite establishments in Madrid. A sausage called *farinato*, made of pork, onion, and bread, is a typical tapa; so is *picadillo*, a mix of meat, onion, garlic, and tomato served with chopped hard-cooked egg. There is some wine production here, but as yet the results are relatively poor. Stay with the young clarets.

The cultural center of the province is, of course, the historic city of Salamanca, without a doubt a highlight of any visit to Castilla.

THE CITY OF SALAMANCA

Salamanca rises like a dream from a flat golden landscape. It stands beside the Río Tormes and is approached from a Roman bridge. Its rosy stone buildings (Salamanca is "the Rose of the Desert" in the words of Edward Hutton) glow in the light of day and are gloriously illuminated by night.

> Tall grove of towers gilded
> by rays of its fire,
> behind the oaks that color the sky
> the father Sun of Castilla.
>
> Miguel de Unamuno

Under the Romans, Salamanca prospered as the juncture of the roads from Zaragoza and those from Asturias. It was also the link between the cattle land to its south and the agriculture of the north, and therefore became a prosperous commercial and marketing center. Of its Moorish occupation there are scant reminders; the city's most significant history began with the Christian repopulation under Count Raimundo de Borgoña. He brought in a heterogeneous group of Castilians, Mozarabs, Jews, even French and Germans, sowing the seeds for a great cultural flowering. Many Romanesque churches were built after the Reconquest, but because Salamanca was prosperous and had a diverse population, the city enthusiastically embraced later styles, and these early churches were often abandoned or remodeled. Fortunately, the exceptional twelfth century Old Cathedral (Catedral Vieja) was left intact when the New Cathedral (Catedral Nueva) was begun next to it in 1513.

THE GREAT UNIVERSITY OF SALAMANCA

First and foremost, Salamanca was Spain's center of learning and had a wide-ranging reputation. "Don't be angry with me, master, for you know that I was not brought up at Court, nor did I study at Salamanca," says Sancho Panza to Don Quijote. At the time *Don Quijote de la Mancha* was written and ever since its founding in the early thirteenth century Salamanca has been a world-acclaimed university center, on a par with the Sorbonne, Oxford, and Bologna. You can still visit the once-celebrated Colegio de Irlandeses, established just to accommodate the large number of Irish students who came here to study.

In Salamanca Spain's most illustrious figures of the fifteenth, sixteenth, and even the early twentieth century studied and sometimes taught: Fray Luis de León, mystic poet and professor of theology; sixteenth century music professor Master Salinas; students Miguel de Cervantes and mystic San Juan de la Cruz; and professor, philosopher, and poet Miguel de Unamuno, who lived all of his adult life in Salamanca—to name but a very few. In its heyday it had more than 10,000 students, and some referred to it as the "New Athens." Today La Universidad de Salamanca continues to be a hub of student life, and its tradition of attracting foreigners endures; Europeans and Americans come by the thousands to study for a summer, a semester, or a year.

Students are today, as they have always been, a vibrant and integral part of city life, and you will find them congregating day and night at the city's focal point, the stately Plaza Mayor. They and many other Salamantinos spend their spare time here sitting at outdoor tables or just walking to and fro; the plaza is in a state of perpetual motion, "a true fiesta for the eyes," as Miguel de Unamuno said. You are also likely to find university minstrels, La Tuna (see box, p. 219), enlivening the atmosphere still further with their music and song. When you come to Salamanca, allow yourself time for an unhurried walk through the streets of the Old Quarter, around the Plaza Mayor, and most especially the leisure to sit down in the plaza, have a drink and tapas (this is a tapas town), and watch the bubbly street life.

Reminders of the students of centuries past and of the importance and prestige of studying in Salamanca are all over the city.

> At the foot of your stones, Salamanca,
> from the crops of tranquil thought
> that year after year matured your classrooms,
> remembrance sleeps.
>
> —*Miguel de Unamuno*

Ever since the fourteenth century, for example, students have spent the night before a final exam in prayer and study in the Capilla de Santa Bárbara of the Old Cathedral, facing the tomb of the learned Bishop Lucero, their feet resting on his sculpted feet; they hoped in this manner to absorb some of his knowledge. Those who were given the passing grade, *vítor*, left the cathedral triumphantly through the main portal and went directly to the Capilla del Cristo de las Batallas in the New Cathedral to give thanks to San Expedito, Patron of Passing Grades. They celebrated at the bullfights and afterward painted their names and a victorious V on building walls in bull's blood (their graffiti are still there). It is said that the unfortunates who failed were taken out a back door in disgrace, herded into oxcarts, and paraded around the city while the townsfolk taunted them and threw water and dirt in their faces.

Salamanca's professors and priests (traditionally, learning and religion went hand in hand) left their literary and political stamp on Spain. In the fifteenth century Catholic King Fernando consulted Salamanca's learned men about the wisdom of supporting Columbus's venture (all voted nay except the Dominican priests). Mystic poet and university theologian Fray Luis de León (see box, p. 87) incurred the wrath of the Inquisition in the sixteenth century and was removed from his post, only to return some years later. And Miguel de Unamuno, elderly rector of the university at the outbreak of the Civil War, escaped execution by a hairbreadth for his outspoken opposition to the war and to the military supporters of Generalísimo Franco.

In the presence of Franco's wife and his generals, assembled in the college hall, Unamuno was giving a speech in commemoration of Columbus Day (El Día de la Raza), when suddenly a general in the audience interrupted him, shouting "Long live death!" and "Death to intellectuals!" To which Unamuno replied that the Nationalists might win the war, but they would never win over the people, for their hatred left no room for compassion. Had it not been for the intervention of Franco's wife in the melee that ensued, the incident would have turned to bloodshed. She personally escorted the frail Unamuno out of the hall. He died shortly thereafter, crushed by forebodings of the fate that was to befall Spain.

Two ground-breaking literary works of the sixteenth century, *La Celestina*, written in 1499 by Fernando de Rojas, who had studied in Salamanca, and *Lazarillo de Tormes*, published anonymously some fifty years later, were set in Salamanca. The first is a tragic love story in which a sly go-between, Celestina, plays a major role. In the second the protagonist, Lazarillo, is born in a Salamanca village (thus his name, de Tormes, in reference to the river), and part of the story takes place in the city.

These two stories gave birth to an original Spanish genre, the picaresque novel, and heralded the coming of the Golden Age of Cervantes, Calderón de la Barca, and Lope de Vega. In contrast to the somewhat remote and idealized figures of earlier literature, *La Celestina* and *Lazarillo de Tormes* revolve around earthy characters—antiheroes—who live by their wits and in sometimes unsavory ways.

By the sixteenth century Salamanca was enveloped in the spirit of the Renaissance. At the university study of the humanities took preference, and Salamanca, with the enthusiastic support of Archbishop Fonseca, became a showcase for current architectural styles. The innovative Salamanca arch, a curve divided into five segments, was one of the city's contributions to Renaissance architecture. The new style that developed, Plateresque, could not have been more Spanish.

SALAMANCA: CAPITAL OF PLATERESQUE

Plateresque derives from the Spanish word for silver, *plata*, because its detailed carving looked more like the work of silversmiths than something sculpted from solid stone. Although there are Plateresque works in many parts of Spain (most notably the Colegio de San Ildefonso in Alcalá de Henares, Hostal de San Marcos in León, and Hostal de Los Reyes Católicos in Santiago de Compostela), it is in Salamanca that the art reached its height; there you will find many of its most dazzling examples.

The presence of the university and the support of Archbishop Fonseca helped the development of the style, but another reason for its success here was purely practical. The building stone quarried near Salamanca is relatively soft and damp (Miguel de Unamuno wrote, ". . . that stone gentle and pliant that when just removed from the quarry can be cut like cheese . . ."), thus lending itself to extensive molding. But when it dries and hardens in the sun it becomes extremely durable, and as it weathers its beauty increases and it acquires subtle gold and rosy hues.

Isabel La Católica paved the way for Plateresque with her preference for excessive adornment and for the Moorish style that so charmed her in Sevilla and Granada. The intricate designs that the Moors had shaped in plaster molds were now transposed into stone in seemingly impossible, minuscule patterns. The style was christened Isabelline (some of its best examples are in Burgos and Valladolid) and was a direct forerunner of Plateresque.

As Renaissance style came into fashion, ornamentation became more structured and self-contained within geometric frameworks. Taking Isabelline as its base and adopting Renaissance designs, Plateresque was born. It was more balanced and less passionate than Isabelline, but no less profuse and capricious. The overall effect was what some art experts describe as a Moorish tapestry. Cherubs in motion, solemn busts of important persons (sometimes enclosed in medallions), foliage in sinuous patterns, scrolls, and royal crests vie for space in this confused yet surprisingly orderly concentration of patterns that lack a focal point. The contrast between the classic look of Renaissance architecture and the exuberance of Plateresque facades just intensified the startling effect. The supreme achievement of Plateresque is the facade of the Old University building in Salamanca.

Plateresque translated effortlessly into metalwork, from which it perhaps had originally derived, and Spaniards also became masters of decorative wrought-iron grilles, gates, and balconies. In Salamanca Plateresque in all its manifestations is at every turn: it is in the facades of the Old University, the New Cathedral, San Esteban church, and the Palacio de Monterrey, but you will see it as well in many other churches, mansions, and palaces, and in the elegant patios that also characterize Salamanca Plateresque.

> forest of stones that history pulled
> from the heart of mother earth
> island of tranquillity, I bless you,
> my Salamanca!
>
> *Miguel de Unamuno*

Seeing Salamanca

◆ You will need at least a full day and a night in Salamanca. All the sights listed below are within easy walking distance of one another.

OLD UNIVERSITY   From the Patio de las Escuelas you can calmly study the Old University facade, the city's jewel of Plateresque from the beginning of the sixteenth century, so heavily decorated that you might think it was stucco instead of stone (see text). It is divided into three levels in which three themes stand out: The lower part shows a large medallion surrounding a portrait of the Catholic Kings, the second has the elaborate coat of arms of Charles V, and the upper represents the pope and his cardinals. Filling every available space around these figures is a maze of stone ornamentation: busts on pedestals, head carvings enclosed in medallions, crests, arabesques, monsters, cherubs, scales of justice, serpentine foliage. A figure of a small frog, reputed to bring luck on exams, is difficult to find: Follow the far-right column up to a skull on which the frog sits.

Inside the university, visit the legendary classroom of Fray Luis de León (see box), untouched since the sixteenth century; the Paraninfo, where the famous incident involving the university's rector, Miguel de Unamuno, took place (see text); and the chapel, where students at the end of their studies were required to pray and where the coffin of Fray Luis de León is kept.

The **LIBRARY** contains close to 50,000 volumes, many written on parchment and bound in Cordoban leather, and is reached by way of a grand stairway with a beautiful stone-carved balustrade. The ceiling is a fine *artesonado* in Moorish style, and the patio in its upper gallery shows the singular Salamanca arch. Only a part of the fascinating fifteenth century fresco on the vaulted ceiling, *The Sky and the Constellations*, survives. Its author, Fernando Gallego, was a highly regarded artist in the Flemish tradition whose work is concentrated in Salamanca. It shows golden stars scattered in a pale-blue sky over which the constellations have been painted. They take human form, in reference to mythological figures. The patio of the *Escuelas Menores*, or lower schools, within the university has fine examples of the Salamanca arch and is especially beautiful.

THE CATHEDRALS

Salamanca has two cathedrals, one beside the other, because by the sixteenth century the Old Cathedral was considered unbearably dark and cramped. It is, however, the older one that I consider a prize for its artistic interest and its lack of ostentation.

OLD CATHEDRAL

Except for the cupola, covered with overlapping stone slabs in the fashion of the Zamora cathedral (it is called "Rooster Tower" because of the figure of a rooster that stands over it), you can't see much of this twelfth century Romanesque cathedral from the outside. The cathedral is effectively hidden from view by the New Cathedral (walk

"AS I WAS SAYING YESTERDAY"

Despite the great architectural works of Salamanca University, one of the places I like best has little artistic worth. It is a classroom that beautifully evokes the memories of centuries of students and of one very special professor of the sixteenth century, Fray Luis de León.

The room is impressively austere, dim, and, I would surmise, icy cold during harsh Salamanca winters. Students, in fact, had the right to stamp their feet for five minutes at the beginning of class to warm up. Split logs served as benches and desks, and they stretch across the width of the room. The desks are deeply marred by centuries of student graffiti and doodles, some of it in Latin.

Fray Luis was a professor of theology who wrote mystic poetry of profound beauty and was dedicated to his classroom. But his religious mysticism and his translation of the biblical Song of Songs, a work some interpreted as a glorification of Judaism, led rival professors to denounce him to the Inquisition. He was jailed for four years, acquitted, and then returned to the university, where his beloved classroom and his chair of theology awaited him. He approached the lectern and serenely began his lecture: "Gentlemen, as I was saying yesterday . . ." With that, he continued his discourse at the point where he had been interrupted four years before.

THE CHURRIGUERESQUE STYLE

The Spanish fascination with architectural extremes continued to evolve beyond Plateresque. Salamanca Baroque, represented by the three Churriguera brothers—José, Joaquín, and Alberto, of Catalan heritage but natives of Salamanca—brought about another original Spanish style named after them, Churrigueresque. It relied on Plateresque detail and Moorish influences but imposed them over the already ornate Baroque style of the late seventeenth and early eighteenth centuries. The result was an utterly wild, flamboyant look of restless motion that could hardly be carried a step further.

The style is seen all over Salamanca, sometimes in building exteriors (like the church of La Clerecía), but most often in church interiors and altarpieces. All the Churriguera brothers worked in similar styles during overlapping periods of time, and it is difficult to determine who did what. Indeed, even today many Churrigueresque works are attributed to the wrong brother.

around the New Cathedral to the Patio Chico for better views). Inside, the altarpiece, composed of fifty-three separate paintings that show the life of Christ, is a wonderful work of a fifteenth century artist, Nicolás Florentino. The venerated Virgen de la Vega, in copper and enamel, is at the center of the scene.

To the right of the altar, magnificent coffins are set in niches decorated with fresco paintings. In the Capilla de Santa Bárbara (see text) a fifteenth century triptych of Santa Catalina is by Fernando Gallego. The Capilla de Anaya holds the beautifully carved alabaster tomb of Bishop Diego de Anaya, surrounded by richly worked wrought iron. The church museum concentrates on works by Fernando Gallego.

NEW CATHEDRAL   A French-influenced late Gothic structure with an impressive and refined Plateresque facade. The Baroque choir is a work by Alberto Churriguera, and the impossibly ornate Capilla del Cristo de las Batallas, designed by his brother Joaquín, holds a Romanesque Christ mounted on a cross and said to have been carried by El Cid into battle.

SAN ESTEBAN   The highlight of this church is a stunning Plateresque facade, recessed and crowded with statues of saints, medallions, and other decorative detail.

CASA DE LAS CONCHAS   The most important work of civil Gothic in Salamanca. Its owner, Talavera Maldonado, was a Knight of Santiago; thus the scallop shells decorating the house (see box, p. 220). It has exquisite wrought-iron window gratings and unusual stone carving, including coats of arms above and below the windows. The patio is a superb example of the Salamanca style.

PLAZA MAYOR   Built in the eighteenth century, this is, along with the Plaza Mayor of Madrid, among the most elegant and harmonious of Spain's monumental plazas. There are medallions representing figures from Spanish history on two sides, university and noble crests on the others. In accordance with tradition, bullfights were held here until the nineteenth century, and markets took place under its arches.

CONVENTO DE LAS DUEÑAS   The upper gallery of the cloister of this convent has wonderfully sculpted capitals in a unique design.

MONTERREY PALACE   If this palace had been finished, it would possibly be the largest palace in the world. As it stands, however, its upper gallery is among the grandest works of civilian Plateresque.

COLEGIO DE IRLANDESES (COLEGIO DEL ARZOBISPO FONSE-CA)   The facade looks like a miniature of the university's plateresque design, and its patio is one of the finest examples of the Salamanca Renaissance style.

FONSECA PALACE   Today a government building, this palace has an exceptional patio with an upper gallery supported by enormous brackets carved with Atlas-like figures.

STAYING IN SALAMANCA

PARADOR DE SALAMANCA   Teso de la Feria 2   tel. (923) 26 87 00   The parador is modern and unexciting and has the inconvenience of being outside the city (within walking distance). But it has the distinct advantage of sensational views of the city, perfectly framed in the picture windows of the public and guest rooms (request, of course, a room with a view). (Moderate; pool.) You can eat well in the restaurant.

GRAN HOTEL   Plaza del Poeta Iglesias 3   tel. (923) 21 35 00   Not nearly so grand as it once was, but well located right next to the Plaza Mayor. (Expensive.)

EATING IN SALAMANCA

CHEZ VICTOR   Espoz y Mina 26   tel. (923) 21 31 23   Despite its French name, the chef, Victor Salvador, is a native of Salamanca (his wife, Marguerite, is French). With a sure hand he creates dishes of exquisite subtlety and delicacy. Among my favorites, *Ensalada de Enrique*, a mixed-green salad with prawns, cheese pâté (*Tartare de Quesos*), and *Magret de Pato*, duck breast with berries. Save room for dessert—there is a separate listing just for chocolate fantasies. (Moderate–expensive.)

EL CANDIL VIEJO   Ruiz Aguilera 14–16   tel. (923) 21 72 39   A Salamanca classic, serving fish and roasts. A good selection of tapas at the bar. (Moderate.)

RÍO DE LA PLATA   Plaza del Peso 1   tel. (923) 21 90 05   A very popular restaurant that concentrates on simple fish and meat dishes. (Moderate.)

◆ Tapas activity centers on the Plaza Mayor. You might try **PLUS ULTRA** on Calle del Concejo and **EL ARCO** and **IMBIS** on Rúa Mayor. Fried tapas, like *Gambas en Gabardina* (batter-fried shrimp), and *croquetas* are especially popular.

SEEING THE PROVINCE OF SALAMANCA

CIUDAD RODRIGO   Contained within seven thousand feet of walls that are forty feet high, this town was named after its conqueror, Count Rodrigo González. It feels like the fifteenth and sixteenth centuries here; the Old Quarter and the Plaza Mayor are quite unspoiled and filled with golden-stone mansions and palaces. Of special interest in the twelfth century **CATHEDRAL** are the alabaster altar, the exceptionally carved choir stalls, the Gothic cloister, and the west portal, over which beautifully detailed and well-preserved statues of the Apostles, each in a separate niche, stand in a row.

PARADOR ENRIQUE II   Plaza del Castillo 1   tel. (923) 46 01 50, is a four-teenth century castle built by Castilian king Enrique II next to the ivy-covered town walls. A central tower rises above the town, and there are excellent views of the Salamanca countryside. (Moderate.)

♦ **CARNAVAL**, approximately forty days before Easter, is a wild affair in which bulls are released and run at will through public streets, bringing young men out to confront them, and other townspeople scurrying for cover.

LA ALBERCA   Because of the singular beauty of this mountain village of roughly cobbled streets and stone and wood-beam houses with wood balconies, all of La Alberca has been declared a national monument, ensuring that not a stone will be touched without government permission. Regional costume is especially rich, sometimes worn on Sundays but always on local religious holidays of August 15 and 16, when you can see men and women in their full ancestral dress (see text).

LA PEÑA DE FRANCIA is a rocky mountaintop, more than 5,000 feet above the sea in the extraordinary setting of the Peña de Francia range. During the Arab occupation, Christians brought cherished religious statues here for safekeeping, and this subsequently became a place of pilgrimage (a Dominican order, which has just two brothers left, is here for that reason). The views are panoramic, and from the overlook you can see cities, towns, and mountain peaks all over the province of Salamanca (indicators point to highlights). There is a bar, but a picnic lunch on a fine day is ideal.

VALLE DE LAS BATUECAS   The road that descends through a lush valley from La Alberca and La Peña de Francia into Extremadura is enveloped in greenery, a forest of vegetation. Mountain peaks loom in the distance.

MIRANDA DEL CASTAÑAR   This wonderful village of stone houses with sloped tile roofs and decorative wrought-iron balconies laden with flowers looks very much like La Alberca (see above) but feels more "lived in" and less like a museum piece.

ALBA DE TORMES   Following the banks of the Río Tormes, this town is undistinguished (it once attracted monarchs, nobility, and artists to the sumptuous palace of the Dukes of Alba, demolished during nineteenth century warfare) but continues to be an active center of pilgrimage: The remains of mystic Santa Teresa de Jesús (see Index) are venerated in the Carmelite convent she founded. Besides her ornate coffin, which sits high above the altar, display cases to either side contain relics of the saint ("Form two lines, please," announces a priest, "arm on the left, heart to the right"). The illustrious Dukes and Duchesses of Alba were originally from here.

CANDELARIO   A quaint town hidden in the mountains of Béjar and not visible until the last turn in the road. Wood balconies overhang narrow, steep, cobbled streets, and crystalline water rushes through street channels as mountain snow melts. Candelario is famous for its excellent *chorizo*.

THE PROVINCE OF VALLADOLID

VALLADOLID (va-ya-doe-*leed*) is physically, politically, and economically at the center of Castilla-León. For centuries the province played host to the royal courts of the Castilian kings, and after the unification of the country, Spanish monarchs continued to come. Pedro el Cruel kept his mistress María Padilla cloistered in a convent here in the fourteenth century (see box, p. 98), and Juana la Loca, daughter of the Catholic Kings and heir to the throne, spent almost fifty years of her life in the same convent. A castle in a town of Valladolid was Queen Isabel's preferred residence (she also died in the province), and kings Philip II, III, and IV all made Valladolid their capital for at least part of their reigns.

Today Valladolid is the capital of Castilla-León and its hub of economic development. And in centuries past, hard as it may be to believe, the town of Medina del Campo was one of Europe's leading banking centers. Three routes that took wool of La Mesta (see box, p. 63) to northern ports joined here, and a major marketing and manufacturing center took shape in the sixteenth century. Buyers came from all over Spain (especially Catalans) and from Europe (the Flemish and Italians were important clients), and the Medina bill of exchange was as good as cash all over Europe.

At the center of the northern meseta, Valladolid is all plains, unbroken by any major mountain ranges. Like Zamora, it is bisected east to west by the Río Duero: To the north of the river, Tierra de Pan (Land of Bread) produces grains and cereals; from Tierra de Vino in the south comes some of the country's best wines and fine-quality pine nuts from the round, squat *pinos piñoneros* that cluster in the plains. The Pisuerga and Eresma rivers also flow through the province and carve valleys deep into the meseta. There are delightful villages in Valladolid, in the typical style of Castilla, and a fair share of outstanding castles, like Peñafiel, La Mota, and Simancas, many of which were important military posts at the time of the Reconquest.

Although Valladolid is well known for its roasts of lamb and suckling pig, it also has exceptionally good bread and two more dishes that you might want to try: *Gallina en Pebre* (chicken stewed in egg and garlic sauce) and, one of my favorites, batter-fried lamb's feet (*Manitas de Cordero Rebozadas*). Fresh sheep's milk cheese from Villalón de Campos, also called *Pata de Mula* because its cylindrical shape resembles a mule's foot, is a prized item, but limited production makes it hard to find.

From Valladolid's Tierra de Vino comes what many consider the Rolls-Royce of Spanish wines, the celebrated Vega Sicilia. It falls under the Ribera del Duero designation, and takes its place among the world's best, although by no means does it stand alone in Valladolid. Besides other out-standing reds, like Pesquera and Yllera, the province is well known for its Rueda white wines. Young and fruity, they are of high quality and great pop-ularity. Of lesser fame but well regarded nevertheless are the wood-aged claret and rosé wines of Cigales that are generally consumed locally.

Valladolid has an extraordinary wealth of polychrome sculpture, and to me this is the feature that makes the province most exciting. It is a typi-cally Castilian art form, produced by the finest artists of the times, whose artistically fertile years centered on this province. The Museo Nacional de Escultura has collected such artwork from around the province, and the museum is as unusual as it is electrifying. And yet in so many of Valladolid's village churches, you will find more great works by the artistic geniuses of this genre: Alonso Berruguete, Gregorio Fernández, Juan de Juni, and Diego de Siloé.

THE CITY OF VALLADOLID

Valladolid, on the banks of the Río Pisuerga, was founded by the Romans and regained from the Moors in the eleventh century. Count Pedro Ansúrez, given a grant from the king, commenced Christian repopulation of the province. Very little is left of the Romanesque architecture from that period, except the tower and porch of the Santa María La Antigua church, and there are fewer traces still of the Moorish-influenced Mudéjar style, so common after the Reconquest. Valladolid was favored by the Catholic Kings, became an important political center, and under their tutelage some spectacular works of art and architecture were created.

Valladolid saw several momentous events in Spain's history: the birth of Queen Isabel's half brother, King Enrique IV, who ruled when she was still a child; the marriage of Fernando and Isabel in 1469, after their meeting in Dueñas (see box, p. 120); and the birth of their great-grandson Philip II and of his grandson Philip IV. Columbus died in Valladolid (but is interred in Sevilla), and Miguel de Cervantes spent his last years here in a house that has been preserved as a museum.

Valladolid was the capital of Spain in the early part of the reign of Philip II, before he chose Madrid as government headquarters. Under Philip

III and Philip IV the capital reverted to Valladolid until Madrid finally became the permanent capital. But in the almost two hundred years during which Valladolid was a nucleus of power, it evolved into a cultural center. There was a flourishing university, and the dazzling Valladolid school of sculpture left its imprint on the city and on all of Castilla.

A broad esplanade, Paseo de Zorrilla, runs parallel to the river and leads you into the old quarter of the city, where there are several spacious plazas. Valladolid has a certain verve associated with a university town, and you can feel the city's heartbeat in the busy Plaza Mayor. But otherwise, the city's points of interest are scattered, and I suggest limiting your visit to the musts: San Pablo, the Colegio de San Gregorio, and its Museo Nacional de Escultura. Include other sights if time permits or as your special interests mandate. For me, another must is lunch at La Fragua, and we have detoured several times from our route just to eat here and to visit once again the above-mentioned sights.

There is no need to spend the night in the city unless you come at Easter for the renowned evening processions on Good Friday. Otherwise, it is far better to continue to the parador in Tordesillas, about forty-five minutes away.

ᔕAN PABLO CHURCH, SAN GREGORIO COLLEGE, AND THE SPLENDID VALLADOLID MUSEUM OF POLYCHROME SCULPTURE

Valladolid's Museo Nacional de Escultura is not a name that springs to your lips, nor to those of most Spaniards, when considering the great collections of the world. But it is a wonder and, for me, stands out as one of Spain's greatest museums.

The museum's concentration of polychrome wood sculpture is outstanding in its own right, but it gains immensely when contemplated in the context of the Colegio de San Gregorio that houses it and San Pablo, with which it was historically connected. The church and college stand back to back, and their artistic splendor is due to one determined and egocentric man, Fray Alonso de Burgos. He was bishop of Palencia, art lover, and confessor to Queen Isabel; his see was San Pablo.

Fray Alonso dreamed of a burial place for himself of unthinkable richness, and with that in mind he built an addition to San Pablo that would be a grand chapel dedicated to his memory. His plan broadened to include the San Gregorio School of Theology, where today the Museo Nacional de Escultura is installed, and he also redesigned the facade of San Pablo.

Over the portal of the church a figure of Fray Alonso kneels in prayer. Above and around him the church facade explodes with stone carving, marvelously detailed and lavish. It provides a unique opportunity to see in juxtaposition the Isabelline and Plateresque styles (see Index), so similar and so easily confused, but here so clearly defined: the lower two-thirds of the facade, designed by Simón de Colonia, who also worked on the Burgos cathedral, is free-flowing, unbridled Isabelline, and the upper third, added at a later time, is Plateresque, clearly more uniform and serene. Both, however, show a love for ornamentation inherited from the Moors.

The facade of San Gregorio became even more sumptuous than San Pablo's. Over the portal Fray Alonso once again prays, this time kneeling before Saint Gregorio. Queen Isabel was patron of this project, and the facade, thought to be a work of her favorite sculptor, Gil de Siloé, who also designed under her commission the monastery La Cartuja de Miraflores in Burgos, is a wonderfully opulent rendition of the Flamboyant Gothic Isabelline style and includes a wealth of design elements. Stylized pomegranate trees bear the fruit that symbolizes the city of Granada (an allusion to Isabel's Reconquest of that city); there are Spanish coats of arms, the largest displayed by two fierce lions; yokes and arrows represent the Catholic Kings; and fanciful figures of savages refer to the Indians discovered in America. Wherever you look there are cherubs, cavorting or clinging to curlicue pomegranate branches; there are monsters and soldiers. So much is happening that the facade seems to have a life of its own.

The patio of San Gregorio is equally remarkable and a fascinating marriage of Gothic and Mudéjar styles. The arches of the upper gallery are partially closed by "curtains" of stone so finely chiseled that the work appears to be tapestry or embroidery. A stone balustrade is as delicately conceived as wrought iron.

The museum's collection is predominantly wood sculpture from the thirteenth through the eighteenth centuries, gathered from churches and monasteries that were abandoned because of the nineteenth century Law of Disamortization (see Index). The works were poorly stored and in a state of decay until several decades ago, when they were rescued and restored to create this peerless museum. This is an anthology of Castilla's best sculpture under one roof, and is all the more arresting because of its single medium (wood) and its exceptionally intelligent and artistic display and faultless lighting. In some cases huge church altarpieces have been separated into sculptural units, and each is individually exhibited. To see such remarkable works up close and at eye level, instead of at a distance in dim and dusty churches, is a rare pleasure indeed.

The museum's two floors are joined by a grand Renaissance stairway, and the fleur-de-lis, symbol of Fray Alonso, appears ad infinitum. Considering the glorious works this man has left us, however, it's hard to begrudge him his vanities.

Featured in the museum are works by Diego de Siloé, Alonso Berruguete, Juan de Juni, and Gregorio Fernández. Through the medium of wood, often gilded for added luster, then polychromed, the beauty of the human form and the passion of the spirit emerge. The artists convey tremendous emotion; you feel suffering, pain, and serenity as well; and you see in their sculptures amazing fluidity, as if the figures were in motion, propelled by an inner fire.

Alonso Berruguete and Diego de Siloé, sons of the famous artists Pedro Berruguete and Gil de Siloé, and Juan de Juni practiced their art in the mid-sixteenth century and were under one another's influence. Diego de Siloé was perhaps the first to work in the sensual pre-Baroque style that predominates in the museum. The enormous vitality of his work is best shown in his depiction of *Saint John the Baptist*, carved in the choir stalls brought from the Convento de San Benito.

Although Alonso Berruguete was strongly influenced by Siloé, it is Berruguete who is considered the true master of this art form. He was a man of strong convictions, and his sense of drama, passion, and strength of character comes across in such works as *Abraham and Isaac*. Juan de Juni was a contemporary of Siloé's and Berruguete's, but he did not come to Spain (probably from France) until he was about forty years old. His work is distinguished by the manner in which he carves wood to resemble draped cloth, clearly evident in *Santa Ana* and in the *Burial of Christ*.

Gregorio Fernández, another of the museum's prominent sculptors, worked in the late sixteenth and early seventeenth century, well after these three masters of polychrome had died. His style is less theatrical and more serene, and his sculptures, such as the *Baptism of Christ*, *San Bruno*, and *La Pietá*, show a quiet sadness. Less represented and from the latter part of the seventeenth century is Pedro de Mena, who worked principally in Andalucía and whose works are more subtle and emotionally subdued. Perhaps my favorite piece in the museum is his statue of *La Magdalena*.

The dramatic, at times melodramatic, quality of the sculpture in this museum is not, of course, to all tastes, but if the visit whets your appetite, you can see more treasured works by these same sculptors in several of the city's churches: in San Miguel a statue of San Ignacio by Gregorio Fernández; in Santiago the altarpiece by Alonso Berruguete; several works by Gregorio Fernández in the Iglesia de la Cruz; the *Virgin of the Knives* by Juan de Juni in Las Angustias; the altarpiece by Gregorio Fernández and a crucifix by Juan de Juni in the convent of Las Huelgas Reales; and the main altarpiece in Valladolid's cathedral by Juan de Juni. There is much more in churches around the province, and more still in Paredes de Nava in the province of Palencia.

Seeing the City of Valladolid

COLEGIO DE SAN GREGORIO   This magnificent structure, once a theology school, where Fray Bartolomé de las Casas in the sixteenth century wrote his ground-breaking treatise, *Historia de Las Indias*, which pleaded the cause of the Indians, is the home of the **MUSEO NACIONAL DE ESCULTURA** (see text). In the chapel built for the founder, Fray Alonso de Burgos, there was once an exquisite alabaster sepulcher with his remains, along with an equally rich altarpiece, but they were destroyed by the French during the War of Independence. We are left with the stupendously carved organ pulpit and an outstanding altarpiece by Alonso Berruguete that replaces the original.

SAN PABLO   The wonderful facade of this church is its principal point of interest. It graphically illustrates the differences between the Isabelline and Plateresque style (see text). Inside the church, see the minute carving of the north portal, designed by Simón de Colonia.

CATHEDRAL   Designed by Juan de Herrera, whose supreme achievement was El Escorial, this was intended to be one of Spain's grandest cathedrals. But progress was slow, and the cathedral was never finished according to the architect's plans. The lower facade shows Herrera's utterly sober style, but the upper part, concluded much later, is a Baroque work by Alberto Churriguera (see box, p. 88). Without a cupola and with thick stone arches, the interior of the cathedral has the heavy yet majestic Herrera style. The altarpiece, although originally in Santa María La Antigua church, is a masterly polychrome work by Juan de Juni. The cathedral's splendid wrought-iron choir screen is today in New York's Metropolitan Museum of Art.

SANTA MARÍA LA ANTIGUA   The thirteenth century porch and graceful tower of this otherwise Gothic church are among the few reminders of Romanesque in Valladolid.

OTHER CHURCHES OF VALLADOLID   In the dozens of historic churches in the city, there are many more works of polychrome art so prevalent in Valladolid (see text).

CASA DE CERVANTES   Among the several houses in Spain where Cervantes supposedly lived, this is the only authenticated one. He was in Valladolid at the beginning of the seventeenth century and wrote several of his lesser works here. Furnished in the style of the period, the house includes a small Cervantes museum. Although not of great historic or artistic value, the Casa de Cervantes gives you a clear sense of the simple life of the great writer.

SANTA CRUZ PALACE   The facade, seen from the patio, is another extraordinary example of the lavish Isabelline style.

UNIVERSITY   If you like the Churriguera Baroque style, the facade of the main university building is a fine example, done by two disciples of Churriguera.

MUSEO ORIENTAL (in the Convento de los Filipinos)   An oddity in Spain, this museum contains pieces from China, the Philippines, and South America.

STAYING IN VALLADOLID

None of the city's hotels is exciting, and, as previously mentioned, there is little need to spend the night. If you do, **OLID MELIÁ**   Plaza San Miguel 10   tel. (983) 35 72 00 (moderate–expensive), is well located in the Old Quarter.

EATING IN VALLADOLID

LA FRAGUA   Paseo de Zorrilla 10   tel. (983) 33 71 02   One of my favorites, this restaurant provides an elegant yet country setting for first-rate roast lamb and suckling pig cooked in a wood-burning oven, lamb chops, and the best *morcilla* (black sausage) you will find anywhere. Slow-cooking dishes like oxtail or beef stew are also popular, as is the fine fresh fish. Their bodega is excellent. (Moderate–expensive.)

MESÓN PANERO   Marina Escobar 1   tel. (983) 30 16 73   A restaurant decorated in rustic style that is known for good eating. I like *Langostinos Gran Mesón* (prawns in garlic sauce), *Conejo con Tomate* (rabbit in tomato and green pepper sauce), and stuffed partridge. (Moderate–expensive.)

MESÓN CERVANTES   Rastro 6   tel. (983) 30 85 53   A friendly atmosphere for Castilian fare. Try *menestra* (medley of fresh vegetables), roast lamb, river crabs, and delicious *Natillas con Nueces* (sugar-glazed soft custard with walnuts). (Moderate–expensive.)

✦ For tapas, head to the area around the Plaza Mayor, especially to bars like **PAN CON TOMATE**   Plaza Mayor 18, and **CABALLO DE TROYA**   nearby at Correo 1.

FIESTAS

HOLY WEEK   There are processions this entire week, but the big day is Good Friday, when the brotherhoods and the public gather in the Plaza Mayor for a huge open-air Mass. The processions continue well into the night, and the dramatic polychrome floats representing some of Spain's greatest sculptors, like Juan de Juni, Gregorio Fernández, Diego de Siloé, and Alonso Berruguete, are slowly and solemnly paraded to the sound of funereal trumpets and drums.

VISITING THE PROVINCE OF VALLADOLID

TORDESILLAS   The importance of Tordesillas dates to the Reconquest, when the town formed part of the Christian defense line at the Río Duero. In the fifteenth century the royal court sometimes convened here, but more important, in 1494 the Treaty of Tordesillas was signed, dividing overseas lands and future explorations between Portugal and Spain. The pope (Alexander VI, a Spaniard from the Borja family; see box, p. 382) acted as arbitrator and chose a line of longitude to separate Portuguese and Spanish possessions. This gave Portugal overseas land east of the line (including Brazil and Africa); everything to the west went to Spain (the rest of Latin America and the Pacific islands).

Two famous women from different periods of Spanish history, María Padilla, lover of Pedro el Cruel of Castilla, and Juana la Loca, daughter of the Catholic Kings, were confined in Tordesillas under most unusual circumstances (see boxes, p. 98 and p. 99).

The town is reached by a ten-span Roman bridge, which reflects in the still waters of the Duero, and has an exceptional Plaza Mayor that beautifully conserves its Castilian flavor. The porticoed houses and the columns on

THE PASSIONATE AFFAIR OF MARÍA PADILLA AND KING PEDRO EL CRUEL

In 1352 Castilian king Pedro el Cruel was introduced to María Padilla, and for nine years he was unable to resist the considerable charms of this daughter of a Sevilla nobleman. María was by all accounts a great beauty with a warm personality. But politics forced the king to marry French princess Doña Blanca (see Index). He abandoned her on their wedding night to return to María Padilla and kept Doña Blanca incarcerated for the rest of her life in several castles. His behavior scandalized the public and brought down the wrath of the pope, and to placate him Pedro devised a clever compromise. He would return to his queen if the pope agreed to establish a monastery where María would become a nun. The pope assented, and the Real Monasterio de Santa Clara was built in Tordesillas.

The convent, however, was merely a pretext; Pedro never intended to make María a nun, or to return to Doña Blanca. María did live in Santa Clara for a time, however, and to make her feel at home, the king designed a charming and cheerful Moorish patio that would remind María of Sevilla. He left her in the convent at his convenience to pursue other amorous adventures, but repeatedly returned to María. They had four children.

When María died, Pedro seemed genuinely moved and asked that she be recognized as his legitimate wife and queen (Doña Blanca had passed away within days of María). His request was granted, and María was interred in royal fashion in the Royal Chapel of Sevilla's cathedral.

which they stand vary in height to adjust to the gentle slope of the cobbled square. Bullfights still take place here occasionally.

In the **REAL MONASTERIO DE SANTA CLARA**, formerly a palace, María Padilla and Juana la Loca resided. A diminutive patio, designed for María Padilla, who was Andalusian, has horseshoe arches, delicate plaster tracery, and lively ceramic tilework on the walls and is unexpectedly Moorish in this austere Castilian setting. Arab baths, punctured with starburst skylights and painted with geometric frescoes, and the unusually large and magnificently executed *artesonado* ceiling of the chapel, once the throne room, also remain from the old palace. In the Capilla de los Saldaña a fine Flemish triptych demystifies the life of Christ, almost in comic-book style. We see, for example, Christ ascending, but only the bottom edge of his robe and his feet are visible. Also in the convent is the spinet brought by Charles V from Flanders and used by his mother, Juana la Loca.

♦ By way of a revolving shelf, the cloistered nuns of Santa Clara sell simple cookies and excellent candied egg-yolk empanadas.

PARADOR DE TORDESILLAS Carretera de Salamanca, km 155 tel. (983) 77 00 51, is just outside of town, a sprawling Castilian-style country house, porticoed like the town plaza, beautifully appointed, and nestled in pine groves. (Moderate; pool.)

MESÓN VALDERREY Carretera N-VI tel. (983) 77 11 72, at the entrance to town, next to the river, has typically Castilian décor and serves fine suckling pig and baby lamb chops. (Inexpensive–moderate.)

EL BUSETO   Plaza Mayor 15, has an unusual selection of handcrafted gift items.

MEDINA DEL CAMPO   Centuries ago this town was a major marketing and financial hub. Activity centered on the Plaza Mayor, where deals made in front of the Colegiata after Mass were given juridical validity. Palaces and noble residences from those times still stand. The well-preserved La Mota castle (it's worth your while to drive up in order to appreciate its immense size and beautiful Mudéjar brick construction) was the favorite residence of Isabel la Católica. She died in Medina del Campo—some say in the castle, others in a palace that no longer exists.

SIMANCAS   The center of attention here is the castle, once Moorish and rebuilt in the thirteenth century. Since the times of Charles V and through the eighteenth century this has been the repository for the National Archives, preserving millions of documents of incalculable worth and attracting serious researchers from all over the world. See a fascinating selec-

JUANA LA LOCA:
TRAGIC QUEEN OF CASTILE

The life of Juana the Mad was a series of unfortunate events. Daughter of Fernando and Isabel, sister of English queen Katherine of Aragón, and heir to the throne of Castilla, she married Philip the Fair, son of King Maximilian I, Emperor of the Holy Roman Empire, and from then on nothing but unhappiness came her way.

With good reason Philip was called "the Fair" (el Hermoso), for he was a bon vivant whose vanity knew no bounds. Leaving Juana in Spain, he returned to Germany to pursue a life of pleasure. Juana, madly in love with him, began to show signs of mental instability.

While visiting her mother, Queen Isabel, in Medina del Campo, she refused food and rest and stood out in the cold until Isabel agreed to let her follow Philip to Germany. When Queen Isabel died, the couple hastily returned to Spain; the following year Philip fell ill from fever and died in Burgos. Because of Juana's delicate state of mind, her father, Fernando, became regent until Juana's son, Carlos, the future Charles V, came of age.

Juana, in the meantime, had her husband's body embalmed and regally clothed, refused to have him buried, and stayed beside him night and day. Finally she agreed to inter him in the Royal Chapel of the Granada cathedral, and during the trip to Granada she never let the coffin out of her sight. When the entourage arrived in Granada, Juana was once more incapable of parting with her husband's body, and she about-faced and headed north again with the body to the Real Monasterio de Santa Clara in Tordesillas, where her father had decided she should live. Eventually Philip was buried in the convent in such a way that Juana from her chambers always had his grave in sight.

During the next forty-seven years, Juana la Loca never left the convent, but she received visits from her father, Fernando; her son, Carlos, who would inherit the throne; and even her grandson, who became Philip II. When she died, her remains and those of Philip the Fair were taken to the Royal Chapel of Granada and buried beside the Catholic Kings.

tion of some of Spain's most important documents: an agreement between the Catholic Kings and the last Moorish king, Boabdil, for his exile from Spain; a letter from Columbus to the kings; the decree of Pope Alexander dividing up the New World between Spain and Portugal; the marriage contract of the Catholic Kings; a detailed sketch of Don Juan de Austria's battle plan for Lepanto; and a personal letter from Fernando to Isabel addressed to "My Princess." (Morning visits only.)

PEÑAFIEL   An unusual castle, seven hundred feet long and only eighty feet wide, looms like a beached battleship at the juncture of three valleys and forms a backdrop for the town's pretty, typically Castilian Plaza Mayor. If you climb into the higher quarters of Peñafiel you will come upon the sand-covered Plaza del Coso, where quaint houses have balconies to watch bullfights and other festivities that from time to time take place here.
ASADOR MAURO   Atarazanas s/n   tel. (983) 88 08 16, has a long-standing reputation as one of the finest *asadores* (restaurants for roasts) in the province. (Moderate.)

SAN CEBRIÁN DE MAZOTE   The church in this village is one of the few examples that still exist in Spain of tenth century Mozarabic architecture, a Christian style of Moorish influence. The wood ceiling, three aisles, horseshoe arches, and carved capitals are typical of the style.

MEDINA DE RIOSECO   Still a prospering market center, this town's picturesque, narrow, arcaded main street, Calle de la Rúa, has been declared a national landmark, and the Holy Thursday processions that pass here are especially stirring. Evidence of the town's notable past can be seen in its churches, among them, **SANTA MARÍA DE MEDIAVILLA**; its altarpiece is by Juan de Juni and Esteban Jordán, and the Capilla de Benavente is richly decorated and crowned by a polychrome stucco cupola. **SANTIAGO** church has a Churrigueresque (see box, p. 88) altarpiece of typically unbridled design. A large antique store at the entrance to town on the road to Valladolid has a good collection, and you can have tapas or lunch at **MESÓN LA RÚA**   San Juan 25   tel. (983) 70 07 83.

VILLALÓN DE CAMPOS   The multilevel village plaza here is a delight, its houses delicately poised on wooden supports. The star attraction is the sixteenth century pillory, a stone execution post carved with vicious dogs and monsters that must have hung menacingly over the unlucky victims. Fresh goat's milk cheese is typical of Villalón.

URUEÑA   We came here by chance and found massive adobe walls encircling a hilltop town, entered through one of two gateways. Local legend, although historically incorrect, says that Doña Urraca (p. 103) was imprisoned here after the conquest of Zamora by El Cid.

THE PROVINCE OF ZAMORA

ZAMORA (tha-*mor*-a) is in western Castilla, and its border with Portugal is formed by the Duero river (Douro in Portuguese). As the river exits Spain, it cuts Zamora into two distinct regions: to the north, Tierra de Pan (Land of Bread), and to the south, Tierra de Vino (Land of Wine). As Zamora approaches Galicia, at its northwest corner the landscape turns lush and mountainous (in the Sierra de la Culebra live the greatest concentration of wolves in Spain), and the customs and architecture begin to be Galician. Nevertheless, the color that predominates in Zamora is the monochromatic ocher-brown of its fields and of the stone used to construct its cities and villages.

The sights of special interest in Zamora are few; three—Toro, the Visigothic church at El Campillo, and, at Easter, Bercianos de Aliste—can be visited from a base in the city of Zamora. The paradors in Puebla de Sanabria and Benavente are convenient resting places en route to Galicia.

The Romans populated Zamora because it was along the important Vía de la Plata commercial route (see Index) from Galicia and Asturias to Mérida, and here that road joined another from Zaragoza. Zamora did not succumb easily, however, to foreign rule and was the scene of heroic struggles against Roman might, led by a brilliant strategist, Viriato (see box, p. 105). The Visigoths and the Moors followed, until finally Fernando I of Castile fought off the terrible Almanzor (see box, p. 137) and returned Zamora to Christian rule.

With the Reconquest came a wave of church building, and Zamora gave its own peculiar imprint to the Romanesque style. Whereas in Segovia porches distinguish the early churches, in Zamora it is the church facades that stand out for their extreme austerity. They spurn even the simple figurative carvings that are typical of Romanesque, opting instead for an utterly minimalist approach. Plant and geometric designs or just a single simple motif, such as a capsule, punched hole, shell, or even unadorned ribbing, may be repeated over an entire portal. Most church interiors in Zamora were restyled in later centuries and do not generally reflect the outer severity.

Holy Week is celebrated with exceptional solemnity in Zamora and is a much more sober (in the full sense of the word) occasion than in, for example, Sevilla. A key place to watch the religious processions is the city of Zamora, but the reenactment of the death and burial of Christ in Bercianos de Aliste, a tiny community of dirt streets and crude stone houses with slat doors, slate and red tile roofs, transports you to the ingenuous world of the Middle Ages, when the profundity of this event had to be graphically conveyed to an uneducated population.

In the village square on Good Friday afternoon, male town elders sit wrapped in the heavy brown wool capes and long black scarves that are customary in Zamora. Women begin to sing religious folk songs, echoed by more men who arrive and are followed by younger men dressed in all-white, from their hoods to their long stockings. The tunics they wear were traditionally woven by their brides-to-be, and would become shrouds for the men when they died.

A dramatic, articulated statue of Christ on the cross in the plaza is the focus of attention as two priests in cardinal-red robes climb two ladders, remove the crown of thorns, and release the figure from the cross into a glass coffin. The young men carry the coffin up a steep hill to the cemetery, and it is followed by a grief-stricken figure of the Virgin. There the event, an emotional one for many villagers and for me a fascinating look at a simple and enduring tradition, comes to an end with song and a return to the village. Eating is the next business of the day.

Besides the typical Castilian cuisine that is found here (the roast lamb is particularly good), Zamora has several characteristic dishes. You wouldn't think that a rice dish would be a specialty so far from rice country, and yet *Arroz a la Zamorana*, prepared in an earthenware casserole and relying on pork products, has a long tradition. It is said, in fact, that the famous Maragato muleteers of León (see Index) brought rice to Zamora from their trips to Valencia. Spain's best chickpeas come from the Zamoran village of Fuentesaúco, and besides being a part of traditional chickpea stew (*cocido*), from which the broth becomes Wedding Soup (*Sopa de Boda*), they are also coupled with cod (*Bacalao a la Zamorana*). Trout from the rivers may be prepared "Jewish style" (*a la judía*), with plenty of onion and garlic.

There are claret wines from Benavente and Fermoselle, but the most prestigious wines of the province are those of Toro, well known since the Middle Ages. The reds are fruity and robust, and appropriate to Zamora's meat-based cuisine.

THE CITY OF ZAMORA

On a hill above the north bank of the Río Duero and approached by a twelfth century bridge of sixteen pointed arches, Zamora was once defended by three castles (ruins of one remain) and in history was the scene of many fierce battles between Arabs and Christians. King Fernando I repopulated the city after the Reconquest, and when he died Zamora passed to his daughter, Doña Urraca. Under her rule the city endured seven years of siege (see box, p. 103).

Zamora is a small city, and its Old Quarter smaller still; it can easily be visited in an afternoon. You could begin at the parador, a fifteenth century palace with a magnificent sixteenth century Renaissance patio and a noble stairway. I would spend a night in Zamora just to stay here. Take a turn to the left as you leave the parador and begin a short tour that ends at the cathedral, the highest part of the city. On the way there are three Romanesque churches, all illustrating the peculiar Zamoran style: **SAN CIPRIANO,** one of the oldest, built in 1025; **LA MAGDALENA,** its portal richly but simply carved, with a rose window above it; and **SAN ILDE-FONSO,** remodeled but keeping its very simple, lobed archivolt portal.

As you continue walking, the dome of the cathedral appears, and it is unlike anything else in Spain (although the dome of the Old Cathedral in Salamanca bears some likeness), covered with overlapping stone slabs that resemble fish scales. It is decidedly Byzantine, but the reason is apparently unknown. You will have to go around to the south portal to see the entrance that has been conserved in its original Zamoran simplicity, and from here there are also extensive views of the river and the surrounding countryside. Inside, you can see the dramatic height of the beautiful dome, the fifteenth and sixteenth century Flemish tapestry collection, representing, among other themes, the Trojan Wars and the risqué, almost pornographic scenes on the choir armrests and upturned seats.

Just beyond the cathedral are the remains of the castle and the famous gate, Portillón de la Traición, where King Sancho was assassinated (see box). Four more ancient gateways, once part of the city walls, still stand in Zamora.

You could extend the tour, doubling back to the parador, then crossing the Plaza de Cánovas and continuing to **SANTA MARÍA LA NUEVA,** which was set afire during the "Trout Riot," when a trout was grilled inside the church to protest noble powers. The church has an impressive polychrome Christ by seventeenth century sculptor Gregorio Hernández (see Index). The massive gate of Doña Urraca, which led to the queen's palace, is just down the street, and there

QUEEN OF ZAMORA: DOÑA URRACA

Doña Urraca was not a major figure in Spanish history, but certainly a colorful one who captured the fancy of writers and became the subject of many Spanish poems and plays. A contemporary of El Cid's, and in some poetic accounts, in love with him, Doña Urraca was the daughter of Fernando I, who reconquered Zamora from the Moors. On his death he unwisely divided his kingdom among his five children; Doña Urraca's share was Zamora, where she ruled as queen, on the condition that she not marry.

Her rule proceeded peacefully until her brother, Sancho, in a grab for power, declared war on his siblings and with the aid of El Cid, threw all of them out of power—except Doña Urraca. She fought on and advised her deposed brother, Don Alfonso, a favorite of hers, to seek haven with the Moors in Toledo until the war was over.

After seven grueling years the siege of Zamora came to a sudden end when a man named Bellido Dolfos, some say with the blessing of the queen, went to the enemy camp just outside the city walls in the guise of a deserter. He told Sancho about a secret entrance to Zamora that could win him the war. Sancho followed him there, and Bellido Dolfos drew his sword and assassinated the king. The event took place at the door to Zamora that is today called Traitor's Gate.

Brother Alfonso returned from Toledo and took control of the kingdom, but in deference to his sister, who had been so supportive, he allowed her to keep Zamora. She reigned until her death at the age of sixty-seven.

The prolonged attack on and tenacious defense of Zamora gave rise to an expression that is immortalized in the city's coat of arms: *"Zamora No Se Ganó en Una Hora"* (literally, Zamora was not won in an hour), which has come to mean "Some things take time."

are two more eleventh century churches near the Plaza de Sagasta: **SAN VICENTE** and its tower, unusually tall for Zamoran Romanesque, and the finely proportioned **SANTIAGO DE BURGO**. Proceed down to the river and you will find **SANTA MARÍA DE ORTA,** which has conserved a primitive altar, and twelfth century **SANTO TOMÉ,** with three square chapels and beautiful but severe capitals. The walk completed, you have seen Zamora's most interesting sights unless, of course, you can arrange to be here for the Holy Week processions.

They are special occasions indeed, solemn and dignified, and they go on for a week, accompanied by hooded penitents in vivid robes and scores of musicians. But what really impressed me was the 11:00 p.m. Holy Thursday Procession of Silence, which begins at the Santa María La Nueva church. Hundreds of white-robed, purple-girded, hooded penitents slowly make their way down the hill, Cuesta de Pinedo. They carry torches and move in total silence until the dead figure of Christ passes, and deeply resonant drums roll. The procession finally enters the Plaza de Cánovas in front of the parador, lights are extinguished, and a hush falls over the crowd that is here to witness the spectacle. A choir from Santa María sweetly sings *Miserere,* and the procession returns to its church.

SEEING THE CITY OF ZAMORA

CATHEDRAL   It took just twenty years to build Zamora's twelfth century cathedral. The exterior has an unusual unity of style, although the interior was remodeled in Gothic fashion, and the main altar and some chapels are Baroque (see text).

THE ROMANESQUE CHURCHES   There are more than a dozen eleventh to thirteenth century Romanesque churches in Zamora, and their main interest lies in the characteristic Zamoran architecture and decorative style of the exteriors (see text).

STAYING IN ZAMORA

PARADOR CONDES DE ALBA Y ALISTE   Plaza de Viriato 5   tel. (988) 51 44 97   This was the palace of the Counts of Alba and Aliste, and it is a parador that I particularly admire. The elegant double-arched Renaissance patio displays medallions of biblical, mythological, and historical figures in its lower portion, the crests of the counts along the upper level. (Moderate–expensive; pool.) Reserve well in advance for Holy Week.

EATING IN ZAMORA

Eat at the parador, or try the locally fashionable **PARÍS**   Avenida de Portugal 14   tel. (988) 51 43 25, for creative and traditional cooking.

(Moderate.) Or make the rounds of the tapas bars along Calle Los Herreros, among them **BODEGA EL CHORIZO** and **BAR LOS ABUELOS.**

SHOPPING

ARTESAL   Ramos Carrión 32   One of my favorite antique stores in Spain. Its exceptional collection is attractively presented and carefully identified, and I especially like the turn-of-the-century Zamoran jugs.

FIESTAS

HOLY WEEK   The most important Easter-week processions take place on Holy Thursday during the day and at night (see text).

VISITING THE PROVINCE OF ZAMORA

EL CAMPILLO   In this tiny town is an unusually large seventh century Visigothic church of three aisles called **SAN PEDRO DE LA NAVE.** It

VIRIATO AND THE BIRTH OF GUERRILLA WARFARE

He was a simple shepherd from the environs of Zamora, but for nine years he was the nemesis of the mighty Roman Empire. Audaciously resisting the Romans with his ragtag supporters, he knew nothing but success.

His battle plans were ingenious and left the Romans bewildered. Viriato knew the local terrain like the back of his hand, and stood his ground only when he knew he could win. His men would appear, fight, and disappear before the enemy knew what had happened. The Romans were, of course, much better equipped, but their heavy armor and unwieldy numbers limited their mobility. Because of his style of fighting, it is said that Viriato was the first to practice guerrilla warfare. The word, in fact, is Spanish and means "little war."

Viriato continued to ambush Roman troops and kill their generals until Rome finally took decisive action to contain this embarrassing situation. Heavy reinforcements were sent, but Viriato was overcome not by the Romans, but by the treachery of three of his men. Lured by Roman promises of rich reward, they passed a sword through the throat of Viriato while he slept.

Viriato's successors were no match for the Romans, and the region finally submitted to their power. But the heroic resistance of Viriato was never forgotten. Today the flag of Zamora has eight red stripes, representing the ribbons that Viriato attached to his lance for each major victory. To this, Catholic King Fernando added a single bright-green stripe in recognition of Zamora's support for him in the Battle of Toro (see "Toro," p. 106), which paved the way for Spanish unity.

was once on the route to Santiago before it was moved to its present location when the Río Esla was dammed and the land flooded to create a reservoir. The church is primitively constructed of large stone blocks of irregular size. Inside, the arches are horseshoe-shaped, supported on columns whose capitals are exceptional, carved so deeply that they appear pierced; the animal, human, and floral designs are detailed and sophisticated. On the walls are decorative friezes in patterns of stars and swirls.

TORO   Standing proudly above a brown landscape by the side of the Río Duero, Toro is known as the Land of Bread and Wine because it straddles the wheat- and wine-producing regions of Zamora. Although not especially important today, Toro, under the rule in the eleventh century of Doña Elvira, sister of Doña Urraca, was a very prominent place. It was later the scene of some major events in Spanish history. Juana la Beltraneja, popularly perceived as illegitimate, challenged her aunt Isabel la Católica for the throne of Castile, and established her court here with her husband Alfonso V of Portugal, until the decisive Battle of Toro established Isabel as legitimate heir. Years later at Toro, in 1505, Fernando el Católico proclaimed his daughter, Juana la Loca (see box, p. 99), Queen of Castile, and Toro was for a long time the seat of the royal court.

Today the old Plaza Mayor, supported by stone columns, is a delightful center of town, and the medieval houses of narrow rough brick and wood beams give Toro a Moorish appearance. Toro's main attraction, the thirteenth century Pórtico de la Gloria of the Colegiata (currently in restoration), is heavily carved and polychromed with scenes of the Last Judgment in the style of the Cathedral of Santiago de Compostela, some say by the same Master Mateo. See also the fifteenth century Palacio de las Leyes, where the Spanish legislature once met, unusually decorated with crests and floral designs in a semicircle over the entrance.

The wines of Toro are sometimes strong and somewhat crude, but the better bodegas produce some nice bottles. Try the local wines with tapas at the bars around the Plaza Mayor.

HOTEL JUAN II   Paseo del Espolón 1   tel. (988) 69 03 00, is in a fine setting at the edge of town overlooking the Duero and the countryside (request a room facing this way). (Inexpensive.) The restaurant is pleasant, and the food quite good.

♦ Holy Week in Toro is solemn and impressive as the processions squeeze through the narrow streets. They follow an unusually long route, setting out from their churches at midnight on Holy Thursday and not returning until midday on Good Friday.

VILLALPANDO   Once a stronghold of the Templars, this simple Castilian town looks much grander than it is because of the imposing crenelated Puerta de San Andrés, made from the ruddy clay of the land and once part of the town walls. The churches in Villalpando have a Moorish air.

BENAVENTE   The "Town of the Counts," on a hill between the Órbigo and Esla rivers, has two Romanesque churches, Santa María del Azogue and San Juan del Mercado, both with fine Zamoran-style portals, but the main reason for being here is to stay at the **PARADOR FERNANDO II DE**

LEÓN   Paseo Ramón y Cajal s/n   tel. (988) 63 03 00. The elegant sixteenth century Torre del Caracol (Snail Tower) of the parador, with its stunning Mudéjar ceiling, is all that remains of a reputedly luxurious palace-castle of the Counts of Pimentel. It stood here high above the town but was burned by Napoleon's troops in the War of Independence (see Index).

BERCIANOS DE ALISTE   The events of Holy Friday begin at 4:30 p.m. and coincide, it is said, with the actual hour of Christ's death. This is a spectacle well worth seeing (see text). Arrive at least one hour in advance to stake out a good viewing post in the plaza.

PUEBLA DE SANABRIA   At cliff's edge and near the border with Galicia, this slate-roofed village is five thousand feet above the sea and is a charming combination of Galician and Castilian styles that incorporates brightly painted glass-enclosed wood balconies, in the Galician tradition. The Galician-green surroundings are scenic and include the largest glacial lake in Spain, El Lago de Sanabria.

PARADOR PUEBLA DE SANABRIA   Carretera del Lago 18   tel. (988) 62 00 01, is a modern parador, neat and well serviced, as paradors always are. (Moderate.)

THE PROVINCE OF LEÓN

LEÓN (lay-*own*) is the largest province of Castilla-León and its link with Galicia and Asturias. Situated at the northwest extreme of Castilla-León, the province shows a marked change in terrain, and no other Castilian province can claim so much variety. While to the south of the city of León the landscape is still typically Castilian, the plains become much greener. León's numerous rivers rush down from the high northern ranges, watering the fields and providing sport for fishermen, who can find 3,000 kilometers of trout rivers in the province. In León you will also find a great variety of large and small game, even the nearly extinct brown bear and the curious large bird called the *urogallo* (see p. 231).

North of the city of León the scenic change is more abrupt, and the pastoral, mountainous countryside begins to look like neighboring Galicia and Asturias. You will see *hórreos*—wood or stone granaries characteristic of northwestern Spain—grazing cattle, and lush greenery that ends in the looming peaks of Picos de Europa; some spectacular sites and sensational views of that range are in León. It is, in fact, the mountainous northern sector of León that I love, especially the forgotten rural villages of thatched- or slate-roofed houses that nestle in the valleys and sit along the rivers; those in the Ancares range, a national reserve near the border with Galicia, are especially isolated and primitive.

Many of these villages were once requisite resting points along the Way of Saint James, for León was directly along the pilgrimage route to Santiago de Compostela (see box, p. 220). That path encompasses the fertile and serene Bierzo valley in the northwestern part of León, known today for the good, although unsophisticated, El Bierzo and Cacabelos wines and for superior fruits and vegetables. Also in this valley in an isolated area called La Maragatería live the Maragatos. They belong to a curious subculture of uncertain origin, and their lives still often follow ancestral, almost tribal, ways. Once prosperous muleteers, they were highly respected for their hard work and absolute honesty. They never robbed, nor did anyone dream of robbing them: Reported George Borrow in the nineteenth century, "No one accustomed to employ them would hesitate to confide to them the transport of a ton of treasure. . . ."

Railroads and trucks have today replaced the Maragatos' traditional occupation, and many have been reduced to the meager life that the land provides and to living in medieval villages not yet touched by the twentieth century (Castrillo de los Polvazares is one of the few where an influx of city dwellers has brought prosperity). Maragatos still, for example, dress in unique costume on festive occasions—"Their garb differs but little from that of the Moors of Barbary—" (George Borrow)—and celebrate weddings in elaborate ceremonies. Maragatos keep to themselves, but the fame of their *Cocido Maragato*, a variation, or perhaps the origin, of Castilla's traditional chickpea stew, has traveled far and wide.

The kingdom of León, which included what is today the provinces of Zamora, Salamanca, Valladolid, and Palencia, played a significant role in the foundation of the Spanish nation. As the Asturs (see Index) pushed the Moors south from Asturias, León became the focus of warfare, and as the Moors were forced still farther south in the tenth century, León became the capital of Christian Spain. In recognition of its important contributions to the Reconquest, the lion in León's coat of arms (León is Spanish for lion) was incorporated into the crest of the united country of Spain. León, however, became Christian before the dawn of the Romanesque style and therefore often relied on Mozarabic design for their churches, blending Christian themes with Moorish style. Several outstanding examples of this art have survived in the province of León.

The food of León corresponds to the mountainous terrain, and hearty dishes predominate. You will find plentiful game and excellent beef, which is especially popular when air-dried and transformed into *cecina* (venison, kid, and boar are dried in a similar fashion). The province's fresh-milk products have a fine reputation in Spain, and from the León sector of the Picos de Europa comes Picón cheese, similar to Cabrales blue cheese from the Asturian side. In Oseja de Sajambre, also in the high mountains, a cylindrical, pungent semisoft cow's milk cheese known as *Queso de León* is made.

Since trout is so abundant in León, it is prepared in a variety of ways, among them *Trucha en Arcilla*, enclosed in clay that hardens as the fish grills, and *Trucha al Estilo del Bierzo*, grilled and served with prized *pimientos* of the Bierzo valley. The wines of El Bierzo and Cacabelos are satisfying with the foods of León, and there are a number of local pastries, like *Mantecadas de Astorga* (sponge cupcakes) and *Nicanores de Boñar* (puff pastries).

THE CITY OF LEÓN

León is today, as it was for generations of travelers, a logical stopping point on the way to Galicia. Medieval pilgrims sought refuge in its hospices, care in its hospitals, and spiritual inspiration in its splendid cathedral and its other churches; they even took time to do some sightseeing ("One has to visit in León the venerable remains of San Isidoro," proclaims the pilgrims' twelfth century guide, *Codex Calixtinus*). You will still find in this city all the things that brought the pilgrims here, and I would add to the guide's imperatives, "You must see the cathedral and stay at the Hostal de San Marcos." Of course, a modern city of more than 100,000 residents has much more than this, but I think that spending one night in León and a morning or afternoon seeing the sights, will uplift your spirits, if not bring the spiritual fulfillment that the pilgrims experienced.

Founded by the Romans in A.D. 68, León grew up along the Río Bernesga and gained importance when the capital of Christian Spain was transferred from Oviedo, in Asturias, to León. Throughout medieval times León was closely entwined with the cult of Santiago, and the city's three major sights are all related to the pilgrimages. The tightly enclosed streets of the Old Quarter have the flavor of those times, in sharp contrast to the wide boulevards, monumental plazas, and ornamental fountains built during the nineteenth century expansion of the city.

I have passed through León many times for no other reason than to stay the night in the Hostal de San Marcos, former pilgrims' hospice and today a deluxe hotel that is part of the parador system. It also happens to be one of the city's principal historic attractions. Ever since the twelfth century a monastery and a hospital for pilgrims stood here, overseen by the knightly Order of Santiago. But in the early sixteenth century King Fernando embarked on a much more ambitious project, building a new monastery and a hospice better suited to the care of pilgrims. Construction took place over a period of two hundred years, and the church, completed in Gothic style, was finished first, and its interior was lavished with decorative detail. The monastery, however, arose later in the sixteenth century, and its facade is a brilliant rendition of the Plateresque style (see Index).

Profusely carved with a variety of design motifs, the monastery is more than three hundred feet long, and its gracefully low line is broken only by a Baroque pediment that was added much later. Its most lavish ornamentation is concentrated over the main entrance. Here is Santiago Matamoros— Saint James in his role as warrior—along with the scallop shells that are the symbol of Santiago. Busts of great figures of history are portrayed along the length of the facade: Roman emperors Augustus, Trajan, and Caesar, the Spanish hero El Cid and the Spanish monarchs—Isabel and Fernando, Emperor Charles V, and Philip II, among them. The overall effect is a combination of freedom of design with the symmetry typical to the Plateresque style. Notice the balcony over the portal and the two balconies to either side. They are all part of one extraordinary guest room, in which the beds are canopied, the bathroom deep green marble, and the salon laden with antiques.

In the monastery cloister of San Marcos remains from the city's Roman past are on display, and an adjoining gallery, converted into a small but select museum, features the superb eleventh century ivory *Cristo de Carrizo*. His mournful eyes, crafted in black and white enamel, the delicately draped loincloth, and the carefully sculpted locks of his hair are unusual details that create a work of stunning impact.

I have hardly touched on San Marcos as a hotel. Dominated by the monastery's regal stone stairway and fashioned around the cloister, San Marcos is sumptuously decorated with antique Castilian furnishings, gleaming brass and copper pieces, period paintings and museum-quality tapestries. In one salon an exceptional gilded wood-carved ceiling has been preserved.

León's cathedral, begun in the thirteenth century, was obviously designed under French influence and perhaps employed French craftsmen in its execution; it is a masterpiece of Gothic art. An airy, delicate creation of exquisite proportions, this joyous work must have filled pilgrims with renewed religious fervor. Even today it is a wonder; keeping walls to a minimum, the cathedral is enclosed by an amazing 19,000 square feet of stained glass, so much that it was feared the cathedral would collapse from lack of solid support. Inside, the sensation is ethereal, as if you had left the earth and were floating in a sea of multicolored light.

Although the cathedral is dramatically lit each night, I will remember it most vividly as I saw it one crisp fall evening, when, as I stood outside, the spotlights were extinguished and the interior flooded with light, flaunting to full advantage the brilliant colors and extraordinary sweep of the stained glass. You could almost hear a celestial chorus singing hallelujahs.

For pilgrims, the Basílica de San Isidoro was a required stop because in this early Romanesque church San Isidoro's remains, brought from Arab-occupied Sevilla, are in a silver urn at the church altar. But for visitors today the basilica's most striking feature is the pantheon of the kings of León. Its domed ceiling, supported on low, finely sculpted capitals, displays in brilliant color perfectly preserved frescoes that are a whirlwind of activity, representing scenes from the Bible for which local people of the twelfth century were apparently used as models. Rarely is Romanesque art seen in such free-flowing form.

You would do well to spend your evening in León tapas hopping in the lively Barrio Húmedo, where almost every doorway leads to a bar. You might settle down to dinner at an old tavern, El Racimo de Oro, formerly a seventeenth century inn for pilgrims, or return to the Hostal de San Marcos and dine elegantly in its restaurant.

Seeing the city of León

HOSTAL DE SAN MARCOS   This extraordinary structure, once a monastery and pilgrims' hospice and now a luxurious hotel, incorporates a fine Gothic church, a cloister, and an excellent museum (see text).

BASÍLICA DE SAN ISIDORO   An early Romanesque basilica (see text). The church museum has some fine pieces, such as a blue enamel and gold chest and a dazzling chalice of agate, gold, and precious stones.

CATHEDRAL   Of pure and straightforward lines, the cathedral crisply rises into a tower and delicate spire. The main interest, however, is not the cathedral's architecture, or its altar or other works of art, but the sensational stained glass of the windows and of three giant rose windows, some of it original from the thirteenth century (see text). The cathedral has three triple-arched entrances, all extravagantly decorated with carved stone showing biblical and historical figures. A column at one entrance that portrays Santiago is worn away from the millions of pilgrim hands that have touched it.

♦ The cathedral is occasionally lit from within, sometimes in connection with religious holidays. Inquire at the Hostal de San Marcos on the chance that your visit might coincide with one of these special occasions.

CASA DE BOTINES (Plaza de Santo Domingo)   This curiosity is an early work of Catalan architect Antonio Gaudí (see Index), built in neo-Gothic style at about the same time as the bishop's palace he designed in Astorga.

STAYING IN LEÓN

HOSTAL DE SAN MARCOS   Plaza de San Marcos 7   tel. (987) 23 73 00 One of Spain's great hotels, as well as a work of art. It is a bit disappointing, however, to find that most of the guest rooms are in a new wing. (Expensive.) I urge you to reserve one of the rooms that belongs to the magnificent old structure and faces the front of the building. They are enormous and decorated in grand style. You'll feel like a king. (Very expensive.)

EATING IN LEÓN

The **DON SANCHO** dining room of the Hostal de San Marcos serves an elegant menu with international and regional specialties (expensive) and **ADONÍAS POZO**   Santa María 16   tel. (987) 25 26 65 prepares good traditional foods (moderate). For more casual fare, sample tapas in the Barrio Húmedo (in and around the Plaza de San Martín). Try **LA BICHA** and **EL TIZÓN,** among many other tapas bars. Or you can dine nearby at **EL RACIMO DE ORO**   Caño Vadillo 2   tel. (987) 25 75 75 (moderate), and have local foods like chickpea stew, frog's legs, and lamb.

THE ROUTE TO SANTIAGO DE COMPOSTELA IN LEÓN

Pilgrimages to the tomb of the apostle Saint James reached massive proportions in medieval times (see box, p. 220) and stimulated the construction of churches, monasteries, and hospitals along the route. The province of León was the last leg of the journey before reaching Galicia, and it is here that I find the most palpable reminders of those times and of the pilgrims' passage. Perhaps it is because much of the route in León goes through villages so little changed since then, or that the mountains of León represented the most grueling lap of the pilgrims' journey. You can almost sense the urgency to reach Santiago de Compostela after months of travel. Ominously, the pilgrim hospitals become larger and more numerous, and although today some of the villages are abandoned, you still see the wide, straight cobbled thoroughfares, called the Calle Real (Royal Road), so out of proportion in these tiny villages, along which the pilgrims walked, and along which churches and hospitals to care for them were built.

My idea of an exceptional day trip (by car) is to follow the stretch of the pilgrimage route in León that ends at the border with Galicia and begins just beyond the city of León in the small stone village of **HOSPITAL DE ÓRBIGO,** set in the fertile Órbigo valley. The hospital for which it was named is in ruins, but the narrow, twisting thirteenth century bridge over the Río Órbigo is still the main road out of town and evokes a celebrated

A PAGE FROM THE PAST: PEÑALBA DE SANTIAGO

A secondary and somewhat forbidding pilgrimage route passes through Peñalba de Santiago, one of the most startling villages you may ever see in Spain. It is an excursion meant for those with an adventurous spirit. To get there by car we braved a very narrow and steep mountain road that climbs through the mossy-green mountains of the appropriately named Valle del Silencio (Valley of Silence); the road comes to a halt in Peñalba. We felt we had reached the end of the world. In Peñalba the women are so sturdy that they sometimes perform tasks similar to those done by their work animals. They dress in black and tie black bandannas across their foreheads; they speak archaic Castilian.

The balconies of the slate-roofed, unmortared stone houses form a continuous line along the main street, and outdoor stairways leading from the dirt streets to the upper floors indicate that deep snows fall here in winter. Peñalba de Santiago, thus named because of its connection with the pilgrimages, is indeed a rare glimpse of medieval life. What a surprise to find in this isolated setting the Santiago church, a jewel of tenth century Mozarabic (see Index) design, distinguished by the perfect lines and the symmetry of its double-horseshoe-arched portal.

event that took place here in the fifteenth century. A Leonese knight, Don Suero de Quiñones, in love with a damsel who showed nothing but scorn for him, decided to battle anyone who attempted to cross the bridge. His objective was to collect three hundred broken swords as proof of his conquests and as a sign of his undying love. News of the jousts traveled far and wide, and when he reached his goal, Don Suero journeyed to Santiago de Compostela to give thanks to Saint James; we can assume that he won the heart of his fair lady.

Beyond the city of Astorga, a major center for the pilgrims and today the province's second most important city, the road enters into the region of El Bierzo; for those traveling on foot, the way became extremely arduous. As you climb into high desolate mountains, the pilgrimage route diverges slightly from the main road, passing through the thatched villages of **RABANAL DEL CAMINO** and **EL GANSO,** now quite deserted but still powerfully recalling the days when churches and hospitals greeted the pilgrims.

FONCEBADÓN has only two inhabitants now, a widow and her son, who gain their living caring for sheep. There was once a church, hostelry, and hospital in Foncebadón, but what remains just beyond the village at the windy 4,500-foot height of the mountain pass is a strange sight indeed: a mound of stones from which an iron cross (*Cruz de Ferro*), placed on a thick, fifteen-foot pole, emerges. The cross was brought here by French pilgrims, and perhaps was used as a signpost when snow obscured the pilgrims' path. Following an old pagan ritual of unknown origin, pilgrims carried stones—the bigger and more cumbersome to carry, the better—and deposited them here, hoping their act of penance would bring good fortune. After centuries (the tradition continues today) the pile contains millions of stones, many of them signed and engraved, and has grown to an impressive height. It's moving to think that each stone represents a person on his way to Santiago.

ACEBO, four kilometers beyond, is tiny, but it too has its Royal Road, bordered by houses with overhanging slate roofs and long wooden balconies. At the western side of Acebo on a road to the left, we take yet another step back in time, descending a beautiful twisting road into the valley, enclosed by mountains that rise on all sides, and to the forgotten village of **COMPLUDO.** Free-range chickens patter about the unpaved streets, and we pause on the wide main street for a country lunch at **EL BODEGÓN,** run by María and José María Acebo. Tree-trunk slabs serve as tables, and the meal is wonderfully simple: a potato omelet (*tortilla*), garden-fresh salad, crusty country bread, grilled *chorizo*, the local wine of El Bierzo, and a dessert from one of María's family recipes (p. 114).

Just outside Compludo on the way back to Acebo, a sign indicates "Herrería," and we make our way along a footpath, accompanied by the sound of swiftly running water, to find an ingenious seventh century iron forge, still functioning today. With the pull of a lever, a rush of river water enters a vertical pipe, sucking in air that fans the fire. At the same time, the river powers a wooden waterwheel that raises and lowers an enormous tree trunk, at the end of which a hammerhead forges the iron.

It was a relief for the pilgrims to reach **MOLINASECA,** for the Royal Road leads downhill and across a Roman bridge into this town, at once seignorial and humble. The going got rough again as the weary pilgrims approached **PONFERRADA,** for they had to detour around a huge gorge—until, that is, a bishop in the eleventh century built a bridge for them that gave the town its name, "Iron Bridge." From here, those of you seeking a truly uncommon experience could detour to **PEÑALBA DE SANTIAGO** (see box, p. 112).

Just outside **VILLAFRANCA DEL BIERZO,** near the Galician border and standing forlornly on a hilltop next to the cemetery, is the Romanesque Santiago church. Pilgrims too sick to complete the journey to Santiago de Compostela came here to the Door of Pardon (Puerta del Perdón), where they were offered the same papal indulgences (waiving some of the punishments of purgatory prerequisite to reaching heaven) that they had hoped to receive at the cathedral in Santiago de Compostela.

ᗰARÍA ACEBO'S APPLE YOGURT CAKE

María uses a 6-ounce yogurt cup to measure ingredients. To do the same, reserve the yogurt (lemon flavor) and dry the container. Otherwise, calculate that a yogurt container equals ¾ cup.

Sift together 3 (yogurt) cups of flour with 4 teaspoons baking powder. In a bowl beat 3 eggs and 2 (yogurt) cups of sugar until light and lemon-colored. Beat in the lemon yogurt and 1 (yogurt) cup of oil. Stir in the flour. Pour half the batter into a greased 9-inch cake pan. Cut two peeled and cored apples into ¼-inch slices. Arrange half of them over the batter and spoon on the rest of the batter. Cover with the remaining apple slices. Bake about one hour at 350°F, remove from oven, and brush with apricot marmalade.

ᔕEEING THE PROVINCE OF LEÓN

SAN MIGUEL DE ESCALADA   The tenth century monastery, of which the church remains, blends the Asturian and the Mozarabic styles (see Index). It has blind horseshoe arches, enclosing the church apse, and capitals decorated with floral motifs, both of Moorish influence.

SAHAGÚN DE CAMPOS   Many Moslem craftsmen stayed here after the Reconquest and applied their skills to Romanesque churches, using Moorish brickwork and horseshoe arches. The twelfth century church of San Lorenzo, with its elegant belfry and porched entrance, and the church of San Tirso (also twelfth century) are fascinating examples of this Mudéjar style.

VALENCIA DE DON JUAN   On a rise beside the banks of the Esla River, this town's fourteenth century Gothic castle rises impressively to its Torre del Homenaje, which is surrounded by other towers that are tall, slender, and cylindrical. The castle's delicacy and finesse are unusual.

HOSPITAL DE ÓRBIGO   Along the route to Santiago (see text).

ASTORGA   The fifteenth century Flamboyant Gothic cathedral, which has a Renaissance facade and fine Renaissance choir stalls and altarpiece, stands near the neo-Gothic Episcopal palace, a fantasy designed by Antonio Gaudí in the nineteenth century in accordance with the wishes of a fellow Catalan, the bishop of Astorga. The interior is a poor example of Gaudí's early attempts at modernism, and the tilework, although intricately designed, is, I think, somewhat gaudy. The palace houses a pilgrims' museum, unfortunately of scant interest. The city had twenty-four hospitals at the height of the pilgrimages to care for travelers. At the Baroque town hall a figure in the traditional dress of the Maragato (see text) strikes the hour.
LA PESETA   Plaza de San Bartolomé 3   tel. (987) 61 72 75, owes its fame to a description by James Michener in *Iberia* that praises the chickpeas and marinated pork (they are, in fact, quite good). The restaurant also serves *Cocido Maragato*, chickpea stew. (Moderate.)

◆ Be sure to try *Mantecadas de Astorga*, spongecake cupcakes, which are the specialty of Astorga and can be purchased all over town.

CASTRILLO DE LOS POLVAZARES   Just off the Santiago route, the wide, cobbled main street of this town is faced with beautifully restored stone houses built in traditional Maragato style; the stone is set in cement and the windows framed in white. On Sundays at midday everyone is eating the local chickpea stew, *Cocido Maragato*, and drinking chilled Cacabelos claret wine, at either of the two charming village restaurants on the main street.

FONCEBADÓN   Here is the celebrated Cruz de Ferro from the times of pilgrimage to Santiago (see text).

ACEBO   A delightful village on the Santiago pilgrimage route (see text).

COMPLUDO   A tiny village in a valley surrounded by high mountains that has a still-functioning iron forge (see text).

MOLINASECA   A pretty town on the Río Meruelo along the route to Santiago (see text).

PEÑALBA DE SANTIAGO   An isolated village living in the past (see box, p. 112).

PONFERRADA   The Templars, a powerful medieval religious military order, established themselves here to protect pilgrims to Santiago. Their imposing crenelated castle, built upon the ruins of a Roman one, is a fine example of thirteenth century military architecture.
HOTEL RESIDENCIA DEL TEMPLE   Avenida Portugal 2   tel. (987) 41 00 58, is designed to look like the Templars' castle. It's a bit overdone but otherwise quite nice and well cared for. (Moderate.)
SANTO TOMÁS DE LAS OLLAS, just outside the city (take the first exit on N-VI to Madrid and follow the signs), is a tenth century Mozarabic (see Index) creation. Its unusual apse has nine blind horseshoe arches in Moorish style.

CACABELOS   Slate-roofed porticoed houses gather around the large main plaza of this village, which was a place of passage for pilgrims (it had five hospitals). The extensive vineyards you see upon entering town announce the pleasant wines of Cacabelos.

VILLAFRANCA DEL BIERZO   In the fertile Bierzo valley, this town was founded by French pilgrims (see text)—thus its name, "French Village of Bierzo." On the curving Calle del Agua are several palaces with coats of arms.
PARADOR VILLAFRANCA DE BIERZO   Avenida Calvo Sotelo s/n   tel. (987) 54 01 75, is a modern parador but with wonderful views of the town and the valley and a good restaurant. (Moderate.)

BALOUTA   In this out-of-the-way Celtic village in the Sierra de Ancares near Galicia, many houses are primitively thatched.

CUEVA DE VALPORQUERO   Caves of surprising length and color tones, with spectacular stalactite formations.
+ The nearby **HOCES DE VEGACERVERA**—gorges hugged by bare white cliffs—provide sensational scenery en route to the cave.

POSADA DE VALDEÓN   See Picos de Europa.

DESFILADERO DE BEYOS   See Picos de Europa.

THE PROVINCE AND CITY OF PALENCIA

PALENCIA (pah-*len*-theea) is a province of contrasts, from the endless wheatfields of its southern tableland aptly named Tierra de Campos (Land of Fields) to the green elevations in the foothills of the Picos de Europa that end in a rocky wall separating Palencia from the Cantabrian coast. In Palencia there is ample trout fishing and game in abundance, from partridge and quail to bear, boar, wild goat, and deer.

The rivers Carrión and Pisuerga, which originate in the mountains of northern Spain and traverse Palencia from north to south in parallel lines, converge at the province's southern limits and bring desperately needed water from the mountains to the plains. Palencia's sights generally follow the course of the rivers, and I have therefore organized the highlights of the province around the rivers. You can, however, easily cross from one river valley to the other.

Palencia was first populated by the Celtiberians; the Romans called it Pallentia, and made it an important city of their Tarraconense province, which extended to Tarragona on the Mediterranean coast. From the Visigoths, Palencia retains a seventh century church—the oldest in Spain— as well as the remains of other Visigothic places of worship, often incorporated into later churches that were built over or around them. After the Reconquest, when Palencia returned to Christian rule, monasteries and churches sprung up in large numbers. They were built in Romanesque style, and Palencia has one of Spain's greatest concentration of such churches.

Church building in this area of Castilla gained added impetus from the presence of the Santiago pilgrimage route (see box, p. 220). Pilgrims were grateful for this easy stretch of flat land on their otherwise arduous journey. The Romanesque style takes a special twist in Palencia, characterized by distinctive facades that have lightly adorned portals, above which intricately carved stone friezes, generally showing Christ and the Apostles, sometimes stretch the entire length of the building.

Reminders of legendary hero El Cid (see Index) echo through Palencia. In the capital, he married Jimena at the San Miguel church, and both his sons-in-law were princes from the town of Carrión de los Condes. When El Cid reprimanded them for cowardly behavior in battle, they sought revenge by abusing his daughters, Dona Elvira and Doña Sol, an event described in the anonymous twelfth century poem *El Cantar de Mío Cid*:

> So hard did they hit them that they lay unconscious;
> bleeding in their slips and their silken dresses.
> They were tired of striking them.
> They competed to see who could hit harder.
> Doña Elvira and Doña Sol can no longer speak,
> They left them for dead in the oak forest of Corpes.

El Cid, always anxious to follow the diplomatic path (at least in poetic accounts), appealed to the king to punish the men and restore his daughters' honor. The girls soon remarried, this time with much happier results.

It was Alfonso VIII of Castile, however, who gave prominence to the province when in the thirteenth century he established in the city of Palencia Spain's first university (short-lived though it was). A century later the city's exceptional Gothic cathedral arose, and south of the city in the tiny village of Dueñas future Catholic Kings Isabel and Fernando met for the first time (see box, p. 120), an event that would change the course of Spanish history. Two of the finest artists of the late fifteenth and early sixteenth centuries, Pedro Berruguete and Juan de Flandes, worked extensively in the city and province of Palencia. Nevertheless, Palencia was in the past and continues to be now a small provincial capital that lazily unfolds along the northern bank of the Carrión river, and whose slow-paced life revolves principally around agriculture.

Except for the cathedral in the city of Palencia and some interesting Romanesque churches in the province, Palencia has few major sights and is generally ignored by foreign visitors and Spaniards alike. Seeing its quaint villages, its Romanesque churches, and the impressive mountain scenery to the north, however, will certainly provide pleasant diversion as you pass through Palencia, perhaps en route to the Picos de Europa and the Cantabrian coast. I would come this way if only to see one of Spain's most acclaimed Romanesque churches in the town of Frómista; visit a fascinating twelfth century church built into a cave in the hills of Olleros de Pisuerga; and spend an evening at the Cervera de Pisuerga parador, set in a natural amphitheater of uncommon beauty, facing the glorious mountains of the Picos de Europa.

SEEING THE CITY OF PALENCIA

CATHEDRAL   Be sure to see the magnificent crypt of a sixth century Visigothic temple built here to honor martyred San Antolín. It remains below the cathedral, as does the nave of an eleventh century Romanesque church built by King Sancho El Mayor in recognition of the apparition of the Virgin on this site (both are reached by a stairway inside the cathedral).

Otherwise this cathedral and its elegant portal are fourteenth century Gothic, but the main interest is artistic rather than architectural. The cathedral is commonly called "La Bella Desconocida" (the Beautiful Unknown One) because of its scant appreciation. The altarpiece is a monumental Renaissance work of several tiers, in which sculpture alternates with noteworthy paintings by Juan de Flandes, and carved scallop shells, symbol of the apostle Santiago, are a repeated motif.

The *trascoro* (the wall behind the choir) shows the Isabelline style (see Index) favored by Queen Isabel and is in part attributed to her favored sculptor, Gil de Siloé. In the octagonal Capilla del Sagrario, profusely decorated in Gothic style, are the remains of Doña Urraca, daughter of Alfonso VII of Castilla. The cathedral museum has valuable Brussels tapestries, commissioned by Bishop Fonseca in the fifteenth century, paintings by Pedro Berruguete, and one by El Greco.

STAYING AND EATING IN PALENCIA

CASTILLO DE MONZÓN   Carretera de Santander, km 11, Monzón de Campos   tel. (988) 80 80 75   Twelve kilometers outside Palencia, this tenth century castle is in a beautiful setting overlooking the valley of the Carrión. It's small (just ten rooms), cozy, and well cared for, and you can eat well in its restaurant. (Moderate.)

There are two good restaurants in the city of Palencia, **CASA DAMIÁN**   Ignacio Martínez Azcoitia 9   tel. (988) 74 46 28, and **LORENZO** Avenida Casado del Alisal 10   tel. (988) 74 35 45, both serving simple, well-prepared foods like *Menestra de Verduras* (vegetable medley), *lechazo* (roast lamb), fish from the Cantabrian Sea, and homemade custard desserts. (Moderate.)

For tapas, try **TABERNA PLAZA MAYOR** in the Plaza Mayor, where the selection is large and the atmosphere lively.

ƲISITING THE PROVINCE OF PALENCIA

The Pisuerga River Route

BAÑOS DE CERRATO   According to a lapidary, in this town's diminutive Visigothic church of San Juan Bautista, King Recesvinto built this church in 661, making it the oldest church still standing in Spain. The capitals are older still, belonging to a Roman temple that was once here. The church has three naves separated by horseshoe arches and covered by a wood roof. Sculptural detail abounds, especially the plant motifs typical of Visigothic art.

FRÓMISTA   In this pretty town of Roman origins that was an important stop for pilgrims on their way to Santiago de Compostela, the San Martín church, built in 1035, is generally considered one of the purest and most perfect manifestations of Spanish Romanesque and a model of its times. The interior has unusual height and an airiness uncommon in Romanesque. Light enters through a pierced octagonal lantern tower, which forms a dome inside. The capital carvings are remarkable. Outside, under the cornices that run around the church, are hundreds of richly carved figures of man and beast. Binoculars are helpful to see the detail.

OLLEROS DE PISUERGA   Just outside this village, next to the Río Pisuerga, a church steeple inexplicably emerges from a hillside. It is the only sign that here, built into the earth, is a unique church. It is thought to be pre-Romanesque, perhaps an ancient pagan place of worship (excavated tombs nearby also suggest this), then a hermitage. What we see today is a twelfth century Romanesque church in a cave, some of its columns and arches carved from the living rock. A primitive altar recently uncovered is thought to be seventh century (to visit, ask at the last house before the church).

MOARVES   The San Pedro church and its exceptional Romanesque frieze of Christ and the Apostles over the portal are in this town.

AGUILAR DE CAMPOO   Although it is the center of Spain's cookie industry (try Fontaneda cookies, freshly made), Aguilar de Campoo manages to keep its small-town charms. Located in the foothills of the Cordillera Cantábrica, the town is also a center for alpine activities. This is a place of palaces and mansions with coats of arms. A long, wide Plaza de España, dominated by San Miguel church, and the streets that radiate from it have houses that follow one another in a continuous line and are deeply porticoed. Glass-enclosed balconies recall La Coruña in Galicia.

CERVERA DE PISUERGA   This town of quaint streets and heraldic mansions is so named because of the many deer (*ciervos*) found here. There is no better place to stop on your way to the Picos de Europa than at the **PARADOR FUENTES CARRIONAS**   Carretera de Resoba, km 2.5   tel. (988) 87 00 75 (moderate), a modern structure in an incomparable mountain setting. From its ample terrace you can admire the distant peaks and the Ruesga reservoir.
◆ Take a scenic road called the "Route of the Reservoirs" that hugs the Ruesga, Camporredondo, and Compuerto reservoirs and passes amid gentle slopes filled in early summer with bushes of glowing yellow flowers and carpeted with tiny purple, pink, white, and periwinkle-blue blossoms.

The Carrión River Route

DUEÑAS   In this otherwise nondescript Castilian village, Fernando and Isabel, future Catholic Kings, met (see box, p. 120), and their daughter, Isabel, was born.

AMPUDIA DE CAMPOS   The arcaded houses along the main street of this village, declared a national monument, rest on crude tree-trunk supports. Some of the houses date to the thirteenth century, and its grand medieval castle, flanked by massive towers, is well preserved.

LOVE AT FIRST SIGHT? THE MEETING OF FERNANDO AND ISABEL AT DUEÑAS

Isabel, heir to the Castilian crown, had many pretenders, among them the king of Portugal and the brother of Louis XI of France. But because of her independent spirit, she threw prudence to the wind and made her own selection: Fernando, successor to the powerful throne of Aragón. The opposition of her half brother, King Enrique IV, and the bad relations between Castilla and Aragón failed to deter her.

Her choice may have been pure political acumen, although it is said that Isabel carefully investigated as well the personal attributes of her pretenders. Isabel and Fernando had never met, and Dueñas, not far from Valladolid, where the princess was living, was chosen for this significant occasion. Fernando's trip from Aragón was an adventure worthy of James Bond.

Fernando knew that those opposing his marriage to Isabel would create serious obstacles en route. But he was an enterprising and determined young man. Disguised as a muleteer, he was spirited past frontier guards who had orders to kill or kidnap him. After several more close calls he finally reached Dueñas, and the meeting more than compensated for the hazardous journey. Isabel and Fernando were delighted with each other. It is said, in fact, that they secretly married in Dueñas before the official ceremony that took place at the Viveros palace in Valladolid several months later on October 19, 1469.

Although the first years were politically rocky for the monarchs, by all accounts they were a perfect couple, and Isabel's outgoing nature and limitless energy were a perfect foil to the somewhat wily and suspicious character of her husband. Throughout their thirty-five-year marriage they showed unfailing support, respect, loyalty, and love for each other.

BECERRIL DEL CAMPO This town was once an important cultural center, and its churches reflect that past with works of art that include paintings by Pedro Berruguete in the Santa María church. The houses in the beautiful main plaza stand on timber supports.

BOADILLA DEL CAMINO Come just to see the elaborately worked pillory behind the church, covered with carvings of beasts and of the scallop shells of the pilgrims to Santiago de Compostela.

PAREDES DE NAVA Three great figures of the Spanish arts were born here: fifteenth century poet Jorge Manrique, whose *Ballad on the Death of His Father* is a classic of Spanish literature; the painter Pedro Berruguete, born in 1450, who brought the Renaissance style to Spain; and his son, master sculptor Alonso Berruguete, known for his powerful and dramatic work. In the Santa Eulalia church there is a small but wonderful museum, occupying several rooms of the church, that has paintings by Pedro Berruguete and Juan de Flandes and a collection of polychrome statues from the hands of Alonso Berruguete and several of his disciples. The church altar paintings are by Pedro Berruguete.

CARRIÓN DE LOS CONDES The royal court was once here and the town was the seat of counts (thus its name). Two princes of Carrión married the daughters of El Cid, with unfortunate results (pp. 116–17). There are three churches of note: in **SAN ZOILO** the counts of Carrión are interred, and although this church and monastery is tenth century, its highlight is an exceptional sixteenth century Gothic-Renaissance cloister with gracefully ribbed arches; the porch of the Romanesque **SANTA MARÍA DE LA VICTORIA,** also called Santa María del Camino because of its location on the route to Santiago, protects the portal, above which is an extraordinarily worked stone frieze; and **SANTIAGO** church is an exceptional example of Romanesque and also has an impressive frieze over the portal with figures carved in finest detail.

SALDAÑA   In the ruined castle of this noble town, Queen Doña Urraca (see box, p. 103) died. Just outside Saldaña a third century Roman villa with a perfectly conserved mosaic floor has been uncovered.

EL MOLINO   Carretera de San Martín del Obispo, km 1   tel. (988) 89 05 74, is an old mill next to the Río Carrión transformed into a charming inn specializing in roast meats made in a wood-burning oven. (Inexpensive–moderate.)

THE PROVINCE OF BURGOS

BURGOS (*boor*-gos) is a large Castilian province and one in which the landscape takes on a pale golden color. We are in the heart of the wheat belt, and yet the valleys of the Río Duero, which just touches the province at its southern limit, and of the Río Ebro, at the northern extreme, bestow a refreshing greenness. The local cuisine is enriched with trout, river crabs, fruits, and vegetables.

Burgos was a crossroads of the Roman Empire, and there are traces of Visigothic civilization as well, but Burgos did not become powerful until the ninth century, when a castle was built here to defend the region from the Moors. The nobility, flush with victory, moved south from Cantabria, and a prosperous city grew up around the castle. The Counts of Castile made Burgos their residence, and their leader, Fernán González, chafing under the rule of León, declared Burgos a kingdom. Because Burgos held the reins of Christian power early in the Reconquest and because it had become by the eleventh century the capital of this Kingdom of Castile, Burgos is often called the "Cradle of Castilla." Nevertheless, attacks by the fearsome Arab warrior Almanzor (see box, p. 137) persisted. His wantonness and continuing victories fired the legendary hero Rodrigo Díaz de Vivar, better known as El Cid, who was born in the province of Burgos in the eleventh century, to become a warrior and fight for the complete return of Spain to Christian rule.

Once the Reconquest was secured in northern Spain, the pilgrimages to Santiago de Compostela (see box, p. 220) began, and Burgos, directly along the main route, gained additional prominence and prestige. The province was one of the most important segments of the journey; in the city of Burgos and in the town of Castrojeriz, pilgrims were assured lodging and hospital care. San Juan de Ortega, after whom a village in Burgos is named, collaborated with Santo Domingo de la Calzada, who gave his name to a village in La Rioja, in constructing bridges and roads to lighten the sufferings of the downtrodden pilgrims. Later, in the fifteenth and sixteenth centuries yet another push to greatness came from La Mesta (see box, p. 63); Burgos was a center for the flourishing wool production and export business and became the residence of those who made their fortunes from the European demand for Spanish Merino wool.

Burgaleses, as the people of Burgos are called, have long been known in Spain for the purity of their Castilian speech, much as the speech of the people of Oxford is the standard by which proper English is measured. Their pronunciation and rhythmic inflection are music to the ears, and their vocabulary and phrasing are simple, clear, and precise.

Burgos is known for hearty cooking that concentrates on meats (especially good are lamb and a marinated pork called *picadillo*), beans, and tripe. Many consider the *chorizo* from Villarcayo the best in Spain, and the black sausage (*morcilla*) from Briviesca, mixed with rice and stuffed into sausage skins, is beyond compare. I love *morcilla*, so it is always on my mind when I come to Burgos. The name of Briviesca also shines for its honey-coated almonds (*almendras garrapiñadas*) and its outstanding sheep's milk rennet pudding (*cuajada*). Although Burgos produces many cheeses, it is most closely identified with one that is simply called *Queso de Burgos*. Made from sheep's milk and eaten when just days old, it is somewhat like a fresh mozzarella and often served as a deliciously simple dessert, drizzled with honey and sometimes sprinkled with walnuts.

Among the most celebrated Spanish wines, receiving rave reviews from wine critics around the world, are those designated Ribera del Duero. They come from vineyards in the vicinity of the Río Duero, and although the region extends into Valladolid, Segovia, and Soria, the bulk of the production is in Burgos. Fruity, crisp, and complex, these red wines naturally complement Castilian lamb, game, and other meat-based dishes, but are proving just as popular when paired with other Spanish and international foods.

Although the city of Burgos is unquestionably the focus of Burgos province and its cathedral is one of the great sights of Spain, when we come here we are more likely to spend our time in the countryside, exploring ageless villages and investigating churches that are sometimes more than a thousand years old. We concentrate on the eastern sector of the province, from south to north; Aranda de Duero, Peñaranda de Duero, Santo Domingo de Silos, Covarrubias, Quintanilla de las Viñas, Frías, and Puenteday are the names that come to my mind when I think of Burgos. Despite my preferences, however, you will certainly not want to miss the city and the cathedral of Burgos.

THE CITY OF BURGOS

Burgos appears like a mirage on the flat Castilian landscape, its cathedral of soaring spires almost absurd in this setting of wheatfields. Built in a valley on the northern banks of the Río Arlanzón, Burgos is a city of gray stone buildings with a wonderful Old World atmosphere unmarred by modern intrusions. You can be here and hardly realize that a new city lies just beyond the fringes of the original town. Eight bridges cross the river, and if you take the Puente de Santa María you will find yourself right in the Old Quarter, face to face with the commanding Puerta de Santa María. There are several gates that remain from the city walls, but this one is the most famous, redesigned in the sixteenth century in honor of Emperor Charles V.

The history of Burgos is condensed in the dark stone of the Puerta de Santa María. It was part of a fortress that defended the city against the Moors, and the statues over the arch represent, among other figures, two men who were key in the history of Burgos and also shaped the destiny of Spain: El Cid and Fernán González.

The name Fernán González may not be instantly recognizable, but it was he who in the tenth century initiated the union of Castile by bringing many feudal estates under his rule. El Cid, on the other hand, was glorified in one of the finest works of early Spanish literature, the epic poem *El Cantar de Mío Cid*, written in the twelfth century. He is also, for better or for worse, immediately associated with Charlton Heston's portrayal of the legendary warrior. The portrait of El Cid on the Puerta de Santa María is just the first of many reminders that Burgos is the city most closely associated with El Cid. In the Plaza de Miguel Primo de Rivera, a statue of El Cid on his horse, Babieca, looms larger than life, a work created in this century by noted Spanish sculptor Juan Cristóbal. In the cathedral El Cid and his wife are buried, and his coffer is on display.

By most accounts, he was born in Vivar, outside of Burgos, in the mid-eleventh century and became a page in the court of King Sancho of Castile. Because of his talents and his ambitious nature, El Cid rapidly rose to trusted adviser and celebrated army commander. When the king was murdered, El Cid lost no time shifting his allegiances to the brother of King Sancho, Alfonso VI. But Alfonso, unsure of El Cid's loyalties, listened to malicious gossip and ordered El Cid into exile. El Cid left his wife and two daughters at the monastery of San Pedro de Cardeña, just outside the city (this was also the first place of burial for El Cid and his wife; their sepulchers are still here).

Having lost the confidence of Castilla's leaders, he traveled east to Zaragoza and sought support from Arab rulers there. Conveniently overlooked in the grand saga of El Cid is the fact that the warrior was a mercenary, as fierce in battle against Christians as against Arabs, and just as likely to burn a church as a mosque. His allegiances shifted several times before he conquered Valencia for the Christians and secured his place in the annals of Spanish history.

It was from the Puerta de Santa María in Burgos that El Cid began his exile. He had sought lodging in Burgos, but although the people of the city admired him, they feared the king's wrath and refused to lodge him or even speak to him.

> He left through the door, leaving Burgos in haste,
> he reached Santa María and then dismounted;
> he fell to his knees and fervently prayed.
> His prayers ended, he remounted his horse;
> He went out through the door and crossed the Arlanzón.
>
> *El Cantar de Mío Cid*

The Río Arlanzón is right next to the Puerta de Santa María and bordered by El Espolón, a densely shaded tree-lined promenade that is a favorite place for Burgaleses to stroll. It's a perfect place for you to unwind (in one of the many cafés) after spending a morning at the cathedral.

Once you pass to the other side of the Puerta de Santa María, a Gothic world unfolds. It was King Alfonso III in the ninth century who ordered Count Diego Rodríguez Porcelos to build a fortress and a town here, and the ruined castle that stands over the city is a reminder of those times. There are churches and mansions of the thirteenth, fourteenth, and fifteenth centuries up and down the streets, built in the dark austere stone that lends so much character to the city. Narrow streets, quiet squares, and a round Plaza Mayor encircled by porticoed houses suggest the city's simple beginnings. But above all it is the cathedral that symbolizes Burgos's centuries of greatness and the cathedral that will capture your attention.

> Walking down one of these avenues beyond the river,
> one sees, really for the first time, the true Burgos,
> its heart, as it were, the centre of its being—the
> cathedral.
>
> *Edward Hutton*

The spires of the cathedral rise like dainty filigree above the houses, and the sight is striking from afar. But when you come up close and see the cathedral from the Plaza de Santa María, you can appreciate what a grand feat of engineering it is. Built on a multilevel plot of land, the cathedral has a north door that is several stories higher than the south entrance. To build something of this size on such irregular terrain would be a challenge even for today's sophisticated architects, but in the thirteenth century, when the work commenced, detailed architectural plans were minimal. Skilled craftsmen, relying on past experience and proceeding by trial and error, were entrusted with the task. There were, in fact, collapses before stability was finally achieved.

What emerged was an elegant but fairly simple early Gothic structure, designed in the style of the León cathedral and of marked French influence. By the fifteenth century, however, something more lavish was desired; German, French, and Dutch craftsmen came to Spain and transformed the cathedral, giving it the grace, elegance, delicacy, and drama that was the European fashion. But both German architect Juan de Colonia, who created the cathedral spires, and Flemish sculptor Gil de Siloé, who provided some spectacular work inside the cathedral, quickly assimilated Spanish styles, and the cathedral began to have a uniquely Spanish appearance. They fell under the spell of Moorish design, and Gil de Siloé, a favorite of Queen Isabel's, was partly responsible for the emergence of the Isabelline style (see Index).

Embellishment upon embellishment followed, and much of this subsequent work on the cathedral was done by the offspring of these European artists, Diego de Siloé and Simón de Colonia, born and bred in Burgos. The Burgos cathedral became a showcase for some of the most talented artists of the times; their works triumphantly and exuberantly crowd the cathedral and would influence styles in Spain for generations to come.

The interior of the cathedral is dazzling and quite overwhelming, a never-ending display of Gothic and Renaissance art. The only way to give your visit some structure, I think, is to take a selective tour, focusing on some of the cathedral's highlights. You can always return another day or on another trip, but it is counterproductive to see more than you can absorb. A personal guide—several are usually in wait in the Plaza de Santa María—is a great help.

So many sights compete for your attention, beginning with the portals: the Real, which faces the Plaza de Santa María, reformed in the eighteenth century, but flanked by two grand towers by Juan de Colonia; the Sarmental door, a fine example of thirteenth century Gothic; the Coronería, richly decorated Gothic; and the Pellejería, a work of Francisco de Colonia (son of Simón de Colonia) in Plateresque style.

Inside the cathedral the immense central nave soars 150 feet to an elaborately carved, lacy Mudéjar octagonal cupola, pierced with windows that flood the cathedral with light. The main altar is a grand work of polychrome sculpture, but no grander than the thirteen stupendous chapels that fill the side naves (the chapels of Santa Ana, Santa Tecla, and the *Presentación* are among the finest). A sixteenth century choir is impressively rich.

The sumptuous hexagonal Capilla del Condestable (Chapel of the High Constable) is like a cathedral within a cathedral. It has its own splendid cupola, rebuilt in 1539 after the original one collapsed. From outside the cathedral it forms airy, ornate pinnacles. The chapel—designed, some say, by Juan and Simón de Colonia along with Gil and Diego de Siloé, and enclosed by magnificent grillwork—is a vast space in which the constables repose, their tombs skillfully carved in Carrara marble.

Elsewhere in the cathedral, an exquisitely elegant marble and gilt diamond-shaped stairway (a work of Diego de Siloé) looks purposeless until you remember the uneven terrain on which the cathedral rests. The sacristy museum houses some fine sculpture (see a powerful work by Diego de Siloé, *Christ Tied to the Column*), Spanish and Flemish paintings (and a Magdalena attributed to Leonardo Da Vinci), and fifteenth and sixteenth century tapestries.

After this relentless assault on your senses, the silly Papamoscas, a clock high up in the nave, struck by a comic figure who opens his mouth at each gong (thus the name, Flycatcher), provides comic relief.

In fact, although the Burgos cathedral is generally considered one of the world's greatest, and I do appreciate its enormous artistic worth, I find it, at the same time, somewhat overdone. It makes me yearn for the innocent beauty of the Romanesque churches in the Castilian countryside. That is why I gravitate toward those things in the cathedral that are on a more human scale, like the simple tomb in the floor beneath the cupola, where El Cid and his wife, Jimena, lie, and the weatherbeaten coffer of El Cid that he weighed down with sand from the Río Arlanzón when he went into exile, in lieu of the gold that the moneylenders Vidas and Raquel were expecting:

> He has two chests filled with fine gold.
> You see that the king is angry with him.
> He has left behind properties and houses and palaces.
> Those he can't take with him, and doesn't want to sell them;
> El Cid is leaving them in your hands,
> So that you lend him what is necessary.
> Take the chests and keep them under your protection. . . .
>
> *El Cantar de Mío Cid*

Once you have completed the cathedral visit, take a walk along the Espolón to clear your mind, then take a break for tapas or lunch. But do reserve some strength for the splendid Cartuja de Miraflores, just outside of Burgos.

Seeing the City of Burgos

CATHEDRAL   There was originally a Romanesque structure on the site of the present cathedral which is considered one of Spain's finest examples of Gothic architecture. You will need the better part of a morning for the visit (see text).

CASA DEL CORDÓN   This palace belonged to the Grand Constables of Castilla, and its most outstanding feature is the doorway, carved with the constables' coats of arms and the sun-and-rope motif that are symbols of the Franciscan order. The kings received Columbus here when he returned from his second voyage.

SAN NICOLÁS   The focal point of this fifteenth century church is the astonishing altarpiece carved in stone in minutest detail by Simón de Colonia.

MUSEO PROVINCIAL   Occupying two historic houses, the museum's treasures are the gilded copper-and-enamel altar front from the Santo Domingo de Silos monastery in the province of Burgos and the stupendous Gothic sepulcher of Juan de Padilla, beloved page of Isabel la Católica, by Gil de Siloé.

MONASTERIO DE LAS HUELGAS   The Catholic Kings showered this twelfth century monastery with favors, and its abbess, to the dismay of some churchmen and high officials, became a powerful woman (if the pope were to marry, it was said, he would have to marry the abbess of Las Huelgas). The fine Romanesque cloister shows the influence of the Santo Domingo de

Silos monastery; in the chapterhouse is the famous embroidered standard of the Moors captured in the decisive battle of Navas de Tolosa (see box, p. 472); the church has some fifty tombs of Castilian royalty and other nobility and a curious revolving pulpit that permitted a priest to face the entire congregation. The Cloth Museum is unique, displaying sumptuous fabrics and clothes from the Middle Ages.

CARTUJA DE MIRAFLORES   Although this monastery was founded by Juan II, father of Isabel la Católica, it was she who engaged Juan de Colonia and his son Simón to design the church and Gil de Siloé to do the astonishing interior. His altarpiece is a sight to behold, drenched in gold (some of which was brought from America by Columbus) and designed in an unusual circular pattern. The tombs of Isabel's parents, also by Gil de Siloé, which rest in front of the altar, are a sculptural masterpiece, lavishly carved in alabaster and forming an eight-sided star. Off to one side and also profusely carved is the standing figure of Don Alfonso, who, had he not died at a young age, would have ruled instead of his sister Isabel. The deftly carved seventeenth century polychrome statue of San Bruno has wonderfully expressive face and hands and a sense of restraint uncommon in sculpture of that period.

STAYING IN BURGOS

LANDA PALACE   Carretera Madrid-Irún, km 236   tel. (947) 20 63 43   Even though it is a five-minute drive from the city, this is my choice when I come to Burgos. A tower of a castle, transported stone by stone from its original location, is the centerpiece of this deluxe hotel, laden with antiques that are arranged into collections of clocks, carts, cribs, cradles, chests, irons, brass scales, and bed warmers. (Expensive; indoor-outdoor pool.) Tastefully decorated rooms and excellent breakfasts. For a singular experience, reserve the Royal Suite, available to you when the king is not in town. Bathroom fixtures are gold plate, and the brass bed culminates in a crown. (Very expensive.)

HOTEL DEL CID   Plaza de Santa María 10   tel. (947) 20 87 15   Conveniently located in the Old Quarter, right across from the cathedral—you couldn't ask for a better setting. Some rooms in this simple hotel have views of the cathedral's spectacular nighttime illumination. (Moderate–expensive.)

EATING IN BURGOS

LANDA PALACE   The restaurant of the above-mentioned hotel, in an elegant setting of Gothic arches, stone block walls, and huge hand-wrought chandeliers, serves local specialties (*chorizo* and black sausage, baby lamb, Burgos trout, fresh Burgos cheese) along with some more inventive dishes. (Moderate–expensive.)

CASA OJEDA   Vitoria 5   tel. (947) 20 90 52   You can come to this classic establishment for sit-down tapas in abundant variety or for a fine dinner.

Good choices are *chorizo* and black sausage with *pimientos*, marinated trout, roast lamb, potted quail, and garlic chicken. (Moderate.)

MESÓN DEL CID   In the Hotel del Cid, this rustic restaurant has similar, well-prepared regional specialties. (Moderate.)

♦ Although I particularly like tapas at **CASA OJEDA,** there are many other possibilities, especially in the area around the cathedral.

FIESTAS

CORPUS CHRISTI is particularly colorful. The religious procession is preceded by "giants" and "bigheads" two stories high, each "danced" by a single person hidden under the skirts.

SANTO DOMINGO DE SILOS

Set in a beautiful countryside of gentle green hills, the monastery of Santo Domingo de Silos can be the centerpiece of a lovely one- or two-day excursion that might include a visit to one of Spain's oldest churches in Quintanilla de las Viñas; a stop to see the castle, the palace, and the village of Peñaranda del Duero; lunch in Aranda de Duero; and a night in the delightful town of Covarrubias.

The church of Santo Domingo de Silos has undergone many changes over the centuries and is not the reason to come here. The cloister, on the other hand, is a jewel of the medieval world. This monastery was founded by Castilian count Fernán González, destroyed by Arab warrior Almanzor (see box, p. 137), and rebuilt in the eleventh century by a monk who became Santo Domingo (Saint Dominic). Handcuffs are his symbol, for he freed many Christians from Arab oppression and in turn imprisoned many Moslems in the monastery. The fame of the saint made this monastery a stopping place for pilgrims making their way to Santiago de Compostela from points south.

The monk who shows us Santo Domingo de Silos, Brother Juan Carlos, greets us in English, but prefers to speak Spanish. He is tall, slim, and boyish, despite his gray hair, and we are surprised to find out that he is American, and his surname is Ross. A longtime resident of Madrid, where he had what he describes as a "quite ordinary" job, he has been a monk here for the last sixteen years, and takes great pleasure in showing us the monastery's renowned cloister.

"This is the only Romanesque cloister you will see in Spain that has two floors," he explains. The cloister, a slightly irregular square, indeed has a grace, unity, and finish we had not seen before. "The floor-to-ceiling stone-carved panels at the cloister corners that show scenes from the life of Christ are also unique," he continues, with more than a touch of pride in his voice. The panels are crowded with figures, carved in a simple, winsome manner and with an energy and sense of motion uncommon in Romanesque. In a scene of *The Doubt of Saint Thomas*, the flowing, harmonious composition of Christ with the Apostles is brilliant. Blackened eye pupils give depth to the stone and increase the emotional impact. In another panel, *Descent from the Cross*, Christ rests on the cross in a pose of utter serenity; there is not a hint of suffering or pain. Even Christ's navel is perfectly sculpted. "Notice the excellent state of preservation of these panels," remarks Brother Juan Carlos. "Even the noses and toes are intact."

Our attention turns to the extraordinary capitals on the double columns supporting the cloister arches. Our guide leads us to the earliest ones, on the north and east sides. They are carved by an unknown sculptor in the kind of minute detail that you would associate not with stone but with ivory or with plaster tracery. The themes are often original, bearing little relation to other works of the times and demonstrating decidedly Moorish influences. This has led some experts to claim that the work was done by Moslems held prisoner in the monastery. Be that as it may, we see an astonishing and complex array of scenes. There are purely ornamental plant designs that swirl intricately and real and imaginary birds and beasts: eagles, peacocks, dragons, serpents, and griffins, sometimes in fierce combat with one another. You could spend a lifetime studying the complex themes and the technical skill.

The capitals on the south and west sides of the cloister are thought to have been carved by a second artist, probably some time later in the thirteenth century. They show religious subjects and are generally considered of lesser worth. To the nonacademic eye, however, they are still quite special.

In the grassy courtyard of the cloister, an old cypress tree rises, a symbol of immortality and itself immortalized in a poem by Gerardo Diego:

> Mast of solitude, isolated wonder;
> Arrow of faith, lance of hope,
> Today he came to you, on the banks of the Arlanza,
> pilgrim of chance, my wandering soul.
>
> When I saw you, proud, sweet, strong,
> what anxiety I felt to dissolve
> and rise like you, changed into crystals,
>   like you, dark tower of straight edges,
> example of vertical raptures,
> silent cypress in the fervor of Silos.

THE MONASTERY'S MUSEUM

I love several unusual pieces in the small monastery museum, among them a dove of gold-plated silver from the late twelfth century; the chalice of Saint Dominic, Moorish-influenced and covered in delicate gold filigree; and a stunning copper chest decorated with brightly colored enamels and bathed in gold that depicts Christ and the witnesses to the crucifixion (in the

Museo Provincial of Burgos, see the altar front from Silos with similar decorative work).

Also in the monastery is an interesting early eighteenth century pharmacy displaying ceramic medicine jars and pharmaceutical books.
◆ Tours are guided by the monks. Ask for Brother Juan Carlos.

TRES CORONAS DE SILOS   Plaza Mayor 6   tel. (947) 38 07 27, is an eighteenth century manor house decorated in Castilian style. It is a good place to spend the night (moderate)—although I would rather stay in nearby Covarrubias—or at least to have lunch.
◆ Near Silos, on the road to Salas de los Infantes, is the awesome **YECLA GORGE,** which you can see best if you venture along the walkway.

$\mathcal{V}$ISITING THE PROVINCE OF BURGOS

ARANDA DE DUERO   Crossed by the Río Duero, this is a big town, but you will find at its heart an Old Quarter and seignorial houses.

I could make a meal of the sensational bread served at **MESÓN DE LA VILLA**   Plaza Mayor 3   tel. (947) 50 10 25, but I would not want to miss their excellent roast lamb, river crabs, or game birds in escabeche. Good homemade desserts. See their magnificent bodega. (Moderate.)
EL ROBLE   Plaza Primo de Rivera 7   tel. (947) 50 29 02, is great for tapas; behind the bar is a huge wood-burning oven where lamb roasts. Try *morcilla* (black sausage), roast red peppers, and *picadillo* (grilled marinated pork).
◆ On Easter Sunday morning, in front of the Santa María Church, distinguished by an outstanding Plateresque facade, an interesting ceremony takes place. A child dressed as an angel descends on ropes from the church towers and removes the black veil of mourning from a person who represents the Virgin, thus signaling the celebration of the resurrection.
◆ If you take the C-114 road that begins three kilometers south of Aranda and continue about twenty-five kilometers (just over the province line in Segovia), a wood sign indicates Refugio de Rapaces. A deep canyon opens up, framed by ruddy red cliffs cut by the Río Riaza. Slowly circling, swooping vultures and other birds of prey make their nests here in this singular setting.

PEÑARANDA DE DUERO   The Plaza de los Condes is the highlight of this wonderful tawny-colored town of historic designation, crowned by a castle. A Gothic pillory stands at the center of the main plaza, and the sixteenth century church of Santa Ana is to one side. Don't miss a visit to the splendid Renaissance **MIRANDA** palace, also in the plaza; the *artesonado* ceilings are extraordinary.
◆ A turn to the left when you exit the palace, then left again, takes you to an eighteenth century pharmacy, filled with more than two hundred original ceramic medicine jars.

SALAS DE LOS INFANTES   It is said that the father of the Seven Princes of Lara founded this town, and according to an old Castilian ballad, his seven sons were assassinated and decapitated here in an act of revenge. Their heads are supposedly interred in an urn in the Santa María church.

COVARRUBIAS   Named for the nearby red caves (*cuevas rubias*), this is a charming town of noble homes and cobbled, porticoed streets by the banks of the Río Arlanza. Fernán González, responsible for the unification of Castilla, and many other Castilian dignitaries of the past are buried in the fifteenth century Gothic collegiate church, shaded by a porch and protected by a delicately worked wrought-iron gate. Covarrubias is a most pleasant place to spend a night.

PARADOR COLABORADOR ARLANZA   Plaza Mayor 11   tel. (947) 40 30 25, is associated with the paradors and occupies a historic building. Accommodations are simple. (Moderate.)

CASA GALÍN   Plaza de Doña Urraca 4   tel. (947) 40 30 15, across from the hotel, serves home-style Castilian fare. (Inexpensive–moderate.)

QUINTANILLA DE LAS VIÑAS   An exceptional seventh century Visigothic church of three aisles, primitively constructed. Three friezes using flower and animal motifs enclosed in spheres run around the outside of the church, and inside is a stone tablet of Christ and two angels, exquisitely carved.

SAN JUAN DE ORTEGA   This town is named after a twelfth century saint who founded a church and hospital here for pilgrims to Santiago. The saint was a disciple of Santo Domingo de la Calzada and also built bridges and roads to ease the pilgrims' journey. Here in the Romanesque church, San Juan is interred in a sepulcher enclosed within a magnificent Gothic shrine that shows, carved in stone, scenes from the saint's life.

BRIVIESCA   You might stop here to see the Baroque altarpiece of the Colegiata de Santa María and perhaps to try the town's food specialties: black sausage (*morcilla*), sheep's milk rennet pudding (*cuajada*), and crackly honey-coated almonds (*almendras garrapiñadas*).

   At **EL VALLÉS**   Carretera Madrid-Irún, km 260   tel. (947) 59 00 25, you can find these specialties plus the beans and the hake for which the restaurant has achieved fame. Or go next door to **CASA TERE**   (947) 59 08 22, for similar food and homemade *almendras garrapiñadas*.

OÑA   Next to the impressive gorge of Horadada, this is a pretty Castilian village with palaces and an interesting multilevel plaza.

SANTA GADEA DEL CID   A little village where the red tile-roofed houses, crisscrossed by wood beams, stand on wood columns. The plaza is charming.

FRÍAS   A Roman bridge takes you over the river and into a steep ascent to this wonderful cliffside village of flower-filled whitewashed houses on crude timber supports. The twelfth century castle emerges like a needle from a narrow rocky spur.

SAN PANTALEÓN DE LOSA   In the Losa valley, next to the Río Jerea, a gently ascending hill ends abruptly in a straight-out cliff, and a twelfth century church with an unusually carved portal is there. The scene from afar resembles a stranded ocean liner.

PUENTEDAY   This village is rarely mentioned, but we were struck by the magnificent scene: a massive natural stone bridge, cows grazing at waterside below it, and above it, an old stone village, from which plants cascade down the rocks. As a backdrop, there is a wall of white cliffs running in a straight line across the sky.

LERMA   The palace of the Duke of Lerma, who was a favorite of Philip III, is a grand work of the seventeenth century and just one of the projects that this powerful duke undertook in his hometown. He laid lineal streets in the seignorial upper town that are in striking contrast to the narrow, more inviting streets of the old town below it.

CASTROJERIZ   The many churches in this very small town are one sign that at the height of the pilgrimages to Santiago, Castrojeriz was much more important than it is today. From the Burgos road there is a beautiful view of the village and its castle.

THE PROVINCE AND CITY OF SORIA

Soria, cold, Soria, pure,
Head of Extremadura,
with its warlike castle
in ruins, above the Duero;
with its corroded walls
and its blackened houses!

Dead city of gentlemen
soldiers or huntsmen;
of doorways with shields
from a hundred generations of nobles,

...

Soria, cold! The bell
of the courthouse rings one o'clock,
Soria, Castilian city
so beautiful! under the moonlight.

WITH THESE WORDS, Antonio Machado, one of Spain's finest twentieth century poets, immortalized the Castilian city of Soria (*sor*-ee-a). When he wrote the poem at the beginning of this century, Soria was forgotten, its mansions and churches the only signs of its past greatness. Harsh in his criticism, Machado nevertheless loved Soria, and the influence of the city and the Castilian countryside moved him to heights of lyricism. Although Sevillano by birth, he lived here five years with his beloved wife, Leonor, and when she died, Machado found in Soria the solitude and the sense of eternity that he craved.

Many poets have sung the praises of Soria, often considered the epitome of Castilian beauty and austerity, but the poetry of Antonio Machado in particular stamped on the Spanish mind images of the province's nobility, its bright light, pure crisp air, and subtle shades of brown, gold, and rust.

The province of Soria, adjoining Aragón on the mountainous fringes of Castilla, saw Roman domination, as the ruins of Numancia and the grand triumphal arch in the charming town of Medinaceli clearly show. The Moors left their mark as well, particularly palpable in the village of Calatañazor. This is a province of physical contrasts. The Río Duero winds its way through Soria. It begins high in the mountains, near the awe-inspiring Laguna Negra (Black Lake), one of Machado's favorite places ("Pure and silent water/ that copies eternal things;/ Impassive water that holds/ in its breast the stars"). The Duero flows through land thick with resinous pines, oaks, and beech trees and waters the ever-present plains of Castilla, where grain grows and sheep graze. But because of Soria's supply of water and its closeness to green mountain land, cattle is abundant and Soria is known for its excellent meats and famous in Spain for the fine taste and purity of its butter.

In Soria you will find the foods typical of Castilla-León, but its sweets stand out: *Brevas de Soria* (custard-filled pastries), *yemas* (egg-yolk candies, see box, p. 398), sponge cakes (*mantecadas*), and *Paciencias*, cookies that use egg whites left over from the *yemas*.

Because the earth of Soria is rich in clay and limestone and evergreen oaks pepper the landscape, the province yields impressive quantities of black truffles. The bulk of the production is shipped over the border to France to supplement that country's diminishing supply. Strangely enough, truffles were rarely a part of Spanish cooking (a notable exception is *Faisán al Modo de Alcántara*, see box, p. 187) until the enthusiasm for nouvelle cuisine sent Spain's chefs scrambling for Soria's truffle supply. And thanks to the efforts of two young Sorianos, Millán and Virgilio Maroto, owners of Maroto restaurant, truffles have finally achieved a starring role in the capital city of Soria. When we ate here recently, we tried truffle soup covered with puff pastry, pâté with truffles, and dove in truffle sauce, and Millán, who is the chef, showed me some magnificent specimens of truffles the size of baseballs.

Not only are Soria's "black diamonds" sniffed out by trained dogs, but after many years of experimentation, around the village of Navaleno the impossible has been achieved: truffle farming. Naturally, secrecy and the protection of lucrative truffle fields are a priority. Truffle markets take place in the dead of night in utmost privacy; no one wants to reveal his sources. Only Spanish saffron (see box, p. 152) approaches truffles in its astounding price and in the protective atmosphere in which it is collected.

Although the golden city of Soria is not usually a principal destination of ours, we often stop here on our way from Madrid to Navarra or Aragón, and we never tire of admiring once again the intriguing cloister of San Juan de Duero, on the banks of the Duero river. From here Soria rises to the heights of its ruined castle, where we spend the night at the parador that has been built next to it.

Soria is no longer the ruined town that Antonio Machado knew, but it does remain a quiet place, a shadow of what it was in the sixteenth century. Castilian king Alfonso VII returned Soria to Christian rule in the twelfth century, and several exceptional churches were built at that time. The king conferred nobility on Soria for its role in the Reconquest and gave the city a coat of arms that included the words *Soria Pura* (Soria, Pure), which Machado incorporated into his poem. In the fourteenth century Soria was capital of a broad region.

Sheep of La Mesta (see box, p. 63) passed by here, and the city, near the northeast limits of the migrations from Extremadura (thus the other words of its crest, Cabeza, or Head, de Extremadura), became a commercial center specializing in the wool industry. Wealth came to its citizens, and they built palaces and noble residences, many of which you can see on and around the Calle Real. Soria reached its height in the sixteenth century (the sumptuous Renaissance palace of the Condes de Gómara is from that period) and has since diminished in importance, living a peaceful small-town existence, but saved from oblivion by Machado's poetry.

Machado loved to take solitary walks to the Hermitage of San Saturio along the banks of the Río Duero, lined with poplars, which passes in the shape of a crossbow around the city of Soria. This is still a pleasant place to stroll and to recall Machado's poems.

> Poplars on the white road, poplars on the riverbanks,
> froth on the mountain
> against the distant blue,
> day of sun, clear day!
> Beautiful land of Spain!

Seeing the City of Soria

OLD QUARTER   A uniformity of style and stone construction and golden color characterize Old Soria. The Plaza Mayor, wide and bare, leads on one side into porticoed Calle de Collado and on to the crested houses of Aduana Vieja. Northeast of the square are the palaces and noble residences of the Calle Real.

SANTO DOMINGO   An oddly square-set twelfth century church of French influence with geometrically matched sides, two levels of blind columns, and above them a rosette window, but no belfry. The Romanesque portal, among the finest in Castile, is richly sculpted in minute detail with hundreds of figures crammed into four semicircles, and depicts scenes from the New Testament.

SAN JUAN DE RABANERA   A twelfth century church, Romanesque but unusually Byzantine in appearance with its especially beautiful tall and narrow apse.

CATHEDRAL OF SAN PEDRO   The facade is Plateresque, the interior Gothic, but the beautiful cloister of double-columned arches is pure Romanesque.

ERMITA DE SAN SATURIO   Improbably built on the steep rocky incline along the Duero in eighteenth century Baroque style, this church grew up around the cave where hermit San Saturio, patron saint of Soria, once lived his ascetic life.

MUSEO PROVINCIAL   This museum is dedicated to the objects uncovered at the Roman ruins of Numancia, such as ceramics that show vivid scenes of men and animals in motion.

SAN JUAN DEL DUERO   Little remains of the Romanesque church that stood here on the banks of the Duero to aid pilgrims on their way to Santiago. What is left, however, is most unusual. Two *baldaquinos*—square, canopied shrines of oriental appearance—to the sides of the altar and close to the congregation, rest on quadruple columns with finely carved capitals. Their purpose, apparently, was to allow three priests to perform Mass simultaneously.

The highlight here, however, is the unique free-standing arches that remain from the thirteenth century cloister. Each side represents a distinct architectural style; two sides have rounded arches typical of the Romanesque period, but the remaining arches loop and crisscross in a complex design that shows Moorish influence and yet is unlike any other in Spain. The arch over the south gateway seems to float in midair, for it dips but has no column under it for support.

STAYING IN THE CITY OF SORIA

PARADOR ANTONIO MACHADO   Parque del Castillo   tel. (975) 21 34 45 Set on a hill overlooking the city, where the ruins of Soria's castle still stand, this modern parador has stunning views and a good restaurant. (Moderate–expensive.)

EATING IN THE CITY OF SORIA

MESÓN CASTELLANO   Plaza Mayor 2   tel. (975) 21 30 45   A typical Castilian tavern serving regional food like beans with *chorizo*, chickpea stew, and roast lamb. (Moderate.)

MAROTO   Paseo del Espolón 20   tel. (975) 22 40 86   The brothers Maroto have created a spark of culinary excitement in Soria with a menu delving into *nueva cocina*. Fine local truffles find their way onto the menu (see text), and game dishes, in season, are excellent. (Moderate.)

$\mathcal{V}$ISITING THE PROVINCE OF SORIA

◆ Take note that monuments and museums in the province of Soria are closed Mondays and Tuesdays.

BERLANGA DE DUERO   This fifteenth century castle, ruddy red like the earth of Castilla and surrounded by two circles of defensive walls, looks out over a town of Renaissance palaces and a quaint Plaza Mayor. Follow the signs to the town's Gothic pillory.

SAN BAUDELIO DE BERLANGA, nine kilometers away in Casillas de Berlanga, is a Mozarabic church (built by Christians in Moorish style) from the eleventh century whose walls were once covered with wonderful twelfth century Romanesque frescoes (now in the Prado Museum). A fascinating architectural detail is the church's tall, thick central column from which the supports of the church dome radiate. Horseshoe arches, two and three deep, stand to the side.

GORMAZ   Over this simple village stand the ruins of an enormous tenth century Arab castle that was part of the defensive line along the Duero. The castle is said to be the largest, or at least the longest, castle in Europe. It is entered through a Moorish arch of grand proportions.

EL BURGO DE OSMA   A town with a long history that was important in Visigothic times, this was a Christian stronghold along the Duero during the Reconquest. It was merely a burgh (*burgo*) of the nearby little village of Osma until granted a bishop's seat in the thirteenth century. The town's porticoed streets and Plaza Mayor maintain a medieval flavor.

The **CATHEDRAL** and its cloister have pure and harmonious lines and are fine examples of Spanish Gothic, even though many changes have been made over the centuries. Exceptional grillwork stands in front of the choir, and the altarpiece is a masterly creation of sixteenth century sculptor Juan de Juni. Be sure to visit the cathedral museum, and see especially the tomb of San Pedro, with its profuse decorative detail that includes an unusual frieze of warriors on horseback. The miniature paintings based on manuscripts of the eighth century monk Beatus from Liébana in Cantabria are a treasure, and show the union of Moorish and Christian styles and themes.
VIRREY PALAFOX   Universidad 7   tel. (975) 34 02 22, is known for good cooking, traditional as well as creative. The quality, variety, and excellent preparation of their pork products and game dishes has gained them a fine reputation throughout Spain. (Moderate.)

CALATAÑAZOR   A walled village of noticeable Arabic flavor and an Arabic name meaning "Castle of the Eagle." Here a momentous event in Spanish history took place: the defeat of the feared Arab chieftain Almanzor (see box, p. 137). Calatañazor, with its cobbled streets (porticoed with wood posts), houses of wood beams and adobe and wood eave overhangs, and a crumbling castle at the summit, is an evocative page from the past. Sunsets are magnificent.

LA LAGUNA NEGRA   This spectacular glacial lake, icy and clear, is like an amphitheater, surrounded by walls of mountains and by tall pine forests of the Urbión range that cut off the light and give the water a dark appearance (probably the reason for its name, Black Lake).

NUMANCIA   There's more to imagine than to see in this little town that so tenaciously and heroically fought off Roman attack for twenty years and made a joke of the Roman military command. Numancia eventually succumbed in 133 B.C., completing the Roman domination of Spain, but the town was destroyed and its population annihilated. The Romans rebuilt the town, and the foundations we see today are of that later period. Decorative objects found here are in the Museo Provincial of Soria.

ÁGREDA   Poised at the edge of a cliff, a castle above it and walls surrounding it, Ágreda commands wide views of a deep, fertile valley. It is near the frontier with Aragón and looks very much like an Aragonese village. Although small, Ágreda has numerous old churches, palaces, and a once-flourishing Jewish quarter that all indicate a far richer past.

ALMAZÁN   Naturally fortified on a hilltop, Almazán keeps its Arabic name and some of its Moorish character, although it is the Romanesque style that predominates in several local churches. The town walls are gone, but the massive gateways remain and lead to the Old Quarter and the porticoed Plaza Mayor. There, a fine Renaissance palace presides. Also in the square is the twelfth century church of San Miguel. Its interior cupola looks sur-

"IN CALATAÑAZOR, ALMANZOR LOST HIS TAMBOR"

No one was more feared in tenth century Christian Spain than the great Arab warrior Almanzor (also known as Al Mansur), who spread terror through the country for twenty-six years. Of noble ancestry, Almanzor was born near Algeciras in Moorish-controlled Andalucía, and after studying in Córdoba, rapidly rose through government ranks until he became acting caliph, in place of an heir too young to rule. He was a man with a passionate interest in the arts, and in Córdoba he surrounded himself with learned men. It is said that Almanzor's palace was like a university to which he welcomed scholars from all over the world.

But twice a year Almanzor set out to battle the Christians. He was fearless and invariably victorious. He seized Zaragoza and devastated León, Astorga, and Barcelona, among many other cities and villages. He even reached Santiago de Compostela, where he leveled the city but, cultured man that he was, left the sanctuary of Saint James untouched. Many thousands of captured Christians became slaves.

Almanzor finally met his Waterloo in Calatañazor, where the battle raged for a full day and left the earth bloodied with corpses. Defeated and wounded in battle, Almanzor retired to Medinaceli, where he died three days later. He was buried in battle gear and dusted with earth from the battlefields of his victories, which he kept in a perfumed box. Almanzor, in the style of the time, would go into battle accompanied by a flourish of drums, but "in Calatañazor," so the saying goes, "Almanzor lost his tambor."

prisingly like those to either side of the mihrab in the Arab Mosque of
Córdoba.

♦ Almazán is known for its egg-yolk candies, *yemas* (see box, p. 398), and
their by-product, *Paciencias*, egg-white cookies. Buy them at **CASA DE LAS
YEMAS**   Arco de la Villa 4.

MORÓN DE ALMAZÁN, thirteen kilometers away, has a lovely multilevel
golden stone plaza that is faced by a sixteenth century palace and a simple
church with a beautiful Renaissance belfry. At the center is a pillory.

SANTA MARÍA DE HUERTA   Named for the orchards (*huertas*) of the
Jalón valley, this austere monastery is a grand example of twelfth to thirteenth century Cistercian (see Index) Gothic architecture. Especially magnificent is the refectory, of lofty height and harmonious design. The kitchen
next to it has a huge chimney and fireplace.

MEDINACELI   This delightful town of old palaces and seignorial houses
was once abandoned, but is now restored thanks to city dwellers seeking
weekend homes in the country. Distinguishing Medinaceli is a Roman triple
triumphal arch some 27 feet high that dates to the first century A.D., the
only one of its kind in Spain. Through the arch a vast panorama of the Jalón
valley appears. Although there are apparently many Roman remains in
Medinaceli, until now only a large mosaic floor has been uncovered in the
Plaza Mayor. The grand palace of the Dukes of Medinaceli is also here.
MESÓN ARCO ROMANO   Portillo 1   tel. (975) 32 61 30, is a charming
country house of rough-hewn stone walls and a heavily beamed ceiling, decorated with artwork and rustic ceramics. Cooking is country style: *migas*
(sautéed bread bits), beans, lamb chops, and garlic soup. (Moderate.)

THE REGION AND PROVINCE OF LA RIOJA

LA RIOJA (lah-ree-o-ha) was not always an autonomous region, but a
province of Castilla-León named after its capital, Logroño (lo-*groan*-yo). But
because La Rioja's historic ties have been with Navarra as well as with
Castilla, the solution, when regional restructuring took place in the last
decade, was to separate Logroño from Castilla-León and form La Rioja.

The great Río Ebro flows through La Rioja, and its vast and fertile valley was a natural gateway through Spain for Romans on their way from the
coastal colony of Tarraco (today Tarragona) to León. They established a
colony called Calagurris in what is now the town of Calahorra.

One of the most celebrated battles against the Moors took place in La
Rioja at Clavijo, where legend says Saint James himself appeared on horseback and routed the Moors (see box, p. 144). Coincidentally, we once more

rejoin the Way of Saint James and find the churches, monasteries, hospitals, and hospices that typically grew up to aid pilgrims. This gentle green land pleased the pilgrims, who were perhaps unaware of the harsh climate and rough terrain that still awaited them on their long journey to Galicia.

For centuries La Rioja was a disputed border territory, claimed by both the kingdoms of Castilla and Navarra, and control swung from one to the other before Alfonso VI definitively made it a part of Castilla at the end of the eleventh century. It became a vital frontier-defense line, and although Navarra repeatedly attempted to reclaim it, La Rioja remained in Castilian hands. Today the culture and the cuisine of La Rioja reflect both regions.

Scant attention has been directed to a simple event that took place in La Rioja more than a thousand years ago, but its ramifications were extraordinary: Here in the monastery of San Millán de la Cogolla the first evidence of the Castilian language was put to paper. A tenth century Latin manuscript was uncovered in which a priest had penned marginal notes in primitive Castilian and then translated several lines of a sermon by Saint Augustine into the vernacular. We can assume common folk spoke a language among themselves that had evolved from Latin several centuries before, but cultured men did not deem it suitable for print. This famous document is today in the library of El Escorial. The literary firsts of San Millán monastery continued. Gonzalo de Berceo, a thirteenth century church deacon and native of the village of Berceo in La Rioja, was the first poet to write his works in Castilian and affix his name to them ("I do not have the culture to write in Latin"). Although his verses are not generally considered supreme poetic achievements, his spontaneity and sincerity are quite charming.

The broad Río Ebro is the lifeblood of La Rioja and forms its northern border with Navarra and with the province of Álava in the Basque Country. Seven tributaries flow through La Rioja and water what is, in essence, one vast fertile valley, edged to the north and south by mountain ranges. One branch of the Ebro, the Río Oja, gave the region its name. Couple this abundant water supply with a benign climate and you have conditions that are ideal for agriculture. It is said that to fill your table in La Rioja you need only extend your hand. When you are here you feel the effects of this relatively easy living, discover the region's warmth and friendliness, and revel in its soft colors. The valleys are so lusciously green and inviting, especially in late afternoon when the light takes on extraordinary subtleties, that we stop frequently to capture it on film.

To most people, both foreigners and Spaniards, the name Rioja means just one thing: wine. Indeed, the largest production of quality red wines in Spain falls under the Rioja designation of origin, which is divided into three subregions: La Rioja Baja (Lower Rioja), which has a moderate climate and yields the largest quantities of wine; La Rioja Alta (Upper Rioja), colder and wetter, where the production is less but of generally higher quality; and La Rioja Alavesa, which also has the continental climate of La Rioja Alta, and although it is in the province of

QUAIL A LA RIOJANA

Roast as many red peppers as you have quail, slit the peppers, remove the skin, and discard the seeds. Rub the cavities of the quail with a mixture of olive oil and black pepper. Brown in olive oil and sprinkle with salt. Place each quail inside a pepper, and arrange in a baking pan. Brush with olive oil and pour in ½ cup white wine. Bake at 450°F about 25 minutes.

Álava in the Basque Country, its wines still have the Rioja designation. Rioja wines are blended to create unusually smooth and pleasant products.

When exceptional harvests are aged to become Reservas or longer still to be Gran Reservas, Rioja wines can reach poetic heights. The wines of Rioja are found all over Spain (and are increasingly common in the United States), and you will inevitably be thinking about wine when you are in La Rioja. Vineyards are everywhere; there are dozens of bodegas from which the earthy aromas of wine aging in wood barrels drift forth; in bars and restaurants clients are drinking it (you rarely find anyone ordering beer); stores all over La Rioja sell it; and local festivities are often wine-related.

La Rioja's gastronomy is naturally based on the celebrated produce of the land, especially sweet red peppers, so good that I can eat them every day and never tire of them. Strings of them hang to dry from balconies and roof eaves, providing an added note of bright color. In the fall, women sit at their doorsteps, roasting and peeling peppers over charcoal grills. Any dish designated *a la riojana* more likely than not will include red peppers in some form, just as in Navarra *al chilindrón* implies the same.

Vegetables are generally exceptional, particularly the baby vegetables of early spring. My thoughts often turn to a meal I had at Beethoven restaurant in the town of Haro during an Easter visit. It began with an exciting vegetable medley (*Menestra de Verduras*) of fresh-picked tiny artichokes, carrots, green beans, cauliflower, leeks, and peas, some of them steamed, others fried to provide contrast, and spiced with a touch of cured ham. This was followed by tiny lamb chops grilled over vine shoots.

I also recall other typical dishes of La Rioja, like *Patatas a la Riojana*, potatoes with *chorizo* and red peppers; *Codornices con Pochas*, a stew of oversized dried lima beans and quail; red peppers stuffed with meat or fish (the Cantabrian sea, after all, is not so far away); and snails, abundant in the orchards, prepared with peppers and tomatoes (*Caracoles a la Riojana*). There is excellent trout and crab from the rivers. Dessert may be local peaches steeped in Rioja wine, *Rosquillas Riojanas* (anise-scented doughnuts), or goat's milk cheese from the nearby mountains of Cameros.

I never like to make the capital city of Logroño my base when I visit La Rioja; I prefer to spend a day or two in the town of Santo Domingo de la Calzada. From there I can absorb the country flavor of the region, and it is easy to travel to Logroño, to Haro and its wine country, to some very interesting monasteries, and to cross into Álava to the beautiful town of Laguardia and then perhaps continue into the Basque Country or into Navarra.

THE TOWN OF SANTO DOMINGO DE LA CALZADA AND ITS FAMOUS SAINT, SANTO DOMINGO

Santo Domingo de la Calzada (its melodious name means Saint Dominic of the Road) is set in a wide, fertile meadow of vegetable gardens, poplar groves, and trickling streams. Only a few sections remain of the town walls that Pedro the Cruel built in the fourteenth century. In this cobbled village of covered passageways, arcaded streets, small squares, and tile-roofed gold-colored houses and mansions emblazoned with coats of arms, quiet reigns and a medieval spirit hangs suspended in the air.

Santo Domingo de la Calzada owes its existence to pilgrims passing this way on their journey to Santiago de Compostela and to an eleventh century religious hermit, Santo Domingo, who lived here. Santo Domingo is a saint who appeals to me; he was apparently a simple and unpretentious man, genuinely kind and sympathetic. He lived an extremely ascetic life by the banks of the Río Oja, and observing the difficulties of the pilgrims as they attempted to cross the river, built a bridge of twenty-five spans to ease their way. Pleased with his efforts, he then founded a hospice over the ruins of a palace that once belonged to the kings of Navarra, and there he provided lodgings and medical care for the pilgrims. Even more ambitiously, he cleared forests to create a roadway twenty-five kilometers long, all, according to legend, with his bare hands. His construction projects were expanded by his disciple, San Juan de Ortega, who lengthened the road into the province of Burgos.

King Alfonso V was so impressed with Santo Domingo's good works that he granted him land, on which the saint built a church in 1106. One century later, the travelers' guidebook, *Codex Calixtinus*, advised pilgrims, "In Spain

"SANTO DOMINGO DE LA CALZADA, THE HEN SANG AFTER ROASTING"

Santo Domingo's abilities to work miracles rests on the following event, which tradition tells this way:

In the fourteenth century an eighteen-year-old boy named Hugonell was on a pilgrimage to Santiago de Compostela in company of his parents. They stopped at an inn to eat, and a young girl falsely accused the boy of robbery. He was sentenced and hanged for the crime. But his parents began to hear the voice of their son telling them he was alive, saved by Santo Domingo. They rushed to tell the town magistrate, who was just sitting down to a roast chicken dinner. He laughed at their absurd claims. "Your son is as alive as this hen that I am about to eat," he said. With that the bird hopped from his plate and began clucking and strutting about (and the boy, indeed, was also alive). From the miracle of the hen came the rhyming refrain, "*Santo Domingo de la Calzada, que cantó la gallina despues de asada*" (Santo Domingo de la Calzada, the hen sang after roasting). And that is why ever since then, a hen and a rooster have resided in the cathedral of Santo Domingo de la Calzada. Visitors take their fallen feathers as good-luck souvenirs.

you must visit the body of Santo Domingo, . . . who built a stretch of the road. . . ."

From its beginnings merely as a bridge on a portion of the Royal Road to Santiago, Santo Domingo de la Calzada became a village of humble and heraldic houses. And almost nine hundred years after the saint's death, the memory of Santo Domingo stays alive: the village's name, of course, brings him to mind; his hospice is still here, transformed into a parador; his church has become a cathedral in which the saint is buried in a rich sepulcher; and a tiny chapel by the bridge marks his hermitage. A hen and a rooster, enclosed in a gilded cage, live in the cathedral in remembrance of the miracle performed by Santo Domingo (see box, p. 141).

SEEING SANTO DOMINGO DE LA CALZADA

CATHEDRAL   Don't be surprised to hear clucking and crowing and to see feathers fly in the cathedral, for a hen and a rooster really do live here in a golden Gothic cage. What little remains of the Romanesque church built by Santo Domingo is masked by Gothic embellishments and dominated by a Renaissance altarpiece, a late work of the Valencian Damián Forment, who was also responsible for the altar of the Basílica del Pilar (in Zaragoza) and of the Poblet monastery (Tarragona province). The cathedral's tower is Baroque, its facade neoclassic. Santo Domingo is buried in an alabaster mausoleum designed in Flamboyant Gothic style.

STAYING AND EATING IN SANTO DOMINGO DE LA CALZADA

PARADOR SANTO DOMINGO DE LA CALZADA   Plaza del Santo 3 tel. (941) 34 03 00   This is one of my favorite paradors. Formerly Santo Domingo's hospice for pilgrims, the parador has grandeur in its Gothic stone-arched salon and village simplicity in its wood-beamed and wood-pillared dining room. (Moderate.) The restaurant has well-prepared regional specialties—I especially like the *Pochas con Codorniz* (beans with quail).

EL RINCÓN DE EMILIO   Plaza de Bonifacio Gil 7   tel. (941) 34 09 90   A cozy and friendly setting for simple dishes like lamb chops and *menestra* (vegetable medley). (Inexpensive–moderate.)

MESÓN EL PEREGRINO   Zumalacárregui 18   tel. (941) 34 02 02   Set in a historic house with rustic décor, here the food is typical of La Rioja: trout, stuffed peppers, lamb. (Inexpensive–moderate.)

⟨V⟩ISITING THE REGION OF LA RIOJA

LOGROÑO   Capital and economic center of La Rioja, Logroño is a thriving city on the Río Ebro, but frankly not very exciting culturally or in physical appearance. The river is crossed by a stone bridge, over which the pilgrims to Santiago once passed, and it leads to the Rúa Vieja. That's where you will find **SANTA MARÍA DE PALACIO** church with its unusual thirteenth century pyramidal tower, and the **SANTIAGO** church, where over its upper portal a heroic Santiago on horseback slays the enemy. Nearby the Gothic portal of **SAN BARTOLOMÉ** depicts the life of San Bartolomé (the scene continues like a frieze along the front of the church), and the **CATHEDRAL**, although from the fifteenth century, has an ornate eighteenth century Baroque exterior.

CARLTON RIOJA   Avenida del Rey Don Juan Carlos I, no. 5   tel. (941) 24 21 00, is an ordinary hotel that does not approach the elegance of its name, but Logroño offers few alternatives. (Moderate–expensive.)

LA MERCED   Marqués de San Nicolás 109   tel. (941) 22 11 66, receives raves from some, and certainly its locale and décor are irreproachably elegant, and the food, tending to nouvelle, is well prepared and based on fine ingredients. I prefer to eat at the owner's other establishment, across the street, **MESÓN LORENZO**   Mayor 136   tel. (941) 20 91 40, for regional dishes in a tavern setting (moderate) or go tapas hopping along **CALLE LAUREL,** a narrow street in the Old Quarter, jampacked with bars. There are several stores in the city to buy wine and canned and bottled Rioja fruits and vegetables. **RIOJA SELECCIÓN**   República Argentina 12, is one of them.

♦ Logroño has an unusual number of antique stores, clustered in the cathedral area.

NÁJERA   A quaint town on the broad Río Najerilla, Nájera was capital of the region under the kings of Navarra and later under La Rioja's Castilian rulers and part of the route to Santiago de Compostela. The eleventh century **SANTA MARÍA LA REAL** monastery is built around a cave in which an image of the Virgin miraculously appeared (a Gothic representation of the Virgin stands at an altar in the cave, the original statue at the main altar). In the Pantheon are rows of tombs of the kings of Navarra and other royalty; especially magnificent is the sepulcher of Doña Blanca de Navarra, mother of Alfonso VIII of Castile, decorated with scenes that are a vivid record of twelfth century apparel and customs.

The cloister, called "de los Caballeros" because so many tombs of noblemen are there, has pointed arches over slim columns and unique Plateresque stone tracery inserts that form delicate curtains between the arches. The two-tiered choir stalls in Flamboyant Gothic style are carved in wonderful detail. Most unusual are the seat supports, each a free-standing carving of a single figure. The much larger abbot's seat shows in high relief King García III of Navarra, who founded the monastery.

SANTO DOMINGO DE LA CALZADA   A delightful town with a colorful history (see text).

SAN MILLÁN DE LA COGOLLA   In a pastoral setting, almost hidden in a deep valley, this village is named after a hermit, San Millán, who lived here in the sixth century. Like Santiago, he miraculously appeared mounted on a white horse and assisted the Christians in their battle with the Moors. Pilgrims to Santiago de Compostela detoured from their route to pay their respect to the saint.

There are two monasteries near each other, **SUSO** and **YUSO,** which functioned as one religious community and a great center of learning. Suso is the older one, built in the simple style of the tenth and eleventh centuries and set against a mountainside from which caves were dug out to form chapels (in these caves, it is thought, San Millán and his followers lived). The interior is Mozarabic (see Index), noticeable in the Moorish-influenced arches. Priest and poet Gonzalo de Berceo (p. 139) studied and wrote his poetry at the monastery. San Millán's tomb is a magnificent twelfth century funerary sculpture showing the saint surrounded by pilgrims pleading for his help.

Yuso, also known as the "lower" monastery, is designed in the Renaissance style of El Escorial, although the original monastery was centuries older. Be sure to see San Millán's reliquary chest, once covered with gold and silver (removed by the French in the War of Independence) but still retaining its extraordinary inlaid ivories, which are a treasure of the eleventh century. They tell the story of the life of the saint and concentrate on human figures almost to the exclusion of ornamental work. These ivories had a powerful influence on future Romanesque designs.

THE MIRACULOUS CHRISTIAN VICTORY AT THE BATTLE OF CLAVIJO

For some historians the Battle of Clavijo is pure legend, and yet the battle has a precise date, May 23, 844. It happened when Christians took up arms rather than submit to demands of the Arab emir in Córdoba, Abderrhamán II, for one hundred young girls as tribute. The battle took shape in La Rioja at Clavijo, and the Christians were outnumbered and forced to retreat to the castle on the hill. As King Ramiro slept that night, a vision of Santiago came to him, promising victory the next day.

During the ferocious battle that ensued, Santiago appeared dressed in a white tunic, on a white steed, and carrying a white flag imprinted with a red cross. He slew Moors right and left; with his help the Christian forces were victorious, and 70,000 of the enemy littered the battlefield. King Ramiro, in tribute to the saint's valor, vowed to bring him each year's first wines and crops and booty captured in subsequent combats. Because of his prowess in battle, Santiago became known as Santiago Matamoros—Moor Slayer—and received the rank of general in the Spanish army. He also became patron saint of Spain.

CLAVIJO   A castle, dramatically set atop a rocky promontory and surrounded by a fertile valley, is all that remains of the times of the legendary battle in which Santiago led the Christians to victory (see box).

HARO   There are many bodegas around Haro that make this town a prosperous wine center. The pretty Plaza de la Paz is faced with mansions from earlier times, and the recessed portal of the Santo Tomás church on the same square has especially nice Plateresque work.

BEETHOVEN I AND II   restaurants facing each other on Calle Santo Tomás 3 and 5   tel. (941) 31 11 81, are so called because the owner's deaf grandfather was nicknamed Beethoven. Both restaurants are decorated in rustic style; one is an old tavern, the other just a bit more stylish. The *Menestra de Verduras* (vegetable medley), made with early-spring vegetables, is memorable, the partridge in wine sauce exceptional. (Moderate.)

LOS AGUSTINOS   San Agustín 2   tel. (941) 31 13 08, is a new hotel in an old convent, tastefully restored. (Moderate.)

LAGUARDIA   See "The Proud Basque Country."

SIERRA DE LA DEMANDA   Crossing these mountains is undoubtedly the long route to the province of Burgos, but the road winds through an untamed and unusually beautiful landscape.

Just off this route is **VINIEGRA DE ABAJO,** a charming rough-stone village by the side of the rushing Río Najerilla that is popular in summer.

𝒱ISITING THE BODEGAS

Most bodegas welcome visitors but require appointments (one that generally does not is Bodegas Riojanas in Cenicero, northeast of Nájera, weekdays only). Ask your hotel to help you make necessary arrangements to visit others.

♦ Many Rioja wines are available internationally at similar or even lower prices than in Spain, so unless you find an exceptional year or a brand not commonly exported, don't burden yourself with bottles.

FIESTAS

WINE HARVEST FESTIVAL (LA VENDIMIA)   September 20 to 27   A week of colorful events: fireworks, bullfights, parades, dancing, food and wine tastings. Festivities are centered on Logroño.

BATALLA DEL VINO   On June 29 a pilgrimage takes place to San Felices de Bilibio to honor Haro's patron saint, San Felices. The event becomes a wild free-for-all in which participants are doused with wine.

CASTILLA–LA MANCHA: A RICH, COLORFUL MOSAIC

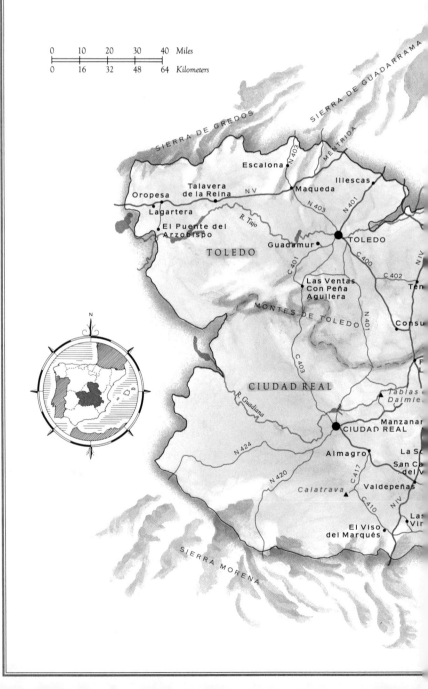

Atienza

Sigüenza

C 101

C 204

C 114

ludo

GUADALAJARA

N 211

Molina
de Aragón

N II

LA ALCARRIA

Brihuega

R. Tajo

Barranco
de la Virgen
de la Hoz

R. Gallo

GUADALAJARA

C 200

C 202

Entrepeñas

Beteta

Pastrana

R. Cuervo

Priego

R. Escabas

SIERRA
DE CUENCA

Tragacete

C 202

Ciudad
Encantada

N 400

CUENCA

R. Huécar

Uclés

N 420

Las Torcas del Palancar

N 320

N 420

Segóbriga

N III

Valeria

CUENCA

N 420

oboso

Belmonte

Mota del Cuervo

Alarcón

N III

San Clemente

npo de
otana

N 320

N 322

Tomelloso

R. Júcar

Alcalá del Júcar

amasilla
lba

N 301

Jorquera

Ruidera

ALBACETE

Chinchilla de
Monte Aragón

N 321

Almansa

anueva
os
ntes

ALBACETE

Alcaraz

N 301

INTRODUCTION

IT IS NOT EASY to categorize Castilla–La Mancha, for it is a region of great variety and complexity. On the one hand there is the ruddy red earth, the windmills, and simple whitewashed villages of the province of Ciudad Real (which encompasses most of the area commonly called La Mancha), where the spirit of Don Quijote (Don Quixote, in English) roams. But there are also the strangely sculpted cliffs and Hanging Houses of Cuenca; the plains and astonishing clefts of Albacete; hilly woodlands of Guadalajara; and the dark mystery and ancient cultures of Toledo.

Madrid was once part of Castilla–La Mancha, but when the city became capital of Spain in the sixteenth century and received the royal court, enjoying power, prestige, and high-style living, its history and traditions diverged. Now Madrid is so different that although historically a part of the region, it is considered an entity unto itself. But because of the accessible distance, a visit to Castilla–La Mancha works well in combination with a trip to Madrid and can also be a part of travel to eastern Andalucía and the Levante.

You might think it unlikely that five such distinct provinces could have anything in common, but they are, in fact, closely related in several ways. Principally, geography is the common tie. Castilla–La Mancha is a vast meseta some 1,500 to 2,000 feet above the sea, although when I'm there all I see is endless flatness stretching to the horizon, and I often forget just how high it is. It can be so flat here that roads run as the crow flies, one town's church belfry directly in line with the next. In contrast, around the fringes of the meseta, mountains loom large: Gredos and Guadarrama to the north, the mountains of Cuenca to the east, and Sierra Morena to the south.

The agriculture of Castilla–La Mancha is typical of a climate so extremely dry, the land yielding cereals, olives, and grapes. A good part of Spain's wheat and other grain crops come from here. Of much smaller proportions is the microclimate of Ciudad Real, which is responsible for the world's best saffron, painstakingly harvested and processed by hand (see box, p. 152).

FOODS AND WINES OF CASTILLA–LA MANCHA

GENERAL

Lamb, pork, cured meats, game, dried cod

SPECIALTIES

Pisto Manchego—vegetable stew
Mojete—dried cod and tomato salad
Ajo Arriero—dried cod and potatoes
Morteruelo—meat and bread pâté
Perdiz Estofada—stewed partridge
Flores Manchegas—fried pastries with honey
Queso Manchego—sheep's milk cheese

WINES

Vega de Moriz from Valdepeñas
Castillo de Almansa, Marius from Almansa
Torres Filoso, Castillo de Alhambra, Señorío
de Guadianeja from La Mancha

Wine is produced in immense amounts in all five provinces of Castilla–La Mancha and accounts for 50 percent of Spain's already enormous output. Known by the names of the wine-growing regions Valdepeñas, Méntrida, Almansa, and La Mancha—these wines are not as sophisticated as those found farther north in Spain. Traditionally they were somewhat crude, unscientifically made products—a bit acidic, fruity, high in alcohol—but in recent years the quality has steadily improved. Poor-quality wines of the past probably explain the reason for a typical drink called *la cuerva* or *la zurra* that mixes local wine with water or seltzer, sugar, and fruits. It resembles sangría and may indeed be the origin of this internationally popular summer wine cooler.

The aridness of the land belies the fact that three of Spain's greatest rivers originate in Castilla–La Mancha: the Tajo (Tagus), which has been dammed into lakes to create the so-called Sea of Castile (Mar de Castilla); the Guadiana, beginning at the Ruidera lakes, then disappearing and reappearing in its course south to the Atlantic, creating the marshy pools of Las Tablas de Daimiel; and the marvelous turquoise Júcar, which in its path to the Mediterranean has sculpted startling cavities and weird rock formations deep into the meseta and is responsible for some amazing scenery and spectacular village architecture.

All five provinces had in the twelfth century a common history of warfare, and their frontiers oscillated between Moorish and Christian Spain. The Knights of Calatrava (see box, p. 159), warriors with a religious mission, dominated military operations against the Moors and worried the king, who feared they were too powerful and a threat to the unity of the country. Once the Moors were expelled, eastern Castile became a bone of contention between the kingdoms of Castile and Aragón, both of which claimed sovereignty. To these long and continual hostilities we owe the numerous castles and fortresses and the region's name, Castilla.

Castles, of course, require elevation to function as defensive positions—and that is hard to come by in this flat terrain. Nevertheless, there were enough strategic and naturally defendable places in Castilla–La Mancha, and there castles were raised to dominate the plains. Today such great castles as Calatrava, Molina de Aragón, Almansa, Sigüenza, Alarcón, and Belmonte are powerful reminders of the tumultuous history of Spain. Two of them—Sigüenza and Alarcón—have become splendid paradors.

In all five provinces food has always lacked variety, and gastronomy is not a highlight of travel in Castilla–La Mancha. Even if you have grown up with such dishes as *morteruelo* (a bready pâté that has been called "bestial foie gras"), *Gazpacho Manchego* (a mush of game meats and bread bits), and *zarajos* (grilled lamb intestines), I venture there are many other things you prefer to eat. Just the fact that there is a dish called "Sorrow and Suffering," and another called "Rotten Pot," (p. 151) tells you something about the state of gastronomy here. Then again, I do like the foods based on vegetables, salt cod, or game; appealing desserts of nuts and honey; and incomparable *Manchego* cheese.

A lively crafts tradition, mostly of Arab origin, continues in Castilla–La Mancha. Entire towns and villages are sometimes dedicated to creating embroidery (Lagartera), pottery (Talavera de la Reina and El

Puente del Arzobispo), lace (Almagro), leather (Las Ventas Con Peña Aguilera), damascene (Toledo), and fine knives (Albacete).

Diversity and unity are the hallmarks of the great lands of Castilla–La Mancha. This is peasant country, simple and close to the earth, yet mixed with sites of royal grandeur. The landscape may be bare, but it is never bleak or austere, as it can be to the north in Castilla-León. There is a cheerfulness here that I like to attribute to a spiritual inheritance from the ever-optimistic Don Quijote de la Mancha.

ꝒIUDAD REAL AND LA MANCHA: LANDS OF DON QUIJOTE

THE PROVINCE OF CIUDAD REAL (thee-oo-*dahd* ray-*ahl*) comprises the bulk of the region known as La Mancha (there are just a few small portions in the provinces of Toledo, Cuenca, and Albacete), and for this reason Ciudad Real and La Mancha are terms often used interchangeably. The Arabs called this region Manxa, meaning dry land, but the translation from the Spanish (*mancha* is a stain) applies just as well to the patchwork of plots that alternate green crops with pale yellow wheat, purple fields of saffron crocus (see box, p. 152), and fallow, ruddy red earth. Here the meseta is so endlessly flat and parched that there are vast stretches with hardly a tree in sight.

> The plain . . . , red, yellowish, gray in the untilled stretches, an almost imperceptible green in the seeded sections. You travel an hour, hour and one half; you don't see a tree nor a puddle nor even a spot of succulent green . . . a maddening monotony.
>
> Azorín

Ciudad Real is a land long ignored, and yet I find its history and unique beauty a source of great interest and pleasure. There are no grand monuments (one reason why La Mancha is often overlooked), but intimations of history are all around you. During the Reconquest, Ciudad Real was a continual battleground and headquarters for the omnipotent Knights of Calatrava, who fought the Moors in the name of Christianity and were showered with wealth (see box, p. 159). Their brazen and shameless use of power eventually brought their demise.

La Mancha has a singular appearance, and I immediately know when I am here by the color of the earth and its flatness, the sparseness of villages and the distinctive village architecture. Construction in La Mancha spreads outward rather than upward. You'll not see many high-rise buildings in this area, for there is plenty of room to grow horizontally. That's why the *quinterías*—sprawling whitewashed granges that accommodate farmers and their

families, seasonal workers, and livestock—are
still so common, even within urban
confines. In this same style you find
occasional "*ventas*," or inns, which
were so prevalent in past centuries
when travel across these broad
plains was time-consuming and still
somewhat of an adventure.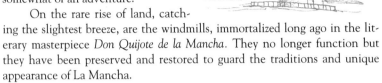

On the rare rise of land, catch-
ing the slightest breeze, are the windmills, immortalized long ago in the literary masterpiece *Don Quijote de la Mancha*. They no longer function but
they have been preserved and restored to guard the traditions and unique
appearance of La Mancha.

Cuisine by modern standards is not impressive in La Mancha, and
good dining is hard to find. Stuck in the Middle Ages, the food is somewhat
heavy, ingredients are few, and traditional dishes have the oddest names.
We are prone to endless jokes when eating in La Mancha. When I read *Don
Quijote de la Mancha* in my college Spanish literature class, I saw no reason
why one of Don Quijote's daily dishes would be called "Sorrow and
Suffering." Now the meaning is perfectly clear, even though the dish of eggs
scrambled with ham and *chorizo* happens to be one that I like.

Consider other recipes with equally picturesque titles: *Atascaburros*
(mule stopper), a mix of potato, egg, cod, and bread crumbs; *gachas* (pap), a
paste of flour, water, and spices; and *Olla Podrida* (Rotten Pot), a long-sim-
mering stew in which just about anything available is thrown in. But we no
longer complain; instead we plunge right in, trying everything and drinking
plenty of hearty Manchegan wine—to digest and forget. We look at it this
way: How better to imagine the humble life of Alonso Quijano, transformed
by Cervantes into the famous Don Quijote, and to gain insight into one
aspect of his austere life (which perhaps contributed to his madness) than to
place ourselves in the times and ambiance of our "Knight of the Woeful
Countenance."

> Three parts of his income were consumed in food—a stewpot of
> beef one night, leftovers on other weeknights, "sorrow and suffer-
> ing" on Saturdays, lentils for Fridays and perhaps a pigeon on
> Sundays.

But there are, of course, other, far more appetizing things to eat in La
Mancha: the famed marinated baby eggplants of Almagro, lots of small game
dishes, *pisto* (vegetable stew), *Flores Manchegas* (fried pastries with honey),
and the crowning glory of La Mancha, *Manchego* cheese. Still often produced in the artisan manner, *Manchego* is made from sheep's milk and tastes
best when well cured. Consumed all over Spain, it is appealing at any time
of day, as a tapa with bread, and with quince preserves or honey for dessert.
Because the saffron from La Mancha is of such high quality and is more than
worth its weight in gold, it is exported rather than used in local cooking.

The wines of La Mancha, accounting for a large part of Castilla–La
Mancha production, are easy to drink and inexpensive, and for these reasons
red wines from La Mancha are the typical wines sipped with tapas—what is

SAFFRON: GOLD OF LA MANCHA

There are few sights comparable to the violet blanket of saffron crocuses that covers certain areas of the generally dry and colorless landscape of La Mancha in mid-October. And there are few stories as fascinating as that of saffron.

Saffron has been the world's most highly prized spice since ancient times, when it was used in Egypt and other Middle Eastern countries to season food and to dye cloth. The Moors brought it to Spain (the Spanish word *azafrán* means yellow in Arabic) and found the ideal environment to grow saffron in La Mancha.

There are other areas in Spain where saffron is grown, but only in a small microclimate around the Manchegan village of Membrilla are conditions perfect. The chalky soil has just the right composition, and the weather is sunny and predictable. In this limited area, more than 60 percent of the world's saffron is produced.

The price of saffron is astonishing—more than $6,000 a pound and forever climbing. "The people of La Mancha don't have bank accounts," explains saffron king Fernando Morillo. "Their nest egg is saffron stashed under the mattress." So valuable is the crop that men stand guard round the clock in the fields when the flowers begin to appear.

Fernando took us through the saffron fields one glorious October morning and gave us a rare look at the process of producing saffron, which is a clue to its price. "The crocus flowers all bloom within a two-week period. They push through the dry, cracked earth during the night and, even before the morning dew has dried on their petals, are hand-picked. The flowers are extremely fragile and admit no mechanical harvesting."

We saw young men in the fields carrying straw baskets filled with the fragrant flowers. Back home in the local villages, women, children, and the elderly waited; since time is critical, everyone, no matter how young or old, is called to assist. Immediately they expertly pluck the three stigmas of each flower (that is the saffron) and roast them without delay to ensure optimum flavor. Tens of thousands of flowers yield just an ounce or two of saffron.

A few strands of saffron in cooking transforms an ordinary dish into a work of art. Its subtle color and exquisite flavor are greatly esteemed in a variety of fish, soup, and rice dishes (paella is the most celebrated). Even desserts take on new dimensions with the "gold of La Mancha."

---

called "*vino de chateo.*" They are ideal with the hearty regional foods, perfect with *serrano* ham and *chorizo,* and stupendous when paired with *Manchego* cheese. All over La Mancha you still see the huge earthenware containers, called *tinajas,* in which the wines were aged and stored, although today their function is largely decorative.

Although a town like Almagro provides an interesting historic aside to life in La Mancha, there is no escaping the fact that this is the land of Don Quijote. The recollections of his adventures—even if they be fictitious—and his unshakable idealism spring to life and pervade any visit to this region. The association of the land and the legend is certainly what I enjoy most about being here.

THE ROUTE OF DON QUIJOTE: "KNIGHT OF THE WOEFUL COUNTENANCE"

In a place of La Mancha, whose name I do not choose to recall, lived a gentleman who owned a lance, an old shield, a weak horse and a hound.

Thus begins the wonderful tale of *Don Quijote de la Mancha*, by Miguel de Cervantes, considered one of the greatest literary achievements of all times. If you have ever been intrigued by the novel or wondered about the meaning of "quixotic" and of the expression "tilting at windmills," both part of our language today, perhaps the words of Cervantes that I have woven into this route through La Mancha will give you a further taste of the novel and of La Mancha in the sixteenth century.

> . . . his judgment gone, he came up with the strangest idea only a madman could invent. He thought it necessary for his personal honor and as a service to his country to become a knight errant and go through the world, armed and on horse-back, seeking adventure and engaging in all that he had read knight errants should undertake: undoing wrong and search-ing for dangerous situations in which he could gain eternal renown.

Cervantes develops this simple theme into a deft satire, a critique of Spanish and world society, of the knight-errant literature then in vogue, and gives us a compendium of sixteenth century Spain.

Cervantes fought with the Spanish navy in the Battle of Lepanto, lived in Italy, and traveled widely in Spain, yet he chose to base his novel in La Mancha. It was probably because knights had been powerful here during the Reconquest and were at the same time absurd in this arid, forsaken land, and also because of the mosaic of people from all walks of life that gave color to La Mancha. For although Don Quijote was a product of Cervantes's fertile imagination (perhaps based on a real personage—see Argamasilla de Alba), the novel's setting was very real.

Modern scholars have taken clues from *El Quijote* to seriously investi-gate the actual sites Cervantes had in mind when writing the novel. Often he was purposely vague, but there are enough indications to uncover just where in La Mancha Don Quijote was knighted, where the inns at which he stayed were found, in what town his beloved Dulcinea lived, and where he tilted at windmills. And since La Mancha today is so much like La Mancha of the sixteenth century, no great stretch of the imagination is required to relive the adventures of Don Quijote.

Seated on his decrepit horse, Rocinante (which he transforms in his mind into the glorious steed of legendary hero El Cid), Don Quijote travels in the company of his "squire," Sancho Panza, the most practical man alive and the perfect foil for Don Quijote's idealism. They wander through La Mancha, meeting all the lowlife, who badly mistreat this trusting soul, so absurdly dressed in armor. But through it all Don Quijote wins hearts and preserves his honor.

We follow the Knight of the Woeful Countenance as he sallies forth from his home, unbeknownst to anyone in his village, and we see him heading for the open plains. He travels all day, seeking knightly adventures, but is gravely preoccupied because he has not officially been dubbed a knight.

> . . . his first adventure was that of Puerto Lápice. . . . He and his horse were exhausted and weak from hunger. . . . Not far from the road he saw an inn. . . .
>
> At Don Quijote's request, and to the great amusement of all present, the innkeeper dubbed him knight . . . he commanded Don Quijote to kneel . . . raised his hand and hit him smartly on the neck, and then with the sword, struck him on the shoulder.
>
> "May God make you a successful knight and give you fortune in fight," declared a country wench [a beautiful damsel in Don Quijote's eyes], stifling her laughter.
>
> This unheard-of ceremony completed, Don Quijote hastened to mount his horse and set off in search of adventure. . . .

Puerto Lápice, a traditional resting point on the road from Madrid to Andalucía in the sixteenth century, had many ventas, and **VENTA DEL QUIJOTE** may not be the very same inn at which these chivalrous events took place, but it is a typical big, sprawling Manchegan inn. Centered on a patio, charmingly decorated in country style, it features dishes from the days of Don Quijote. Sipping a glass of Valdepeñas wine in the bodega, lined with enormous wine jugs and pervaded by earthy aromas, and perhaps eating some "Pain and Suffering," is enough to put you in situ.

Don Quijote soon encounters his next adventure, when he sees in the distance a cluster of windmills.

> ". . . you see there, friend Sancho Panza, thirty or so towering giants with whom I will do battle and take their lives. . . ."
>
> "What giants?" asks Sancho Panza.
>
> "Those that you see over there, with the long arms," his master replied.
>
> ". . . What you're seeing over there," replies Sancho, "are not giants but windmills, and what looks like arms are their sails."
>
> "It may seem so to you," responds Don Quijote, "because you know so little about such things: those are giants, and if you are afraid, step aside and start praying while I enter into fierce and perilous battle with them."
>
> He charged the windmill before him, throwing his lance into the sail, which the wind spun with such fury that it broke the lance and caught the horse and horseman, sending them rolling down the hillside.

By some accounts, windmills were introduced to La Mancha in the sixteenth century by the Flemish, who also brought their lacemaking skills to
Spain. Windmills became a common tool to turn millstones, but in the
times of Cervantes they were still a novelty, and Don Quijote might very
well be seeing them for the first time.

No one is quite sure whether Don Quijote encountered his evil
giants in Consuegra, Mota de Cuervo, or Campo de Criptana. Many
think it was Campo de Criptana, which centuries ago had more than
thirty windmills. No matter. In the hills over any of these three villages
you will find many windmills, unmenacing, and lending great character
to the landscape.

Don Quijote had not yet laid eyes on his fair lady, Dulcinea, and
ordered Sancho to lead him to her "palace" in the humble town of El
Toboso.

> It was precisely midnight, more or less, when Don Quijote and
> Sancho left the mountain and entered El Toboso. The town was
> in deep silence. . . . The night was clear. . . . Nothing was heard
> except the barking of dogs. . . . Occasionally an ass brayed, a pig
> grunted, cats meowed, their voices magnified by the silence of
> the night.
> "Sancho, my son, guide us to the palace of Dul-
> cinea. . . . Either I am not seeing well, or that big shadowy bulk
> before us must be the palace. . . ."
> Don Quijote led the way and after a while came upon the
> bulk that was casting the shadow and saw a grand tower and real-
> ized that the building was not the castle but the village church.
> ". . . I told you, sir . . . ," said Sancho, "that the house of
> this woman is on a very narrow dead end street."
> "Damn you, liar," said Don Quijote. "When have you ever
> seen a castle or royal palace built on an alleyway?"
> "Sir," replied Sancho, "To each his own."

With these clues from Cervantes, the "house of Dulcinea" was determined to be a large whitewashed structure on a narrow street of El Toboso.
Today at the entrance to this small simple town, signposts quoting from
the novel guide you to the house. It is preserved as a museum and is a typical Manchegan grange with a spacious central patio and furnished
throughout with Castilian antiques. Although the house is in town, it was
also a farm, so it includes primitive olive and grape presses and the quarters for the livestock.

"Madness," says Sancho, "is always better received and has more followers than wisdom ever had." And yet, there is great wisdom in the madness of Don Quijote.

$\mathcal{V}$ISITING DON QUIJOTE'S COUNTRY

◆ You will find few hotels and restaurants in La Mancha of Don Quijote, but the area is small and you can cover it in a day, then stay the night at the parador in Almagro.

MOTA DEL CUERVO, CAMPO DE CRIPTANA, CONSUEGRA
Three towns that keep the flavor of La Mancha and have many well-conserved or reconstructed windmills. Those at Campo de Criptana are the best; at one, El Infante, you can see the intricate system of wood gears, once used to mill grain (look for the caretaker with the key).
◆ In Consuegra on the last Sunday in October, La Rosa del Azafrán festival celebrates the saffron harvest with folkloric events.
◆ Mota del Cuervo is known for its fine and unusually elongated pottery jugs.

EL TOBOSO   Besides seeing the house of Dulcinea (see text), in the Town Hall there is a substantial collection of editions of *Don Quijote* in more than thirty languages.

PUERTO LÁPICE   This town was once filled with ventas, but few remain. See the quaint village plaza of two levels with lacy, deep-red wood balconies that run around the plaza and are covered with tile roofs—in the style of Tembleque (see Index).
VENTA DEL QUIJOTE   El Molino 4   tel. (926) 57 61 10, uses the Don Quijote theme to create a large and busy but charming restaurant based on regional cuisine. (Moderate.)

ARGAMASILLA DE ALBA   This is supposed to be the "place of La Mancha," of which Cervantes speaks in the opening sentence of his novel. The author was incarcerated here and perhaps conceived the novel at that time, although historians dispute the story. Visit the Casa de Medrano, a traditional Manchegan country house, and in it, the cave where Cervantes stayed. In the church of San Juan Bautista, see the sixteenth century portrait of Domingo Pacheco, on whom the character of Don Quijote is presumably based.

$\mathcal{L}$ACEMAKING AND FLEMISH ARCHITECTURE OF ALMAGRO

The first time I came to Almagro, I could immediately see that it was not like other Manchegan villages. It was more seignorial, more architecturally rich, with a more sophisticated look. But I did not know why until I investigated further.

Part of Almagro's noble appearance is related to the powerful Knights of Calatrava (see box, p. 159). Once the Reconquest was completed, they abandoned their fortress and established base in Almagro, where they built grand palaces adorned with personal coats of arms and founded numerous churches. But the crown feared the knights and stripped them of their power, and with that the town of Almagro went into decline.

Almagro's singular Plaza Mayor, unlike any other in Spain, is from a later period and reflects Almagro's new lease on life in the sixteenth century. The plaza has a certain Central European air, and clearly relies on influences not completely Spanish. But the explanation still surprised me: in the sixteenth century emperor Charles V needed large sums of money to consolidate his European empire and turned to a German banker, Jacob Fugger, who was so wealthy that he had also advanced money to Charles's predecessor, Emperor Maximilian I, to the pope, and to many more of the rich and powerful of his era.

To repay his debt to Fugger, Charles V gave him exploitation rights to mercury mines in Almadén, near Almagro, and the banker established his base of operations in Almagro, breathing new life into the decaying town and bringing it renewed prosperity. With him came his fellow countrymen, and a curious mix of Flemish and Manchegan architectural styles developed. New palaces and churches rose, adding to the already grand look of Almagro. The solemnity of elaborate carved stone doorways contrasted with cheerful whitewashed facades in the Manchegan tradition.

The unusually long Plaza Mayor, for example, has stone colonnades and glass-enclosed wooden galleries trimmed in green, which is most uncharacteristic of the Spanish style. The Fugger family may also have been responsible for the sixteenth century theater, the Corral de la Comedia, just recently uncovered and the only one of its kind in Spain. Originally a patio of an inn, this theater was where the Golden Age works of Cervantes and Lope de Vega were performed, and today classic theater is staged on special occasions.

Without doubt, the lacemaking tradition in and around Almagro also dates from the sixteenth century and the influx of Flemish families. The native women of Almagro quickly learned the craft and loved to trim their clothes with touches of lace. Ever since, they have dedicated their time to this intricate art and have achieved fame for the quality of their workmanship. You will see them seated at their doorsteps in the bright Manchegan light, their bobbins clicking at a furious pace.

STAYING AND EATING IN ALMAGRO

PARADOR DE ALMAGRO   Ronda de San Francisco s/n   tel. (926) 86 01 00 A beautifully restored sixteenth century Franciscan convent, with several pleasing interior patios. (Moderate.) You can eat well here, or try **MESÓN EL CORREGIDOR**   Plaza Fray Fernando Fernández de Córdoba 2   tel. (926) 86 06 48; both specialize in regional dishes. Be sure to try the famous *Berengenas de Almagro*—marinated baby eggplants.

SHOPPING

Shops in the Plaza Mayor sell local lacework, and there is often someone in the patio of the parador making and selling lace. Prices are reasonable.

$\mathcal{V}$ISITING CIUDAD REAL

LAS TABLAS DE DAIMIEL   A marshland of the Guadiana river where the river mysteriously travels underground, capriciously surfacing into ponds, called the "eyes" of the Guadiana. This is today a peaceful wildlife preserve, principally for migratory and other aquatic birds, with an unusual landscape of tall reeds and gnarled trees. Follow the marked paths to the various islands and lookout points.
◆ Best times to visit are early morning and late afternoon and in the spring. Bring binoculars. If you drive and take a left turn on a road as you enter the reserve, you can picnic by the side of a pond and watch the birds come and go.

TOMELLOSO   A large wine center, where in the Plaza Mayor there is a sixteenth century posada—once a resting place for muleteers—and just beyond town (road to Pedro Muñoz) an antique carriage museum (request a visit at town hall).

RUIDERA LAKES   There are seventeen lakes formed by the Guadiana river, many joined by canals and popular with summer vacationers.

LA SOLANA   A town in typical whitewashed Manchegan style, with a porticoed Plaza Mayor and many noble homes bearing coats of arms.

SAN CARLOS DEL VALLE   The brick plaza with wooden galleries is the town's centerpiece and quite delightful, reflecting something of the Flemish style of Almagro but on a small, intimate scale. The plaza doesn't look like a public square because it was originally the courtyard of a small village church, built here in recognition of a miraculous apparition of Christ.

VILLANUEVA DE LOS INFANTES   A little-known and underappreciated town filled with noble stone homes (displaying 120 coats of arms), in addition to more modest whitewashed houses with wrought-iron gratings covering the windows. The stately Plaza Mayor is built of honey-colored stone.

> ### $\mathcal{P}$ICKLED EGGPLANT, ALMAGRO-STYLE
>
> Cut a 1-inch lengthwise slit in 8 small eggplants (¼ pound each). Cook in salted water until barely tender; drain. In a bowl combine 1 cup red wine vinegar, 2 cups water, 5 tablespoons olive oil, salt, pepper, dried red chili pepper, 2 minced cloves of garlic, 1 teaspoon crushed cumin, and ¼ teaspoon oregano. Add the eggplants, cover, and marinate for several days.

VALDEPEÑAS   Center of a vast winemaking region of La Mancha, with dozens of bodegas, most of which can be visited, usually by previous appointment.

CIUDAD REAL   The Knights of Calatrava were so powerful in La Mancha that King Alfonso X El Sabio became alarmed and decided to establish an outpost of the crown here. Thus this provincial capital, named Royal City, was created. There is little to see in Ciudad Real except the fourteenth century Puerta de Toledo—two thick, square towers flanking delicate Moorish horseshoe arches. It is all that remains of the original walls, 130 towers, and eight gateways of the old city.

CALATRAVA   The massive thirteenth century castle and monastery sits imposingly on a lonely windswept clifftop. In history this was one of Spain's most strategic locations (an important pass between Castilla and Andalucía) and was headquarters of the Order of Calatrava. This castle replaced a previous one, Salvatierra, that was in turn instrumental in the decisive battle against the Moors at Navas de Tolosa (p. 472). It's worth your while to drive up to the castle for a closer look.

THE FEISTY KNIGHTS OF CALATRAVA

The Moorish occupation of Spain created a spirit of religious crusade, and men of the cloth were as much a part of the Reconquest as the common foot soldier. Especially influential were the twelfth century Knights of Calatrava, the first of these military-religious orders. Fearless warriors, they were rewarded for their achievements with reconquered land, and their wealth and power became immense. They were exempt from local law and answered only to the Holy See in Rome; kings pampered and feared them. But the Knights of Calatrava became drunk with power.

Their grand master lived at court or in his palace in Almagro, and members flagrantly disregarded the doctrines of the Catholic Church. Unable to stem their excesses, the pope awarded them special privileges that permitted them to do what, in fact, they were already doing: eating exquisite foods, dressing regally in expensive and colorful robes, and keeping prayer to a minimum. The pope even allowed them to marry—his only recourse in view of the many illegitimate children the knights had already sired.

After the thirteenth century the order went into steep decline, and the power of the Knights of Calatrava passed to the king of Spain.

LAS VIRTUDES   Some say this village's square bullring from the twelfth century is the oldest in Spain, and one side of the bullring incorporates a sixteenth century hermitage. The elegant wood galleries are reminiscent of the Flemish style of Almagro.

EL VISO DEL MARQUÉS   In the midst of landlocked La Mancha, this curious palace—once the home of sixteenth century naval hero Álvaro de Bazán (Marqués de Santa Cruz)—guards the archives of the Spanish navy. It is a sumptuous residence in sixteenth century Italian Renaissance style, with frescoed walls, a majestic staircase (Philip II liked it so much that he used the same architect to design one for El Escorial), an elegant patio, and lush gardens, in which a collection of boat prows is displayed.

THE PROVINCE OF ALBACETE

CALLED AL BASIT (the Plain) by the Arabs, Albacete (ahl-bah-*theh*-tay) is just that—a vast, flat expanse that becomes hillier to the east and south as it meets the mountains of the Levante and Andalucía.

Albacete is primarily agricultural, and its wine production is substantial. Known for its pottery, especially that of Chinchilla de Monte Aragón, Albacete has for centuries also been famous for the outstanding quality and craftsmanship of its knives, many of them artisan products with handles of bull horn and deer hooves.

I would not give particular importance to the cooking of Albacete were it not for the efforts of a very special lady from Albacete, Carmen Useros. A one-woman show, she crisscrossed the province, visiting every one of its villages and seeking out the best cook in each. Her tenacity produced a comprehensive cookbook of one thousand recipes called *Cocina de Albacete*, an exceptionally handsome and exhaustively researched cookbook that I treasure and consider a unique achievement. The recipes are simple peasant foods of the kind that returns us to our roots, and they have influenced the menu of Nuestro Bar, a delightful restaurant in the city of Albacete, where we sampled some of Carmen Useros's delicious discoveries. Among her other accomplishments is the creation of a ceramics museum in Chinchilla de Monte Aragón that exhibits pottery from all over Spain.

Despite my great admiration for the efforts of Carmen Useros, in Albacete there are few places of major interest for the visitor. But don't let this discourage you—if you came only to see Alcalá del Júcar, I think your time would be well spent.

THE ASTONISHING VILLAGE OF ALCALÁ DEL JÚCAR

We came to Alcalá del Júcar for the first time from Alarcón, passing through the lush Júcar valley. Bordered by sheer, bare white striated cliffs of fantastic formations, these canyon walls were in sharp contrast to the green land and blue-green waters of the Río Júcar, and it was a beautiful sight.

But we could hardly believe what suddenly appeared to our left: Several hundred feet up a cliff we saw round and square openings punched out of the rock like portholes, and specks of people were looking down to the river. Not until we rounded the tight bend in the Júcar and the town of Alcalá del Júcar appeared, as white as the cliffs against which it nestles, did we fully realize that the windows belonged to the village houses.

Jutting out over the river like a ship's prow, Alcalá del Júcar was once an Arab town and later a dependency of the powerful Marqués de Villena.

But the history of Alcalá is the least of its allure. So narrow are the streets and so steep the climb that Alcalá del Júcar can only be reached on foot or by burro. The ascent begins at the stone bridge over the river, where a small beach attracts village children. Twisting streets, lined with whitewashed houses, led us toward the Arab castle that stands tall at the summit. These were not ordinary village houses, however, but mere facades opening into networks of rooms hollowed from the cliff. The streets we climbed were built on top of the houses, and the entire village was a part of this amazing subterranean world.

We were a bit winded and in need of refreshment when we reached the upper village. Bar La Cueva was a welcome sight, and its gregarious owner, Juanjo, twirling his devilish Daliesque mustache, added an exotic touch to the scene. The wonder we had experienced when we saw the portholes in the cliff increased as we entered the bar and found ourselves in a long dark corridor with irregular whitewashed walls, perhaps three hundred feet long. We groped our way toward a spot of daylight—the proverbial light at the end of the tunnel—and emerged into a cozy, cavelike room with large openings overlooking the countryside. We had traversed the entire mountain and were now gazing from those portholes.

With gin-and-tonic and some tapas in hand, we looked down to the road, now absurdly reduced in size, and appreciated the incredible situation of Alcalá and its dizzying height, and we marveled at the human ingenuity it took to create it.

VISITING THE PROVINCE OF ALBACETE

ALCARAZ   The best of this village in the Sierra de Alcaraz is its Plaza Mayor—a national monument—much too grand and majestic, it would seem, for a place so small and isolated. From the fifteenth to the seventeenth centuries, however, this was a famous and wealthy rugmaking center—its rugs were found all over Europe—and one of the most important cities of the region. Renaissance architect Andrés de Vandelvira (see Index) was born here, and the town monuments have something of his style, from the arcaded *lonja* (merchants' exchange) to the two Renaissance churches whose similar towers come unusually close together at one corner of the plaza and are said to be designed by Vandelvira.

ALMANSA   Up a long flight of steps from the village is the elongated, very narrow, and beautifully preserved Moorish castle sitting on one of the few rocky spikes in the plains of Albacete. An eleventh century palace, Casa Grande would be quite plain were it not for the elaborate chipped stone bands trimming the portal and an oversized coat of arms above the doorway, flanked by two larger-than-life figures.

CHINCHILLA DE MONTE ARAGÓN   Situated on a high hill over the plain, the village, entered through a gateway in the town hall that leads to the beautiful Plaza Mayor, wraps around its wide, squat castle in descending tiers. This was once the provincial capital, which explains the seignorial homes and palaces in the upper town. Around Chinchilla are man-made caves hollowed from the hillside, which are used to grow and store wild mushrooms (some other caves have been charmingly converted to private homes).

The **MUSEO DE CERÁMICA** (stop at Calle de Los Médicos 4, near the plaza, to find the museum caretaker), founded by Carmen Useros, is set up in a whitewashed village house and exhibits an enormous variety of pottery pieces from all over Spain. Notice the *cuerveras*—large bowls holding around their rim miniature pitchers from which to serve the regional wine drink, la cuerva.

♦ There are a few pottery makers still in their workshops in the caves, continuing their traditional craft.

ALBACETE   This capital of the province is a crossroads for routes to the south, the Levante, and central Castile, and a convenient point to stop en route. My recommendations in Albacete center on food, lodgings, and crafts, for little of Old Albacete has survived, and the new city is not particularly attractive. Knifemaking here is a tradition that goes back at least to the fifteenth century, and few travelers pass through town without purchasing the city's famous knives, of high-quality steel blades with beautifully handcrafted handles. There are several reputable shops at the eastern entrance to town on Calle La Feria.

The **MUSEO ARQUEOLÓGICO** has an interesting display of ancient Iberian stone statuary and an unusual collection of articulated Roman dolls of amber and marble from the third century.

PARADOR DE LA MANCHA   Honda de la Morena, Carretera 430, km 220 tel. (967) 22 94 50, is a typical Manchegan grange, beautifully appointed, just outside the city and always a pleasant and relaxing stopover. (Moderate; pool.)

NUESTRO BAR   Alcalde Conangla 102   tel. (967) 22 72 15, is one of my favorites for tapas and has an overwhelming selection of them (close to one hundred). The restaurant features Manchegan cooking—try *Nuestras Cosicas*, a tasting of various specialties. (Moderate.)

JORQUERA   On the road from Albacete to Alcalá del Júcar, which winds through canyons of the Río Júcar, this town is in a spectacular setting, high above the river and encircled by a deep river gorge.

LAGUNAS (LAKES) DE RUIDERA   See "Visiting Ciudad Real."

THE PROVINCE OF CUENCA

CUENCA (*cuen*-cah), a large, underpopulated province, known as Conca to the Romans and ruled by the Arabs until the twelfth century, was once exceptionally prosperous. Besides the cattle that were raised and the wool that was produced in Cuenca, impressive forests created an important paper and wood industry, the latter being particularly significant for boatbuilding during the times of the discovery and exploration of America.

Cuenca has a look distinctly its own. Bound by the Tagus river to the north and cut north to south by the tranquil Río Júcar, it is situated at the eastern extreme of the Castilian meseta. Plains give way to the gentle hills of La Alcarria (p. 168) and then to the Serranía de Cuenca, low mountains of pine forests and massive rock formations. Here the scenery takes on awesome, almost Dantesque proportions.

Eons of erosion, generated by wind and by water slowly dripping or madly rushing over soft limestone, has etched a fantasyland that appears carved by a sculptor's chisel (in an area known as the Enchanted City, the rock configurations, indeed, look man-made). In Cuenca you will find deep canyons and gorges colored ocher, sand, and gray—as if by a painter's brush—and astounding ravines, called *hoces*, over which the famous Casas Colgadas (Hanging Houses) of the city of Cuenca are built at the edge of the precipice. Strange rocks mushroom from flat land into phantasmagorical shapes; there are gaping chasms and stunning vertiginous abysses dropping to the rivers. In several cases rivers have so persistently carved their routes that towns like Cuenca and Alarcón are virtual islands.

Enough has already been said about the cooking of La Mancha (see the introduction to Castilla-La Mancha). You'll find all the typical dishes here—*morteruelo* (especially popular in this province), *mojete*, *ajo arriero*, *zarajos*, etc, but add to this appealing river trout and red partridge, as well as excellent lamb chops and some fine desserts like *Alajú* (an Arab sweet of honey and nuts), a cake called *Pellizco de Monja* (literally, a "Pinch" of Nun), and figs confected with honey and nuts. Cuenca has two typical drinks: *la cuerva* (p. 149), served from a special bowl called *la cuervera*, and *resoli*, sweet coffee liqueur spiked with anisette.

Food, however, is the least important aspect in this province of unique landscape and of the astonishing Hanging Houses of the city of Cuenca.

THE HANGING HOUSES OF CUENCA

Cuenca hangs at the edge of a rocky spur, ringed by gently rounded cliffs and flanked by two rivers—the Júcar and the Huécar—that join at one extreme of the city after cutting the town into a shell shape (Cuenca originally was named Conca, meaning shell). In ancient times Cuenca was an impenetrable fortress, approachable only by way of a narrow bridge crossing a shallow natural moat that drops off into chasms on either side. That strip of land was the only point where Cuenca needed man-made protection, and was defended by thick fortified walls, which in part are still standing. A map and an aerial photograph helped me appreciate the topography of Cuenca, for as provincial capital, the city has expanded considerably, and its original outlines are somewhat obscured.

Rising from the rock, at the very tip of the precipices, are Cuenca's unforgettable fourteenth century Casas Colgadas, or Hanging Houses, impossibly poised at cliff's edge and soaring straight up from vertical ravines, their terraces projected over emptiness. The houses have been described as suspended in midair, motionless, like hovering, long-winged predatory birds on the hunt. Sometimes characterized as predecessors of modern skyscrapers, the houses of Cuenca, backed by the cliffs, rise more than a dozen stories over the rivers, but from the medieval city streets that wind and twist up and down from the central Plaza Mayor, the houses are just three and four floors high. You must see the Hanging Houses from afar, by the banks of the rivers or from the Hanging Bridge (Puente Colgante), but to sense their height you should also view the setting from the houses themselves.

While Cuenca is unique in Spain today, there is substantial evidence to indicate that as far back as Roman times (see Valeria, p. 167), hanging houses were an ingenious solution to the architectural challenge posed by the small, protected enclosures that characterize the province's landscape. To utilize limited space to the maximum, houses had to reach the very edge of the cliffs and grow taller than would normally be necessary.

But by the turn of this century, lack of space was no longer a problem. Bypassed by major railway lines, Cuenca had become a forgotten city, on the verge of ruin. Fortunately, in recent decades it was recognized as an architectural treasure and revived by Spanish artists. Houses were lovingly restored, and Cuenca became an important enclave for painters and sculptors. When the time came to establish a Spanish museum of abstract art, the unusual but not completely unexpected choice of location was Cuenca, and the specific site selected was one of the choice Hanging Houses.

The main sights in Cuenca are, predictably, the town's setting and the Hanging Houses that border both the cliffs over the Río Júcar and those above the Río Huécar. But there is still more to Cuenca: a cathedral of note, two fine museums, and the Old Quarter—exceptionally well preserved and wonderful for meditative walks.

Seeing Cuenca and its Environs

PLAZA MAYOR   Large and harmonious, the plaza includes the cathedral, and the eighteenth century town hall, the arches of which form the entrance to the plaza.

CATHEDRAL   With obvious Gothic traits in its exterior, the cathedral has a nave inside that takes on the austere, unadorned appearance of Anglo-Norman architecture and is unique in Spain. The central bell tower collapsed at the beginning of the century and was never rebuilt—thus the chopped-off, unfinished look of the facade. See the wrought-iron altar screen, so intricate it almost looks like embroidery; the delicately designed upper balcony, or triforium, an unusual feature in a Spanish church; the chapterhouse doors carved in the sixteenth century by master sculptor Alonso Berruguete; and in the Diocesan Museum, next to the cathedral, a thirteenth century Calvary and two El Greco paintings (one is the highly regarded *Prayer in the Garden*).

MUSEO DE ARTE ABSTRACTO ESPAÑOL   Set in one of the Hanging Houses, the modern interior design (nevertheless preserving the *artesonado* ceilings and murals originally there) is appropriate to display some unusual works of well-known twentieth century Spanish abstract painters and sculptors, perhaps less known to the visitor than to Spaniards. Represented are Feito, Canogar, Zóbel, Tàpies, Chillida, and Saura, among many others.

MUSEO ARQUEOLÓGICO   In a fourteenth century house that was once the city granary, see on the second floor Roman coins and statuary from the ancient city of Segóbriga and remains of Valeria (you can also visit the sites of both cities; see p. 167). A Roman kitchen has been carefully re-created.

HOZ DEL HUÉCAR   Descend from the town through an archway of the Casas Colgadas to the **PUENTE COLGANTE** (Hanging Bridge), a nineteenth century iron bridge built over the supports of a medieval stone bridge. Disconcertingly high above the Huécar ravine, the bridge leads to the Convento de San Pablo (soon to be a parador); from mid-span are the best views of the Hanging Houses.

HOZ DEL JÚCAR   You can see these other, less famous (but I think more representative) Hanging Houses of Cuenca, which rise from the poplar-lined Júcar river, on the road heading to the Ciudad Encantada. Also along this route is the **VENTANO DEL DIABLO,** a rocky enclosure that forms a natural lookout point with splendid views of the river as it flows through a gorge.

LAS TORCAS DEL PALANCAR   These uncommonly deep conical depressions are formed by underground springs that cause the ground to collapse. Some are filled with water, forming lakes; in others dense vegetation grows. One is more than 2,000 feet across.

CIUDAD ENCANTADA   Traveling a short distance from Cuenca through pine forests brings you to this natural wonder, thus called because the rock formations look somewhat like the ruins of a city. Colossal boulders form all kinds of vaguely familiar shapes, and an unknown hand has named some of them Head of Man, City Streets, Roman Bridge, The Toboggan, and Elephant Fighting a Crocodile. It's a real workout to cover the entire route, and unless such curiosities interest you, just see a few examples near the entrance, then turn back.

◆ If your itinerary takes you to Alarcón (a place you should not miss; see p. 166), be sure to take the road toward Tórtola. It leads through stunning scenery of gorges and ravines and passes next to the Roman town of Valeria, which is next to the present town of Valeria de Arriba.

STAYING IN CUENCA

POSADA DE SAN JOSÉ   Julián Romero 4   tel. (966) 21 13 00   Simple accommodations in a cozy and most charming hotel (really an inn) that is beautifully kept and furnished with antiques. The hotel occupies a sixteenth century Hanging House in the heart of the Old Quarter with wonderful views over the Hoz del Huécar. A very pleasant bar. (Inexpensive.)

EATING IN CUENCA

MESÓN CASAS COLGADAS   Canónigos s/n   tel. (966) 22 35 09   Ideally located in a prize Hanging House. A varied menu includes local specialties like partridge, excellent lamb chops, *Sopa Manchega* (garlic soup), and a variety of local desserts. (Moderate–expensive.)

FIGÓN DE PEDRO   Cervantes 13   tel. (966) 22 68 21   Same owner and menu as the above, but less expensive because it is in the newer part of Cuenca and does not have a view. (Moderate.)

SAN NICOLÁS   San Pedro 15   tel. (966) 21 22 05   On a beautiful street in a centuries-old house, San Nicolás concentrates on regional specialties— pickled partridge, rabbit, *Pisto Manchego* (stewed vegetables), and trout. (Moderate.)

SHOPPING

Cuenca is known for its ceramics, particularly in the form of small black bulls.

Two well-known shops for ceramics are **ALFARERÍA DE LUIS DE CASTILLO,** in the Plaza Mayor, and **ALFARERÍA PEDRO MERCEDES** Benito Pérez 22.

$\wp$ ISITING THE PROVINCE OF CUENCA

ALARCÓN   This tiny village is situated very much like Cuenca, encircled by the Júcar, which snakes in a double S around the village. Joined to the mainland by a strip of land just wide enough for a car to pass, Alarcón is practically an island. But unlike Cuenca's, Alarcón's astounding site is easily appreciated from the cliffs across the river. You are not likely to find a more sensational setting, nor a place that reflects a greater peace. Life revolves around the walled eighth century Arab castle, which is today an exceptional parador.

PARADOR MARQUÉS DE VILLENA   Avenida Amigos de los Castillos 3 tel. (966) 33 13 50, in Alarcón's castle, has just thirteen rooms (ask for one in the tower), and a fine restaurant in a medieval setting. Spaniards like to escape here for a quiet weekend. (Moderate–expensive.)

SAN CLEMENTE   Although dating from the twelfth century, this village has Renaissance character and an unusually attractive Plaza Mayor.

MOTA DEL CUERVO   See "Visiting Don Quijote's Country."

BELMONTE   In this typical Manchegan village, the great sixteenth century mystic poet and humanist Fray Luis de León was born. But the main attraction is an excellently preserved castle-palace, built by the Marqués de Villena in the fifteenth century, far above the town. In that same century Juana la Beltraneja, who contested the right of Isabel La Católica to the Castilian throne, was imprisoned here.

The castle consists of three rectangular structures that have rounded towers at each exterior corner. The structures join to form a triangular patio at their center. There are many exceptional *artesonado* ceilings of walnut and gold leaf, some keeping their bright colors. The most beautiful is in the former bedroom of the marqués—octagonal, with colored-glass skylights; it used to rotate so that the light flashed and bells tingled. Delicate stone tracery around window alcoves and other interior details give an idea of the former luxury of this castle. There are extensive views of the Castilian plains and the village of Belmonte below.

VALERIA   Because this Roman city, still in the process of excavation, is rarely visited, you feel a special closeness to the distant past. Founded by Valerius Flaccus in the first century, Valeria was once quite grand. You'll see the columned basilica, a public meeting place, and the remains of an ornamental fountain called the *ninfeo*, unique in Spain and the largest ever found in the Roman Empire. The fountain buttressed the ravine, over which the first known Hanging Houses of Cuenca were built.

SEGÓBRIGA   Four kilometers from Saelices, the main attraction of these Roman ruins is a well-preserved Roman theater. A small museum displays some of the objects uncovered here.

MONASTERIO DE UCLÉS   An imposing sixteenth century monastery above the town of Uclés, designed in the style of El Escorial, although the facade is posterior.

TRAGACETE   A well-known base for trout fishing, near the place where the Río Cuervo is born, amid lush vegetation and waterfalls. From here you can continue to where the Río Tajo originates and on to Albarracín in the province of Teruel.

PRIEGO, HOZ DE BETETA   A wonderfully scenic route that begins in Priego, passes the ravine (Estrecho de Priego) of the Río Escabas, continues to the deep Beteta gorge (Hoz de Beteta), lined by massive ocher cliffs streaked with gray that follow the Río Cuervo, and ends at the small town of Beteta, set over a cliff. Another stunning stretch of road north of Beteta, direction Molina de Aragon, follows in part deep pine-covered gorges from which bare rocky promontories dramatically emerge.

THE PROVINCE OF GUADALAJARA

THE LITTLE-KNOWN PROVINCE of Guadalajara (gwa-da-la-*ha*-ra) has a most beautiful name (from the Arab Wadi-Ihajra, meaning River of Stones) but few major sights and no important cities. Nevertheless, I think a visit to Sigüenza, one of my favorite Castilian towns, is time well spent, and its castle-cum-parador is beyond compare. The city of Guadalajara and the villages of Atienza and Pastrana also merit a pause as you pass through the province, most likely en route to Madrid, west of Guadalajara, or to Aragón, east of the province. And the huge Entrepeñas reservoir—part of what is known as the Mar de Castilla (Sea of Castile) and watered by the mighty Río Tajo—offers possibilities for swimming and relaxation.

Guadalajara looks unlike the plains of La Mancha; it is much hillier and includes the bulk of an area called La Alcarria, famous for its rosemary-, thyme-, and marjoram-scented honeys, which was brought to public attention by Nobel Prize winner Camilo José Cela, who described his travels through here. You will begin to see gorges and ravines similar to the spectacular ones that will appear in the adjoining province of Cuenca.

As for food, trout from the Tajo and other rivers is found in many restaurants of Guadalajara, and river crabs (*cangrejos de río*) are a gastronomic highlight. Game is abundant, especially partridge and quail, and *cabrito* (kid) takes preference over lamb, although I usually do not find it as tasty or tender. A variety of simple cakes and pastries are bathed with the fragrant honeys of La Alcarria.

THE TOWN OF SIGÜENZA

The pure medieval ambiance of the streets of Sigüenza (see-*gwen*-tha) is enough inducement to bring us to this small Guadalajara town, but two outstanding monuments are particularly enticing. Sigüenza is ancient, conceived, it is thought, more than two thousand years ago in Celtiberian times near the banks of the Henares river and called Segontina (meaning "place dominating the valley"). It was also appreciated by the Romans, but its real importance developed in later centuries when it became a bishops' see. It remained so for eight centuries, accounting for the presence of a grandiose cathedral in what seems like a forgotten village. Sigüenza's strategic position between warring Aragón and Castilla made fortification essential, and the cathedral looks as much like a fortress as the town's castle up on the hill.

In Sigüenza we like to follow a simple walking route, beginning on the hill above the city where we stay at the bishops' palace-castle—now a stunning parador. We cross the wood-planked bridge over the castle moat and wind our way down to the Plaza Mayor and end at the cathedral.

The parador was once an Arab fortress, then for centuries a residence for bishops who were also the feudal lords of the region. Poor Doña Blanca, beautiful blond French princess and wife of Pedro el Cruel, was imprisoned here in the fourteenth century. The king abandoned her for his Andalusian mistress, María Padilla (see box, p. 98), just three days after the wedding and kept her imprisoned, here as well as in other castles, for the rest of her brief life. Doña Blanca had many supporters among those who disapproved of the king's behavior and among his political enemies. She died when only twenty-five years of age.

From the towers of the parador we look down on the cobbled streets and red-tile rooftops of Old Sigüenza and out over straw-colored fields and the pine-forested countryside in the distance. The old Jewish quarter is near the parador, centering on Sinagoga street. From there we descend into the village, passing, among other noble homes, the purely Gothic Casa del Doncel, named after the beloved page of Catholic Queen Isabel whose celebrated tomb is in the cathedral. We reach the beautifully porticoed Plaza Mayor and enjoy its sixteenth century atmosphere. The cathedral adjoins the square, and its massive fortified square towers are immediately striking. Looking closely, we could see that the towers are peppered with gunshot holes, reminders of the Civil War battle between Republican militiamen holding the cathedral and attacking Nationalist forces. The cathedral was begun in the twelfth century, right after the Reconquest (the Romanesque triple portal is from that era), and continued to evolve for several more centuries.

The cathedral's interior is in Gothic style, and what mostly attracts us is the statue known as *El Doncel,* an exquisitely but simply carved reclining figure of Queen Isabel's young page, Don Martín Vázquez de Arce, who died at age twenty-five in her service during the Reconquest of Granada. He rests on his elbow in a natural pose, reading a book. His face, gentle and kind, reflects the special affection the queen felt for this young man and her great sorrow over his untimely death. It is an incomparable work of Gothic funerary art and is why Sigüenza is called "City of *The Doncel.*"

◆ In the cathedral museum are works by El Greco, Morales, Ribera, Zurbarán, and the Murcian sculptor Salzillo.

STAYING AND EATING
IN SIGÜENZA

PARADOR CASTILLO DE SIGÜENZA   Plaza del Castillo s/n   tel. (911) 39 01 00   A twelfth century castle magnificently restored; its furnishings are in perfect harmony with the architecture. Request the upper floor overlooking the village. (Moderate–expensive.) The restaurant is elegant, and the food very good.

♡ISITING THE PROVINCE OF GUADALAJARA

THE BEAUTIFUL ONE-EYED PRINCESS OF ÉBOLI

Pastrana, a mere fifty kilometers from Madrid, is even today but a pueblo. How remote it must have seemed to the princess of Éboli, banished from the opulent court of Madrid and imprisoned here in her palace. A barred palace window, which you can see today, was her only view of the outside world.

She was considered the beauty of the court of Philip II, this despite a black eye patch she always wore following a childhood duel with her page (perhaps a child's game gone awry) in which she lost her right eye. Married at thirteen, she acquired the title of Princess of Éboli through her husband, a trusted adviser of the king's, and bore ten children. When widowed at thirty-six, in a moment of madness she entered the Carmelite convent in Pastrana, where she lived as a nun for several months. But so disruptive was she, according to most accounts, that Santa Teresa herself ordered her out, and the princess quickly discarded the monastic life.

At the insistence of King Philip, a personal friend (some say her lover), the princess returned to Madrid and became linked romantically to her husband's good friend and secretary to the king, Antonio Pérez. When the affair was uncovered, the scandal brought down the wrath of the deeply religious and ascetic king, and the princess was ousted from Madrid and imprisoned in her castle in Pastrana, where she remained confined for the rest of her life, occasionally appearing, it is said, at the barred palace window facing the square.

The visitor shudders to think that on the other side of those walls that enigmatic, beautiful, one-eyed, and apparently fun-loving lady, who had so much influence and drove powerful men mad, spent such difficult times and finally died.

Camilo José Cela

PASTRANA The sober sixteenth century Renaissance palace of the infamous Princess of Éboli, also called the Duchess of Pastrana (see box), occupies one-quarter of Pastrana's attractive three-sided Plaza de La Hora (the fourth side is open to the valley). Both exits from the plaza lead upward—one street (to the right when you face the palace) climbs to the old Albaicín district, which still has a Moorish flavor and was a silkmaking center in the days of the princess. At the opposite side of the plaza another street enters into the twisting streets of the old Christian town. In the Colegiata church the Dukes of Pastrana are entombed, and also here is an exceptionally beautiful collection of Gothic tapestries depicting in fine detail the victories of King Alfonso V of Portugal in Arzila and Tangier.

HOSTERÍA PRINCESA DE ÉBOLI Convento de las Monjas de Abajo tel. (91) 261 56 86, occupies part of the sixteenth century convent of San José, founded by Santa Teresa and the Dukes of Pastrana (it is still inhabited by a religious order). The restaurant is delightful—at street level there is a rustic tavern, on the upper floor a dining room that embraces the primitive convent kitchen. Regional fare: sautéed *chorizo* and black sausage, trout escabeche, roast lamb, lamb chops, *Leche Frita* (fried custard). Open only at lunch hour and only on Saturdays, Sundays, and holidays. (Inexpensive.)

ENTREPEÑAS   A reservoir in a pleasing mountainous setting, part of several lakes known collectively as the Sea of Castile, which is a popular summer resort.

GUADALAJARA   Although capital of the province, this small city's chief interest lies in the Palace of the Duque del Infantado, a fifteenth century structure that is a skillful blend of Renaissance, Gothic, and Mudéjar styles. Its unusual facade is covered by protruding diamond-cut stones and elaborately decorated balcony turrets. The interior patio has a heavily carved double gallery, and the salon ceilings are *artesonado*.

BRIHUEGA   An ancient fortified town (parts of the walls remain) over which an Arab castle presides. The streets are narrow—some porticoed— and lined with whitewashed houses and an occasional stone palace. On August 16 the town celebrates the Virgen de la Peña by setting bulls loose in the streets.

COGOLLUDO   Distinguishing this village are a fifteenth century Plaza Mayor and the palace of the Dukes of Medinaceli, which bears a resemblance to the ducal palace in Guadalajara, although somewhat less ornate.

ATIENZA   Dating back to the times before Christ, this village is impressive when seen from the Sigüenza road: a mound almost 4,000 feet high dominating the richly green and undulating land, with an imposing castle at its height. A delightful Plaza Mayor is flanked on one side by a massive church, and delicately porticoed houses complete the plaza. Beautiful views from the heights of the castle.

BARRANCO DE LA VIRGEN DE LA HOZ   The Río Gallo, a branch of the Tajo, has cut majestic walls of stone here. From the hermitage at the highest point, a wonderful vista unfolds.

MOLINA DE ARAGÓN   The houses and the twelfth to thirteenth century castle of this town have the same color as the ruddy Castilian earth. Ancient walls, steeply descending down the mountainside from the castle, are massive, and the main road cuts right through a crumbled sector, giving you an unusually close look at their height and thickness.

THE PROVINCE OF TOLEDO

TOLEDO (toe-*lay*-doh) is on the fringe of La Mancha and begins to resemble austere Castilla-León, to the north. Construction materials change to stone, in the same shade of brown as the land from which the towns and villages arise.

The strategic location of Toledo province—a crossroads near the center of Spain and traversed by the historically important Río Tajo—made Toledo an essential stronghold for whichever culture reigned in Spain. Not only was it an economic and communication hub, but it was a cultural showpiece as well, where arts and crafts flourished. Toledo was once Roman, and in the sixth century became the opulent capital of Visigothic Spain. It was an important Moorish center during the Arab occupation, and when reconquered in 1085 by King Alfonso VI, Toledo became the capital of Castile, a thriving Jewish center, and for the next few centuries the focus of Spanish history and culture.

Because of Toledo's strategic location, it was naturally a battleground, in need of fortresses. The famous castles of Castilla are common here: Maqueda, Guadamur, Oropesa, Escalona, and Orgaz are but a few that have survived.

In Toledo the rustic farmhouses of La Mancha become the more sophisticated *cigarrales*, which although often serving agrarian purposes, are more likely to be luxury villas on the outskirts of the city of Toledo. They are named, it is said, for the well-modulated symphony of the cicadas (*cigarras*) in spring and summer.

Hunting is pursued with enthusiasm in this province. The landscape of low mountains and scrub bushes is ideal for small game like the highly prized red partridge, and in the fall, gamesmen gather from all corners of the world. So it should come as no surprise that the food most closely associated with Toledo is partridge, the most famous dish being *Perdiz a la Toledana*—partridge slow-cooked with plenty of onion, garlic, bay leaf, and wine. Méntrida wines of Toledo are the perfect complement to such a dish. Also inseparable from Toledo—a product of its rich Jewish and Arab past—is marzipan, the Eastern sweet of almond paste and sugar.

Why crafts prosper in Toledo while dying out in many other regions may be attributable to its long-lasting Arab heritage. Surely we can credit the Moors with bringing to Spain the art of damascene (inlay of gold and silver threads in a grooved sheet of metal in Moorish patterns) and influencing the design of the blue ceramics of Talavera de la Reina and the green pottery of El Puente del Arzobispo; with perhaps introducing embroidery skills, now a specialty of Lagartera (see box, p. 180); with the craft of tooled leather and the art of woodcarving, which has made Toledo a center for furniture made in the Castilian style.

The splendid city of Toledo is, of course, the indisputable highlight of this province and will undoubtedly be your main motivation for traveling here.

THE MYSTICAL CITY OF TOLEDO

Toledo is the city that offers the most complete and characteristic assemblage of genuinely Spanish land and civilization. It is the most brilliant and suggestive summary of our national history. For this reason, if a traveler has just one day in Spain, he should spend it, without thinking twice, seeing Toledo.

Manuel B. Cossío

Years before I seriously began to explore Spain, Toledo fascinated me, particularly because of its association with El Greco. The first time I visited Toledo I felt the mystery that permeated the air. The streets of the old city whispered the past. The Jewish quarter was labyrinthine, twisting, hilly, with intimate, dimly lit squares, humble homes, an air of melancholy. And yet Toledo was at the same time a city of grandeur: mansions with coats of arms, triumphal gateways, convents, monasteries, churches, synagogues, mosques. I could picture lean, moneyless but dignified hidalgos and shrewd, wily picaros prowling the streets; I could see Jews, Christians, and Moors going about their daily lives, undisturbed by religious or racial discord; and most of all, I could imagine El Greco himself assimilating Toledo's unique atmosphere.

Toledo at that time meant El Greco to me, and it still does, for the city seems imbued with his spirit. But Toledo is so much more than that. No other city in Spain was the focus of so many civilizations, with so much concentrated in such a small space. Toledo may be only a short ride from Madrid, but it is a world unto itself and a microcosm of Spanish history and culture.

Toledo is not only interesting historically, but geographically it is a marvel as well. To properly appreciate its site, drive into the hills across the Río Tajo (where the parador is situated) to see the all-encompassing view and to experience, by day and again by night, the changing lights and colors that were captured so beautifully by El Greco in *View of Toledo.*

Toledo sits in isolated splendor on a rocky crag that is a natural fortress, tightly encircled by the Río Tajo, which carves a deep moat around the town. Thick walls on the city's north side guard the only entrance not protected by the river. In the distance, mountains loom: to the north the Sierra de Gredos, to the south the Montes de Toledo. The city itself, built on seven hills, is seen in unreal clarity and intensity, a monochromatic blend of austere brown hues, punctuated by towers, steeples, and on the highest hill, the imposing Alcázar.

Compare, as I have often done, El Greco's *View of Toledo,* which hangs in the Metropolitan Museum in New York, with what is before you. Allowing for artistic license and a typical El Greco spiritual surge toward the heavens, you will see a city frozen in time. The entire city of Toledo is a national monument that cannot be altered.

Looking at the lay of the land, one can understand why in Toledo three of the world's major religions—Christianity, Islam, and Judaism—and the different cultures they represented so successfully coexisted: There was simply no room to expand, and accommodation and tolerance became the means of survival. Even architecture had to conform, sometimes imposing one style over another. After all, this was a thriving city, the most important of Spain, and required cultural and architectural embellishments worthy of its prominent position.

Even Toledo's grand cathedral is squeezed between narrow streets and built on the foundations of a mosque; one of Toledo's synagogues became the Church of Santa María La Blanca, and the Alcázar, an Arab fortress, was converted into a royal palace for Emperor Charles V. Jewish, Arab, and Christian structures are often indistinguishable from one another (the craftsmen for all three were usually Moorish). Plaster tracery and decorative writing on the synagogue walls of Toledo, for example, are the same that you will find in a mosque, except the message is in Hebrew.

Christian churches and monasteries in Toledo, even when built in Gothic, Renaissance, or Baroque style, show markedly Moorish influences. San Juan de los Reyes monastery is the best example of an effortless and harmonious Moorish and Christian architectural blend. And El Tránsito synagogue has reminders of all three cultures: Moorish architecture and plasterwork, decorative reference to King Pedro El Cruel of Castile, and Jewish inscriptions—in Arabic style—on the walls. Curiously, even today Sephardic temples around the world often preserve a Moorish appearance.

THE TOLEDO OF ALFONSO EL SABIO

Although Toledo was returned to Christian rule in the eleventh century—relatively early in the Reconquest—some Arabs converted, remained in the city, and continued to practice their crafts. But the rest departed, and the crown, eager to repopulate cities emptied by the retreat of the Arabs, and to replace their erudition and artistic knowledge, turned to the Jews. Fleeing unrest in Moorish cities of southern Spain, Jews heeded the call, and by the thirteenth century Toledo had the largest Jewish community in Castilla—and perhaps in all of Spain—and the city supported dozens of synagogues. In southern Spain the Arabs and Jews were deposed or expelled simultaneously in the fifteenth century, but in Castilla the Arabs left much earlier, and the Jews took their place.

The elite of the Jewish community, who gathered in Toledo, attained extraordinary power and influence: they became administrators, financiers, and creditors to the royal court, as well as doctors serving kings, noblemen, and clergy. Jewish scholars and interpreters preserved and transmitted the accumulated knowledge of three civilizations. Culturally, Toledo became the Christian-controlled equivalent of Moorish Córdoba, and between them they produced some of the most learned men and influential literary and scientific works of the times.

Even before he was crowned king in 1252, Alfonso X, better known as Alfonso the Wise (el Sabio), spent much of his time in Toledo, gathering astronomers and other scholars, most of them Jewish and Arab, to work on a compilation and revision of Greek astronomical information—what has become known as the Alfonsine Tables. In his early youth the king had acquired a profound respect for learning and was well versed in mathematics, astronomy, and physical sciences. In his effort to promote and preserve Greek and Roman science and letters (much of it had survived the Dark Ages only in Arabic manuscripts), as well as Eastern cultures, he established in Toledo the famous School of Translators, where works from around the world and across the centuries were translated from Latin, Greek, Hebrew, Arabic—even Sanskrit—into the modern Castilian tongue.

By most accounts, Alfonso the Wise was politically inept, but European culture is in his debt; through his efforts a massive amount of scientific and literary knowledge was salvaged, translated, compiled, and subsequently retransmitted to the Western world.

Even after the expulsion of the Arabs and Jews and the death of Alfonso the Wise, Toledo conserved their cultural legacy, and the city never lost its Hebraic and oriental flavor. The Catholic Kings subsequently built the grand monastery of San Juan de Los Reyes in Toledo, and their grandson, Emperor Charles V, made Toledo the Imperial City (you are immediately reminded of this on entering the massive Bisagra Gate, above which the majestic two-headed eagle crest of the Hapsburgs attracts the eye). And although the emperor's attention was distracted to many other parts of his empire, his home base was Toledo, and it continued to be a city of great splendor, with no equal elsewhere in Spain.

Great writers of the sixteenth century Golden Age—Lope de Vega, Cervantes, and Garcilaso de la Vega—visited and often used Toledo as a theme. The anonymous author of *Lazarillo de Tormes* set part of his famous picaresque novel in Toledo. Sixteenth century saints Santa Teresa and San Juan de la Cruz spent time in Toledo. And the culture and luxury associated with court life was here. Once Philip II moved the royal residence to Madrid, Toledo's importance began to wane, but when El Greco arrived here in the sixteenth century this was still an exciting and vibrant city.

THE TOLEDO OF EL GRECO

When Domenico Theotocopoulos, or El Greco (the Greek), came to Toledo from Italy he was close to forty, an accomplished yet undistinguished Renaissance painter. Perhaps it was the oriental air of the city and the Jewish and Arab intermix of its people that inspired him and changed him into an artist unique in the world and the first of many extraordinary painters that Spain would produce. The strong spiritual and mystical bent of this highly cultured man seemed to mesh perfectly with Toledo. And contrary to some popular theories, El Greco did not suffer from astigmatism, but was merely depicting the people of Toledo as he saw them, then spiritually elongating them.

El Greco did not have the personality nor the inclination to be a court painter, but Philip II, then commissioning artwork for El Escorial and hearing of El Greco's talent, asked him to illustrate the Martyrdom of Saint Maurice and the Theban Legion. El Greco painted a masterpiece, but the monarch, a fan of realism, so disliked the painting that it was never hung, and El Greco was not called to court again.

But he did have a considerable following, especially among the people of Toledo. Single-handedly he seems to have decorated the cathedral, the churches, and the palaces of the city. What a dazzling concentration of El Greco works we still find here today.

> It is impossible to imagine his work, if he had ended his days in Rome or Venice, or in any other place except Toledo, achieving the impetus and the esthetic and psychological transcendence that it reached in the city on the Tajo.
>
> *Gregorio Marañón*

Seeing the City of Toledo

♦ Toledo is perhaps Spain's number-one attraction, conveniently close to Madrid and generally much too crowded—especially in the cathedral and Santo Tomé church. Visit after 5:00 p.m., when tour buses have left. And wander the streets away from the major sights to absorb Toledo's full medieval flavor (I especially like the area around Plaza Santo Domingo El Antiguo). Plan to stay at least one night, for it is difficult to see even a small part of the sights in a day.

CATHEDRAL   Asymmetrical, with one slender, ceramic-inlaid tower, Toledo's massive cathedral of five aisles and grand heights (some of its chapels are as large as churches) is the result of many architectural styles. Begun in the thirteenth century, it did not reach completion for almost three centuries, and continued to be remodeled into the seventeenth century. Thus what we see is essentially Spanish Gothic with Mudéjar influence and Renaissance and Baroque additions.

The main altar, around which the kings of Castile are entombed, is astonishing, completely bathed in gold that drips like icicles and has extraordinary detail (it looks like a rich gilt tapestry). Behind it, the **TRANSPARENTE** alcove, cut out of the cathedral wall and known as the "apotheosis of Baroque," is a massive flow of marble, a storm of figures in Gaudíesque fashion, streaming into one another and flooded with natural light (thus its name, "*transparente*"). The work provokes vehement pros and cons.

The choir, set in typical Spanish style in the middle of the cathedral, is enclosed by an elaborately carved stone frieze telling the story of the Bible (it was there to teach the illiterate) and by unusually open wrought-iron work. The choir stalls are magnificent; the lower ones depict the Reconquest of Spain by the Catholic Kings. Above the choir stalls are porticoed arches and a unique Renaissance alabaster frieze of saints.

The **SALA CAPITULAR** has a wonderful Mudéjar ceiling and minute plasterwork in the style of the Alhambra. The cathedral treasures are unsurpassed: a glittering monstrance—some 400 pounds of elaborately worked gold and silver by Enrique de Arfe—that is carried through the narrow streets for Corpus Christi. In the sacristy (which looks more like an art gallery) hangs an extraordinary collection of El Greco paintings (seventeen of them, including the famous *Expolio*, commissioned, designed, and proportioned for the place it occupies). Clerical vestments of gold and silver thread demonstrate the exceptional embroidery skills of the province.

EL ALCÁZAR Originally a Roman fortress, then Moorish, the Alcázar became the residence of conquering King Alfonso VI. The architect of Charles V, Covarrubias, made the Alcázar regal, and Philip II continued the work of the Alcázar with his El Escorial architect, Juan de Herrera, and gave the palace the severe look of his monastery. Much of the Alcázar was reduced to rubble in a fierce siege during the Spanish Civil War. It is now restored—except for the rooms where the wartime events took place (see box).

SANTA MARÍA LA BLANCA A twelfth century synagogue, Toledo's oldest, built as a synagogue but in a very original design of five aisles divided by brick horseshoe arches, recalling the Córdoba Mosque. The plaster tracery is pure Moorish (the Jews relied on Arab craftsmen). The synagogue later became a

"EL ALCÁZAR NO SE RINDE"

The defense of El Alcázar is a supreme symbol of courage and of a heroic fight against overwhelming odds. "The Alcázar will never surrender" became a rallying cry for the Nationalists in the Spanish Civil War.

Trapped by the Republicans at the beginning of the war, Franco's supporters—some 1,800 men, women, and children and a stock of horses—took refuge in Toledo's Alcázar and for two months withstood bombardment from the air and shelling from land. Ammunition was plentiful, but food was meager, and soon all that was left was horsemeat and grain, crudely baked into bread in a makeshift oven.

When the twenty-four-year-old son of the Alcázar's commander, Colonel Moscardó, was captured by Republicans, an ultimatum arrived by telephone: Surrender the Alcázar in ten minutes or your son will be shot. The boy took the phone:

". . . they say they will shoot me if you don't give up the Alcázar."

To which his father replied, "Then give your soul to God, shout ¡Viva España! and die like a patriot."

"Love you, father."

"Love you, son."

With that, Moscardó waived the ten-minute warning, declaring, "The Alcázar will never surrender." The Alcázar was eventually liberated, but left in total ruin.

The underground living quarters of the defenders and their families, the makeshift hospital, and the shell-pocked office with the famous telephone of Colonel Moscardó can be seen just as they were left at the end of the siege.

THE BURIAL OF COUNT ORGAZ: A PICTURE OF TOLEDO SOCIETY

The colors are still fresh, the painting breathes life, and the characters are powerfully realized. This is the painting that El Greco considered his supreme achievement, and it is spellbinding.

The Burial of Count Orgaz occupies the altar of the Santo Tomé church, the place for which it was designed, and is a painting of intense contrast in which black and white predominate. It is calm, and yet so much is taking place. In the sky is a swirling celestial scene; below, completely separate, is the terrestial event. The nobility of Toledo, members of the Order of Santiago, wear black garments with white ruffs and bear the red cross of Santiago. There are priests and monks of Toledo, all thought to be portraits of real people of the time. The young boy is probably El Greco's son, and the man looking straight out at us with his large soulful eyes is thought to be El Greco himself. Notice the elegance of the upturned hands that seem to float in midair.

A miracle is taking place as Saint Augustine and Saint Stephen come to earth to transport the soul of the count to heaven. Yet everyone on earth is seemingly unaware of or unperturbed by the momentous occasion and the turmoil in progress above them. Uniting the two scenes is the embryo-like soul of the count, lifted by angels into the flowing world above.

The subject of the painting was commissioned, but El Greco transformed the event into a complex statement of his religious beliefs and a penetrating look at Toledo society in the sixteenth century.

Catholic church, thus its Christian name.

EL TRÁNSITO   A splendid fourteenth century synagogue of Mudéjar decoration: an impressive wood ceiling (once painted with silver stars, which by candlelight looked like the night sky) and plasterwork—some of it is Hebrew writing—so dainty that it looks like lace; traces of the original polychrome remain.

SAN JUAN DE LOS REYES Grand Gothic monastery with Moorish touches, built by the Catholic Kings to commemorate an important victory at Toro in 1476. It is a blatant but beautiful mix of religion and politics. The stone carving to the sides of the altar—of crowns, coats of arms, and royal eagles—is incredibly rich. There are symbols of the monarchs everywhere: the letters F and Y for Fernando and Ysabel (her name in Old Spanish), yokes and arrows, and the inscription "*Tanto monta, monta tanto, Ysabel como Fernando*" (a declaration of each monarch's equal rights). An exceptional cloister, deeply carved in stone, looks like filigree, and there is a noble stairway designed by Covarrubias.

CASA-MUSEO DEL GRECO Probably not his actual house, but similarly elegant and spacious, with attention to period detail and furnishings. The large collection of his paintings includes a view of Toledo and portraits of saints and the Apostles, similar to those in the Prado, but from a later period.

SANTO TOMÉ   This church is noteworthy essentially because El Greco's supreme achievement, *The Burial of Count Orgaz,* is here (see box, p. 178). The chapel where the painting hangs is very small, and it is important to come at an off-hour, without the crowds, to fully appreciate the work.

HOSPITAL DE SANTA CRUZ   An outstanding museum, as much for its sixteenth century Plateresque design as for the eighteen El Greco paintings on exhibit, among them his celebrated *Assumption of the Virgin.*

CRISTO DE LA LUZ   A tenth century mosque, the only building in Toledo from before the Reconquest that has survived. Its interior horseshoe arches and cupolas have designs derived from the Córdoba Mosque, but these are wonderfully primitive and simple, with little ornamentation. The mosque was later converted into a church.

HOSPITAL DE TAVERA   This was first a hospital, then residence of the Dukes of Medinaceli and later of the Dukes of Lerma, of which the Plateresque patio by Covarrubias is especially noteworthy. Today it is a museum with a private collection of antique furnishings and twenty El Greco paintings (extraordinary are the vibrant colors of *San Pedro,* the tranquillity of the Virgin in the *Holy Family,* and the somber brown tones of *San Francisco*). The church altar is designed by El Greco.

SAN ROMÁN   The red-and-white-striped horseshoe Moorish arches of this Mudéjar church look like those of the Córdoba Mosque. The church today is a Visigothic museum.

PLAZA DE ZOCODOVER   Busy main square of the Old Quarter, once a marketplace and today filled with stores, restaurants, and tapas bars.

PUERTAS DE BISAGRA   Monumental entrances to Toledo; the older tenth century gate (Puerta Antigua de Bisagra) is solid and unadorned, with horseshoe arches showing its Moorish heritage. Here Alfonso VI entered the reconquered city with El Cid (see Index). The "new" gate is sixteenth century and much more grand, with its oversized Hapsburg coat of arms.

PUERTA DEL SOL   A thirteenth century gateway that is an unusual example of Moorish military architecture, with beautiful horseshoe archways.

TALLER DEL MORO   A fourteenth century Mudéjar mansion—a particularly rich example of Moorish decorative arts—that today displays Moorish crafts.

STAYING IN TOLEDO

PARADOR CONDE DE ORGAZ   Cerro del Emperador s/n   tel. (925) 22 18 50   An elegant parador, but slightly inconvenient, just outside of Toledo. The panoramic views of the city, however, are splendid. Request a room with a view. (Moderate–expensive; pool.)

HOSTAL DEL CARDENAL   Paseo de Recaredo 24   tel. (925) 22 49 00 Located at the entrance to Toledo and built into the city walls, this eighteenth century palace was once the residence of Toledo's archbishop. Beautiful gardens, and an excellent value. (Moderate.)

HOTEL PINTOR EL GRECO   Alamillos del Tránsito 13   tel. (925) 21 42 50   A simple new hotel in an old noble home, ideally situated in the Jewish quarter. (Moderate.)

EATING IN TOLEDO

The Parador Conde de Orgaz and the Hostal del Cardenal are both known for good dining. I also like **VENTA DE AIRES**   Circo Romano 25   tel. (925) 22 05 45, a roadside inn from the last century (unfortunately considerably modernized) on the outskirts of town. Their *Perdiz a la Toledana* (stewed partridge) is famous (have it with local Méntrida wine).

For tapas, try **BAR LUDEÑA,** Corral de Don Diego (near the Plaza de Zocodover), for *Carcamusas,* a typical beef-stew appetizer that Toledanos love.

SHOPPING

Typical Toledo crafts are damascene and swordmaking.

For general shopping the **CALLE DEL COMERCIO,** as its name suggests, is the main business street.

For Toledo marzipan, **CASA TELESFORO** and **SANTO TOMÉ** are both in the Plaza de Zocodover.

FIESTAS

CORPUS CHRISTI   Nine weeks after Easter, a full week of processions and ceremonies, culminating in the colorful procession of the cathedral's spectacular gold-and-silver monstrance through the city's narrow streets, which are covered with canvas for the occasion.

$\mathcal{V}$ISITING THE PROVINCE OF TOLEDO

MONTES DE TOLEDO   Low mountains of oak, cork, and scrub bush with areas of wooded groves, between the Guadiana and Tajo rivers. Known for an abundance of deer, wild boar, and partridge.

TEMBLEQUE   The dark, delicate woodwork of this town's two-tiered plaza is striking, especially in contrast to the otherwise bare square. Inlaid in the balconies are colorfully painted representations of the Cross of Calatrava.

LAS VENTAS CON PEÑA AGUILERA   An undistinguished town except for its fine leatherwork, which shows up in the elegant Loewe shops of Spain's major cities. Along the street called 28 de Marzo and Calle Arroyo there are several stores.

GUADAMUR   A perfectly preserved palace-fortress of the fifteenth century stands tall over this village.

OROPESA   A town of medieval character set on a hilltop. Its main attraction is an outstanding parador, once the fifteenth century castle of the Counts of Oropesa. Charles V stopped here on his way to retirement in Yuste; San Pedro de Alcántara (see box, p. 197) slept here (see his cell), as did Santa Teresa de Ávila.

PARADOR VIRREY TOLEDO   Plaza del Palacio 1   tel. (925) 43 00 00   See above. (Moderate.) The restaurant of the parador is quite good, if somewhat overpriced.

LAGARTERA   A traditional center for fine embroidery (see box below).

PEPITA ALIÁ   Ramón y Cajal 10, is among the most highly regarded craftswomen and has a full range of fine quality Lagartera work. Prices range

Needlework of Lagartera: Fit for Kings

The countess of nearby Oropesa castle in the sixteenth century had her trousseau made in Lagartera. More recently Prince Bernhard of the Netherlands, the British royal family, and the king of Spain have all been clients. In Lagartera just about every village woman produces fine linen sheets and tablecloths in delicate drawn-thread work as well as casual tablecloths and pillows in colorful peasant embroidery. It is said that the girls of Lagartera are born with needles in their hands, but no one will boast of culinary skills; the women of Lagartera have little time or inclination for the kitchen.

Elderly village women regularly wear the traditional black dress, apron, embroidered shawl, and thickly embroidered high red socks of the past. To see a family's heirloom chest with the heavily embroidered and gold-encrusted holiday and wedding clothes of their ancestors is to see work of museum quality. "Not even the king of Spain," declares Lagarterana Pepita Aliá, "has the richness of work that each of us in Lagartera keeps in our family chests."

from a few dollars for a pillowcase to more than 100,000 pesetas for a table-cloth representing untold hours of labor.

TALAVERA DE LA REINA, EL PUENTE DEL ARZOBISPO
Famed since the twelfth century for pottery of Arab origin and design. Talavera specializes in blue ceramics, El Puente del Arzobispo in green.
CERAMICA MAURO Y CORRACHANO, Avenida de Portugal 22, in Talavera, has an overwhelming selection of pottery made in its own work-shop.
The **MUSEUM RUIZ DE LUNA**   Plaza General Primo de Rivera 5, has Talavera pieces as old as the sixteenth century.

ILLESCAS   El Greco came to Illescas to paint on commission for Nuestra Señora de la Caridad church-hospital. Five of his paintings are here.

CONSUEGRA   See "Visiting Don Quijote's Country."

EL TOBOSO   See "Visiting Don Quijote's Country."

PARTRIDGE, TOLEDO-STYLE

In a deep casserole heat 2 tablespoons olive oil and brown 4 trussed partridges. Add 2 chopped onions, 1 whole head of garlic, separated and peeled, sauté 5 minutes. Stir in 1 cup dry white wine, 2 tablespoons vinegar, 2 bay leaves, salt, and peppercorns. Cover and cook slowly about 1 hour.

EXTREMADURA:
LAND OF THE CONQUISTADORES

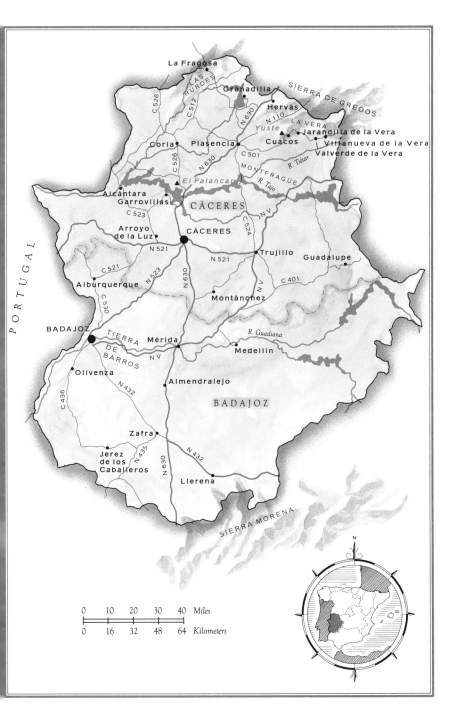

INTRODUCTION

THE NAME EXTREMADURA, meaning "extreme" or "farthest out," accurately describes the nature of this western region of Spain that borders Castilla and Andalucía and is separated in part from Portugal by the wide Guadiana river. It is a broad plain enclosed by the snowcapped mountains of Gredos to the north and the forests of cork and oak of the Sierra Morena range to the south, and crossed by two major rivers—the Tajo and Guadiana. Extremadura was indeed at the very edge of Spain, a frontier land, an isolated outlying territory, parts of which were not integrated into Spain until modern times. The weather is also extreme, most notably in summer when excessive heat and dryness make a bottle of water your constant companion.

The look of the land, the architecture, and the character of the people of Extremadura take on a little bit of both Castilla and Andalucía, mixing Castilian austerity with Andalusian liveliness. And a visit to Extremadura will most likely be in conjunction with travels through Castilla or Andalucía.

Extremadura was traditionally somewhat of a wasteland. Poor land and a meager existence scratched from raising pigs and sheep herding (this was the southern "extreme" of the Merino sheep's migratory route; see box, p. 63) led to emigration, depopulation, exploitation, and defoliation of the land. Las Hurdes, a beautiful but remote area, was well into this century a prime example, almost a byword, for the legendary backwardness of Extremadura. The harshness of the land bred austere men: the men of the Reconquest of Spain and the conquest of America, with the toughness and inner strength to accomplish unheard-of feats against the Moors and endure inconceivable hardships in the New World; religious figures like San Pedro de Alcántara, who founded a monastery so extremely ascetic that its likes were unknown in the Christian world (see box, p. 197). Emperor Charles V chose Yuste in Extremadura to live a life unthinkably severe for a man of his power and wealth.

FOODS AND WINES OF EXTREMADURA

GENERAL
Lamb, kid, game, *serrano* ham, trout

SPECIALTIES
Gazpacho Extremeño—white gazpacho
Caldereta de Cordero—lamb stew
Frite—potted lamb with garlic and paprika
Cocido Extremeño—chickpea stew, Extremeño-style
Faisán al Modo de Alcántara—pheasant with truffles and foie gras
Tencas—tench (freshwater fish)
Queso de los Ibores—aged goat's milk cheese
Queso Torta del Casar—semisoft sheep's milk cheese

WINES
Trampal from Montánchez
Lar de Barros from Tierra de Barros

Today Extremadura continues to be "outlying," generally unexciting scenically (with notable exceptions) and culturally spare. Zurbarán was born in Extremadura, but worked quite exclusively in Sevilla. Only Luis de Morales, "The Divine," a sixteenth century mystic painter of considerable fame and achievement, established a presence here. And yet, some of my favorite places in Spain are in Extremadura: the valley of La Vera and its tiny quaint villages are very special; so too are the incomparable diminutive monastery of El Palancar and the village architecture of Garrovillas. The monumentality of Mérida and Cáceres, the evocative reminders of the conquest of America in Trujillo, and the colorful history of Emperor Charles V in Yuste are all unique to Extremadura.

I must admit, however, that cooking in Extremadura lacks variety, finesse, and sophistication. It reflects the region's poor past and relies on hearty dishes served in large portions, some with the oddest names. *Zorongollo* (lamb's tail stew) and *Lagarto en Salsa Verde* (lizard in green sauce) are two unusual examples, but there are other tasty dishes like *Caldereta de Cordero* (lamb stew with paprika), *Frite* (potted lamb with paprika and garlic), *Cocido Extremeño* (a version of the Castilian chickpea stew), *migas* (crisp bread bits), rabbit stews and *Gazpacho Extremeño,* a cold soup without tomato but otherwise very much like the gazpacho of neighboring Andalucía. A restaurant in Badajoz, El Tronco, takes Extremeño gastronomy with a grain of salt, announcing on its menu, white beans "lightly scattered with *chorizo* and swine ear," and Extremeño chickpea stew, "including all the cholesterol."

Cured meats like *chorizo* and ham are especially good in Extremadura, made from famed Iberian black pigs that are fed on acorns. In the northern reaches of the region there are trout and game in abundance, and although it is hard to believe, one of the great classic dishes of French cuisine comes from the monastery of Alcántara, near the Portuguese border (see box, p. 187). Well known are the red wines of Tierra de Barros—hearty, high in alcohol, and appropriate to the cuisine.

The two provinces of Extremadura, Badajoz and Cáceres, share a common glorious past (according to your point of view, you might also call it inglorious or vainglorious). Rome first brought glory to Extremadura in 25 B.C., when it established Mérida as a major city. After that, Extremadura fell into oblivion until the Reconquest, at which time the powerful religious-military orders of Santiago and Alcántara were established here to counteract the Moors. The king granted their warrior priests noble titles and generous pensions, and fortified homes on a grand scale became characteristic of several Extremadura towns.

A thousand years would pass, however, between the brilliant centuries of the Roman Empire and Extremadura's next period of real greatness: the exploration and conquest of America. Almost without exception the legendary names of the conquest—Vasco Núñez de Balboa, Hernando de Soto, Hernán Cortés, and Francisco Pizarro, to mention just a few among hundreds of others—were from Extremadura. Countless New World towns and cities adopted the names of their Spanish counterparts, like Trujillo, Medellín, Guadalupe, Mérida, and Alburquerque. A trip through Extremadura provides the opportunity to follow what has been called the Route of the Conquistadores.

Why were so many of these bold men Extremeño, when the initial voyages were made almost exclusively by Andalusians and the boats continued to sail from Cádiz and Sevilla? There are some clues: An early governor of the Indies, Fray Nicolás Ovando, was Extremeño and surely favored his countrymen; Extremadura was so abjectly poor that its men would risk anything for a chance at wealth; and men of this unforgiving land had learned to survive by their wits, tenacity, and defiance, and they had experience and knowledge of a harsh countryside. These qualities were of greater worth than the seafaring experience of Andalusians. But I have one more theory: Andalusians were having such a good time eating tapas of *pescado frito* and *langostinos*, sipping *fino* sherry, and enjoying their fiestas that they had no inclination for such hardships; I can see them gathered at outdoor cafés and tapas bars along the banks of the Guadalquivir river poking fun at the wild Extremeños who hopped boats to the New World, risking disease and death in exchange for dreams of riches and glory.

Indeed, many of the conquistadores returned to their hometowns wealthy men. They raised grand palaces and were granted royal privileges, titles, and coats of arms by the Spanish kings. The reminders of such glorious—or if you prefer, inglorious and vainglorious—times color any visit to Extremadura.

THE PROVINCE OF CÁCERES

CÁCERES (*cah*-ther-es) is a large province, more fertile, more wooded, and much greener than Badajoz. Mountainous to the north, somewhat flatter to the south, and well watered by the flow of the mighty Tajo, the landscape is of oak and cork trees, wheatfields, and granite outcroppings. Merino sheep and white cows graze in the abundant pastures.

Cáceres is known for its wildlife and as a natural reserve for native and migratory birds. Year-round you will find partridge, quail, dove, woodcock, duck, and bustard— the largest bird of Europe—in residence. In spring you are likely to see the comforting sight of returning storks nesting in every church belfry. The Montfragüe reserve harbors hare, wild boar, deer, lynx, wolf, and fox.

This is a province with wonderful towns of great character and beauty and unusual charm. Many are living reminders of the exciting times of the Reconquest of Spain and of the subsequent conquest of America. And primitive *verracos* (bulky stone carvings of ancient bulls or boars) and life-size granite bulls found around the province attest to prehistoric civilizations as well.

The food is generally like that in the rest of Extremadura, but there are some specialties: *prueba de cerdo* (literally "test of the pork"), pork seasoned

like *chorizo*, with garlic and
paprika, but eaten uncured,
especially during slaughter
season; the celebrated
Faisán al Modo de Alcántara
(see box); and the cured
hams that bear the name of
the village of Montánchez.

Local crafts have sur-
vived, especially lacemaking—delicate open work as
well as simple, brightly colored folk embroidery that
village women typically
work on while sitting at
their doorsteps. It is similar
to what you will find in
Lagartera, in the neighboring province of Toledo. In
Cáceres these handiworks
are sometimes made by convent nuns, who also support
themselves selling pastries
and candies. Still made in
the traditional manner are
the colorful straw-and-wool-
yarn hats of Cáceres, decorated with mirrors and once
worn on festive occasions by
young women in search of
husbands. Married women

HAUTE CUISINE FROM CÁCERES: FAISÁN AL MODO DE ALCÁNTARA

As improbable as it may seem, one of the all-time great dishes of French haute cuisine, Pheasant Alcántara-Style—stuffed with foie gras and cooked in a sauce of truffles and port wine—comes from the province of Cáceres, and more specifically, from the Alcántara monastery. The recipe is recorded in the bible of French cooking, *Le Guide Culinaire*, by Auguste Escoffier.

In the nineteenth century the invading troops of Napoleon sacked the Alcántara monastery and used library manuscripts to make cartridges. Miraculously a book of the monks' recipes survived, was taken by a French officer to his wife, the Duchess of Abrantes, and she in turn included the recipe in her memoirs, where Escoffier found it. The recipe, declares Escoffier, "represents, perhaps, the only good thing the French derived from that unfortunate campaign, and it would tend to prove that foie gras and truffles . . . were also known in Extremadura, where, even at the present day, tolerably good truffles are to be found."

also wore them, but exchanged the colors for black and shattered the mirrors, indicating, alas, that they were no longer available.

THE VALLEY OF LA VERA AND ITS FAMOUS DENIZEN, EMPEROR CHARLES V

It doesn't seem possible that a valley so beautiful and so unspoiled as La Vera could be so close to Madrid. The contrast was particularly striking in early spring when we set out from the capital one morning and in no time found ourselves in the luxuriant valley of La Vera. Cherry trees were in full blossom, and the foliage was luminously green. Wildflowers splashed brilliant colors across the woods and fields, and the scent of rockrose hung suspended in the air. The only sounds were of singing birds. Having just arrived from a harsh New York winter, we felt we had entered Elysium.

La Vera is primarily agricultural, known for its fruits and vegetables, tobacco, and cotton. Especially good are the red peppers, from which the paprika *pimentón de la Vera*, synonymous with the best, is made. I always take some home with me.

Villages are as lovely as their names, which roll off the tongue with great resonance (Villanueva de la Vera, Valverde de la Vera, Jarandilla de la Vera, for example). All have similarly charming architectural style, centering on small plazas graced with stone fountains and surrounded by centuries-old whitewashed and timber houses with wood balconies, porticoed ground floors, tile roofs, and timber eaves. Invariably they are laden with potted flowers that add a note of color. Black-clad women gather at doorsteps and take advantage of the brilliant light to embroider and darn. Narrow channels in the cobbled streets harness spring mountain runoff, and you are never far from the sound of rushing waters.

> The houses, of wood beams, with wooden overhanging eaves . . . the lines and contours that at each step break the profile of the street, give the sensation of something organic . . . spontaneously created, not made by man. The narrow street twists . . . like the course of a snaking river. You feel the intimacy of the shade.
>
> *Miguel de Unamuno*

I am particularly attracted to the villages of Cuacos, where the illegitimate son of Charles V, later to become Don Juan de Austria, was raised in company of peasants, ignorant of his royal birth (see box, p. 189), and Jarandilla de la Vera, near where the emperor himself lived the last years of his life.

In 1555 Emperor Charles V, Europe's most powerful ruler, his empire in disarray, in failing health (he suffered from gout), and eager to return to Spain, made a momentous decision: He abdicated his throne in favor of his son, Philip II, and embarked on the long journey to retirement at Yuste Monastery in La Vera. Today this is a secluded site, and in the sixteenth century, I imagine, absolutely remote. La Vera had been recommended to the monarch by his aide, the Marquis of Mirabel, a native of Extremadura, who thought La Vera's tranquillity, mild climate, pure air, and excellent water ideal for the emperor's fragile health.

Awaiting completion of his palace, contiguous to the monastery, Charles lived in the palace of the Count of Oropesa in Jarandilla (now the parador). Several months later he moved to his permanent quarters and began a life in most respects as rigorously austere and ascetic as that of the monks. It is intriguing to visit his palace, for it appears untouched by the intervening centuries: Here is a cramped and surprisingly uncomfortable covered litter that brought Charles on a forty-day trip, on the shoulders of his servants, from the northern coast of Spain, where his ship from Holland made port. You will see also a rosy suede chair, specially designed so that Charles could lift his leg and alleviate the pain of his gout. His bedroom, depressingly shrouded in tattered black drapery put up to mourn the death of his mother, Juana la Loca (see box, p. 99), was designed to overlook the church so that he could follow the Mass while in bed (his son adopted the idea at El Escorial). When he rose, he could go to his balcony at the other side of the room and contemplate the majestic mountain scenery or fish for trout in the reservoir below.

Although the life of Charles in Yuste was generally austere, the king was not inclined to cast aside all the trappings of power. He kept up on politics, advised Philip, and retained a retinue of fifty servants, almost all Flemish—barbers, laundresses, beer brewers, bakers, and coopers, as well as two doctors, two surgeons, and his personal confessor. And he continued, in spite of gout and to the dismay of his physicians, his renowned gastronomic excesses. Fine foods were brought to his remote retreat from all corners of the Iberian Peninsula: savory eel pies from Valladolid, veal from Zaragoza, game from Ciudad Real, sausages from Denia, anchovies from Cádiz, oysters from Sevilla (rushed to him by mule teams), sole from Lisbon, olives from Extremadura, marzipan from Toledo.

DON JUAN DE AUSTRIA: FROM BASTARD TO WORLD FAME

Juan, or Jeromín, as he was affectionately known in La Vera, was the illegitimate son of Emperor Charles V and a woman from a noble Nuremberg family, Barbara Blomberg. The boy was secretly raised by a steward of Charles V, Luis de Quijada, and when the emperor retired to Yuste, his servant brought Jeromín, then eight years old, to nearby Cuacos, where he grew up among countryfolk. Charles met his son for the first time in Yuste and employed him as a page. He thought the child should become a priest, but Juan had more ambitious plans and convinced his half brother, Philip II, to use him in the military.

Juan de Austria distinguished himself in battle against the Turks and Berbers. Back in Spain he subdued the Morisco uprising in Las Alpujarras (see Index) before returning to fight the Turks, this time off the coast of Lepanto, Greece. His spectacular victory in the Battle of Lepanto ensured Spanish supremacy of the Mediterranean. He became one of Philip's most respected and successful military leaders, but his career was cut short by illness, and he died at the age of thirty-three. Since Philip had previously recognized him as a brother, Juan de Austria was interred in El Escorial with the royal families.

Charles survived just a year and a half at Yuste, and was interred according to his wishes below the church altar. The head of his coffin protruded from its niche so that priests holding mass would always be directly above his head. And when Philip completed El Escorial, almost two decades later, his father's remains were transferred there (to be similarly positioned beneath the church altar). La Vera's brief period in the Spanish limelight came to an end.

VILLAGES OF LA VERA

The villages of La Vera are all quite similar, to be visited for their charm and character rather than for any specific sights (see text). However, do look for the thirteenth century pillory in **VALVERDE DE LA VERA** and in **CUACOS** the Casa de Jeromín—the house where the future Juan de Austria spent his childhood (see box).

STAYING AND EATING IN LA VERA

PARADOR CARLOS V   Carretera de Plasencia s/n, Jarandilla de la Vera   tel. (927) 56 01 17   A fifteenth century palace flanked by towers and centered on a distinguished courtyard; Charles V stayed here before moving to Yuste. (Moderate–expensive.) An attractive restaurant with good food.

At the bar **CUEVA DE PUTA PARIÓ** (literally, the Cave of the Whore Who Bore Me), on Calle Francisco Pizarro 10 in Jarandilla, watch the antics of owner Pedro, who may spray himself with seltzer on a hot day or expertly enact a dance with primitive wooden dolls on a plank of wood (request a performance). Good tapas of cured ham and Manchego cheese and simple meals. (Inexpensive.)

In Losar de la Vera, **CARLOS V** restaurant, Avenida de Extremadura 45, tel. (927) 56 07 36, serves home-cooked foods based on local ingredients: trout, roast kid, vegetables. (Inexpensive.)

FIESTAS

PERO PALO   Villanueva de la Vera (during Carnival, about forty days before Easter)   In a night of merrymaking, an effigy of the devil is carried through town, tossed around, punched, beheaded, and finally buried.

LOS EMPALAOS   Valverde de la Vera (Thursday before Easter)   In re-creation of the Calvary, villagers bind their outstretched arms to thick wood branches in the form of a cross and proceed through the streets.

THE UNEXPECTED MONUMENTALITY OF CÁCERES

Old Cáceres, enclosed by ancient walls, has an assemblage of honey-colored Gothic and Renaissance stone mansions and palaces on quiet cobbled streets that is without equal in Spain. It is a living museum of the fifteenth, sixteenth, and seventeenth centuries.

In my view, Cáceres is one of the great undiscovered sights of Spain. I wondered how the old town, founded by Romans, destroyed by Vandals, rebuilt by the Arabs, and reaching its height in the sixteenth century, managed to survive the twentieth century in its medieval guise. A young Cacereño, Francisco Mangut Ramiro, uncommonly enthusiastic and knowledgeable about his city, gave me the answer. "Cáceres," he explained, "was saved because it was built on a hill, and the newer town developed on the plains. And since most of the old mansions were continually occupied, many by descendants of the original owners, they never fell into disrepair."

The mansions of Old Cáceres are massive and surprisingly close together. They reach right to the street's edge, have few windows, and are separated from one another only by narrow streets through which a small car can barely squeeze. The town feels somewhat like the canyons of Wall Street, on a medieval scale. You would expect buildings of such grandeur to stand on stately plots, perhaps surrounded by gardens. Francisco once again had an explanation. "In the sixteenth and seventeenth centuries Cáceres was veritably bursting with power and money, and its nobility jealously scrambled to outdo one another. But a war mentality still persisted, even though the fight against the Moors in central Spain had long ended. The earliest mansions were close together and lacking windows to increase protection, and they were fortified against attack."

CASA DE CARVAJAL, for example, incorporates a watchtower that is built into the town walls. And the balcony of the **CASA DEL SOL** was designed to hurl arrows and pour scalding oil on aggressors, although it was never used for such purposes. Houses were huge not just to impress but also to accommodate dozens of servants and their families, who all lived there. Life took place within the confines of the palaces; large interior courtyards provided light and open space and served to collect rainwater.

The latter part of Cáceres's glorious centuries took place under a different philosophy. Nobles no longer sought to flaunt their wealth with fortifications but with elaborate ornamental Plateresque decoration. And yet the mansions continued to be austere. "Ostentation had not yet come into style," explained Francisco.

A visit to Cáceres means walking its streets, for few houses can be visited. In any case, it is not the interiors or the individual structures that make Cáceres so special; rather, it is the completeness and fine preservation of the old town that are remarkable.

S EEING CÁCERES

◆ The tourist office in the Plaza Mayor can provide maps and additional information on Cáceres.

PALACIO DE LOS MOCTEZUMA-TOLEDO   A palace in Renaissance style, the result of the marriage of Moctezuma's daughter with an Extremeño who fought with Cortés, Juan Cano de Saavedra.

PALACIO DE LOS GOLFINES DE ABAJO   One of the outstanding facades of Cáceres, Gothic-Moorish with later Plateresque additions (in honor of the Catholic Kings, who resided here during their visits to Cáceres).

CASA DE LAS VELETAS   Built over an Arab fortress, this is today the local museum. Here you can see one of the two remaining Arab *aljibes* (cisterns) in the world; the only other, according to Francisco, is in Istanbul. This one is enclosed by Moorish horseshoe arches.

CASA DE LAS CIGUEÑAS   When the Catholic Kings, in recognition of the completion of the Reconquest, ordered all battlement towers removed from castles and palaces to show their supremacy over the nobility, the tower of this mansion was spared, perhaps because the house belonged to the governor of the Indies, Fray Nicolás Ovando.

PLAZA MAYOR   Stone-paved and unusually large, this square is surrounded by quaint four-story porticoed houses.

STAYING IN CÁCERES

PARADOR DE CÁCERES   Calle Ancha 6   tel. (927) 21 17 59   A fourteenth century palace, once Moorish, beautifully restored, as paradors are wont to be. (Moderate–expensive.)
 ◆ Next door, find **EL PALACIO DE LOS VINOS,** where among other wines, a very pleasing acorn liqueur called Licor Bellatrán, created here, is sold.

EATING IN CÁCERES

EL FIGÓN DE EUSTAQUIO   Plaza de San Juan 12   tel. (927) 24 81 94   A longtime Cáceres restaurant serving traditional food. (Moderate.)

BODEGA MEDIEVAL   Orellana 1   tel. (927) 24 54 58   Set in a medieval house in upper Cáceres; the food here is typical tavern fare. (Moderate.)

SHOPPING

Shops in the Plaza San Jorge sell traditional Cáceres handcrafts, like embroidery and colorful straw hats (p. 187).

TRUJILLO: CRADLE OF THE CONQUEST AND HOME OF FRANCISCO PIZARRO

The town of Trujillo, walled and studded with more than thirty-two towers, is a gem of a town and the direct result of the discovery and conquest of America. Hundreds of Trujillanos went to the New World, and many returned wealthy men. Among them were Francisco Pizarro, conqueror of Peru, and his half brothers Hernando, Gonzalo, and Juan, all but Hernando illegitimate; Francisco de Orellana, who discovered and explored the Amazon; Diego García de Paredes, founder of Ciudad Trujillo in Venezuela; Nufrio de Chávez, warrior in Paraguay and founder of Santa Cruz de Bolivia; and Francisco de las Casas, participant in the conquest of Mexico, along with a variety of governors, mayors, and bishops of the New World. In all, Trujillanos participated in founding twenty new nations and gave their hometown name to numerous New World cities.
    Francisco Pizarro, although the son of a noble family of Trujillo, was born out of wedlock and abandoned on the doorsteps of a Trujillo church. He survived, so the story goes, suckled by a pig—a presage, perhaps, of his adult life as an illiterate swineherd. The tale continues that one day he was out minding the

pigs when they all suddenly ran off. Afraid to return to town without the pigs, Pizarro left for Sevilla, where he hopped a boat to Santo Domingo. He lived twenty years in the New World, participating in various perilous expeditions (including the discovery of the Pacific with Vasco Núñez de Balboa, an Extremeño from Jerez de los Caballeros). His obsession, however, was to find the fabulous empire he had heard about in the remote mountains of Peru. No one believed him, except the legendary "Twelve in Search of Fame." When Pizarro dramatically drew a line in the sand and announced, "This way is the road of hardship, but it takes us to Peru to be rich men. That way you go to rest . . . and to be poor men. You choose," these twelve stepped over the line. Against almost insuperable odds they found what they were looking for. But lacking funds to continue on, Pizarro took the bold step of returning to Spain and requesting an audience with Emperor Charles V, who was flush with the recent news of the conquest of the Aztec Empire. Impressed by the Extremeño's convincing presentation, the king granted all that Pizarro asked.

Pizarro passed through Trujillo to recruit his four half brothers, then went back to America. Displaying insatiable ambition and astounding courage, Pizarro accomplished his mission and obtained unimaginable quantities of gold and silver, but in the process ignobly murdered the Inca king Atahualpa, spawning anarchy among the Indians and within his own ranks. He remained in the New World, and many years later was murdered in his palace in Lima. His brother Hernando, however, returned to Trujillo a wealthy man, and married Pizarro's daughter, offspring of the conquistador's relationship with Atahualpa's daughter.

Despite its more than two hundred coats of arms, Trujillo lacks the majestic air of Cáceres, and in some ways I like it better. It is less austere, more intimate, down to earth, and approachable. The town centers on a striking **PLAZA MAYOR—**one of Spain's finest, irregular in shape, porticoed and multilevel, and dominated by a statue of Pizarro by American sculptor Charles Rumsey (its twin is, appropriately, in Lima, Peru). The plaza is ringed with palaces; the San Martín church and the beautiful porticoed town hall are also there. The **PALACIO DEL MARQUÉS DE LA CONQUISTA** (the name refers to the royal title conferred on the Pizarro family) has a distinguished corner balcony that displays the Pizarro coat of arms and portrays the palace's four protagonists: Francisco Pizarro and his Inca princess, Hernando Pizarro and his wife-niece. It also depicts Atahualpa and his Indian servants in chains.

From the plaza, Trujillo climbs steeply through narrow cobbled streets and past many noble homes, with defensive towers in Reconquest style. Many have been purchased and lavishly restored, albeit in a most understated manner, by moneyed Spanish and international gentry. Trujillo ends at the rocky heights of its Moorish castle.

ЅEEING TRUJILLO

As in Cáceres, the visit to Trujillo is mainly walking and seeing the exteriors of its noble homes and palaces (see text). In the upper quarters is the church of **SANTA MARÍA,** with its exceptional Flemish-style altar paintings by Francisco Gallego (see Index) and tombs of families of the conquest.

STAYING IN TRUJILLO

PARADOR DE TRUJILLO   Santa Clara s/n   tel. (927) 32 13 50   A former sixteenth century convent, beautifully restored. (Moderate–expensive.) It has a fine restaurant (the frog's legs are particularly good).

EATING IN TRUJILLO

HOSTAL PIZARRO   Plaza Mayor 13   tel. (927) 32 02 55   An immaculate restaurant facing the Plaza Mayor. Extremeño fare, like *Gallina Trufada* (pâté), potted lamb (*Frite*), freshwater fish (*tencas*), and fine local cheeses. (Moderate.)

LA MAJADA   Seven kilometers from Trujillo on the N-IV road to Mérida, km 259   tel. (927) 32 03 49   Upscale for this area, with traditional dishes like partridge, but also serving hake and other fresh fish. (Moderate.)

♦ Try tapas in the Plaza Mayor at **CAFETERÍA IMPERIO** and around the corner on Calle de Domingo de Ramos at **LA PATA.** Typical tapas are asparagus tortilla and marinated pork (*prueba de cerdo*).

SHOPPING

The nuns of Santa Clara, who now reside across the street from their former home (now the parador), sell a variety of convent sweets. At the Convento de San Pedro the nuns make hand-embroidered tablecloths, napkins, pillowcases, and the like.

GUADALUPE: SPIRITUAL CENTER OF EXTREMADURA

Guadalupe is two distinct worlds. On the one hand, its grandiose monastery is the spiritual center of the Hispanic world, and on the other, it is a quaint village that is among my favorites. I love its quiet timelessness—so unlike the commotion visitors create around the monastery. Curving and primitively porticoed streets—tree trunks are sometimes the supports—sustain fragile balconies laden with flowers. Guadalupeños watch the world go by seated in the shade of their verandas.

Of course, Guadalupe has not gained renown for the charm of its village, but rather for its monastery and its connection to the discovery, conquest, and settlement of America. Columbus named an island after the

Virgin of Guadalupe, and there are numerous towns and cities in Latin America and western United States called Guadalupe. On his return from the New World, Columbus himself came to Guadalupe to honor a vow he made to the Virgin during a ferocious storm at sea that he did not expect to survive. With him he brought Indians for baptism. The conquistadores followed, praying to the Virgin before their voyages (many documents authorizing expeditions were signed here) and returning afterward to give thanks, pausing first to pray near the road at the Humilladero (literally, the "place to bow your head"), where the monastery first comes into view.

The story of Guadalupe is a familiar tale that goes back to the Moorish occupation, when priests buried an image of the Virgin for safekeeping. The statue disappeared; in the twelfth century, a herdsman went in search of a lost cow and, finding it dead, began to quarter the carcass. The cow came to life, and the Virgin appeared, instructing the herdsman to fetch the clergy. The long-lost image of the Virgin was found where the cow died, and word of the miracle spread; pilgrims began to come, and in the fourteenth century the monastery was built. Donations poured in from kings (the Catholic Kings made a pilgrimage), royalty, and the newly wealthy conquistadores. And in this century King Alfonso XIII crowned the Virgin Queen of the Hispanic World. Today she is the symbol of Hispanic unity, binding the New World to Spain.

THE MONASTERY

The delicate Gothic-Mudéjar entrance to the monastery is set off by two massive towers—in the fortress style typical of Reconquest architecture—and by a monumental flight of steps. The Mudéjar cloister, with its horseshoe-arch gallery, has at its center a one-of-a-kind Moorish-Gothic chapel.

The monastery centers on the Camarín, where the image of the Virgin resides. A small twelfth century statue with a blackened face, adorned in the richest of robes, and possessing a prodigious wardrobe, the Virgin is surrounded by the flags of the American nations and is dramatically revealed to the visitor by a monk who solemnly revolves the statue into view.

Of greatest cultural interest are the monastery treasures: eight magnificent Zurbarán paintings in the sacristy; eighty-six profusely decorated, oversize choir books from the fifteenth through eighteenth centuries, weighing some 100 pounds each; and a fabulous display of antique religious vestments lavishly embroidered by the monks in gold and silver thread.

STAYING AND EATING IN GUADALUPE

PARADOR DE GUADALUPE   Marqués de la Romana 10   tel. (927) 36 70 75   In an ideal setting, across the plaza from the monastery, it was in the fifteenth century a hospital for pilgrims (where the first autopsy in Spain was performed) and a school. (Moderate; pool.)

HOSPEDERÍA DEL REAL MONASTERIO   Plaza Juan Carlos I s/n   tel. (927) 36 70 00   Sparse accommodations, as befits a hotel that adjoins the Gothic cloister of the monastery, but the setting couldn't be better. (Inexpensive.)

♦ Both hotels have good restaurants but I prefer the Hospedería's for its monastic atmosphere, its well-prepared food (stick to simple things like fresh vegetables, garlic chicken, salad) and reasonable prices. Another alternative is **MESÓN EL CORDERO**   Convento 23   tel. (927) 36 71 31, for Extremeño home cooking. (Inexpensive.)

SHOPPING

Copper, brass, and tin utensils, like cauldrons and mortars, and decorative pieces (braziers, jars, pitchers) are traditionally hand-crafted in Guadalupe and sold in local shops around the main square.

Seeing the province of cáceres

ARROYO DE LA LUZ   This typically dusty village of western Cáceres has the Spanish-Portuguese Manueline look (see box, p. 200). In the Asunción church, which sits in the center of the main plaza, are beautifully restored altar paintings—the most complete collection anywhere—by sixteenth century Extremeño mystic painter Luis de Morales, "The Divine," one of the least known of the Spanish masters.

GARROVILLAS   The houses around the dusty, bare, unpaved Plaza Mayor look like the work of a crazed or drunken builder. Pillars tilt every which way, as do the walls of the glaringly white houses. But nothing is propped up or in danger of falling; the town was actually designed this way to compensate for the natural slope of the land. It has a certain Dalí-like beauty.

ALCÁNTARA   An important and imposing half-mile-long second century Roman bridge over the Río Tajo in the town of Alcántara is much more massive and monumental than others from that period. The surprising height is accentuated by an added arch over the center span, and the bridge stones are set in decorative designs. It merits a detour.

CORIA   A town of perfectly conserved walls, punctuated by gateways and towers, has a fifteenth century castle and many noble homes. See the one immense nave of the cathedral, the detailed carvings of the choir stalls, and a beautiful wrought-iron altar screen.

GRANADILLA   An abandoned but completely walled village in a beautiful setting encircled by the Gabriel y Galán reservoir. It has a turreted castle and a pretty plaza.

LAS HURDES   For a sense of what the primitive life of this area once was, travel to La Fragosa in the heart of Las Hurdes. The area's dramatic verdant mountains and narrow valleys somewhat resemble the Picos de Europa. Along the banks of the Hurdano river, which rushes around gulleys carved from limestone, on terraced land there are primitive stone-and-mortar houses with flat slate roofs that look almost like Celtic huts. Elderly women all dress the same—black-and-gray-plaid aprons over black skirts and sweaters and black bandannas tied behind their heads.

EL PALANCAR   The world's smallest monastery (see box). To reach El Palancar from the Plasencia-Cáceres road, turn off in the direction of Coria, continue about six kilometers, then turn left to Pedroso de Acím. Shortly beyond the village is the monastery. Ring the bell and wait a few minutes for a priest to answer your call and to show you around.

MONFRAGÜE   At the western extreme of the valley of La Vera, a beautiful wildlife reserve of dense vegetation at the juncture of the Tajo and Tiétar rivers. If you're willing to get up very early and be very patient, you may see such wildlife as Imperial eagles, black storks, lynx, deer, boar, and fox. But at any time of day, circling and nesting vultures can be observed (better with binoculars), and you can enjoy the scenery while picnicking. Spring is the optimum time to visit.

THE MINI-MONASTERY OF SAN PEDRO DE ALCÁNTARA

Call him mad, if you will, but if anyone deserves to be called "saint," surely it is the sixteenth century patron saint of Cáceres, San Pedro de Alcántara, not only because of his good deeds, but also because of the manner in which he chose to live.

His monastery is so small that its church is a mere eight feet by six feet, and its cloister just nine feet square. The kitchen has dollhouse proportions, with tiny benches and a Lilliputian fireplace and sink.

San Pedro's life was so austere that he slept just one and a half hours each night, seated on a stone and resting his head on a stone niche. He ate nothing but bread, sometimes sprinkled with herbs, then dusted with ashes to kill any taste deemed too pleasurable. His great admirer, Santa Teresa de Ávila, describes him as so thin that he looked like "tree roots."

San Pedro began life comfortably in Alcántara, son of a noble family. By sixteen he had decided on the priesthood and rose swiftly through the ranks. Despite his high birth, San Pedro was always concerned for the poor and downtrodden. He was uncomfortable with church wealth and yearned for the simple life of Saint Francis of Assisi. Finally papal approval was granted for his mini-monastery, El Palancar, where San Pedro retired for the remaining seven years of his life (he was sixty-three when he died) in company of eight or ten religious brothers, all engaged in penitence, abstinence, contemplation, and prayer.

A new monastery was later built around the old, and the monks here today live in comparative luxury. But the original monastery has been preserved as a testimony to the extreme yet noble life of San Pedro de Alcántara.

PLASENCIA   An immediately pleasing city (its name, in fact, means pleasure) on the Río Jerte. The arcaded Plaza Mayor, with a clock tower and a life-size figure that rings the hour, leads into the lovely Old Quarter, with numerous palatial homes and many more whitewashed dwellings. A striking Plateresque cathedral (really two cathedrals of different periods that are joined), in which some of the greatest architects of the fifteenth and sixteenth centuries, like Covarrubias and Diego de Siloé, participated, has delicate spires and an exuberant Plateresque facade. The lavish interior features finely carved Gothic choir stalls and a grand Baroque altar. Graceful ribbed pillars mushroom into a dome ceiling.

◆ In the Plaza Mayor are several popular tapas bars like **EL ESPAÑOL. BAR GABI,** just off the plaza on Calle Pedro Isidro, serves good snails in a spicy paprika sauce.

◆ The Tuesday market in the Plaza Mayor has taken place since the twelfth century, and keeps much of its rural charm.

HOTEL ALFONSO VIII   Alfonso VIII 32   tel. (927) 41 02 50, is clean and well cared for, simple yet elegant. Request a back room: the street side is too noisy. (Moderate.) The hotel's restaurant is one of the city's best.

HERVÁS   An ancient Jewish enclave that unfortunately was renovated and in the process lost much of its Hebraic character. Still, it makes for an interesting visit.

THE PROVINCE OF BADAJOZ

BADAJOZ (bah-dah-*hoeth*), Spain's largest province, forms a frontier with Portugal and is separated from its neighbor by the broad and mysterious Río Guadiana, which sometimes flows underground in its course through western Spain.

Despite its size, Badajoz has few scenic attractions and, aside from Mérida, little cultural appeal; the province undoubtedly takes a back seat to its more attractive and interesting sister province of Cáceres. It's astoundingly hot here in July and August, dry and dusty to the extreme. But I come anyway, to continue the Route of the Conquistadores I began in Cáceres and to visit the hometowns of Hernán Cortés, Vasco Núñez de Balboa, and Hernando de Soto, three of the greatest adventurers in the New World. I also travel here to admire the Manueline architecture (see box, p. 200) of towns that were not incorporated into Spain until the nineteenth century. But principally I come—and recommend that you do too—to the city of Mérida and see what are perhaps the best-preserved remains of the Roman Empire outside of Rome.

⒨ÉRIDA: EMERITA AUGUSTA OF THE ROMAN EMPIRE

Why was one of Rome's greatest outposts in, of all places, Badajoz? Certainly the area was not rich agriculturally nor well endowed with mineral deposits, nor was its quality of life high. Rather, Badajoz was artificially selected to become the center of a major Roman region called Lusitania because of its strategic and central location; it was ideal to bridge the gap between the southern colonies of Bética (Andalucía), Rome's Portuguese territories to the west, and the northeast coastal settlements stretching from Ampurias to Tarragona.

The principal city of Lusitania was christened Emerita Augusta—"Emerita" because veterans of the Roman legion retired here, "Augusta" in honor of the Roman emperor Augustus. The name Mérida was given to the city by the Moors. In Roman times Mérida was a nexus of roads that radiated throughout Roman Spain. One began in Asturias and continued through Salamanca and Mérida, then south to Sevilla. This was the so-called Vía de la Plata, along which silver from the mines of Asturias was transported, and sections of the original stone road still exist in Ávila in the mountains near Gredos (see Puerto del Pico). Other routes went south to Córdoba; west to Lisbon; north to Cáceres; east to Ciudad Real, Toledo, Zaragoza, and Tarragona.

Conceived in 25 B.C.

> # ⒯HE MANUELINE STYLE
>
> Named after fourteenth century King Manuel I of Portugal, under whose reign the style flourished, Manueline architecture is seen in Spain quite exclusively in Extremadura, for the region was geographically close to Portugal and not yet culturally united with Spain. Described as a blend of oriental influences (especially Indian) coming from the Portuguese empire, European Gothic, and a touch of Moorish, Manueline is distinguished by twisted stone design around doorways and windows, exposed supports for vaulted ceilings, and delicate stone carvings. Some say the style produced works that would have been decadent monstrosities were it not for their beautiful ornamental detail.

at a time when the Roman Empire was well consolidated in Spain and enormously prosperous, Emerita Augusta was designed to be an impressive monument to Rome's grandeur and richness that would be the talk of the Roman world, the mecca of Lusitania, and the Rome of Spain. The sumptuous marble theater, the amphitheater, and circus were spectacular in size, each accommodating many thousands of spectators; the circus, where chariot races were staged, held 30,000 people. In the huge elliptical amphitheater seating 14,000, Roman gladiators battled fierce wild beasts, and sometimes the arena was flooded with water to enact mock sea battles. The theater provided entertainment for countless citizens of the city and the surroundings. Impressive bridges, aqueducts, monumental arches, temples, and baths completed this marvelous complex. Many of the city's star attractions and most admirable structures survived the tumultuous centuries that followed the fall of the empire and can be admired today. You can easily spend a full day in Mérida.

Mérida fell to the Vandals in A.D. 5 and later to the Moors. As a frontier territory along the Christian-Moorish line, it became a focal point for rebellion and warfare, and much of the city crumbled. It would never again regain greatness, for when finally the Christians took control of Extremadura, the capital of the province was transferred to the city of Badajoz.

SEEING MÉRIDA

TEATRO ROMANO   Taking advantage of a natural hollow in the land, this semicircular theater (one of the most exceptional of the Roman world) is built on several levels. As the remains attest, this indeed was a splendid theater, constructed with the finest materials and richly decorated with works of art. Its ingenious design provided a two-tiered stage, supported on tall marble columns, and unusually free circulation for some 6,000 spectators. Today the theater is the site of a classic drama festival.

MUSEO DE ARTE ROMANO
Although an ultra-modern structure, the grand proportions of this exciting museum (its brick arches are the same height as Mérida's Arco de Trajano, see below) perfectly complement the display of extraordinary Roman mosaic floors (displayed on the walls) and heroic statues of gods, emperors, and warriors that remain from ancient Mérida. The museum is built over the ruins of Roman houses and tombs, which are also on view, and an underground tunnel joins the museum to the Roman theater and amphitheater.

ACUEDUCTO LOS MILAGROS   Serving an essential function in these dry lands, this aqueduct is almost 2,500 feet long and 75 feet high. It brought water to the city from a reservoir that was in itself a major feat of hydraulic engineering. Although a practical structure, the aqueduct was designed to be elegant as well, and was originally sheathed in marble.

ANFITEATRO and **CIRCO ROMANO**   See text.

ROMAN BRIDGE   With sixty spans and a length of about 2,400 feet, this stone bridge was among the largest of its kind.

ARCO DE TRAJANO   A triumphal arch 45 feet high, built during the reign of Augustus and today incongruously set among humble whitewashed houses.

STAYING AND EATING IN MÉRIDA

PARADOR VÍA DE LA PLATA Plaza de la Constitución 3 tel. (924) 31 38 00 A sixteenth century convent that is an exceptional parador (moderate–expensive) with a fine restaurant.

FIESTAS

INTERNATIONAL CLASSIC DRAMA FESTIVAL This is held in Mérida's Roman theater at the end of June and beginning of July.

ᕫISITING THE PROVINCE OF BADAJOZ

MEDELLÍN On a tall column, dramatically set off against the backdrop of Medellín's fourteenth century castle, stands the likeness of native son Hernán Cortés, brave and brash conqueror of Moctezuma's Mexican Empire (see box). A stone tablet in this plaza displays on one side the coat of arms from the palace of Cortés, on the other an inscription marking this spot as the location of the bedroom where Cortés was born.

ALBURQUERQUE Near the Portuguese border is one of Spain's great castles, built in the thirteenth century, long and narrow and occupying a rocky spike that stands guard over the walled village of Alburquerque. The town and its dukes gave their name to a city in Brazil and to another in New Mexico (spelled Albuquerque).

BADAJOZ Capital of the province and on the main route to Portugal, this city has kept little of historic character except the Puerta de Palmas, the sixteenth century gateway to the city, and the Torre Espantaperros, a tower that was once part of an Arab fortress. The principal reason for coming here is that it is a convenient resting point in Extremadura.

ᗷURNING HIS BRIDGES: CORTÉS'S EXPEDITION OF NO RETURN

Hernán Cortés, unlike many other conquerors from Extremadura, was of noble birth and even studied law briefly at Salamanca University. But he longed for adventure and embarked for the New World. Although a clever, pleasant, and good-looking man, his actions were bold and often cruel.

Determined to conquer the Aztec Empire and strip it of gold and silver, he established a base on the Mexican coast at Veracruz. His expedition was unauthorized, and some of his men were in a mutinous frame of mind. Cortés hoped to avoid word of his plans reaching his home base in Cuba, so after sending one boat to Spain to gain support from the king, he sunk or burned—the accounts differ—the rest of his ships and continued on his daring venture with his soldiers, who now had no choice but to aid him in the conquest of Mexico and fight to the finish.

GRAN HOTEL ZURBARÁN   Paseo del Castelar s/n   tel. (924) 22 37 41, is modern and unexciting but the best in the city. (Moderate; pool.)

MESÓN EL TRONCO   Muñoz Torrero 16   tel. (924) 22 20 76, is small and pleasant for simple fare. Especially good is hand-sieved gazpacho (as opposed to blender-made) and baby lamb chops. Hefty breakfasts are served in the style of Badajoz (such as fried eggs with crispy bread bits, or *migas*, and hero sandwiches. (Inexpensive.)

If you hunger for Galician food, **LA TOJA**   Avenida de Elvas 22   tel. (924) 23 74 77, serves well-prepared specialties of that region. (Moderate.)

♦ For tapas, try **AZCONA,** also on Avenida Elvas, at number 21.

OLIVENZA   A village of marked Portuguese flavor. See the doorway of the whitewashed town library done in intriguing Portuguese Manueline-Gothic style (see box, p. 199), its flowing stone sending out shoots as if this were a delicate royal crown. In the Magdalena church, see the surprising spiraling stone columns.

JEREZ DE LOS CABALLEROS   Four church towers of richly worked golden stone and bright blue ceramic inlay (especially those of San Bartolomé and San Miguel) contrast with the simple whitewashed village. At 12 Capitán Cortés is the home of Núñez de Balboa, still occupied at my last visit by an elderly woman, who graciously showed us around and pointed out the bedroom where, "they say," he was born. Hernando de Soto, an audacious and supposedly charming adventurer, who was instrumental in the conquest of Peru, explored Florida and the Mississippi River and traveled as far as Texas, was also from this village.

ZAFRA   A town with two continguous plazas, joined by an archway: the Plaza Chica, charmingly simple (once a marketplace), and the eighteenth century Plaza Grande, on a much larger scale, surrounded by mansions with coats of arms. Both have a lively atmosphere and plenty of tapas bars (try **CRESPO,** Arco de San Antonio).

PARADOR HERNÁN CORTÉS   Plaza Corazón de María 7   tel. (924) 55 02 00, is a fifteenth century castle, where Cortés lived for a time before setting off for America. Its large and elegant white marble patio is said to be a design of Juan de Herrera, architect of El Escorial. (Moderate; pool.)

LLERENA   An interesting village (declared a national historical complex) of noble homes with the somewhat Portuguese look of western Extremadura. Its center of interest is the Plaza Mayor, dominated by a bulky lime-washed church topped by two levels of graceful and airy arcades, and finished with a brick Baroque tower. The rest of the intensely white plaza echoes the arcades of the church.

THE GENTLE
GREEN LANDS
OF GALICIA

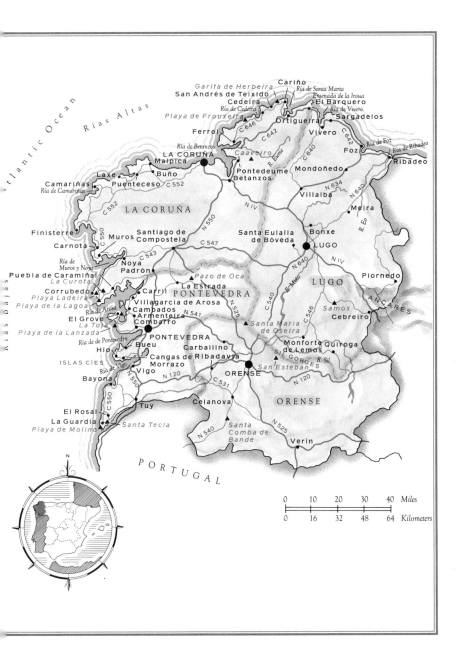

INTRODUCTION

GALICIA . . . the melodious sound of its name (pronounced ga-*lee*-thea) is enough to evoke the soft breezes, the silent mists, the white sands, and the gentle people of this singular area of Spain that I have long loved and that frequently calls me back. It is a lush green land fragrant with the scent of eucalyptus and covered with chestnut trees and pine forests. Horses roam free as they have throughout the ages (see box, p. 205); fjord-like shallow waterways, called *rías*, bring the Atlantic Ocean inland to towns and cities and create some of the most memorable scenery you will ever see in Spain.

Galicia covers a relatively small area, but its four provinces—Pontevedra, La Coruña, Lugo, and Orense—provide ample opportunity for exciting travels. Plot your course around the region's unusual concentration of paradors. And be sure to reserve sufficient time in Galicia (perhaps a week) to fully absorb its special character.

FOODS AND WINES OF GALICIA

GENERAL
Fish, shellfish, young beef, breads, vegetables

SPECIALTIES
Empanadas—savory meat or fish pies
Vieiras con Jamón—baked scallops with cured ham
Pulpo a Feira—octopus with oil and paprika
Merluza a la Gallega—hake with paprika and potatoes
Pimientos de Padrón—fried tiny green peppers
Lacón con Grelos—boiled ham hocks, potatoes, and greens
Caldo Gallego—beans, greens, and potato soup
Filloas—dessert pancakes
Tarta de Santiago—almond cake
Queso de Tetilla—semisoft cow's milk cheese
Queso de San Simón—smoked cow's milk cheese

WINE AND SPIRITS
Pazo from Ribeiro
As Laxas, Fillaboa (Albariño wine) from Rías Baixas
Orujo—brandy distilled from grape skins, such as Ruavieja

Galicia divides into two worlds, that of the sea and that of the interior. Both have a reputation for being rainy, but at least in summer, the weather is splendid. Life along the coast is more modern, more lively, more open to the world. The interior is one of the most unchanged areas of Spain, very rural and somewhat underdeveloped, but hauntingly beautiful. Here is where age-old pottery methods and the art of hand-carved wooden shoes refuse to give way to the twentieth century.

Galicia is culturally unique, with a pronounced Celtic heritage that goes back almost 3,000 years. The Celts arrived here on their westward migrations through Europe, and finding that the sea barred them from going farther, they remained. For ancient peoples, in fact, Galicia represented the End of the World, or Finisterre.

It comes as a great surprise to first-time visitors that Galicians are fair-skinned and that the land is not unlike Scotland; a dance resembling a jig is performed to the sound of bagpipes, the traditional instrument of Galicia that brings life to innumerable local festivities.

Accompanying the bagpipes are other ancient instruments that you would not usually associate with Spain, like the hurdy-gurdy, harp, and laud. Even the festive costumes for men—kiltlike cropped trousers, black leggings, white shirts, and brilliant red sashes—remind me of the Highlands. There are, in fact, so many pilgrimages and festivals in Galicia that you are sure to come upon one or another at almost any time of year.

True to its Celtic past, Galicia has a culture that is pervaded by fantasy, and today the land remains enveloped in legend and mystery. Paganism and Christianity intertwine; tales of witches stirring magic brews (see box, p. 208) in misty forests mesh with accounts of miracles performed by Santiago—the apostle Saint James—whose tomb and the cathedral built in his honor in Santiago de Compostela have been focal points for Christendom since the Middle Ages. Today the city of Santiago de Compostela continues to be the highlight of a visit to Galicia.

Three outstanding Spanish writers were shaped by the climate and traditions of Galicia: the poet Rosalía de Castro, who wrote of nature, of Galician

A RAPA DAS BESTAS: GALICIA'S HORSE ROUNDUPS

Horses roam free in the most rural areas of Galicia, a custom that began, it is said, in the Middle Ages when citizens offered their horses to saints in exchange for immunity from the plague. You can see the horses close up at any time in sparsely populated higher elevations (especially at La Curota, on the road to Cariño from Cedeira, in the mountains of La Estrada, and around Vivero; see Index). They are not confined by corrals or fences, and they live on the wild grasses of their natural habitat. But once each year, in summer, there are roundups, which are exciting events that begin early in the morning.

Hundreds of horses appear, silhouetted against the distant hills, and horsemen direct the unsuspecting herds to corrals, where young horses are branded and horsetails are cut for counting purposes and to sell the horsehair. Other horses are sold at auction. Then the event turns into a country fair, as bagpipes play and stands sell equestrian articles and all kinds of foods—from breads, empanadas, doughnuts, and *churros* to sardines grilled on smoky barbecues.

Get there early (before 9:00 a.m.) to sip garlic soup, which takes the chill from the damp morning air, and to watch what I think is the most exciting moment of the day: the tumultuous arrival of the galloping horses. Stake out a viewing post near the corral entrance. Later on you can shift your attention to the event's other festivities.

Two key places to witness the roundups are at San Lorenzo de Sabucedo (see Monte Lobeira, p. 213) and Monte Buyo (see Vivero, p. 235), the latter in a more remote location and therefore less congested.

THE PRIVATE WORLD OF JOSÉ CAO

José Cao spends long solitary hours chipping at stone and creating massive sculptures that flow from the depths of his fertile mind. He is not an educated man; his love for artistic beauty originates deep in his rural Galician character. Like so many of his countrymen, his task in life was to care for cows, and he might have spent a lifetime of routine and monotony had he not stopped one day to consider the beautiful stone carvings of Christ and the Apostles over the portal of his local parish. He wondered how such delicacy could come from granite blocks, and while his cows grazed, he unearthed some turnips and set about carving figures from them. He progressed to wood, then to stone. He now spends every waking hour making his dreams a reality.

He has not yet achieved stardom, and his works spill out onto the grounds of his ramshackle workshop, his ideas coming faster than his selling capabilities: here a figure of a young girl combing a doll's hair and a Virgin stirring a pot of hot chocolate; over there, an enormous stone table and an oxen-drawn cart. (To visit José Cao, see p. 224.)

customs, and of the difficult life of Galician peasants; Ramón de Valle Inclán, whose works are pervaded by the mystery and legend of Galicia; and iconoclast Camilo José Cela, recent Nobel Prize winner, who sets many of his stories in his native land.

Because of Galicia's historic and geographic separation from the rest of Spain (it sits in the northwest corner of the country, bordered by Portugal to the south and the Atlantic Ocean to the north and west), the region evolved in relative isolation. The charming archaic lilt of the Galician tongue is one good example of Galicia's solitude. In the past it was easier and more profitable to take a boat to America (chart a beeline from Galicia across the North Atlantic, and you'll reach Boston) than to make the arduous journey to Madrid, and that is why Galician immigrants populate all corners of the New World.

Emigration is still in progress. Don't be surprised to see humble homes in tiny Galician villages with a bright red or yellow Mercedes-Benz proudly parked outside, the badge of the triumphant Indiano who has returned home for vacation or retirement (Indiano means he who went to the "Indies"). The names of commercial establishments are also clues to where their owners have been: Hotel Mexico, Comercial Caracas, El Caribe, Taberna Venezuela, Café New York. So great, in fact, is the return flow to Galicia in summer that Iberia Airlines adds nonstop New York–Santiago de Compostela 747 flights to accommodate the overwhelming demand.

Yes, everyone has an uncle in New Jersey, but the folks left behind continue to live immersed in the past. And for that reason, Galicia retains its rural character, its pristine appearance, and its comforting timelessness.

Galicia has incredible natural beauty, but the Galician people have also contributed to the land's unique appearance. Towns are subdivided into parishes, and the land is carved into small plots crammed with cornstalks (originally brought from America), local greens called *grelos* that grow tall and ramrod straight, and vegetable gardens. Fields of rye and grass nourish the typically honey-colored cows of Galicia.

The air becomes fragrant with aromas of hay,
And the open furrows wait for the rye,
And in the humid depths of the green pastures
Ruddy cows graze, among strong young shepherds,
When in the saintly blue of the morning,
Damp with dawn, the village church bell peals.

Ramón de Valle Inclán

Galicians have taken the region's most abundant building material—granite—and erected humble homes and elegant palaces (called *pazos*), stately churches, and imposing monasteries (Galicia has an unusually large concentration of monasteries, in varying states of preservation). But they have also shaped stone into unusual works of popular art that contribute to Galicia's distinctive look. Thin stone slabs placed one next to another mark property lines, and stone pillars support grape vines. Most striking of all are the countless *hórreos*, curious granaries of slitted stone raised on stilts (to keep moisture and rodents out) and topped by crosses, and the *cruceiros*, elaborately carved crosses on tall stone columns that are seen along roadways or in town squares. Galicians, it is said, have patience to dominate stone and give it a fine feminine skin. Patience and dedication certainly mark the life of sculptor José Cao (see box, p. 206) and of the Galician craftsmen before him who have struggled to give warmth to cold hard granite.

The Galician people (called Gallegos) are warm, hospitable, hardworking, simple, and down to earth. Land means everything to them, even if it's just a small patch. Their close relationship to the land and to their animals creates a certain symbiosis. You will find robust women walking by the roadside, each with a single cow on a lead or carrying on her head an immense bundle of hay or a ten-kilo sack of potatoes. In the rural interior, it is not unusual for humans and animals to live under the same roof.

The coast of Galicia divides into the Rías Bajas and Altas, the lower and upper estuaries. Most visitors concentrate on this coastline, and for good reason: The scenery is spectacular, the eating extraordinary. You see shellfish in astonishing quantities and varieties, and I never get enough of it: lobster, spiny lobster, *nécora* crabs, small *santiaguiño* crabs (a red cross mark on their heads resembles the cross of the Order of the Knights of Santiago, thus the name), giant spider crabs (*centollas*), tiny *quisquilla* shrimp (eaten shell and all), scallops in their shells (you will rarely see them elsewhere in Spain), *zamburiñas* (diminutive, highly prized members of the scallop family), mussels, oysters, clams, cockles, razor clams, squid, *sepia*, barnacles, langoustines, and *pulpo* (octopus), boiled and sprinkled with oil and paprika *a feira* style, and often found in special bars called *pulperías*.

In fact, more than forty varieties of shellfish alone are found in Galicia (but do, as a precaution, avoid eating uncooked clams and oysters), not to mention fish of every description, like the exquisite hake (*merluza*), typically cooked *a la Gallega* with oil, paprika, and potatoes, sardines, turbot (*rodaballo*), monkfish (*rape*), grouper (*mero*), and salmon. Shellfish is especially expensive, although not nearly what it will cost in Madrid. But Spaniards have their priorities in place: Put a dollar or two in the gas tank, then blow everything else on shellfish.

Pizza-size savory pies called empanadas, found in just about every bar and restaurant, are special to Galicia and have such fillings as lamprey, eel, pork, tuna, scallops, or clams. And although vegetables are not seen in great variety, how good they are: small flavorful potatoes (*cachelos*); *grelos* (greens similar to Swiss chard), used primarily in combination with meat, beans, and potatoes in *Caldo Gallego* soup and in *Lacón con Grelos* (a boiled dinner of *grelos* with ham hocks and potatoes); and tiny green peppers of Padrón that are fried and sprinkled with coarse salt and served as tapas. Eating the peppers is like Russian roulette—some are mild, others fiery, and both kinds often grow on the same plant with the hotness accelerating as the summer season progresses. And you'll find wonderful breads in Galicia, unlike any others that I have tasted in Spain. Made with corn, rye, wheat flour, or a mix of all three, the big round loaves—deliciously moist and crusty—are formed with characteristic twisted caps.

Since cows are so common in Galicia, cheese is most often made from their milk (*Tetilla*, in the typical breast shape, is most popular). The fine young beef called *ternera*, which comes from the interior of Lugo, is considered the best in Spain. Desserts here are unusually varied for Spain, featuring *filloas* (dessert pancakes, often custard filled) and an interesting array of cakes and tarts. Most famous of these is the *Tarta de Santiago*, a dense confection of eggs, ground almonds, and sugar.

I am always fascinated by Galicia's traveling markets, which make weekly appearances in Galician villages, selling fresh produce and local rough-hewn pottery. Perhaps they once existed all over Spain, but today these markets, so rustic and full of character, have survived principally in Galicia. When you come across one, stop to browse and use the opportunity to buy picnic supplies.

Wines, young, fresh, and fruity, most from the Ribeiro region and the Rías Bajas, are traditionally served in white porcelain cups called *cuncas*. The best are the whites (the reds tend to be dark and syrupy), especially the exceptional ones from the native Albariño grape, and they complement Galician seafood like no others. Forget about beer and Rioja wines while you are here. And at the end of a meal, try the potent *orujo* liqueur, an ideal *digestivo* made from grape skins and served chilled. When mixed with sugar and flamed in a footed

QUEIMADA: A FIERY BREW

On typically foggy nights in Galicia, when the mist hangs low over forest and sea, it is said that witches gather under magical oak trees to brew flaming Queimada, made from a grappa-like liquor called *orujo*. They stir the pots to the accompaniment of ancient Celtic chants, which echo through the forest.

To make Queimada, combine in a wide, shallow casserole or bowl 2 cups *orujo* or grappa, 3 tablespoons sugar, and half an apple, cut in wedges, the zest of a lemon or 10 coffee beans (or both). Put 2 more tablespoons of sugar into a ladle, add some of the *orujo* and ignite the ladle. Burn until the sugar is caramelized, then lower the ladle into the pot, igniting the remaining *orujo*. Continue burning until as much of the alcohol as you wish has been consumed. Cover to extinguish the flames, and serve in small cups.

earthenware bowl called a *queimadera*, it becomes Queimada (see box, p. 208).

In short, simplicity is the byword in Galician cuisine. Don't be tempted by restaurants that seem chic and serve "creative" cooking. You will more than likely be disappointed.

Come to Galicia ideally in late spring, early summer, and in September—but do come. It is another Spain that you may not have imagined existed.

T HE PROVINCE OF PONTEVEDRA

PONTEVEDRA (pone-tay-*vey*-dra), one of the southern provinces of Galicia, is separated from Portugal by the gently flowing Río Miño, which empties here into the Atlantic. "The land around the mouth of the Miño, in Spain and in Portugal," said Miguel de Unamuno, "opens like a vision of a dreamworld firmly anchored to the land." The climate of Pontevedra is moderate all year round, and it is among the drier and warmer regions of Galicia. In all my visits, spanning many years, I have never experienced a rainy day in Pontevedra.

Pontevedra, like the other coastal provinces of Galicia, is celebrated for its seafood—a shellfish paradise it is often called, honored as such during curious local festivals like the Exaltation of Shellfish at El Grove; the Exaltation of the Mussel at Villagarcía de Arosa; of the Octopus at Bueu; of the Eel at Tuy; and of the Sea Lamprey in Arbo. I invariably eat my way through Pontevedra, ordering spiny lobster and *nécora* crabs at every possible opportunity and lingering over each and every claw. How beautifully Pontevedra's light, fruity white wines accompany its seafood: those of O Rosal (*o* is the soft Galician replacement for the Spanish article *el*), grown in the Miño Valley, and the prestigious and somewhat scarce Albariño wines, grown in vineyards near the coast of Cambados. These are young wines that, as the saying goes, do not "travel" well, but they are without equal in their native land (and, quite frankly, quite good even when purchased in another country or carried home from Galicia).

Pontevedra has a great concentration of *hórreos* (granaries) and *cruceiros* (stone crosses), and a good many of them are along the Pontevedra coast. The fishing town of Combarro, for example, is a national monument because of its numerous *hórreos*, and Galicia's most complex *cruceiro* is near the water's edge at Hío. In fact, just about everything you will want to do in Pontevedra centers on its river estuaries, or *rías*, and around the oceanfront, although you may also want to drive through some beautiful mountain roads or through the valley of the Río Miño.

Las rías bajas in pontevedra

The coastline is particularly gentle and peaceful in these lower Galician estuaries, known as the Rías Bajas, where scenic wonders unfold at every turn in the road. Here are two of the largest and most beautiful *rías*—those of Vigo and Arosa (Arousa)—crystal-clear and lined with miles of fine beaches. Filling these natural harbors are odd floating platforms with an oriental appearance, called *mejilloneras*, under which mussels cling to ropes and grow to maturity.

These *rías* are also among the most accessible (the Rías Bajas continue to Finisterre in La Coruña province and become more rugged), and, as might be expected, their popularity has steadily risen among vacationers. I don't think the coast of Pontevedra will ever see high-rise resorts (its difficult accessibility and greater distance from the rest of Europe prevent that), but it is, nevertheless, the most developed part of Galicia. During the summer months there can be traffic backups and crowded beaches (especially on weekends), and it is best to avoid coming in the busy month of August.

I love exploring the Pontevedra coastline; distances are short, even though to see the nicest scenery you must wind your way around the *rías*. You might begin in the southern extreme of the province at Tuy and leisurely work your way up to Cambados, near the northern limit of Pontevedra, choosing lodgings from four exceptional paradors and one deluxe hotel.

Visiting the rías bajas in pontevedra

SANTA TECLA   A single steep mountain at the southern tip of Galicia that commands precious views of the Atlantic, the mouth of the calm Río Miño, the village of La Guardia, and of northern Portugal. Celts once populated Santa Tecla, and archaeological finds are in a museum at the top of the mountain. A Celtic hut, as it might have looked, has been reconstructed.

EL MOLINO beach, at the foot of Santa Tecla, faces the Atlantic and invites you to spend the day in this exceptional setting.

EL ROSAL (O Rosal)   The wines of El Rosal are produced here, but no need to come for that reason. Come instead to visit the nuns of the Convento de las Descalzas and buy their homemade goodies—scarce and highly regarded mirabelle plums in syrup (available only toward the end of summer), candied squash (*cabello de ángel*), marmalades, and honey. The king of Spain is among the clients.

TUY (Tui)   A frontier town across the river from Portugal with a well-conserved Old Quarter and an unusual thirteenth century fortress-cathedral; its elaborately carved portal is covered by a Gothic porch.
PARADOR SAN TELMO   Avenida de Portugal s/n   tel. (986) 60 03 09 Built to resemble a castle, this parador is in a restful setting overlooking the Miño River and with views of the cathedral. Its terrace is a delight for leisurely drinks and tapas. (Moderate; pool.)
◆ The drive through the wine-growing region of the **MIÑO**, a lush valley between Tuy and Salvatierra, is easy and pleasant.

BAYONA (Baiona)   It was here that one of Columbus's ships, the *Pinta*, landed with first word of the New World. A most pleasant but busy summer town that is stylish and full of life along the waterfront, while the quaint porticoed passageways of the back streets are dim and Old World, even though crowded with popular bars. See the beautiful Roman bridge as you pass into or out of town.
PARADOR CONDE DE GONDOMAR   Monte Real   tel. (986) 35 50 00, is a double-walled medieval castle on a promontory overlooking the sea. In all respects, an outstanding parador. (Moderate–expensive; pool.)
MOSCÓN   Alférez Barreiro 2   tel (986) 35 50 08, is still your best bet in Bayona for fine seafood (we like to feast here on spiny lobster). (Moderate, except for shellfish.)

VIGO   Pontevedra's foremost industrial city, but not without its charms. Rising from the beautiful Ría de Vigo on a steep hill, it has an Old Quarter with noble stone mansions and wonderful views from the heights of the Castro hill, where there is a castle with a park.
PUESTO PILOTO ALCABRE   Avenida Atlántica 194   tel. (986) 29 79 75, has classic Galician cooking in simple surroundings. (Moderate.)
SIBARIS   García Barbón 122   tel. (986) 22 15 26, is considered one of the best restaurants in Galicia, featuring, of course, seafood, in traditional and creative preparations. (Expensive.)
◆ Vigo is a popular city for tapas (try **BODEGÓN CENTRO**   Manuel Núñez street) and young people flock to its many pubs and bars.
◆   **LAS ISLAS CÍES**, several small islands at the mouth of the Ría de Vigo have been preserved in their natural state and provide an inviting day in the outdoors. It's a lovely boat ride from Vigo (there is frequent service in summer). The islands can also be reached from La Toja.

CANGAS DE MORRAZO, HÍO   On a small peninsula between the *rías* of Vigo and Pontevedra. It is worthwhile coming here for two reasons: to indulge in seafood debauchery at friendly, family-style **CASA SIMÓN**, featuring a huge open kitchen (one kilometer past Cangas de Morrazo, direction Hío, and to the left at a sign indicating the restaurant), tel. (986) 30 00 16 (Moderate–expensive); and to see the extraordinary Baroque *cruceiro* at **HÍO**, depicting Christ's descent from the cross. The detail and fluidity of its figures are remarkable.

COMBARRO   This is a national monument because of its unusual concentration of *hórreos* along the waterfront. Walk left from the port to see the *hórreos* along wonderful little streets that are hardly more than alleyways. Living rock erupts from tiny plazas, and the houses are built of stone and supported on stone pillars.

ARMENTEIRA is an isolated twelfth century monastery, reached from a thickly wooded road near Combarro. It is artistically interesting for its portal and cloister (the interior of the church is eighteenth century and of lesser worth). The ancient legend of the monk San Ero is charming (see box, p. 213).

LA TOJA (A Toxa)   Over a quaint bridge that links this island to the town of El Grove, La Toja occupies a paradisaical setting on the Arosa estuary. It's been a spa ever since, according to legend, a man abandoned a dying donkey here, and when he returned, found the animal the picture of health. You can still take "the baths" or perhaps visit the casino.

GRAN HOTEL LA TOJA   Isla de La Toja   tel. (986) 73 00 25—not as grand as it once was, but still a hotel with class and turn-of-the-century style. Its terrace bar, overlooking the water, is the stylish place to be before dinner. A waterfront room is a must, preferably in the older quarters of the hotel. (Expensive; pool.) A less expensive alternative, also on the waterfront, is **LOUXO**   Isla de La Toja   tel. (986) 73 02 00, which has been stylishly renovated. (Moderate–expensive.)

CRISOL   Hospital 10   tel. (986) 73 00 29, is a friendly, attractive restaurant in El Grove serving fine fish. (Moderate.)

♦ La Toja produces a black soap with a wonderful fragrance that is a favorite of mine. Made with the health-giving salts of the spa, this soap, called Magno, is surprisingly inexpensive and available at shops on the island and elsewhere in Spain.

♦ If you have little girls on your gift list, buy them painted shell jewelry from country women who display their wares in big baskets.

♦ Nearby, open to the Atlantic, is the magnificent fine sand beach of La Lanzada.

CAMBADOS   A little village that has grown, but its colorful houses in the oldest neighborhood still look like dollhouses, and the seventeenth century Fefiñanes palace, occupying two corners of the beautiful Fefiñanes square, is impressive. Notice the palace's unusual circular balcony.

♦ The Fefiñanes wine bodega can be visited (by appointment), and the fine Albariño wines can be purchased here.

PARADOR DEL ALBARIÑO   Paseo de Cervantes s/n   tel. (986) 54 22 50, occupies a lovely stone manor house right in town, in a garden setting. (Moderate.)

O ARCO   Real 14   tel. (986) 54 23 12, is a delightful antique-filled restaurant that features local fish dishes, fresh shellfish, Galician veal, and an excellent *Tarta de Santiago*. (Moderate.)

♦ The July 11 **SAN BENITIÑO DE LÉREZ** fiesta is most colorful in Cambados. A procession of hundreds dressed in vivid red and black costumes carry five-foot candles and a collection of votives—plastic legs, arms, heads—in hopes of miraculous cures. They pass through town carrying an image of San Benitiño, who is covered in paper money from all over the world. There are bagpipe music and dancing to the jiglike *muneira*.

♦ Near Cambados, in an old graveyard are the ruins of **SANTA MARINA** church. There is little left except the suspended arches, which, surprisingly, are intact, and float eerily in space.

VILLAGARCÍA DE AROSA (Vilagarcía de Arousa) A summer town with an exceptionally pretty waterfront promenade. Writer Ramón de Valle Inclán was born here and often wrote about his homeland of Galicia.

PAZO O'RIAL El Rial 1, in nearby Vilaxoan tel. (986) 50 70 11, is a seventeenth century house, now a hotel, set among pine trees. (Moderate; pool.)

MONTE LOBEIRA is a steep car climb from Villagarcía. You must cover the final stretch on foot, but you are rewarded by panoramic views of pine-covered mountains and giant rock formations, the Salnos valley (where Albariño wines grow), and the Arosa estuary.

♦ The **RAPA DAS BESTAS** wild-horse roundup takes place in San Lorenzo de Sabucedo (La Estrada) on the first Saturday, Sunday (the key day), and Monday in July (see box, p. 205).

∫AN ERO OF ARMENTEIRA: GALICIA'S RIP VAN WINKLE

San Ero, first abbot of Armenteira monastery, yearned for a glimpse of eternity. One beautiful spring morning he went walking in the forest and paused to rest under a tree. The utter quiet was suddenly broken by a bird singing the sweetest song imaginable, and San Eros became lost in ecstasy, suspended in time, as he watched the bird in flight and listened to its ethereal music.

When San Eros finally set off for the monastery, he saw to his amazement that the trees were much taller than before, the path overgrown, and the chestnut tree he had planted just a few days before in the church atrium had long thick branches that shaded the entire square. He did not recognize the priest who opened the door, nor did the priest know him. The fathers gathered and checked monastery records; they found that an abbot named Ero had gone off into the woods to pray one fine morning—three hundred years ago—and never returned. . . .

A miracle, they all agreed, as they warmly greeted the long-departed abbot, who stubbornly insisted that he had not spent more than three minutes listening to the bird's song. But he also knew that he had experienced eternity and died shortly after, at peace with the world. A white dove representing his soul flew off into the heavens. A sculpted white dove rests on the church pulpit in Armenteira in recognition of this singular event.

CARRIL Famed for its clam beds, which can be seen at low tide.

LOLIÑA Alameda 1 tel. (986) 50 12 81, a quaint restaurant of red-checkered tablecloths and antiques, serves, of course, clams of Carril among many other fish dishes. (Moderate–expensive.) **PANELA,** also on the waterfront, has a large selection of tapas, including incredibly tasty grilled squid with garlic and parsley and a cornmeal-clam empanada.

PAZO DE OCA See p. 223.

THE CITY OF PONTEVEDRA

You're not likely to read very much about Pontevedra in guidebooks, for it is a has-been city, important in Roman times (its name refers to the city's old Roman bridge, Pontis Veteri) and in later centuries still a prosperous port city until an attack by Sir Francis Drake sent it into decline. When the Pontevedra estuary silted, Pontevedra's harbor disappeared, and the city was robbed of its raison d'être.

I admit we have bypassed Pontevedra many times. But then we discovered its small manor-house parador, now one of my favorites, and the city's Old Quarter, among the most complete, untouched, and picturesque of any Spanish city, and I began to understand the popular Galician refrain *"Pontevedra e boa vila / Ninguen a ve que n'o diga"* (Pontevedra is a pleasing city / No one who has seen it will disagree). There are few squares that can match the charm of the Plaza de la Leña (around which the Jewish quarter once thrived) and the Plaza de Teucro. Under their arches a country market takes shape in the mornings. And few streets are as delightful as these that are porticoed and paved in stone blocks (just about everything in Pontevedra is made from granite).

On a subsequent visit to Pontevedra I discovered the Museo Provincial, set in two eighteenth century manor houses, and wondered how I could have missed it before. Its collections are eclectic and far from comprehensive, but the jet, or *azabache* (see box, p. 222), is exceptional and represents Spain's finest collection of this fossilized carbon. It is fashioned into jewelry of many-faceted beads, into statuary and crucifixes (a thirteenth century Christ is especially impressive), and carved to resemble the scallop shells used by pilgrims to Santiago de Compostela.

The original stone kitchen of the manor house is still here, there is an interesting exhibit of Bronze Age gold jewelry, and a fine display of antique Sargadelos ceramics is on view (you will see the stark white and royal blue modern designs of Sargadelos in gift shops all over Galicia). Most surprisingly, the captain's quarters of the ship *Numancia*, wrecked as it returned to Spain from the American colonies, have been set up here. Enter through a basement hatch, just as if you were descending into a ship's hold.

SEEING PONTEVEDRA

MUSEO PROVINCIAL   Plaza de la Leña   See text.

SANTA MARÍA LA MAYOR   A sixteenth century church constructed by the wealthy merchant guilds. It has an extremely rich Plateresque facade that details religious figures as well as scenes showing Galician fishermen.

LA PEREGRINA   This church takes the shape of a scallop shell, symbol of the pilgrimages to Santiago de Compostela. Above the entrance the

Virgen Peregrina, patron saint of Pontevedra, is portrayed as a pilgrim with scallop shells on her hat.

◆ Eight kilometers south from Pontevedra is the lookout of **COTORRE-DONDO,** with splendid views of three *rías:* Pontevedra, Vigo, and in the distance, Arosa.

STAYING IN PONTEVEDRA

PARADOR CASA DEL BARÓN   Plaza de Maceda s/n   tel. (986) 85 58 00 An exceptional, centuries-old manor house with its original and unusually graceful staircase. Small-scale and charming. (Moderate.)

EATING IN PONTEVEDRA

O MERLO   Santa María 4   tel. (986) 84 43 43   This restaurant occupies one of the beautiful old stone houses of Pontevedra's Old Quarter. Over the bar thousands of key chains hang, and owner Alfonso Merlo and his wife, Marisol, are aiming for a Guinness record. The atmosphere is warm and friendly at O Merlo, and the restaurant specializes in delicious tapas in portions that are often complete meals (don't miss the quail and the meatballs), and offers a variety of excellent salads. (Inexpensive.)

DOÑA ANTONIA   Soportales de la Herrería 9   tel. (986) 84 72 74   In a lovely house facing the Plaza de la Herrería, this restaurant presents an elegant menu based on Galician seafood. (Moderate–expensive.)

CASA SOLLA   tel. (986) 85 26 78   Located just two kilometers outside Pontevedra on the road to El Grove, this fine restaurant, in an old stone manor house, serves classic Galician cuisine. (Moderate–expensive.)

FIESTAS

SAN BENITIÑO DE LÉREZ is celebrated in Pontevedra from July 11 to 25, with a pilgrimage on July 11 to the monastery of San Salvador de Lérez.

THE PROVINCE OF LA CORUÑA

OCCUPYING THE NORTHWEST CORNER of Spain, where the Atlantic joins the Cantabrian Sea, La Coruña (lah core-*oon*-ya) (the article *la* is part of its proper name) is for me the most interesting and most varied of the four Galician provinces.

The history of La Coruña is dominated by the sea. For ancient man, Cape Finisterre was "land's end," as far west as you could go: beyond that, only the immense sea. The Carthaginians and Romans arrived in La Coruña by way of the sea; the body of the apostle Saint James was brought by boat from Palestine to the coastal town of Padrón in La Coruña; Sir Francis Drake attacked La Coruña from the sea; the "invincible" Spanish Armada departed in 1588 from the port of the city of La Coruña, and its tattered remains later returned here. The sea is the province's lifeblood, and few places are far from it.

Food in La Coruña also concentrates on the sea—wonderful fish like flounder, fresh sardines, and lamprey. Prized shellfish are scallops and rare goose barnacles, or *percebes* (see box, p. 230). There are also addictive tiny green peppers from Padrón and simple tortillas of egg and potato that surpass any others I have ever eaten.

The soothing coastal scenery of lower Galicia undergoes a change in La Coruña, becoming more abrupt, more wild and rocky, and consequently less exploited. Wild horses have plenty of free range in these uncultivated elevations. The beaches, among the finest in Spain, are vast and uncrowded; the fishing villages that dot the shoreline, picturesque and unspoiled; the scenic overlooks, splendid. And time-honored crafts like pottery, weaving, and lacemaking have survived as artisan labors.

Although the city of La Coruña is the capital and industrial center of the province, and a city of great charm that I wholly enjoy, there is little doubt that what has over the centuries brought the eyes of the world to the province of La Coruña is the wondrous city of Santiago de Compostela.

THE CITY OF SANTIAGO DE COMPOSTELA

Santiago de Compostela is a city unlike any other in Spain and created for just one purpose: as a place to worship the apostle Saint James (known as Santiago in Spanish). In the twentieth century this continues to be the city's most compelling attraction; Santiago de Compostela is a city imbued with the past and enveloped in a religious aura. Pilgrims come as they have since the Middle Ages, to be at the hallowed grounds where Saint James is buried. Even those who travel here without religious motivation, such as myself, find the beauty of the city, its medieval atmosphere, and its artistic treasures reason enough to come. I like to make Santiago my base whenever I travel in Galicia.

To understand the genesis of the city of Santiago de Compostela, we must go back to the dawn of Christianity when fact and fiction effortlessly mingled. Intent on Christianizing Spain, Saint James came from Jerusalem and spent perhaps a year or two traveling around Spain and preaching the Christian doctrine (in Zaragoza the Virgin Mother miraculously appeared to him, p. 312). We don't hear about him again until his return to Jerusalem, where he was martyred by decapitation.

Although his body was spirited back to Spain, the grave site was lost during the years of Christian persecution until, as the story goes, in 813 a supernatural light shone from the heavens, directing shepherds to the spot where the saint was buried (consequently, according to one theory, the city's name, Compostela, comes from Campus Stellae—Field of the Star). At roughly this same time, Spain was engaged in warfare against Moorish invaders, and Santiago is said to have appeared in battle at Clavijo (see box, p. 144), near Logroño, on a white steed and carrying a red cross, and slew the enemy, thus winning the battle for the Christians. He is today nick-named "Matamoros"—Moor Killer—and his cross became the distinctive symbol of the Knights of Santiago. In his dual role as saint and warrior, Santiago became patron saint of Spain.

Word quickly spread throughout the medieval world of these miracu-lous events. King Alfonso II ordered a chapel built at Santiago's grave site, which eventually developed into a Romanesque church of great beauty, then blossomed into a sumptuous Baroque cathedral. The city of Santiago was born and became a place of pilgrimage. In the Middle Ages millions endured incredible hardship to travel on foot from all parts of Europe to pay homage to the saint and to ask for miracles (see box, p. 220).

Despite the fame of Santiago de Compostela in the Middle Ages, it is surprising how few visitors to Spain today are aware of, or choose to visit, this wonderful city. In fact, one of the most gratifying tours of Spain follows the pilgrimage route, The Way of Saint James, through northern Spain and culminates in a visit to Santiago (See Itinerary 6, Appendix); there is no better way to re-create the awe that arriving pilgrims experienced when they finally reached their destination.

Santiago retains a medieval air that old streets and historic stone buildings alone cannot convey. Compostelanos, as the people of Santiago are called, seem to fall effortlessly into a way of life that is worlds away from, for example, stylish fast-paced Madrid, in spite of some high-rise buildings and sleek boutiques in its newer neighborhoods.

You must walk to see and feel Santiago, and distances are quite short. There are noble golden granite homes, grand public buildings, and churches of architectural beauty everywhere. Streets (they are called *rúas* in Galician) are paved in stone block and porticoed—a most practical device in a city that rarely goes a day without at least a passing shower—and crowded with pedestrians. Many are students at Santiago's university, an important center of learning for centuries. I would imagine that tapas bars were as popular in the early years of the university as they are today, for they fill the students' need for quick, inexpensive food in casual surroundings. Tapas bars are everywhere in Santiago.

Charmingly old-fashioned stores announced by quaint wrought-iron signs reinforce the spirit of the past that reigns in Santiago. There is a bas-ketry shop on the Plaza Toral that also sells Galician wooden shoes (in stan-dard shoe sizes); a store painted bright green displays all the wonderful cheeses of Galicia; the tantalizing pastry shop Mora features the typical almond cake, *Tarta de Santiago*, with the familiar cross of Santiago burned in sugar on top; and there are a surprising number of old-fashioned hardware stores. Then there are the crafts shops carrying on the tradition of the guilds that existed when Santiago de Compostela was a major center of artisan activity. Jewelry and other finely crafted objects of silver and jet in antique and modern designs are still popular items, as they were among early pilgrims (see box, p. 222).

There is nothing to compare with Santiago's rustic open-air morning market that takes place under the arches and in the area of the Plaza de Cervantes. Vendors pour in from the surrounding countryside, carrying on their heads huge handcrafted baskets, which they set down to display their wares: luscious fruits and vegetables; farm-made cow's milk cheeses (some in the familiar breast shape of Galician *Tetilla* cheese) that tilt in helter-skelter piles; crusty unrefined wheat breads (in the same breast shape), huge corn and rye loaves; and dewy, just-picked flowers. It is, in short, a feast of color and activity and a welcome taste of bygone times.

Crafts, religion, and food all intertwine in Santiago's symbol, the scallop shell. Pilgrims carried holy water in jet receptacles carved to resemble scallop shells and returned to their homelands with real shells pinned to their robes as evidence that they had indeed reached the holy city (Santiago, Rome, and Jerusalem are the three cities that the Catholic church officially designates "holy"). And you will see fresh scallops, still attached to their shells, in food displays all over the city. If you stop to consider the famed French dish, *Coquilles Saint Jacques*, you will realize that its translation is none other than scallops of Saint James.

All streets in Santiago eventually lead to the Plaza del Obradoiro, named for the stone carvers who once worked here and created the elaborate stonework of the cathedral's facade. This is the very heart and soul of Santiago, and one of the world's most splendid squares, framed by buildings of diverse styles that somehow merge into a perfectly harmonious whole. The long, low, and massive neoclassic town hall (Raxoy palace) occupies one side; the stupendous cathedral, bishop's palace (Palacio de Gelmírez), and Reyes Católicos hotel line two more. In counterpoint to the plaza's stone monumentality, a row of small white houses with glassed-in balconies lends a special charm to the fourth side of the square.

For me, Hostal de los Reyes Católicos is the *only* place to stay in Santiago. That's been true for centuries, ever since the Catholic Kings ordered the construction of this glorious hospital-hospice for ill and dying pilgrims to reside (that's why the hotel's elaborately carved Plateresque facade depicts Life and Death and shows a doctor healing the infirm).

From my room at the Reyes Católicos (need I say that rooms facing the square are privileged?), I love to watch the constantly shifting activity of the Plaza del Obradoiro. I awake in the morning and never know what will greet my eyes. Perhaps busloads of tourists, some obviously from small Spanish villages, on a trip of a lifetime; bagpipe players; the pomp of a papal visit. *Tunos*, university troubadours (see box, p. 219), are always there. They serenade in the evening under the arches of the Raxoy palace. On the Día de Santiago (Day of Saint James), July 25, horsemen in peacock-feathered helmets enter the square; dancers in headdresses that appear tribal move to the beat of huge wood drums and the tinkle of scythes being tapped; giants (men on stilts covered by oversized heads and robes) cavort; and city folk dance the Galician jig.

The grandiose cathedral, on the east side of the Plaza del Obradoiro, is the focal point of the plaza (and of all Galicia) and incorporates an entire world of tradition, legend, and devoutness. It is a magnificent structure, beginning (or ending, chronologically speaking) with the Baroque eighteenth century facade, which is quite impressive and theatrical, especially when illuminated at night. It cannot, however, compare with the beauty of the Romanesque entrance, Pórtico de la Gloria, that it masks, and through which by tradition every pilgrim must enter the cathedral.

This twelfth century portal is the supreme creation of Master Mateo. It is said to mark the beginning of sculpture's modern age, transforming the stiff and unnatural figures of earlier art into real people. At its center on the tympanum, a warm, human, and larger-than-life Christ figure is surrounded by evangelists, angels, and forty everyday people, carved in miniature, who represent the redeemed. There is Saint James the Pilgrim directly below Christ, who seems to say, "Welcome." He is supported on a column where centuries of pilgrims have placed their fingers, creating deep indentations that have taken the shape of a hand.

Santiago mediates between Christ and the people (he is variously portrayed in the cathedral as warrior, pilgrim, and saint). To either side of him a bevy of smiling polychromed saints benevolently look down in greeting. Notice particularly rosy-cheeked Daniel, to the left, with his cherubic smile.

> Saints and Apostles, see them! it seems
> that their lips move, that they are talking quietly
> one to another.
>
> Are they alive? Could they possibly be made of stone
> those lifelike figures
> those marvelous robes
> those eyes brimming with life?
>
> *Rosalía de Castro*

LA TUNA: MODERN TROUBADOURS WITH AN ANCIENT TRADITION

You can't miss *la tuna*: in university towns such as Madrid, Salamanca and most especially Santiago de Compostela, these modern-day minstrels can be found serenading, as much for their own pleasure as for that of their enthusiastic public. They are exuberant students, full of energy and loaded with charm, making music with mandolins, guitars and tambourines, then passing the tambourine for contributions, or selling tapes of their music to finance tours that bring their lively music to the rest of the world.

The name *tuna* once referred to people who led a vagabond life, and indeed *la tuna* members, called *tunos*, have a devil-may-care outlook on the world. They dress as their predecessors did, in sixteenth century garb: knickers, black stockings, buckled shoes, and black capes covered with badges, each representing a city or country where they have performed. The multicolored ribbons that stream from their robes are gifts from young female admirers. Their hearty and infectious songs, whose themes revolve around university life, uplift the spirits and are sure to set toes tapping and hands clapping.

THE WAY OF SAINT JAMES

It was a medieval phenomenon: throngs of Europe's sick and weary, gathering at designated French cities (mainly Paris, Vezelay, Le Puy, and Arles), then walking across the formidable Pyrenees, even in the dead of winter, on a cruel journey that took months to complete. It was at first a movement initiated by the masses, but eventually bishops, priests, kings, Saint Francis of Assisi, even twelfth century Pope Calixtus II, joined the peregrination to Santiago.

Pilgrimages to Santiago became a major impetus for expansion of the clergy and construction of churches and hospitals to care for pilgrims en route, and resulted in an exchange of ideas and a mingling of concepts and cultures on a grand scale. Today if you follow the route from the French border (see Itinerary 6, Appendix), you will find early churches and hospitals (that gave rise to towns and cities with wide lineal roads to accommodate the masses) every thirty kilometers or so, the average distance a pilgrim might cover in a day.

One of the world's first travel guidebooks, compiled by a French priest, Aymeric Picaud, tells the pilgrim where to find the best food and lodging en route ("Estella, rich in fine bread and excellent wine, as well as fine meat and fish and supplied with all manner of goodnesses"), even where they should avoid drinking the water ("Take care not to drink nor let your horse drink from it [the Río Salado in Navarra], for it will be fatal!").

The costume of the pilgrim was standard: a thick coarse wool cape, a stave with a gourd atop to store water, sturdy sandals, a wide-brim felt hat turned up in front, and on the return (for those who had the health to return) scallop shells pinned to the shoulders of their robes as evidence that indeed they had reached Santiago.

The pilgrimages reached their height in the twelfth century, then declined but never disappeared. The devout and those merely seeking adventure backpack today along the Way of Saint James (Pope John in his younger years was one of them) and are still cared for by the clergy as they tenaciously make their way to Santiago.

♦ You can get to Santiago de Compostela in July and August on Al Andalus (see box, p. 397), a vintage train that begins its two- to three-day trips in Barcelona and travels along The Way of Saint James.

Crowning the portal's complex biblical scene, twenty-four Elders of the Apocalypse appear engaged in lively dialogue while tuning traditional Galician instruments: the harp, viola, and the unusual *zanfonía*, a keyboard instrument with crank and tuning pegs, similar to the hurdy-gurdy.

Just behind the column supporting Santiago, a kneeling figure looks to the altar. It is Master Mateo himself, who is popularly called the Santo dos Croques (Head-Knocker Saint), for it is tradition to bang your head against his in hope of absorbing a small measure of his genius.

Inside the cathedral the aisles sublimely soar, and the chapels, especially the main altar, are awash in gold, silver, and precious jewels, accumulated over the centuries. To some art connoisseurs, the glitter is in gaudy excess, masking objects of limited artistic value, but there is no denying its dazzling impact. Most visitors will file past the figure of Saint James, who sits in majesty behind the altar, then descend a flight of stairs to see his silver-encrusted coffin.

The cathedral is today very much the way medieval pilgrims found it. To complete the picture one has only to visualize the thousands of downtrodden pilgrims camping here (although they were generally confined to the upper balconies) and to imagine the stench from their unwashed bodies. Then you will understand the original purpose of the huge *botafumeiro*, or incense burner, that today is put to use only on ceremonial occasions and otherwise kept in the cathedral museum. If you are fortunate to see it in action, the spectacle is memorable indeed. Hanging on a pulley in front of the main altar, the *botafumeiro* gathers terrifying momentum as clerics swing it until it finally reaches the upper balconies—the original goal—before swooshing low over the heads of onlookers. Stay out of its path.

Leave the cathedral through the south portal to the Plaza de las Platerías, named, by some accounts, for the Plateresque style (see Index) of its doorway, and by others for the silversmiths who traditionally worked under the arches of the square. Today there are jewelry stores here that specialize in silver and jet (see box, p. 222). Just to the left of this plaza, on the Plaza de la Quintana, is the Puerta Santa, the eastern entrance to the cathedral that opens only in Holy Years (that is, when July 25, the Day of Saint James, falls on a Sunday). It is adorned with more extraordinary sculptures by Master Mateo. The Plaza de la Azabachería, facing the cathedral's north portal (this cathedral, quite unusually, has plazas on all sides), continues to specialize in stores carrying objects of jet (*azabache*).

When you leave Santiago—I'm sure with a desire to return again—take a parting view of the city from the Paseo de la Herradura. It's an image of this esteemed and eminently likable city that will remain with you for a long time to come.

Seeing Santiago de Compostela

CATHEDRAL   The exterior and the Pórtico de la Gloria are the highlights of this cathedral (see text). Inside, there are many beautiful chapels (the oldest one is right behind the altar), but the Baroque main altar with its Romanesque image of Santiago is of overwhelming richness and unquestionably the center of attention. Follow a hallway at the front of the cathedral to a ninth century Romanesque hermitage to see its exquisite portal and inside, to the left, an image of Christ in the Olive Grove. The ground is littered with scraps of paper petitioning favors, an old tradition in Santiago.

The **CATHEDRAL MUSEUM,** besides displaying the *botafumeiro* (see text), has impressive treasures of gold, silver, and jewels. It also has one of Spain's richest collections of tapestries (by Goya and Rubens) and exhibits the frayed battle flag from the decisive Battle of Lepanto (see Index).

♦ Be sure to find out if and when the *botafumeiro* will be functioning.

PALACIO DE GELMÍREZ   The residence of Santiago's first and most powerful archbishop and one of the finest examples of twelfth century civil Romanesque architecture in Spain.

HOSTAL DE LOS REYES CATÓLICOS   A sixteenth century hospice, in the shape of a cross and organized around four courtyards, this magnificent structure was built by the Catholic Kings, who on a visit to Santiago were appalled by the atrocious conditions under which the pilgrims were living. You can see inscriptions carved in the stone walls that relate to the building's medical function, like "Leech Deposit" and "Observatory for the Dying."

SAN MARTÍN PINARIO   A regal and very unusual outdoor stairway leads you *down* to the church entrance of this monastery. The facade and especially the altar are grand examples of highly ornate Galician Baroque.

CONVENTO DE SANTO DOMINGO DE BONAVAL   In the building adjacent to the church see the unique triple free-standing snail stairway. Also here is the Galician Folk Museum (Museo do Pobo Galego).

SANTA MARÍA DE SAR   On the eastern outskirts of the city, this church has columns all askew, generally tilted inward at their base and producing a disconcerting "drunken" sensation. Some think the church is the work of a genius, who by minute calculation actually planned the columns this way. But the explanation is really quite matter-of-fact and a result of design error. The church was built over the soft shifting earth of a riverbed, and, adding to this problem, the side aisles were raised too high to provide adequate support for the central nave, which collapsed in the sixteenth century. In the seventeenth and eighteenth centuries massive stone buttresses were added to prevent any further slippage, and in this

---

JET: A QUINTESSENTIAL GALICIAN CRAFT

Jet, or *azabache* as it is called in Spanish, is petrified coal that traditionally comes from the mines of Asturias. Throughout the ages it was reputed to possess magical powers: It repelled the evil eye, made serpents flee, kept devils at bay, and even ascertained a woman's virginity.

In Santiago powerful guilds supervised the quality of crafted jet objects and maintained ironclad monopolies. Scallop shells carved from jet became an important craft in the Middle Ages and were among the world's first souvenirs. Also popular with pilgrims were jet rosaries and amulets. A cupped hand with the index finger extended gave protection from the evil eye, evil gossip, curses, and excess pride. An open hand placed on doors and walls dispelled enemy powers.

Jet jewelry is still commonly purchased by many visitors to Galicia.

condition Santa María de Sar has survived. The Romanesque arches of the cloister again show the genius of Master Mateo.

MONTE DEL GOZO (Monxoi)   From this height as you approach Santiago de Compostela from the Lugo road, the city first comes into view, and thus this spot was called by the pilgrims the Hill of Pleasure.

PAZO DE OCA, some twenty-five kilometers from Santiago (just over the province line in Pontevedra), is a stone mansion sometimes called the Versailles of Galicia for its stateliness and its magnificent gardens.

STAYING IN SANTIAGO DE COMPOSTELA

HOSTAL DE LOS REYES CATÓLICOS   Plaza de España   tel. (981) 58 22 00   This resplendent former pilgrims' hospital, centering on four interior courtyards is lavishly appointed. Reserve well in advance, and rearrange your travel dates, if necessary, to obtain reservations. (Expensive.)

EATING IN SANTIAGO DE COMPOSTELA

In Santiago you can concentrate on tapas and local wines—Rúa del Franco has more bars than you could possibly need. I particularly like **O CHARCA** for typical Galician tapas like empanada, octopus, *calamares*, seafood vinaigrette, and *pimientos de Padrón*.
For more serious eating:

VILAS   Rosalía de Castro 88   tel. (981) 59 10 00   A bit inconveniently located just outside the heart of Santiago, but well worth the walk or short cab ride. Scallops, *Merluza a la Gallega* (hake in paprika sauce) or *a la Vasca* (in green sauce), fresh shellfish, and *Tarta de Santiago* are all outstanding. (Moderate–expensive.)

DON GAIFEROS   Rúa Nova 23   tel. (981) 58 38 94   Housed in the former stables of a lovely old stone building on the main street of Old Santiago. The food is for the most part typically Galician and well prepared. (Moderate–expensive.)

EL ASESINO   Plaza de la Universidad 16   tel. (981) 58 15 68   An institution in Santiago, unchanged in a hundred years (even the owners seem to be the originals). Simple Galician fare. (Moderate.)

SHOPPING

Jet (see box, p. 222) is found all over the city, usually in combination with silver. Buy from certified jewelers to ensure authenticity. **MEYER**   (Plaza de las Platerías 2) has a great variety of pieces, from necklaces and bracelets to stickpins, hair clips, amulets, and small statuary, many in interesting and original designs.

If you can't get to the village of Buño, find some of its pottery (casseroles and other cookware items) at **CACHARROS**   (Rúa del Villar 16). There is also some in stores near the market.

OBRADOIRO   Azabachería 12, has granite carvings and statuary—the smallest piece is an ashtray.

◆ For serious works of art in stone, some small enough to possibly carry home with you, visit **JOSÉ CAO** (see box, p. 206) outside of Santiago at Monte del Gozo (road to Lugo, past the San Lázaro bridge, second street on the right). Prices begin at about 50,000 pesetas.

FIESTAS

DÍA DE SANTIAGO (*Day of Saint James*), July 25   See text.

THE CITY OF LA CORUÑA

Although La Coruña (A Coruña in Galician) is the capital of the province, it has always been upstaged by Santiago de Compostela. What I saw when we arrived at La Coruña for the first time was not at all promising, for the city is an industrial center. But once we reached the waterfront, my impression completely changed. Here was a maritime city very much like Cádiz, which I so dearly love: located on an isthmus and cut off from the mainland except for a narrow neck of sand. Then we reached the Avenida de la Marina and saw the long stretch of three- and four-story white houses with glass galleries, La Coruña's pride, and I was thoroughly charmed.

That night we visited the Old Quarter. Its streets were dark, hilly, and evocative, the vast Plaza de María Pita (heroine of La Coruña, who saved the city from the attack of Sir Francis Drake) brightly lit and animated. We continued on the Calle Real, thronged even after business hours with lively, fast-moving crowds, then we doubled back onto Olmos street, a bar hoppers' paradise, and we felt very much at home. At Fornos we joined everyone eating octopus that had been boiled in cauldrons and served *a feira* style, sprinkled with oil and paprika and accompanied by potatoes, on wooden plates. Local barrel wines could not have tasted better.

Later that evening we visited inveterate showman "El Barbas" (The Bearded One), who, depending on how the mood strikes him, dresses as a Viking or an Orthodox priest and prepares flaming Queimada (see box, p. 208), all the while reciting incantations, in the tradition of the witches who stirred their magic brews in Galician forests.

In daylight the city was equally bustling, and we set out on a walking tour to see the city's Gothic and Romanesque churches; the castle of San Antón, with its wonderful views of the city; and what is for me the most delightful corner of La Coruña, Plaza de Santa Bárbara—cobbled, tranquil, and faced on one side by a convent (where the nuns sell excellent cookies) and on another by homes that look like dollhouses. Six venerable trees fill the small square and lean toward a *cruceiro* at the center.

La Coruña is a pleasant city in which to spend a day and an excellent jump-off point for excursions farther up the coast.

SEEING LA CORUÑA

OLD QUARTER   Some streets recall artisan times—Zapatería (street of the shoemakers), Herrerías (street of the metalworkers), Tinajas (barrel makers' street), Cortadura (tailors' street). Amargura and Sinagoga streets, once part of the town's Jewish quarter, have some of the city's oldest houses, their windows framed in heavy dark wood.

TORRE DE HÉRCULES   This is the world's only functioning Roman lighthouse, dating from the times of Trajan in the first century A.D. It is more than 300 feet tall, and you can climb up for views of the city and the sea.

PLAZA DE SANTA BÁRBARA   See text.

SANTIAGO   A twelfth century Romanesque church, the city's oldest, with unusual sculptures of Saint John and Saint Mark done in profile at the portal.

SANTA MARÍA DEL CAMPO   A Romanesque church with a lovely portal, set on a popular square.

JARDIN DE SAN CARLOS   In these gardens Sir John Moore, who aided the Spanish in their war against French invaders, lies buried, killed by Napoleonic troops in a fierce struggle. Wrote George Borrow, in 1842 in *The Bible in Spain:* "Yes, there lies the hero, almost within sight of the glorious hill where he turned upon his pursuers like a lion at bay and terminated his career. Many acquire immortality without seeking it, and die before its first ray has gilded their name. Of these was Moore."

EATING IN LA CORUÑA

EL RÁPIDO   Estrella 7   tel. (981) 22 42 21   A restaurant unchanged in all the years it has been here. Amiable service and good simple Galician food—shellfish croquettes, *Caldo Gallego, Lacón con Grelos*, grilled flounder. (Moderate.)

POLO   Rodríguez Yordi 2   tel. (981) 27 61 10 succeeds a classic of the city that has closed, Viuda de Alfredín. It carries on the tradition, serving those famous ham-and-potato tortillas and chickpea and tripe stew. (Inexpensive.)

Eat tapas-style at any or all of the following:

FORNOS (Olmos 25)   For octopus, *empanadillas* (savory turnovers), and grilled sausage (see text).

JAMONERÍA LA MARINA (Avenida La Marina)   Serves huge hero-style sandwiches on great Galician bread, and tapas as well. It also has cheeses and cold cuts for takeout.

MESÓN DE LAS CAZUELAS (Calle de la Estacada 1)   Typical *mesón* with all kinds of little-casserole tapas and Galician wines.

◆ At **TABERNA BOHEMIA,**   Orilla Mar 16, described as "401 meters from the cemetery," see the late-night performance of "El Barbas," who dramatically flames Queimada. Not much food except cheese omelets, also in flames.

STAYING IN LA CORUÑA

Choices are slim, but the best bet is **FINISTERRE**   (Paseo del Parrote 20 tel. (381) 20 54 00), nicely located on the water and near the Old Quarter, but in need of renovation. Request a high floor overlooking the water. (Moderate–expensive; pool.)

SHOPPING

OBRADOIRO   (Plazuela de los Ángeles 7)   Silver and jet jewelry, antiques, stone statuary.

THE END OF THE RÍAS BAJAS AND THE BEGINNING OF THE RÍAS ALTAS IN LA CORUÑA

There's just a short stretch left of the Rías Bajas in La Coruña, and they come to an end at the desolate cape of Finisterre (no wonder it was thought to be the end of the world). The landscape begins to change now; the *rías* are smaller, tighter, lined with cliffs; beaches are especially beautiful and pristine; there are more forests; and the *hórreos* change from granite to wood and slate. Around Cedeira the coast takes the name Costa de la Muerte—Coast of Death—certainly not an appealing name in tourist terms, but most descriptive of this harsh and inhospitable, yet extraordinarily commanding coast where many have lost their lives prying goose barnacles (*percebes*) from the rocks (see box, p. 230).

You'll have to take it slow and easy on these hilly narrow roads that circle

A GALICIAN REFRAIN

Non te cases cun ferreiro
que ten moito que lavar.
Cásate con mariñeiro
que ven lavado do mar.

Never marry one who forges iron
for you will have too much to wash.
Marry a mariner
who is cleansed by the sea.

around *rías* and inlets, but to me this is in many ways the best of Galicia, and I wouldn't miss it for the world. There are interesting crafts, charming legends, wild horses, wonderful beaches, and spectacular scenery that is ever changing as the shallow *rías* empty and fill with the tides. The only thing lacking is hotels: North of La Coruña one possibility is the parador at El Ferrol.

THE BEST OF THE RÍAS BAJAS AND RÍAS ALTAS IN LA CORUÑA

PADRÓN   It was here that the body of the apostle Saint James was brought from Jerusalem by his Christian disciples. The boat anchored at a stone mooring (displayed under the altar of the village church), and the name Padrón refers to the stone. This was also the home of Galician poetess Rosalía de Castro. It is a pretty town with a lushly shaded waterfront promenade, and in the surroundings, the tiny green peppers of Padrón are grown.

LA PUEBLA DE CARAMIÑAL (Poboa do Caramiñal)   Distinguished chiefly by its procession of Las Mortajas, the Shrouds, in which those who have come close to death during the year are paraded in coffins (third Sunday in September).
◆ None of Galicia's many scenic overlooks is as astonishing as **LA CURO-TA,** reached from La Puebla de Caramiñal. Don't stop at the lower viewing area, but continue as far as the road goes for an almost aerial, maplike view of all the Rías Bajas. Clear skies are, of course, essential.

CORRUBEDO   A small town on a horseshoe bay looking out on two of the most beautiful beaches I have ever seen, **PLAYA LADEIRA** and **PLAYA DE LA LAGOA.** They are of smooth white sand, protected by mountainous sand dunes and separated from each other by a small rocky island and a stream of water that flows in and out of a small lagoon.

PLAYA AGUEIRO, between Noya and Corrubedo, is a long curving beach of fine sand facing the Ría Muros y Noya and backed by beautiful mountain scenery.

NOYA (Noia)   An ancient town on the Muros *ría*, well known to the Romans and once an important port before the *ría* silted. In the attractive Old Quarter is the beautiful San Martín church of the school of Master Mateo, its portal scene of Apostles and musicians inspired by Santiago's cathedral. Above the portal is an intricate rose window. See also the exceptional *cruceiro* at the northern entrance to the town.
TABERNA TÍPICA, Cantón Bajo, is in the town's most historic house (built in 1339). Good for simple tavern food: fried squid, cured ham, cheese, etc. (Inexpensive.)

MUROS   A delightful seaside village with Gothic-arched arcaded streets and a bay full of mussel-breeding platforms.

BAZAR PEPITA, on the waterfront, sells the charming straw hats of Carnota (see below).

DON BODEGÓN, also along the waterfront, specializes in seafood. Excellent steamed mussels, grilled sardines, spider crab (*centolla*), and *nécora* crabs. (Moderate.)

CARNOTA   The town's chief attractions are Galicia's longest *hórreo*, some 110 feet and belonging to the village priest, and a lovely four-mile-long curved beach.

◆ In and around Carnota, notice the straw hats with black streamers and flat brims designed to transport bundles and other packages on the head, which are paradoxically feminine on the squat, solidly built women working in the fields. The hats are intricately assembled from spirals of narrow straw braid and laboriously stitched together. The hats can be purchased at **COMERCIAL CARACAS**, in the main plaza of Carnota, or in Muros (see above).

FINISTERRE   A lighthouse sits on this lonely site, once the most westerly land known to Europeans. It is a setting that certainly looks like the End of the World. Borrow wrote: "It was a blue shiny waste. . . . On all sides there was grandeur and sublimity. . . . Even in the calmest day there was a rumbling and a hollow roar . . . which fills the heart with uneasy sensations."

CAMARIÑAS   This town and the surrounding villages have been dedicated to lacemaking since the sixteenth century. We can thank nobleman Fernando de Andrade and his contingent of Galicians, who fought with Philip II in Flanders, for this odd circumstance: Many returned with Flemish brides, who in turn brought their lacemaking skills.

Buy exquisite handkerchiefs from **MARÍA LUISA QUINTANA,** who works outdoors by the waterfront, or visit her parent shop, **PALILLEIRA MELANIA,** at the entrance to town (Avenida Coruña).

◆ The road to Malpica, between Laxe and Puenteceso, is particularly beautiful, skirting the cliffs of the Ensenada (inlet) de la Insúa.

MALPICA   Closely protected by cliffs, this pretty fishing harbor has mounds of fishnets piled up at the water's edge and several bars and restaurants for seafood.

BUÑO   Dedicated since Roman times to pottery, this is my favorite place to pick up wonderfully rough-hewn items like open or covered casseroles, chestnut roasters, garlic and onion jars, wine jugs, and *queimadera* bowls hung with cups for the traditional Queimada (p. 208).

Shop at **CASA AMALIA "LA CACHARRERA,"** at the eastern entrance to Buño on the main Santa Catalina street, at number 35. Exiting the town, see pottery being made by **APARICIO AÑÓN CAAMAÑO**   Rúa Nova 4.

BETANZOS   Another former port that silted up, this city is built on a lofty mound with concentric streets from which steep radial streets branch out. Many houses have wood balconies, thought to have been added to dry the corn introduced from America. The main plaza of Betanzos is expansive, its streets narrow and well cared for. There are three Gothic churches:

SANTA MARÍA DEL AZOGUE (it has an unsymmetrical facade from which a bell tower rises to one side); **SANTIAGO**, whose portal is modeled after Santiago's cathedral; and my favorite, **SAN FRANCISCO**. Its most interesting feature is the tomb of Fernán Pérez de Andrade, a member of this region's powerful medieval Andrade family. His likeness is beautifully carved in stone, and his loyal dogs rest at his feet. Detailed hunting scenes run around the coffin, which rests on the backs of a bear and a boar, both uncustomarily sculpted in great anatomical detail.

♦ Betanzos has the best tortillas in Spain, and that's quite a statement in a country where this egg-and-potato omelet is a national dish and available almost anywhere. It is the quality of the potatoes and the cooking technique (the omelet stays deliciously juicy) that make it special. **LA CASILLA** (Carretera de Castilla 30 tel. (981) 77 01 61) serves a fine tortilla, along with other down-to-earth Galician foods, like a chickpea and tripe stew.

TONELERÍA LAGOA Calle Ribera 12, has full-size or decorative-size wood and brass containers called *sellas*, traditionally used to hold milk, wine, or water.

PONTEDEUME An old town of arcaded streets and quaint plazas, named for its bridge over the Río Eume.

MUEBLES TENREIRO Real 7, is an interesting shop, jampacked with basketry.

♦ I wouldn't miss **MONASTERIO DE CAAVEIRO,** some twenty minutes away, stunningly set above the Eume in a dense eucalyptus forest. A short climb on foot takes you to the remains of the monastery—a Romanesque apse and coat of arms are intact—and from there the views are phenomenal.

FERROL Known in years past as Ferrol del Caudillo (of the Chief) because it was birthplace of Francisco Franco, this is a major city and home port to the Spanish navy. I recommend it mainly for its pleasant **PARADOR DEL FERROL** (Plaza Eduardo Pondal s/n tel. (981) 35 67 20), near the waterfront. (Moderate.) Eat at the parador or make the rounds of some of the city's many tapas bars.

PLAYA DE FROUXEIRA, a wonderful beach, can be reached from the nearby town of Valdovino.

CEDEIRA An immaculate town (the hand of its most exigent mayor, Leopoldo Rubido, is evident) in an idyllic and incomparable setting, surrounded by pine-covered mountains and within the narrow neck of the Ría de Cedeira. It has one of the most beautiful bays in Galicia, and its waterfront promenade is a delight.

TABERNA DA CALEXA (Tras da Eirexa 7), fastidiously restored, is a great place for an aperitif.

Be sure to lunch at **EL NÁUTICO** Almirante Moreno s/n tel. (981) 48 00 11, on clams *marinera*, exceptional lobster salad, monkfish with peas, Galician bread that is extraordinarily moist and flavorful, and finish with the *Tarta de Ortigueira*. (Moderate.)

SAN ANDRÉS DE TEIXIDO A tiny village, long isolated, where many risk their lives to scrape *percebes* (see box, p. 230) from forbidding rocks (try

Goose Barnacles: Delicacy of the Sea

Percebes—goose barnacles—are among the sea's most unsightly creatures, have pearly white shells that extend into blackened leathery necks, and bear a grotesque likeness to human fingers. And yet Spaniards adore them, and they command sky-high prices. Sweet, succulent, with something of the consistency and flavor of lobster, this shellfish, say fans, captures the very essence of the sea.

Percebes cling to the rocks along the Galician "Coast of Death," where the Atlantic Ocean confronts—often violently—the Cantabrian Sea. Fishermen must work at water's edge, attached at their waist by ropes held by a companion who stands vigil atop the rocks. The danger of being smashed against the rocks or swept out to sea is very real and a constant preoccupation. But no matter—fishermen will take the greatest risks and diners will pay any price to get *percebes* to the table.

percebes at the village bar), while others eke a living from the pilgrims who come to worship San Andrés, guardian of fishermen. Be careful not to trample insects or small lizards! They may be, legend tells, reincarnated pilgrims, unable to pay homage to the saint in their lifetimes. Buy the herb of love (*herba de namorar*)—guaranteed to give results—and drop bread pieces in the fountain below the church; if they float, your wish is granted, if not, you will have to return another time to San Andrés.

Crafts are among the most primitive you will find in Spain. Charming dried bread figures, childlike in design and coloring, tell the story of San Andrés. Naïve dolls and unassuming wall hangings of wood, shell, plaster, and pebbles, also portraying San Andrés, are for sale in a rustic crafts store on the main square.

♦ The road to Cariño hugs the rugged seaside cliffs and has views of startling precipices (stop at the windy **GARITA DE HERBEIRA** lookout, the highest point of the Galician coast). Wild horses populate these mountains.

ORTIGUEIRA   A large town on the enormous inlet of Ría de Santa Marta. The landscape is gentle, and wharves along the *ría's* edge form attractive walkways. Ortigueira, some say, resembles a Swiss town on a lake.

EL BARQUERO   A tiny slate-roofed village built steeply up the mountainside from its fishing port and enclosed by pine-covered mountains. This is a great place for calm and rest.

ESTRELLA DEL MAR BAR-RESTAURANT   tel. (981) 41 41 05, has rooms (no private baths). The owners are extremely cordial, and all is immaculately kept. (Inexpensive.)

THE PROVINCE OF LUGO

I NEVER SEEM to linger long in Lugo (*loo-go*)—there's just too much that attracts me in the provinces of Pontevedra and La Coruña—and I always run out of time. Nevertheless, it is a region that stays in my mind, for it is so gentle, green, and beautiful, and so very remote from modern Spain. I would love to see it stay that way forever.

There is much untouched territory in Lugo. The Ancares mountains are luxuriantly virgin, and the protected *urogallo* (capercaillie), a beautiful bird somewhat resembling a cross between a turkey and a modest peacock, loudly announces its presence in song and puts on elaborate courtship displays in mating season. Horses roam with few restrictions, and in early summer several *rapa das bestas*—horse roundups—take place (see box, p. 205).

Villages in Lugo look as they have for centuries: houses with walls of stone and thin stone-slab roofs, and property lines marked by stone "monoliths." In many isolated farm areas, wooden shoes are still part of everyday dress ("So much more practical and comfortable," country folk like Feliciano Gallego of San Cosme parish will tell you, "drier, warmer in winter, cooler in summer"). The people and their animals sometimes still live together in primitively thatched houses, in the style of their ancient Celtic ancestors. Pottery is typically formed and fired just as it was in Roman times, although the Sargadelos chinaware made here and for sale in shops all over Galicia is unexpectedly modern.

But archaeological evidence suggests a much richer history. Lugo was along an important Roman road through Spain, and in the tiny village of Santa Eulalia de Bóveda the remains of a sophisticated sanctuary have brought specialists from all over the world to try to decipher their significance (see box, p. 234). In medieval times the Way of Saint James cut right across Lugo province: In the high mountains of Cebreiro, some 4,000 feet above the sea, the pilgrims walking to Santiago de Compostela first set foot in Galicia, completing one of the most arduous crossings of their journey. There, they sought refuge in the church that was established to provide lodgings and food and to instill in them renewed religious inspiration.

Lugo has a short coastline and, like its interior, is the least exploited province in Galicia. Vacationers seeking to escape summer crowds choose Lugo, and its three estuaries are exceptionally beautiful, particularly the Santa Marta *ría*, which divides into cozy lakelike areas. Seafood is, of course, prevalent along the coast, but the grazing land of the interior produces young beef that is unusually tender and flavorful. *Chuletón de Lugo*, a thick chop of impressive size, is the cut most frequently served. Also highly regarded are the fine capons of the town of Villalba, in demand during the Christmas season. Salmon and trout are plentiful in Lugo's rivers, and the sweets of the province of Lugo, especially the complex tarts made in the town of Mondoñedo, lure motorists away from their chosen paths.

THE CITY OF LUGO

Lugo is low key, so much so that it has been described as the ideal place for an ill poet. I presume this is a compliment, referring to the peace of mind one may find here, but the message may just as well reflect the rather unexciting life of this provincial capital. In any case, there are just a few sights to keep you in the city of Lugo before moving on.

A major crossroads in ancient times, Lugo was founded by the Romans and built upon a Celtic *castro,* or fortified hilltop. The Roman walls (accounts of their age vary from third century B.C. to second century A.D.) completely encircle Old Lugo and are an amazing sight. They extend more than a mile, are thirty to forty-five feet high, fifteen feet thick, and have ten entry gates. Unique in Spain is the sentry path that runs around the top of the walls. It's great for a stroll and for contemplating the city, the Ancares mountains, and the Río Miño; it's also a good jogging circuit.

The Old Quarter of Lugo is somewhat neglected, but its quaint plazas and porticoed streets are nevertheless quite attractive. They become animated at the evening tapas hour, and on Cruz and Rúa Nova the bars seem to burst at the seams with customers who spill out onto the streets. But after 9:00 p.m. the city quiets down quickly as everyone goes home for dinner.

You need not stray far from these central streets to see the sights of Lugo. The cathedral, a mélange of styles, is most impressive at its oldest entrance, porch-covered and graced by an unusual Romanesque Christ in Majesty that seems to float in midair. Nearby in the old convent of San Francisco is the Museo Provincial, with archaeological objects displayed in the cloister (some from Santa Eulalia), several Baroque altars, a very complete collection of antique Sargadelos chinaware, and a fine example of an old stone Galician kitchen where the priests of the convent once cooked.

EATING IN LUGO

Tapas in Lugo are abundant and varied and can easily constitute a meal. Otherwise, visit **MESÓN DE ALBERTO**   Cruz 4   tel. (982) 22 83 10, or **VERRUGA**   Cruz 12   tel. (982) 22 98 55, both well regarded and both with busy tapas bars. Their *Chuletón de Lugo* is properly tender and a treat in Spain, where beef is not often up to par. Very good custard-filled *filloa* crepes. (Moderate.)

STAYING IN LUGO

Choose either the modern **GRAN HOTEL LUGO**   Avenida Ramón Ferrerio 21   tel. (982) 22 41 52 (moderate–expensive), in the newer sector of Lugo or the ancient **MÉNDEZ NÚÑEZ**   Reina 1   tel. (982) 23 07 11 (moderate), outdated in a kind of creepy way (oversized black telephones from the 1940s, overstuffed furniture, an ancient staff) but just steps away from the sights, the bars, and the restaurants of the Old Quarter. I chose the latter, but another option is to spend a few hours in Lugo and continue on.

♦ Tuesday and Friday mornings a lively market takes place in the Plaza de Santo Domingo.

◊ISITING THE PROVINCE OF LUGO

The Interior

MONFORTE DE LEMOS   If you happen to be passing through this large city on the exceptionally beautiful road from Lugo to Orense, **J.M.**   Campo de la Compañía 41   tel. (982) 40 09 26, has excellent simple fare. We had a great lunch at the bar: *Gambas al Ajillo* (garlic shrimp), tortilla (potato omelet), salad, and *Pincho Moruno* (miniature shish kabob). (Inexpensive.)

QUIROGA (Queiroga)   A charming rustic restaurant, **REMANSIÑO DE PAZ**   tel. (982) 42 80 07, specializing in game and wild mushrooms, is what will bring you to this town. (Inexpensive.)

CEBREIRO   Entrance into Galicia for millions of medieval pilgrims. That's why a church was built here in the ninth century, and why in 1072 Alfonso VI put it in the hands of French monks from Saint Geraud d'Aurillac, who could better attend to foreign pilgrims. Legend tells of a fifteenth century miracle: A monk, somewhat lacking in faith, was celebrating Mass while a blizzard raged outside. How absurd, he thought, that pilgrims should come so far in such abominable weather just for the bread and wine of the Eucharist. To his astonishment the bread and wine turned to flesh and blood, and it has stayed as such ever since. These supposedly uncorrupt remains are on display (although the area's too dark to see it very well) behind the church altar.
♦ There are Celtic thatched huts here; one can be visited, furnished and equipped in the primitive style of the country folk who once lived there.
♦ The **HOSPEDERÍA SAN GIRALDO DE AURILLAC,** former pilgrims' hospital and monks' residence, is now a *mesón,* and the only place nearby to find food and drink.

SAMOS   This massive monastery with the look of a fortress has been in existence since the seventh century, although its present facade is eighteenth century. In the ninth century, when the Arabs dominated the south of Spain, monks from Córdoba came here to take refuge. Enrique Navarro, an old friend of ours, was commissioned by the monks to paint wall frescoes for an upper gallery of the monastery to replace those that had been destroyed by fire. A lover of beautiful women, he used likenesses of women he knew or admired as models for the angels; one you might recognize is Ava Gardner.

PIORNEDO   Of great ethnological interest, its thatched houses, some still inhabited, are built in the Celtic tradition.

SANTA EULALIA DE BÓVEDA   An extraordinary archaeological find of mystifying origin (see box).

BONXE   An out-of-the-way parish of solid stone homes, once totally dedicated to pottery, but today only two artisans remain. They still use wood-burning firing ovens of stone and foot-operated pottery wheels. Traditional, unsophisticated pottery all marked with the half-moon symbol of Bonxe: jugs, plates, and the *jarra bruja,* the bewitched jug (because you never know from which of its three spouts liquid will flow). Ask for the house of pottery maker Indalecio Lombao Gómez.

MEIRA   In the heart of Lugo's primitive interior, Meira is a detour I suggest for those looking for an intimate taste of this rural world and wanting to purchase Feliciano Gallego's hand-crafted wooden shoes, painted black and etched in lacy designs. To reach his farm from the Lugo-Ribadeo road, pass Meira and turn left at Marco, then take the first left to San Cosme. The house is the first one on the left.

THE MYSTERY OF SANTA EULALIA

Santa Eulalia de Bóveda, just fourteen kilometers from the capital city of Lugo and yet locked in a primitive countryside, was probably an ancient place of worship, but its exact origins and its purpose baffle experts. An exterior stone wall shows puzzling reliefs of a bird, a woman holding an arc (or perhaps a rainbow or a garland), and a group of five young girls dancing. A Moorish brick arch—suggesting some Arab connection—leads to the interior, most of which is occupied by a central pool, once filled with heated water and perhaps used for curative purposes (suggested by a carving of a crippled man nearby). To add to the mystery, remarkable wall frescoes—most likely Roman and as such among the most important finds from the western Roman Empire—show detailed, anatomically precise portraits of colorful birds: roosters, peacocks, doves, ducks, pheasant, and partridge, singly and in pairs, all in natural poses and framed by lines in a diamond pattern.

Celtic? Roman? Mozarabic? Pagan? Christian? A burial site or place of cult worship of the Spanish priest Priscillian, accused of heresy and executed in the fourth century? Ancient spa? Theories for all of the above have been proposed, and until the final word is in, if ever it is, the enigma of Santa Eulalia will persist.

VILLALBA   In this town is the **PARADOR CONDES DE VILLALBA** Valeriano Valdesuso s/n tel. (982) 51 00 11 (Moderate–expensive), in a single octagonal tower, all that remains of the medieval castle of the powerful Counts of Andrade. This is a parador that I have always liked. It has only six rooms (all in the tower) and an unusually good restaurant (try the Lugo chop, *Caldo Gallego,* and *filloas*). The capons of Villalba are known all over Spain and are especially bred for Christmas feasts.

MONDOÑEDO   A city that was once a capital of Old Galicia. We visit Mondoñedo to see the impressive thirteenth century Gothic cathedral, with its unusual Baroque towers and the exceptional arcaded plaza it faces. Three-story slate-roofed houses in whites and pastels with wrought-iron balconies line the remaining sides of the plaza.

Another reason we come here is to pay our respects to the **REY DE LAS TARTAS** (King of Tarts), Obispo Sarmiento 2, and sample his *Tarta de Mondoñedo*, a moist confection of ground almonds and candied squash in a pastry shell. The shop, hung with dozens of honorary medals and plaques, is plastered with photo blowups of owner Carlos Fogueira with Julio Iglesias and with a really regal king—Spain's Juan Carlos. I like to think of him as the Famous Amos of Mondoñedo.

The Coast

VIVERO   Somewhat like La Coruña in miniature, the houses of glassed white balconies face the waterfront. Narrow twisting streets come out from an attractive two-level Plaza Mayor, also with enclosed balconies and lovely wrought-iron work. However, the town has been neglected, and my main reason to be here is to witness the **RAPA DAS BESTAS** (see box, p. 205), which takes place nearby in Monte Buyo.
HOTEL EGO   Playa de Área   tel. (982) 56 09 87, is simple but quite pleasant. Ask for a room with water view. (Moderate.) **NITO** restaurant, belonging to the hotel, is well known in town for its fine seafood. (Moderate.)
♦ A huge selection of chinaware and jewelry of **SARGADELOS** is on sale at the factory store (Vivero-Ribadeo road, right turn at Riocorvo to Sargadelos). The factory can also be visited.

FOZ   A beach town with a tightly enclosed harbor and a splendid beach. Nearby see the unusual early Romanesque (eleventh century) **SAN MARTÍN DE MONDOÑEDO** church, formerly a cathedral and, as such, the oldest in Spain. Note the wood roof and richly carved capitals.
XOIÑA   Corredoira s/n   tel. (982) 14 09 44, is an elegant villa at the entrance to Foz, specializing in Galician seafood. (Moderate.)
O CARRO, at the beachfront, is a tapas bar and restaurant, both serving Galician seafood. (Moderate.)

RIBADEO   The town is not special, but the views from the waterfront of the Ría de Ribadeo and of the Asturian town of Castropol on the other side are wonderful (this is the last coastal town before crossing into Asturias).
PARADOR DE RIBADEO   Amador Fernández s/n   tel. (982) 11 08 25 (moderate), is in a choice location overlooking the *ría*, which is narrow at its mouth but widens within to form what appears to be an enormous lake.

THE PROVINCE OF ORENSE

ORENSE (or-*en*-say) (Ourense) is Galicia's only landlocked province, but water is so abundant in its rivers and reservoirs that you will hardly feel deprived. Because of its mighty rivers, Orense is Spain's largest producer of electricity and a major source of bottled spring water. Mountains and valleys trace the rivers' paths (the Miño and Sil rivers join here). Forests are thick with pine, and deer, partridge, boar, martens, and ermines abound. The Orense–Lugo road is, in fact, one of the most beautiful we have come across. The tranquil dammed waters of the Sil Gorges look unreal, cutting a blue swath through the lush green mountains. We are startled to come upon a marvelous complex of church and cloisters enveloped in dense vegetation that make up the ruins of the San Esteban monastery, founded in the tenth century. Three splendid and monumental cloisters speak eloquently of a vanished but rich past.

As in Lugo, the beef of Orense is excellent, and the pork—in particular *serrano* ham—is of high quality. Although Orense has no coast, the rivers give forth trout and eel, and fresh seafood is never far away. Octopus *a feira* is a popular and very tasty dish of Orense, and the Festival of the Octopus is held each year in the town of Carballino.

The greatest production of Galicia's Ribeiro wines is in Orense, mainly in the Miño valley. A wine well known even in ancient times, when the Romans carried it back to Rome, it is today what everyone drinks in Galicia, and the fruity whites are particularly praiseworthy. From the grape skins the powerful liquor *orujo* is made.

Although the scenery of Orense is undeniably beautiful, there are few attractions in the province to single out, and even fewer quality hotels (with the exception of one interesting parador), and I would expect that you'd be in Orense mainly en route from Galicia to other destinations in Spain.

Lest I incur the wrath of Orensanos (and there are a surprising number of them who live in the United States, many from the small town of Celanova), let me tell you about the things that I have enjoyed in Orense.

THE CITY OF ORENSE

Built in a valley along the Miño river, Orense is a small provincial capital that existed in Roman times, and its name, by varying accounts, derives from the word *oro* (gold)—because of the ancient gold mines nearby—or from the Germanic Wum See, meaning warm, referring to Orense's hot springs. Those springs continue to produce water that is close to the boiling point and emerges from Orense's neoclassic fountain of Las Burgas.

You reach Orense by way of a modern bridge over the Miño. Next to it is the old bridge, built over Roman foundations in the thirteenth century to accommodate pilgrims on their way to Santiago. With its seven arches, it is one of the longest stone bridge in Spain. The Old Quarter of Orense is a patchwork of seductive little plazas and porticoed streets, charming humble homes and seignorial dwellings, centering on the cobbled, trapezoidal Plaza Mayor.

The cathedral—originally Romanesque, but with many later additions—is the center of cultural interest in Orense. Its altarpiece is an elaborate Gothic work, and in the exceedingly Baroque chapel of Santísimo Cristo a much-venerated statue of Christ, Santo Cristo, is thought to perform miracles. The pièce de résistance, however, is the portal, Pórtico del Paraíso, fashioned in design and subject after the Pórtico de la Gloria in Santiago. Its polychrome coloring is vividly preserved.

A popular refrain sums up the attractions of the city of Orense:

Tres cosas hay en Orense / Three things has Orense
que no las hay en España: / that Spain does not have:
El Santo Cristo, la Puente, / The Santo Cristo, the bridge,
y la Burga hirviendo el agua. / And the Burga [*Las Burgas*] boiling water.

S EEING ORENSE

MUSEO PROVINCIAL   In the Plaza Mayor, housed in the former bishop's palace, this museum has an important collection of Celtic and other prehistoric remains, local antique pottery, and altarpieces from the Romanesque, Gothic, and Baroque periods.

SAN FRANCISCO   The cloister of this thirteenth century Romanesque church (now, unfortunately, a military barracks, but still open to the public) has an impressive sixty-two arches, each resting on double columns.

EATING IN ORENSE

SAN MIGUEL   San Miguel 12   tel. (988) 22 12 45   There are of course many tapas bars in Orense, but for serious eating, busy San Miguel is the top choice in the city. Hake and salmon preparations are excellent, as is the scallop empanada, the fresh shellfish, and the *cañas*—custard-filled cannoli-like pastries. (Moderate–expensive.) At the bar you can have either tapas or a full meal.

♀ISITING THE PROVINCE OF ORENSE

VERÍN   A pleasant stone-hewn village, known mainly for its spring waters, in particular those sold as Fontenova and Cabreiroa. The thirteenth century castle of Monterrey, once of strategic importance because of its proximity to the Portuguese border, is a complex of church, castle, and fortress (and three rings of defensive walls) that dominates the valley and, farther on, the Castilian plains of Zamora.

PARADOR DE MONTERREY   Verín   tel. (988) 41 00 75, is built over the ruins of a sixteenth century Jesuit college. The parador is on a hill looking toward the castle of Monterrey (see above) and with splendid views of the valley. (Moderate.)

SANTA COMBA DE BANDE   A primitive seventh century Visigothic church that is a jewel of pre-Romanesque Galician art and unique in Galicia.

CELANOVA   This town, which hundreds of Galicians in New York call home, in summer proudly accommodates expensive foreign cars of emigrés enjoying their vacations back home. Celanova took shape around the imposing **MONASTERIO DE SAN SALVADOR DE CELANOVA** which is sixteenth century with ornate touches from later times. Emperor Charles V considered retiring here, before ultimately choosing Yuste (see Index). The cloister of the monastery is designed in exuberant Baroque style. Be sure to see in the garden the tiny Mozarabic chapel from the tenth century, with horseshoe arches, that is one of a kind in Galicia.

RIBADAVIA   In the heart of Ribeiro wine country, this stone village has steep, narrow streets; homes with overhanging wood upper balconies; and a narrow, arched, and porticoed plaza. Ribadavia also has one of the best-preserved Jewish quarters of Galicia, dating from the twelfth to sixteenth centuries.

SANTA MARÍA DE OSEIRA   A Cistercian monastery sometimes referred to as the Escorial of Galicia for its austere but grand Renaissance style. See particularly the fifteenth century sacristy with its surprising contorted columns that burst open as they reach toward the vaulted ceiling. The room looks almost Gaudíesque.

GARGANTAS DEL SIL   Along the beautiful Sil gorges, almost hidden among the trees and vines, is the **SAN ESTEBAN** monastery, and its ruined cloisters are still a glorious sight. One has Romanesque arches and a lacy stone balustrade; another, the largest, consists of three arched levels in Renaissance style; the third and smallest has Doric columns supporting Gothic arches. See also the refectory and the old monastic kitchen—with cupboards, sinks, and a huge chimney.

USII ASTURIAS AND CANTABRIA

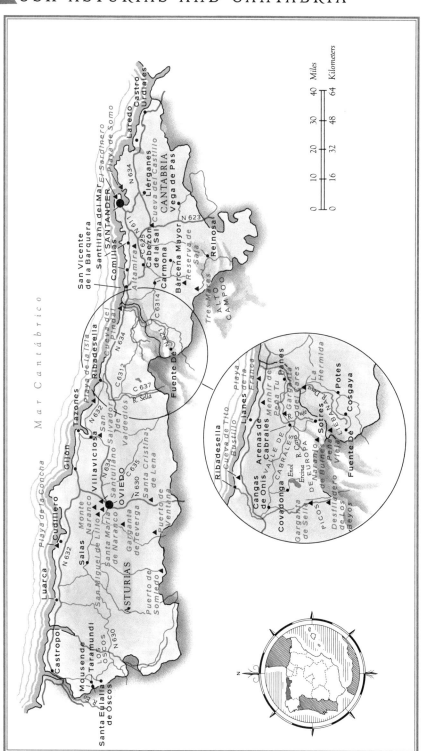

THE PROVINCE AND REGION OF ASTURIAS

ASTURIAS (ahs-*tour*-ee-ahs) is an intensely green land, dear to its people, both those who live here and the generations that found new homes abroad but still yearn for the verdant beauty, the endearing traditions, and the wonderful foods of their homeland. I've seen how the Asturian song "Asturias, Patria Querida" (Asturias, Beloved Homeland) brings tears to emigrant eyes.

Many Asturian expatriots eventually return to the *patria* (writer José Ortega y Gasset says, ". . . I find in all Asturians hidden just below the surface a rural spirit. Beneath their city ways beats the heart of a peasant"). The enterprising come back with hard-earned money that in decades past was used to build what is still known as the *casa del Indiano*—the house of the one who returned from America (the Indies). You'll see these decaying symbols of wealth and pride all over Asturias.

A delightful Asturian speech pattern that adds the affectionate, diminutive *ín* to many words reflects a special love for the land and for all things Asturian. Thus, one special church near Villaviciosa becomes El Conventín, monkfish is called *pixín*, and an old village woman once told me her cat was *muy buenín*—so very well behaved.

You'd hardly know that Asturias is a major mining region; overwhelming greenness is all you ever seem to see from the rocky coast to the gloriously mountainous and mossy, green-covered interior. I have read that artists have great difficulty capturing the Asturian countryside on canvas, so endless are the shades of green, one ever so subtly different from the next.

Asturias is delineated by the Cantabrian Sea to the north, with its craggy coves and unusually wide and beautiful beaches; the impressive snowcapped peaks of the Picos de Europa to the south; and the Deva and Eo rivers to the east and west, respectively, famed for their trout and salmon. This is one of the rainier regions of Spain, and in the high interior precipitation provides an abun-

---

FOOD AND DRINK OF ASTURIAS

GENERAL
Seafood, salmon, trout, beans

SPECIALTIES
Fabada Asturiana—Asturian bean stew
Fabes con Almejas—clam and bean stew
Pulpo con Patatines—stewed octopus and
  potatoes
Sardinas asadas—grilled sardines
Merluza a la Sidra—hake in cider sauce
Entrecote con Queso Cabrales—steak with blue
  cheese sauce
Arroz con Leche—rice pudding
Casadielles—walnut turnovers
Queso Cabrales—Asturian blue cheese

DRINK
Sidra—hard apple cider

dance of winter snow. The Asturian landscape is dotted with haystacks, and, as in neighboring Galicia, where the climate is similar, *hórreos* are practical for storing grain and potatoes, although here they are made of weather-beaten wood planks instead of stone. Like the Galicians and a product of common Celtic heritage, Asturians play their traditional music at local festivities on bagpipes. Both culturally and scenically, a trip to Asturias blends well with travel in Galicia.

Asturias has a long and eventful past. Stone Age man left evidence of his culture in the many cave paintings of the region, and the early Asturs, for whom the area was named, contributed their stubbornly independent spirit. Invaders had great difficulty dominating the Asturian people; when the Romans had most of Spain under their control, they still had to struggle through years of warfare to subdue the Asturians.

Rome's rewards were the gold and iron of Asturias and the native horse, called the Asturcón, that Asturs held in godlike reverence and that the Romans prized for their power, bravery, and agility (they could apparently climb rocky cliffs like mountain goats). The Asturcón was exported to Rome in such quantity that the word Asturconarius evolved, meaning those who cared for these horses. Writers like Pliny sang the praises of these remarkable animals and commented on the singular white star that marked their foreheads. Descendants of the horses roam the remote interior of Asturias today and also bear the white star, and the heirs of the Asturs continue living in sparsely populated regions of the province, sometimes harnessing river power to turn the wheels that forge and sharpen metal tools.

With a history of defiance and bravery, Asturias in the eighth and ninth centuries was the focal point of resistance to Moslem control. Asturians under the leadership of legendary Don Pelayo were the first to beat back the Moorish invasion.

The Moors had swept through the Iberian Peninsula from south to north in less than a year and brought it under their control. But in 718 Don Pelayo gathered a small band of Asturians and inspired them to revolt (he was supposedly motivated by his desire to avenge an affront to his sister by a Moorish official). The Moors attempted to crush the rebellion but met with fierce resistance, and in 722, just eleven years after the Moors' spectacular entrance into Spain, they were overcome by Don Pelayo's forces at Covadonga. The story is told that the Virgin of Covadonga, whose image was secretly worshipped by the Christians in a remote mountain cave of Covadonga, spurred the Asturians to victory. Another story recounts a terrible storm that flooded the Deva river and drowned the infidels—124,000 of them, according to one account.

It would be many centuries before the Moors were expelled from the rest of the country and Spain became a nation. In the meantime, Don Pelayo, in reward for his achievements, was named the first king of Asturias, and when all of Spain finally returned to Christian rule, Covadonga became a place of pilgrimage and a symbol of the rebirth of Spain (it is said that a good Asturian should make a pilgrimage, on foot, to Covadonga at least once in his lifetime). Don Pelayo is entombed in the same cave where the Virgin of Covadonga is worshipped.

The centuries that followed the Reconquest of Asturias were ones of splendor, both for the region and for such early Asturian kings as Alfonso II and Ramiro I. Asturias became a bastion of Christian culture and an example to those still under Moorish domination. And while the Moors were leaving their imprint on architecture and on the decorative arts in the central and southern portions of Iberia, Asturias, well before the dawn of Romanesque, developed its own peculiar art style.

Based on the classic forms of ancient Rome, modified by Byzantine overtones, and championed by the so-called Master of Naranco (a prolific but nameless craftsman), Asturian architecture featured vaulted ceilings, decorative (nonsupporting) columns, a profusion of stone-carved adornment, in geometric and plant motifs, and elaborate murals in vivid colors. Toward the tenth century some Moorish influence, inevitably, began to creep in.

SAN MIGUEL DE LILLO

Certainly we do not see the exquisite languor, sensuality, and luxury of the Moorish style, but Asturian architecture represented a huge step forward from the severity and austerity of the Visigothic period and had a profound influence on the development of Romanesque.

As other northern regions of Spain gained liberation in the tenth century the Romanesque style began to take hold. As the center of power shifted south to León, Asturias became isolated, and its early artistic flourishing was arrested. Several fine examples of Asturian architecture still stand, however, and they are unique in the world.

Food and drink in Asturias are an integral part of the culture and encompass a diversity of ingredients and preparations. There is wonderful seafood from the coast; I particularly seek out delectable spider crabs (*centollas*), grilled sardines, and a typical dish, *Pulpo con Patatines*—octopus with potatoes. I am also partial to the wonderful salmon and trout from the region's many great rivers, and to desserts like *Casadielles* (walnut-filled turnovers) and rice pudding coated with crackly caramelized sugar that surpasses any other I have tasted. But Asturian gastronomy really revolves around three themes: Cabrales blue cheese (p. 252), *fabes* beans, and *sidra*—Asturian hard cider. Although all three usually appear in the most classic forms—*fabes* in the peerless *Fabada Asturiana* bean stew, Cabrales for tapas, and *sidra* to accompany traditional Asturian foods—these ingredients also appear more creatively: *entrecote* with Cabrales cheese, hake in cider sauce, and a surprisingly delicious bean stew with clams (*Fabes con Almejas*).

Fabada Asturiana has traveled the world over by way of nostalgic Asturian emigrés, but like paella, this stew of dried fava beans, sausage (*chorizo* and Asturian blood sausage), and meats (pig's ear, ham hocks, and salt pork) tastes just right only in Asturias.

I usually think of bean stews as dishes that simmer for an indeterminate time on a back burner. But when we reserved a table at the "temple" of *fabada*, La Máquina, just outside Oviedo, we were asked to arrive promptly. For in Asturias cooking the dried bean is an art in itself; it has to be exactly *en su punto*—buttery soft, but never mushy. *Fabada* is, also like paella, considered a heavy meal suitable only for lunchtime consumption, and most restaurants will not serve it in the evening (La Máquina does not even open for dinner).

Luis Gil Lus of Casa Fermín restaurant in Oviedo also produces a laud-
able *Fabada Asturiana* and relishes the tale of the conquering Moors, pausing
to lunch on *fabada* prepared by the defeated Christians. So hearty and satisfying was the meal that the Moors promptly fell asleep, and the Christians
effortlessly regained control of the city.

Asturias is not a wine-producing region, but the climate is ideal for
growing apples: thus hard cider, which goes back to Celtic times, is the
quintessential Asturian drink.

> Sang a blackbird in an apple tree,
> He who cider does not drink,
> An Asturian cannot be.
>
> *Anonymous*

Drinking cider, like eating *fabada,* has its rules. To observe the ritual of
cider—or *sidrina,* as it is lovingly called—and to understand its congenial
messiness, I can make no better suggestion than a visit to a busy *sidrería* like
El Cantábrico in Oviedo. The pungent aroma of cider fills the air; noise and
confusion reign as barmen and customers raise the green-tinted, unlabeled
cider bottles above their heads and pour it into wide-mouthed glasses the
size of flower vases. The traditional cider pouring pose (back straight, feet
firmly planted on the floor) resembles that of a bullfighter preparing for a
verónica. Bad aim, and the cider ends up on the sawdust-strewn floor—not
an uncommon occurrence, except when in the hands of an expert. And
that's why you will rarely find cider served in elegant restaurants.

The odd rite has its logic: Fermented cider must be aerated for added
sparkle. Despite the large glass size, only an inch is poured, just enough to
consume in one gulp. Any remaining in the glass is discarded, for the cider
"dies" in a matter of seconds. When the cider is accompanied by crusty
bread, pungent Cabrales cheese, and some *chorizo,* slowly simmered in cider,
I cannot think of a more ideal marriage of tastes or a more enjoyable way to
pass the time in Asturias.

THE CAPITAL CITY OF OVIEDO

I don't expect you to fall in love with Oviedo, but you will find it an agree-
able city with many appealing features. An exceptional hotel in a magnificent eighteenth century former hospice-hospital is not a bad beginning.
And eating is excellent too—Ovetenses revere fine food, be it at elegant
restaurants serving creative cookery and refined renditions of regional dishes, at down-to-earth restaurants providing hearty foods from the land or
fresh fish from the sea, or at the casual tapas bars that proliferate in the capital. University students go for the last, congregating by the hundreds on the
Calle del Rosal in the Old Quarter, inside and in front of countless bars and
taverns (called *chigres* in Asturias). This is the city of *bocaditos,* miniature
rolls filled with anything from squid or ham to potato and vegetable salad
(*ensaladilla*).

I think this Old Quarter of Oviedo, beautifully and lovingly conserved, is one of the most delightful in Spain. Lively by day, at night its palaces, seignorial houses, university buildings (the university began here in the sixteenth century), and picturesque squares (especially the Plaza Daoiz y Velarde) take on a somber and mysterious mood.

Among Oviedo's other strong points is the cathedral's splendid Cámara Santa, extravagantly endowed with gold- and jewel-encrusted treasures. It was constructed under Alfonso II, the ninth century "Great Builder" of Asturias, who set out to emulate the grandeur of Toledo and who transferred the court from Cangas de Onís to the new capital of Oviedo. Here, in the foothills of Monte Naranco (also called Ovetao), a monastery had existed since the eighth century. He built sumptuous Santullano and several other churches that no longer exist. This was a ruler who chose luxury as a symbol of power, lavishing marble and a wealth of other decorative elements on all his projects.

Despite the briefness of the seven-year reign of Ramiro I, Alfonso's successor, his accomplishments were also grand and of lasting import. He claimed victory over the Moors at the decisive Battle of Clavijo (p. 144), and elegance reached new heights under his rule. A summer palace (today the church of Santa María) was built on Mount Naranco, the likes of which had never before been seen; San Miguel de Lillo rose nearby; and Santa Cristina de Lena appeared south of the city. All were showered with expensive and profuse artistic detail. The next king, Alfonso III, continued his predecessors' building programs, adding such great works as San Salvador de Valdediós.

Artistic treasures from these early monarchs are preserved in the Cámara Santa of the cathedral, but they have suffered more than their fair share of vicissitudes. The chamber was demolished by a bomb during the Spanish Civil War, and surprisingly the treasures survived (as did the Cámara's exceptional portal. Then in 1977 a daring jewel heist left many pieces defaced or dismantled. Most of the missing gems have since been recovered and the works restored, and although the collection is small, its rarity and its artistic worth make it priceless.

Because of the ambitious building projects of the early Asturian monarchs, who were based in Oviedo, you will find important monuments of Asturian architecture in the environs of the city. For their unusual style and for their interest as precursors of Romanesque, you should not miss seeing at least some of them.

SEEING OVIEDO

CATHEDRAL AND CÁMARA SANTA   The cathedral, begun in 1388, is of Gothic style and has a magnificent wood-sculpted sixteenth century altar covered in gilt and polychrome painting. The cathedral's only tower was added in the sixteenth century.

The **CÁMARA SANTA** predates the cathedral but was incorporated into it. Built in the ninth century, reformed in the twelfth, and reconstructed after the Civil War bombing, it holds several of the world's great jeweled creations, of overwhelming richness and detail, studded with priceless gems and encrusted with gold: La Cruz de Los Ángeles (ninth century), a cross miraculously created, it is said, by two angels, thus its name; La Cruz de la Victoria (tenth century), which supposedly encloses the original cross Don Pelayo victoriously raised at Covadonga; the Caja de Ágatas, a gold- and agate-inlaid box of the tenth century; and the ninth century Arca Santa—a cedar chest that was coated and minutely carved in silver in the eleventh century to become a prized work of early Romanesque art. It once guarded valuable relics salvaged when Toledo fell to the Moors—those objects are now separately on display. The exceptional portal of the Cámara Santa is framed with twelfth century statues of saints, smiling and in conversation with one another, in the style of the Pórtico de la Gloria of the cathedral in Santiago.

MUSEO ARQUEOLÓGICO   Examples of works of pre-Romanesque Asturian art from Santa María de Naranco, San Miguel de Lillo, and from other monuments in the province.

CAMPO DE SAN FRANCISCO   A park of grand proportions in the center of Oviedo, densely shaded and a very popular pedestrian thoroughfare.

OLD QUARTER   See text.

STAYING IN OVIEDO

HOTEL DE LA RECONQUISTA   Gil de Jaz 16   tel. (985) 24 11 00   A former hospice of the eighteenth century in Baroque style, arranged around a huge central courtyard. Elegant and deluxe. (Expensive.)

GRAN HOTEL ESPAÑA   Jovellanos 2   tel. (985) 22 05 96   Conveniently located downtown and recently restored to its former elegance, it is an alternative but by no means a substitute for the above-mentioned Reconquista. (Moderate–expensive.)

EATING IN OVIEDO

RESTAURANTS

CASA FERMÍN   San Francisco 8   tel. (985) 21 64 52   Luis Gil Lus, one of the foremost promoters of Asturian cuisine, has created an ambiance of great elegance and style in which you will find well-prepared creative cooking, but never at the expense of traditional Asturian dishes, like *Merluza a la Sidra* (hake in cider sauce), *Entrecote con Queso Cabrales* (steak with blue cheese), *Fabada* (one of the city's best), and outstanding rice pudding. (Moderate–expensive.)

TRASCORRALES   Plaza de Trascorrales 19   tel. (985) 22 24 41   Decorated with exquisite taste and set in one of Oviedo's landmark houses on the quaint Plaza de Trascorrales. Fine food in nouvelle style, without overlooking traditional fare. (Moderate–expensive.)

LA GOLETA   Covadonga 32   tel. (985) 21 38 47   Among Oviedo's most popular restaurants, specializing in all the great seafood of the Asturian coast. (Moderate–expensive.)

THE BEST OF OVIEDO'S TAPAS BARS

EL CANTÁBRICO   Río San Pedro 11   For Asturian cider and tapas in lively surroundings (see text).

CABO PEÑAS   Melquíades Álvarez 24   Big and busy, this is a fashionable place for a large selection of tapas.

MARCHICA   Doctor Casal 8   Although there is also a dining room here, I prefer the tapas and the ambiance at the bar.

LA GRAN TABERNA   Eusebio González Abascal   A soccer fan was obviously in charge of décor at this popular tavern, serving such tapas as garlic spareribs, chicken in cider, and *empanadillas*.

◆ Along the Calle del Rosal are many crowded bars catering to university students. The specialty is *bocaditos*, little round rolls with a variety of fillings.

SHOPPING

ESCANDA   Jovellanos 5   A good place to find the typical black Asturian pottery made in the village of Llamas de Moura.

ꝅISITING THE ENVIRONS OF OVIEDO

SANTA MARÍA DE NARANCO   Summer palace of Ramiro I, just two kilometers north of Oviedo at Mount Naranco, later converted to a church. A rare and beautiful example of ninth century civil architecture, the structure was far more luxurious, elegant, and artistic than anything else of the time. Spacious airy reception hall and many original and surprising design elements: columns heavily carved in rope designs and rounded arches—embedded in the walls or free-standing—finished with Roman-style disks and carved with oriental motifs.

SAN MIGUEL DE LILLO   Built next to the above and in a similar Byzantine-influenced style during the same period of Ramiro I. The church is too narrow in proportion to its height because two-thirds of the building collapsed centuries ago. The stone carvings, particularly the circus scenes at the entrance, are unusual.

SANTA CRISTINA DE LENA (Vega del Rey)   Built under Ramiro I, here is an intact assemblage of double arches and columns (known as an iconostasis) that were used in early Christian times to elevate and separate the altar from the body of the church and from the congregation. To get here, go to Pola de Lena south of Oviedo and follow the signs. Ask for the key at the last house.

SANTULLANO   Also called San Julián de los Prados, this unusually large ninth century church, to the left side of the Gijón-Avilés thruway as you exit Oviedo, has uncustomary architectural and decorative elements: three naves that form three altars and walls covered with frescoes in geometric patterns and in trompe l'oeil designs that originally covered every inch of wall space (only a small portion has survived; the rest has been partially re-created).

SAN SALVADOR DE VALDEDIÓS   Commonly called El Conventín, this ninth century church on the road to Villaviciosa once adjoined a palace where Asturian king Alfonso III the Great spent his last years. It is done in the Asturian manner—three arched aisles, wall frescoes, and a touch of Moorish influence in the horseshoe-arched windows with delicate filigree. The Romanesque porch on the right side of the church is the first of its kind, a precursor of those that would appear more than a century later.

GARGANTA DE TEVERGA   Southwest of Oviedo, on the road to León by way of Puerto de Ventana, this gorge is especially impressive in the stretch known as Peñas Juntas (Close Cliffs), where two vertical sheets of rock come so near to each other that there is just room for a narrow river and a small road to pass through.

TARAMUNDI: COMMENDABLE EXPERIMENT IN RURAL RESTORATION

The regional government of Asturias has undertaken an ambitious program to promote tourism, especially in remote inland areas where most visitors don't venture and the living for country folk is slim. A restored manor house in the mountains near Panes and a castle at Salas are part of this project. But Taramundi is far more enterprising: Accommodations are first-class, and local crafts have been given a new lease on life, recapturing and preserving a heritage that was on the verge of extinction. It is just the kind of out-of-the-way place that so often attracts me.

While quite close to the sea, Taramundi, a village of dark stone houses with slate roofs, is in one of the most untouched and unknown areas of Asturias. It is a region of high mountains and deep narrow valleys named Los Oscos, after the ancient Oscans of Italy, who at one time populated these mountains. The Romans mined gold and iron here and captured the native horses for export to Rome (p. 241). They left behind their iron-forging skills.

A craftsman in nearby Mousende, Amancio Calvín Mon, hones knives on a lathe powered by river water, just as the Romans used to do; in Taramundi a young country woman, Pilar Quintana, weaves—a craft handed down by her forefathers—and her small shop sells exceptional handwoven rugs, fabrics, and wall hangings. I love the hanging I bought—so primitively conceived, with thick hand-spun wool in earth tones and incorporating pieces of slate, just like the slate of the rooftops. And in Teijós a waterwheel that once made the village self-sufficient harnesses river power as it has for a thousand years. Villagers can mill grains and power a hammer to forge iron (it is said that the nails to build the Spanish Armada were made here).

We enjoyed several restful days in Taramundi, taking a short ride north to the beach, and on another occasion, a road to the south through the mountains where the Asturcón horses freely graze, untouched by civilization (we could also have gone hiking, horseback riding or jeep riding, and fishing in the Turia river). In the tiny village of Santa Eulalia we happened upon a delightful inn, **MESÓN LA CERCA,** where we sat under an *hórreo,* surrounded by squawking chickens, and inexpensively lunched on cheese, salad, eggs, and perfectly fried *calamares.*

STAYING IN TARAMUNDI

HOTEL LA RECTORAL   tel. (985) 63 40 60 (moderate–expensive)   A country manor on a rise commanding sensational views of green rolling hills and haystacks. Rooms are spacious. Ask for a ground-floor room with terrace, the ideal place to sample a wonderful breakfast of rolls, homemade preserves, and sponge cake (heavenly, spread with apple jam). A well-appointed dining room (reserve the corner window table for best views) has excellent food based on local produce: Cabrales blue cheese, *Fabada, Fabes con Almejas* (beans with clams), rice pudding, *chuletón* (steak), as well as fish from the Cantabrian Sea.

◆ Roads are not well marked, so carry a good map (the hotel provides a detailed local road map). Visit nearby Mousende and Teijós, venture into the Oscos mountains to see the horses on the road to Santa Eulalia, and eat at **MESÓN LA CERCA** in Santa Eulalia. Another option is to take a craft tour by jeep organized by the hotel.

𝒱ISITING ASTURIAS

The Coast

CASTROPOL   The first town on the Asturian side of the Ribadeo estuary, built on a promontory. At waterside is a seawall and a thickly shaded walkway that follows the perimeter of the town.

LUARCA   The Negro river snakes through this well-cared-for white town, dividing it in two parts. The riverbanks and the seven bridge spans that cross the river are lined with geraniums in brightly painted pots. Relax over drinks or tapas at **MESÓN DE LA MAR** at the harbor entrance.

CUDILLERO   The town is built on a steep incline that rises abruptly from the tiny port. There are many bars to sample locally caught seafood.

PLAYA DE LA CONCHA DE ARTEDO, as its name suggests, is a beautiful shell-shaped rocky cove more than one kilometer long, enclosed by cliffs and a mountainous green landscape. At **CASA MIGUEL** we had a great lunch of *bocartes* (little fried fish), grilled shrimp, salad, and cider.

GIJÓN   The largest city in Asturias and its industrial capital. It has a good beach, a small peaceful fishing port tucked into the city, and a nice Old Quarter where seafood bars like **EL TIBURÓN** and **LA DÁRSENA** are concentrated and specialize in grilled sardines, cider, and marinated mussels.
CASA VICTOR restaurant, Carmen 11   tel. (985) 35 00 93, has some of the best-prepared fish in the city. (Moderate.)
PARADOR MOLINO VIEJO   Avenida Torcuato Fernández Miranda s/n   tel. (985) 37 05 11, is a converted water mill (there used to be many in Gijón) in the Isabel la Católica park and close to the beach. (Moderate–expensive.)

TAZONES   I come to this port village, built up into the hillside, to feast at **BAR LA NANSA** on *nécora* crabs; sweet and delicate giant *centollas* (spider crabs—be sure to order only Spanish *centollas*, not the less expensive and inferior French imports); and *salpicón* of monkfish. (Moderate.)
♦ A small cider bodega, **LES MESTES,** at the entrance to town, makes cider the old-fashioned way (ask for owner Federico Barro Rodríguez at his bar across the road).
PLAYA DE RODILES, enclosed by lush green mountains, is one of Spain's finest beaches.
MIRADOR DEL FITO provides exceptional views from a mountain lookout of the Asturian coastline to the north and a spectacular panorama of the Picos de Europa to the south.
♦ Descendants of the ancient Asturcón horses are seen in this area.

VILLAVICIOSA   Because of a navigational error, the young emperor Charles V first touched Spanish soil here in 1715. (Tazones, at the mouth of the Villaviciosa estuary, also takes credit for this event.) There are several twelfth century Romanesque churches, but I particularly like **SAN JUAN DE AMANDI** and its unusual semicircular columned porch, in Amandi, just outside of Villaviciosa.
♦ Sparkling cider, low in alcohol, sweeter and more carbonated than the typical hard cider of Asturias, is sometimes used as a substitute for champagne. It is made here at **EL GAITERO,** a large factory that you can visit.

RIBADESELLA   The name refers to this town's location on the banks (*ribera*) of the Río Sella at its exit to the sea. There are many grand houses from another era—tall and awkward with pointy roofs, towers, turrets, and gazebos (some are straight out of Charles Addams's cartoons), and the river gently winds around the town to the open sea. Potentially a great vacation spot but presently in need of refurbishing, it is in the meantime a good base for coastal excursions.
GRAN HOTEL DEL SELLA   Ricargo Cangas 17   tel. (985) 86 01 50, in a former palace (with modern additions) is beautifully set over the beach on a jetty between the river and the sea. (Moderate–expensive; pool.)
♦ The first Saturday in August, the International Competition of the Descent of the Sella in Canoe takes place. Canoeing is popular on the river throughout the summer and fall.

CUEVA DE TITO BUSTILLO, with its prehistoric paintings, is nearby (see box, p. 256).

PLAYA DE LA ISLA is so called because a small island breaks the curve of these three beaches, separated by large boulders. Magnificent.

LLANES   This is a bustling summer resort with a diminutive port—its entry is hardly one boat wide. You can try the spiny lobster, a specialty of Llanes, at **LA MARINA** restaurant, overlooking the harbor entrance.

MENHIR DE PEÑA TÚ, near Vidiago in a beautiful mountain setting, is a megalithic monument with Bronze Age carvings and is thought to be an idol of some sort. There is also a human figure (prehistoric) painted in red. It's a hefty climb to get there.

PLAYA DE LA FRANCA, west of the Río Deva's exit to the sea, is a lovely beach in a small cove guarded by boulders on either side.

The Interior

COVADONGA   A famous shrine to the Virgin of Covadonga (affection-ately called La Santina), who aided Asturians in the fight against the Moors, has made this a well-known place of pilgrimage. These majestic, tightly enclosed green mountains in the foothills of the Picos de Europa were an ideal location for the Christians to lie low, waiting for an opportunity to reconquer Spain. See the statue of the Virgin in the original grotto, a site dwarfed by an elaborate religious complex, incongruous amid the intense greenness of the countryside. In the basilica, donations to the Virgin include a splendid diamond-studded crown.

HOTEL PELAYO   tel. (985) 84 60 00, is an old-fashioned and somewhat depressing place but the only option if you plan to stay overnight. (Moderate.)

◆ Drive into the national parkland of Covadonga on a mountainous road of stunning scenery. Green gives way to rocky peaks as you approach the glacial lakes of Ercina and Enol, where cows graze in broad fields against a snowy backdrop.

CANGAS DE ONÍS   Here was the first court of the Asturian kings and the first capital of reconquered Spain. A beautiful medieval stone bridge is at the entrance to town.

◆ The **DESFILADERO DE BEYOS** leads you to the southern side of the Picos de Europa, exiting at Riaño in León, where the landscape is suddenly Castilian.

SALAS   Throughout history this has been an important town (one of the pilgrimage routes to Santiago passed here), evident in the monumental Old Quarter of palaces and noble homes.

CASTILLO DE VALDÉS SALAS   tel. (985) 83 10 37, a restored medieval castle is today a hotel run by the Asturian government. (Inexpensive.)

TARAMUNDI   Remote village in the primitive region of Los Oscos (see text).

CABRALES VALLEY   See "The Imposing Picos de Europa."

PANES   See "Seeing the Picos de Europa."

THE IMPOSING PICOS DE EUROPA

WE HAVE SPENT wonderful times in the high mountains and deep valleys of the Picos de Europa and have been struck every time by their awesome beauty. The Picos de Europa are in some ways even more impressive than the Pyrenees, for they are concentrated in a small, self-contained area—just 312 square miles—of densely assembled, bare jagged peaks, perpetually snow-covered. Three massifs joined as one, with heights of more than 8,000 feet, the Picos de Europa have been called a geological explosion, a wall created by the hand of God, a mountain climber's dream, the Spanish Alps. This concentration of mountains in virtual perpendicular creates the narrowest and deepest of gorges and powerful flows of icy river waters. And then, in striking contrast, deeply green valleys surround the peaks on all sides and form an amphitheater.

The Picos de Europa, just twenty-five kilometers from the Cantabrian Sea, converge at the borders of three provinces—Cantabria, Asturias, and León—but my favorite places to stay and explore are in the first two, and for this reason I have planted my discussion squarely in the center of this Asturias-Cantabria chapter.

We love to spend our days along the banks of the Deva and Cares rivers. Only the locals who intimately know the flora and fauna ever seem to catch the rivers' famous trout and salmon, but no matter. What counts is casting the line, relaxing, and enjoying nature to its fullest. We picnic, incorporating into our menu earthy Cabrales blue cheese that is made here, take long walks, ride jeeps into the heart of the peaks, and have a field day with our cameras. The "big one that got away" can always be found on local restaurant menus, along with other appealing mountain specialties like the chickpea stew *Cocido Montañés*, most welcome on cool mountain evenings.

We can't take our car through the peaks—only circle around them, cross in a jeep, or hike to the other side—so we like to stay at two different places that bring us closest to where we most love to be: one on the Asturian side in an idyllic setting near Panes, where the Cares and Deva rivers meet, and the other to the south in the Cantabrian sector at Fuente Dé.

Fuente Dé is in the Liébana valley, enclosed on all sides by lofty mountains. From here a sheer cliff, Peña Vieja, suddenly and dramatically rises before our eyes, bringing the road on which we have come to an abrupt end. A cable car takes us still higher—another 2,500 feet in three minutes flat—in an almost vertical path following the face of the mountain. At the summit, noticeably cooler, I feel as though I'm looking down at the world from the heavens.

When a mountaineering spirit overcomes us, we hike an invigorating three kilometers through a lunarlike setting to the Aliva mountain refuge and feast on fried eggs, potatoes, and *chorizo* sausage. Sated, we sometimes return to Fuente Dé in a hired jeep, touring the peaks along the way and perhaps crossing through the heart of the mountains to the remote cheese-producing village of Sotres, in Asturias, on the other side.

Another favorite area in the Picos de Europa is in Niserias near the Asturian village of Panes. Here life revolves around the rivers more than the peaks. At the bar of Casa Julián, a small family-operated hotel on the Cares river, the talk is of lures, flies, hatches, and fishing poles. Day's end finds fishermen in the bar trading success stories (a magnificent salmon stretched out on a table in front of us, tagged and weighed, was proof that these were not merely tall tales).

From our base in Niserias, we drive past the town of Arenas de Cabrales toward the highest mountains of the range on a road that ends in Sotres. My first visit to Sotres was to track down the source of Cabrales cheese for a newspaper article I was preparing. For although this earthy local blue cheese, named after the Cabrales valley, which in turn takes its name from the *cabras* (goats) that graze here, possesses an almost cultish status in Spain, it remains a cottage industry. The cheese is produced by age-old methods in country kitchens and in isolated mountain caves, some accessible only by burro. Sotres, fortunately, can be reached by car.

We had no idea the ride would be so scenically sensational. Before climbing into the high mountains we stopped to fortify ourselves at a bar at the Poncebo bridge, then left the car and took a footpath that followed the cliff's edge, high above the softly green-tinged Río Cares that flows between two walls of stone. We so enjoyed the astonishing beauty of the route that we might have walked the entire twelve kilometers to Caín, on the other face of the peaks in León, but thought better of it (you can, however, hire a jeep in Poncebo or begin at Caín and travel partway by car—see **POSADA DE VALDEÓN**). Back at the bridge we set out for Sotres, at over 3,400 feet, the highest village of the range.

The road winds through a landscape of almost fairyland beauty. Rugged yet gently moss-covered cliffs cut by deep, narrow gorges carved by the clear green rivers, Cares and Duje, produce one stunning view after another. The road ends suddenly in Sotres, a tiny village of dark-stone cottages with rust tile roofs.

Hortensia Fernández González, an enterprising villager who makes Cabrales cheese, spends another part of her day spinning lamb's wool and knitting it into thick, rugged socks and sweaters, which she sells to visitors. She has become somewhat of a local celebrity, interviewed on Spanish radio and television, since I mentioned her name in the *New York Times*. Yet she continues to make just one cheese a day from the milk of the few cows, goats, and sheep that belong to her. Everyone in the village fortunate to own a few milk-bearing animals also makes Cabrales cheese. Hortensia's stock is stored in a cool limestone cave, where it ripens for two or three months. It becomes naturally blue and is then wrapped in leaves until consumed.

We like to purchase a whole cheese from Hortensia, knowing full well that unless we quickly consume it or find a cool place to keep it while we travel, the "pestiferous fragrance," as writer Pérez Galdós put it, will prove overwhelming (it's simpler, but not as much fun, to buy the cheese right before returning home in a Madrid gourmet shop like Mallorca).

When finally the sight of another lofty peak loses its impact and our senses go into overload, we know it is time to move on. Having the sea so close affords us an immediate scenic contrast.

SEEING THE PICOS DE EUROPA

POSADA DE VALDEÓN   On the León side of the peaks, this village has views around it that are stupendous. There are good tapas at the bar Picos de Europa on the main square.

◆ From here a very narrow road continues to the spectacular viewpoint Mirador del Tombo, and, for you fearless drivers (otherwise, walk), on to **CAÍN** and the beginning of the Río Cares gorge. It is one of the most breathtaking routes I have ever traveled. You can continue on foot to Poncebo, across the mountains.

POTES   A pretty mountain village in a lovely setting in the Liébana valley.
SANTO TORIBIO DE LIÉBANA monastery, eighth century but with later additions, is nearby and guards what is said to be a large piece of the Original Cross (Lignum Crucis). The eighth century monk Beato lived here and wrote his religious works on which magnificent miniature paintings were later based.
SANTA MARÍA DE LEBEÑA, between Potes and Panes, dates from the tenth century and shows Moorish influence, most unusual in this region of Spain.

COSGAYA   A small village in typical mountain style next to the Río Deva in the Liébana valley, not far from Fuente Dé.
HOTEL DEL OSO   Carretera de Espinama s/n   tel. (942) 73 04 18 (inexpensive; pool), offers good accommodations in a rustic setting, and you can eat very well at its restaurant—try especially the mountain stew, *Cocido Lebaniego*, steaks, and chops, all in superabundant portions. (Moderate.)

FUENTE DÉ   This cluster of houses, more than 3,000 feet above the sea in a natural amphitheater, is the departure point for mountain excursions—hiking, by jeep (inquire at the parador), or by cable car.
PARADOR RÍO DEVA   tel. (942) 73 00 01, at the foot of the cable car, is the best place to stay in this area. (Moderate.)
REFUGIO DE ALIVA   tel. (942) 76 09 99, in the heart of the Picos de Europa, offers simple accommodations and hearty food. (Inexpensive.)

SOTRES   An isolated mountain village where Cabrales blue cheese is made (See text).

PANES   Not a distinguished town, but nearby are two hotels, either of which makes a good base for trips into the peaks (see text) or to the nearby coast.

CASA JULIÁN   Carretera Panes-Cangas de Onís, at Niserias   tel. (985) 41 41 79, has extremely simple accommodations on the banks of the Cares river (ask for a room facing the river) in a peaceful setting. (Inexpensive.) Proprietor Julián is most gracious, and the restaurant, in the capable hands of wife Vicentina, produces excellent uncomplicated food like grilled trout and marinated pork, baked salmon, fresh vegetables, *fabada,* and Asturian rice pudding. (Inexpensive–moderate.)

LA TAHONA   in Besnes (in the hills above Niserias near Allés)   tel. (985) 41 42 49, is a hotel sponsored by the local government occupying an old country house in a tranquil environment. (Moderate.)

NARANJO DE BULNES   One of the highest peaks, well over 8,000 feet, it is readily distinguishable from many vantage points by its straight sides and almost rectangular shape (the best view is from the Pozo de la Oración, Well of Prayer, near the town of Poo). It presents a formidable challenge to experienced mountain climbers.

COVADONGA   See "Visiting Asturias."

NOTEWORTHY GORGES—since roads in this area tend to trace the natural course of rivers, many follow mountain gorges. Some of the most spectacular are: **LA HERMIDA,** fifteen kilometers long and opening into the Liébana Valley (". . . they call this a gorge . . . they should call it the Hermida esophagus, because when you pass it you feel devoured by the earth": Benito Pérez Galdós); the **SELLA,** which follows the river of the same name (especially the sector of Los Beyos between Cangas de Onís and Oseja de Sajambre); and the **CARES,** an awesome route to follow on foot or by jeep (see text).

◆ Best chances for warm weather and fair skies in the Picos de Europa are in summer and through September and early October.

THE PROVINCE AND REGION OF CANTABRIA

CANTABRIA, (cahn-*tah*-bree-a) once considered a province of Castilla, is today an autonomous region, touching Castile to the south, the Basque Country to the east, and Asturias at its western border. Traditionally referred to as La Montaña, Cantabria is aptly named for its mountainous interior, comprising some of the most spectacular scenery in all of Spain, and for its rocky coastline, considerably softened by long, deep, and gentle beaches (there are no fewer than seventy-two of them, covering more than thirty kilometers). This is one of Spain's rainier regions, but its luxuriant verdure and generally moderate temperatures (except in the high mountains, perpetually covered with snow) more than compensate for some lack of sunshine.

Cantabria has four mountain areas; three of them—Pas, Miera, and Alto Campoo—are certainly of great beauty (Tres Mares in Alto Campoo, in fact, has one of the most astonishing views in Spain), but for me none compare with the wonder and the pleasures of the Picos de Europa, in many ways even more enjoyable and exciting than the great Spanish Pyrenees.

Cantabria, when it was associated with Castile, was that region's only exit to the sea. Trade from the interior flowed north to the port of Santander. Because of this long relationship—and also because the kings repopulated Cantabria with Castilians after the Reconquest—the people of Cantabria have something of the austere Castilian character. For your travel purposes, however, I think Cantabria belongs with Asturias or the Basque Country.

The main economic riches of Cantabria—fishing, cattle, and agriculture—reflect on the region's cuisine. Along the coast eating centers on seafood (especially sardines, anchovy, striped bass, red snapper, and porgy), and in the interior on meat and dairy products. *Cocido Montañés*, a hearty meat-and-chickpea stew similar to the *cocido* of Castile (see box, p. 34) but adapted to the province's produce, is a characteristic dish. As a

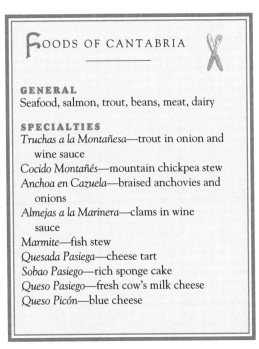

FOODS OF CANTABRIA

GENERAL
Seafood, salmon, trout, beans, meat, dairy

SPECIALTIES
Truchas a la Montañesa—trout in onion and wine sauce
Cocido Montañés—mountain chickpea stew
Anchoa en Cazuela—braised anchovies and onions
Almejas a la Marinera—clams in wine sauce
Marmite—fish stew
Quesada Pasiega—cheese tart
Sobao Pasiego—rich sponge cake
Queso Pasiego—fresh cow's milk cheese
Queso Picón—blue cheese

major milk producer, Cantabria makes excellent cheeses, such as *Queso Picón*, a blue cheese similar to Cabrales, and a fresh cheese called *Queso Pasiego*, from which a cheese tart, *Quesada Pasiega*, is made. This dessert and *Sobao Pasiego*, a cake rich in butter and eggs that is at its best when dunked in thick hot chocolate, are traditionally made in Vega de Pas and are most popular during the Easter holidays. Vineyards do not adapt to the climate of Cantabria, and you will find few native wines.

My husband and I come to Cantabria mainly to spend time in the Picos de Europa and to explore high mountain villages of great character and beauty, but we also like to cruise the coastline whenever possible and pass through the capital city of Santander. Not far from the coast are two places that are recurrently in my thoughts: the caves of Altamira (Cuevas de Altamira) and the village of Santillana del Mar.

THE LIVING PRESENCE OF PREHISTORIC MAN IN THE CAVES OF ALTAMIRA

The mountainous terrain of Cantabria and Asturias—especially in areas not far from the coast, where temperatures are moderate—provided cave shelters for Stone Age man. And there is clear evidence of the existence of prehistoric societies, as seen through the artwork and the tools that have been found. But the cave paintings of Altamira are light-years beyond the simple and primitively sketched line drawings found in other caves, and their discovery in the nineteenth century by the young daughter of a local scholar, Marcelino S. de Sautuola, who squeezed her way through the small entrance, revolutionized scientific thought on the origin and development of man. These were clearly works produced by a people of uncanny ability.

Nothing you may read or hear about the caves of Altamira quite prepares you for the sensitive artistry, the sophistication, the elegance, the spirituality of the cave paintings of Altamira, executed some 15,000 to 20,000 years ago and considered the most important in the world from the prehistoric Magdalenian period. In years past, visiting Altamira was as simple as paying the price of admission. But growing fears of temperature changes and carbon-monoxide damage have led to severely restricted access; the sight is so extraordinary, however, that I urge you to make the necessary effort to arrange the visit (see p. 257).

When I entered that small cave chamber one drizzly August day, the

EXPLORING OTHER CAVES IN CANTABRIA AND ASTURIAS

CANTABRIA

CUEVA DEL CASTILLO, in Puente Viesgo, is important for the human element it introduces—the hand of a prehistoric inhabitant is imprinted on a wall and is thought to have some magical significance.

ASTURIAS

CUEVA DEL PINDAL, west of San Vicente de la Barquera near Pimiango, is of special interest because among other animal depictions is one of an elephant (a mammal that soon after became extinct in Spain), and the animal's heart is clearly drawn.

CUEVA DE TITO BUSTILLO, just outside Ribadesella in Ardines, has a chamber (reached through a cave that is itself beautiful) filled with paintings, done with much of the skill and technique of Altamira but not nearly as well preserved. Most of the paintings are only faintly defined, but you can make out several horses (a large one is shaded in deep charcoal tones), running deer, a reindeer, and a stag. Some are outlined in black; others are colored in red, purple, and earth tones.

magnitude of the beauty I witnessed shattered my notion of prehistoric man as a being of limited artistic skill and intellectual capacity. Here within this relatively inaccessible chamber were dozens of animals (there are another fifty or so elsewhere in the cave), all the animals that the prehistoric people of Cantabria knew well and hunted for food, many of them life-size. They were exuberantly crowded together in a kind of tableau. I saw a bison at rest, comfortably curled up, and deer, horses, goats, bulls, and wild boar, walking, running, galloping, charging, and leaping—like a motion picture passing before my eyes.

All the animals are anatomically precise, drawn so that their bodies conform to the curves, protuberances, and undulations of the cave walls and ceiling. The effect is three-dimensional and very alive, in striking contrast to the awkward, flat, and somewhat childlike paintings produced by many later civilizations. The painting has delicate nuances of texture and shading, a result, I later discovered, of mixing natural pigments and iron oxides and skillfully applying them with pointed sticks, applicators of lichen and moss, brushes, and fingers, or by blowing the paint through tubes. Thousands of years later, the subtle shadings of Altamira art became a feature of such Spanish artists as Zurbarán and Ribera and was known as *claroscuro* in Spain, *chiaroscuro* in Italy.

Altamira is sometimes referred to as the Sistine Chapel of prehistoric art because the artistic skill, the difficulty of painting in a contorted posture, and the problem of achieving proper perspective at such close range are all similar.

> . . . we are confronted with nothing less than the birth of art. . . . From this instant, the history of civilization began. . . .
> José Camón Aznar

TIPS ON VISITING ALTAMIRA

Several months in advance of a visit, you must apply for permission to the Centro de Investigación y Museo de Altamira, Santillana del Mar, tel. (942) 81 80 05. I have been told that a well-placed tip at the door or a last-minute cancellation sometimes gets you in, but I certainly wouldn't count on it. An alternative, definitely not on par with seeing the original, is to see the exact copy of the cave paintings at the Museo Arqueológico in Madrid.

SANTILLANA DEL MAR

A medieval town arrested in time, a treasure without equal in Spain, Santillana del Mar is just minutes from Altamira, and I cannot think of two more rewarding visits. The entire town of Santillana is a national monument, ensuring that no stone be touched. What I love is the way the streets guard the silence of centuries; there are no cars, and the people of Santillana continue to live simple lives of centuries past. At day's end townsmen return from field and pasture leading their cows or oxen pulling carts piled high with hay. They follow the cobbled main street along which a stream flows into a fountain. There the animals pause to drink before retiring to barns that occupy ground floors of village houses.

Santillana was born at the time of the Reconquest, when a monastery was built to guard the remains of martyred Santa Juliana (from her contracted name comes Santillana). Pilgrims arrived in increasing numbers, and a town grew up around the church. Although the monastery eventually disappeared, replaced by the fine Romanesque Collegiata we see today, Santillana continued to grow in importance and privilege. Its aristocracy gained prominence, sustaining noble houses and palaces conspicuously emblazoned with elaborate coats of arms. But power struggles ensued, and Santillana languished, leaving it as we see it today.

There's nothing quite like the sense of eternity created by evening in Santillana. Stay a night, walk its quiet, dimly lit streets, and reap the full flavor of this very special village.

SEEING THE VILLAGE OF SANTILLANA DEL MAR

Santillana is small and meant for walking. See the medieval seignorial homes and, most especially, the Romanesque **COLEGIATA,** built in the twelfth century. Over its entrance is a small statue of Santa Juliana, and inside the church is her tomb. The capitals in the cloister are skillfully carved and unusually beautiful (for more information about Santillana, pass by the tourist office in the Plaza Mayor).

STAYING IN SANTILLANA DEL MAR

PARADOR GIL BLAS   Plaza Ramón Pelayo 11   tel. (942) 81 80 00   An old manor house beautifully set on the town plaza. It is named for the fictitious Cantabrian Gil Blas, protagonist of an eighteenth century French novel by Alain-René Lesage. (Moderate–expensive.) Your best bet is to dine at the parador or at **ALTAMIRA**   Cantón 1   tel. (942) 81 80 25, serving Cantabrian specialties. (Inexpensive.)

THE CAPITAL CITY OF SANTANDER

Santander is located in a privileged position on the Cantabrian Sea at the mouth of a wide bay of gentle, sandy beaches that at low tide join into one uninterrupted expanse. There is a soft look to the landscape—hazy muted colors, almost like an Impressionist painting—created by the misty sea air.

Santander is a city whose life now and always has revolved around the sea, and it was the sea that caused the city to prosper. Romans made it an important port; in the sixteenth century the wool and wheat of Castile were exported from here to northern Europe (this when Santander was still a part of Castile), and in the eighteenth and nineteenth centuries the city carried on trade with America. And yet Santander never evolved into a great city. Attention was concentrated on the port in earlier times, and in recent decades on the beaches, but never on the city itself.

At the beginning of this century Spanish monarchs summered here, and the aristocracy followed. Santander vied with San Sebastián as the north's most fashionable and elegant resort (the two cities are similarly situated along beautiful beaches) but eventually lost out in popularity. When the monarchy fell, the Franco government chose San Sebastián as its summer headquarters. That blow was followed in 1941 by a devastating windstorm, fueling a fire that destroyed much of the city. Fortunately Santander was intelligently rebuilt, and although there is little left of historical importance, we see today a beautiful city of wide boulevards, promenades, and lush gardens encircling the bay.

Santander has gradually regained its city spirit. The Menéndez y Pelayo summer university, named after the city's native son, Marcelino Menéndez y Pelayo, a literary critic and prolific writer of philosophical works, attracts students from all over the world; the summer music and dance festivals are of international fame; the Hotel Real, now restored, has recovered its regal look; and one of Spain's most beautiful and highly regarded restaurants is nearby, along with many other restaurants and numerous tapas bars. Certainly if you come to Santander for a day or two, to attend the music and dance festivals or to relax at the beach, you can once more do so in style.

SEEING SANTANDER

PALACIO DE LA MAGDALENA   Situated in isolated splendor on a peninsula of the Santander bay and surrounded by gardens, this turn-of-the-century Tudor-style palace was built by popular subscription and presented to King Alfonso XIII. Today it is the site of the summer university.

PLAYA DE SOMO   Across the bay from Santander and separated from the city by the narrow harbor entrance, this endless curving beach has fine views of the city and of the Magdalena palace.

EL SARDINERO   The city's principal beach, beautifully situated on the Cantabrian Sea, is enclosed by promenades and gardens.

MUSEO DE BELLAS ARTES   Not one of Spain's great museums, but there are works here by Goya—in particular some etchings—and by Zurbarán.

MUSEO DE PREHISTORIA Y ARQUEOLOGÍA   On display are some of the prehistoric cave finds from around the province.

◆ From the rugged green-covered rocky mound of **PEÑA CABARGA,** a few kilometers south of Santander, there are wonderful views of the Santander bay and the green interior of Cantabria. An absolutely clear day is essential.

◆ There is a ferry from Santander harbor that crosses to Plymouth, England.

STAYING IN SANTANDER

HOTEL REAL   Paseo Pérez Galdós 28   tel. (942) 27 25 50   This grande dame from the turn of the century has recently been restored to its past splendor. Gracious public rooms and outstanding views of the bay. Request a room facing the sea. (Very expensive.)

ROMA   Avenida de los Hoteles 5   tel. (942) 27 27 00   A hotel in turn-of-the-century style not far from El Sardinero beach. (Moderate.)

EATING IN SANTANDER

EL MOLINO   N-611   tel. (942) 57 40 00   In the town of Puente Arce, twelve kilometers from Santander, this well-known restaurant, parent of Cabo Mayor in Madrid, is set in an old mill and charmingly decorated with rustic antiques. El Molino is a pioneer in *nueva cocina española,* but I prefer to stick to their more traditional dishes. (Expensive.)

BAR DEL PUERTO   Hernán Cortés 63   tel. (942) 21 30 01   Overlooking the port, this recently remodeled restaurant with an open kitchen offers the very best of the sea. (Moderate–expensive.)

LA SARDINA   Doctor Fleming 3   tel. (942) 27 10 35   The freshest seafood, expertly prepared. (Moderate–expensive.)

◆ Santander is a town frequented by young people; thus there are countless tapas bars and a lively ambiance. You might try **MAZÓN**   (Hernán Cortés 57), **BODEGAS BRINGAS**   (Hernán Cortés 47), or **CAÑADÍO**   (Gómez Oreña 15).

FIESTAS

The International Festival of Music and Dance is held here from the end of July to the beginning of September, with world-renowned opera companies, ballet troupes, and orchestras participating.

ISITING CANTABRIA

The Coast

SAN VICENTE DE LA BARQUERA   A maritime village, very popular in summer, with a pretty bay and harbor and a quaint porticoed Old Quarter and Plaza Mayor. Under the portals of Avenida del Generalísimo, **RESTAURANTE/BAR EL PUERTO** has a large selection of Cantabrian seafood and a surprisingly good paella.

COMILLAS—a seignorial town of palaces and noble homes, frequented by the Spanish royal family at the beginning of the century. Its main attraction is an odd villa called **EL CAPRICHO** ("The Whimsy"), created by Antonio Gaudí (see Index) and covered with green and yellow three-dimensional flowered tiles of his own design. It recently became a deluxe restaurant. **EL CAPRICHO DE GAUDÍ**   Barrio de Sobrellano s/n   tel. (942) 72 03 65, has an overambitious menu of international and nouvelle food. If you don't eat here, come at least to see this strange creation of Gaudí. (Moderate–expensive.)

LAREDO   A three-mile-long beach has made this a summer vacation spot and, unfortunately, caused overbuilding. But **PLAYA DE LA ISLA,** west of Laredo at Quejo cape, is a splendid expanse of beach with rocky inlets, faced by thick woods and green mountains.

CASTRO URDIALES   Called Flavióbriga by the Romans, set on a cliff by the sea. The "skyline" of Castro Urdiales is dominated by a ruined castle and the Gothic Santa María church, built by Alfonso X in the thirteenth century. The church displays the Santa Cruz, Christian standard of the battle of Navas de Tolosa (see box, p. 472). There are two pleasant beaches. **MESÓN EL MARINERO**   La Correría 23   tel. (942) 86 00 05, is a waterfront restaurant offering excellent seafood specialties. I particularly like its tapas bar and its warm maritime ambiance. (Moderate.)

Nearby, **EL SEGOVIANO**   La Correría 19, serves good tapas in friendly surroundings. (Inexpensive.)

The Interior

TRES MARES peak in the Alto Campoo mountains is named "Three Seas" because three great rivers (the Ebro, Nansa, and Pisuerga) are born here and flow to three separate seas (the Mediterranean, Cantabrian, and Atlantic Ocean, respectively). A chair lift, when in operation, takes you to the summit, where the views are celestial—a full 360 degrees and featuring the Picos de Europa and the Cantabrian Sea. Otherwise, go by car as far as the Fuente del Chivo for an impressive partial view and, if you wish (it is a somewhat strenuous climb), continue on foot. Perfect visibility is a necessity.

Skiers come to Tres Mares in winter, and the hotel **LA CORZA BLANCA** in Brañavieja   tel. (942) 75 40 01 (moderate) accommodates them.

POTES   See "Seeing the Picos de Europa."

FUENTE DÉ   See "Seeing the Picos de Europa."

COSGAYA   See "Seeing the Picos de Europa."

RESERVA DEL SAJA   A mountain reserve of considerable natural beauty comprising the valley of Cabuérniga and the Nansa river. The route through the area begins at Cabezón de la Sal (see below) on a road that passes a series of rural villages, many with simple restaurants: **RESTAU-RANTE EL PERDIS**, in Renedo de Cabuérniga, and **LA CASONA DE FRESNEDA**, in Fresneda, both featuring *Cocido Montañés* and river trout.

The road entering **BÁRCENA MAYOR** comes to a dead end here, but it is well worth the detour to see the oldest and most charming village of the area, so quaint it looks like a toy mockup. It has been preserved as a National Historic-Artistic Complex. Try the rustic **MESÓN RÍO ARGOZ** Manuel González Puente 68   tel. (942) 70 60 33, for simple local foods. (Inexpensive.)

CARMONA   If you would like to spend time in a tiny mountain village, free from tourism and surrounded by high velvety green hills, come here. The houses are golden stone with coats of arms, tile roofs, and second-story wood balconies.
VENTA DE CARMONA   Barrio del Palacio   tel. (942) 72 80 57, is a thirteenth century manor house run as a hotel by the government of Cantabria and an ideal base for visits to the Saja mountain reserve and Bárcena Mayor (see above). (Inexpensive.)
♦ The road from Carmona to Puentenansa and La Hermida is stunning, featuring green, cultivated hillsides that farther on are dwarfed by the steep bare cliffs of the Picos de Europa. The route is a constant delight, with well-kept stone villages of great character dotting the way.

CABEZÓN DE LA SAL   Named for the nearby rock salt mines, this town is a crossroads for excursions into the Saja mountain reserve. **PICU LA TORRE** serves very good tapas, some of them complimentary.
VENTA DE SANTA LUCÍA   in nearby Cos   tel. (942) 70 10 61, is a centuries old post house serving simple food, especially grilled meats, in rustic surroundings.

LIÉRGANES   A pretty mountain town whose old quarter has many palaces of the seventeenth century. **POSADA DEL SAUCE**   José Antonio s/n   tel. (942) 52 80 23   is both a good restaurant and a modest hotel set in a nineteenth century mansion looking toward the mountains. (Moderate; pool.)

VEGA DE PAS   A village in the softly green-covered Pas valley, enclosed by mountains and dedicated to making cheese, *quesadas* (cheesecakes), and *sobaos* (sponge cakes). Try them at any of the village bars.

THE PROUD
BASQUE COUNTRY

INTRODUCTION

THE BASQUE COUNTRY—called El País Vasco in Spanish and Euskadi in the Basque tongue—comprises three provinces in Spain, but when I think of this region, foremost in my mind are its two coastal provinces, Guipúzcoa and Vizcaya, that face the Cantabrian Sea. Subject to sudden and fierce storms, the Cantabrian engenders respect in Basques who base their livelihoods on the sea; they know that its dangerous unpredictability has cost many lives. And seaside villages are constructed on the premise of the sea's violence; they rise abruptly and picturesquely from the rocky coast and rely on their natural harbors and inlets to protect their fishing fleets.

The Basques' prodigious fishing skills against formidable climatic odds have taken them for centuries as far away as Newfoundland to hunt whales and to catch cod, and some say they were in America before Columbus.

A visit to the Basque Country combines well with travel through Asturias and Cantabria. But let's make no mistake about it: We are far from the Costa del Sol. Rainfall is abundant (but at its lowest in summer), and Spaniards, appreciating the cooler temperatures and the welcome respite that clouds and rain afford from the unabated scorching sun of the south, have traditionally vacationed here.

Although most places of interest in the Basque Country are on or near the coast, I also love the interior, a gloriously green land of dense forests and rolling emerald hills that reach to the very edge of the sea. In the meadows cows and sheep peacefully graze. Basques are adept sheep-herders, and Americans are often surprised to discover that there are large communities of Basques in the American West, descendants of emigrants who gravitated there to continue their traditional sheep-related occupations in a similar climate and terrain.

FOODS AND WINES OF THE BASQUE COUNTRY

GENERAL
Seafood, tapas, vegetables, soft-set eggs (*revueltos*)

SPECIALTIES
Angulas a la Bilbaína—baby eels in garlic sauce
Bacalao a la Vizcaína—salt cod in red pepper sauce
Bacalao al Pil-Pil—salt cod in creamy garlic sauce
Kokotxas a la Donostiarra—hake cheeks in green sauce
Besugo a la Bilbaína—grilled porgy with garlic
Merluza Koskera—hake in green sauce
Marmitako—bonito and tomato soup
Txangurro—stuffed spider crab
Pochas—broad bean stew
Judías de Tolosa—red bean stew
Leche Frita—fried custard
Queso de Idiazábal—smoked sheep's milk cheese

WINES
Txakolí—young fruity white wine, such as Txomin Etxaniz
Sidra—hard cider

The houses of the Basque interior, called *baserri* or *caseríos*, also have special characteristics. Families in these self-contained units once lived in an isolated world of hard work and proud subsistence. In these multipurpose structures, farmers and livestock shared quarters and fodder was stored. Today such houses are no longer so solitary, but their charming appearance is unchanged: Whitewashed stone walls, crossed by wood beams, are enlivened by long deep balconies painted in bright reds and greens (they face west to catch the afternoon light); sloped red tile roofs wash away the rain.

Despite such poetic surroundings, the Basque Country is in reality highly industrialized, concentrating on iron-ore mining and metallurgy, and is the center of Spain's steel industry. It gets gray and grimy around Bilbao, but fortunately you can travel through most of the Basque Country and never realize the existence of this other aspect of the region that creates wealth but does little for aesthetics.

The fact that the Basque Country is referred to as a "country" is significant and reflects the Basques' long tradition of self-sufficiency and democratic ways. Although the Romans came here, they found the coast harsh and inhospitable and moved on. Likewise, the Arabs came but never conquered, and the Basques once again managed to preserve their jealously guarded freedom. Independence, however, also had its drawbacks—it meant that the Basque Country was not subject to the powerful and dynamic cultural and artistic influences of Roman and Moorish Spain; in later centuries Basques lacked these traditions to build upon. And for this reason you will not generally find great monuments and works of art in the Basque Country; artistic endeavors have never been an important focus of life.

Who are these hardy and freedom-loving people, recognized worldwide by their characteristic black berets, who lived outside of the Spanish mainstream for most of their history? Experts have been unable to relate them in race or culture to any other Indo-European group, and their origins remain a mystery. Some believe they are indigenous people of Spain; others disagree. Such controversy gives fuel and a certain credibility to one theory that associates the Basques with the survivors of the supposed lost continent of Atlantis. It certainly provides one explanation as to why a good many Basques are Rh negative and why their language, called Euskera, is unrelated to any known tongue in the world.

The Basque language will strike you immediately, for it looks strange in print, strewn with odd consonant combinations like *tx* (as in *txakolí*, the local wine), *tt* (*ttoro*, a fish stew), and with words of unaccustomed sounds, unmanageable length, and unwieldy pronunciation like *etxekoandres* (housewives), *baserritarras* (countrymen), and *eskarrikasko* (thank you). In fact, only about one-quarter of Basques today can speak the language, and far fewer can put it to paper, but still they hold it sacred.

> One is born Basque, one speaks Basque, one lives Basque and
> one dies Basque. The Basque tongue is like a fatherland. I had
> almost said a religion.
>
> Victor Hugo, *The Alps and Pyrenees*

So the Basques went their own way with no formal government, dedicating their lives to fishing, agriculture, and livestock. But they were never truly independent, alternately ruled—but never dominated—by Navarra and Castile. In their isolation Basques developed a unique system of self-government and exacted from their rulers certain rights of independence (called *fueros*) that were generally respected. Representatives of the people met regularly in towns and cities as part of a long Basque tradition—a tradition that sprung to world attention when the town of Guernica was bombed during the Spanish Civil War and, subsequently, when Picasso immortalized the event in his powerful painting *Guernica* (see box, p. 275).

The Basques clung tenaciously to their independence into modern times, even though the monarchy abolished their *fueros* in the nineteenth century when Basques supported the Carlists in the War of Succession (see Index). For a time during the Spanish Republic of 1936–37 those rights were restored, only to be suppressed once again at the close of the Civil War. Today regional autonomy has been reestablished in Spain, undercutting a movement known as ETA that engages in terrorism as a means to regain Basque independence. But don't be put off. I always feel perfectly comfortable, relaxed, unthreatened, and warmly welcomed in the Basque Country and have no hesitancy in encouraging you to come here.

Basques are a hard-working, hearty people who throw themselves into sports based on brute strength, like lifting stones of up to four hundred pounds, splitting tree trunks that may be nine feet thick, and using teams of oxen and men to drag rocks weighing thousands of pounds, as if these activities were just one more part of the workday.

There are Basque sports that have more universal appeal, such as jai alai, which is even practiced in the United States. Then there are the rowing contests in the Cantabrian Sea of the heavy, modified fishing vessels called *traineras*. The origin of this sport is also related to work, for the boats once raced each other to port to try to arrive first with the day's catch.

Basques love song and dance—their dances require great strength and dexterity—and are particularly fond of choral groups, called *orfeones* (as the saying goes, bring together a few Basques and an *orfeón* is instantly born). Their traditional instrument is the *txistu*, a primitive oboe with three holes, from which expert musicians extract the most marvelous and varied sounds. They accompany themselves with a tabor drum.

Perhaps one of the reasons I particularly love the Basque Country is the food. Within the rich and varied culinary heritage of Spain, Basque cooking has long held a unique position. This is a region dedicated to fine eating and known throughout Spain for its great chefs. In otherwise uninteresting Basque towns, it is not unusual to find first-rate eating establishments.

Basque chefs are to Spain what French chefs are to the world: eagerly sought out and recruited by restaurants in other regions. In Madrid especially, the cooking of the Basque region has ardent admirers, and many of the most prestigious restaurants feature Basque chefs, Basque menus, and fish rushed in from the Basque coast.

It was here in the Basque Country that Spain's answer to nouvelle cuisine was born and christened *nueva cocina vasca*—new Basque cuisine. Based on a philosophy similar to that of the French movement, a revitalization of Basque cooking took place. It was based on freshness and, on the one hand, a return to Grandma's recipes, albeit adapted to modern times and tastes; on the other hand, there were the flights of fancy created by skilled chefs, experimenting with new ingredients or using traditional ingredients in more imaginative ways.

And yet, what Basques love best is the wonderfully simple dishes they grew up with, dishes that do not mask the true flavor of the food. Although the interior of the Basque Country provides fine meats, somehow they never arouse the excitement generated by fish; just about all the great dishes of Basque cuisine are based on fish.

Basques are particularly fond of cod, traditionally preserved in salt to survive the long journey from the fishing grounds in Newfoundland. But Basque chefs turn this "survival food" into something splendid in preparations like *Bacalao al Pil-Pil* (cod in an emulsion of garlic and oil) and *Bacalao a la Vizcaína* (cod in a sauce of dried sweet red peppers and onion). Then there are the highly prized hake cheeks (*kokotxas*) and hake *koskera*, both served in green sauces; *Marmitako*, a tuna soup, traditionally prepared by fishermen; *Txangurro*, flaked seasoned

THE ODYSSEY OF THE BABY EEL

The life cycle of the eel is an amazing tale that mystified the ancients. Female eels were never seen carrying roe, leading to the conclusion that baby eels appeared spontaneously. The scientific truth is as startling as the legend.

Adult eels live in the rivers of Spain, but as spawning time approaches they inexplicably leave the rivers, cross the Atlantic Ocean, and gather in the Sargasso Sea near what is known as the Bermuda Triangle (one argument for the existence of Atlantis cites this strange behavior, concluding that at one time there must have been a continent where the eels now congregate). There they are joined by their American relatives. Once they have deposited their eggs, the females die, and their transparent offspring—elvers, as they are called—must fend for themselves. Those of American parentage instinctively find their way back to America, while those of European ancestry undertake a journey of more than three thousand miles and almost three years to return to their homelands. En route, countless elvers are devoured by predators, and those that do survive hardly grow at all during the arduous crossing.

When they finally arrive at the mouths of Spanish rivers, in fall and early winter, they are no thicker and no longer than matchsticks. Especially in the Basque Country, fishermen await their arrival with fine nets, immediately parboil them with some tobacco (for subtle flavor), then rush them to restaurants where they are plunged into very hot olive oil, seasoned with garlic and dried red chili pepper, and brought still sizzling to table. Their price is outrageous, but as is so often the case, Spaniards would mortgage their souls rather than forgo a delicacy of this magnitude.

spider crab, served in its shell; squid in ink sauce; and the greatest delicacy of all, *angulas* (baby eels), which incidentally have a fascinating life story (see box, p. 267).

Note that the emphasis in general is on fish rather than shellfish and that cooking in sauces takes preference over frying and grilling. The ever-present *tortilla* (potato omelet) of Spain takes a back seat in the Basque Country to *revueltos*, soft-set eggs, often mixed with vegetables and seafood. Red beans from Tolosa make luscious stews. Desserts tend to have a custard base: *Leche Frita* (fried milk), *Pudin de Manzana* (apple pudding), *Arroz con Leche* (rice pudding), and *Tarta Vasca* with custard filling. Basque sheep's milk cheese, cured and smoked, is well known all over Spain and called Idiazábal, after the village near the caves where the cheese is made. The landlocked Basque province of Álava proves to be different from its coastal cousins, and the cuisine takes on a distinctly Castilian flavor.

Basques nurture their cuisine. Interest in food is a social preoccupation, not confined to food professionals, and even though in this matriarchal society women are known as fine cooks and successful restaurateurs, it is the men who often take credit because of the mystique surrounding the uniquely Basque, men-only eating clubs.

Clustered in cities, these *sociedades gastronómicas* are alternatives to bars or restaurants. Here members meet for a drink or a meal. They must, however, provide and prepare their own food in the ample, well-organized kitchens of the clubs. When parties are organized, they often turn into raucous affairs of hearty drinking and singing (a club will always have a piano and will often invite an *orfeón* to entertain). But such gatherings also give members a chance to prove their culinary worth, and some great chefs have emerged from the eating societies.

Except for the province of Álava, the climate of the Basque region is not conducive to the production of fine wines. The local white wine, *txakolí*, is dry, acidic, and low in alcohol but nevertheless ideal with Basque seafood. Hard cider also appears as a common tavern drink in conjunction with tapas. And tapas, by the way, are lavished with the same attention as any other food in the Basque Country. Here you are apt to find artfully garnished canapé tapas instead of the fried and stewed tapas of other regions of Spain.

THE PROVINCE OF GUIPÚZCOA

GUIPÚZCOA (ghee-*pooth*-co-a) is the smallest province on the Spanish mainland; it adjoins Navarra, Álava, and Vizcaya as well as France, and faces the Cantabrian Sea. Because it is small and the landscape abrupt, everything in Guipúzcoa is concentrated. Valleys are numerous but narrow and confined (there is little room to grow crops, except some grains to support livestock); the coast is craggy, forming small natural enclosures that become harbors—the only havens from the unforgiving sea. Guipúzcoa fishermen may brave the open seas on journeys to Newfoundland to fish cod, but they know that a safe port awaits them back home. There are two more substantial ports, San Sebastián and Pasajes de San Juan, but they also are so well sheltered that they are hardly visible from the open sea. Because the coast is rocky, beaches are few and tend to be of coarse sand. San Sebastián is a glorious exception.

Although temperatures are moderate, the proverbial rain in Spain does not fall on the plain but on Guipúzcoa, and ranges from a fine drizzle, called *sirimiri,* to *galernas,* storms that arrive unexpectedly, bringing heavy seas and drenching rain. Despite this, San Sebastián is one of Spain's most popular resorts, attracting a mostly Spanish crowd. I've heard stories of intense summer storms, but on the many occasions that I have been to Guipúzcoa, the skies were sunny and the temperatures warm.

Fishing is a major industry in Guipúzcoa, and fish a major culinary pleasure of Guipuzcoanos, although just one aspect of the province's collective preoccupation with food. All of the Basque Country is indeed known for fine eating, but interest in food and quality restaurants concentrates on San Sebastián, and the focus of the entire province of Guipúzcoa is, in fact, San Sebastián.

THE CAPITAL CITY OF SAN SEBASTIÁN

San Sebastián is, I think, one of the most beautiful cities in the world. It is placed like a string of pearls around the shell-shaped bay of La Concha. To one side of the city looms Monte Igueldo, to the other Monte Urgull; and in the bay, Santa Clara island sparkles. At night San Sebastián glows like a multifaceted gem.

For most of its history San Sebastián (called Donostia in the Basque language) was a tiny fishing village. But when Isabel II at the end of the last century was advised by her personal physician to spend the summer in the north by the sea to cure a skin ailment, she chose San Sebastián. Her son, King Alfonso XII, and his queen, María Cristina, followed, as did the court, the government, and the aristocracy. The Miramar palace was built overlooking the bay, and in no time San Sebastián became a fashionable and elegant resort; it has remained so ever since. Today the city retains its turn-of-the-century charm: stately boulevards graced with immaculately white

lampposts; quietly elegant Old World hotels; nineteenth century mansions; and expensive shops catering to the well-to-do. The splendid beach and the waterfront Paseo de la Concha, lined with feathery tamarind trees, are integral parts of city life and a center of activity throughout the day and well into the night.

Apart from its physical attributes, San Sebastián has another unique quality: This city of just 175,000 residents boasts as many highest-rated restaurants as either Madrid or Barcelona—cities almost twenty times as large as San Sebastián. For as long as anyone can remember, fine eating has been a tradition in San Sebastián, particularly in the last fifteen years, during which a new generation of chefs has sparked a food revolution in Spain.

There is no other city in Spain that says "food" quite like San Sebastián, beginning with the city's surprisingly small fishing port, enclosed by Monte Urgull and hardly large enough to accommodate its substantial fleet. Here the fishing boats, gaily painted in the red and green colors of the Basque flag, are in close view, and business is brisk for vendors peddling freshly caught sardines. Family-run restaurants under the wharf's porticoes overflow with customers seeking perfectly fresh fish, simply prepared, at reasonable prices.

The cobbled streets of Old San Sebastián, right off the port, are home to strings of animated tapas bars that feature the characteristic tapas of the city. Emphasis is on canapés and *pinchos* (tapas on toothpicks), both in endless variety and appetizingly arranged on bar counters. A typical canapé is fried bread topped with a mix of tuna, onion, and vinegar and garnished with sieved egg yolk, a slice of pickle, and a dot of mayonnaise. *Pinchos* may combine on a single toothpick a piece of potato, a thick slice of egg, a chunk of tuna, and one shrimp. Since all these tapas are easy to pick up, you take your own—no permission necessary—and keep an honest count.

Each morning finds the city's top chefs at the stupendous San Sebastián market on Aldamar Street, where the fish section is set apart in an impressive stone structure that might easily be mistaken for city hall. On peak days there are more than sixty varieties of fish—flounder, tuna, hake, whiting, red snapper, striped bass, monkfish, porgy, and turbot among them—and by lunchtime almost everything has disappeared.

Basques are experts when it comes to fish. Not content with same-day freshness, they insist fish be eaten only at its peak season. *Angulas* (see box, p. 267), for example, are served in fine restaurants only during the winter months. And buyers in the know look for fish that has been hooked rather than netted, even though they pay twice the price. "The fish fights when hooked and is rapidly scooped from the water by the fishermen, producing a firmer flesh and sprightlier flavor. The netted fish, kept under water for some time until the net is retrieved, 'drowns,' " explains Modesto de Acosta, owner of the Gainza fish stands in the city's other big market on Loyola street. His proudest signs read, *de Anzuelo* (Hooked).

Planning menus according to what the market offers has always been fundamental in Basque cooking, long before *nueva cocina vasca* made it fashionable. With the death of Francisco Franco came renewed recognition of Basque rights and a resurgence of Basque pride and Basque cuisine. Young, exuberant Juan Mari Arzak, of Arzak restaurant, captured Spain with his innovative new cooking.

The food renaissance centered on San Sebastián because here food commands great respect and because the city holds a privileged position, open to both the bounty of the sea and the produce of the interior, while being close enough to France to catch the winds of change wafting across the border. Arzak restaurant, today rating three Michelin stars, continues to be a required stop for anyone interested in food, be it creative or traditional (chef Juan Mari will never give up the time-honored Basque dishes his mother once made).

Food, the beach, and the overall beauty of San Sebastián will hold you here for a day or two. I love the city best as day ends, and I fall in with townsfolk and vacationers who have changed from bathing suits to fashionable attire and stroll the waterfront promenade. After dinner we return to the promenade to see the city, the sea, and the mountains enclosing the bay all gloriously illuminated. It's a sight I never tire of.

$\int$ EEING SAN SEBASTIÁN

MONTE IGUELDO   At the top of this mountain is an amusement park, but the real attraction is the stupendous view of San Sebastián, by day and by night.

ALDAMAR STREET MARKET   I consider this a principal sight in San Sebastián, even for those who are not food buffs (see text).

OLD QUARTER   Little of Old San Sebastián has survived (it was destroyed during the War of Independence [see Index]), but the narrow streets around the port still keep the flavor of the past. Tapas bars are everywhere.

MONTE URGULL   Preserved as parkland, this mountain is a fine place to walk and picnic.

STAYING IN SAN SEBASTIÁN

HOTEL DE LONDRES Y DE INGLATERRA   Zubieta 2   tel. (943) 42 69 89   Located on the waterfront promenade, this hotel offers stunning views of the bay and is convenient to all of San Sebastián. Request a room, preferably with salon, overlooking the sea (try for number 412, 512, 513, or 515). (Moderate–expensive.)

MARÍA CRISTINA   Paseo de la República Argentina s/n   tel. (943) 42 49 00 Situated on the banks of the Urumea river, this majestic Old World hotel has always been San Sebastián's most elegant, and after recent renovations, it is now the most luxurious (although I do prefer the views from the Londres y de Inglaterra). (Deluxe.)

MONTE IGUELDO   Monte Igueldo s/n   tel. (943) 21 02 11   the décor of this modern hotel is mundane, and the location a bit inconvenient, but the panoramic views of San Sebastián and the open sea from the heights of Monte Igueldo are breathtaking. Request a room, with salon, facing the city. (Moderate–expensive; pool.)

EATING IN SAN SEBASTIÁN

ARZAK   Alto de Miracruz 21   tel. (943) 28 55 93   A warm friendly restaurant whose owner and chef, Juan Mari Arzak, pioneered *nueva cocina vasca* and continues to influence cooking all over Spain. Try the tasting menu for a sampling of his creative dishes. Arzak also turns out perfectly prepared traditional Basque dishes; go for the classic *Marmitako, kokotxas,* or *Pochas con Chorizo.* Desserts are superb. (Expensive.)

AKELAŘE   Barrio Igueldo s/n   tel. (943) 21 20 52   Lunchtime is best to appreciate the spectacular views of the sea seen through huge picture windows in this restaurant of ski-chalet décor. Chef Pedro Subijana will often personally take your order. He has a flair for *nueva cocina vasca* and is particularly adept at puff pastries (his father was a baker). (Expensive.)

PANIER FLEURI   Paseo de Salamanca 1   tel. (943) 42 42 05   An airy restaurant with an Art Deco look. Chef María Jesús Fombellida presents a mostly traditional Basque menu with French overtones. I like the mixed fry (of fish and meats), stewed pigeon, and *mero* (grouper) San Sebastián style. A prizewinning wine cellar with more than 25,000 bottles. (Expensive.)

CASA NICOLASA   Aldamar 4   tel. (943) 42 17 62   An institution in San Sebastián. Its elegance and exceptional Basque fare are intact despite new ownership. (Expensive.)

REKONDO   Paseo Igueldo 57   tel. (943) 21 29 07   This is the place for simple grilled foods, such as wild mushrooms, shrimp, beef, and veal. (Moderate.)

♦ If you seek tapas, go to the Old Quarter near the waterfront, and try any tapas bar with an appetizing selection. I particularly like **BAR ARALAR** and **BAR PORTALETAS,** both on Portu Kale street.

FIESTAS

INTERNATIONAL FILM FESTIVAL   Every September this event attracts a glittering crowd of the world's foremost directors and movie stars.

TRAINERA REGATTAS   Rowing races of traditional Basque vessels, called *traineras,* take place the first and second Sundays of September.

♀ISITING THE PROVINCE OF GUIPÚZCOA

ZUMAYA   (Zumaia)   An attractive port town set at the mouth of the Urola river, where the home of artist Ignacio Zuloaga—known for his colorful scenes of the Basque Country and its people, and of bullfighters—has been made into a museum. See also his personal collection of Spanish masters. (Open only Wednesday and Sunday afternoons.)

GUETARIA   (Getaria)   A town noted for its seafood, grilled on the street outside of restaurants; try **RESTAURANTE ELKANO**   Herrerieta 2   tel. (943) 83 16 14. Some of the region's best *txakolí* wines (p. 268) are made here. Just off-shore is an island known as **EL RATÓN** because its shape suggests a large mouse.

PASAJES DE SAN JUAN   (Pasaia Donibane)   The extremely narrow sea entrance to this town ("High tide re-establishes the 'passage.' Hence the name," says Victor Hugo) hides the ample and well-protected harbor that is one of the Basque Country's major seaports. The old village near the exit to the Cantabrian Sea has stone-arched streets and houses of brightly colored wood balconies in typical Basque style. Victor Hugo's residence while he was in the Basque Country is today a museum (San Juan 63).
CASA CÁMARA   San Juan 79   tel. (943) 52 36 99, at the entrance to the port, is a charming, tasteful, antique-filled restaurant with a nautical theme that is the pride of the family that has run it for generations. At its center, below the floor, are the lobster and crab pots, raised on pulleys so clients can make their selections. (Moderate–expensive.)
♦ The Jaizkibel road from Pasajes to Fuenterrabía, especially at the hostal on the Jaizkibel mountain, provides sensational views of the mountains, the French and Basque coasts, and the Bidasoa river.

FUENTERRABÍA   (Hondarribia)   Because of its location near the French border, at the juncture of the Bidasoa river and the Cantabrian Sea, this delightful city was often under siege and therefore is built up steeply, is crowned by a castle, and has many noble homes emblazoned with coats of arms. An expansive beach nearby makes this a popular summer destination.
PARADOR EL EMPERADOR   Plaza de Armas   tel. (943) 64 21 40, is a small and impressive castle from the days of Emperor Charles V. (Moderate.)
HOTEL PAMPINOT   Mayor 3   tel. (943) 64 06 00, in the Old Quarter, occupies a sixteenth century palace and has just eight rooms. (Expensive.)
RAMÓN ROTETA restaurant   Irun s/n. Villa Ainara   tel. (943) 64 16 93, in an elegant villa, is known for high-quality creative cooking. (Expensive.)

IRÚN   All the trappings of a frontier town are here. Visitors stop to shop and catch trains on their way to and from France.

SAN IGNACIO DE LOYOLA MONASTERY   This   enormous monastery, a popular place of pilgrimage, was built in the eighteenth century in honor of Saint Ignatius Loyola. The saint, who founded the Jesuit Order, was born here five centuries ago in a house at the site of the present monastery.

OÑATE (Oñati) A town with history—you can see it in the noble homes, palaces, and churches of golden stone and in its sixteenth century university (no longer in use) designed in Renaissance-Plateresque style.

♦ If you are traveling to Pamplona from San Sebastián, take the beautiful road that runs through Astigarraga and Hernani.

THE PROVINCE OF VIZCAYA

THE MOST WESTERLY of the Basque provinces, Vizcaya (veeth-*cah*-ya) has a coastline on the Cantabrian Sea just as rugged as that of Guipúzcoa and a mountainous interior to match, where livestock is raised and vegetables are grown. Vizcaya is the most densely populated area of the Basque Country, highly industrialized and centering on its most important city, Bilbao, or Bilbo, as it is called in Basque.

Belying the industrial nature of this province (Spain's iron-ore mines and metallurgy production are concentrated here), several of the most colorful villages and most beautiful natural harbors of the Basque Country are in Vizcaya, bearing names typically Basque: San Juan de Gaztelugache, Elanchove, Bermeo. They are not close to the highway that runs from Bilbao to San Sebastián, and perhaps for this reason they have kept their character and charm. To visit them you will have to follow the winding and rugged shoreline road, but the reward is seeing the best and the least explored of the Basque coast, where coves and rocky heights bring one scenic wonder after another.

In gastronomy, several famous Basque dishes take the name of Vizcaya and Bilbao and are so well known that in Spain no further explanation is necessary: Everyone knows that *Bacalao a la Vizcaína* is cod in a sauce of onion and dried sweet red pepper; that *Besugo a la Bilbaína* is porgy simply grilled with olive oil, garlic, and hot pepper; and that *Angulas a la Bilbaína* means baby eels in garlic sauce. Likewise, the town of Santurce is immediately identified with its outstanding grilled sardines.

A historic and tragic event that took place in Vizcaya during the Spanish Civil War stirred world controversy and anger. On that fateful day in the town of Guernica (pronounced gair-*nee*-ka) the civilian population was bombed by German aircraft, setting a sad precedent and presaging a new and more barbarous era of warfare.

For generations the town of Guernica has represented the stubborn independence of the Basque people. Under its venerated oak tree—age-old symbol of that freedom—representatives from Basque towns and cities met, new delegates were elected, and early Castilian monarchs (even they had to bow before the Basques) and later their emissaries, came to swear respect for Basque rights and privileges (*fueros*). Every Spanish king from Alfonso XI in the fourteenth century to Isabel II in the nineteenth century adhered to this ritual.

When the Spanish Civil War broke out, the Basques surprised the nation by pledging their support to the Republicans. Although traditionally a conservative people, Basques believed the liberals were more likely to honor their *fueros*, as the Spanish Republic of 1931 had done.

It was April 26, 1937, when German warplanes appeared in the skies over Guernica, showering bombs on a defenseless civilian population. Casualties were high, and the central city was completely destroyed. The famous oak tree, however, emerged unscathed, and Guernica became a rallying cry for outraged Republican supporters worldwide.

The dastardly event speaks for itself, but it is only fair to add that the reasons why Guernica was

THE POWER OF PICASSO'S *GUERNICA*

The Republican government of Spain in 1937 commissioned Picasso to create a painting for their pavilion at the Paris World's Fair. Before he had begun, however, the bombing of Guernica took place. Picasso was so moved and so angered by the event that he decided to make this the theme of his painting. Although he lived and worked in France, his passions remained Spanish.

All his formidable artistic skills and his personal beliefs were concentrated in this work, painted in stark black and white for added drama. *Guernica* is a statement against man's barbarism and a call for world peace.

What modern work can compare with its sweep, its emotional impact, its terrible timeliness in an era dominated by war? *Guernica* is the Apocalypse of our time, a mighty expression of man's divided pledge to life and to death.
Maurice Raynal

Guernica was on extended loan to New York's Museum of Modern Art until such a time when Spain returned to democratic rule. Today the painting resides in a special pavilion of the Prado Museum in Madrid.

bombed are not at all clear, even with more than fifty years of hindsight. The intent most likely was not to make an example of Guernica; rather, a navigational error caused by bad weather sent the planes off course from their probable military target: a corridor for fleeing Republicans that bypassed Guernica and continued to the sea.

The oak tree remains a powerful symbol of Basque unity and pride, and the horror of April 26, 1937, vividly lives in Pablo Picasso's masterpiece, *Guernica*.

THE CAPITAL CITY OF BILBAO

Bilbao (beel-*bah*-oh) or Bilbo is a prosperous city, big and bustling. It was founded in 1300 as a mere fishing village, but owing to its proximity to mining and its location on the Nervión river estuary near its exit to the

Porgy, bilbao-style

Butterfly a large porgy, removing as much bone as possible, and brush with olive oil. Grill or broil, turning occasionally and brushing with more oil, until browned and cooked through. Meanwhile, heat 4 tablespoons of olive oil in a small skillet. Add 4 sliced garlic cloves and half of a seeded hot red chili pepper, crushed. Drizzle the oil mixture over the fish, sprinkle with minced parsley, and serve.

Cantabrian Sea, Bilbao soon became a major port and commercial center. It grew most rapidly in the nineteenth century and today accounts for most of Spain's steel production. On the east side of the river sits the original city with the cathedral as its nucleus. The dark and narrow section called "Seven Streets" (*Siete Calles*) near the river is the oldest quarter of Bilbao. In contrast, the modern extension, or *ensanche*, on the west bank, has wide boulevards, gardens, and grand plazas. All of Bilbao is enclosed by mountains.

I am sorry to say that my most vivid impressions of Bilbao are of the city's sooty grayness and of massive traffic jams on a single-lane road of endless exasperating curves along which all traffic, including heavy trucks, traveled to reach Bilbao from the west. I know that Bilbaínos who live and work here dearly love their city, but I don't think Bilbao is a place that grabs the heart of a visitor. Its salvation is food: There is a strong tradition of tapas, and several of Spain's top chefs and a remarkable number of Spain's finest restaurants are here.

For me a typical evening in Bilbao begins in the area around Licenciado Poza street and Alameda del Doctor Areilza. With the approaching tapas hour, it is packed with Bilbaínos, many of them university students, making the rounds of the innumerable tapas bars. I have never seen such a concentration of tapas activity as there is here. People spill out of bars onto the streets, glasses and tapas in hand, and impede the flow of traffic—to no one's consternation. Tapas are often canapés or hearty triple-decker sandwiches filled with everything imaginable. If after this you have room to proceed to dinner, Bilbao, true to its Basque heritage, offers many excellent options.

Seeing bilbao

PUENTE COLGANTE   A local landmark, this "hanging" bridge, suspended between two towers, connects Las Arenas, upriver from Bilbao, with the town of Portugalete, on the other side of the Nervión, and is crossed by means of a moving platform that accommodates cars.

MUSEO DE BELLAS ARTES   Some works of the masters (Bruegel, Van Dyck, El Greco, Velázquez, Zurbarán, Ribera, and Goya) as well as Basque painters like Zuloaga and other contemporary artists.

OLD QUARTER The original town, declared a National Historic-Artistic Monument, developed around what is known as the Siete Calles, seven parallel streets that come to an end at the river. It is closed to traffic and is a busy commercial center—a place where farmers come to sell their wares—and bustling with restaurants and tapas bars.

STAYING IN BILBAO

VILLA DE BILBAO Gran Vía 87 tel. (94) 441 60 00 A deluxe hotel, very modern but unimaginative. (Expensive.)

ERCILLA Ercilla 37–39 tel. (94) 443 88 00 Pleasant, busy, and centrally located. (Expensive.)

LÓPEZ DE HARO Obispo Orueta 4 tel. (94) 423 55 00 This new ultra-deluxe hotel, named after the founder of Bilbao, is classically elegant. (Very expensive.)

CONDE DUQUE Campo Volantín 22 tel. (94) 445 60 00 Well situated near the Old Quarter. (Moderate–expensive.)

EATING IN BILBAO

GOIZEKO KABI Particular de Estraunza 4 tel. (94) 442 11 29 Considered today the city's finest restaurant, featuring imaginative and traditional dishes in an elegant but rustic setting. Some say this restaurant alone makes a visit to Bilbao worthwhile. (Expensive.)

GURÍA Gran Vía 66 tel. (94) 441 05 43 A Bilbao classic. This restaurant's forte is the traditional Basque dishes, especially cod preparations like *Bacalao Pil Pil.* (Expensive.)

BERMEO Ercilla 37 tel. (94) 443 88 00 In the Ercilla hotel and a popular spot among Bilbaínos. Its chef takes special care with dishes and products of his homeland of Navarra and prepares excellent Basque dishes as well. (Moderate–expensive.)

JOLASTOKI Avenida Leioako 24 (Neguri) tel. (94) 469 30 31 Set in a pretty villa some fourteen kilometers outside of Bilbao, this top-rated restaurant prepares exquisite innovative and traditional dishes under the command of talented chef Sabino Arana. (Expensive.)

✦ Keep in mind also the tapas bars around Calle del Licenciado Poza. (I especially like **BAR OR-KOMPÓN** and **TABERNA ZIZIPOT.**)

⒱ISITING THE PROVINCE OF VIZCAYA

SANTURCE (Santurtzi) The most famous town in Spain for just-caught sardines, grilled in the streets by the harbor.

SAN JUAN DE GAZTELUGACHE   This bare rocky spike would be an island except for a narrow strip of rock joining it to the mainland. It's a wonderful walk, and there are great views as you climb to the hermitage, where sailors leave votive offerings.

BERMEO   A busy port crowded with hundreds of fishing boats in long straight rows, varying in size from rowboats to vessels capable of braving the roughest seas, all brilliantly colored in reds, blues, and greens.

ARTXANDA   Santa Eufemia 14   tel. (94) 688 09 30, has a terrace overlooking the port and serves excellent seafood in casual surroundings. I loved the *Mariscada*, grilled shellfish sprinkled with coarse salt. (Moderate.) There is also an appetizing tapas bar.

ELANCHOVE   White houses with red tile roofs climb up the hillside from a tiny, tightly enclosed harbor, all surrounded by abrupt, deeply green mountains.

GUERNICA (Guernika)   Site of the infamous bombing during the Spanish Civil War and symbolic heart of Basque independence. The venerated oak tree—more than a hundred years old—stands in front of the Casa de Juntas, where local representatives meet, and the stump of the previous oak tree is on display inside (see text).

ELORRIO   In the interior of Vizcaya, a fortified city of noble homes and palaces from the seventeenth and eighteenth centuries and known for its distinctive stone crucifixes, such as the cross of Santa Ana and those at the entrances to town and in front of the church of the Conception.

♦ If you are traveling from Vizcaya to Castilla, be sure to take the beautiful Orduña pass through the mountains.

THE PROVINCE OF ÁLAVA

ÁLAVA (*ah*-lah-va) is the southernmost region of the Basque Country, adjoining Castilla and in fact sometimes resembling Castilla more than Guipúzcoa or Vizcaya. From the mountainous north, where livestock is raised, Álava flattens into the rich valley of the Río Ebro, where cereals, vegetables, and fruits grow, and I am not surprised that this was the region of the Basque Country in which the Romans chose to live and to cultivate the land. Álava has no exit to the sea, but does have several artificial lakes for recreation.

Álava's fame as a wine producer has blossomed in recent years, for here is the region referred to as La Rioja Alavesa, where some elite Rioja wines are made. If you are familiar with these wines, the village names of Labastida, Elciego, and Samaniego, all in Álava, should ring a bell; they produce several of Rioja's finest reds. The climate here is quite different and the land less fertile than on the southern banks of the Ebro, where Rioja's two other wine regions (Rioja Alta and Rioja Baja) are located (see "La Rioja"), but the added sunshine, hotter summers, and milder winters help to create wines that are fruitier, smoother, and less acidic.

In Álava the Basque tradition of fine eating is honored, although the food tends to be most closely related to the Rioja region. Among its well-known dishes are *Tortilla de Perrechicos* (wild mushroom omelet), *Pochas con Codorniz* (bean and quail stew), and *Habas con Jamón* (fava beans with ham). Of course all the wonderful fruits and famed baby vegetables are grown here, fish arrives fresh from the Basque coast, and excellent lamb comes from Castilla.

I have discovered few villages in Álava that rate a detour, with the notable exception of Laguardia. The capital city of Vitoria is perhaps your most interesting stop in the province.

THE CAPITAL CITY OF VITORIA

Most of the population of Álava is concentrated in and around Vitoria (vee-*tor*-ee-a), which in the last thirty years has experienced Spain's largest population growth. One reason is that Vitoria is the government capital of the Basque Country; another is that it is an important crossroads between the Basque Country and Castilla, as well as an opening to Aragón. As such, ever since the sixteenth century wealthy merchants have concentrated here and built many of the Renaissance mansions that you see today. Vitoria was a city of craftsmen, known especially for weaving and ironwork, and street names reflect this rich past (for example, Cuchillería—Knife Makers' street; Herrería—Ironworkers' street).

Founded in the twelfth century by the king of Navarra, Sancho El Sabio, as an extension of his reign, the town was named Nueva Vitoria (New Victory), although it is still known to Basques by its original name, Gasteiz. Vitoria later came under the rule of Castilla and remained part of its domain for several centuries.

The original city was built on a hill (once the site of a Roman temple), but limited space made expansion a necessity. To bridge the gap between the streets circling the hilltop and the more traditionally designed lineal streets of the lower city, tunnels and steeply descending ramps, such as the Paseo Arquilla, were devised and create an interesting multilevel configuration that is best seen at the town's main Plaza de la Virgen Blanca.

You will want to concentrate your visit in the area from the hilltop to its base. A wonderfully preserved Gothic Quarter is here, greatly admired by Victor Hugo when he visited the Basque Country in the last century. Tile-roof houses of narrow brick and wood beams somehow remind me more of a British Tudor village than anything else I have seen in Spain. There may be no connection, but it is curious that the Escoriaza-Esquibel palace in Vitoria once belonged to Fernán López de Escoriaza, physician to King Henry VIII of England and his wife Catherine of Aragón (who in turn was daughter of the Catholic King Fernando of Aragón and Queen Isabel of Castile). The doctor also took care of Catherine's nephew, the emperor Charles V of Spain.

Vitoria is a city with a sweet tooth that has gained fame in Spain for the quality and variety of its candies and pastries and for its charming, old-fashioned bake shops.

SEEING VITORIA

EL PORTALÓN   Once a medieval trading house, this admirable fifteenth century brick building of heavy wood beams and eave overhangs today encloses an elegant restaurant.
♦ From here to the Plaza de España on quaint Calle Correría there are many antique shops.

MUSEO DE NAIPES (MUSEUM OF PLAYING CARDS)   Located in the mansion of the Fournier family, foremost manufacturer of Spanish playing cards (their name appears on almost every Spanish deck). The collection includes playing cards from all over the world.

CASA DEL CORDÓN   A sixteenth century house with an interesting rope motif carved in stone around the entryway. Inside there is a wonderful Gothic salon and medieval tower.

MUSEO ARQUEOLÓGICO   Remains of the ancient town of Iruña, discovered in this region, are displayed here.

MUSEO DE BELLAS ARTES   There are several paintings by José Ribera in this museum, including his famous *Christ on the Cross*.

STAYING IN VITORIA

PARADOR DE ARGÓMANIZ   Carretera Madrid–San Sebastián, km 3, Argómaniz   tel. (945) 28 22 00   On a hill overlooking the plains of Álava, this former palace of the seventeenth century is a parador that I particularly like, especially the eaved and heavily beamed dark-wood dining room. Although it is fifteen kilometers from Vitoria, I would choose it over the city's otherwise ordinary accommodations. (Moderate.)

EATING IN VITORIA

IKEA   Castilla 27   tel. (945) 14 47 47   Set in a beautiful old house, this restaurant is especially adept at fish preparations. (Moderate–expensive.)

DOS HERMANAS   Madre Vedruna 10   tel. (945) 13 29 34   Traditional fare, concentrating on Basque seafood and Rioja vegetables prepared with top-quality ingredients. (Moderate–expensive.)

EL PORTALÓN   Correría 151   tel. (945) 14 27 55   Come to this elegant restaurant to admire its landmark building and antique collection as well as for its food, which features Basque and Navarra cuisine. (Moderate–expensive.)

◆ You can buy the famed sweets of Vitoria at **BOMBONERÍA GOYA** (Calle Dato 6 and 20 and Avenida Gasteiz 45 and 78) and at **CONFITERÍA ALBERDI** (San Prudencio 27).

♥ISITING THE PROVINCE OF ÁLAVA

IRUÑA   Roman and pre-Roman finds from this ancient city are on display here in a small museum (there are more remains in the Museo Arqueológico of Vitoria).
◆ Nearby is the Roman bridge of Trespuentes, more than 120 feet long, with thirteen arches.

PEÑACERRADA   Massive side-by-side rounded towers give the town its name and leave just a narrow arched opening for access to the village.

LAGUARDIA   High above the Ebro valley, lovely Laguardia is encircled by walls. From its park, at the edge of the hill, the views are panoramic. The town is medieval, and its extremely narrow streets, happily, do not accommodate cars. During wine harvest, Laguardia is redolent with the earthy scent of fermenting grapes, and red peppers that hang to dry on wood balconies in the fall add a vibrant touch of color.
◆ Be sure to see the fourteenth century covered portal of the Santa María de los Reyes church, impressive with its larger-than-life polychrome statues of the Apostles.

MARIXA   Sancho Abarca 8   tel. (945) 10 01 65, is a popular restaurant with
pretty views over the valley. Marixa serves fruits and vegetables from the
Ebro valley, along with roasts of lamb and kid and, of course, wines of La
Rioja. (Inexpensive–moderate.)

♦ Some Álava-Rioja bodegas that can be visited by previous appointment,
and where you can also purchase wines, are: **BODEGAS PALACIO,** at the
entrance to Laguardia; **BODEGAS ALAVESAS,** just outside of Laguardia;
and **REMELLURI,** in Labastida.

♦ If you are traveling on the main road toward Pamplona, take a detour
(road Alsasua–Estella) to the Puerto de Urbasa for exciting, untamed
scenery of huge boulders, cliffs, and rocky gorges.

PEACEFUL, PASTORAL NAVARRA AND THE MADNESS OF SAN FERMÍN

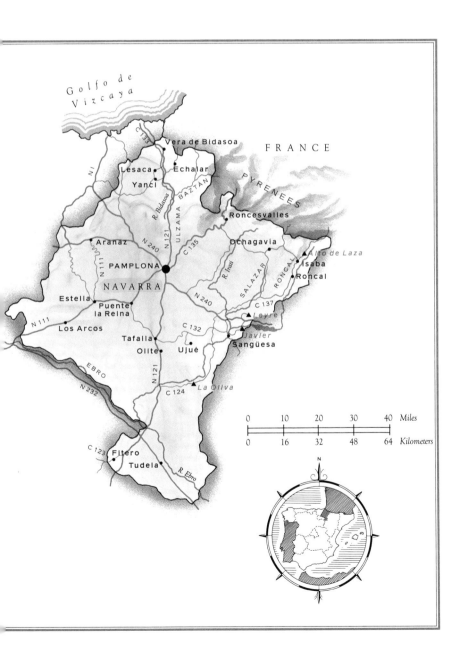

Introduction

THERE IS ONLY ONE province in Navarra (nah-*vah*-rah), so the region and the province are one and the same. Navarra shares borders with the Basque Country, Aragón, and France and has historical and cultural links to all three. But Navarra's personality is distinct and so deserves a chapter of its own. However, I suggest that you combine a visit to Navarra with one to the Basque Country or Aragón or both.

Navarra's history has been a long tug-of-war among rival powers. In its earliest history, Navarra was linked to the Basques; then it was conquered by Charlemagne in the eighth century (northern Navarra adjoins France), and shortly afterward achieved a hard-won independence. Notably absent were the Moors, who spent only a few brief years in Navarra and never gained a foothold, thus allowing the early development of the region's Romanesque style. Medieval pilgrimages to Santiago de Compostela (see box, p. 220) passed through Navarra—the first stop on Spanish soil once the Pyrenees were crossed—and exceptional Romanesque churches sprang up in abundance to accommodate the needs of the fervent masses. Consequently, Navarra's towns have great monuments and are rich in history.

The eleventh century brought a golden era to Navarra under powerful King Sancho III, who achieved control over most of Christianized Spain. Subsequently Navarra fell under the domination of Aragón, and then for almost three hundred years, from the thirteenth to the sixteenth century, belonged to the French crown (the colorful Charles III el Noble ruled during this period—see box, p. 292) until finally Navarra was annexed to the newly formed Spanish nation of the Catholic Kings (the uppermost portion of Navarra, however, reverted permanently to France).

A proudly independent people—a product of geographical isolation—

FOODS AND WINES OF NAVARRA

GENERAL
Lamb, trout, game, sausage, vegetables (white asparagus)

SPECIALTIES
Trucha a la Navarra—trout with cured ham
Bacalao al Ajo Arriero/Ajo Arriero con Langosta—cod/lobster with pimento and tomato
Cochifrito—lamb stew with garlic and lemon
Pichón a la Cazadora—pigeon in wine sauce
Chistorra—variety of *chorizo* sausage
Canutillos—custard-filled pastry rolls
Queso del Roncal—cured sheep's milk cheese
Queso de Ulzama—fresh sheep's milk cheese
Queso de Urbasa—lightly smoked sheep's milk cheese

WINES AND SPIRITS
Agramont, Gran Feudo, Viña Marcos from Navarra
Pacharán—bilberry-and-anise liqueur

Navarros have always jealously guarded their *fueros,* or local liberties and rights, which gave them special privileges and governing autonomy. They demanded that all rulers respect these traditions, and the rulers generally did. The brilliant red berets worn by local police today, once part of the uniform of the *requetés*—Navarrese soldiers who fought in the Carlist Wars (see Index)—symbolize the region's pride and free will. The jota dance and its accompanying stirring songs are another manifestation of regional self-esteem. Now that Spain has been divided into many autonomous "states," Navarra has come full circle and once more enjoys a great measure of self-rule.

Navarra is exceptionally beautiful, especially to the north where it meets the high Pyrenees, creating a land of soaring peaks, deep valleys, tranquil pastureland, swift-flowing rivers and streams, chasmic gorges, and thick forests of oak and beech. It is a pastoral landscape with many luxuriant green valleys like the Bidasoa, Baztán, Ulzama, Roncal, and Salazar, each evoking for me images of the gentlest virgin beauty: cattle lazily grazing; quaint villages of distinctive architecture—stone houses with tile roofs and wood-balustraded balconies that in summer are crowded

TROUT NAVARRA-STYLE

Fill the cavities of 4 trout with slices of cured ham. Sprinkle with lemon juice. Dredge the trout in flour and salt. Heat 3 tablespoons of olive oil in a skillet, and sauté the trout until golden and cooked through.

with pots of pink and red geraniums; and glorious rivers in extraordinary number flowing untamed southward, linking the well-watered highlands with the thirsty central plains of Spain. Navarra gradually levels off to the south in the Ebro valley, where the climate is drier, producing crops more typical of La Rioja, such as wines and vegetables.

Whether the name Navarra has a familiar ring or not, it has become a part of our American literary heritage. For this was Ernest Hemingway land; he loved fishing here along the Río Irati, and he immortalized Navarra, specifically, the Running of the Bulls in Pamplona, forever engraving this event on the world's mind in *The Sun Also Rises.*

Gastronomically Navarra has ties both to the Basques and the Aragonese, and although Navarra is landlocked, you begin to feel the influence of the sea, only a few miles to the northwest. Basque-related dishes like fish-filled red peppers (*Pimientos de Piquillo Rellenos*), *Merluza a la Koskera* (fresh cod in parsley, garlic, and wine sauce), *pochas* (a Basque bean variety), soft-set eggs with shellfish (*revueltos*), and *canutillos* (custard horns) will often be found in Navarra, along with dishes like *Cordero Chilindrón* (lamb stew with red peppers), influenced by the cooking of Aragón and La Rioja.

On the other hand, Navarra has several dishes and food products to call its own: *Bacalao al Ajo Arriero* (dried cod in tomato and red pepper sauce—a sauce that frequently appears in upscale restaurants with lobster); pigeon (captured in nets placed in narrow gorges as they migrate in October) in a variety of preparations; *Cochifrito* (lamb stew with garlic and lemon); and its most famous dish, *Trucha a la Navarra*—trout with cured ham. The region is noted as well for its delicate white asparagus. It is found fresh in spring, but otherwise is bottled or canned. Many Spanish asparagus lovers actually prefer conserved white asparagus, typically served with may-onnaise or a vinaigrette thick with minced pimento and onion. Add to all these foods the outstanding sheep's milk cheeses of Roncal, Urbasa, and Ulzama, as well as two special types of *chorizo* (long skinny *chistorra* and *chorizo de Pamplona*), and you have a cuisine sure to please a variety of tastes.

As is often the case, local wines taste best with these foods, especially refreshing *claretes* and rosés, served slightly chilled. There are also heavy-bodied high-alcohol reds similar to those of Aragón, but these are less appropriate with the somewhat more delicate cuisine of Navarra. Also, try *Pacharán*, a delicious and most unusual liqueur of bilberries and anise—served straight up or iced—that is a specialty of the region; it has gained popularity in Madrid as well.

THE CAPITAL CITY OF PAMPLONA

Despite Pamplona's antiquity (it was supposedly founded by Pompey, which explains its name) there is surprisingly little sightseeing to do here, although I must say there are an inordinate number of fine restaurants to attract your attention. You don't come to Pamplona (pahm-*ploe*-nah) with culture per se in mind; very simply, you come here for the Running of the Bulls.

At least once in your lifetime you should witness the Fiesta de San Fermín, as this eight-day celebration, July 7 to 14 (opening ceremonies on July 6), is called, although that is easier said than done. The fiesta is addic-tive, and I know many Americans, myself included, who came once and can never again be free of San Fermín. Even when we are unable to go to Pamplona, we're always there in spirit. If we happen to be somewhere in Spain during the fiesta, we unfailingly awake each morning before eight, affix ourselves to the TV, and follow the day's Running of the Bulls.

Surely such a fiesta, in which untamed bulls run after the public on city streets, is a barbaric anachronism that should have faded with the twen-tieth century. But no, if anything the fiesta is more vigorous than ever.

It starts at noon on July 6, when an enormous crowd squeezes into the small square facing the Ayuntamiento, Pamplona's Baroque city hall, and can hardly suppress its excitement. The mayor appears on a balcony and declares, "Fellow citizens, ¡*Viva San Fermín!*" A rocket fires, and Pamplona erupts with delirious merriment, as if a charge of electricity had suddenly jolted the town. ". . . the 6th of July, the fiesta exploded. There is no other way to describe it," Hemingway writes in *The Sun Also Rises*. The week-long excitement of San Fermín has begun.

The entire town of Pamplona, joined by thousands who come from elsewhere, take to the streets and cast aside daily cares and everyday clothes for what has become the uniform of the fiesta: white shirt and pants, a fringed red sash knotted low at the waist, and a small red scarf rakishly tied around the neck. Even infants in strollers echo their parents' dress with the most charming results. Nor are animals and city statuary excluded; they too sport red scarfs.

Cafés and bars, especially around the porticoed Plaza del Castillo—
named for the medieval castle that once stood nearby—will be crowded and
lively for the duration of the festivities. Dozens of local bands, followed by
elaborately dressed "giants" and "bigheads" (*gigantes y cabezudos*) that gracefully twirl to the accompaniment of rat-a-tat drums and the haunting sound
of the oboe-like *txistu*, circulate through the streets playing the infectious
"*riau riau*" music of Navarra, and few can resist the urge to get up and dance.
Suddenly the plaza will be a mass of bobbing heads with hands held high. As
one band passes, followed in Pied Piper fashion by those still dancing,
another arrives and the dancing continues.

> The dancing kept up, the drinking kept up, the noise went on.
> The things that happened could only have happened during a
> fiesta. Everything became quite unreal finally and it seemed as
> though nothing could have any consequences.
> *The Sun Also Rises*

Despite the notoriety the *feria* gained through *The Sun Also Rises* and
the thousands of young foreigners who flock here for the week, *los sanfermines* is much more than the running of the bulls; it is a fiesta that for many
Pamploneses is as much a deeply felt religious event as an occasion to party
all through the night. San Fermín, after all, is the patron saint of Pamplona
(his saint's day is July 7), and during this week there are frequent church services and religious processions.

Navarrese youths, many of whom belong to clubs, or *peñas*, dedicated
to *los sanfermines*, have saved money all year for this event and descend on
Pamplona from the countryside. And although everyone joins in the street
dancing, the singing, and general uninhibited joyfulness, the actual run with
the bulls is an exercise in machismo from which women are explicitly
excluded (feminists have recently appeared on TV, demanding the right to
run).

Short, slight Gerónimo Echagüe, a legend in Pamplona and known to
all simply as "Gerónimo," ran the bulls every day of the fiesta for more than
seventy years. "When July arrives, my blood boils," Gerónimo was fond of
saying. "It's been like this ever since that day decades ago when I met the
great torero El Gallo. He rumpled my hair and said, 'Hi, kid.' That's when
the mania struck me."

At 6:45 each morning (it has only been an hour or two since the city
settled down for the night), everyone is rudely awakened by crisply dressed
marching bands playing invigorating reveille. Nobody minds, however, for
this is the alarm clock that signals the approaching *encierro*, the Running of
the Bulls. A full night's sleep is out of the question for the next week; it is
time to practice the fine art of catnapping.

> "My gosh! I'm sleepy now," Cohn said. "Doesn't this thing
> ever stop?"
> "Not for a week."   *The Sun Also Rises*

We roll out of bed and rush to old, narrow Calle de la Estafeta, which
is now boarded up and closed off to all but runners, and we join the crowds

that gather behind barricades. Lucky are those who know someone with a balcony overlooking the street. Runners stake out their favorite spots, some at the gate where the bulls are released, others along the route and still more near the entrance to the bullring and in the bullring, where the run ends.

The event begins as the *mozos*—young male runners in their white and red outfits—lustily sing to the statue of San Fermín, punctuating their words by gesticulating vigorously with rolled newspapers (carried to direct wayward bulls) and practically demanding that the saint deliver them from danger. Suddenly a rocket explodes and the gates open. Six huge bulls, bred for fighting and accompanied by steers who point the way, stare determinedly ahead, intent on staying together. The streets are unknown territory for them, and they are just as scared as the hundreds of men who run with them. You can't imagine the size of these beasts until you see them close up, and the insanity—whether alcohol-induced or not—of voluntarily putting yourself in their path.

> Then people commenced to come running. . . . The crowd was running fast now. . . . [The bulls] were going fast and gaining on the crowd. . . . There were so many people running ahead of the bulls that the mass thickened and slowed up going through the gate into the ring, and . . . the bulls passed, galloping together, heavy, muddy-sided, horns swinging. . . .
>
> *The Sun Also Rises*

Usually the run takes place without serious injuries, but the danger is very real: If a bull separates from the herd, he panics and strikes out at anything in his path. That's why runners and onlookers wait for the sound of the second rocket, which means that all six bulls have reached the corral behind the bullring. These are the same animals that will be fought in the afternoon by professional bullfighters.

We now shift our attention to the Plaza del Castillo, where the morning events are excitedly discussed over big cups of strong, steaming *café con leche*. Runners straggle in, clutching their rolled newspapers like so many badges of courage; relief from the early-morning tension is almost palpable. American aficionados (and there are many) like to gather at the Café Txoko, and hasten to offer their congratulations to their runner compatriots. It has been more than sixty years since the publication of *The Sun Also Rises*, yet Americans still seek to emulate the personal style of Hemingway, even though those who knew him insist he never participated in the morning runs.

A relative lull sets in during the afternoon hours as some catch up on sleep, others make the rounds of the tapas bars on Estafeta, which has quickly returned to normal, and many more watch the parades and processions. The excitement builds for the daily 6:30 p.m. bullfight. Bands sweep through town again, rounding up everyone in their wake and leading them—dancing, of course—toward the bullring. There is little doubt that this is primarily the Festival of the Bull, and that this noble creature is the key to the fiesta's tremendous vitality and worldwide appeal.

I enjoy watching the people at these bullfights, for they too are a show. The stands pulsate with exuberant dancing, ear-splitting music, lusty singing, and rhythmic swaying. Bags of flour shower on the crowd, cooled by sudden spritzes of champagne and seltzer (if you have expensive seats in the shade, you can watch all this at a safe distance), and huge picnic baskets of food and drink are happily consumed while the death-defying spectacle takes place. Remains from these snacks rain on the unfortunate torero or picador who fails to live up to expectations.

Evening brings activity back to Estafeta, and at the Plaza del Ayuntamiento, hundreds dance themselves into a frenzy until the wee hours of the morning. And yet despite so much liberty and alcohol consumption, a certain self-control is apparent, and there are few problems.

For eight successive days, the events of San Fermín are repeated. Exhaustion settles in, mixed with the sadness that San Fermín must end and the routine of everyday life return. The last evening is one of lament to the sound of "Pobre de Mí" ("Poor me / Poor me / San Fermín is over") sung in dirge-like measures. By the next morning San Fermín has vanished into thin air—no more crowds or merriment—but many are already making their plans for the following year.

TIPS FOR THE FIESTA

Reserve hotel rooms well in advance. Try to arrive the afternoon of July 6, and stay at least two more days. Avoid Saturday and Sunday, if possible, when the crowds noticeably swell. Hotel prices double during San Fermín, but are still relatively reasonable. This is one instance when you will want to request an interior room that does not face the noisy streets.

You can usually get bullfight tickets by giving a good tip to the hotel concierge. Prices will be high (regular-price tickets are sold by subscription), but not so high as those charged by scalpers outside the ring.

SEEING PAMPLONA

CATHEDRAL   Built over a Romanesque church, the cathedral is Gothic from the fourteenth century, although the facade is eighteenth century neoclassic. See the lovely alabaster tombs of Carlos III el Noble and wife Leonor (see box, p. 292) and the exceptional Gothic cloister.

MUSEO DE NAVARRA   Once a pilgrims' hospital, the remains of the original Romanesque church around which the cathedral was built are preserved here, along with archaeological finds and a collection of Gothic and Renaissance paintings.

CIUDADELA   This pentagonal citadel was built in the sixteenth century by Philip II, and is surrounded by an ample park.

STAYING IN PAMPLONA

NUEVO HOTEL MAISONNAVE   Nueva 20   tel. (948) 22 26 00   An adequate hotel in the heart of the city on a relatively quiet street. I always stay here during San Fermín. (Moderate–expensive.)

LA PERLA   Plaza del Castillo 1   tel. (948) 22 77 06   This is the nineteenth century hotel described in *The Sun Also Rises*. It is modest, but *the* place to stay during the fiestas, if you can get a reservation. (Moderate.)

TRES REYES   Jardines de la Taconera s/n   tel. (948) 22 66 00   In appearance the best of the hotels, but it is a bit out of the way and during San Fermín often requires full pension—certainly not the best way to eat in Pamplona. (Very expensive during San Fermín; other times moderate–expensive; pool.)

EATING IN PAMPLONA

◆ Reservations are imperative at most restaurants during San Fermín.

JOSETXO   Plaza Príncipe de Viana 1   tel. (948) 22 20 97   The city's number-one restaurant, although I preferred it when it was on Estafeta street in less elegant surroundings. First-rate preparations of local specialties, in particular fish dishes. The frozen dessert truffles are wonderful. (Expensive.)

HOSTAL DEL REY NOBLE   Paseo de Sarasate 6   tel. (948) 22 22 14   More commonly known as Las Pocholas, this is an institution in Pamplona, run by the remaining of nine sisters, who have managed the restaurant since 1938. The menu centers on seafood and other Navarrese dishes. Try *canutillos* for dessert. (Expensive.)

CASA MARCELIANO   Mercado 7–9   tel. (948) 22 14 26   A most popular 200-year-old restaurant for simple meals or tapas, accompanied by Navarrese wines. Extremely crowded during San Fermín. (Moderate.)

RODERO   Arrieta 3   tel. (948) 22 80 35   In a newer section of town in a modern setting. Traditional Basque dishes like *Chipirones en su Tinta* (squid in ink sauce), *pochas* (beans), and *Leche Frita* (fried milk) for dessert. (Expensive.)

HARTZA   Juan de Labrit 19   tel. (948) 22 45 68   Top-quality seafood in the simple preparations that Pamplona favors. Try also the red beans (*Alubias de Tolosa*) and cheese from the mountains of Urbasa. (Expensive.)

♦ Tapas are well prepared and varied along Estafeta and Nicolás streets, where one bar follows another: batter-fried or grilled shrimp, *chistorra* sausage, croquettes, fried squid, and fresh white anchovies (*boquerones*) are some of the specialties. I especially like **BAR FITERO** on Estafeta street.

SEEING HISTORIC NAVARRA

PUENTE LA REINA   On the pilgrimage route to Santiago, this village was named for its splendid eleventh century arched bridge over which the pilgrims traveled, which in turn was named for the queen (Doña Mayor) who ordered the bridge built. See the town's main street, with its noble residences that evoke the times of the pilgrims; the Romanesque portal of the **SANTIAGO** church; and at the **CRUCIFIJO** church, a German crucifix uniquely mounted on a Y-shaped cross.

ESTELLA   Today a prosperous city, Estella was also a busy place in medieval times because of its strategic location on the way to Santiago. From here to Galicia all routes from France became a single road, and for this reason the city has an unusual number of Romanesque and transitional Gothic churches. Since most are along the main street that the pilgrims trod, next to the Río Ega, the city lends itself perfectly to a short walking tour.

In the San Pedro de la Rúa historic district, of narrow streets and medieval flavor, see a wonderful concentration of twelfth century buildings: **SAN PEDRO DE LA RÚA** church, atop a rocky mound and reached by a long elegant flight of steps, its portal of sweepingly clean lines yet rich in scenes of dragons and other monsters; **SAN MIGUEL ARCÁNGEL** and its unusually lavish sculpture over the portal; and the **PALACIO DE LOS REYES DE NAVARRA,** a singular example of civil Romanesque architecture and facing **PLAZA DE SAN MARTÍN,** a square of great Navarrese flavor and unusual beauty. Just across the river is **SANTO SEPULCRO** church, whose portal is immensely graceful.

SANGÜESA   The town, also along the Santiago pilgrimage road, is nondescript, but don't miss the remarkable Romanesque portal of **SANTA MARÍA LA REAL,** with its superabundance of detailed stone carvings, touching on a wide variety of themes and characters. There are musicians, warriors, craftsmen, fighters, and scenes from the New and Old Testaments. The hand of the Master of San Juan de la Peña, responsible for the magnificent cloister of San Juan de la Peña monastery in Huesca is evident.

MONASTERIO DE LEYRE (Yesa)   In its exceptional setting above the stunning turquoise waters of the Yesa reservoir, this was the first great Romanesque structure in Navarra, already existing in the ninth century. The church portal is eleventh century and richly carved (that is why it's called Porta Speciosa), depicting scenes of local saints and biblical figures, along with the monsters representing temptation, sin, and hell. The interior of the church is primitive but of unusual height and design (note the three archways at the altar and their irregular shape). Tombs of several of Navarra's early kings are here.

The crypt below, which supports the weight of the church and where the pantheon once was, is the oldest part of the church and one of the most extraordinary works of Spanish Romanesque—primitive columns of massive stone blocks and uncommonly low capitals, of varying heights, some only one foot from the ground.

The monastery sponsors an inn, **HOSPEDERÍA DE LEYRE** Monasterio de Leyre, Yesa tel. (948) 88 41 00 (inexpensive), that is beautifully kept and in most peaceful surroundings. The restaurant has wonderful *Pimientos de Piquillo* (local red peppers), Roncal cheese, *Merluza a la Koskera* (fresh cod in green sauce), and *canutillos* (custard horns). (Moderate.)

YESA RESERVOIR is a huge expanse of calm aquamarine water. Crowning a hilltop over the reservoir is the once-proud village of Tiermas, abandoned and crumbling. Summer water sports.

CASTILLO DE JAVIER The mountain setting is beautiful for this the birthplace (later converted to a castle) of the celebrated sixteenth century Spanish missionary to India and Japan, Francis Xavier. The castle is a mix of styles and periods.

OLITE Overshadowing the town of Olite is its superb thirteenth century castle, rectangular in shape and flanked by four square towers. In the fourteenth century a palace was added

---

THE COLORFUL COURT OF CARLOS III EL NOBLE AND QUEEN LEONOR

The end of the fourteenth century was a peaceful time in Navarra, allowing King Carlos III to attend to administrative reform and to engage in many building projects, such as the palaces of Tafalla and Olite. The king and his queen, Leonor, daughter of Enrique II of Castile, took up residence in Olite.

The queen found this massive edifice much too "cramped" for her liking and much too somber, so the king agreed to build an elaborate addition, the exterior in French château style, the interior of sumptuous Moorish design, with plaster tracery, ceramic floors, and *artesonado* ceilings. The queen's chamber overlooked a lush Valencian garden of fountains and lemon and grapefruit trees. There were hanging gardens on the upper terraces, supported by pointed arches; spiral stairways; tapestry-covered walls; even a lion's den where the king kept his extensive menagerie. He organized fiestas, bullfights, and musical events and planned to build a gallery connecting this palace with the castle of Tafalla some three miles away. In short, all was luxury, and the whims of his beloved queen were satisfied.

But alas, Leonor was not happy. She suffered from what has been described as "melancholy"—perhaps a mix of depression and homesickness—and although the king implored his beloved queen to stay, she gathered her children and went to live at the Castilian court of her brother. King Carlos missed her enormously, but she refused to return. Only when her brother died nine years later did she go back to Olite and to the open arms of the king.

Carlos III el Noble and Queen Leonor are buried in the cathedral of Pamplona.

to satisfy the whims of Queen Leonor (see box, p. 292), and it was done in elegant French Gothic style (the king was related to the rulers of France) with multiple slate-roofed, cone-shaped turrets. You will have to imagine its once lavish décor. The Santa María La Real church is part of the complex; see its floridly carved fourteenth century portal.

PARADOR PRINCÍPE DE VIANA   Plaza Teobaldos 2   tel. (948) 74 00 00, is installed in the Olite castle and provides accommodations in a peerless setting. (Moderate–expensive.) The dining room serves regional food accompanied by the fine rosé wines produced in Olite.

TUDELA   With a decidedly Moorish flavor (the Arabs stayed here into the sixteenth century), this city has an old quarter of narrow streets, Moorish archways, and brick houses graced with bulging coats of arms. Benjamín de Tudela, a famous Jewish writer of the twelfth century, was born here. He traveled extensively through other lands and wrote one of the world's first guidebooks. The entrance to the **CATHEDRAL,** called the Door of Judgment (Puerta del Juicio), is on a narrow street, which makes it difficult to gain enough distance for proper perspective. Give yourself time to decipher its complex and amusing scenes, showing the glories of heaven to the left (everyone looks exceptionally angelic) and the horrors of hell to the right (gory portrayals of monsters, decapitations, burnings, boilings, people hanging by their feet, tongues being yanked from mouths, etc.).

The main square, **PLAZA DE LOS FUEROS,** is adorned with coats of arms of Navarrese cities and numbered balconies—the plaza was once used as a bullring. **CHOKO**   tel. (948) 82 10 19, on the square, is good for tapas or a meal and is well known for its bite-size frog's legs and fresh vegetables, especially just-picked white asparagus in season.

RONCESVALLES   Literally "Valley of the Thorn Trees," this beautiful area is a place of great symbolic significance and an inspiration for poets, artists, and novelists. It was here that the old Roman road entered Spain, that Charlemagne's forces were defeated (see box, p. 294), that millions of pilgrims to Santiago first touched Spanish soil and were given hospital care. You may wish to see the Sancti Spiritus chapel, the oldest construction from the twelfth century, under which, it is said, Roland and Charlemagne's Twelve Peers and many pilgrims who did not survive the mountain crossing are buried. See also the thirteenth century chapel of Santiago, which once rang its bells to orient pilgrims crossing from France. In the thirteenth century Colegiata church is a much-venerated statue of the Virgin, bathed in gold and silver, and a museum displaying church treasures. All that is left of the Royal Pantheon (entered through the church cloister) is the tomb of King Sancho VII, who fought in the battle of Navas de Tolosa (see box, p. 472). Near him are the chains from the battle which enclosed the camp of the Moorish king, and a stained-glass window showing a scene from that fierce confrontation. I like to stretch out with a picnic on a grassy knoll above Roncesvalles at the Alto de Ibañeta, take in the glorious view, and envision the stirring events that took place here so many centuries ago.

UJUÉ   The village climbs to a well-preserved castle-church of the eleventh century, a national monument, which looks out onto a sea of green terraced land.

THE DEFEAT OF CHARLEMAGNE AT RONCESVALLES

It is impossible to sort legend from the facts of the events that took place at Roncesvalles more than 1,200 years ago. Emperor Charlemagne crossed into Spain in 778 with the intention of pushing back the Arab invasion. He reached Zaragoza, thus liberating part of northern Spain, but there a fierce Arab attack forced him to retreat to Navarra. His troops destroyed everything in their wake and took booty and hostages, thus angering the Navarros, who were not in any case kindly disposed to the presence of foreign forces on their soil.

Charlemagne safely crossed the pass at Roncesvalles into France, but the Navarros then cut off the retreat, ambushing the French rear guard, commanded by Roland. At this point the great tale of *Chanson de Roland* (written three centuries after the events) begins to take over. The attackers are transformed from Navarros into the much more hateful Moslem infidels, and there is treason and heroism of epic proportions. Roland, although finding himself in an impossible situation, delays blowing his famous horn to summon help from Charlemagne, and when the emperor finally arrives, Roland is dead, his troops defeated.

The *Chanson de Roland* became a kind of battle hymn recited by medieval pilgrims, who entered Spain at Roncesvalles en route to Santiago de Compostela, and a symbol of the still-ongoing battle against anti-Christian forces.

Try **MESÓN LAS TORRES** tel. (948) 73 81 05, for typical fare of lamb chops and *migas* (Spanish seasoned bread cubes) and end with excellent candied almonds. (Inexpensive.)

MONASTERIO DE LA OLIVA A grand example of the extremely sober, austere, and massive transitional Gothic architecture of the Cistercian religious order, encompassing the twelfth through fourteenth centuries. The monastery was abandoned, but has once again been occupied by a community of monks.

LOS ARCOS A town often passed by, but you'll be amazed at the interior of the Gothic **ASUNCIÓN** church. I have never seen such a wealth of decorative elements: gold-leaf sculpture everywhere and two walls, wood-paneled floor to ceiling, densely painted in muted flower designs.

FITERO Noteworthy mostly for its Cistercian monastery, **SANTA MARÍA LA REAL,** built in the thirteenth century in that typically austere style. See especially the Sala Capitular (chapterhouse) and the monastery treasures.

TAFALLA The Renaissance altarpiece by Pamplona sculptor Juan de Ancheta in the **SANTA MARÍA** church is one of Navarra's most beautiful, but little remains of the famous castle of Carlos III (see box, p. 292). There are two fine restaurants here, **HOSTAL TAFALLA** on the Carretera Pamplona-Zaragoza, km 38 tel. (948) 70 03 00, and **TUBAL** in town at Plaza de Navarra 2 tel. (948) 70 08 52. Both serve traditional fare of Navarra and add a touch of nouvelle. (Moderate–expensive.)

SEEING SCENIC NAVARRA

Most of these sights are in the mountainous north of the region.

BIDASOA VALLEY   The road through the valley hugs the gentle Río Bidasoa (which forms a natural border with France) and runs near some charming Navarrese villages that form a unit called Las Cinco Villas: In **VERA DE BIDASOA**, high green mountains serve as a backdrop for this town of Swiss appearance with whitewashed dark-wood-trimmed houses, cheerfully adorned with geraniums. Here is the former home of renowned twentieth century Spanish writer Pío Baroja. It is kept by his nephew—also a highly regarded writer—just as it was when Don Pío lived, and although it is not open to the public, visits are sometimes granted—try knocking on the door. **LESACA** has a similar quaint appearance. In the beautifully verdant gorges of **ECHALAR** pigeons are captured during their fall migrations. The road to **YANCÍ** is narrow and winds through a countryside of grass-covered hills and haystacks. The woods become dense as you approach **ARANAZ**.

RONCAL VALLEY   This is the valley where Roncal cheese is made and a good place to buy some, either to picnic or to take home.

   The village of **RONCAL** has steep cobbled streets graced by several stone palaces with elaborate coats of arms.

ISABA is an ideal place to relax in the Roncal valley and take advantage of mountain-related activities. **HOTEL ISABA**   Carretera Pamplona s/n   tel. (948) 89 30 00, is adequate but undistinguished. However, the surroundings with their sightseeing possibilities merit a visit. (Moderate.)

   At the stunning heights of the Puerto de Belagua near the French border, a mountain refuge, **VENTA DE JUAN PITO**   Puerto de Belagua   tel. (948) 89 30 80 (inexpensive), serves solid country fare, like grilled lamb chops and *migas* (crisp bread bits).

ULZAMA VALLEY   Yet another valley of deep-green mountain scenery. The views from Puerto Velate pass looking out over the Bidasoa valley are quite extraordinary. Ulzama cheese is made here.

VENTA DE ULZAMA   Carretera Pamplona-Irún, km 31   tel. (948) 30 51 38, is a small inn (once a stagecoach stop), clean and comfortable, in lovely tranquil surroundings and just forty minutes from Pamplona. (Inexpensive.) Its large airy restaurant, through which a breeze always flows, overlooks the lushly green mountains. The menu is appealing and the food very well prepared. (Moderate.)

RÍO IRATI   There are wonderfully scenic spots along the length of this river for trout fishing and picnicking (we particularly enjoyed the area around Orbaiceta).

SALAZAR VALLEY   The gorge, Hoz de Arbayón, of awesome proportions, and the sheer cliffs blanketed in green distinguish this valley. The banks of the Río Salazar also have dense vegetation.

The immaculately kept and most attractive village of **OCHAGAVÍA** spans both sides of the rapidly flowing Salazar and is crossed by bridges at regular intervals.

♦ At the **ALTO DE LAZA** a fantastic scene of the high Pyrenees unfolds—jagged snowcapped peaks in the distance contrast with the mossy green covering of the mountains in the foreground. Utter silence except for cowbells and buzzing flies.

THE RUGGED BEAUTY
OF ARAGÓN

INTRODUCTION

WE ALWAYS SEEM to be in Aragón on our way to someplace else (you too might consider combining a visit to Aragón, as we do, with travel to eastern Castilla-León or to the Levante), so I have seen the region in bits and pieces. But it seems to me that Aragón has the best of the Pyrenees, a compelling Arab legacy, and villages of unparalleled beauty that have not changed for centuries.

"Passing through" also reflects the history of Aragón, which was a crossroads between eastern and western Spain, between Spain and France, and the link joining Catalunya and the Levante with central Spain. Because it was necessary to travel across the region to reach many other destinations, Aragón became a powerful kingdom in medieval times, and for the very same reason it was pivotal, its control vital, during the Spanish Civil War.

Despite its proximity to major vacation areas, Aragón is sparsely populated and probably the region of Spain least visited by both foreigners and Spaniards. I can't imagine why, for it has an untamed, untouched beauty without equal, and summer brings fine warm days and refreshingly cool evenings. Aragón is one of the last great undiscovered regions of Spain, and I will happily keep it a secret for me and for those of you who choose to follow in my path.

No fewer than three great mountain chains cross Aragón—the Pyrenees, the Maestrazgo, and the Montes Universales. The Pyrenees are the most spectacular because of their startling height, but the Maestrazgo possesses an awesome beauty of its own, and the austere Montes Universales attract in yet subtler ways. The area of Los Monegros, a desert setting of eery silence, forms another world, unlike anything else in northern Spain.

From the elevations of the Pyrenees to the north in Huesca down to the green valley and grand Río Ebro of central Aragón (Zaragoza) and to the arid southern lands of Teruel, Aragón is full of surprises.

FOODS AND WINES OF ARAGÓN

GENERAL

Lamb, pork, rabbit, Teruel ham, trout, salmon, truffles, fruits

SPECIALTIES

Ternasco—roast lamb
Chuletillas de cordero—baby lamb chops
Cordero or Pollo Chilindrón—lamb or chicken and red pepper stew
Ajo Arriero—dried cod and red pepper stew
Melocotón al Vino Tinto—peaches in red wine
Cuajada—rennet pudding
Queso Tronchón—semisoft sheep's milk cheese

WINES

Monte Ducay from Cariñena
Abuelo Nicolás, Borsao from Campo de Borja
San Lorenzo, Señorío de Lazán from Somontano

You somehow know when you are in Aragón: There is a special ruddy coloring to the earth and to the rock formations. Low trees and bushes cover the mountains, and villages of stone and slate have an original architecture and unique medieval atmosphere. In the province of Huesca, houses are built of stone blocks and set in rolling green valleys; in Zaragoza a reddish adobe finish gives an entirely distinct look, while in Teruel villages tend to blend into the rocky mountain scenery.

Aragón was the northernmost limit of the Arabs' Al Andalus, attached to the caliphate of Valencia. Moorish influence remained strong many centuries after their expulsion, and most pronounced in the provinces of Zaragoza and Teruel. Arab horseshoe arches, construction of narrow brickwork, and ceramic inlay can be seen all around the region. The arched upper galleries of noble homes and palaces have a Moorish flavor and are characteristic of Aragónese architecture. The ceramic pottery made in Aragón today looks just like museum pieces from Arab times, and the region's song, the jota, sounds somewhat like an Arab wail. Aragón's villages bear exotic Arab names like Albarracín, Calatayud, and Alcañiz. The Moors left Huesca in the eleventh century, allowing early Romanesque architecture to flourish in northern Aragón. Its churches became guardians of Christian documents, and a distinctive ornamental style developed, characterized by stone carved in checkered patterns and decorative ball motifs.

Along came Jaime the Conqueror, reclaiming the rest of Aragón and Valencia for the Christians, and Aragón became one of the most powerful kingdoms of medieval times. When a later king, Fernando, married Queen Isabel of Castilla and thus for the first time united Spain as one country, Aragón gradually lost its importance and its independence to a centralized Spanish state.

The Aragonese people, however, never lost their spirit of independence, resisting tooth and nail any intrusions of central power and insisting on keeping their age-old tradition of local privileges and rights (called *fueros*). In the twelfth century, for example, local noblemen defied the efforts of ruler Ramiro II to usurp their power (with tragic results; see box, p. 323); some of the fiercest fighting of the Spanish Civil War took place here (see box, p. 306); and even today towns like Albarracín are self-contained and retain their ancestral rights to govern communal property.

Aragoneses are a hardy lot, and their character is as rugged as the landscape. Men tend to be tall and muscular; their dance is an exercise in athletic prowess. And there is always occasion for an outburst of song. Once, with a group I led to Albarracín, a late evening in a village restaurant became a rowdy joust between Aragonese song and "Oh! Susanna." On another occasion, in a restaurant outside the city of Huesca, a hundred or so Aragonese men, attending a company luncheon, spontaneously serenaded us, to their and our great pleasure, with jota music.

Food in Aragón is equally robust, based on simple meats, like roast lamb and cured ham, and stews like *Ajo Arriero* (made with dried cod and red peppers) and the typical *chilindrón* preparations of chicken or lamb, also made with red peppers. I pass on *Gazpacho Turolense*—not the refreshing cold soup of Andalucía, but a thick mixture of bread, rabbit, potatoes, pork liver, and spices. Portions are enormous in Aragón. Don't ask for a *bocadillo* and expect a small roll with a dainty filling. It will more likely be a whole loaf of bread bursting at the seams with cheese, *chorizo,* or ham (even though for the Aragoneses this sandwich is merely a snack). A portion of locally smoked salmon I once ordered was not the paper-thin slices I was accustomed to, but a thick slab of fish. Of course you can always turn to trout, salads, baby lamb chops, healthy rennet pudding (*cuajada*), and the region's famous peaches, home-preserved in local red wine, for lighter fare.

The wines of Aragón, such as the well-known Cariñenas, are as lusty as the food, all the better to help digest gargantuan food portions. They are typically dark, heavy-bodied reds with up to 17 percent alcohol and are traditionally considered a man's drink. When we were in Cariñena one year with another couple and ordered in a local bar four glasses of Cariñena wine, we were served two glasses of red and two of white. The explanation? The red was not suitable for ladies! In recent years, however, lighter reds have begun to appear in response to the current preference for such wines.

THE PROVINCE OF TERUEL

I HAVE SPECIAL affection for Teruel (teh-roo-*el*), the southernmost province of Aragón; so many of the things that I love in Aragón are here— extraordinary mountain ranges and wonderful villages of unique medieval architecture. The houses seem to spring forth from the living rock, while distant rock formations sometimes mimic man-made structures.

Modern times have not come to rural Teruel; its villages are losing their populations to the cities, for winters are harsh and isolating and the living eked from the dry and rocky earth meager. But fortunately such villages are attractive to a special breed of tourist looking for peace of mind and a sense of timelessness (and, as an added benefit, prices far below what you find in most of Spain).

Moorish influence is still palpable in Teruel. You will see Moorish towers in many cities and towns, and find craftsmen who forge iron and decorate pottery—the typical green-and-black design of the province—in much the same manner as the Arabs once did (potters must also know some well-kept secrets, for this is the most durable and chip-resistant pottery I have ever used).

We divide our time in Teruel between two regions, the Maestrazgo mountains in the northeast and the Montes Universales to the south, from which three of Spain's mightiest rivers emerge: the Turia, the Júcar, and the Tajo. We come to Teruel to take it easy—to trout-fish (with surprisingly little competition), and to walk in the mountains, take leisurely drives, explore enticing villages, and enjoy a climate that is ideal in summer, when days are hot (but a cold clear stream is never far away) and evenings deliciously cool.

THE ENCHANTMENT OF ALBARRACÍN

It is precisely for relaxation and simple pleasures that we come to Albarracín, a village that, besides its magnificent setting in the Montes Universales next to the rapidly flowing Guadalaviar (as the Turia river is called here), is the epitome of a Teruel village and a national treasure.

The road to Albarracín twists through a mountain landscape of scrub trees and massive striated rocks of a rosy hue. Quite suddenly Albarracín and its hanging houses appear, rising dramatically over the rocks and blending in color and construction with the natural surroundings in a most perfect harmony.

Albarracín is a natural amphitheater, enclosed on three sides by the Río Guadalaviar, which snakes around the town. On a steep rise are the original walls (from the times of the Arab caliphs), which form a semicircle that effectively closes off the town. For this reason, in its history Albarracín never experienced an armed invasion.

Although it was inhabited since prehistoric times and once a Roman town, Albarracín has an importance that dates to the times of the Moorish occupation of Spain and more specifically to the eleventh century, when Aben-Razin (from whose name Albarracín is derived) made this the capital of his reign. Albarracín eventually passed to the Christian feudal rule of the Azagra family, which for well over a century managed to keep Albarracín independent from the rival kingdoms of Aragón and Castile. Even today some of that autonomy persists. The surrounding mountains are community property, and the profits from the lumber industry and the lease of grazing land go to local municipalities.

Albarracín has a Moorish flavor that casts a spell. Crudely cobbled streets are dim and winding, and there is a hush broken only by the sound of rushing water. High walls and tightly grouped houses envelop you in the medieval atmosphere of a fortified town.

Few cars brave the steep streets of Albarracín, and walking is the only practical means of getting around. If you are staying overnight (and I can't imagine not doing so), you will most likely stay at a sixteenth century mansion that is the Hotel Albarracín, perched over the river gorge and commanding wondrous views of town and mountains.

Hardly a ray of light penetrates Azagra street, which begins near the hotel, and it is not hard to understand why students of architecture are so attracted to Albarracín. This street is just nine feet wide at its base, but its houses, built upon boulders, slant out over the street and practically touch at the tile rooftops—a brilliant architectural device that utilizes space to the maximum in a village where space is a precious commodity. My eyes always travel upward in Albarracín, at once to capture scarce light and to appreciate unusual architectural detail and varying geometric planes. There is elegant woodwork under roof overhangs and wrought-iron decorative work, of which Albarracín is justifiably proud.

Streets, houses, even flights of steps in Albarracín appear misshapen and contorted as they strive to conform to the natural contour of this rocky spike. Sharp angles, not curves, are the distinguishing feature of the town;

stone and stucco houses (in the tones of the red and
pink rocks of the surroundings) are supported by
vertical, horizontal, and diagonal timber frameworks that create Albarracín's characteristic
appearance.

   This is essentially a town of simple houses
that are often multipurpose: sheltering animals
and storing wine and tools on the street level,
providing living quarters on the second floor
and ventilated granaries above. But there are
also mansions from the sixteenth and seventeenth centuries, emblazoned with intricately carved coats of arms. Elaborate iron
window gratings and fanciful door
knockers and handles in shapes of lizards

CASA DE LA JULIANETA

and serpents bearing grotesquely human teeth and ears catch my attention.
One of these lizards, copied in hand-wrought iron by craftsman José Luis
Jarreta, is now on display in our home.

   I like to get up late in Albarracín, but my husband, Luis, is sometimes
awake at the crack of dawn,
donning his fishing gear
and heading for the
Guadalaviar. By the time I
am ready to start the day,
he has already sent his
morning's catch to the
hotel kitchen to be cleaned
and fried *a la navarra* (see
box, p. 285) and served to

LAMB CHOPS *EL CHORRO*

Grill baby lamb chops to taste. Sprinkle with
salt, lemon juice, minced garlic, and minced
parsley and serve immediately.

us for breakfast. We have lunch on the banks of a river or in a pine forest,
and it typically consists of *chorizo*, Teruel ham, olives, cheese and fruits from
a village grocery, and incredibly good bread, just out of the oven, from the
bakery on the other side of the river.

   As darkness falls, we watch hundreds of swallows circle and swoop by
our hotel terrace at dizzying speeds, snatching in midair insects that rise
from the river. Dinner will most likely be at friend Pedro's El Chorro restaurant, and we'll eat down-to-earth food—wonderful lamb chops and salads;
fried eggs with locally made *chorizo* and blood sausage; fried trout filled with
a slice of ham; local peaches steeped in red wine; and of course hearty
Aragonese jug wine. Once you've become slightly tipsy, ask Pedro to show
you his hilariously vulgar and indecent bodega.

   After dinner we wander the village streets, deserted, dark with mystery. We venture into the old Jewish quarter beyond the cathedral, and
imagine the friendly ghost of Doña Blanca, a beautiful Christian princess
upon whom a spell was cast because she wished to marry a young Jewish
man. She died in her castle, and since then, at midnight and at full moon,
villagers have seen a woman dressed in a fluttering white tunic descending
from the castle to bathe in the waters of the Guadalaviar. It is a tribute to
the medieval beauty and timelessness of Albarracín that a legend such as
this so easily comes to life.

We end the evening with a short drive just outside the town, stop the car, turn off the headlights, and contemplate the astonishing number of stars that crowd the clear mountain sky.

Seeing Albarracín

PLAZA MAYOR   Once a moat outside the town walls, this main square, faced by town hall and a beautiful assemblage of sixteenth century houses, is one of Albarracín's few open spaces and a site for theater, bull-fights, and dancing of the jota. Stop by the tourist office here for walking-tour information.

CASA DE LA JULIANETA   A remarkable structure, the most pho-tographed in town, that appears about to topple because it is built at the juncture of an ascending and a descending street.

PLACETA DE LA COMUNIDAD   Popularly known as the Little Corner of the Fan (Rincón del Abanico), this diminutive plaza is a rare architectural unit of houses crammed together into a striking number of angles and corners; its houses look out onto the plaza from at least eight dif-ferent directions.

TOWN WALLS   Built by the Moors, the walls are intact, rising 36 feet and punctuated by lookout posts. Climb up for formidable views of Albarracín and the countryside.

CATHEDRAL   The most notable feature of this sixteenth century Gothic structure is its carved-wood altar dedicated to San Pedro. There are several valuable pieces in the Cathedral museum, such as a pyx (box to guard the Host) attributed to Cellini; a beautifully worked crystal container for incense, in the form of a fish; and Flemish tapestries.

◆ About three miles from Albarracín, over the bridge at the foot of the town, are caves with prehistoric paintings. Some are easier to reach than others.

STAYING IN ALBARRACÍN

HOTEL ALBARRACÍN   Calle Azagra s/n   tel. (974) 71 00 11   In a his-toric building, very simple but comfortable. The restaurant is quite good. Request a room overlooking the river. (Moderate; pool.)

EATING IN ALBARRACÍN

EL CHORRO   Calle del Chorro s/n   tel. (974) 71 01 12   Choose tapas at the bar or hearty meals in the upstairs dining room (see text). (Inex-pensive.)

SHOPPING

ARTESANÍA JARRETA   Across the street from the Hotel Albarracín, this shop features a large selection of beautiful Teruel pottery and wrought-iron work made by owner José Luis Jarreta.
◆ By the river, just beyond the town and through the tunnel, Mr. Jarreta's elderly father, Adolfo, has his workshop, where he displays and sells his wrought-iron creations.

$\mathcal{V}$ISITING OTHER VILLAGES IN THE MONTES UNIVERSALES

ORIHUELA DEL TREMEDAL   A prosperous well-kept village with noble residences and elaborate wrought-iron grillwork everywhere.

SALDÓN   There are few inhabitants left, but the setting is special, ringing a mountain and surrounded by yellow fields of grain that undulate in the wind.

MORA DE RUBIELOS   On the banks of the Fuenlozana river, the village center is a National Historic-Artistic Complex with lovely eighteenth century seignorial houses that have overhanging eaves and beautiful wrought iron balconies. Above the village is a thirteenth century castle encircled by a moat.
JAIME I   Plaza de la Villa   tel. (974) 80 00 92, is a small hotel occupying an old mansion. (Moderate.)

RUBIELOS DE MORA   A village in the charming style of Teruel province that has received prizes for its beauty, distinguished by fifteenth to seventeenth century noble homes and palaces and an unusual number of churches and convents.
PORTAL DEL CARMEN   Glorieta 2   tel. (974) 80 41 53, in an old convent, serves simple fare like beans, lamb *chilindrón*, and the typical Spanish dessert *Tocino de Cielo* (rich caramel flan). (Inexpensive–moderate.)

$\mathcal{T}$HE CITY OF TERUEL

Just a few minutes from Albarracín is the provincial capital of Teruel, set on a cliff over the Turia river and joined to the surrounding land by a series of bridges. Much of the city was demolished in the fierce battles of the Spanish Civil War (see box, p. 306), but the beautiful Mudéjar towers, with their green-and-white ceramic inlay and decorative brickwork, miraculously escaped destruction, and the narrow winding streets in the Old Quarter keep their Moorish flavor. The city is home of the legend (and probably of the actual characters) of the Lovers of Teruel (see box, p. 305).

Seeing Teruel

CATHEDRAL   Don't miss the astonishing Mudéjar ceiling, painted in minute detail and unusual in its depiction of human faces and figures (rarely seen in Moorish art). From the upper balcony you can appreciate the exceptional work at closer range.

SAN PEDRO   In a chapel of this church are the tombs of the Lovers of Teruel, sculpted of alabaster in this century by Juan de Ávalos (the same artist who worked on El Valle de los Caídos, in the province of Madrid). The lovers' hands symbolically reach, one for the other, but do not touch. The tombs are more interesting for what they represent than for great artistic worth, and visitors seem to get ghoulish pleasure in viewing the spotlighted mummified remains of the lovers as seen through windows in the sarcophagi.

PLAZA DEL TORICO   An odd nineteenth century statue (replacing one from the sixteenth century) of a miniature bull, no more than a foot high and with a star on his forehead, stands atop a tall thick column at the center of this porticoed plaza. It is said that a sacred bull determined the site of the present city, and the bull has been the symbol of Teruel ever since.

MUDÉJAR TOWERS   Five towers, constructed in the thirteenth to fifteenth centuries as church belfries by Moors living under Christian rule, have survived (San Martín and San Salvador are the finest examples). The delicate brickwork is set off by colorful ceramic tiles, and city streets uncustomarily pass *through* the towers.

Spain's Romeo and Juliet: The Lovers of Teruel

Isabel de Segura and Diego Garcés de Marcilla grew up together in Teruel in the thirteenth century, she from a family of means, he without money to his name. They fell in love, but because he was poor, Diego was denied her hand. Isabel's family, however, gave him exactly five years to prove his worth, and he set off in pursuit of fame and fortune. Five years to the day later, he returned to Teruel flush with success, only to find that on that very day Isabel, in accordance with her parents' wishes, had married a powerful nobleman from Albarracín (Diego neglected to count his day of departure, so his time had expired the day before).

Diego secretly visits Isabel on her wedding night and tells her that he is leaving Teruel forever. All he asks is a kiss, which she, as a proper bride, must deny him. He drops dead, as if struck by lightning.

The funeral is celebrated the following day in San Pedro church (see above). Isabel, grief-stricken, throws herself on the corpse of Diego, gives him the kiss she had withheld in life, and dies on the spot. In death they are united, buried next to each other, but at a respectable distance; after all, they were not married.

The debate goes on over whether the lovers of Teruel actually existed, but in the meantime the appealing tale has been the basis for novels, plays, operas, and film the world over.

THE FIERCE BATTLE FOR TERUEL IN THE CRUEL WINTER OF 1937

Teruel was in the hands of the Nationalists at the outbreak of war in 1936, but was continually under siege from the Republicans, who soon captured the city. In an attempt to regain Teruel, the Nationalists launched a final battle. It was December 29, 1937.

> Teruel, maintaining its reputation for bad weather, registered a temperature of 18 degrees below zero. Men who, at Brunete, had cursed the remorseless sun of Castile, now went down with frostbite. A blizzard lasted four days, leaving behind four feet of snow and cutting both armies off from their supply depots.
> Hugh Thomas, *The Spanish Civil War*

Losses on both sides were spectacular, and in the end the Republican defenders of Teruel were all killed or captured.

A makeshift cemetery just off the Teruel-Zaragoza road (about six kilometers from Teruel, on the left side as you head towards Zaragoza) is a site of complete tranquillity where the tall wheat waves in the breeze. It brings the tragedy of civil war to life as no battle accounts can possibly do. Here the execution of 1,005 Republicans who defended Teruel against the victorious Nationalists is commemorated. But these are not formal graves. There is a deep pit into which the massacred victims were tossed. All around are mounds of stone and earth, some with headstones, others with handwritten messages, in an effort by surviving family to personalize a loved one's death. Particularly heart-rending is one written by a young widow: "I searched and searched for you, only to find you here. What a senseless death that has left me and your four-year-old child utterly alone!"

More than fifty years have passed, but the wounds are still unexpectedly fresh.

STAYING AND EATING IN TERUEL

PARADOR DE TERUEL   Carretera de Zaragoza   tel. (974) 60 18 00   Just outside Teruel in a quiet setting, this is a fine parador. (Moderate–expensive; pool.) But with Albarracín so close, I prefer to stay there. The parador is a pleasant place for a drink, and the restaurant serves good regional specialties, like Teruel garlic soup and grilled rabbit.

EL MAESTRAZGO

What makes one mountain range different from another? It's hard to pinpoint, but I do know that the Maestrazgo is not like anything else in Spain.

A mountain road that cuts through the Maestrazgo from Cantavieja to Villarluengo showed me the Maestrazgo in its greatest glory. Startling vistas of great majesty unfold in a stark setting of bare mountains, deep ravines, astounding precipices, gorges, and clefts. Rocky spurs soar from between cliffs, and the landscape resembles a series of ships stranded in most uncharacteristic surroundings. Rounded rock formations that often crown mountains look deceptively like castle ruins (and occasionally that is just what they are). Similarly, the circular patterns of terraced land blend effortlessly into the land's natural lines.

> The region between Mirambel and Morella is arid, rugged, desolate, bristling with barren hills. There are grand ridges of limestone, massive red and yellowish formations like ruins of immense palaces and castles, like citadels of Cyclops or giants that, at times, mimic details that seem for a moment to be of human construction.   *Pío Baroja*

The Maestrazgo was of vital importance during several periods of Spain's history and was already populated in prehistoric times, as cave drawings attest. The Greeks and Romans were here; during the Reconquest, El Cid (see Index) crossed the Maestrazgo en route to the conquest of Valencia (he gave his name to villages like Villafranca del Cid and La Iglesuela del Cid), and the region saw the forces of Jaime I El Conquistador bring control back to Christians. The Knights of Montesa—Aragón's equivalent of those of Calatrava, Santiago, and Alcántara (see Index)—protected the region from further Moorish intrusions by fortifying the towns (their leader was the master, or *maestre;* thus the mountains became known as the Maestrazgo, Land of the Maestre).

The Middle Ages was a period of greatest splendor for the Maestrazgo: Nobles who were given privileges and titles in reward for their efforts against the Moors established their feifdoms in the Maestrazgo, often asserting their independence from the Aragonese kings. And with the antipope nearby in Peñíscola in the fourteenth century (see Index), a great deal of traffic passed through the Maestrazgo, keeping Pope Pedro de Luna in touch with the rest of Spain. During the Carlist Wars of the nineteenth century (see Index), the Maestrazgo was a stronghold of the Carlists and the scene of repeated warfare.

The villages of the Maestrazgo, often enclosed by walls and crowned by castles, are of haunting beauty. Their medieval appearance is intact and their silence overwhelming, and were it not for the friendly, hospitable inhabitants, such towns would seem museum pieces or stage sets. Streets are cobbled and multilevel with unusual angles and often with long flights of short steps that connect one level of the town with another. There are seignorial houses of golden stone with impressive coats of arms and palaces that date to the times when the Maestrazgo was still a major route through Spain. But there are humble homes as well that equally speak of pride, elegance, and nobility unrelated to wealth or title.

To see the Maestrazgo and its unique villages, I suggest establishing your base at the parador in Alcañiz and spending one day touring Calaceite, Cretas, Valderrobres, Beceite, and Peñarroya de Tastavins. Another day might focus farther south on Forcall, Mirambel, Cantavieja, Iglesuela del Cid, Ares de Maestre, and Castellfort (several of these villages are actually over the border, in Castellón province, but the Maestrazgo unites them, and they more appropriately belong here). Rest that night in Morella. Rubielos de Mora and Mora de Rubielos, farther to the south, fit more comfortably into a Teruel-Albarracín visit. Each route has at least one good place for lunch, and a picnic is of course always an option. If your interests run to trout fishing, I highly recommend a stop in Villarluengo.

*V*ISITING THE EXCEPTIONAL VILLAGES OF EL MAESTRAZGO

ALCAÑIZ   Center of lower Aragón; its Old Quarter is a national monument. See particularly the stately Plaza de España and its sixteenth century town hall and the Lonja—fifteenth century commodities exchange—that is a fine example of civil Gothic architecture. Nearby, the Colegiata church has an exceptional Baroque portal.

PARADOR LA CONCORDIA   Castillo Calatravos tel. (974) 83 04 00, is set in the town castle and one of my favorite paradors, commanding stunning views of Alcañiz and the Río Guadalope far below. It incorporates a Romanesque portal and cloister from a twelfth century church. The restaurant is good, with such specialties as *Pollo Chilindrón*. Request room number 1. (Moderate–expensive.)

MESEGUER restaurant   Avenida del Maestrazgo 9   tel. (974) 83 10 02, is neat and clean and serves simple, well-prepared food, like lamb chops, *menestra* (vegetable medley), beans with partridge, and for dessert, *orejones*—stewed dried apricots in red wine. (Inexpensive.)

JESÚS LEJ ROMEO   Plaza Cabanero 6   tel. (974) 83 24 61 or 83 07 47, has what I think is one of the great collections of antique pottery jugs of the Aragón region. It's a good idea to telephone ahead since the store is not always open, but will open upon request.

CALACEITE   Climbing the slopes of a bald hill and practically indistinguishable in color from the earth, this is a town of noble stone houses (some with the Romanesque arched upper galleries seen in Aragón) and elegant balconies of wrought iron and intricately worked stone. An exceptional Plaza de España has Gothic arches, underpasses, and streets that rise and descend from its center.

CRETAS   In a lovely setting overlooking valleys and fields and a wall of mountains beyond, the streets and the plaza in this town have the typical look of Aragón.

VALDERROBRES   A stone bridge leads to the gateway where the old town begins. Steep cobbled streets ascend to a fourteenth century castle-church. I like the unadorned sweep of its Gothic portal and the huge rosette window above it. Town hall, in the Plaza de España, has wonderful wrought-iron work on its balconies.

HOSTAL QUEROL   on the main street   tel. (974) 85 01 92, has no décor to speak of—a TV in one corner, paper tablecloths, and no menu—but you can't go wrong with fried eggs, *chorizo*, peppers, and the bean stews. (Inexpensive.)

BECEITE   In an exceptional setting, the road to Beceite runs between high cliffs that drop precipitously to the Río Matarrana, where this pleasing little town is situated. Nearby is a reserve of Capra Hispanica.
ANTIGUA POSADA DE RODA   Villanueva 19   tel. (974) 85 02 54, is a tiny old inn of genteel appearance that serves simple home cooking. (Inexpensive.)

PEÑARROYA DE TASTAVINS   Very narrow, steep streets (with steps carved into them for easier walking) lead to the upper limits of the town where the whitewashed houses have crude wood balconies.

FORCALL   The village has an unusually elongated and most attractive plaza. On it, **MESÓN DE LA VILLA** has a substantial selection of tapas.

MIRAMBEL   There is nothing to distract you from the pure medieval ambiance of this silent walled village, declared one of Europe's most beautiful. Exquisitely kept stone houses (two twin mansions are especially noteworthy), cobbled streets, and overhanging rooftops of wood-carved eaves.
    At the village bar, **LAS TEJAS,** you can get tapas, like local *chorizo* and *longaniza* sausage.

CANTAVIEJA   The charm of this cobbled whitewashed village centers on the Plaza de Cristo Rey, a harmonious assemblage of Romanesque and Gothic arched buildings with delicate wrought-iron balconies. The plaza is unpaved, to use for bullfights during local fiestas. Here were the headquarters of General Cabrera during the Carlist Wars.
BUJ   Avenida Maestrazgo 6   tel. (964) 18 50 33, is a real find in such out-of-the-way surroundings. Doña Francisca and her two daughters run this simple, immaculate restaurant serving uncommonly good food, lovingly prepared. (Inexpensive.)

VILLARLUENGO   Trout-fishing fans will find the Pitarque river of rushing water and deep, still ponds great for angling—uncrowded and with easy access all along the course of the river. Two days of the week fishing is prohibited—call the hotel for more information.
HOSTAL DE LA TRUCHA   Las Fábricas   tel. (974) 77 30 08 (moderate), although in a splendid setting, this hotel, former site of a paper factory, is not all that it could be. But you do have a restful terrace where you can order drinks, contemplate the mountains that loom nearby, and listen to the serenade of the river. The restaurant is a pleasant surprise—I have never eaten better roast quail, generously sprinkled with garlic and parsley. (Inexpensive–moderate.)
 • On the road between Cantavieja and Villarluengo, see La Cañada de Benatanduz, a village set over a deep rocky gorge, and the Órganos de Montoro, two miles of massive rock formations that derive their name from their resemblance to organ pipes.

IGLESUELA DEL CID   The name "Little Church of El Cid" is identified with El Cid (see Index), hero of the Reconquest either because his daughter was married here in a fourth century hermitage (it is just beyond the town and was enlarged in the sixteenth century) or because El Cid prayed here en route to Valencia. The village, built of flat golden stone, is set over an impressive canyon.

ARES DEL MAESTRE   This village has an extraordinary appearance, flowing down a hillside from its castle, which is incorporated in a massive circular rock that looks somewhat like an oversize brioche.

CASTELLFORT   From this village there are stupendous views of laboriously terraced land that forms swirling tiers in the mountains.

MORELLA   Once an important Roman town, Morella centers on an immense rock more than 3,000 feet above the sea, over which a castle was raised many centuries ago (you have to look carefully to separate the castle from the rock). More than a mile of walls and fourteen towers enclose this town of medieval character (a national monument), which because it follows the round shape of its rocky base, is circular and tiered. It's hard to get anywhere without climbing flights of short stone steps. A highlight is the arcaded main street, its stone pillars huge in contrast to the narrow streets and small houses. Be sure to see the view approaching from the south on the Alcañiz-Morella road and the town's aqueduct. The thirteenth century Gothic church Arciprestal de Santa María La Mayor has two elegant portals (it is said that the sculptor and his son carved in competition), and the choir is uncustomarily elevated and richly decorated. Papa Luna, the antipope who lived in Peñíscola, held Mass here.

HOTEL CARDENAL RAM   Cuesta Suñer 1   tel. (964) 16 00 00, is in a sixteenth century mansion of rustic Castilian decor. (Inexpensive–moderate.) At the restaurant here or at the **MESÓN DEL PASTOR**   Cuesta Jovaní 5 tel. (964) 16 02 49, try the *Sopa de Buñuelos Morellense* (a chicken-vegetable soup served in squat pottery bowls in which tiny *pâte à choux* float), *Ternasco Trufado* (lamb with truffles—this is truffle country), and excellent *cuajada*, rennet pudding garnished with squares of almond sponge cake. (Inexpensive–moderate.)

♦ Since the fifteenth century Morella has been a textile center and is still known for its bright-colored woven blankets and hand-knit sweaters.

FIESTAS

LOS TAMBORES   An unusual Easter tradition principally in the villages of Híjar, Calanda (where celebrated Spanish film director Luis Buñuel was born), and Alcañiz. The insistent beat of hundreds of drums begins at midnight on Holy Thursday and never ceases until Saturday evening.

THE PROVINCE OF ZARAGOZA

THROUGHOUT HISTORY Zaragoza (thah-rah-*go*-thah) province has been for the Romans, Arabs, and then the Christians a major crossroads through Spain, by land and by way of the Río Ebro, and it has prospered both economically and culturally. Zaragoza united the Cantabrian coast with the Mediterranean, and the Pyrenees with the Castilian plain, so control of Zaragoza was essential to whoever ruled the country. This is why Zaragoza was a major battleground in the nineteenth century War of Independence and the Carlist Wars and in modern times during the Spanish Civil War. Once the Nationalists dominated Zaragoza and its Ebro valley, their total victory was for all purposes a fait accompli.

For similar reasons Zaragoza was an important Moorish center that joined the Valencian and Andalusian caliphates and allowed the Arabs to keep a foothold in north-central Spain long after they had been expelled from other northern regions. Zaragoza became the capital of Upper Al Andalus.

Most of Zaragoza province lies in the broad valley of the great Ebro river and is therefore the least mountainous area of Aragón (although one of Spain's highest peaks, El Monte Moncayo, 7,630 feet above the sea, is in western Zaragoza). Its villages have a different look too. Rather than being constructed with the stone so prevalent in Aragón, the houses are built in a crumbly ruddy adobe that blends into the natural terrain.

The most productive land of Aragón is also in Zaragoza, now that irrigation (first introduced by the Arabs) has converted once-arid areas into fertile ground, where grape vines (from which popular Cariñena and Campo de Borja reds are made), wheat, and fruit trees flourish. In striking contrast, the Monegros region is for all purposes a desert—a unique microclimate— quite unexpected this far to the north.

THE CITY OF ZARAGOZA

I can't say that Zaragoza is one of the cities I prefer in Spain, but its venerable history and several interesting sights certainly provide a gratifying visit. On the banks of the Río Ebro in the Ebro valley, the city of Zaragoza is more than two thousand years old. It was originally an Iberian settlement, and in 24 B.C. was established as a Roman colony, named Caesar Augusta in honor of the Roman emperor Augustus, as a place for Roman legionnaires to retire (some Roman walls from the third century remain). The city of Zaragoza is today, as it has been throughout history, the center of the bustling crossroads that is the province of Zaragoza.

Prized by the Arabs, who called it Sarakosta (several monuments remain from those times), Zaragoza was claimed by the Christians in the twelfth century. Surprisingly, they made little effort to eradicate vestiges of the Arab past, as commonly occurred elsewhere. Romanesque style developed side by side with Mudéjar, and Arab craftsmen were held in highest esteem. In the nineteenth century War of Independence (see Index), however, the city was devastated by the French siege and the fierce resistance of Zaragozanos. Much of the Old Quarter and its great monuments were destroyed. Yet others survived, and today the old palaces, churches, towers, and mansions that remain have the decidedly Mudéjar flavor of the city's past.

Quite apart from its strategic location, Zaragoza has come down in history for quite another reason: It is a place of mass pilgrimage to the shrine of the Virgen del Pilar. It is said in Zaragoza that he who doesn't believe in God believes in the Virgen del Pilar. And in fact her temple here rivals, and some think surpasses or at least eclipses, the cathedral.

It seems as though every other woman in Spain bears the name Pilar, which literally means pillar and refers to a momentous event that presumably took place on January 2, in the year A.D. 40. The apostle Saint James (see Index) was traveling across Spain, preaching the Christian doctrine and gathering Christian converts. He had stopped in Zaragoza and was praying with his disciples one evening by the banks of the Río Ebro when suddenly the Virgin Mary dramatically appeared on a marble column amid choirs of angels. Since then miraculous sightings of the Virgin have occurred by the thousands all over the world, but this account is of singular significance and extraordinary impact: The elderly Virgin Mother of Christ was still *alive* and living in Jerusalem when Saint James saw her vision in Zaragoza. At this very site a chapel was erected to enclose the sacred column, and a grandiose church eventually developed around it.

The cult of the "Virgin of the Pillar" persisted through centuries of Moslem domination, and soon after the Reconquest, Zaragoza's bishop asked for monetary aid from all Christians to restore the somewhat neglected temple. Pilgrimages began, and donations flowed in from commoners (who were promised special indulgences), from Spanish and European royalty, and from popes. Catholic King Fernando, a native of Aragón, was a devotee of the Virgen del Pilar's, claiming that she had saved him from a crazed, knife-wielding Catalan, and his gold collar, which had deflected the blow, was offered to the Virgin. He also constructed a chapel in her name in the cathedral of Granada.

By the seventeenth century the chapel of Pilar in Zaragoza had become a sumptuous place of worship. And although October 12 is universally known as the day Columbus sighted land, it became as well the Día del Pilar. As Hispanic nations adopted her, the date was celebrated as El Día de La Raza or El Día de la Hispanidad—the Day of the (Hispanic) Race. October 12 is marked by major festivities in Zaragoza during which the figure of the Virgin is deluged with flowers, floats parade through the streets, bullfights take place, and the jota is joyfully danced.

SEEING ZARAGOZA

BASÍLICA DEL PILAR   The temple as seen today is a graceful seventeenth century structure that incorporates works from earlier periods. There are many representations of the Virgin here, but most meaningful is the one in the Santa Capilla, a large chapel that encloses the space where the apparition occurred and the jasper column (a pilgrim's ritual includes kissing the column) on which an image of the Virgin rests. A crown resplendent with jewels adorns her head, and her costly robes are changed frequently to show off her rich and varied wardrobe. Valencian Damián Forment, who worked extensively in Aragón, executed the basilica's beautiful main altar in alabaster.

LA SEO DEL SALVADOR   The city's cathedral (known as a *seu* in Aragón and Catalunya) is perhaps artistically superior to the Basílica del Pilar, but has for centuries struggled for attention and recognition in the face of the Virgin's enormous popularity. Although ostensibly Gothic, this huge cathedral of five aisles is an interesting mix of styles, including Mudéjar, Baroque, Plateresque, and neoclassic, and was built on the site of a former mosque. See in particular the Mudéjar cupola and a wonderful tapestry collection.

ALJAFERÍA   A celebrated eleventh century Arab palace of brick and delicate plaster ornamentation, magnificently restored, which evokes the beauty and poetry of the Moorish south and was the setting for the tower scene of Verdi's *Il Trovatore* (an unusual choice when you consider that almost all operas with a Spanish theme take place in Andalucía).

PATIO DE LA INFANTA   A sixteenth century patio of impressive Plateresque style, today it is located within a bank building, La Caja de Ahorros, but formerly it was attached to a palace.

TORREÓN DE LA ZUDA   This tower in traditional Mudéjar brick construction is all that remains of a tenth century residence of Moorish rulers. The tourist office is located here.

LA LONJA   A former commercial exchange that represents civil Renaissance architecture at its best. The exterior has the typical Aragonese upper gallery and eaves. Inside, pillars mushroom into a vaulted strapped ceiling punctuated by rosettes.

STAYING IN ZARAGOZA

GRAN HOTEL   Costa 5   tel. (976) 22 19 01   Recently renovated, this deluxe hotel is in a landmark building and centrally located. (Expensive.)

MELIÁ ZARAGOZA   Avenida César Augusto 13   tel. (976) 43 01 00   A modern, well-appointed hotel of unexciting design, especially popular with businessmen. (Expensive; rooftop pool.)

THE TRAGIC DEMISE OF BELCHITE

There are few things in Spain that have made a more lasting impression on me than the ruins of the small town of Belchite. In the stunningly hot summer of 1937, Nationalist supporters fiercely clung to Belchite, even though the town was surrounded by Republican-controlled territory. Belchite finally succumbed, and the spirits of the weary Republican army, aided by the International Brigades, were temporarily lifted. But just five months later, the battle for Belchite raged anew and the town returned to Nationalist control. Destruction was so great that instead of attempting to rebuild, a new town was constructed nearby.

But the remains of old Belchite were not bulldozed; they have been preserved as a reminder—a kind of monument—to those terrible times. Today you see the crumbling buildings and feel an overwhelming silence and sadness. The only signs of life are the birds that flutter in and out of artillery shell holes and the black beetles that slowly make their way along the parched soil. On the door of the bombed-out church, someone has handwritten this memorial:

Village of Belchite, no more
Do strong young men gather around you,
Never more will you hear the jotas
That our fathers sang.

EATING IN ZARAGOZA

I am more at home in Zaragoza with down-to-earth Aragonese cooking than with the French- and Basque-influenced cuisine of the city's expensive restaurants. I think you will enjoy **BODEGÓN TÍO FAUSTINO** Don Teobaldo 14 (behind La Magdalena church) tel. (976) 39 69 52, a barn-size tavern with the patina of centuries, even though it has only been a restaurant for about twenty years (before that, it was a distillery). Earthy smells of hanging hams, wine barrels, and peppers and olives marinating in earthenware pots and casseroles permeate the air. At the fireplace lamb chops, *chorizo*, *longaniza* (a long, narrow sausage), *morcilla* (black sausage), and rabbit (my favorite) are grilled to order. (Moderate.)

LA RINCONADA DE LORENZO La Salle 3 tel. (976) 45 51 08, has regional cooking, like roast lamb and *chilindrón* dishes, and a good tapas bar. (Moderate.) **MESÓN DE CARMEN** Hernán Cortés 4   tel. (976) 21 11 51, has a wide selection of tapas along a dark wood bar and a restaurant featuring Aragonese fare. (Moderate.)

♦ For more tapas, make the rounds of the dozens of bars along the narrow street known as El Tubo (the Tube).

FIESTAS

VIRGEN DEL PILAR   The week of October 12 (see text).

ꝓISITING THE PROVINCE OF ZARAGOZA

FUENDETODOS   Birthplace of Francisco de Goya (see box).

BELCHITE   A town in ruins, destroyed during the Spanish Civil War and preserved as a reminder of the horrors of warfare (see box, p. 314).

DAROCA   Declared a national monument, this village of steep winding streets has more than two miles of walls of a soft, red crumbly stone, punctuated by dozens of defense towers. Of interest is the church of Santa María, where altar cloths, objects of a miracle at the time of the Reconquest, are on display in a beautiful chapel.

The story is told of several army captains about to receive Communion in Daroca when the Moors staged a surprise attack. The priest hid the Communion hosts in the altar cloths, and when the captains victoriously returned, Mass continued. The host, to their amazement, had turned to flesh and blood. Each wanted to take the miraculous cloth to his hometown. Instead it was placed on a donkey that was set free at a point equidistant from all the towns. The donkey headed for Daroca, and the altar cloths have been in the Santa María church ever since.

MONASTERIO DE PIEDRA   In a peaceful green oasis around the Río Piedra, hidden below the bare red hills of Aragón, are the remains of the twelfth century Piedra monastery. A beautiful hotel has been created around a grand Renaissance stairway of impressive proportions (a later addition) and the original monks' cells are guest rooms. Abandoned on the grounds, but very interesting to explore, are the remains

ꝭUENDETODOS: BIRTHPLACE OF GOYA

Francisco de Goya y Lucientes was born and lived until his teenage years (at which time the family moved to Zaragoza) in the tiny village of Fuendetodos in a barren desolate Aragonese setting. His mother had inherited some land and a noble title, and his father administered the land. The village and its setting provide a glimpse of Goya's formative years.

The lasting impression this arid country made on Goya is clear in the landscape backgrounds of his work—especially his etchings. They are remarkably empty, with only a gnarled tree or a jagged outcropping of rock breaking the low line of a featureless horizon. The look of the land perfectly matches the bleak lives of the people pictured in the foreground of many of the etchings, but this is more than a stylistic device; it is also a realistic interpretation of the landscape in which, as a boy, Goya was imprisoned.

Richard Schickel,
The World of Goya

Despite the family title, Goya's home was humble and has been preserved with its primitive kitchen and furnishings as a museum.

RESTAURANT OF THE THIRTY-SEVEN DISHES

While searching for recipes for my book *Tapas: The Little Dishes of Spain*, I kept hearing about a place in a little Aragonese village that had sensational tapas. But no one seemed to know exactly where it was or why it was so special. Further detective work brought us to the little town of Almonacid de la Sierra, where we asked for this bar of tapas fame. "You mean El Mesón, the Restaurant of the Thirty-seven Dishes?" all would ask.

El Mesón was an ordinary village bar, where dozens of local retirees gathered. We saw no tapas, so headed for the plain, bustling dining room. A harried waitress delivered a huge tureen of steaming soup to our table. Perplexed, we nevertheless served ourselves (the soup was very tasty), and the tureen was immediately whisked away and replaced by a big bowl of garbanzos.

These dishes, it turns out, were not tapas at all, but part of twenty-six separate meals and eleven desserts, served in mammoth portions from which you were welcome to take as much or as little as you pleased (all for a modest price that varied according to how many dishes you tried). In rapid succession came (I'll only list a few) bean stew, paella, grilled sausage, shrimp in their shells, fried peppers, lamb stew, rabbit stew, baseball-size meatballs, salad, chicken, mushrooms, lamb chops, sausage, snails, pork loin, fried eggs, and of course plenty of local wine. As a finale, a whole *serrano* ham, a Manchego cheese, desserts, coffee, brandy, and champagne came to the table.

Indulge selectively—unless you are Zaragozano, you will not likely be capable of eating everything.

---

of a twelfth century Tower of Homage, the austere abbatial palace, and the monastic kitchen and dining room.

In the nineteenth century a park of grottoes, waterfalls, and lakes set among lush vegetation was created next to the monastery. It is wonderful for quiet walks.

HOTEL MONASTERIO DE PIEDRA   Nuévalos tel. (976) 84 90 11 (Moderate.)   Request a second-floor room facing the countryside. The hotel restaurant is quite good, serving simple local fare such as *longaniza* sausage, partridge in *escabeche,* grilled steak, and fresh vegetables.

CARIÑENA   The center of a region producing robust wines of the same name. Come here to sample these wines on site, in local bars, or at a bodega.

ALMONACID DE LA SIERRA   Just another little village, were it not for El Mesón, the "Restaurant of the Thirty-seven Dishes" (see box, tel. (976) 62 70 14; reservations necessary on weekends).

CALATAYUD   Its name reflects the clear Arab origins of this town, named after its castle (Calat-Ayud, castle of Ayud). The streets are distinguished by numerous Mudéjar towers, especially those of the San Pedro and San Andrés churches.

◆ Located on the main road from Madrid to Zaragoza, Calatayud provides travelers with many bars serving fine tapas.

MONASTERIO DEL VERUELA   In the foothills of Mount Moncayo, this twelfth century monastery became known as the place where Spain's great lyric poet of the nineteenth century, Gustavo Adolfo Bécquer, retired to a life of simplicity, and where he composed one of his outstanding works, *Cartas Desde Mi Celda* (Letters from My Cell). The Romanesque portal is utterly sober and severe, almost devoid of unnecessary ornamentation, but superbly designed in Aragonese style. The interior is equally severe, vast, and grand.

TARAZONA   The old town rises steeply from the Queiles river and is reached by several bridges. Tarazona's rich Moorish heritage is apparent in the brickwork of its towers, arches, and passageways and in the intricate plasterwork of the cathedral cloister. At the foot of the old town and across the river is a charming octagonal bullring, painted in pastels and converted into simple apartments.

LOS MONEGROS   An area of desert-like hills, unique in northern Spain.

UNCASTILLO   A dramatic elongated castle crowns a hilltop over this village through which the Río Riguel flows. Many small bridges pass over the river, each one leading to a house on the other side. **SANTA MARÍA** church has an unusual heavily carved and turreted belfry with the checker-and-ball decoration that is typical of Aragón, but what I like best is a sensational Romanesque portal, elaborately decorated, its statues uncustomarily angled toward the viewer.
+ The village bakery, near the church, makes wonderful sugar cookies.

SOS DEL REY CATÓLICO   A jewel of a town, immaculately kept and of true medieval flavor. Walled, with countless noble homes of golden stone, this town is constructed on not one, but several hills (be careful—it's easy to lose your sense of direction). All streets, however, eventually join at the Plaza del Ayuntamiento, where several low arches form an unusual porch.

The reason there are many seignorial houses in this seemingly isolated and unimportant town is that it was the birthplace in 1452 of Catholic King Ferdinand; his mother often traveled here to oversee the frontier wars with Navarra and was a guest of nobleman Martín de Sada when she gave birth. In recognition of this event, Ferdinand's father bestowed on all families of Sos the noble title of hidalgo.

See the frescoed cupola of the crypt and the outstanding choir stalls of the Romanesque **SAN ESTEBAN** church, reached by a delightful covered passageway beneath the church (the king-to-be was baptized here). Visit also the Palacio de Sada, where the king was born.

PARADOR FERNANDO DE ARAGÓN   Sainz de Vicuña 1 tel. (948) 88 80 11 (moderate), is a new parador that blends perfectly into the medieval ambiance of the town and commands wonderful views; the Pyrenees appear like a wall in the distance. Spacious dining room with very good food.

YESA RESERVOIR   See p. 291.

THE PROVINCE OF HUESCA

WE ARE NOW in upper Aragón in a province adjoining France and dominated by the highest peaks of the Pyrenees, which gradually give way to the gentle foothills of fertile verdant land and innumerable rivers, streams, and cascades. As you might imagine, Huesca (wes-ca) is an ideal summer and winter vacationland of incredible natural beauty, and possibilities for outdoor sports are boundless. Yet the region is lightly visited, and that is all the more reason to come.

Moorish domination of upper Aragón was substantially shorter than that of Zaragoza and Teruel; indeed, many Christians never left, hiding in almost impenetrable regions of ravines, gorges, and dense vegetation and continuing their religious practices. And when Christianity officially returned, some outstanding churches, monasteries, and castles were built in a Romanesque style distinctive to this medieval pocket of Christianity that was enclosed on one side by the Pyrenees and on the others by Moorish Spain. We see the checker-and-ball motif of Aragonese Romanesque and, particularly in Huesca, perceive the hand of a sculptor known only as the Master of San Juan de la Peña. His craftsmanship and unusually expressive style are part of what makes the eleventh century monastery of San Juan de la Peña such an exciting complex.

Since the Moors were quickly driven from Huesca, there was little need for fortified towns embraced by walls, except on the province's southern borders with Moorish Spain. Villages were constructed in broad and gently rolling valleys, not at the summits of rocky defensive spikes. The look is typical of high-mountain architecture, similar, in fact, to what you would see in alpine regions of other European countries: stone houses, wood balconies, and pointed slate roofs to shed the snow.

The isolation of Huesca bred self-sufficiency and created a fervidly independent people—a serious obstacle for early Christian kings like Alfonso el Batallador and Ramiro II el Monje, who encountered fierce resistance in their attempts to centralize power. Local nobility was particularly rebellious, arrogant, and adamantly opposed to outside control. As a result a stunning event, known in history simply as the incident of the "Bell of Huesca" (a pallid name indeed for an event so grisly), took place in the city of Huesca (see box, p. 323).

Huesca takes pride in several food specialties: roast lamb (referred to as ternasco, rather than cordero, and not so young as the lamb of Castile), stewed lamb a la pastora, and "mountain asparagus," a quaint euphemism for lamb's tails boiled, then sautéed, and served with peppers and tomato. Huesca produces a variety of pork products, several of which enter into a bean stew made with the region's special beans, called boliches. Vegetables include wild mushrooms, wild asparagus, and cardoons (cardos) served in a creamy almond sauce.

THE SUBLIME SPANISH PYRENEES IN ARAGÓN

The Pyrenees have been called Spain's glory, because of their beauty, as well as her downfall, for historically they were practically impenetrable and stood as a political and cultural barrier between Spain and the Western world. A common expression (and valid well into this century) was that Africa began at the Pyrenees, referring both to Spain's Moorish character and to the isolation created by the mountains.

Although today the Pyrenees still present a formidable geographical impediment, modern roads, tunnels, and bridges have eased problems of communication, especially in summer when the heavy snows have melted from mountain passes. Winter brings skiers, while milder weather attracts fishermen, hikers, and nature lovers. And yet the villages of the Pyrenees have retained their pastoral charm and sense of character.

We count ourselves among the summer visitors, and a trip to the Pyrenees of Huesca (see also "The Pyrenees in Lérida") gives us a chance to immerse ourselves in their awesome natural beauty. We like to focus on two areas: the national parks of Ordesa and of Monte Perdido. On a map the two appear side by side, but no road crosses between them; you have to travel south, then north again—a total of 100 kilometers—to get from one to another. In the Pyrenees, east-west travel is generally arduous because that is the direction in which the mountains run. On the other hand, river valleys point north-south and are your easiest route. There are times, however, when you have to take the more difficult roads, but the exceptional scenery makes the effort more than worthwhile.

I first came to Ordesa in early summer, and I always remember the Pyrenees as they were at that time of year. The weather was glorious—pleasantly warm days, brilliant sunshine, and deep-blue skies through which small puffy clouds drifted serenely. Mountain flowers were in full bloom, and crystalline rivers, swollen by melting winter snows and teeming with trout, cascaded down narrow ravines and waterfalls, cutting through forests of pine, spruce, beech, and boxwood in their hurry to fill the riverbeds and continue their journey south through Spain. The valleys were verdant, even though the high peaks remained snow-covered. Signs of rebirth were everywhere, enough to convince even the resolute atheist of a godly presence.

The weather suited everyone, from the young men in shorts we saw returning from higher altitudes, their skis flung over their backs, to the climbers in mountain gear, to the ordinary visitors, such as we, out for an invigorating jaunt. Cars are not allowed in Ordesa, walking is often uphill, and the air is thin, but you will be rewarded by sights of heights and depths of incalculable proportions, jagged snowcapped mountains appearing in the distance through Vs in the nearby mountains, and colors so dazzling and vivid and in such stark contrast to the sky that the landscape loses its third dimension.

Our days in Ordesa were dedicated to walking, and we would pause for picnics along the rivers, where cows grazed with their newborn calves. In the evenings we either dined at our hotel and retired early or took a short ride "into town" for dinner in the little village of Torla.

In Monte Perdido we spent our time a little differently. This natural reserve is a great place to do absolutely nothing, and there's not a town for miles around. Yes, there are pleasant walks (but certainly not so spectacular as those in Ordesa), and there's a hair-raising jeep ride that I highly recommend if vertigo does not affect you. But what I remember most in Monte Perdido is sipping a gin-and-tonic on the parador's wide veranda, a good book in hand, listening to the perpetual music of cascading water, and contemplating a veritable wall of mountains that rose before me in dramatic perpendicular from the Cinca river.

$\mathcal{V}$ISITING THE HIGH PYRENEES IN ARAGÓN

PARQUE NACIONAL DE ORDESA   See text. An ideal time to visit this nature reserve is mid-June to early July.

HOTEL ORDESA   Carretera de Ordesa s/n, Torla   tel. (974) 48 61 25 (moderate), is ideally located at the entrance to the park, but aside from that, quite ordinary. It will have to do, since there is little other choice. Ask at the hotel for a walking map and information on jeep excursions.

TORLA   This village of stone and slate-roofed houses, with an interesting thirteenth century Plaza Mayor, is the closest to Ordesa. In the pleasant dining room of the **EDEL-WEISS HOTEL**   tel. (974) 48 61 73 you can eat well-prepared simple foods. I particularly enjoyed *Pollo al Ajillo* (garlic chicken; see box). (Moderate.)

> ## $\mathcal{P}$OLLO AL AJILLO (GARLIC CHICKEN)
>
> Cut a chicken into small serving pieces and sprinkle with salt. Heat 6 tablespoons olive oil in a skillet, and fry the chicken until golden and cooked through. Add 10 cloves of garlic, unpeeled and lightly crushed, and continue cooking until they have browned

MONTE PERDIDO   See text. Good accommodations at **PARADOR MONTE PERDIDO** Valle de Pineta, Bielsa   tel. (974) 50 10 11 (moderate), located almost 4,000 feet above the sea in the Pineta valley. Inquire at the hotel for information on jeep excursions and walking routes.

♦ The road **BIESCAS-BROTO-BOLTAÑA** is especially lovely, winding through rocky gorges and passing through a series of delightful villages in lush pastoral settings that follow the course of the rapidly flowing Ara river.

GARGANTA DE AÑISCLO   I have never seen a gorge in Spain that quite compares with this one, reached by turning west on the road just north of Escalona, a town eleven kilometers north of Ainsa. If these mammoth sheer cliffs of ocher, white, gray, and black blotches and striations were any closer, there wouldn't be space for a road. The car ride is impressive, although if you prefer you can reach Añisclo by jeep from either Ordesa or Monte Perdido.

ANSÓ AND HECHO VALLEYS   These two beautiful valleys follow the Veral and Aragón rivers, respectively. The views of soft green meadows alternate with those of narrow gorges, like the impressive Boca del Infierno, in Hecho Valley. The highest peaks of the Pyrenees are always within sight.

CANDANCHÚ   Near the French border, this is the most celebrated ski resort in Huesca. There are several hotels clustered around the ski lifts on the Zaragoza-France road, all moderately priced like **EDELWEISS**   tel. (974) 37 32 00; pool.

BENASQUE   A village of narrow winding streets, distinguished by palaces and noble homes. The **ANETO PEAK,** highest of the Pyrenees, is nearby.

THE MONASTERY OF SAN JUAN DE LA PEÑA

Medieval monks had an uncanny knack for finding remarkably secluded locations for their monasteries. San Juan de la Peña is no exception. Begun by hermits, it soon became a bastion of Christianity, a refuge, a spiritual center, and a focus of resistance to Moslem rule. The Moors never uncovered this monastery. How could they? For although San Juan de la Peña is high in the mountains, the original monastery was built far below in a canyon, completely hidden from view. So sure were the Christians of their camouflage that the Holy Grail (or at least what many presume to be such) was left here in safekeeping for three centuries and used by the monks until Papa Luna (see Index) had it removed to Zaragoza, and from there to the cathedral of Valencia, where it now resides.

What an astounding site this is. As you descend (preferably leaving your car above and walking) along a winding road surrounded by thick vegetation, enveloped by the sounds of singing birds and gurgling streams, a mammoth, semicircular rose-colored boulder (or *peña*—thus the monastery's name) appears quite unexpectedly. It hangs alarmingly close to your head as you approach the monastery, which, because of the rock overhang, is almost a cave.

There are really two monasteries, called the upper and the lower monasteries (there's a third, at the top of the road from which you have come—it is eighteenth century and not of primary interest). The lowest is underground, carved in the tenth century from living rock and a very rare example of early Mozarabic construction (Moorish style—with horseshoe arches, for example—but built by Christians).

The upper church is an eleventh century pantheon for the kings of Aragón and Navarra (from the times when the two kingdoms were joined) and one of the most complete in Spain, with twenty-seven niches. Note as you exit from the church to the cloister the "signed" stones, lines etched by medieval construction workers to calculate the money owed them for their labor.

But what is most stunning in this monastery is the cloister, sheltered and covered like a dome by the monastery's massive boulder. It is a cloister like none other in the world. Quite aside from the wonder of its location is the extraordinary design of its columns. Alternately they are single, then grouped two or four together and uniquely free-standing. The capital carvings, among the finest anywhere, are of astonishing richness and artistic quality.

Represented are scenes of mankind from the Creation to the coming of the evangelists and the life of Christ from his infancy through public career, death, and resurrection. Notice the bulbous and oversized eyes on the faces and the sensitivity and profound tranquillity that they convey. This was the signature detail of the anonymous "Master of San Juan de la Peña," who left his mark around the region and carved especially beautiful work on the facade of the Sanguesa church in Navarra in the twelfth century.

◆ As you come up from the lower monasteries, take a path to the left to a lookout point for fine views of the Pyrenees (indicators point to various peaks).

◆ Another approach to the monasteries is on a small winding road that emerges on your left, about nine kilometers west of Jaca. There are vulture-breeding grounds en route, and it is surely the more impressive way to get here.

ᴠISITING THE FOOTHILLS OF HUESCA

JACA   The first capital of the ancient kingdom of Aragón and a major crossroad to and from France and south to Zaragoza—it was also along one of the major routes to Santiago de Compostela (see box, p. 220)—Jaca is today a busy nucleus for travel into the Pyrenees. See the sixteenth century pentagonal Ciudadela, the only complete citadel remaining in Spain, and the eleventh century cathedral, one of the first and finest example of Romanesque architecture from the times of the Santiago pilgrimages. Notice particularly the finely worked capitals of the portal.

GRAN HOTEL DE JACA   General Franco 1   tel. (974) 36 09 00, is a modern, characterless hotel but with adequate services. (Moderate; pool.)

CONDE AZNAR   General Franco 3   tel. (974) 36 10 50, is a simple family-run hotel, in rustic mountain style. (Inexpensive.)

Within the Conde Aznar hotel is **LA COCINA ARAGONESA** Cervantes 5   tel. (974) 36 10 50, a restaurant decorated with local antiques and focusing on a large stone fireplace, once part of an old country kitchen. Aragonese specialties like wild mushrooms (*setas*), cardoons (*cardos*), roast lamb, and bean stew. (Moderate.)

SAN JUAN DE LA PEÑA— See text.

AINSA Surrounded by walls, this medieval town of brown stone construction has a wonderful arcaded and cobbled Plaza Mayor, highlighted by a twelfth century Romanesque church. It is one of Huesca's most exceptional villages.

BODEGAS DE SOBRARBE Plaza Mayor 2 tel. (974) 50 02 37 (moderate), is charming, built into two wine cellars that are centuries old. Game is a specialty, and in the bar area you can order simple tapas (closed September through Easter).

LOARRE The castle of Loarre is surrounded by walls punctuated by cylindrical towers that climb the hillside. It is the most important Romanesque church-fortress in Spain and served as defense against the Arabs until the eleventh century. Loarre looks like a crown, completely covering a rocky

THE TERRIBLE TALE OF THE BELL OF HUESCA

Few serious historians give truth to the appalling revenge Ramiro II el Monje took on Aragonese nobility. Be that as it may, the story is of stunning impact and enormous popular appeal.

Ramiro II el Monje (the Monk) came to power in Aragón in 1134 on the death of his brother Alfonso el Batallador (the Battler), thus giving up his chosen monastic career. His rule was turbulent: The Aragonese nobility, loath to give up its considerable power, persistently challenged his authority and his right to the throne. Although a somewhat weak ruler of a vacillating nature, Ramiro finally reached the limits of his tolerance and took decisive action.

On the pretext of witnessing the casting of a huge bell, so big that its ring would be heard throughout his kingdom, the king united more than a dozen of the most influential noblemen. Little did they know the trap they had walked into: All were decapitated, their heads placed in a circle and cast into the bell's rim. The head of the most notorious of the group was hung in the center as a bell clapper.

If the famous bell ever existed, it has since disappeared, but a painting that hangs in Huesca's town hall vividly portrays the event, and the room where the event took place can be visited.

spike and looking toward the spectacular vistas of the Ebro valley. During the eleventh century Loarre became the palace of Aragonese king Sancho Ramírez, and later an Augustine monastery. Many rooms are intact, including the monastic kitchen and its chimney and a toilet that surely is without equal for its sensational panoramic views.

♦ Between Loarre and Huesca, in a town called Esquedas, is a restaurant that I greatly enjoy, **VENTA DEL SOTÓN** tel. (974) 27 02 41. In the cozy bar area, centering on a huge hearth, you can have marvelous *chorizo, longaniza,* and *morcilla* sausages grilled *a la brasa,* over the open flame. (Inexpensive.) This part of the current establishment was the roadside inn that originally brought the restaurant fame, and is still what I prefer, although the formal restaurant, where regional specialties vie for attention with more creative and complex dishes, is most highly regarded. (Moderate–expensive.)

LOS MALLOS   These reddish-brown rock formations somewhat resemble giant fingers. The setting is reminiscent of the American West, and the road that passes through here is one of singular beauty.

♦ **AGÜERO** is a small tile-roofed village overshadowed by an enormous *mallo* (see above). An unusual Romanesque church of three distinct bodies and roofs stands forlornly at the top of a hill.

♦ At the juncture of the Jaca-Huesca and Pamplona roads, at Santa María, **RESTAURANTE GALÁN** is a simple, family-run operation with excellent home-style cooking. We once enjoyed here delectable potted quail with onions. (Inexpensive.)

HUESCA   Wrested from the Moors by Pedro I of Aragón in the eleventh century, Huesca is the provincial capital, but is not an especially exciting city. Do see the thirteenth century cathedral, built in Gothic style, and its portal with fourteen life-size statues. The alabaster altarpiece is a magisterial work of the Valencian Damián Forment, who executed the altar of the Basílica del Pilar in Zaragoza. If the story of the Bell of Huesca (see box, p. 323) catches your fancy, see the painting depicting the dastardly deed at the town hall; visit in the Museo Arqueológico, formerly the Old University, the room where this event supposedly took place; and see the tomb of the protagonist, Ramiro II el Monje, at San Pedro church.
HOTEL PEDRO I DE ARAGÓN   Avenida del Parque 34   tel. (974) 22 03 00, is thoroughly unexciting, but adequate if you find yourself in Huesca for the night (Moderate–expensive). I can, however, wholeheartedly recommend the previously mentioned **VENTA DEL SOTÓN** restaurant, just outside of Huesca.

ALQUÉZAR   A village of picturesque nooks that is a national monument, and among my favorites. The eleventh century collegiate church-castle perches on the edge of sheer cliffs over the village. Speleologists love the magnificent canyons here, and the Río Vero, from which many of the caves emerge, is great for trout fishing.

GRAUS   Another village of medieval flavor with a beautiful Plaza Mayor.

BARBASTRO   An important town in Roman and Arab times and still a bustling center of the Pyrenees.
ANTIGUEDADES ISMAEL ANGULO   Boltaña 20, has a wonderful collection of jugs and other rustic antiques.

CATALUNYA:
INNOVATION AND TRADITION

INTRODUCTION

IT'S EXCITING, it's alive, it's fascinating, it's contradictory, and it can be maddening. Catalunya is a land of extremes, both scenic and cultural, and is designed by nature and by man to provoke, incite, and instill wildly

---

THE BAROQUE WORLD OF CATALAN CUISINE

GENERAL
Fish, fowl, vegetables (wild mushrooms), pasta, rice, and fruits

SPECIALTIES
Bacallà a la Llauna—salt cod with beans
Bacallà amb Mel—salt cod with honey
Butifarra—white cooked sausage
Fuet—salami-like sausage
Canalons—rolled pasta with meat, fish, or vegetable filling
Empedrat—codfish and bean salad
Escalivada—grilled peppers, tomato, eggplant and onion
Esqueixada—cod with peppers, tomato and onion
Escudella—mixed boiled pot
Espardenyes—sea cucumbers, fried or sautéed
Fricandó amb Moixarnons—veal stew with wild mushrooms
Faves a la Catalana—fresh fava beans with mint
Llagosta amb Pollastre—lobster with chicken
Múrgules Farcides—stuffed morels
Oca amb Peres—baby goose with pears
Rossejat de Fideus—baked pasta with seafood
Rovellons—wild mushrooms
Suquet de Peix—fish stew
Sarsuela—mixed seafood stew
Romesco—sauce of nuts, garlic, dried red pepper, for fish or vegetables
Crema Catalana—custard glazed with caramelized sugar
Mel i Mató—honey and cheese
Formatge Llenguat—strong-flavored cow's milk cheese
Mató—fresh sheep's milk cheese

WINES
Naveran, Vall Fort, Can Feixes, Gran Coronas, Gran Sangre de Toro (red wine) from Penedés
Jane Ventura, Gran Viña Sol, Ramón Balada, Jean León (white wine) from Penedés
Hill, Mas Rabassa, Juvé y Camps, Vallformosa (*cava*) from Penedés
Marqués de Alella from Alella
Masía Barrel, Cartoixa, Novell Scala Dei from Priorato
Joan D'Anguera from Tarragona
Castillo de Perelada from Ampurdà

mixed emotions. Yes, this region is undeniably beautiful; it is staunchly traditional and at the same time outlandishly avant-garde, receptive to visitors and yet self-absorbed and self-indulgent.

To Catalans, Catalunya is not another region of Spain but a different country, a world unto itself. By psychologically separating Catalunya from Spain, Catalans have created a certain provincialism that contradicts Catalunya's reputation for being poised on the cutting edge of what is new or about to happen. Be it by intention, by historical circumstance, or by nature, Catalunya, in fact, does not feel like Spain; you may love it, but what you love will be different from what attracts you to the rest of the country.

Catalunya is in northeast Spain, bordering France to the north, Aragón to the west, the Levante region to the south, and the Mediterranean along its eastern coast. Composed of four provinces—Lleida, Tarragona, Girona, and Barcelona—Catalunya is a land of extraordinary contrasts. Flatter toward the south, where vineyards and olive groves are concentrated, jaggedly rocky along the stunning Costa Brava, and reaching soaring heights in the Pyrenees, Catalunya boasts some of Spain's most memorable scenery.

In addition to its breath-stopping beauty and its fine food, Catalunya is home to artistic achievements ranging from grand Greek and Roman monuments and a wealth of exquisitely simple Romanesque works to some of the most exciting modern art of the twentieth century. Several of the great creative geniuses of our time (Gaudí, Dalí, Miró, Picasso) are either from Catalunya or spent important formative years here (Picasso was born in Málaga but moved to Barcelona when he was a teenager). Even the cuisine of Catalunya represents a tug-of-war between traditional cooking and the forces of "nouvelle." There is indeed so much variety in Catalunya that you could easily spend a week or two here without ever stepping beyond its borders.

Catalunya's cultural legacy dates back to antiquity, gaining importance under the Greeks and then the Romans. Ancient civilizations thrived along this northern Mediterranean coast, and the Romans made Tarragona a nucleus, especially important for sea commerce. The Arabs conquered Catalunya but never gathered much strength, and were quickly pushed south with the help of Charlemagne. The ninth century brought Wilfred the Shaggy to power (see box, p. 351), and the region's unique character began to develop and the Romanesque style took root.

Despite Catalunya's political alliance with Aragón in the Middle Ages, the region kept its own laws, traditions, and language, and the Counts of Barcelona became a formidable power, for a time ruling the entire Catalunya-Aragón region. Once Aragón joined Castile under the Catholic Kings, the center of influence shifted south, and maritime interest became focused on the Atlantic and on the New World colonies. So Catalunya lost much of its power and influence.

The union of the Spanish kingdoms into one nation only fueled Catalunya's traditional desire for independence. The Catalan pride and separatism that we see today is nothing new, but merely a continuation of an age-old problem that grew even more vexing in modern times when Catalunya's support for the Republicans in the Spanish Civil War led to

𝒞ATALAN TO SEE YOU THROUGH

Bon día Good morning
Bona tarda Good afternoon
Bona nit/bon vespre Good evening
Avui Today
Ahir Yesterday
Demà Tomorrow
Ara Now
Bon viatge Have a good trip
Quan val? How much is it?
Adéu Goodbye
Moltes gràcies Thank you
Quina hora es? What time is it?
Com aném? How are you?
Com es diu?/Quin es el seu nom? What is your name?
Si us plau Please
De rès You're welcome
Perdoneu/perdoni Excuse me
Ón es/ón està . . . Where is . . .
Molt de gust/encant Nice to meet you
No comprenc I don't understand
Parla Català, Castellà? Do you speak Catalan, Spanish?
A la dreta To the right
A l'esquerra To the left
Can Restaurant
Magatzem Store
Desdejuni Breakfast
Esmorzar Early lunch, snack
Dinar Late lunch
Sopar Dinner
Tancat Closed
Cambrer Waiter
Nota Bill

official postwar suppression of Catalan language and customs. Now in Spain's relaxed political mood, Catalan traditions once more flourish.

Catalans are a hard-working people, intent on success, and they have won grudging admiration from other Spaniards for the diligence, persistence, and sense of mission with which they pursue their goals. Fiercely proud of their cultural heritage, Catalans take special care to preserve their past. Every Sunday, for example, in cities and villages all over Catalunya the group dance *la sardana* is performed by Catalans as if it were a defiant declaration of independence. The Catalan language, a tongue with traits of both French and Spanish, but most closely related to Provençal, has reemerged stronger than ever.

Catalans speak to one another in Catalan; road and street signs, billboards, books, newspapers, television programs, even restaurant menus are commonly in Catalan, without Spanish translation, even though Catalans are bilingual. In Catalunya you will most likely be greeted with the Catalan *bon día*, but that greeting generally shifts to *buenos días* if you are obviously more comfortable with Spanish (see box for Catalan vocabulary).

Food plays a spirited role in the life of Catalunya, for good eating has a long and venerable tradition. Catalunya is one of the few regions of Spain where you find small family-owned inns in some of the most unlikely places, providing cozy lodgings and excellent food. Fine produce grows here in fertile soil—vegetables, fruits, and the region's famed wild mushrooms, which come in dozens of delectable varieties. Olive trees yield first-rate virgin oils, and a significant acreage devoted to vineyards brings forth quantities of quality wines. From the Priorato wines of Tarragona province to the Alella and Penedés wines of Barcelona to the Empordà wines of Girona, Catalan wines have steadily gained prestige and admiring fans. And there is nothing quite so satisfying as a Catalan wine to accompany Catalan cuisine.

I think of Catalunya as the gastronomic cradle of Spanish cuisine. One of the earliest European cookbooks, *El Llibre del Cuiner*, was published in the Catalan language in 1520 (then later translated to Castilian). Author Ruperto de Nola, chef to King Fernando of Naples (Naples was then a Spanish kingdom), produced recipes featuring unusual food combinations that are still characteristic of modern Catalan cooking.

The use of honey, fruits (especially pears and figs), and nuts (almonds, pine nuts, and hazelnuts) in main-course dishes appear in his book and in current Catalan cuisine. Dried cod with honey, sweetened sausage (*botifarrón dolça*), goose with pears, chicken with figs, pork with chestnuts, and rabbit with quince and honey all trace their origins to medieval times, although the use of chocolate, tomato, and peppers typical of Catalan cooking today awaited the arrival of these products from the New World. Because of Catalunya's close political association with Italy in the sixteenth and seventeenth centuries, Italian chefs went to Catalunya and Italian-influenced dishes (especially those made with pasta) became part of the Catalan repertory. Italian cooking is once more fashionable in Catalunya today.

By favoring stews and "composite" dishes featuring more than one main ingredient, and by joining the most unlikely and disparate elements, Catalans have created an imaginative, almost baroque-style cuisine that is one more example of the Catalan love for shock and surprise. I consider Catalan cooking to be one of Spain's greatest regional cuisines, but you may have to familiarize yourself with a new food vocabulary to get by gastronomically in Catalunya (see box, p. 326).

Culturally, however, the word *baroque* hardly enters my mind in connection with Catalunya. I see two exceptional periods in Catalan art and architecture: first, the Romanesque and then, seven centuries later, the era of modernism. The Romanesque style (see Index) flourished from the eleventh to the thirteenth century and is found in most of northern Spain, but it is particularly prominent in Catalunya. With religious pilgrimages to Spain attracting millions of Europeans in the Middle Ages, ideas traveled easily. Catalan Romanesque absorbed new trends, then developed its own peculiar style (polychrome altar fronts, for example, are unique to this area). Apse frescoes, first introduced into Spain by way of Catalunya, polychrome wood sculpture, and the aforementioned altar fronts decorated tiny country churches of the northernmost regions of Catalunya.

Romanesque artwork has been preserved with painstaking care, and much of it is on display in Catalan museums, especially in Barcelona, Solsona, and Vic. On heavily traveled pilgrimage routes you will find the grander works of Catalan Romanesque, such as the monasteries of Ripoll and Sant Joan de les Abadesses. If you love the purity and lack of pretension of the Romanesque style, as I do, there is nothing more pleasing than to travel from village to village in Catalunya exploring its Romanesque heritage and savoring those simpler times.

The mad leap in Catalunya from Romanesque to modern and avantgarde (intervening works of Gothic, Baroque, Renaissance, and neoclassic are relatively scarce) necessarily leads me to Barcelona, where new artistic visions blossomed in the twentieth century. By no means does this imply that Barcelona is my principal destination in Catalunya. Mountain villages, majestic mountain scenery, and bright Mediterranean coasts are what I love most, but it is to Barcelona that one turns for excitement and innovation.

THE PROVINCE OF BARCELONA

THIS IS CATALUNYA'S most developed, industrial, and populous province, and for these reasons, it doesn't compare in natural beauty with the other three provinces. Of course, a star attraction like the city of Barcelona (bar-say-*low*-nah) more than compensates for whatever the rest of the province may lack. But the weather is fine along the coast and attracts *Barcelonins* and tourists alike to its beaches, and its mountainous interior can be beautiful. Despite the bigness of the city of Barcelona and its industrial satellites, there is still plenty of open land, much of which is devoted to wine production.

The limestone soil, temperate climate, and moderate rainfall in the area called Penedés create ideal conditions for vineyards. For thousands of years Penedés has produced wine, and although some red Penedés wines have won international awards, production centers on white wine. The whites are light, fruity, and plentiful and have justly achieved worldwide recognition.

Since fine champagne necessarily begins with excellent white wine, Penedés has become the largest producer in the world of sparkling wines made by the *méthode champenoise*. Called *cavas*, to distinguish them from Champagne made in the French region of that name, they are every bit the equals of the French product.

THE CITY OF BARCELONA

Barcelona began as a Roman city (called Barcino) and had considerable importance—there were once a forum, circus, and theater here. The city became increasingly influential in the sixteenth and seventeenth centuries as Spain's main contact with its Italian possessions and one of Spain's most important ports on the Mediterranean. Thus the city grew into a commercial hub, its people developed a keen business sense, and a textile industry grew up as early as the twelfth century and reached its height in the fourteenth. Many of the Gothic mansions standing today were proudly built with the riches of commerce. Alas, power moved away from Barcelona, and it became a second-rate city, until once more growing to greatness in the nineteenth century.

I have warmed to Barcelona slowly but steadily over the years. At one time the architectural achievements of Antoni Gaudí were my overriding motivation for coming here, and his works still hold a powerful attraction for me. But I see Barcelona in much broader terms now, and have come to consider it among the most gracious cities in Spain.

Barcelona has a privileged location on the shores of the Mediterranean, enclosed by the mountains of Tibidabo and Montjuïc, which help to create a consistently benign climate. Its beauty has not been damaged by modern development, for its citizens have taken inordinate care in preserving the city's past (unlike Madrid, which has grown chaotically). While a sleek high-rise world of glass and steel has sprouted beyond the city's core, an Old World atmosphere prevails downtown, and block associations lavish affection on their small domains. Barcelona is therefore meant for strolling: wide tree-lined boulevards, where street junctures have beveled corners that transform intersections into mini-plazas, are the city's hallmark; they are graced with elaborate antique street lamps (some designed by Gaudí), decorative inlaid sidewalks, outdoor cafés, and startling modernist architecture.

It's a little difficult to get your bearings in Barcelona until you understand the city's layout. Barcelona begins at its port, where a statue of Columbus on a tall, narrow column authoritatively points to the sparkling Mediterranean. The city progresses up Las Ramblas, one of the city's most famous and busiest boulevards, which was once a riverbed running along the city walls. The commercial, cultural, and culinary life of Barcelona revolves around the plane-tree-shaded Las Ramblas, but it is just one of many boulevards that invite you to slow your pace and take in the beauty of Barcelona.

Las Ramblas is the scene of unending activity. There are outdoor cafés everywhere. Chirping canaries, cooing doves, and squeaking white mice fill cages at outdoor marts and delight passing children. Flower stalls are awash in color, and florists busily arrange bouquets of red and pink rosebuds; they water huge bunches of daisies and chrysanthemums and put the final touches on elaborate funeral displays. Suddenly the scene on Las Ramblas changes, and book stands appear (this stretch of the street is called La Rambla del Estudis).

Just blocks from Las Ramblas is the Gothic Quarter (Barri Gòtic)—a tangle of medieval streets, where nothing jars you from thinking you have entered a medieval world. The city's great cathedral is at the limits of the quarter, and continuing northwest you reach the immense Plaça de Catalunya, the geographical and spiritual heart of the city. It is forever lively with everything from mime groups, fire eaters, jugglers, and dancers to those who just like to sit in the shade or feed the pigeons.

The Plaça de Catalunya is the link between the city's oldest neighborhoods and what is known as L'Eixample, the nineteenth century expansion of the city. As late as 1850 Barcelona was still tightly girdled by its medieval walls and literally bursting at the seams. Finally the walls came down and a new neighborhood was created in the fashionable gridiron design of the nineteenth century, bordered by broad boulevards running diagonally to the rigidly squared blocks (these diagonal cuts are what disorient you). The building boom provided a unique opportunity for modernism to take flight, and L'Eixample is where you will see the singular and daring architecture so characteristic of Barcelona. As its name suggests, the Passeig de Gràcia is a gracious boulevard with elegant boutiques and is a highlight of this neighborhood. Beyond L'Eixample are still newer neighborhoods that grew up in later decades.

Like the rest of Catalunya, only more so, Barcelona is a surprising and irresistible mix of tradition and the avant-garde. When you couple a love for the past with a flair for the outrageous and ultramodern, the result is a city of remarkable vibrancy.

To experience a tradition still very much alive today, go to Barcelona's Gothic Quarter, where on Sunday afternoons between twelve and two the *sardana* is danced in front of the cathedral. An eleven-piece band, costumed in taupe trousers and plaid shirts and shaded by candy-striped umbrellas, assembles on the cathedral steps. Its players tune an odd assortment of instruments—a recorder, a miniature drum, and some primitive relatives of the horn and oboe—and begin to play the lilting melody of the *sardana*, which recalls a jig. Barcelonins, as if on cue, drop their packages and handbags, join hands, raise their arms high, and begin to bob up and down, toes pointed and feet crossing, to the rhythm of the simple, almost childlike music. Everyone, even amateurs like us, are welcome to join in.

Barcelona loves classical music; its concert halls are lovingly maintained, and hometown performers are treated with the greatest respect and admiration. Opera stars such as Victoria de los Ángeles, Montserrat Caballé, and José Carreras, and piano virtuoso Alicia de Larocha have made the city proud. Where else would you see, as I did, a young, bearded man pushing an upright piano through the streets, stopping behind the cathedral, setting an upturned top hat on the ground and sitting down at the keyboard to tackle *Iberia* by Spanish composer Isaac Albéniz?

In the realm of art, it is not mere coincidence that Picasso, Dalí, Miró, and Gaudí all worked and developed their styles here. There is something about this city that foments cultural excitement, that warmly embraces all the latest trends and movements, then sometimes picaresquely carries them one step beyond into the realm of the ludicrous. I can't imagine another city that would have conceived of, much less sponsored, the "marriage" of Barcelona's statue of Christopher Columbus and New York's Statue of Liberty, and prepared wedding clothes and a complete trousseau in the gargantuan size of the groom and bride for New York City's 1992 Columbus Day Parade.

You will, of course, visit Barcelona to see the cathedral, the Gothic Quarter, and the city's fine museums, to climb to its hilltops, walk the broad boulevards, and absorb the city's lively atmosphere. But what particularly capture my imagination and admiration are the city's modernist architectural creations, its collection of Romanesque works of art (see Museu d'Art de Catalunya), and the city's love for fine food—perhaps seemingly unrelated attributes but intimately reflective of Barcelona's curiously compatible mix of tradition and innovation.

At the turn of the century, Modernism flourished in Barcelona, characterized by buildings of flowing, lavalike concrete, set off by tortuous wrought-iron grilles, grates, and gates, and one-of-a-kind brightly colored

Looking for Gaudí

CASA MILÀ Passeig de Gràcia This strangely undulating apartment house, with outrageously complex wrought-iron balconies and twisted ceramic chimneys, was pejoratively known in its time as the "Stone Pit." Be sure to see the lobby and visit the surreal rooftop.

CASA BATLLÓ Just a few houses down from Casa Milà and sometimes described as evoking a carnival (because of its colorful, capricious air; its softly molded wrought-iron balconies resembling festive masks; and the skeletal look of its lower portion). You might mistake the building next door for another Gaudí. It is not, but it is from the same modernist period.

PARK GÜELL North of downtown Barcelona, this park, originally conceived as a suburban housing complex, is an incredible flight of fancy, a fairyland of unexpected passageways, strange mosaic animals, and park benches of ceramic bits and pieces in a wild array of colors and patterns. Colorful rooftops end in soft peaks like meringue pie. There is not a straight line anywhere, for the park follows the natural roll of the land.

FINCA GÜELL All that remains of the country estate of Eusebio Güell (just off the Diagonal on Pedralbes avenue) is a fantastic wrought-iron gate that takes the form of a lifelike, slithering serpent with exposed fangs. The creature brings the hard cold metal to life.

COL·LEGI DE LES TERESIANAS Ganduxer street A facade strangely austere for Gaudí, but inside is a dizzying maze of parabolic arches.

CASA VINCENS, Les Carolines 24 An early Gaudí house, more traditionally structured. Its brick and ceramic work creates a somewhat Moorish appearance.

PALAU GÜELL Conde de Asalto The only downtown Gaudí work, it looks austere from the exterior, and not very distinguished, but the interior is exuberantly Gaudí.

COLÒNIA GÜELL, thirteen kilometers west of Barcelona in Santa Coloma de Cervelló A project never completed; all that stands is a crypt-chapel of amazing design, with a complex interplay of stone, brick, ceramic, stained glass, and wrought iron. The curves, arches, and angles show the mastery and genius of Gaudí.

LA SAGRADA FAMILIA Gaudí's grand religious and artistic statement, still unfinished (see text). You will need to spend some time looking skyward to take it all in. Binoculars are helpful.

♦ See the small museum with Gaudí's architectural plans, and climb the church spires for wonderful views.

♦ Gaudí also designed his interiors, which, as might be imagined, are of extraordinary originality. If you're a real Gaudí fan—and with money to spare—visit **BD EDICIONES DE DISEÑO** (see SHOPPING).

ceramic tile. All required highly skilled artisan labor and meticulous architectural planning, and although Antoni Gaudí's eccentric style is a highlight of this movement, he did not work in a void; several other architects developed similar styles at about the same time, most notably Lluis Domènech i Muntaner and Josep Puig i Cadafalch. Walk almost any street in the L'Eixample neighborhood with eyes raised and admire the buildings constructed in this elaborate manner that resembles Art Nouveau. You'll wager they all show the hand of Gaudí, but in fact his works in Barcelona number fewer than a dozen.

Gaudí spent his entire professional life in Barcelona, but his creations, startling even to our worldly eyes, were in his time considered eyesores and ridiculed by a majority of citizens. His supporters were astute students of art, in particular Eusebio Güell, who became his benefactor and sponsored some of his most sensational works.

Once Gaudí turned his complete attention to the church of the Sagrada Familia, however, he ceased all other projects. The church became his obsession, the culmination and synthesis of his architectural philosophy and of his deepest religious beliefs. Its impact is powerful, its detailed work extraordinary, its flow otherworldly. The exterior stonework drips like stalactites, and towers topped by weird ceramic pinnacles soar. Without doubt, it was Gaudí's magisterial work, occupying his last forty years, until he was tragically killed by a trolley in 1926.

The church is today unfinished, a mere facade, but work has recently resumed at a quickened pace, following the detailed plans Gaudí left behind. It is a mammoth undertaking and a constant polemic, for many believe that new additions, even if they follow Gaudí's vision, are of lesser craftsmanship and unworthy of the architect's grand design.

Some years ago we organized a trip to Spain expressly to see everything ever designed by Gaudí. Our quest led us not only to Barcelona but as far afield as Astorga, Comillas, and León. It was quite an adventure, for the almost godly aura that now surrounds Gaudí did not then exist, and it was sometimes no easy task to locate his works. Barcelona was no exception— some of Gaudí's most astonishing creations are in far-flung areas of the city and not always noted on maps or in guidebooks. But I can think of no better way to spend a day in Barcelona than "Looking for Gaudí" (see box, p. 333).

FINE DINING IN BARCELONA

And now to a subject that preoccupies most of us and is a particularly impassioned theme in Barcelona: food. The love for quality produce, which approaches reverence, has always been a feature of Catalan cuisine and is now at an all-time high. To give you some idea of the important role of food in the lives of Barcelonins, I cannot think of a more telling tale than the suicide of a famous restaurateur that took place in the city's grand central market, La Boquería.

He had been a habitué of the market since the age of seven, and was a flamboyant, gregarious sort, beloved by all and known as the "Gentleman of the Boquería." The market was his very life, but personal problems overwhelmed him, and when he chose to take his own life, the market became his stage. Dramatically, he drank a lethal brew before the eyes of his admirers. The following day, his funeral cortege paused before the doors of La Boquería, and a huge crowd showered his coffin with flowers, then burst into a prolonged and emotional ovation.

The suicide at La Boquería was a symbolic act of a man who loved fine food to the extreme, revered Catalan cuisine, and regarded the six-hundred-year-old La Boquería as one of the great marketplaces of the world. That it certainly is, and it is where most fine restaurateurs do their daily shopping. I like to visit the market with my friends José María Llach and Martí Forcada, both of Quo Vadis restaurant, just around the corner from the market, and follow their keen eye as they choose ingredients for that day's menu. Not only is the produce superabundant and top-quality, but also the care and artistry with which everything is displayed indicate the importance of food in Barcelona.

In spring the vegetable stands are a riot of color—white asparagus, tiny green peppers, and morels are the stars. In the fall dozens of varieties of wild mushrooms—a highlight of Barcelona cuisine—and fresh truffles make their appearance at the market, then show up in all the best restaurants. In any season fish appears in astounding variety and is carefully arranged on bright green leaves. Especially rare and considered a great delicacy are *espardenyes*, or sea cucumbers, a seafood with a delicate flavor resembling lobster.

> ## Pa amb Tomàquet
>
> There are many variations of this simple accompaniment to Catalan cooking. Cut a round loaf of dense country bread in long, ¾-inch-thick slices. Use slightly stale bread, or toast fresh bread lightly, rub it on both sides with a cut garlic clove and then with a halved, very ripe, flavorful tomato. Drizzle with fruity olive oil, and sprinkle with coarse salt.

Although there are many restaurants in Barcelona loyal to their Catalan roots (and traditional Catalan cuisine is of course what you will find in family kitchens), in the most fashionable restaurants nouvelle cooking has run rampant. It ranges from subdued, sophisticated, and highly imaginative food to the outrageous (are you ready for Roquefort cheese ice cream bathed in raspberry purée?). Yes, gastronomy in Barcelona is alive and in high spirits and ready to surprise you. If, on the other hand, time-honored Catalan country cooking is what you seek, as I do, there are always well-prepared classics on even the most determinedly inventive menus.

Seeing Barcelona

Getting Around Barcelona

It is best to tour central Barcelona on foot. For longer distances there are buses, subways, and taxis. A special "museum bus" begins at the Plaça de

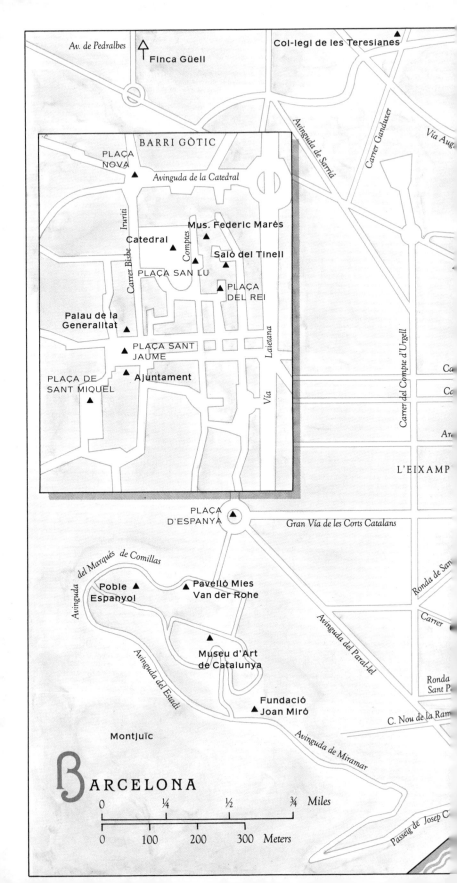

Av. de Pedralbes

Finca Güell

Col·legi de les Teresianes

Avinguda de Sarrià

Carrer Ganduxer

Via Aug.

BARRI GÒTIC

PLAÇA NOVA

Avinguda de la Catedral

Iruritii

Carrer Bisbe

Catedral

Comptes

Mus. Federic Marés

Saló del Tinell

PLAÇA SAN LU

PLAÇA DEL REI

Palau de la Generalitat

PLAÇA SANT JAUME

PLAÇA DE SANT MIQUEL

Ajuntament

Laietana

Via

Carrer del Compte d'Urgell

Ca

Ca

Ar

L'EIXAMP

PLAÇA D'ESPANYA

Gran Vía de les Corts Catalans

Avinguda del Marqués de Comillas

Avinguda

Poble Espanyol

Pavelló Mies Van der Rohe

Ronda de San

Carrer

Avinguda del Estadi

Museu d'Art de Catalunya

Avinguda del Paral·lel

Ronda Sant P

Fundació Joan Miró

C. Nou de la Ram

Montjuïc

Avinguda de Miramar

ʙARCELONA

| 0 | ¼ | ½ | ¾ | Miles |

| 0 | 100 | 200 | 300 | Meters |

Passeig de Josep C

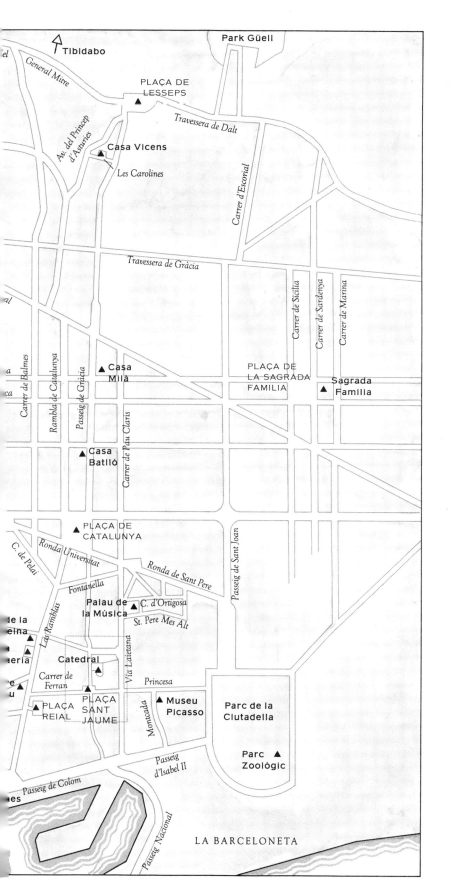

Catalunya and follows a route that takes you to most of the city's major sights. Get on and off as you will, paying one flat fee.

✦ Museums are closed Mondays and at lunch hour, unless otherwise noted.

Montjuïc

Literally "Mountain of the Jews" (here was the ancient Jewish cemetery), this is one of the hills that encloses Barcelona. The panorama of the city, its harbor, and the Mediterranean are heady. You can come to Montjuïc by cable car (from La Barceloneta), automobile, or bus and could spend the better part of a day here.

MUSEU D'ART DE CATALUNYA   This is one of my favorite museums in Spain, and I like to concentrate on the Romanesque department. It is a formidable treasure of wall frescoes, polychrome wood altar fronts, and statuary that have been brought from churches all over Catalunya (they were in many cases uncared for and rapidly deteriorating). The colors are still brilliant; the primitive, almost childlike qualities are endearing. I especially love the extraordinarily sensitive polychrome statue *Crist de Battló*; the brilliantly colored Soriguerola altar front; and the apse fresco from Sant Climent de Taüll in the province of Lleida. If you travel elsewhere in Catalunya, it is interesting to match these works with the churches from which they came. (Mornings only.)

POBLE ESPANYOL   This "Spanish Village" was built for the 1929 World's Fair, and although a bit kitschy, it is an interesting assemblage of houses, churches, and plazas reproduced from towns and villages all over Spain. Although only facades (sometimes there are gift shops or craftsmen at work inside), you are led on a brief tour of Spain, seeing characteristic structures of each region. If you have seen the originals, or plan to see them, this exhibit takes on added meaning. (Open daily; no lunch-hour closing.)

FUNDACIÓ JOAN MIRÓ   An extensive collection of paintings and drawings by the artist. (No lunch-hour closing.)

PAVELLÓ MIES VAN DER ROHE   Built for the 1929 World's Fair, this is a landmark of twentieth century architecture.

Old Quarter and Downtown

PLAÇA DE CATALUNYA   Barcelona's vast main square (see text).

BARRI GÒTIC   The oldest section of the city, site of the original walled Roman town, where there is a concentration of thirteenth, fourteenth, and fifteenth century gargoyled Gothic mansions with coats of arms. It is like an outdoor museum, fascinating but somewhat lacking in everyday street life. For more of that, cross the Vía Laietana to a popular old neighborhood, where alleylike streets teem with activity.

PLAÇA DEL REI is a small but elegant square faced by two palaces, the church of Santa Àgata, and the Saló del Tinell (a magnificent arch-covered royal reception area).

PLAÇA DE SANT JAUME, site of the Roman Agora, is still today a center of activity; the Catalan central government (Generalitat) and the city hall (Ajuntament) occupy two Gothic palaces.

CATHEDRAL   A mélange of architectural styles and periods (the facade is nineteenth century), its most interesting feature is the dramatic and unusual height of its side naves. In the lovely cloister gardens geese live under the blessing of Santa Eulalia, patron saint of the city. The cathedral is beautifully illuminated by night.
◆ An antique market takes place in front of the cathedral every Thursday.

MUSEU PICASSO   A fourteenth century palace on Montcada street (a pedestrian street lined with medieval mansions) is the site for this museum, which concentrates on early drawings and paintings by Picasso. Some are from the end of the nineteenth century, when he was only a child, some "mere" doodles, and all provide a rare glimpse into the artistic roots of the painter.

MUSEU FREDERIC MARÉS   Set in a palace once belonging to the Counts of Barcelona (p. 327), the museum makes its focus the polychrome sculpture of Catalunya from the twelfth to the seventeenth century.

PALAU DE LA MÚSICA   Amadeo Vives   A work of Modernism gone mad, this is one of my favorite places in Barcelona, a creation of architect Domènech i Montaner. You *must* see the interior—either take a tour (Mondays and Fridays at 11:30) or, better still, attend a concert (avoid summer; there is no air conditioning).

MUSEU DE LES ARTS DECORATIVES (in the Palau de la Virreina) This museum concentrates on antique furniture but also has the fine Cambó collection of paintings by Botticelli, Titian, Tintoretto, Zurbarán, and Goya.

LA BOQUERÍA   Barcelona's central market right off Las Ramblas on Carrer del Carme street (see text).

LAS RAMBLAS   Barcelona's busy boulevard (see text). Be careful here with wallets and handbags.

WORKS BY ANTONI GAUDÍ   See box, p. 333.

Around the Waterfront

LA BARCELONETA   A small triangle near Barcelona's harbor that feels like a tiny Mediterranean fishing village (thus its name, "Little Barcelona"). Here is Barcelona's beach, but the main interest is dozens of seafood restaurants along the waterfront and plenty of tapas bars. Cable cars to Montjuïc are nearby.
PACO ALKALDE   Almirall Aixada 12   tel. (93) 319 30 26, is a congenial bar (and restaurant) serving excellent tapas in dozens of varieties. For more sub-

stantial fare, the *Rossejat de Fideus*—baked pasta with seafood—is extraordinary. (Moderate.)

At beachfront, **CAN SOLÉ**   Sant Carles 4   tel. (93) 319 50 12, is wildly popular for seafood and for rice dishes. (Inexpensive–moderate.)

DRESSANES REIALS   The center of interest in this royal shipyard, which produced many of Spain's great galleons, is a full-size reproduction of the command ship of Don Juan de Austria (see box, p. 189), which saw action in the famous sixteenth century Battle of Lepanto (the battle was won, but the ship lost).

♦ Nearby in the harbor is a reproduction of the *Santa María*, which sailed with Columbus from Huelva in Andalucía to America.

PARC ZOOLÒGIC   One of the world's finest zoos, with lovely shaded acres near the waterfront in the Parc de la Ciutadella, where the animals are uncaged. I wouldn't miss the world's only blue-eyed white gorilla, Copito de Nieve (Snowflake).

STAYING IN BARCELONA

CONDES DE BARCELONA   Passeig de Gràcia 75   tel. (93) 487 37 37   Ideally located on the elegant Passeig de Gràcia, this outstanding "new" hotel is a beautifully renovated mansion, small and seignorial. (Expensive.)

HOTEL RITZ   Gran Vía de les Corts Catalans 668   tel. (93) 318 52 00   Exquisitely appointed, luxury hotel, a landmark since its inauguration at the beginning of this century and recently restored to its former splendor. (Ultra-deluxe.)

HOTEL MAJESTIC   Passeig de Gràcia 70   tel. (93) 215 45 12   We often use this comfortable hotel because of its excellent location. (Expensive.)

HOTEL COLÓN   Avinguda Catedral 7   tel. (93) 301 14 04   Directly across from the cathedral in the heart of the Gothic Quarter, this is a favorite of many visitors; request a room overlooking the cathedral square. (Expensive.)

GRAN HOTEL HAVANA   Gran Vía de les Corts Catalanes 648   tel. (93) 412 11 15   Barcelona's most talked-about new hotel, in an elegant turn-of-the-century building. (Very expensive.)

RAMADA RENAISSANCE   Las Ramblas 111   tel. (93) 318 62 00   Too glitzy for my taste, but right next to Las Ramblas and known for its rock-star clientele. (Ultra-deluxe.)

REGENTE   Rambla de Catalunya 76   tel. (93) 215 25 70   A simple hotel, well located in an animated area on the northern extension of Las Ramblas. (Expensive.)

GÓTICO   Jaume I 14   tel. (93) 315 22 11   In the heart of the Old Quarter, this hotel is small, comfortable, and ideally located. (Moderate–expensive.)

BALMES   Mallorca 216   tel. (93) 451 19 14   An excellent location, in L'Eixample and not far from shopping and sightseeing. (Moderate–expensive; pool.)

ELDORADO PETIT   Dolores Monserdá 57   tel. (93) 204 51 53   Housed in a stately mansion, this is one of the most chic and sophisticated restaurants in town, under the expert direction of owner Lluís Cruanyas, whose first restaurant in Sant Feliu de Guíxols still thrives. The ultimate in *nueva cocina,* with several traditional dishes as well. (Expensive.)

FLORIÁN   Bertrand i Serra 20   tel. (93) 212 46 27   The look of an elegant *masía* (Catalan country house), with a lively menu that is at once nouvelle and traditional. There are Italian overtones, in tribute to the Italian ancestry of one of its owners and in accord with the current rage in Barcelona for food with an Italian flair. (Expensive.)

QUO VADIS   Carme 7   tel. (93) 302 40 72   Right off Las Ramblas and one of my favorites. A no-nonsense classic restaurant with a warm, friendly atmosphere. I am crazy about the potpourri of wild mushrooms. (Moderate–expensive.)

AZULETE   Vía Augusta 281   tel. (93) 203 59 43   A trendy and very beautiful restaurant in an enclosed garden that attracts a spirited and stylish young crowd. An eclectic menu. (Expensive.)

VÍA VENETO   Ganduxer 10   tel. (93) 200 70 24   An exceptionally elegant restaurant that typifies the Art Nouveau Catalan style. Impeccable service and a menu that tends toward the traditional, with more than a passing nod to nouvelle. (Expensive.)

RENO   Tuset 27   tel. (93) 200 91 29   *The* classic restaurant in Barcelona, similar in prestige and longevity to the legendary Jockey in Madrid. Irreproachable ingredients, service, and preparations, be they classic, Catalan, or of recent creation. (Expensive.)

CAN ISIDRE   Flors 12   tel. (93) 241 11 39   In the Old Quarter of Barcelona, this charming and petit restaurant feels like an old-fashioned parlor and is a favorite of local celebrities and theatergoers. A traditional menu features fine, honest food. (Moderate–expensive.)

SIETE PUERTAS   Passeig Isabel II 14   tel. (93) 319 30 33   A tradition for well over a century, a port restaurant serving what you might expect: fish and Catalan seafood stews. (Moderate.)

CHICOA   Aribau 71   tel. (93) 253 11 23   With warm brick walls, a fireplace, and red-checked tablecloths, this is a haven for diners seeking refuge from nouvelle. A great selection of traditional Catalan dishes (with an unusual selection of dried-cod recipes), all perfectly prepared. (Moderate.)

LOS CARACOLES   Escudellers 14   tel. (93) 301 20 41   It's kind of touristy and not very Catalan, but the atmosphere is lively and the ambiance inviting. Have snails—*caracoles,* the restaurant's specialty—for starters, then try the chicken, roasted outside on a spit. (Moderate.)

BARCELONA'S TAPAS BARS

Some popular tapas areas are along Las Ramblas; around the port (especially a renovated wharf area called Moll de la Fusta); in La Barceloneta; in the Plaça del Rei; and along the Passeig de Gràcia and Mercé street.

ꓥ TASTE OF THE BUBBLY: BARCELONA CHAMPAGNE BARS

Champagne bars, known in Catalan as *xampanyeries*, have in the last few years brought *cava*—as Catalan champagne is called—to center stage. Sporting a fresh, clean, stylish, and thoroughly contemporary look, *xampanyeries* are a great way to get acquainted with dozens of boutique *cavas*, served by the glass. Sophisticated tapas, like smoked fish, caviar, pâtés, and selected cheeses, or rich desserts like frozen chocolate truffles, admirably complement these *méthode champenoise* sparkling wines.

Some of the best *xampanyeries* (open from about 7:00 p.m. until 2:00 a.m.) are: **LA XAMPANERÍA** Provença 236; **XAMPÚ, XAMPANY** Gran Vía 702; and **LA CAVA DEL PALAU** Verdaguer i Callis 10.

CASA TEJADA Tenor Vinyas 3 In an elegant residential neighborhood of upper Barcelona, an extremely popular bar with an abundant selection of excellent tapas.

ALT HEIDELBERG Ronda Universitat 5 Despite the name, an extensive variety of Catalan tapas, with some German specialties as well.

PINOCHO, In La Boquería A forever-changing menu of tapas, based on the fine daily produce of the market.

CRISTAL CITY Balmes 249 A combination bookstore and tapas bar with a great variety of tapas.

ELS QUATRE GATS Montsío 5 In a Modernist building, once a hangout for Picasso, Miró, and Dalí.

EL GRAN COLMADO Consell de Cent 318 Tapas bar, restaurant, and grocery store in a modern casual setting.

♦ Keep in mind as well the "champagne bars" for tapas (see box).

OTHER FOOD EXPERIENCES

BOPÁN, LA BOUTIQUE DEL PAN Rambla de Catalunya 119 A large variety of traditional Catalan breads and sweet rolls.

BAIXÁS Calaf 9 Famous for pastries and also for savory pies and turnovers.

DRUGSTORE Passeig de Gràcia and Mallorca Always open and carrying just about anything you might need at an off-hour.

CASA PEPE Balmes 337 A grand variety of cheese, wines, and prepared food. Also a tapas bar.

MAURI   Rambla de Catalunya 102 and Provença 241   Known for its pastries, but also carrying prepared foods, excellent sandwiches, and sausage. It has a small café.

SHOPPING

There are several principal shopping areas in Barcelona: the **PASSEIG DE GRÀCIA,** the **RAMBLA DE CATALUNYA,** and the **AVINGUDA DIAG-ONAL.** The city is known for unusual jewelry and excellent bookstores.

LOEWE   Passeig de Gràcia 35   Deluxe leather goods.

CENTRE D'ANTIQUARIS   Passeig de Gràcia 55   An antique center with dozens of fine stores. There are also many antique stores in the Gothic Quarter.

EL CORTE INGLÉS   The city's main department store, on the Plaça de Catalunya, carrying everything from Woolworth items to designer accessories.

BD EDICIONES DE DISEÑO   Carrer Mallorca 291   Exquisitely hand-crafted Gaudí reproductions, especially chairs and mirrors. Most are in the range of 200,000 to 300,000 pesetas. You can also buy doorknobs and handles for under 10,000 pesetas.

ISITING THE PROVINCE OF BARCELONA

♦ The elegant Al Andalus vintage train (see box, p. 397) has two-to-three-day tours that begin in the city of Barcelona, cross Catalunya, follow part of the Way of Saint James, and finish in Santiago de Compostela.

ARENYS DE MAR   A port town, not far from Barcelona. We travel here to dine at **HISPANIA**   Real 54   tel. (93) 791 04 57 (moderate–expensive), a spacious country-style restaurant featuring fine down-to-earth Catalan seafood specialties—sea snails, *Suquet de Cloisses* (clam stew), and striped bass baked with potatoes, all accompanied by *Pa Amb Tomàquet* (see box, p. 335).

ARGENTONA   A summer place at the foot of a mountain, this town deserves a special visit to dine at **RACÓ D'EN BINU**   Puig i Cadafalch 14   tel. (93) 797 01 01 (moderate–expensive), an elegant yet rustic restaurant made cozy by a central brick fireplace, filled with plants in the summer. Its cuisine is modern, yet based on traditional cooking. *Amanida de Llagostins* (marinated prawns), red peppers in puff pastry, pheasant, and wild duck are among their specialties.

VILAFRANCA DEL PENEDÈS and **SANT SADURNÍ D'ANOIA** Around these towns is the prestigious wine-producing area of Penedés, known for its still wines, especially its crisp fruity whites, and also for its acclaimed sparkling wines made by the champagne method.

◆ You can usually visit the larger bodegas, like Torres in Penedés and the stunning old headquarters of Codorniú in San Sadurní, without previous appointment.

SANTA COLOMA DE CERVELLÓ   Site of Gaudí's Colònia Güell (see box, p. 333).

MONTSERRAT   It sometimes seems that nearly every woman in Catalunya is named Montserrat (Montse for short) in honor of this shrine, where the twelfth century La Moreneta, or "Black Virgin" (so called because of the dark wood from which the statue is carved), is worshipped. The monastery is set in the unique frame of the barren and jagged ("serrated") Montserrat mountains that look like so many pointing fingers. The monastery was once the glory of the monastic world, but fire destroyed it, and the monastery you see today is nineteenth century. Its principal interest is as a place of pilgrimage, and unless your inclinations bend in this direction, the lines awaiting a glimpse of the Virgin are unnerving. You can come also for the views—the most scenic approach is from Santa Cecilia.

CARDONA   This town is high on a conical hill, surrounded by salt mines; one of its main attractions is its castle and collegiate church, which together have been transformed into a magnificent parador, **PARADOR DUQUES DE CARDONA**   Castell de Cardona   tel. (93) 869 12 75. (Moderate.)

VIC   A large industrial city, worthy of a visit to see its neoclassic cathedral, covered with twentieth century murals and incorporating an eleventh century tower from a previous church; next door the **MUSEU EPISCOPAL** has a substantial collection of Romanesque polychrome altar fronts and statuary.
PARADOR DE VIC   14 kilometers from Vic   tel (93) 888 72 11 (moderate–expensive; pool), is splendidly set in pine forests overlooking a lake. Fine Catalan cooking.

MONTSENY   An area of densely green-covered mountains and forests that include Mediterranean as well as alpine species—even some rare sequoias. The road from Sant Celoní to the Hermitage of Santa Fe is of uncommon beauty and finishes with panoramic views that include the area's highest peak, Turó de L'Homme.

THE PROVINCE OF GIRONA

GIRONA (juh-roh-nah) enfolds the eastern limits of the Pyrenees and never gives way to the sea until its cliffs abruptly drop down in sharp jagged formations to the Mediterranean coast. But it is also an area of fertile flatlands, and can claim two distinguished gastronomic regions, the Empordà and the eastern half of La Cerdanya (the rest is in Lleida), both producing the fruits and vegetables so essential to Catalan cooking—the famous Catalan dish *Oca amb Peres* (goose with pears), is a creation of Girona. Combine such great produce with the exceptional seafood found along Girona's coast, and it would be surprising indeed if this were not a great province in which to enjoy fine food. It certainly is a place where I always look forward to eating.

Some of the most unusual dishes characteristic of Catalan cuisine originated in Girona: *Llagosta de l'Estil de l'Empordà* (lobster with tomato, almonds, and hazelnuts), *Conill a l'Empordanesa* (rabbit in chocolate, hazelnut, and pine nut sauce), *Fricandó* (veal stew), *botifarrón dolça* (sausage cooked in caramelized sugar), and the above-mentioned goose with pears.

Girona's name rings of history, for it was here that the Phoenicians, Greeks, and then Romans first landed in Spain and from where their empires spread through the Iberian Peninsula. Girona's coastline was ideal for foreign invaders: It was unusually fertile (the Empordà region is named after the Greek settlement of Empúries, or Emporium, meaning market) and was protected from the native populace by a veritable wall of mountains.

Girona gained great importance once again in medieval times because of its prominent situation along the well-traveled pilgrimage route to Santiago de Compostela (see box, p. 220). The monasteries of Ripoll, Sant Joan de les Abadesses, and Sant Pere de Rhodes—major works of Romanesque art and architecture—are a result of the pilgrims' passage.

Today Girona, and most especially its Mediterranean Costa Brava, is one of Spain's major vacationlands, enormously popular with Spaniards and equally attractive to foreign visitors.

THE CITY OF GIRONA

At the juncture of the rivers Ter and Onyar, Girona was once a well-fortified, walled city (the walls still remain), thought to have been founded by the Greeks and named Gerunda by the Romans. To me, its Old Quarter, completely separated from the new town by the rivers, is among the most beautiful and evocative of any Spanish city. Getting there is part of the pleasure; you cross one of the bridge spans, preferably on foot, and see the quaint pastel houses of blue, pink, and green, hazily reflected in the still waters. The ancient city, climbing steeply from the riverbanks, reveals a world of alleys and twisting streets that daylight struggles to penetrate.

Girona's strategic location, midway between the Pyrenees and Barcelona, made it an important center of commerce and culture in ancient and medieval time. Although its Arab flavor is often noted (you can still visit the Arab baths), in truth the Moors were here for a relatively brief time; it was the six-hundred-year era of Jewish influence that is most pronounced and that is, to me, the most fascinating period of Girona's history, only now being fully explored.

As you climb up to old Girona—I do mean climb, in what sometimes seems a pure vertical—you pass the Baroque cathedral, which is noteworthy for its dramatic ninety-step ascent. You are now on Forca street and in the heart of the Call, as the Jewish quarter was called. The streets are dark, mysterious, precipitous. Girona's great Jewish past is almost palpable. A hollow in a doorpost on the Placeta de L'Institut Vell vividly tells a story of the symbolic Jewish mezuzah—a tube containing biblical verses—that once filled that space and protected a Jewish home here; it vanished when the Jews were forced to leave.

From the ninth century until 1492, the Jewish community thrived in Girona, and its life revolved around a long-gone synagogue, which had been near the cathedral. Jewish communities were typically contiguous with cathedrals (or mosques, as the case might be), because the commercial heart of a town was there.

Jews in Girona enjoyed a privileged status under the Spanish crown, protected by the king himself in exchange for payments made directly to the crown, bypassing Girona officials. The lack of local jurisdiction over the Jews led to times of good relations and others of tension, violence, and persecution. But the community survived six centuries and was a vital part of the local economy. Culturally the influence of Girona Jews extended to the international Jewish community, for in Girona the Cabala, or mystic philosophy of Judaism, was developed, and to this day many Jewish surnames, such as Gerondi, find their roots in the ancestral home of Girona.

SEEING GIRONA

CATHEDRAL   A Gothic structure built over a Romanesque one, with a Baroque facade, this cathedral is not distinguished for great beauty but for technical feats: It has the widest nave of any Gothic cathedral in the world. Unfortunately, it lacks side aisles, so its Gothic heights never achieve grace, and the cathedral is very dark (the ability to build larger windows had not yet been mastered). Don't miss the finely worked and originally conceived twelfth century *Tapestry of the Creation* in the cathedral museum.

SANT PERE DE GALLIGANS   An important twelfth century monastery in Catalan Romanesque style. The original chapel is charming, the carved capitals in the church quite beautiful, and in the cloister is a collection of funerary pieces with Hebrew inscriptions and local works of Romanesque art.

CENTRE ISAAC EL SEC   A center for Jewish studies with interesting exhibits related to the Jewish presence in Girona. Within the center are the remains of the ancient Jewish baths, or mikvah.

ARAB BATHS   From the twelfth century, one of the few remaining reminders of Girona's Moorish past.

EATING IN GIRONA

L'HOSTALET DEL CALL   Travessía Oliva I Prat 4   tel. (972) 21 26 88   While exploring the Jewish quarter we decided to lunch here because the dining room had an invitingly cozy, Old World look. Our instincts were good—the menu includes several specialties of Girona, such as frog's legs, cod-stuffed zucchini, and duck with pears. Chef Antonio proudly tends the fires while his cheery red-headed wife, Nuria, takes charge of the dining room. (Moderate.)

LA COSTA BRAVA

It is named the "Untamed Coast," and for good reason. Cliffs drop sharply to the aquamarine waters of the Mediterranean; secluded, tightly enclosed coves with small beaches are stunning and dramatic. "Untamed," however, does not apply to the weather, which is docile most of the year. Certainly this is one of the most beautiful sectors of the extensive Spanish coastline. But it is convenient to France and to Barcelona and attracts too many visitors during the summer. Ugly construction has marred many stretches, especially in areas of flat beachfront (a rule of thumb: The rockier a coastline and the less beach it has, the more unspoiled it will be). We must pick and choose carefully to find peace and relative privacy here, but we always manage to do so. Besides, the water is as crystal clear as ever, and this is a great place for snorkeling and for boat cruises along the coastline.

The Costa Brava was home to the great Salvador Dalí, and one can feel his Surrealist presence here—in his birthplace, Figueres, where he established a startling museum for his private collection and has since been entombed, and in his summer residence, Port Lligat, where his eclectic house is the focus of attention in the small village.

There is plenty of good eating along the Costa Brava, but also some disgraceful concessions to the supposed bad taste of foreign visitors. We were very disappointed to find that L'Escala, for example, once a tiny fishing village and still famous for its anchovies, now has its waterfront filled with pizza places and ice cream stands, and precious little fish is to be found. On the other hand, the crowded beach areas like Platja d'Aro, Roses, and Sant Feliu de Guíxols have several of Spain's finest restaurants, serving all the wonderful fish (especially firm-textured rockfish like *salmonete*, called *moll* in Catalan, ideal in fish stews) and shellfish of the Mediterranean prepared in Catalan style. I wouldn't choose to vacation in these overgrown towns, but I would go out of my way to eat in them. Distances are manageable on the Costa Brava, and you can easily incorporate side trips for such dining experiences while keeping a home base at, for example, Aiguablava.

THE BEST OF THE COSTA BRAVA

TOSSA DE MAR   We used to love Tossa, but now its waterfront is over-built and overpopulated. However, the medieval walled quarters, high on a rocky promontory with lovely vistas of the Mediterranean, have been preserved and still make Tossa worth visiting.

S'AGARÓ–PLATJA D'ARO   A busy tourist center, which I suggest principally because of its fine hotels and their restaurants:
CARLES CAMÓS–BIG ROCK   Fanals 5, Playa de Aro   tel. (972) 81 80 12, a luxurious hotel with five suites installed in a sixteenth century Catalan country house (very expensive; pool), and its beautiful top-rated restaurant, specializing in fine Catalan cuisine (expensive); and the very elegant **HOSTAL DE LA GAVINA**   Plaza Rosaleda s/n   tel. (972) 32 11 00, considered one of Spain's finest hotels (very expensive; pool), and its equally luxurious restaurant (very expensive).

CAP ROIG (Palafrugell)   Established in this century by a Russian general who lived here for almost fifty years, these gardens of Mediterranean flora with terraces over the Mediterranean are splendid. We spent an enjoyable afternoon in this shady, flower-filled retreat.

AIGUABLAVA   Because it is so hilly, this precious cove and its small fine-sand beach have escaped large-scale construction. Aiguablava is almost exclusively an enclave of expensive summer homes that scale the face of the hills. It is where we choose to stay on the Costa Brava.
    There are two hotels that we like very much: the **PARADOR COSTA BRAVA**   Platja d'Aiguablava   tel. (972) 62 21 62 (moderate–expensive; pool), a modern parador in a prized location at cliff's edge, with vertiginous views and a good restaurant featuring local fish; and **HOTEL AIGUA-BLAVA** Platja de Fornells   tel. (972) 62 20 58 (moderate; pool), set by the beach in the cove, charmingly decorated, very well run, and also serving fine food.
    On the road to Pals, **SA PUNTA**   Platja de Pals   tel. (972) 63 64 10 (moderate–expensive), is in a beautiful setting and offers well-prepared specialties of the Empordà, like *Rossejat de Fideus*, a baked pasta dish, and *suquet*, a stew of rockfish, as well as creative cooking.

PALS   A walled feudal town, dating back to the tenth century, probably the residence of the lords who controlled the fertile Ampurdà region, which surrounds Pals. Today the medieval mansions are all fully restored and used mostly as weekend and vacation retreats, and although I find Pals exceptionally beautiful, it is also curiously lifeless.

EMPÚRIES   The Greeks landed here and set up one of their first Iberian settlements at water's edge in 550 B.C. and named it Emporium. The

Romans first touched Spanish soil here when Scipio's army came to fight the Second Punic War against the Carthaginians. Julius Caesar brought Romans to colonize Empúries in 49 B.C. Empúries was a sizable town, and its ruins, among the most extensive in Spain, give a graphic account of these early civilizations. The building foundations, the mosaic floors, the sculpture, and other remains to be seen in the archaeological museum make it easy to reconstruct the importance of this town in its times.

ROSES   On a beautiful gulf with fine-sand beaches, this town was founded in the ninth century B.C. by the Greeks, who would be surprised to see how it has changed since then. Plenty of flatland has led to excessive high-rise construction.

Worth noting, however, is the top-rated **HACIENDA EL BULLI** restaurant   Cala Montjoi s/n   tel. (972) 25 76 51 (very expensive), beautifully set on a promontory over the sea and featuring a creative menu (the tasting menu gives you an ample selection of the restaurant's specialties) and outstanding desserts.

CADAQUÉS   A perfectly stunning setting: a hilly bright-white village, bursting with flowers, on a Mediterranean cove set against the dark backdrop of the Black Mountain. Access is not easy, but nonetheless Cadaqués has become very popular with an offbeat, somewhat bohemian European crowd. Because of sensible planning, Cadaqués has kept its architectural integrity while accommodating art galleries and shops and presenting a kind of circus atmosphere at night, as many visitors don their most outrageous outfits. Don't come to Cadaqués for the beaches; they are poor and few.

There are two hotels here, **LLANÉ PETIT**   Dr. Bartomeus 37, tel. (972) 25 80 50 (moderate), and **PLAYA SOL**   Pianc 3 tel. (972) 25 81 00 (moderate–expensive; pool). We've stayed at both, and neither is exciting, but they are waterfront and all there is in Cadaqués.

PORT LLIGAT   The house of Dalí was at one time on a completely secluded cove, but now, next to the only road running through town, it is surrounded by activity and construction. It is a rambling, whitewashed house with a garden engulfed by fishnet. Atop the roof are two enormous sculpted heads, one with a wide black slash dividing the face into two parts. The road continues to Cap Creus, a wilderness of rocks and blue and yellow flowers punctuated by occasional craggy coves. There is little civilization in this magnificent setting, except for a Club Med.

SANT PERE DE RHODES   On our first visit we had to make the climb to this monastery, from which the Costa Brava is visible in the distance, on foot. Now you can go by car, but you might prefer the beautiful walk. Founded in the seventh century, the present building is tenth century. Legend says that the remains of the apostle Saint Peter were taken from Rome during a time of turbulence, destined for France. Rough weather brought an unexpected change in course, and the priests carrying the body landed here, hid the relics in a cave, and were later unable to find them. A cult grew at the site of this cave, and thus the monastery came to be. It is one of the purest Romanesque structures of medieval Spain.

VISITING THE PROVINCE OF GIRONA

FIGUERES   Birthplace of Salvador Dalí and home of the Dalí museum. There's no mistaking that this museum is a Dalí creation: a massive mauve building dotted with hundreds of bread loaves (the artist was supposedly much taken with the idea of a building made of bread) and topped by gigantesque white eggs. The works within are equally bizarre—in general, more outrageous than of high quality, but nonetheless, all products of an incredibly imaginative and creative mind.

On the death of Dalí, the museum received the ultimate Dalíesque touch: the artist, with his characteristic sense of showmanship, requested burial, center stage, in the glass-domed patio of the museum.

DALÍ IN HIS OWN INIMITABLE WORDS

"Spain is the verticality best represented by the helicopter and the submarine. In the past, to be an artist was to be leftist. Now one must be a monarchist and work for the return of monarchy to Romania." (Dalí's answer to a totally unrelated question posed by a Spanish journalist.)

BESALÚ   I found this town so much more interesting than most accounts led me to believe it would be. Besalú dates to the sixth century B.C., and its streets preserve a wonderfully medieval air. There is a wealth of Romanesque architecture concentrated in the Old Quarter. See a Jewish mikvah, or ritual bath (go to the local tourist office to request entry), that is unique in Spain and one of only three still remaining in Europe. A massive twelfth century bridge was once the only gateway to Besalú, and it is quite unusual, twisting at odd angles as it approaches the entrance to town.

ANTONIO LOBERA, Portalet street, has a fine selection of local antiques.

CASTELLFOLLIT DE LA ROCA   From the road below, see this village, amazingly situated on the edge of a narrow, sheer 180-foot cliff of lava rock. Beautifully illuminated at night.

SANT JOAN DE LES ABADESSES   A twelfth century monastery that traces its origins to the ninth century, when it was founded by an early Catalan ruler with the intriguing name of Wilfred the Shaggy (see box, p. 351). His daughter Emma became its first abbess, and her tomb is here. The monastery church has an unusual Romanesque design with five impressive front apses that seem out of character next to the great simplicity of the rest of the church (an earthquake and economic hardship may have curtailed more ambitious plans for the monastery). But it is the exceptional thirteenth century wood polychrome sculpture *The Descent from the Cross* that brings me to this monastery. The seven principal figures of the Calvary are life-size, carved with great realism and emotional power. Note that the Good Thief is a restoration; the original was burned during the Spanish Civil War, and a thirteenth century host hidden in the forehead of the Christ figure—said to have been found miraculously intact in the fifteenth century—was also destroyed during that war.

RIPOLL   The very same Wilfred the Shaggy (see box) who founded the Ripoll monastery in the ninth century made it his base for the reconquest of the Pyrenees, and later under his grandson, Abbot Oliva, Ripoll became an impressive center of learning with a world-renowned library that was a clearinghouse of foreign knowledge entering Spain from Europe. The eleventh century monastery, replacing the original ninth century structure, was a grand example of Romanesque art, but was unfortunately destroyed by fire in the nineteenth century. The rebuilt monastery we see today is of scant interest. But the surviving Romanesque portal is enough to make Ripoll a fascinating visit.

Looking somewhat like a triumphal arch and often referred to as the "Stone Bible" (it tells the story of mankind in sculpture), this portal is so rich in human and animal figures and decorative detail that you must allow plenty of time to take it all in. A plan (ask for it here) identifies each stratum of carvings from the lowest level, where man fights against temptation (in the form of monsters), to the highest, occupied by God, angels, and saints.

THE IMPROBABLE WILFRED THE SHAGGY

Guifre el Pilós (in Catalan), a ninth century count, led Catalunya in its fight against the Moors and against Charlemagne, and for this reason he has been called the founder of the Catalan nation. It was not, however, his considerable accomplishments that sparked my curiosity, but his unlikely name, "The Shaggy One."

A portrait of Guifre shows a man of aquiline features, piercing, intelligent eyes, and indeed, a long, full, droopy mustache that becomes one with a short thick beard. But scholarly investigations into the source of his odd nickname (I, obviously, was not the first to wonder about it) only increased my perplexity. One account refers to his "capillary exuberance." Another learned work opines that Guifre owned forests, and that the name referred to the dense foliage of his land. My favorite is an explanation uncovered by an erudite French study, which found that Wilfredo was "very hairy in parts of the body not normally hairy."

In reaction to years of Moorish rule, Wilfred the Shaggy immersed the region in a frenzy of church building, founding the monasteries of Ripoll, where his grandson became abbot, and Sant Joan de les Abadesses, where his daughter was abbess. There is no record indicating a hairy inheritance.

VISITING LA CERDANYA IN GIRONA

Note: Most of La Cerdanya is in the province of Lleida and is described in that section.

PUIGCERDÀ   Capital of La Cerdanya; the city's quaint pedestrian commercial center in the Old Quarter has narrow streets and special Old World charm. Just outside town is a large lake used for boating and surrounded by turn-of-the-century mansions that were once the summer homes of the well-to-do.

LLIVIA   An accident of history, this lovely town of cobbled streets and stone houses with wood balconies is Spanish, but is buried in French territory and connected to Spain by a "neutral" road. The unusual situation is a result of the seventeenth century Treaty of the Pyrenees, which settled age-old border disputes between France and Spain, awarding the small villages of La Cerdanya to France, but the "villas," or larger towns, to Spain; Llivia was considered a villa. A fifteenth century pharmacy, said to be the oldest in Europe, was in the hands of one family for more than five hundred years and is now a museum. There is a delightful old restaurant, **CAN VENTURA** Plaça Major 1   tel. (972) 89 61 78, furnished with antiques, which serves food based on products of the region (inexpensive–moderate).

MERANGES   In a remote and incomparable mountain setting, Meranges is a pure pueblo, right down to the pervasive odor of cows. And yet it has an exceptional restaurant and hotel, **CAN BORRELL**   Retorn 3   tel. (972) 88 00 33 (moderate). One part of a large village house has been converted into eight diminutive rooms (the biggest are room numbers 1, 4, 5, 8). Around a charming central patio overlooking the mountains are the dining room, the kitchen, and a sitting room and reception area that are cozy and personal. Under a constant flow of pristine mountain water, a *porrón* of red wine chills and dried cod desalts for dinner. The winsome country dining room of slate floor, beamed ceiling, and stone walls has fine Catalan food indeed. Can Borrell is a unique opportunity to savor rural life at its best.

THE PROVINCE OF LLEIDA

LLEIDA (yey-ee-dah) is the largest Catalan province and the only one that does not exit to the sea. Adjoining Aragón on its western frontier and France and Andorra to the north, it is the nexus between those lands and Catalunya, has seen rule by Romans and Arabs, and was historically close to France. The frontier was long in dispute; Lleida at times was a French province, and indeed, today a French influence is still noticeable. The bishop of the city of La Seu d'Urgell and the president of France are still the symbolic rulers of Andorra.

The charms of Lleida have nothing to do with the Mediterranean and everything to do with stunning mountain scenery, woods, wildlife, mountain fauna, rushing rivers (the lovely Segre and the two branches of the Noguera—Noguera Pallaresa and Noguera Ribagorçana), trout fishing, gentle valleys, placid lakes of icy water, perpetual mountain snows, hunting, skiing, kayaking, and wonderful little Romanesque churches tucked away in diminutive alpine villages. Here is where you will find some of Catalunya's most primitive and, for me, most cherished examples of Romanesque art.

Lleida is primarily agricultural and overwhelmingly rural. It is known for its fine fruits, a great variety of cheeses—many of Catalunya's best, like Llenguat, come from here—and its high-quality and subtly flavored olive oils, which have carried Lleida's name (Lérida in Spanish) around the world. The food-producing area of La Cerdanya, which follows the Segre river as far as La Seu d'Urgell, has become legendary for its peerless produce and for good eating, although in general, Lleida has few famous dishes unique to the province. This is mountain food of meats, vegetables, and river fish, but with a refined touch.

Lleida's cities are not exceptionally interesting, not even its capital. The Pyrenees dominate the landscape to the north and are my principal reason for being here.

THE PYRENEES IN LLEIDA

It is the Pyrenees in Lleida that bring many here exclusively to ski, among them the king of Spain, who is a regular at the winter resorts. I frankly enjoy the Pyrenees the most in summer, when the valleys are lushly green and the living is easy—and I can stretch out along riverbanks with a good book or walk through the mountains while my husband spends long quiet hours angling for trout.

Perhaps the Pyrenees in Lleida are not so awesome as the Aragonese Pyrenees, but they are nonetheless exceptional. And the pastoral villages nestled in the river valleys make these eastern Pyrenees much to my liking. Forget Catalunya's innovative nature while you are here: In the Lleida Pyrenees everything is tradition, a place where ancestral ways effortlessly endure. No, there is not a great deal of variety, but the villages, one following another at short distances, built of stone with sloped slate roofs, dwarfed by the looming Pyrenees, and each centering on a Romanesque church with tall belfry from the twelfth or thirteenth century, are out of a storybook.

I am invariably intrigued by the nameless Romanesque masters who gave their personal touch to these village churches. These artists come down to us only as the Master of Aràn, or the Master of Taüll, for example, but their styles are distinct and their works identifiable. Sculptors or painters in the twelfth century were only craftsman, never thinking to "sign" their works. They were probably simple countrymen, but they demonstrated a surprising command of fresco painting and sculptural skills. The Master of Taüll left us frescoes in the Sant Climent church that are considered masterpieces of Romanesque, and the Master of Aràn created polychrome sculptures of extraordinary beauty and sensitivity in the Valle de Aràn.

I particularly enjoy the Valle de Aràn, in the highest part of the Lleida Pyrenees (Alt Aràn), a verdant valley that follows the Garona river, where bucolic villages dot the landscape and cows graze. Isolated for centuries from the rest of Spain by a barrier of mountains, the Valle de Aràn formed firm French connections (it is the only Spanish valley that opens directly into

France), perhaps most noticeable in the cooking and in the local dialect. Even today there are just two ways to reach the valley from Spain, both of them remarkable: the five-kilometer tunnel of Vielha, which cuts right through the mountains; or if you like beautiful roads and views, as we do, and don't mind a fair share of hairpin curves, take the Bonaigua pass, once the *only* way to get to Aràn from Spain.

At the invigorating height of Bonaigua, wild horses live undisturbed (we keep a carrot or two in the car for them to nibble). But in winter heavy snows close the pass; imagine the isolation of this valley centuries ago, or even in past decades, before the tunnel made Valle de Aràn accessible year-round. So isolated was it that in the 1940s an army of exiled Spanish Republicans from the Spanish Civil War crossed from France into the valley in winter with the intention of staging a coup against the newly instated government. To the frustration of Generalísimo Franco, there was no way to send troops from Spain to the Valle de Aràn in winter to expel them, and he was forced to wait until spring. He vowed that this embarrassing situation would never recur, and construction began on the Vielha tunnel.

My first choice in the Valle de Aràn is the tiny stone village of Artiés, with just four hundred inhabitants. It skirts both banks of the Garona, and reflects the typically quaint style of the Spanish Pyrenees. But more important, it is the only village around that provides fine accommodations at a parador or at a newly opened hotel, and outstanding dining at one of my longtime favorite restaurants, Casa Irene (see box, p. 355). Besides, Artiés is a good point from which to visit other Pyrenees villages that I think are exceptional, like Taüll and Rialb, and to engage jeeps for excursions along high mountain trails. Also nearby is the beautiful Aigües Tortes national park and the spectacular lake Sant Maurici, enclosed by dramatically abrupt, rocky peaks that are splashed with snow and covered with pines that spill down to the lake. Water cascades all around.

I have wonderful memories of a delicious early summer afternoon spent at Sant Maurici, reading and sunning on a grassy knoll and fishing by its banks, while the wine and just-picked cherries for our picnic lunch of bread, cheese, *butifarra* sausage, and tortilla cooled in the lake's icy clear water. That day pretty well sums up for me the glories of the Lleida Pyrenees.

VISITING THE PYRENEES IN LLEIDA

♦ Remember that in the Pyrenees north-south roads follow the river valleys and are relatively straight. In the east-west direction, however, roads twist and curve through high mountains and are very time-consuming, although often exceptionally beautiful.

ARTIÉS A unique town that unites great natural beauty, charm, fine eating, and good accommodations (see text).
HOSTAL VALARTIÉS Mayor 3   tel. (973) 64 09 00, belongs to Casa Irene and is a friendly, well-kept new hotel. (Moderate.) **PARADOR DON GAS-PAR DE PORTOLÀ** Carretera Baqueira-Beret s/n   tel. (973) 64 08 01, is named after a native son who became governor of California in the eighteenth century. The parador is a part of what was once Don Gaspar's home. (Moderate.)
CASA IRENE (Mayor 4   tel. (973) 64 09 00; see box)   The prix fixe menu has four courses plus appetizer, an aperitif, and after-dinner homemade liqueurs. (Moderate.)

BAQUEIRA A new town, done in mountain-chalet style, which is the region's major ski resort. Skiing is reputedly excellent.

SALARDÚ Five minutes from Artiés and quite similar in appearance. See a simple but endearing Romanesque Christ over the church altar, attributed to the Master of Aràn (see text). Find someone to switch on the lights, or bring along a powerful flashlight.

VIELHA Capital of the Aràn Valley and a commercial center for the region. There are many stores catering to skiers and other visitors, and from here jeep excursions take you into the heart of the Pyrenees (I particularly like the route Barrados Vilamòs—Cascada Deth Pitx). Don't miss what is perhaps the best of the Master of Aràn's works: the polychrome wood-carved *Crist del Mig-Aràn* (a fragment of what was originally a complete scene of the Descent from the Cross). Unlike most Romanesque works, this Christ is highly expressive and breathes a profound sense of peace and sorrow.

THE PLEASURES OF CASA IRENE

Why is one of Spain's finest restaurants tucked away in the remote village of Artiés? Simply because owner and chef Irene España grew up here and loves the simplicity of rural life. And as isolated as this village may seem, Irene has loyal fans who travel out of their way just to eat at her inviting restaurant and experience her warmth and her love of fine food. We are among them. And so is the king of Spain.

The food at Casa Irene is a taste of the Lleida Pyrenees, with the French influence that is implied. A meal begins with complimentary appetizer and aperitif and progresses to a first course that may be anything that strikes Irene's fancy, based on the produce available that day. You choose the main course (my favorite is fresh cod in almond and creamed garlic sauce) and dessert (I like Irene's frozen yogurt drizzled with honey in an almond cookie shell).

You might find on display in the restaurant a slightly wrinkled copy of our version of the lyrics to "Good Night, Irene," which we sang to Irene when we passed here with a group of Americans ("High up in the Pyrenees/In a valley called Aràn/Our good friend Irene/Has a fabulous restaurant . . ."). How proud and touched she was to be thus celebrated. Casa Irene is as good a reason as any to visit Artiés and the Valle de Aràn.

The circular **PARADOR DEL VALLE DE ARÀN**   Carretera del Túnel s/n   tel. (973) 64 01 00, has the look of a ski lodge and is in the hills overlooking Vielha. (Moderate.)

♦ To arrange jeep trips, go to the **SKI ARIAS** agency   Edificio "Creu de la Neu"   tel. (973) 64 10 27.

EL PONT DE SUERT   The old sector is a maze of tunnel-like cobbled streets and arcaded porticoes that lead into the Plaça Major and down to the river. The sun never penetrates, and the atmosphere is truly medieval.

TAÜLL   A delightful village of rustic stone houses with sloping black slate roofs and wood-balustraded balconies. The church of **SANT CLIMENT** is a jewel from the Romanesque period, and although its brightly colored dome frescoes—among the most famous of all Catalan Romanesque works, by the Master of Taüll—now reside in the Museu d'Art de Catalunya in Barcelona, there is an exact replica in the church.

There is good simple food at **BAR-RESTAURANT SANT CLIMENT.** I will never forget the lamb-and-garlic meatballs in brandy sauce that I once ate there. (Inexpensive.)

BOSSOST and **VILAMÒS**   Two beautiful slate-roofed villages in mountain settings above Vielha. See the excellently preserved and finely designed Romanesque church of Bossost.

AIGÜES TORTES   This national park is reached by the beautiful twisting road to Espot. In Espot you can hire a jeep to tour the park, or, preferably, take your car, as we did, as far as Sant Maurici lake and spend a relaxing afternoon in this idyllic setting. Bring along a picnic lunch—your hotel can put it together for you.

LA SEU D'URGELL   Seu means Seat of Archbishops, and this town was just that since the fifth century. Jointly, the bishop of La Seu d'Urgell and the president of France exercise honorific sovereignty over Andorra. The **CATHEDRAL** is among the purest of Romanesque works, severe in appearance because of its fortress-like style, with massive twin octagonal defense towers. At the same time, four apses give unusual beauty and grace to the cathedral.

There is a quaint arcaded shopping street in the Old Quarter where I especially liked a stylishly cluttered shop selling natural products. We bought wonderful lozenges flavored with a variety of wild herbs and honeys of the Pyrenees.

EL CASTELL   Carretera Lleida-Puigcerdà, km 129   tel. (973) 35 07 04 (expensive; pool), is high over the city, commanding exceptional views of the countryside and of the old Castell fortress. This hotel is a prime example of a well-cared-for, well-appointed, and smoothly run hotel, always under the watchful eye of Jaume Tàpies and his wife, Ludi. I think Castell's restaurant is among the finest and most beautifully appointed of Catalunya. (Expensive.)

PARADOR DE LA SEU D'URGELL   Sant Domènec 6   tel. (973) 35 20 00, is next to the cathedral and has just been remodeled. It incorporates a sixteenth century cloister in its salon. (Moderate; pool.)

ESTERRI D'ANEU   We love lunching here at **CASA POLDO** on delicious homemade pâté, a strong local cheese called Llenguat, *butifarra* sausage, and the like. (Inexpensive.)

RIALB DE NOGUERA   Cats abound in the primitive, stone-arcaded old quarter, which is just one long street at the edge of town. The bakery on the main square turns out crusty round loaves of bread that are good enough to make into a meal.
♦ On the Noguera Pallaresa river between here and Sort, white-water rafting has gained popularity. Information in Sort.

SOLSONA   An ancient town, especially distinguished for its fine collection of Romanesque frescoes and wood polychrome at the Museu Diocesa.

Ĺa CERDANYA IN LLEIDA

La Cerdanya is a region on the southern slopes of the Pyrenees, where the landscape becomes gentler and the climate drier and warmer under the influence of the Mediterranean. Running along the length of the pastoral Segre river valley, La Cerdanya yields fine fruits and has a reputation for gastronomic greatness. Indeed, there are several fine restaurants of traditional and creative cookery as well as some delightful food shops. La Cerdanya in Lleida is just a part of La Cerdanya, which also includes La Cerdanya in Girona and, farther on, Le Cerdanye in France.
♦ If you approach La Cerdanya from the south, particularly from Barcelona, the impressive new Cadí tunnel can substantially cut travel time.

MARTINET   What I like best about this town is the **FORN JORDI,** which bakes a sourdough country loaf (*pa de pagès*), only slightly sour, and also excellent *cocas*, breads resembling brioche, moist and tender, filled with candied spaghetti squash (*cabell de àngel*).
    Just down the road, the **HOTEL BOIX**   Carretera Lleida-Puigcerdà tel. (973) 51 50 50 (moderate–expensive), may not look like much, but its rear rooms have terraces right over the Segre river (you can even fish here if you like), and the hotel's restaurant has won many culinary awards. There are local specialties, like trout and river crabs, and creative cooking as well (sometimes just a bit too creative). For a diverting finale, ask for the coffee menu or for the "*carrito de infusiones*," a cart of some thirty herbs and teas, each accompanied by a full description of its medicinal powers. Your hot water may get cold before you figure out what to choose. (Expensive.)

PRULLANS   In a lovely mountain setting looking over the Cadí mountains, the **HOSTAL LA MUNTANY**   Puig 3   tel. (973) 51 02 60, is very inexpensive, neat, and clean, with a simple restaurant. Home-style cooking is featured. (Inexpensive.)

BELLVER DE LA CERDANYA   Steeply stepped streets and a stone arcaded plaza make this village especially attractive.

We ate inexpensively and wonderfully well in the rustic bar of the **JOU VELL** restaurant, Plaça de Sant Roc, tel. (973) 51 01 39, in the town plaza: grilled rabbit with *alioli* and *Ensalada Catalana,* a salad that includes *butifarra* and *fuet* sausage. (Inexpensive–moderate.)

BORN   There would be no reason to detour to this simple village (take the Bellver–Túnel de Cadí road, turning south at the sign for Born) were it not for an unusual and, yes, quite sophisticated shop, **EL TUPÍ DE LA CERDANYA.** A young "refugee" from the wear and tear of Barcelona dedicates his time to collecting the best wild produce of the land and attractively packaging it. You can pick up many small gifts to take home—dried herbs, flavored olive oils, jams, and preserved fruits are among my favorites.

𝒱ISITING THE CITY OF LLEIDA

LLEIDA   Situated on a hill next to the Segre river, the ancient Roman town of Ilerda, where Julius Caesar conquered the troops of Pompey, is in the southwestern portion of the province and not likely to be on your route if you are going to the Pyrenees. The city was the scene of numerous battles throughout history, ending with those of the Spanish Civil War. For this reason, over the centuries Lleida has experienced extensive destruction and reconstruction, leaving little of note for the visitor to see.

The **CATHEDRAL,** known as the Seu Vella, is at Lleida's highest point, built on the site of an Arab mosque. It was begun in the thirteenth century in Romanesque style and finished in Gothic. The cloister—placed uncharacteristically in front of the cathedral—and the church capitals are unusually beautiful.

LA PAHERÍA is a rare thirteenth century Romanesque civilian structure, covered in the eighteenth century with a neoclassic facade. Today it is the town hall.

There are several fine restaurants in Lleida, among them:

FORN DEL NASTASI   Salmerón 10   tel. (973) 23 45 10, is a cordial, well-cared-for classic Lleida restaurant, serving Catalan specialties and some personal creations. The restaurant features wines of Lleida, such as Raimat from the Costers del Segre region. (Moderate–expensive.)

MOLÍ DE LA NORA   Carretera de Puigcerdà, km 6   tel. (973) 19 00 17, just outside Lleida in Vilanova de la Barca, occupies an elegantly restored mill and specializes in seafood plus classic Catalan dishes. There is outdoor dining in the garden in summer. (Moderate–expensive.)

THE PROVINCE OF TARRAGONA

THE SOUTHERNMOST PROVINCE of Catalunya, Tarragona (tah-rah-*go*-nah) is somewhat transitional, marking the end of Catalunya and the beginning of the Levante. It is also the least mountainous part of Catalunya, distinguished by the Costa Dorada of wide golden-sand beaches and the marshy, pancake-flat Delta del Ebro basin, where the mighty Río Ebro empties into the Mediterranean, depositing rich alluvial earth as it goes, and every year extending the breadth of the landscape by some thirty feet. This is rich agricultural land yielding crops you would expect in a dry, sunny, and mild climate: olive oil, wines (the reds of Priorato are particularly well regarded today as they were in Roman times), almonds (essential to Tarragona's unique *Romesco* sauce), hazelnuts and *calçots*—tender young leeks that are eaten as an early-spring ritual.

At the mouths of large rivers such as the Ebro, prawns breed, and those from Tarragona are considered among the best in Spain. If you love this exquisite crustacean, as I do, you can indulge freely here. Tarragona waters produce a wealth of other seafood, some of it peculiar to this region, like *espardenyes* (sea cucumbers) and *pulpitos* (tiny octopus no bigger than a thumb joint)—other delicacies of the sea that I always look forward to.

Tarragona reached its greatest glory with the arrival of the Romans, who made the city of Tarragona an important Mediterranean port and the region a center for the Roman colonization of northern Spain. From medieval times there are two of Spain's most historically and architecturally important monasteries, Poblet and Santes Creus, built when the Catalan monarchy was at its peak.

THE CITY OF TARRAGONA

In Tarragona, always remember the two Rs: Roman and *romesco*, for this city was a principal Roman overseas capital and is the home of *romesco* sauce, to me a remarkable culinary creation. Writer Josep Pla puts it this way: "I doubt there are many cities in the world that, besides an incomparable past, an incredible history, and a location of rare beauty, can boast a sauce of its own, so special and unique."

On a hill rising from the Mediterranean, Tarragona was established by the Romans in 218 B.C. and named Tarraco. It served as a stronghold against the Carthaginians during the Second Punic War and seems to have instilled fond thoughts in Romans ("... when hoar December and wild winter shall moan with the hoarse northern blast, you will repair to Tarraco's sunny shores," wrote Martial). By decree of Julius Caesar, Tarraco became a

Roman capital, and under Emperor Augustus the city was the centerpiece of Tarraconensis, an area that comprised more than half of the Iberian Peninsula. Emperor Augustus visited the city, as did Emperor Hadrian, who further expanded Tarragona's power and prestige.

The accounts, however, of Tarragona's founding and its occupation by Rome are somewhat meager; surprisingly few firsthand or contemporary reports of Tarraco have come down to us, and there are far fewer remains of ancient Roman civilization here than, for example, in Mérida. In Tarragona the reminders of the past are scattered and somewhat lacking in impact. It is common to see houses built over Roman foundations, the marble in the cathedral is Roman, and some Roman town walls still stand. Although you have to piece together the scant information and use a lot of imagination, what does exist within Tarragona and on the outskirts of the city will give you some idea of Tarragona's vital position in Roman Spain. This was, after all, one of the few Roman cities honored with a circus, a theater, and an amphitheater.

Have your fill of past glories, then be sure to try Tarragona's other big R, *romesco*, which also traces its origins to Roman times. This is a sauce—or a dish made with that sauce—using the ingredients typical of the Tarragona countryside: almonds, garlic, olive oil, and a special variety of dried sweet red pepper (called *romesco*) that imparts a unique flavor, essential to *romesco*. *Romesco* is used as a dip for *calçots* or other vegetables, and with the addition of seafood and diluted with broth it becomes a fish stew (*Romesco de Peix*). It is a dish that fishermen prepare when at sea.

Today the tradition of preparing *romesco* is carried on by Tarragona's *romesco* maestros; for me one of the best is Simón Tomás, at the Sol Ric restaurant. We beat a path to his door whenever we pass through Tarragona, and it is many hours before gregarious chef Simón and his unflappable, suave brother Antonio, who attends to the dining room and outdoor terrace, will let us continue on our way. Although we're at Sol Ric for the company of the brothers Tomás and for the *romesco* that we crave, they will not hear of so "light" a lunch and will ply us with other delicacies—those *pulpitos*, baby squid, tiny fish, and the exquisite cod puffs! By the time we've enjoyed all this and a taste of Simón's latest creations, we have to take a breather before tackling the pièce de résistance, *Gran Romesco de Peix*, brought bubbling in an earthenware casserole and brimming with the best of the coast's fish and shellfish.

We first came to Tarragona to see the sights, but frankly our principal reason for repeated returns to Tarragona is this nonpareil dish. But so late do we usually emerge from lunch that it was years before we ever got to see what we always had scheduled for the afternoon—a visit to the Poblet monastery.

Seeing Tarragona

BALCÓ DEL MEDITERRANI   An overlook from a 150-foot height with sweeping vistas of the Mediterranean.

OLD QUARTER   Enter through the old gate of San Antonio near the Balcó del Mediterrani into a small world of arcaded streets, far removed from the bustle of New Tarragona and the beachfront summer-resort atmosphere. There are remains here of Roman towers and walls.

Tarragona once had a prospering Jewish quarter, and you can still see Jewish inscriptions carved into stone facades; one example is the window lintel (once a tombstone) of the Casa del Degá at Carrer Escrivanies Velles 6.

CATHEDRAL   Tarragona was a major center for the transmission of Christianity into northern Spain—thus the great size and imposing presence of its cathedral, begun in the twelfth century and finished in the fourteenth century. The apse incorporates some Romanesque works, but the major part of the building is Gothic. Particularly beautiful is the richness of detail of the main altar depicting the life of Santa Tecla, among the best works of the fifteenth century. The turbulence of the lower section gives a sense of her torture and martyrdom and contrasts with the serenity of the upper part.

MUSEU ARQUEOLÒGIC   Installed next to the ancient praetorian, or magistrate's tower, it has important pieces from the city's Roman past, such as the marble sarcophagus of Hippolytus and a magnificent mosaic head of Medusa.

PASSEIG ARQUELÒGIC   An interesting walk through city gardens to observe close up the massive stone construction of the old Roman walls, which in turn were built upon megalithic Iberian foundations.

ANFITEATRE ROMÀ   (Roman Amphitheater)   The remains can be seen near the beachfront.

EATING IN TARRAGONA

SOL RIC   Vía Augusta 227   tel. (977) 23 20 32   On a rise above the Rabasada beach, just north of the city, tastefully decorated with local antiques and appetizing food displays. *Romesco* is the specialty (see text). (Moderate–expensive.)

ROMAN REMAINS JUST OUTSIDE THE CITY

Entering Tarragona from the north along the coast, see the **TORRE DELS ESCIPIONS,** a funerary monument from the first or second century, and the **ARC DE BERÀ,** a typical Roman monumental arch. The perfectly preserved double-arched **AQUEDUCT,** commonly called the Devil's Bridge, can be seen four kilometers from the city on the Lleida road; the fourth century **MUSEU PALEOCRISTIÀ,** a mausoleum, five kilometers from Tarragona (direction Reus at Constantí), is part of a Roman villa (by its grandeur, this must have belonged to someone important, perhaps an emperor), and there are exceptionally beautiful mosaics of oriental influence on its huge vaulted ceiling. (Mornings only.)

VISITING THE PROVINCE OF TARRAGONA

The Coast

LES CASES DE ALCANAR   As we make our way down the coast, this lovely village and fishing port is a place we look forward to. We come for the exquisite fish of Angelina at **EL PESCADOR**   Cádiz 4,   tel. (977) 73 70 93, passing first through her kitchen to see what she has brought from the market and to devise our menu. Then we settle down outdoors in the glass-enclosed restaurant overlooking the port. We might start with little fried fish, squid, and prawns from the nearby delta, then choose grilled fish, like turbot, sole, *salmonetes* (red mullet), or striped bass. It is never cheap, but worth every peseta. (Moderate–expensive.)

SANT CARLES DE LA RÀPITA   With the advantage of a well-protected port, Charles III planned to make this a great commercial center and organized its streets lineally for this purpose. **MIAMI "CAN PONS"** Avenida Constitució 37   tel. (977) 74 05 51 (moderate–expensive), and **FER-NANDEL**   Sant Isidre s/n   tel. (977) 74 03 58 (moderate–expensive), have been here for decades, serving the finest seafood of the delta.

DELTA DEL EBRO   Ride through this vast, rich basin, and see birds everywhere—especially storks—in spring and summer. Travel to the large lagoons at Amposta and continue to the water's edge, where the miles-long, wide, and unspoiled **EUCALYPTUS BEACH** faces calm, shallow waters.

At the beachfront **RESTAURANTE MEDITERRÁNEO** you can feast on excellent seafood (try the casserole of mixed shellfish) in great abundance and at reasonable prices.

CAMBRILS   A resort town with an attractive port and old fishermen's quarters.

An unusual restaurant dynasty, which began with the grandfather's restaurant, now numbers three: **CASA GATELL**   Paseo Miramar 26   tel. (977) 36 00 57   **CAN GATELL**   Paseo Miramar 27   tel. (977) 36 01 06; and **EUGENIA**   Consolat de Mar 80   tel. (977) 36 01 68. All are close together near the waterfront, and each is run by a different branch of the family. They all serve similar fine food based on excellent seafood of the region, and are all exceedingly successful. (Expensive.)

The Interior

POBLET   A stunning religious complex with splendid examples of monastic, civilian, and military architecture from the twelfth to the sixteenth centuries. Since the twelfth century, the Aragón Royal Pantheon has been here, and the great El Escorial pantheon outside Madrid is said to be an imitation of this one at Poblet. Cistercian monasteries are austere, and an exceptional Renaissance alabaster altarpiece by Valencian sculptor Damián Forment was considered shockingly ornate. The abbot responsible for it was accused of misappropriation of funds, removed from office, and imprisoned.

SANTES CREUS   Begun in the twelfth century, this monastery is on a much smaller scale than Poblet, but is a fine example of Catalan Gothic. An extremely simple and austere thirteenth century church contrasts with the intricate and delicate open stonework over the capitals of the cloister. Favored by Catalan nobility, there are several royal tombs here. See also the Sala Capitular; the monks' sleeping quarters; a smaller, simpler cloister; the patio of a former royal palace; and the gardens.

TORTOSA   An ancient city with a fourteenth century Gothic cathedral and beautiful views of the Ebro river and its delta.
PARADOR CASTILLO DE LA ZUDA   Castillo de la Zuda s/n   tel. (977) 44 44 50; is high above the city and commands panoramic views. (Moderate.)

FIESTAS

ELS XIQUETS DE VALLS   June 24 and 25 and the first Sunday after October 21, in the city of Valls, the famed Els Xiquets de Valls (the Boys of Valls) perform as part of local festivities. A few dozen young men climb atop one another in seven, eight, even nine tiers, to create human pyramids.

FESTIVAL OF THE CALÇOTADA   Last Sunday of January, near Valls, a popular country event at which the first leek sprouts of the season are picked up, grilled over open fires, dipped in *romesco* sauce, and eaten in an atmosphere of general merriment.

EL LEVANTE:
LAND OF THE RISING SUN

INTRODUCTION

EL LEVANTE stretches along Spain's eastern shore between Catalunya and Andalucía and greets the rising sun each morning (the name Levante derives from *levantar*—to rise). In ancient times the region attracted Carthaginians, Greeks, Romans, Visigoths, and Arabs, and today it continues to attract millions from foreign lands, although they no longer come as conquerors, but as tourists. In deference to political demands, the Levante has been renamed Comunidad Valenciana—the Valencian Community—and Murcia is no longer one of its provinces. But I prefer to preserve the region's more colorful name and to keep Murcia here where it traditionally belonged. A visit to the Levante combines well with travel to Aragón and Catalunya.

Retaining characteristics of both Catalunya and Andalucía, the people of the Levante are work-oriented, like the Catalans (there is lots of industry here, especially related to ceramics, furniture, shoes, and toys), and their dialect, proudly regarded as a language by Levantinos, in some ways resembles the Catalan tongue. On the other hand, the people of the Levante celebrate fiestas, such as Las Fallas in Valencia, with all the verve, devotion, color, and pageantry (and with the added attraction of spectacular fireworks) that the world expects from Andalucía.

In literature, Vicente Blasco Ibáñez, a son of the Levante, earned international acclaim at the beginning of this century for such novels as *Blood and Sand* (Sangre y Arena) and *The Four Horsemen of the Apocalypse* (Los Cuatro Jinetes del Apocalipsis). In art, Joaquín Sorolla y Bastida dominated the twentieth century in the Levante, Francisco Salzillo and his polychromed reli-

FOODS AND WINES OF EL LEVANTE

GENERAL
Seafood, vegetables, rice, oranges

SPECIALTIES
Paella mixta—rice with seafood, chicken, *chorizo*, and vegetables
Paella a la Marinera—rice with seafood
Paella a la Valenciana—rice with rabbit, snails, and broad beans
Arroz Negro—black rice with squid
Arroz a Banda—rice cooked in fish broth (seafood served separately)
Arroz Murciano—"soupy" rice with fish and dried red peppers
Fideuá—pasta prepared in the style of paella
Fesols y Naps—rice, bean, and turnip stew
Anguilas All-i-Pebre—eels in garlic sauce
Turrón—almond candy, soft (Jijona style) and crackly (Alicante style)
Horchata—tigernut (chufa) refreshment

WINES
Viña Turquesa, Villa Íñigo from Utiel-Requena
Cavas Murviedro, Cantalviento from Valencia
Altos de Pío, San Isidro from Jumilla

gious sculptures the eighteenth, and José Ribera's powerfully realistic religious canvases the seventeenth. Architecture experienced two golden periods: Gothic in the fifteenth century and, three centuries later, an exuberant Baroque style peculiar to the Levante, characterized by ornately carved facades and somewhat squat churches and cathedrals with belfries slightly separated from the main structure.

But perhaps one of the most celebrated works of the Levante is a creation of ancient Iberian art and one of my favorites: the so-called *Dama de Elche* (see box, p. 387), which was unearthed in the province of Alicante and today resides in the Museo Arqueológico in Madrid.

Ceramics have a long and prestigious tradition in the Levante, and like the region's art and architecture, express vivacity in design and color. Although often destined for commercial use (floor and wall tilings, for example), beautiful ceramics of original design continue to be made by local artisans. Those by Lladró have ardent admirers around the world.

The landscape, the food, and the traditions of the Levante always interest me, and we return to the region repeatedly, even though Valencia, the Levante's major city and Spain's third largest, is not among my favorites; most Valencian villages (with a few notable exceptions) also lack charm and character, and there are stretches of overdeveloped coast that we assiduously avoid. You have to weave your way around rampant commercialism to find the region's best and discover its unique attractions.

Gentle climate; endless sunshine; wide, sandy beaches backed by perfectly flat land; and beyond that, scenic mountainscapes (the mountains block the biting winter winds of central Spain) make the Levante a developer's dream. To the north the coast has been christened Costa del Azahar (Orange Blossom Coast), and to the south Costa Blanca (White Coast). Many areas are chaotic high-rise horrors, but the international crowds just keep coming, charmed by the prospect of sunning and swimming when winter envelops the rest of the continent in an icy chill.

And yet despite the tourist blight, I can't resist the Levante. As crazy as it may sound, my main reason for coming here is to eat paella in unending variation. I also enjoy the peculiar and fascinating landscape intimately intertwined with rice production, centuries removed from the activity taking place along the coast.

As you move from north to south, the Levante changes its appearance. A superhighway makes it possible to get an overview of the region in the space of a day, even though you will most certainly want to establish a more leisurely pace. In the northernmost province, Castellón de la Plana, immense orange orchards startle the senses, blanketing the land as far as the eye can see. Sharply contrasting in scale are small family patchwork plots, bursting with such crops as peppers, broad beans, lettuce, tomatoes, and melons. These are the famed huertas, peculiar to this area, that have made the Levante the "Garden of Spain" and that yield three or four crops a year.

Then the swampy rice fields of Valencia appear in endless extensions, giving way eventually to the huertas of Murcia until finally, in the region's extreme south, the land begins to take on the desert appearance of neighboring Almería. All the while, as you move down the coast, arid mountains loom close by in exciting contrast to the green, pancake-flat cultivated land along the Mediterranean. In these hillier reaches many of the region's wines, such as those with the regional designations of Valencia, Utiel-Requena, and Jumilla, are produced. Many are destined to become inexpensive jug wines, although quality wines from the Levante have recently begun to attract attention.

Credit the Moors, who remained in the Levante long after they had been expelled from the rest of the country, for turning the rich alluvial land of the coast, a product of eons of silting by several of the country's major rivers, into this Garden of Spain that is the source of the Levante's wealth and fame. It was they who introduced rice (and gave it its Spanish name, *arroz*), planted almond trees, crowned Levante villages with massive fortresses, and gave them exotic Arab names that have survived the centuries, like Benicasím, Guadalest, and Alboraya.

But most important, the Arabs established an intricate, highly sophisticated, and well-regulated irrigation system of canals (called *acequias* by the Moors) that still waters the Levante and without which the region could not survive. Rain in the Levante comes in downpours, overflowing riverbanks and swelling creeks into raging torrents. It hardly penetrates the dry cracked earth, and were it not for canals and rigid allocation, the water would be lost to the Mediterranean. Which brings me back to my particular passion for rice in Spain, grown thanks to the Levante's special terrain and to Arab ingenuity.

If your only contact with paella has been in America, you may wonder why I make such a fuss about it, and why some call it "a gastronomic miracle." A good dish, you may say, nice on occasion, but certainly not extraordinary enough to merit a trip all the way to the Levante just to eat it at its source. Once you have tasted authentic paella, I'm sure you will agree with me that the atrocities committed worldwide in the name of *Paella a la Valenciana* are appalling: soppy, tasteless rice made in a soup pot, artificially colored, then heaped with seafood sadly transforms a quintessential rice dish into a dish in which the rice is merely an aside. Such paellas are a personal affront, and I prefer to either prepare paella at home or abstain.

But paella in the Levante is another story. From Castellón de la Plana south to Murcia, it can be so spectacularly good and so sensually pleasurable that for me there are few dishes in the world that compare. Rice dominates the diet in the Levante; it is eaten by everyone in some form just about every day, and yet it never ceases to be exciting.

"I grew up on rice," explains Valencian Ramón San Martín, owner of Café San Martín in New York, "and ate it every day of my life. Paella is the most versatile dish imaginable: a poor man's meal when only humble ingredients are used, a deluxe dish when shellfish takes part." Indeed, when I spend a few days in the Levante, I often eat rice day and night—to an occasional raised eyebrow, for Spaniards consider this an afternoon dish, too "heavy" for the evening. Traditionally prepared by men at lunchtime, in the fields over a fire, some of my most memorable paellas have nevertheless been eaten at local restaurants.

Because there are so many elements that contribute to the perfect paella, it is impossible to unite all of them outside of the Levante; paella is a dish that just does not "travel well." Of course, there is always a certain psycho-logical satisfaction in eating a local dish on site, but aside from that, the local rice—short grain and low in starch—and the mineral content of the Levante water supply are crucial elements. Consider also the regional additions to paella like vegetables and snails from the orchards, seafood of the Mediterranean, and ideally, Spanish saffron (see box, p. 152) to color and flavor the rice, even though quite acceptable paellas are possible without this expensive ingredient.

One of the reasons I love sampling paella in the Levante is that here paella is not a single dish, but a variety of subtly different rice preparations made in the same kind of pan—the wide, flat *paella,* or *paellera.* If the ingredients are too diverse to single out, the dish is called paella, while other preparations may be called *arroz* followed by a description of their style or ingredients (*Arroz a la Marinera, Arroz con Pollo,* etc.). While seafood, chicken, and vegetables are common additions to paella, lamb, pork, game, even sausage, meatballs, and chickpeas enter into some lesser-known versions.

I can't think of another region of Spain where one single ingredient so dominates the cuisine, but of course there are other wonderful dishes that depend on the produce of the huerta or the fish of the Mediterranean or both: vegetable medleys, featuring peppers, eggplant, and mixed baby green vegetables; snails in a spicy sauce; simply cooked fish and shellfish; and rabbit and duck preparations (Duck à l'Orange, uniting two typical products of the Levante, must surely have some connection with the region). A great favorite of Levantinos is *Anguilas All-i-Pebre*—eels in a sauce of oil, garlic, and peppers.

THE PROVINCE AND CITY OF CASTELLÓN DE LA PLANA

ALTHOUGH USUALLY associated with its benevolent Mediterranean coast, Castellón de la Plana (cahs-teh-*yown* day lah-*plah*-nah)—even its name, Castellón "of the Plain," refers to its coastal flatness—extends in reality into the harsh, snowy, and spectacularly beautiful mountain interior of the Maestrazgo. Geographically and culturally speaking, however, these areas are closer in character to the province of Teruel, and I have taken the liberty of including them in that chapter. So let's concentrate here on the Castellón known for its beaches, mild winters, and most notably, its huertas and orange groves.

What a spectacular sight are Castellón's orange trees, thousands upon thousands of them, creating a tweedy carpet of light- and deep-green shiny leaves punctuated, according to season, by fragrant white blossoms or bright orange fruit (but just try to find a glass of fresh-squeezed juice!). The groves extend almost to the water's edge and even timidly creep up on terraced land into the foothills of the Maestrazgo mountain range. Tourist developments that take advantage of fine wide beaches sometimes push the orange trees back from the coast, but they remain the lifeblood of the province and its most characteristic feature.

In gastronomy, rice and seafood play major roles (strange that oranges are so little used here in cooking). Two typical versions of paella in Castellón combine rice with fish: *Arroz a Banda* (a two-course affair that begins with poached fish and continues with the rice that has cooked in the fish broth) and *Arroz Negro* (darkened and flavored with squid ink and complemented by an eye-opening dollop of *alioli*—garlic mayonnaise). The prawns of the town of Vinaroz rival those of Sanlúcar de Barrameda in the province of Cádiz for the title of Spain's best.

The capital city of Castellón de la Plana is little more than an overgrown town (about 125,000 inhabitants) that swells in summer with German and French tourists vacationing at the shore and intent on eating paella. Beware! All paellas are not created equal, not even in their native land, and restaurants that cater to foreign visitors often do not make commendable paellas.

Castellón's port, or *grao*, is an extension of the city and is where the best restaurants are found. In fact, my sole reason to include Castellón on my itinerary is to lunch on *Arroz Negro* at Tasca del Puerto, where owner Chimo and his wife, Remi, warmly greet their loyal fans. Words cannot do justice to the pure poetry of the dish.

EATING IN THE CITY OF CASTELLÓN DE LA PLANA

TASCA DEL PUERTO   Avenida del Puerto 13   tel. (964) 23 60 18   A charming, friendly restaurant for the world's best Black Rice. Also, rice stew called *Fesols y Naps; Fideuá*, a pasta dish made in the style of paella; plus a variety of excellent seafoods. (Moderate.)

RAFAEL   Churruca 28   tel. (964) 28 21 85   Crowded with businessmen at lunchtime, this highly regarded restaurant specializes in *Arroz a Banda* and seafood. (Moderate.)

PEÑÍSCOLA: LAST REFUGE OF THE INDOMITABLE POPE BENEDICT XIII

Peñíscola is for me the highlight of the Castellón coast, and although it has grown right along with the rest of the beachside towns (like Benicasím, Benicarló, and Oropesa, which do not at all entice me), Peñíscola keeps its special charm and has a most unusual history.

Enclosed by walls, set atop a rocky peninsula, and tenuously connected to the mainland by a narrow neck (it was in fact once an island), Peñíscola has picturesque lime-washed old quarters that rise sharply along narrow streets. Peñíscola's photographic appeal made it the scene of Charlton

Heston's victorious entrance into Valencia (despite the historical inaccuracy) in the movie epic *El Cid*.

Peñíscola is particularly dramatic in stormy weather, when waves crash thunderously against the town's solid-rock base, sending up huge misty sprays. I love to walk along the waterfront, piled with fishing nets, and see the boats arrive with the daily catch for the afternoon auction. I like to climb the main street (cars not allowed), which circles the perimeter of Peñíscola, revealing stunning views all along the way, and which ends in a castle built at the very top by the Christians as a defense from Moorish invaders. It later became the residence of Antipope Benedict XIII, known in Spain as Papa Luna.

At the time of the Great Schism (1378–1417), when the French king demanded a pope sympathetic to him and residing in France, and Italians clamored for an Italian pope based in Rome, Cardinal Pedro de Luna, a learned man of noble birth, pleased the French and was elected antipope. However, his support waned, and Papa Luna retired to the castle of Peñíscola, chosen because the town was near his native Aragón and because the castle symbolized the Christian victory over the infidel.

Papa Luna stubbornly and tenaciously clung to his belief that he was the rightful heir to the papacy. He lived here in utmost austerity to the age of ninety-four, and never renounced his claims (see box, p. 372). The coat of arms of Papa Luna, a crescent moon (a play on his name, which means moon), has become the symbol of Peñíscola.

At night when moonlight ripples over the Mediterranean and Papa Luna's castle is illuminated, Peñíscola turns magical. Stroll its darkened streets, but walk also along the beach or the promenade and see the stunning scene from afar.

STAYING IN PEÑÍSCOLA

HOSTERÍA DEL MAR   Carretera Peñíscola-Benicarló   tel. (964) 48 06 00   This well-cared-for hotel, associated with the paradors, faces the beach and the rocky heights of the old town. (Moderate–expensive; pool.)

◆ On Saturday nights, elaborate medieval dinners with dishes like fish stew and roast lamb that might have been served in the times of Papa Luna, take place, served by hotel staff in medieval dress and accompanied by music and dance. Finally, Papa Luna himself appears!

EATING IN PEÑÍSCOLA

CASA SEVERINO, in the elegant Las Atalayas urbanization, tel. (964) 48 07 03, has good local fish. I particularly like the mixed grilled shellfish (*Mariscada*). (Moderate.)

◆ In the upper areas of the old quarters of Peñíscola there are several seafood restaurants with wonderful terraces looking over the Mediterranean.

PAPA LUNA'S LEGACY: THE CONTINUING GREAT SCHISM

On the death of Papa Luna in 1423 (by poisoning, some say), two new antipopes appeared—Clemente VIII, the personal choice of Papa Luna, and another secretly selected by Papa Luna's vicar-general who received the name Benedict XIV. Clemente VIII renounced his claim to the papacy, officially bringing the Great Schism to a close. But Benedict XIV, by some accounts, continued a line of antipopes that to this day are regularly elected by an occult society of "anti-cardinals."

The family of Papa Luna, fearing that his refusal to renounce the papacy would lead to excommunication, did not bury him. Instead they brought his body to the family castle and sealed it in the room in which he was born, where it remained for centuries. During the War of Independence in the nineteenth century, the French sacked the castle and the skeleton was discovered and tossed down to the river. The skull was retrieved and is now supposedly kept in a palace in the nearby town of Saviñán.

VISITING THE PROVINCE OF CASTELLÓN DE LA PLANA

DESIERTO DE LAS PALMAS A beautiful barren area about fourteen kilometers from Castellón up a tightly twisting road. It's not really a desert, nor are there so many palms, but from the monastery the views of the coast and sea are exceptional.

LUCENA DEL CID The village itself is not as exciting as its remarkable setting, on the edge of mountains that face a deep valley.

◆ You might try returning to the coast by way of Argelita. It's a more difficult road, but you will see stunning mountain spikes, terraced land with fruit and olive trees, and wonderful panoramas.

CASTELLFORT, MORELLA, ARES DE MAESTRE, and **FORCALL**   See **EL MAESTRAZGO**.

◆ Although I rarely recommend highway travel as the best way to see Spain, in the case of the Levante, A-7 shows you the best of the region while avoiding time-consuming traffic jams through villages of little interest.

THE PROVINCE OF VALENCIA

FROM THE FIFTEENTH through the seventeenth centuries, Valencia (vah-*len*-theea) was an influential province and a link between powerful Aragón and its kingdom of Naples in Italy. Valencia was residence of the noble and notorious Borja family (Borgia in Italian, see box, p. 382), and produced two popes (three if you include Benedict XIII, who was born in Aragón but lived in the Levante) and one of Spain's great seventeenth century painters, José Ribera, nicknamed in Italy, where he produced much of his work, "The Little Spaniard" (Lo Spagnoletto) because of his small physical stature. Born of a Spanish father and an Italian mother, Ribera had a great command of chiaroscuro, and his style was characterized by powerful realism and an emphasis on themes of martyrdom, pain, and suffering.

Despite the presence of one of Spain's major cities, the province of Valencia is still a strange combination of big-city industry with traditional Levante agriculture. It is, of course, the shore that attracts the tourist trade.

The beaches, the Mediterranean, and the exceptional brilliance of the Levantine sky were major influences on the style of twentieth century painter Joaquín Sorolla, born and raised in Valencia. All the gaiety, liveliness, color, and folkloric qualities of the Levante are reflected in his works, which were a breath of fresh air in an art world in the throes of change. And although his later paintings, mostly portraits of world-famous figures done in Madrid and abroad, brought him acclaim, his simple scenes of fishing boats, peasants, and kids frolicking on the beach are those that he seems to have experienced most intimately.

Today Valencia is a province that gives off mixed signals. You need some guidance to find the best and avoid the worst. So let me focus on what attracts me to Valencia: the fiestas and traditions of the city of Valencia and the rice paddies in the outskirts.

THE CITY OF VALENCIA AND ITS ENVIRONS

Valencia is a city of a certain raw, unsophisticated vibrancy that rises from the very borders of the orange orchards, the rice fields, and the sea, which are its sustenance and which were immortalized in such novels by Blasco Ibáñez as *La Barraca* (The Cabin) and *Cañas y Barro* (Reeds and Mud). I cannot think of another Spanish city so large yet so inextricably united to its countryside. One minute you are surrounded by rice paddies and huertas, the next confronted by concrete-block apartment complexes and car dealerships.

In fact, I never consider Valencia proper as the highlight of my visits. I don't even stay in town; instead I chose the parador at El Saler, nineteen kilometers to the south, on the delta between the Turia and Júcar rivers, secluded in the midst of low hills, dwarf pines, and sand dunes on a strip of land called La Dehesa. Serving the important role as a separation between Valencia's vast lagoon, La Albufera, and the sea, La Dehesa is a National Reserve, and commands splendid Mediterranean views. Here I can capture the true country flavor of Valencia, so often overshadowed by the coast's resort atmosphere and the bigness of the city.

In the wedge of marshy land between the rivers I absorb an entirely different Valencia. In spring and summer a sea of delicate green rice shoots appears, and stooped laborers, shaded from the sun by wide-brimmed straw hats, plod the swampy fields, pants rolled to the knee. I visit La Albufera (the word derives from Arabic and means "Little Sea")—pea green, thick with tall reeds, alive with eels, jumping fish, croaking frogs, and aquatic birds. No matter how often I come to Valencia, witnessing the unrivaled sunsets over La Albufera, either from its shores or while lazing in a rented rowboat, is a treat.

Crude single-sailed sampan-like boats glide soundlessly through the waters of La Albufera (there are motorboats too, but I prefer to ignore them). In the rice fields an occasional triangular-shaped whitewashed cottage called a *barraca* (where rice field workers traditionally sought shelter), thatched with straw and reeds, quaintly raises its head. I feel for all the world that I am no longer in Spain but in some far-off exotic land.

> [The boatman] who crossed the Albufera four times a day engendered respect, taking to Valencia the best fish of the lake and bringing from there thousands of objects of a city mysterious and fantastic for those kids brought up on an island of reeds and mud.
>
> Blasco Ibáñez, *Cañas y Barro*

Continue south along the main road that skirts La Albufera, then turn onto a country road that leads to El Palmar, the onetime island described by Blasco Ibáñez. Today it is joined to the mainland but still a world apart and still dedicated to rice production, fishing, and small vegetable plots, delineated by makeshift bamboo partitions. Providing another source of income are simple family-run restaurants serving paella and the traditional dish of La Albufera, *Anguilas All-i-Pebre*, made with the eels traditionally caught in the lagoon.

Beyond El Palmar you are veritably engulfed by rice paddies, and the only solid land is under the road on which you travel. Don't venture too far, however, or you may lose your way, for there is nothing in sight except endless kilometers of marshland.

> . . . to one side the immense flatness of rice fields that are lost in the horizon at Sollana and Sueca, blending into the distant mountains.
>
> Blasco Ibáñez, *Cañas y Barro*

Although this country landscape intrigues me, I do not mean to overlook the city of Valencia, the "light, cloudless" city seized from the Moors by the legendary El Cid (see Index) more than eight centuries ago (it later reverted to Moorish power until definitively taken by King Jaime I of Aragón). El Cid looked proudly upon his conquered lands and saw, in company of his wife and daughters, a view not very different from what you might see today:

> "Enter with me into Valencia
> The city that I have won for you."
> He takes them to the castle heights
> Where they gaze upon the city below,
> The sea beyond, the orchards,
> Lush and grand, and many other pleasures.
>
> *El Cantar de Mío Cid*

Nothing is somber in Valencia. The cathedral is a lively mixture of architectural styles, and its octagonal tower goes by the lighthearted name of Micalet—Little Michael. The old silk exchange, La Lonja, is Flamboyant Gothic and is the city's finest example of the fifteenth century period when Valencia flourished both economically and artistically. An extraordinary ceramics museum in the palace of the Marqués de Dos Aguas is distinguished by an exceedingly ornate Baroque facade of alabaster, in a style called Churrigueresque (see box, p. 88), and its wild design and sensual flow are quite extraordinary (its artist, Ignacio Vergara, was supposedly deranged). Among its extensive collection of antique ceramics, the museum features a magnificently tiled Valencian kitchen, patterned in the colorful designs still used by artisans in Valencia today.

Valencia's privileged location creates a unique culinary environment, and for me many of the city's attractions are food-related. The extraordinary central market, one of the largest in the world, explodes with the colorful bounty of the Valencian huertas—unblemished deep-red and green peppers, tomatoes, oranges, lemons; there is rice displayed in large jute baskets, and fish stands are laden with the day's catch. Small eels are sold live and slither about in tubs of water. Not far away at the immense Plaza del País Valencià, the heart of the city, I like to pause for a tapa or two at Barrachina, a mammoth tapas bar and gourmet shop, and buy a two-kilo burlap sack of *arroz bomba*—Valencia's best rice—and perhaps some saffron to take home with me.

If by chance you happen to be near the cathedral at 10:00 a.m. on a Thursday, you can witness the reunion of the Water Tribunal at the Apostles Door of the Gothic cathedral. Twelve city elders, solemnly dressed in dark smocked robes, hear and settle landholders' water disputes, as they have for centuries. Their decisions are ironclad and admit no legal appeal.

Valencia is one of the great places in the Levante to eat rice dishes. At elegant La Hacienda restaurant I have eaten a simple shrimp paella so good it brings conversation to a halt. But for good rice in a more traditional and casual atmosphere, I head at lunchtime to Valencia's port, El Grao, where La Pepica restaurant, commonly and most appropriately known as the "Cathedral of Paella," opens onto the Levante beach. An institution in Valencia since the nineteenth century, La Pepica was a favorite of Ernest Hemingway when he came to Valencia for bullfight festivals. In this cavernous establishment, which somewhat resembles a converted train station, you can appreciate the importance, the almost religious aura, that surrounds paella in Valencia.

> Dinner at Pepica's was wonderful. It was a big, clean, open-air place and everything was cooked in plain sight. You could pick out what you wanted to have grilled or broiled and the seafood and the Valencian rice dishes were the best on the beach.
>
> Ernest Hemingway, *The Dangerous Summer*

In a large open kitchen, hung with paella pans for two or two hundred portions (even a paella for two requires a sixteen-inch pan to properly cook the rice in a thin layer), chefs labor over stoves fueled by aromatic woods. They produce paellas at a furious pace to feed the several hundred diners that La Pepica accommodates (and they *all* order paella). The chefs follow centuries-old methods and know intuitively just when the rice is *en su punto* (al dente). After resting for several minutes, the paella is rushed to tables ("Paella waits for no man," Valencians are fond of saying) and presented for the diner's approval and admiration.

We are already enjoying our paella—the traditional version of the huerta, with snails, rabbit, and broad green beans (Valencian purists frown upon mixing fish and meat, as is common in paellas made outside the Levante)—when our waiter brings a small dish of golden brown, crunchy rice that has been scraped from the bottom of the pan. This is the quintessence of the paella, presented to us as if we were about to receive Communion or participate in the rites of a secret society. "Ladies and gentlemen," he proudly announces, "here is the *socarrat.*"

Whether there are fiestas or not, nighttime brings a carnival atmosphere to the old quarters of Valencia, for this is a city in which weather permits outdoor activities all year round. Huge outdoor cafés around the Plaza del País Valencià fill beyond capacity with Valencianos enjoying predinner tapas and drinks, then later in the evening sipping Valencia's unique refreshment, *horchata* (see box, p. 380).

Many narrow twisting streets are closed to traffic and crowded with outdoor tables. We savor the breezy night air at El Palacio de la Bellota and indulge in nutty cured ham from Jabugo in the province of Huelva, marinades of red peppers or of shellfish; fried baby *calamares*, no bigger than a thumbnail; and an extravagant platter of shrimp, prawns, langoustines, goose barnacles, and sea snails. Owner Enrique Grau, however, is no slouch when it comes to rice; paella extravaganzas are his specialty, like the paella for thousands that he prepared during a visit by the pope to Valencia.

In a city famed for its pyrotechnics, you never know when the night will light up with fireworks. Valencians seize any opportunity for an elaborate display that can awe even the most jaded observer. But none of this can compare with the spring rite of Las Fallas, when in an orgy of fire and merriment the city is consumed in flame.

THE EXCITING SPECTACLE OF LAS FALLAS

Despite Valencia's size and importance, the city virtually shuts down for the five-day fiesta of Las Fallas. Streets close to traffic and Valencians spend their days and nights strolling from one plaza to another, munching on *churros* (see box, p. 35) and *bunyols* (Valencian doughnuts), which fry in huge vats of oil at street corners, and viewing *las fallas*, the enormous tableaux of remarkable color and detail that soar several stories into the air. They are proudly displayed in every neighborhood and in just about every square. There are hundreds of them.

The event of Las Fallas takes its name first from the Valencian word for torch (*falla*), then from these tableaux (*las fallas*), which are the focus of the fiesta. They are styled by artists whose lives are devoted to this yearly event, and are first made in plaster molds, then papier-mâché (the perfect fuel for fire), and after that, painstakingly painted. *Las fallas* require a full year to plan; months, millions of pesetas, and the efforts of thousands of workers to build; and many days to assemble. But in the space of an hour on the night of San José, March 19, the *cremà,* or burning of *las fallas,* reduces them to ashes. A year's work is gone up in smoke, and an artist's vision forever vanishes; so much planning and anticipation for something so transient, so briefly pleasurable.

But Valencians dearly love the festival of Las Fallas and the fire, smoke, explosions, nightly fireworks, daily bullfights, colorful parades, processions, orchestras, and lively street life that characterize this action-packed week. "I get chills every time I see it," remarks our Valencian friend Cristina de Ibáñez. "It's a purifying experience, a renewal, a cleansing of the spirit."

Las Fallas began quite modestly centuries ago, when guild carpenters burned wood chips and shavings on the day of San José to mark the beginning of spring and to celebrate longer hours of daylight and the end of winter's hardships. Laborers no longer needed the torches (called *fallas*) that were held on long poles to provide extra light to work by. The poles were decorated like scarecrows to amuse spectators and provide added liveliness to the bonfires. This tradition, carried one step further, led to the satirical representations of neighborhood events and the caricaturization of important community members (both these elements are essential to Las Fallas today). Valencians found through *las fallas* a socially acceptable means to publicly express displeasure—and "cleanse" the past year from their minds.

Over the years *las fallas* continued to grow in artistic worth and in physical size, fueled by the fierce but friendly rivalry among neighborhoods. Today the tableaux have reached enormous proportions—a far cry from the child-size mockups (*ninots*), each of which was once an entire *falla.* The *ninots* have not, however, disappeared. You can see them in the lower part of every *falla,* lavished with detail. They are exhibited in La Lonja (see "Seeing Valencia") before the start of Las Fallas, and one of them will become the "*ninot indultat,*" saved from the fire by popular vote and added to the exhibit of *ninots* at Valencia's Museu Faller. The collection serves as a barometer of changing social values and public tastes.

Every *falla* has a theme and generally satirizes political figures in the news (and in the gossip columns) and world events headlined during the year. A major *falla* not long ago showed massive figures of the Three Wise Men—Spain's equivalent of Santa Claus—surrounded by several important political figures who had promised everything and delivered little. The politicians had defrauded the public's expectations, just as the Three Wise Men often leave children's wishes unfulfilled at Christmas. While the theme of this *falla* was relatively benign, *las fallas,* although still artistically and technically skillful, are often cartoonlike, burlesque, erotic, even downright pornographic representations. "You really have to be born and bred in Valencia to appreciate the bad taste of Las Fallas," says another Valencian friend, Ramón San Martín.

The *cremà* that takes place on March 19 during the Night of Fire, or as Valencians say, La Nit de Foc, is the apotheosis. Hours before the main event that ignites the largest and most prestigious *falla* in the Plaza del País Valencià, the city reverberates with bomblike blasts, crackles with fireworks, and acquires a golden glow as lesser *fallas* burn, often in tightly enclosed

plazas, perilously close to the houses (the bonfires will not burn simultaneously, as they once did, because fire regulations now require the presence of
firemen at each location). The air fills with smoke and ash and a haze settles
over the city. Valencia looks like a war zone.

As 1:00 a.m. arrives, the crowd in the Plaza del País Valencià swells
and the scene soon resembles New York's Times Square on New Year's Eve.
Rhythmic applause breaks out, followed by whistles and jeers as the hour
passes and there is still no *cremà*. Then suddenly all the plaza's lights are
extinguished; the crowd roars its approval. Dazzling fireworks illuminate the
night, and the *tracas*—strings of firecrackers—set off brilliant sparks and colored rockets that soar in the air and explode thunderously in a well-orches-
trated concert called the *mascletà*. The *falla* is masked by smoke. The air
clears, the *falla* fiercely burns, and the heat is intense. The summit of the
falla is the last to ignite, then in a flash the structure collapses. The cheers of
the crowd turn to song as the Valencian anthem is heard.

Seeing Valencia

CATHEDRAL   Of Gothic design, but incorporating many other styles,
this cathedral was begun in the thirteenth century to replace the mosque of
the fallen Moorish rulers. Its facade has the short, squat appearance typical
of churches and cathedrals in the Levante and is distinguished by its octagonal tower, El Micalet, a landmark that is the symbol of the city (climb up for
views of the city and countryside). At the cathedral steps, the Water
Tribunal meets every Thursday (see text).

Of chief interest within the cathedral is the Aula Capitular, where the
supposed Holy Grail of the Last Supper is exhibited. Carved from agate, it
has been authenticated as dating from the time of Christ, and when the
pope visited Valencia in 1982 he used the cup for Mass.

LA LONJA   This crenelated and gargoyled fifteenth century Gothic structure with a delicately worked doorway was the site of the medieval commodities exchange. Its interior reaches lofty heights and has interesting
spiral pillars that end in a spray of arches that forms the crisscross *crucería*
ceiling, dotted with medallions.

LAS TORRES DE SERRANOS   These imposing towers are what remains
of the walls of Valencia from the fourteenth and fifteenth centuries.

MUSEO DE BELLAS ARTES   In a seventeenth century building is a
fine collection of Valencian primitive art from the fourteenth and fifteenth
centuries, much of it altar paintings brought from around the region (along
with a smattering of El Greco, Velázquez, and Goya).

MUSEO NACIONAL DE CERÁMICA   A favorite of mine, with a magnificent collection of antique ceramics (see text).

MUSEU FALLER   A provisional installation for the *ninots indultats* of Las
Fallas, but an interesting look at the changing artistry and the changing

political and social concerns that reflect a changing Spain.

PLAZA REDONDA   An unusual round "square" in the old city that is a continuous circle of whitewashed houses surrounding two concentric circles of porticoed stores.

STAYING IN VALENCIA

PARADOR LUIS VIVES   Carretera del Saler   tel. (96) 161 11 86   About ten minutes south of Valencia, a spacious and airy parador with water views, a beautiful beach, and a well-groomed golf course. This is my favorite place to stay in Valencia; most other hotels outside of the city are done in Miami Beach style. Very popular—reserve well in advance. (Moderate–expensive; pool.)

♦ If you are in Valencia specifically for Las Fallas, it is more practical to stay right in town. Reservations are hard to come by, so make your plans as early as possible.

REINA VICTORIA   Barcas 4   tel. (96) 352 04 87   The grande dame of Valencian hotels, recently restored to its former glory (it has had such notable guests as Queen Victoria, wife of King Alfonso XIII, for whom it is named; Dalí; Picasso; and García Lorca. For Las Fallas, reservations are at a premium. (Moderate–expensive.)

EATING IN AND AROUND VALENCIA

LA HACIENDA   Narvarro Reverter 12   tel. (96) 373 18 59   Posh and fashionable, this restaurant has a menu that runs to nouvelle cuisine, but the chef also creates about the best paella that I have ever eaten. (Moderate for paella; otherwise expensive.)

LA TABERNA ALKÁZAR   Mosén Femades 9–11   tel. (96) 352 95 75   A tavern of smart décor for select (and expensive) seafood, as tapas or for dining.

EL PALACIO DE LA BELLOTA   Mosén Femades 7   tel. (96) 351 49 94   Named for its luscious ham from the acorn-fed pigs of Huelva, this tavern has a huge selection of tapas in very animated surroundings.

CERVECERÍA MADRID   Abadía de San Martín 10   A charming multi-level tavern with a lively ambiance. Try their specialty, Rocafull, a mix of iced coffee, egg white, and brandy.

HORCHATERÍA SANTA CATALINA, Plaza de Santa Catalina   For excellent *bunyols*, hot chocolate, and *horchata* (see box, p. 380) in a turn-of-the-century atmosphere. It is busy until all hours of the morning during Las Fallas.

HORCHATERÍA LA ESPAÑOLA, corner Ruzafa and Lauria streets   Fine *horchata* from La Alboraya (see box, p. 380).

Horchata: The Uniquely Refreshing Drink of Valencia

Made from an obscure African root called chufa, *horchata* is a sweet creamy white refreshment that is served chilled; it is rich in protein, vitamins, and minerals. Its nutty flavor bears a faint resemblance to coconut but otherwise defies description, and it is my favorite drink on a hot summer's day.

Horchata came to Spain by way of the Moors, who first planted chufas unsuccessfully in Málaga and finally found the ideal microclimate in Alboraya, just north of Valencia. The origin of the word *horchata* is thought to be Latin, meaning barley (similar drinks are made from barley, rice, and almonds), but this learned explanation pales beside the tale of King James I of Aragón, who wrested control of Valencia from the Arabs in 1238. The monarch was wandering through the orchards of his newly conquered land one steamy summer afternoon. Perspiring and parched from thirst, he rested with his attendants at a farm, where an Arab girl offered him a drink so wonderfully refreshing that he exclaimed (in medieval Spanish) "*Aixo es or, xata*"—This is gold, girl— which became contracted to *horchata*.

Until recently, *horchata*'s fragility (it does not keep fresh for long) meant that the drink was found almost exclusively in the Valencia region. But today you can find fine *horchata* in Madrid and in many ice cream parlors around the country. Its taste, nevertheless, is purest at its source in Alboraya, especially at the palatially proportioned Horchata Daniel, where on a warm summer evening many hundreds of loyal customers will be sipping it, accompanied by a pastry called *fartón*. You can also try it in Valencia from February through October.

RACÓ DE L'OLLA   El Palmar   tel. (96) 161 00 72 This restaurant, just before you reach the town of El Palmar, is quite large, but has the distinct advantage of being on the banks of the Albufera (you can arrange boat rides). Arrive in time to watch the sunset over the lagoon and dine on a selection of tapas (like tiny fried fish and squid and fresh shrimp) and paellas. (Moderate.)

♦ In the village of El Palmar you can choose from dozens of family-style restaurants (such as **CAÑAS Y BARRO**). Avoid visiting El Palmar on weekends, especially on Sundays, when restaurants are jammed with day trippers from Valencia.

LA PEPICA   Playa del Levante   tel. (96) 371 20 25 An institution in Valencia for paellas (see text). Begin with excellent steamed mussels or garden fresh salad, and be sure to watch the chefs at work in the open kitchen. (Moderate.)

FIESTAS

LAS FALLAS   See text. The fiesta runs from March 15 to March 19. On the night of March 18 thousands of Valencian girls in elaborate traditional dress form the Ofrenda de Las Flores procession, which winds its way through the city for over eight hours and ends just behind the cathedral at the "Virgin of the Forsaken" church. Here a towering scaffolded figure of the Virgin receives millions of flowers in bouquets that are arranged as if they were her clothes. March 19 is the key date of Las Fallas; that night the tableaux are burned.

◆ Buy a booklet at a newsstand to guide you to the prizewinning *fallas* and help you decipher the involved symbolism (you'll need a good grasp of Spanish to wade through it, and even then it may still seem to you, as it does to me, a bit perplexing).

BULLFIGHT FESTIVALS take place the second half of July and culminate July 25 (the Day of Santiago) with exciting fireworks.

VISITING THE PROVINCE OF VALENCIA

SAGUNTO   A walled Roman seaport (called Saguntum), once at water's edge but now, because of silting, three kilometers from the sea and towering tall above the Mediterranean. In ancient times it was famous throughout the Roman Empire for its pottery (it is said that there were over two hundred "brand names"). Sagunto's theater, from the third century, was capable of accommodating more than 10,000 spectators. It is well preserved and has exceptional acoustics, and in August festivals of theater take place. Climb to the Acropolis to see its remains and some expansive views of the countryside. Don't miss the old Jewish quarter, on extremely narrow, steep, twisting streets that climb almost perpendicularly to the rocky base of the Acropolis. This was one of the very oldest Sephardic enclaves in Spain. Sagunto's stubborn resistance to Carthaginian assault is legendary (see box).

THE HEROIC STAND AND TRAGIC FALL OF SAGUNTO

The defense of Sagunto is among world history's greatest tales of defiance and bravery. A Roman colony located within the domain of Carthage, Sagunto became a strategic and psychological thorn in the side of Carthaginian general Hannibal. So a siege began, and the people of Sagunto put up fierce resistance. Even after the town walls had been breached and defeat was imminent, they refused to capitulate.

But finally when they knew their cause was hopeless, the people of Sagunto built an immense bonfire and threw into it everything of value (they were determined to leave no bounty for the Carthaginians). As the end approached, another decision was made: All those unable to bear arms were to be sacrificed to the flames. Women, children, and the infirm flung themselves into the blaze, then the city was torched. The remaining defenders fought to the very last man. It was a classic example of a pyrrhic victory.

Cool-headed historians see things a bit differently. They believe Rome glorified the resistance of Sagunto for propaganda purposes (years later Sagunto returned to Roman power, and the tenacity and loyalty of Sagunto's people sent a clear message to the rest of the empire). Nevertheless, I like to remember this great event undiluted by historical polemics and imbued with the grand proportions of high drama and Greek tragedy.

ALBORAYA   Come here exclusively for *horchata* at **HORCHATA DANIEL**   53 Avenida del Generalísimo, and other family-run *horchaterías*.

MANISES   Just outside of Valencia, this town is dedicated to ceramic work, and there are many stores at which you may purchase hand-painted pieces. I especially like **ENRIQUE CASES**   Maestro Guillem, 46 bajo   tel. (96) 154 67 42, where besides individual ceramic pieces, I have found beautiful dinnerware that can be packaged and shipped.

L'ALCUDIA   Here is one of the Levante's most highly regarded restaurants, **GALBIS**   Avenida Antonio Almela 15   tel. (96) 254 10 93 (moderate–expensive), specializing in paellas and other Valencian dishes as well as some nouvelle cuisine.

EL SALER   See text.

EL PALMAR   See text.

CULLERA   A high-rise coastal resort, crowned by a castle and enclosed by rice fields. Set up in two charming *barracas* is **SALVADOR**   Lago del Estany   tel. (96) 172 01 36, specializing in paellas. (Inexpensive–moderate.)

GANDÍA   A bustling business and tourist center, notable in history for its connection to the Borja (Borgia) family (see box). Their lavish fifteenth century Palacio Ducal may be visited.

JÁTIVA   This small city was the birthplace of the great seventeenth century painter, José Ribera, and of two Borja popes, Calixtus III and Alexander VI (see box). Its old quarter is a national monument, and in its Museo Municipal a portrait of King Philip V hangs upside down as it has since the eighteenth century, a sign of displeasure with this king who subdued Valencia during a bitter War of Succession (see Index).

THE BORJAS OF THE LEVANTE

It comes as a great surprise to many that the renowned Borgias of Renaissance Italy were Aragonese and once based in Valencia. The story of their ascent begins with Papa Luna (see Peñíscola), who, to show his appreciation for the support of Alfonso de Borja during the Great Schism, named him canon. Borja rose to bishop of Vic, and then for his efforts in ending the schism, was awarded the post of cardinal; finally he became Pope Calixtus III and transferred his residence to the Vatican. Thus began the Italian branch of the Borja family and the change of name to Borgia.

Pope Calixtus appointed his nephew Rodrigo de Borja, born like his uncle in Játiva, Valencia, to a cardinalate, and while serving in that position, Rodrigo fathered several children, among them Lucrezia Borgia (who became the sensation of Renaissance Italy) and the ruthless Caesar Borgia. Rodrigo eventually became Pope Alexander VI, and the Italian wing of the Borjas achieved such fame and infamy (it was said that the father of Lucrezia's son was none other than her own father, the pope) that the family's Spanish connection faded from public memory.

THE PROVINCE OF ALICANTE

I HAVE VERY SPECIAL and specific reasons for coming to Alicante (ah-lee-*cahn*-tay), different from those of most tourists who flock here by the thousands from all parts of Europe. Northern Europeans especially are enticed by reports of the freewheeling life in resorts like Benidorm (where Swedish beauties may sit topless eating tapas) and by promises of endless sunshine and mild temperatures. Certainly the climate is as advertised, the beaches can be beautiful, the Mediterranean is most inviting, and if all you want is sun and a square foot of sand, Alicante may seem like heaven. But unfortunately, so many have the same idea that building has become chaotic and uncontrolled, and the pristine beauty that originally brought visitors no longer exists. Nevertheless, tourists and retirees pour in en masse, often on cut-rate overnight bus rides from Germany and France. Which just proves that one man's meat is another man's poison.

When we pass through Alicante, as we often do en route between Valencia and Andalucía, we pause only at a handful of places that we know have maintained their attractiveness and character. The parador in Jávea, for example, is isolated on a rocky cape (much of the Alicante coast is craggy, quite different from the flat delta sands of Castellón and Valencia) and has splendid grounds. We also enjoy the lush gardens of Huerto del Cura in Elche and that city's ancient palm groves. And there is one indispensable stop in Denia for the best *Arroz a Banda* that has ever seen the light of day.

Denia is, in fact, quite nice—any town crowned by a castle has a certain amount of character that even tourist developments cannot dispel. But that rice . . . El Pegolí restaurant is at beachside, and jam-packed at lunchtime with businessmen in suits and ties; only an occasional diner comes in from the beach. I have never seen anyone ask for the menu—everyone is eating the same thing: a platter of glistening fresh shellfish, a salad, and then a platter (not a paella pan, mind you, but an ordinary platter) heaped with rice that has none of the fish, meat, or vegetable embellishments usually associated with Spanish rice dishes. Nothing, that is, except a small bowl of a potent *alioli*. The rice may look plain, but its flavor and texture are unsurpassed. The secret lies in the local fish used to make the stock and, undoubtedly, the finesse of a cook dedicated to making this one dish day after day.

As I proceed down the coast of Alicante I will switch to another rice specialty, *Arroz con Costra*, a meat-based paella that often includes tiny meatballs and is covered with a baked egg crust. I'll have *cocas*, resembling small pizzas, and the fine seafood of this rocky coast—rockfish, naturally, such as red mullet (*salmonete*), as well as striped bass (*lubina*), grouper (*mero*), shrimp, and langoustine. I will look for *turrón* in Alicante, for it is a sweet, made from almonds and honey (clearly of Arab influence), that is the specialty of the province and famous worldwide. It comes in two basic varieties—soft "Jijona" style and the crackly "Alicante" variety—and is made principally in the small town of Jijona.

TURRÓN ICE CREAM

Soften a pint of high-quality vanilla ice cream and with a rubber spatula rapidly combine it with ¼ bar of crumbled Jijona (soft) *turrón* (for contrasting texture, use also some Alicante—hard—*turrón*, chopped in small pieces). Return to the freezer immediately. Chill until firm.

Or simply scoop vanilla ice cream into serving dishes and crumble the soft *turrón* on top.

Although most popular during the Christmas holidays, you can find it out of season at airport duty-free shops.

THE CITY OF ALICANTE

Guarded by two hills, one crowned by a castle, the city of Alicante has a certain romance, especially at night. Once a Roman city and appreciated by the Moors (who called it Al-lecant) for its gentle climate and protected bay, the city became prosperous and supported several mosques. Through the efforts of Jaime I el Conquistador, Alicante came under Christian control in 1265.

The old town, comprising the fishermen's and ancient Jewish quarters, still has some charm, and the nighttime ambiance is lively along the lovely promenade, of undulating red, white, and black marble. But the changes wrought by international tourism have been spectacular, and the town now bears faint resemblance to what it once was.

SEEING ALICANTE

SANTA MARÍA   Built on the site of a mosque, this church was designed in the peculiar eighteenth century Baroque style of the Levante. Its ornate altar is a sheet of gold.

CASTILLO DE SANTA BÁRBARA   Almost any photograph you see of Alicante shows its impressive castle, at the top of Monte Benacantil, 500 feet above the sea and commanding stupendous views. It has been an important defense of the city's harbor since the times of the Carthaginians and can be reached by lift.

AYUNTAMIENTO   The three-story City Hall has beautifully carved portals and is flanked by twin towers. It is a harmonious example of civil Baroque architecture.

EL RAVAL ROIG   Picturesque fishermen's quarter of the old town.

STAYING IN ALICANTE

PALAS   Cervantes 5   tel. (96) 520 92 11   A simple hotel in an old palace facing the sea. (Moderate.)

For modern resort hotels on the beach try **SIDI SAN JUAN**   Playa de San Juan   tel. (96) 516 33 46 (moderate–expensive; pool), and **ALMIRANTE** Playa de San Juan   tel. (96) 565 01 12 (moderate; pool).

EATING IN ALICANTE

NOU MANOLÍN   Villegas 3   tel. (96) 520 02 91   An animated restaurant and exceptional tapas bar specializing in local seafood and regional cooking, including, of course, rice. (Moderate.)

DÁRSENA   Muelle del Puerto   tel. (96) 520 73 99   More than two dozen versions of the great rice dishes of the Levante can be found here. (Moderate.)

◆ There are bars and cafés galore, concentrated around the Alicante waterfront. Try El Cantó (Alemania 26) and El Marítimo (San Fernando 42).

FIESTAS

FOGUERES DE SANT JOAN   A celebration similar to Las Fallas in Valencia (p. 376), but on a much smaller scale, that takes place June 21 to 24, culminating on the twenty-fourth, the Day of San Juan.

℘ISITING THE PROVINCE OF ALICANTE

DENIA   A thousand-year-old castle, beautifully illuminated at night, presides over this beach town, which juts out into the Mediterranean. Protected from the cooler interior by Monte Montgó, the Greeks found Denia especially attractive and around 600 B.C. established a colony and port here. Denia's northern beaches are smooth and the waters shallow, while to the south there are many rocky coves.
◆ Don't miss El Pegolí (see text), Playa Les Rotes, tel. (96) 578 10 35 (moderate), for shellfish and *Arroz a Banda*. Reservations often necessary.

JÁVEA   A rocky seaside town with a beautiful Old Quarter. It was here that artist Joaquín Sorolla painted some of his most memorable beach scenes.
PARADOR COSTA BLANCA   Playa del Arenal 2   tel. (96) 579 02 00, is a modern structure with magnificent grounds and views. (Moderate–expensive.)

ALTEA   A fishing village enclosed by mountains that is favored by artists and writers and still preserves some of its original charms. Lots of bars and taverns in the Old Quarter.

BENIDORM   A tourist town that came to be because of its phenomenal climate and its large bay with two fine beaches. But its beauty has gone—

high rises line the bay, and there are bars everywhere. See the views from the area known as the Rincón de Loix.

GUADALEST   Unfortunately, the proximity of this uniquely set village to busy beach resorts makes it a well-known visit in the province, and souvenir shops have sprung up everywhere. Nevertheless, the site is breathtaking. A natural fortress, Guadalest is set upon a rocky spike overlooking a turquoise reservoir and rugged mountains, and its only access is by way of a small hollow in the massive rock.

ALCOY   The principal point of interest in this highly industrialized city is its annual Battle of Christians and Moors on the Day of San Jorge, April 23, when a day-long battle is staged. Elaborately costumed *Moros y Cristianos* depict the victory of the Christians—with the assistance of San Jorge—over the Moors in 1276. The ritual has been performed for more than two hundred years, and three days of parades and merriment culminate in a thunderous battle and the predictable victory of the Christians.

JIJONA   Hidden in the barren Sierra de Peñarroja, this is the center of *turrón* (see text) candy making. There are almond trees all around—they produce the candy's main ingredient—and a nearby village bears the descriptive name Muchamiel, meaning lots of honey (another important component of *turrón*). Visit **TURRÓN EL LOBO** to see how *turrón* is made.

PEÑÓN DE IFACH   (Penyó d'Ifach) A huge rock tenuously attached to the mainland at Calpe that looks like a miniature Gibraltar (imposing in its own right at almost 1,000 feet). Because of tourism's impending encroachment on the Peñón's natural beauty, it has been declared a national park and will be left in its virgin state.

ELCHE   An undistinguished town, except for its extraordinary date palm forest with some 600,000 trees, which is unique in Europe. The first palms were most probably planted by the ancient Phoenicians.

Visit the **HUERTO DEL CURA,** named for a priest with a special love for plants and flowers, who devoted his time to this botanical garden, where some of the finest examples of palms are represented (the huge imperial palm, for example, with its eight astonishing trunklike arms). Among numerous other Mediterranean and tropical plants there is a great variety of cacti. A reproduction of one of Spain's most highly prized works of art, *La Dama de Elche* (see box, p. 387), which was discovered in nearby L'Alcudia, can be seen in the gardens.

HOTEL HUERTO DEL CURA   Porta de la Morera 14 tel. (96) 545 80 40
Nestled in the midst of gardens lush with bougainvilleas, fuchsias, coleuses, and petunias are the cottages that comprise this lovely and tranquil hotel complex, associated with the paradors. (Moderate–expensive; pool.)

ELS CAPELLANS   Porta de la Morera tel. (96) 545 80 40 (moderate) A beautiful pool, lit from below and surrounded by palms, is the setting for this fine restaurant that is part of the Huerto del Cura hotel. Regional cooking— try *Arroz con Costra* (see text).

◆ It should come as no surprise that Palm Sunday is a major occasion in Elche, with a procession displaying palm branches elaborately woven into artisan creations.

L'ALCUDIA *La Dama de Elche*, plus many other examples of ancient Iberian sculpture, was excavated here. Some are on display in the Museo Arqueológico.

THE GRACIOUS LADY OF ELCHE

You will not see her in Elche (she resides in the Museo Arqueológico of Madrid), but her origins are in L'Alcudia, just a mile from Elche, where an ancient Iberian city—part of an indigenous civilization that predated the Romans—was uncovered in the last century. The *Lady*, a life-size stone bust thought to be from the third or fourth century B.C., was found buried in sand that fortuitously conserved her magnificent polychrome coloring. She was on display in the Louvre Museum until 1941, when the *Lady* was returned to her homeland.

How alive she looks with her lightly painted red lips, aristocratic nose, and narrow face (she was apparently carved from life; perhaps she was a priestess). She is bedecked in elaborate necklaces and huge circular hair ornaments not very different from the headdresses you see on Valencian girls during Las Fallas. And yet how otherworldly and mysterious she is—cold, distant, regal, and proud. *La Dama de Elche* looks right through you with her penetrating gaze.

Who is she? Her origins remain obscure, but her magnetism is undeniable.

THE PROVINCE OF MURCIA

MURCIA (*moor*-theea), known for its fruit and garden produce and famous in particular for the intense flavor and vivid colors of its vegetables, is in appearance much like the other Levante provinces, and its huertas and rice fields turn an otherwise arid landscape richly green. A Murcian rice variety called Calasparra is prized in Spain, and rice preparations here take on distinctive characteristics; they are soupier and do not necessarily need a paella pan. *Caldo Murciano*, for example, made with rice, fish, and dried red peppers, traditionally cooks in an iron kettle over an open fire. You couldn't do better than to pair such a dish with the robust Jumilla wines for which the province has a national reputation.

Rincón de Pepe, in the city of Murcia, the finest restaurant of the province, is a showcase for Murcia's produce; some of the most perfect

examples of Murcian vegetables are prominently
displayed and appear in a multitude of dishes. I
have never tasted a vegetable medley quite
like the mix of eggplant, fresh favas, asparagus, carrots, peas, and green beans,
accented by a touch of cured ham, that
makes up the exceptional and most
appropriately named *Festival de Verduras
Frescas* (festival of fresh vegetables), nor a vegetable paella as good as their *Paella Huertana*. Also
focusing on vegetables are the restaurant's vegetable
soups, tortillas with fresh favas, red peppers stuffed with grouper, and a
grilled vegetable salad. Murcia is among the few areas of Spain where a veg-
etarian could be perfectly content.

The huertas and the rice fields of Murcia exist because of the Moors,
who remained in Murcia long after they were expelled from Granada. As in
the rest of the Levante, they established irrigation systems—with the difference that here the land is considerably more mountainous and the water
had to be carried *up* to the huertas. This required an ingenious system to lift
the water from the rivers. In Alcantarilla, for example, you can see a still
functioning waterwheel, turned by the force of the flowing river, that scoops
up the water as it passes and deposits it in aqueducts that lead to the huertas.

Aside from this, however, Moorish vestiges are surprisingly absent
from Murcia, except in the names of villages and cities like Los Alcázares,
Mazarrón, Aljezares, and Aljorra. And despite Murcia's large Arab population in the thirteenth century, the city supported the crown against Moorish
rebellions and so impressed King Alfonso el Sabio (see Index) that in token
of Murcia's loyalty, he chose to have his heart interred in the cathedral of
Murcia (his body lies in Sevilla cathedral).

Murcia penetrates much farther into the mountainous interior of
Spain than other provinces of the Levante, and its coastline is considerably
shorter—although the sandbars of Mar Menor, a huge saltwater lagoon that
is the largest of the European continent, provide many extra miles of beachfront. Within the space of half a kilometer you can choose either the placid
waters of the Small Sea or the open Mediterranean. Salt flats are common
in Murcia, and quite naturally *Pescado a la Sal*, fish baked under a mound of
coarse salt, and a variety of preserved salted fish are two more elements of
local gastronomy.

Once you are past the Mar Menor, from Mazarrón south to Águilas,
there is special beauty in the desertlike mountainous terrain. This is an area
that is transitional, looking more like Murcia's southern neighbor, Almería,
than the Levante.

The people of Murcia and their region have suffered from bad press for
centuries. Although the reputation was undoubtedly undeserved, Murcians
were perceived as crude and uncultured, and the province was among the
least visited. It still is not a popular destination, and unless your travels take
you in this direction, I do not suggest a detour, except perhaps to the city of
Murcia.

THE CITY OF MURCIA

Travelers in the Levante are more likely to follow the coastal route than to turn inland to the city of Murcia, but I recommend this deviation if you wish to eat the produce of the huertas and the excellent rice dishes at Rincón de Pepe; to see the city's rococo cathedral, a grand example of Spanish Baroque; or to visit a museum where many of the best polychrome wood sculptures of native son Francisco Salzillo—a phenomenon of Murcian art—are exhibited.

On the banks of the Río Segura, which flows down from the Segura mountains of Jaén, Murcia was founded in the ninth century by the Arabs— quite early in their conquest of the Iberian Peninsula—and was an important center for them. The city's Old Quarter still has something of a Moorish air, but unfortunately Murcia was extensively rebuilt in the eighteenth century, erasing most traces of its past. The city is today the commercial hub of the province.

SEEING MURCIA

CATHEDRAL   Although begun in the fourteenth century, on the foundations of the city's Arab mosque, the cathedral was not finished until the eighteenth century. Designed in the unusual shape of Baroque Levantine churches (and considered a bold digression from traditional design), the structure has a facade of great elegance and harmony.

Inside, note particularly the profusely carved Capilla de los Vélez, behind the altar, done in what is known as Flamboyant Gothic style with Mudéjar overtones (deposit a coin to illuminate it); in a niche of the main altar an urn holds the heart of Alfonso el Sabio; and in the Cathedral museum there are a splendidly sculpted Roman sarcophagus and sculptures by Salzillo (see below).
◆ You can climb the gracefully designed belfry for views of the city and surrounding orchards.

MUSEO DE SALZILLO   Francisco Salzillo was a prolific eighteenth century Murcian sculptor whose wood polychrome works can be found all over the province, but are concentrated in Murcia at this museum. Many of his sculptures were created specifically for the processions of Holy Week, and while they may be on display at the museum for most of the year, at Easter they take to the streets. Not to everyone's taste, his life-size representations of Christ and other religious subjects are exceedingly dramatic, and his folkloric personages are perhaps overly folkish. (Regular museum hours, plus Monday mornings.)

CASINO   Built in the nineteenth century, the city's casino has a distinctively ornate facade, lovely Moorish patios, and an elegant ballroom.

STAYING IN MURCIA

There are no distinguished hotels in Murcia, and in fact, everything you might want to do and see in the city can be accomplished without spending the night. If you choose to stay, the hotel of Rincón de Pepe restaurant (see below), is well cared for and well located (moderate–expensive).

EATING IN MURCIA

RINCÓN DE PEPE   Apóstoles 34, tel. (968) 21 22 39   An extremely attractive restaurant with a rustic yet elegant ambiance. Excellent fish, Murcian vegetables and rice dishes (see text). (Moderate–expensive.)

◆ Murcia is a good city for tapas. They are abundant at Rincón de Pepe (you can also order at the bar from the regular restaurant menu) and in bars around the cathedral and on the contiguous plazas of Las Flores and Santa Catalina in the Old Quarter.

FIESTAS

ENTIERRO DE LA SARDINA   This curious event, the Burial of the Sardine, takes place midweek after Easter to celebrate the end of Lent. It consists of folk parades (*Bando de la Huerta*), singing, and dancing, and it culminates in fireworks and the burning of a symbolic sardine.

ꝎISITING THE PROVINCE OF MURCIA

ALCANTARILLA   Near this town on the road to Almería, there is an oversized medieval waterwheel from the fifteenth century, called a *noria*. It is still in use, elevating and channeling water to the huertas.

CRESTA DEL GALLO   These craggy reddish mountain peaks are called Cresta de Gallo because of their resemblance to a cock's comb. In the vicinity are exceptional mountain landscapes and views of the huerta.

LOS ALCÁZARES   We stumbled upon this summer enclave quite by chance, and were delighted to find along this touristy coast a town that felt down to earth and very Spanish. The beach is narrow—nothing much to speak of—but there are no high-rises, just one-story houses at beachfront along a small promenade. The town is crowded and lively; there's even an open-air movie house.

CARTAGENA   Founded by the Carthaginians in the third century B.C. as their capital (called Cartago Nova), this was one of the principal ports of antiquity. The city is enclosed by mountains and several defensive castles that date from the fourteenth to the nineteenth centuries. At the waterfront is one of the world's first submarines, designed by Isaac Peral, native of Cartagena, in 1888.

PUERTO LUMBRERAS   The **PARADOR PUERTO LUMBRERAS** Avenida Juan Carlos I 77   tel. (968) 40 20 25 (moderate), is at roadside, but it does have gardens and a pool and, like all the paradors, is clean, neat, and trustworthy.

LORCA   Around the Plaza de España, gracefully designed with double arches of peachy stone, are some fine buildings like the town hall, with its elaborate wrought-iron balcony; the massive Colegiata, also built in peach-colored stone; and the seignorial Casa Guevara. All attest to Lorca's past importance as a crossroads between the Levante and Andalucía. The town is otherwise undistinguished.

THE *ALEGRÍA* OF ANDALUCÍA

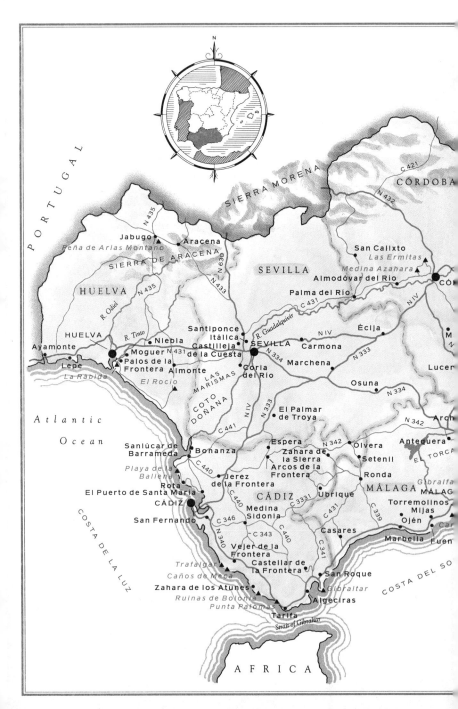

Despeñaperros
Navas de Tolosa

ta María
a Cabeza
La Carolina
Baños de
la Encina

C 321

Segura de
la Sierra

N IV

C 321?

N 332

Hornos

SIERRA DE SEGURA

N 332

Baeza

Úbeda

Iznatoraf

N IV

JAÉN

C 328

JAÉN

Peal de Becerro

La Iruela
Cazorla

ena

N 321

Santa
Catalina

SIERRA DE CAZORLA

C 325

Vélez
Blanco

GRANADA

N 342

N 323

N 324

Purullena

N 321

Montefrío

R. Genil

GRANADA

Guadix

ALMERÍA

oja

N 342

Santafé

SIERRA NEVADA

Lacalahorra

ispiro del Moro

N 323

Capileira

Mulhacén

Trevélez

N 324

Sorbas

Mojácar

LAS

ALPUJARRAS

C 322

Tabernas

N 332

Lanjarón

Bubión
Pampaneira

Níjar

giliana

Salobreña

ALMERÍA

Nerja

N 340

Almuñécar

CABO DE GATA

M e d i t e r r a n e a n   S e a

| 0 | 10 | 20 | 30 | 40 | Miles |

| 0 | 16 | 32 | 48 | 64 | Kilometers |

Introduction

MY HUSBAND, LUIS, was born and bred in Madrid; together we have traveled the length and breadth of Spain, but I must confess that our hearts belong to Andalucía. Each region of Spain has its charms, but Andalucía just seems to have more—more joy (*alegría*), more spontaneity, and more warmth. Andalusians have a sunny disposition, an incisive and infectious

FOODS AND WINES OF ANDALUCÍA

GENERAL
Fish, shellfish, gazpachos, tapas, sweets

SPECIALTIES
Pescado frito—fish fry
Pescado a la Sal—fish baked in salt
Cazón en Amarillo—shark in saffron sauce
Bienmesabe—marinated fried fish
Menudo—chickpea-and-vegetable stew
Rabo de Toro—oxtail stew
Jamón de Jabugo—cured Jabugo ham
Puntillitas de solomillo—beef tenderloin with garlic
Riñones al Jerez—kidneys in sherry sauce
Gazpacho Andaluz—gazpacho
Ajo Blanco—white gazpacho
Huevos a la Flamenca—baked eggs with sausage and vegetables
Habas con Jamón—fresh favas with ham
Tocino de Cielo—rich caramel flan
Yemas—Egg-yolk candies
Polvorones—sugar cookies
Pestiños—fried pastries with honey
Alfajores—nut-and-honey candy

WINES AND SPIRITS
Solear, Eva, San León (dry *manzanilla* sherry) from Sanlúcar de Barrameda
San Patricio, La Ina, Tío Pepe, Tío Mateo (dry *fino* sherry) from Jerez
Quo Vadis, Amontillado del Duque (medium-dry *amontillado* sherry) from Jerez
Sibarita, Apóstoles (medium-sweet *oloroso* sherry) from Jerez
Cuco, Barbadillo Pedro Jiménez (cream sherry) from Jerez
Gran Barquero, Carlos VII (medium-dry *amontillado* sherry) from Montilla
Gran Barquero, Néctar (medium-sweet *oloroso* sherry) from Montilla
Gran Barquero, Alvear Pedro Jiménez (cream sherry) from Montilla
Cartojal (sweet wine) from Málaga
Castillo de San Diego (white wine) from Sanlúcar de Barrameda
Carlos I, Lepanto, Duque de Alba (brandy) from Jerez

sense of humor, and a fierce desire to enjoy life to the fullest: Life is lived for the present, with hardly a thought to the future. Pleasure is the key word, "enjoyed with the rapture of children," says nineteenth century British traveler Richard Ford.

Possessing innate elegance and style, Andalusians carry themselves like nobility. Richard Ford continues, "The better rule is, on landing at Cádiz, to consider every stranger in a long-tailed coat to be a marquis, until you find him out to be a waiter, and even then no great harm is done, and you dine the quicker for the mistake." In Andalucía every waiter, every cab driver, seems to have a touch of the marquis and yet maintains a democratic outlook on the world.

In their rush to talk (there is nothing at which they are more adept), Andalusians have developed their own ingratiating way of speaking "*e'paño.'*" They speak fast as a bullet, with a pronounced lisp and a tendency to drop consonants and even entire syllables. Your high school Spanish may not be enough to understand an Andaluz, but the ease of establishing emotional rapport will more than compensate for any language deficiencies.

Come just once to Andalucía, and the compulsion to return becomes irresistible. It is not only the region's great beauty and cultural wealth that takes hold of you, but also the *alegría* of its people that binds Andalucía together and makes a visit here such a special experience.

The profusely flowering purple bougainvilleas and brilliant red geraniums, blindingly white villages, parched mountains looming over endless beaches, cool patios, fiery Gypsies, soulful flamenco, heart-stopping bullfights, and Moorish mystery that you may have read about are not exaggerated, nor are they clichés. Andalucía is really like that, and that is why it has delighted foreigners for centuries, beginning with the Phoenicians and continuing with the Greeks, Carthaginians, Romans, and most especially the Arabs. In recent centuries writers and composers have set the scenes of novels, theater, and opera here in Andalucía, for the region's color and romance are hard to match.

Andalusian villages are stark white, softened by flowers in profusion. Be they coastal, built into mountain folds, or on mountain crests, they are suffused with light, color, and gaiety.

> Only the Andalusian temperament and its extreme sense of aesthetics is capable of converting a modest corner into a marvel.
> *Enrique Uceta*

In Andalucía you don't speak of whitewashed houses but of The White Towns (Los Pueblos Blancos). There are many villages in Spain that are whitewashed, but here the whiteness takes on more importance and character. First, whitewashing here is a practical device to deflect the blazing sun and ovenlike heat. And although all these white villages may be similar, each is distinct, be it for the wrought iron of its balconies and windows, the artistic arrangement of flowerpots and plants in patios or on house walls, the refinement of architectural style, or the primitive irregularity of houses and chimneys. All, however, speak of Andalucía's long-lasting Arab influence.

We tend to think of Andalucía in terms of its coast (and certainly many of its attractions are on the coast or close to it), but the interior is strikingly beautiful, with vegetation typical of a dry hot climate: cork and oak trees, scrub bushes, and olive groves. Mountains soar to great heights, especially in Granada, and despite the dryness, there are great rivers; the Guadalquivir, laden with history, runs like a unifying thread through most of the region, from the mountains of Jaén to its exit into the Atlantic in the provinces of Cádiz and Huelva. Since Andalucía is one of Spain's largest regions, for travel purposes I would divide its eight provinces into three parts: Cádiz, Huelva, and Sevilla could easily occupy a week of your time; Málaga, Granada, and Almería another; and Córdoba and Jaén in the northern part of Andalucía combine well with travel to Castilla–La Mancha.

El campillo, Andalucía's dry hilly land studded with squat evergreen oak trees, is ideal for raising fighting bulls, and you will often see them behind barbed wire, peaceably grazing or resting in the trees' shade. Bulls are part of Andalusian culture, admired for their sleek beauty and respected for their awesome strength, and most of the legendary bullfighters were and are Andalusian. Those who follow the fights revere the names of Joselito, Belmonte, Manolete, El Gallo, and currently, Espartaco, El Litri, and Ojeda, all from Andalucía. You may remember the mad courage of El Cordobés in the late 1960s, vividly recounted in his life story, *Or I'll Dress You in Mourning*. Like countless other young, poor Andalusians, he saw the bullring as the only escape from poverty. With a friend, he set about gaining experience by jumping fences and fighting bulls in the fields by the light of the moon.

> "There is no road, no field, no village square of this sunburned land of Andalusia that did not know our wandering feet. For months we wandered up and down our land, through every one of its valleys and its plains, to its mountains and its sea, looking for adventure."
>
> . . . the priest understood the lure that was pulling the boy away from his classroom. He was himself an aficionado.

Flamenco music and dance are equally associated with Andalucía, and different forms of flamenco take their names from the towns from which they come: Sevillanas (Sevilla), Malagueñas (Málaga), Granaínas (Granada), and Rondeñas (Ronda), to name a few. Flamenco is an art born of Andalucía's Arab past, of eastern chants and wails, of Gypsies, and of Spanish folk music. It sings of love, pain, and suffering, and of hope and joy as well. It is tragedy, comedy, and eroticism, and the dance is at once deeply sensual and lightly playful. But flamenco is essentially singing by just one voice; guitar accompaniment, whirling dancers, rhythmic hand clapping, and clicking castanets take second place to the beauty and depth of the song.

Although flamenco is generally tied to the large Gypsy population of Andalucía, it is thought more specifically to have originated in Cádiz and Sevilla; to pinpoint it more exactly, it probably began in the Triana neighborhood of Sevilla. No one dances or sings flamenco with such passion as someone of Gypsy heritage, and yet it is an art that effortlessly draws inspiration from other cultures. It has borrowed tap shoes from American jazz, catchy rhythms from Latin America, and a currently popular flamenco group has even adopted one of Frank Sinatra's signature songs, "My Way," and given it a distinct flamenco flavor.

ALL ABOARD
AL ANDALUS EXPRESS

Travel Andalucía in the grand manner on the Art Deco vintage train *Al Andalus Express* that rivals the luxury of the legendary *Orient Express*. Its cars are lavishly appointed with original wood marquetry and antique furnishings, accommodations are deluxe, and during the two-to-three-day trips from Sevilla to Córdoba, Granada, and Málaga (or the reverse) you will be served fine cuisine in a posh dining car and listen to live music. Here's the chance to sample the slow-paced elegance of another era, with time along the way to see some of the great sights of Andalucía. The service is in effect May–June and September–October (there is also a one-night excursion from Málaga to Sevilla). In July and August *Al Andalus Express* heads to northern Spain and follows part of the Way of Saint James (see box, p. 220) from Barcelona to Santiago de Compostela. For more information, consult the Tourist Office of Spain.

Fiestas spring up at the drop of a hat in Andalucía, providing yet more opportunities for fun and camaraderie, and they have captured the fancy of the world: Carnaval in Cádiz, Holy Week and the April Fair in Sevilla, El Rocío pilgrimage in Huelva, the Horse Fair in Jerez are just a sampling of events that fill the calendars in Andalucía. Flamenco music is always an important part of these fiestas, from the laments of the religious songs called saetas at Easter to the gaiety of Sevillanas during the Sevilla Fair. Flamenco is the very soul of Andalucía.

One always senses in Andalucía its compelling and continuing Arab legacy. The Moors first entered Spain through Andalucía in 711 and called the region Al Andalus. They produced splendid works of architecture and helped preserve ancient knowledge at a time when the rest of Europe was immersed in the Dark Ages. The Moors also left Spain through Andalucía when they were expelled from Granada, their last stronghold, almost eight centuries later. Subsequently, most of their great architectural works were destroyed in a wave of religious fervor brought on by the Reconquest.

But while in other regions history books tell you where the Arab quarters were or where a mosque once stood, in Andalucía every nook and cranny still speaks of oriental culture and style. Christian Andalucía succumbed to the charms of gurgling fountains, delicate filigree and mosaic design, the refreshment of enclosed patios and the relaxing privacy they provide. An oriental philosophy of life coupled with Moorish architectural styles persisted long after the Arabs were gone, and the love affair continues to this day.

Spain's masterpieces of Arab architecture—the Alcázar in Sevilla, the Mosque in Córdoba, and the Alhambra in Granada—are all in Andalucía and are as fresh and exciting as they must have been five or more centuries ago.

Arab influence reflects on southern cooking as well. While we generally think of Andalusians as masters at preparing fried fish and icy gazpachos, both exquisite in their simplicity and freshness, in fact Andalucía also produces delicate sauces, seasoned with the saffron, coriander, and cumin introduced by the Arabs. Olive oil is the base for all cooking here, as well it should be in a land often dominated by the impressive sight of endless olive groves. And sweets based on honey and almonds with such Arab names as *alfajores* are still the favorites in Andalucía, today as in past centuries, prepared with loving care by convent nuns (see box).

Tapas are a way of life in Andalucía, perhaps because of the warm climate and because so much daily living takes place out of doors at cafés and tapas bars. Especially in summer, "grazing" has greater appeal than formal dining; fine restaurants, in fact, have never been the rule here. Restaurants were more likely to be ventas, that is, inns, that thrived along well-traveled

Convent Sweets:
AN ENDURING ANDALUSIAN TRADITION

Some of the best sweets to be found in Spain are often the creations of convent nuns, following centuries-old recipes and traditions that more often than not have their roots in Andalucía. Ingredients are simple, but the names of the sweets are exotic and amusing: *Corazón de Obispo* (bishop's heart), *Lengua de Obispo* (bishop's tongue), *Suspiros de Monja* (nun's sighs), *Cabello de Ángel* (angel's hair), *Orejas de Fraile* (friar's ears), and *Huesos de Santo* (saint's bones), to name but a few.

Convent sweets go back to the Arabs, who brought their egg, almond, sugar, and honey-based candies and desserts with them to Spain. The religious fervor brought on by the Reconquest led to a proliferation of convents; newly wealthy noblemen pledged their daughters to the celibate life and made generous gifts to their favored religious orders. The nuns, in thanks to their benefactors, prepared homemade goodies as gifts for holidays and fiestas.

But in the nineteenth century, convents fell on hard times, and to help support themselves the nuns began to sell the sweets for which they already had such fine reputations. The recipes were kept in utmost secrecy, never written down and often known only to the mother superior. Sherry wine producers, who traditionally used egg whites to clarify their wines, frequently donated leftover yolks to the convents. Thus, so many of these sweets, in particular the candies called *yemas* and the rich flan, *Tocino de Cielo*, are based on egg yolks.

Today convent sweets continue to be best-sellers, for they radiate an aura of purity, honesty, and motherly love. Depending on which convent you visit (they are mentioned in appropriate chapters), you may buy a variety of delicious cookies, pastries, cakes, almond candies, jams and marmalades, and the above-mentioned *yemas* and *Tocino de Cielo*, often sold to you by means of a *torno* (revolving shelf) in order to protect the privacy of cloistered nuns. Convent sweets may be rich, but every bite will bring to mind the enterprising nuns who began making them so many centuries ago.

roads as stagecoach stops, and they catered to travelers. Today these inns are popular among city folk, who will drive out of town expressly to eat at a venta. Also traditional in Andalucía is the *merendero,* or *chiringuito,* as it is called here—beachside lean-tos, temporarily set up in the summer season, to prepare foods like fried fish, paella, eggs and peppers that are ideal for the beach.

Tapas and casual eating go hand in hand with the wines of the region, particularly sherry (*jerez*) and its close relatives, *manzanilla* and *montilla,* all of which need the soil and climate of Andalucía to give them their distinctive character. It is thought that the custom of eating tapas originated with sherry; a fortified wine does not sit well in an empty stomach, so bars began offering a complimentary nibble, like almonds or olives, to accompany the sherry.

Andalusian cuisine has *alegría*—in its sprightly appearance and the unmatched freshness, especially of its tapas, and in the special joy that food brings forth in Andalusian cooks. "I put my heart into my cooking," "This is a labor of love," and "His cooking has 'angel' " are expressions I have heard time and time again. Convent nuns add maternal warmth to the sweets for which they are famous (see box, p. 398).

Eating and anticipation of eating are among my favorite pastimes in Andalucía. Cuisine varies from province to province, but look for seafood in most of the region, and you simply can't go wrong. From the sweet *urta* (porgy) of Cádiz and the prawns of Sanlúcar to sweet Málaga shrimp and succulent sole, the range is astounding, and everything tastes so fresh that meat eaters are easily converted into fish fanatics.

You will find beautiful beaches in Andalucía, miles of marshland, majestic mountains, millions of olive trees, stork nests on every church steeple, troglodyte dwellings, fervent fiestas, a continuing Moorish presence, and many reminders of the discovery of the New World. But most of all you will find *alegría,* and you will understand why this land bewitched such writers as Washington Irving and continues to cast a spell, enveloping the visitor in a very special magic.

THE PROVINCE OF HUELVA

HUELVA (*well*-vah)—Ghelbah, or Guelbah, to the Arabs—is a privileged province, a wedge of land, the most westerly of Andalucía, bordered by the Atlantic Ocean to the south and Portugal to the west, and quite cut off from the rest of Spain by marshlands to the east and mountains to the north. In Huelva the Sierra Morena, in this province called the Aracena mountains, reaches its end in Spain (but continues into Portugal). The province flattens as it continues south until it ends in a smooth coastline, a magnificent and uninterrupted expanse of fine-sand beaches stretching the length of the province for more than a hundred kilometers. These are not bare beach-fronts: They are often thickly bordered by pine trees (the short round variety that bears pine nuts), by dunes, cliffs, and, around the river estuaries, by deserted marshlands.

The weather is warm all year round, and the Huelva-Cádiz coast claims the title Costa de la Luz—Coast of Light. The name is not an idle, touristy gimmick: The light is almost surreal in its intensity and clarity, and light-meter readings document what is apparent to the eye. Only the province of Almería can contest Huelva's claim to more hours of sunshine.

Marshlands are characteristic of Huelva, and they are crucial to both European and African wildlife, for it is in Huelva that migratory birds stop on their twice-yearly journey between the two continents. One of the world's most important preserves—an ecological paradise, recognized as such by the World Wildlife Fund—is a triangle of land on the Guadalquivir estuary called Coto Doñana.

Huelva's importance goes back to prehistoric times, and its rich mountain deposits of copper and silver attracted early civilizations. The province was part of the Roman "Silver Route" that passed through Mérida in Extremadura, and some say it was the site of the ancient kingdom of Tartessus, mentioned in the Bible and later by Greek writers and thought to be the first foreign colony in Spain. Its exact location is unclear (but thought to be near the exit of the Río Guadalquivir in Huelva). In ancient times Tartessus was already the subject of legends.

Like all of Andalucía, Huelva lived under Moorish rule for centuries, but here the traces of this cultural heritage are much less apparent than in Sevilla, Granada, and Córdoba. Much of the folkloric charm of other southern provinces is missing, and except for the emotional celebration of El Rocío (see box, p. 406) and the presence of Huelva's fandango flamenco music, life in the province is simpler and more down to earth. Likewise, this is not an area of great artistic treasures. Its charms lie elsewhere—in its climate, its villages, its gastronomy, and, most especially, in its gravitation to the sea.

Huelva has always been a great seafaring province. For me, one of its prime attractions is its association with Christopher Columbus and its decisive role in the "encounter" with America (Native Americans quite rightly claim that he could not discover a place already inhabited). But the province's America connection was short-lived. As travel to the New World increased, the center of operations was transferred first to Cádiz, then to Sevilla, and the province lost its importance. It was not until the nineteenth century, when the British reactivated the mining industry, and in past decades when tourists discovered its gentle climate, its beaches, and its extraordinary food, that Huelva once again came to life.

Food . . . What fine eating there is in Huelva, and what an unusual gamut of products, representing the best of the mountains and of the sea. Naturally, seafood is delicious, particularly shellfish. Even newsstands sell tiny boiled shrimp (camarones) by the bagful, eaten shell and all by strollers, much as one might munch on potato chips. At tapas bars camarones are served in big heaps and are ravenously consumed. There are lobsters and langoustines (cigalas), and there are also fresh tuna in tomato sauce, grilled sardines, skate in paprika sauce, flounder, gilthead, porgy, white bream. . . .

I could happily live on these gifts from the sea, but there is much, much more to taste in Huelva: Spain's best melons and watermelons, from the town of Lepe; ever-so-fragrant strawberries (in May you see scores of workers in what look like Chinese coolie hats busily harvesting the crops); fruity white wines from the Condado region; wild mushrooms and game from the mountains. And then there are the legendary cured hams from Jabugo.

Jabugo hams (and other Jabugo pork products, like *chorizo* and pork loin, or *lomo*) come from silky, taupe-colored pigs with black hoofs—thus the term *jamón de pata negra*—that roam free and exist on a steady diet of acorns. Their flesh acquires an exquisite nutty flavor and a tenderness that makes them unique. Those labeled *JJJJJ* are best, having eaten nothing but acorns in their lifetimes. The hams cure in vast underground bodegas for one to two and a half years. Believe me, this is ham as you have never tasted it before, and even Italians privately admit that it surpasses the finest prosciutto.

Most Spaniards think that tales of free-range pigs in Huelva are nothing more than romantic inventions. Not so! Traveling through the mountains of Huelva from Aracena to Ayamonte we saw them for ourselves. At first we spotted just two, and my husband, Luis, hastened from the car for a photograph before they could run off. By the time his camera was in focus, he had attracted scores of friendly pigs. They were elegant, privileged creatures, a far cry from the proverbial pig in a mud sty. They encircled him, nudged him, and treated him like one of the group. I never knew pigs could be so beautiful.

There is so much worth discovering in this the least explored province of Andalucía. Follow the footsteps of Columbus in Palos and La Rábida, just before he set off into the unknown. Travel by jeep through the Coto Doñana for an unforgettable glimpse of near-extinct wildlife and unique natural scenery. You will never lack for things to do in Huelva.

PALOS, LA RÁBIDA, AND THE "ENCOUNTER" WITH AMERICA

Five hundred years have passed since Columbus brought a fresh breeze to a staid Old World with his revolutionary ideas and dramatic discoveries. And yet despite exhaustive investigation, researchers still don't know much about the early life of Columbus. We are presented with innumerable theories and very little hard evidence of his life before he appeared in Spain and set about convincing the Catholic Kings of the merits of his visions.

By most accounts, he was born in Genoa, but no birth certificate has been found, and there is surprisingly slim evidence to confirm him as Italian. Italians naturally insist he was the pride of Italy, while Spaniards just as vehemently claim him as their own. One Spanish researcher theorizes that he was a Sephardic Jew from Mallorca who only said he was from Genoa to disguise his Jewish heritage at a time when unconverted Jews were being forced to leave Spain. Even his place of burial is a bone of contention (see **CATHEDRAL,** Sevilla). In any case, his name in all known documents appears in Spanish as Cristóbal Colón—never Cristoforo Colombo—and all his written words, including marginal notes he scribbled on many documents, are in Spanish.

Certainly, what is irrefutable is that Columbus's greatest accomplishments were undertaken in the name of Spain and were encouraged, supported, and approved by the priests of La Rábida, the people of Palos, and the crown of Spain.

Let's go back to 1484 when Columbus first appeared at the monastery of La Rábida and revealed to Father Antonio de Marchena (in a small, sparsely furnished room that is today known as the "Cradle of America") his ambitious plans to sail west across the ocean to India. Although such ideas were generally ridiculed by the clergy in the fifteenth century, the Franciscan monks of La Rábida, and Father Marchena in particular, were highly cultured men, quite knowledgeable about science and open to theories that the world was a sphere. Columbus was treated with great respect (he was never an idle dreamer, but a highly experienced and skilled navigator), and through the friars' backing, he finally gained access to the kings.

Columbus stayed at La Rábida with his ten-year-old son, Diego, for several months, then, leaving his son behind with the monks, he set out to seek the financial support he would need to make his dream a reality. He returned to La Rábida in 1491, disheartened by the indecisiveness of the monarchs (they were in financial straits owing to the war against the Moors). He picked up his son and said his goodbyes. He would look for support elsewhere—perhaps, he thought, in Portugal. Now Father Juan Pérez comes into the picture and persuades Columbus to stay, promising a speedy decision from Fernando and Isabel. He is the queen's confessor and uses his influence to encourage her to finance the expedition. Were it not for the efforts of Fathers Pérez and Marchena, the voyage might never have taken place.

The scene now shifts to the little village of Palos, upstream from La Rábida on the Tinto river, where Columbus appears at the church of San Jorge to read the royal decree and to recruit men. Because he is not a villager, he gets little response, and it is the Pinzón brothers from Palos, destined to play a major role in the voyage, whose enthusiasm and promises of riches convince villagers of this desperately poor region that there is little to lose and much to gain. Ninety men, the majority from Palos, decide to take the gamble.

Three local boats were called into service and outfitted for the journey. No one really knows just what they looked like, because in those times boat construction required no architectural plans. It was a skill passed from father to son and refined over the centuries (one theory claims the boats' design was a closely guarded state secret, and for this reason no records remain). We do know that the boats were quite small for such a large crew and such a long journey: The *Niña* was under sixty feet long—but extremely seaworthy.

LA FONTANILLA

Supplies were loaded on board; it is logical to suppose that the wines came from the Jerez-Sanlúcar region, and tradition says that the water was drawn from a Roman well just outside Palos called La Fontanilla—today a national monument.

Having prayed before the statue of the Virgen de la Rábida, Columbus and his crew set sail down the river and into the ocean on the morning of August 3, 1492. The *Santa María* was commanded by Juan de la Cosa; the *Pinta* by Martín Alonso Pinzón with his brother, Francisco Martín Pinzón; and the *Niña* by their brother, Vicente Yáñez Pinzón—all natives of Palos.

> Along the coast a crowd of people, all Palos, watched with emotion as the three light boats disappeared little by little into the caverns of time and space. How many hearts must have felt anguish! How many eyes must have shed tears! . . . There in the west, still dark and mysterious behind the veil of fleeting night, the New World awaited—as distant as the three caravels that searched for it—a vast future that history would suddenly open to humanity.
>
> *Salvador de Madariaga*

The rest is known to every schoolchild the world over. Two boats returned to Spain seven months later (the *Santa María* was wrecked; its crew built a fort and stayed behind in Santo Domingo, but was never heard from again). Columbus returned to America three more times, always setting sail from the Huelva-Cádiz coast, and although the men of Palos continued to travel to the New World (Vicente Yáñez Pinzón, for example, sailed to Brazil, discovered the mouth of the Amazon River, and later became governor of Puerto Rico), the next phase—that of the Conquest—belonged to the men of Extremadura.

℣ISITING LA RÁBIDA AND PALOS DE LA FRONTERA

LA RÁBIDA   A monastery founded in the thirteenth century by Franciscans, it has a lovely Mudéjar brick patio with remains of wall frescoes in Arab geometric design. See here the alabaster statue of the Virgin de la Rábida—the same one Columbus and his sailors prayed before; the room called "Cradle of America," where Columbus first presented his plan to Father Marchena; the Sala Capitular, where concrete plans for the trip were formulated; the refectory where Columbus and his son Diego dined with the fathers; documents signed by Columbus; and detailed reproductions of his sailing vessels.

HOSTERÍA DE LA RÁBIDA   tel. (955) 35 03 12, is next to the monastery with views over the Tinto and Odiel rivers. Only five rooms. (Inexpensive.)

PALOS DE LA FRONTERA   In the plaza in front of the Mudéjar church of San Jorge a plaque commemorates the native sons of Palos who set sail with Columbus. A statue honors Martín Alonso Pinzón—not Columbus—for he, after all, was the hero of Palos. By the waterfront (centuries of silting have significantly increased the distance between the town and the sea), another plaque notes the spot from which the three ships set sail.

℘OTO DOÑANA

Parque Nacional de Coto Doñana, bounded by the shrine of El Rocío, the Río Guadalquivir, and the Atlantic Ocean, is a unique and immense area of virgin sands, dunes, marshland, brush, and pines. It was named after Doña Ana, daughter of the ill-fated Princess of Éboli (see box, p. 170) and wife of the Duke of Medina Sidonia. She built a palace in this wilderness, retired here with her husband, supposedly out of despair over the scandalous conduct of her mother, and eventually died here. Since then the Coto Doñana and the palace have been frequented by royalty and heads of state. Philip IV came to hunt in the seventeenth century; Goya stayed in the spring of 1797 and painted his famous portrait of his presumed lover, the Duchess of Alba. At the end of the nineteenth century the palace and the property passed from the Duke of Medina Sidonia to the Duke of Tarifa in a card game, and in this century the palace was a favorite retreat of King Alfonso XIII. Recently the palace has served as the summer home of Spain's prime minister.

Besides being a place of astonishing beauty, Coto Doñana is a haven for endangered wildlife and an important part of the life cycles of more than half of Europe's migratory birds. Without the Coto Doñana and the vast unspoiled marshes to the east of the reserve, countries as far north as Norway might not see the return of their most cherished bird species.

In spring Coto Doñana teems with ducks, geese, flamingos, storks, spoonbills, egrets, and pelicans, pausing in their long journey from Africa to other parts of Europe. And in the fall they again appear on their trip south. In residence during any season are countless rabbits, wild boar, partridge, quail, deer, vultures, and the prized but nearly extinct Spanish lynx and imperial eagles. Most surprising, the only wild dromedaries in the world reside here. We do have trouble, however, convincing friends that we were not victims of a mirage produced by shimmering sands; we really did see on several occasions these one-humped creatures with their offspring.

Just as some species inhabiting the Coto Doñana are threatened by extinction, so too was the reserve itself once in danger of disappearing when ever-greedy land developers plotted to replace it with more of the skyscraper condominiums that have blighted the Costa del Sol. But the World Wildlife Fund, under the direction of Prince Bernhard of the Netherlands, came to the Coto's rescue, contributing financial aid and convincing the Spanish government of the importance of what was about to be lost.

Thus, today this irreplaceable treasure has been preserved, and those people who traditionally inhabited the Coto, living their primitive lives in thatched huts, have also remained. A projected road through the reserve was never built, and the only trace of civilization is a sprawling tourist complex called Torre de la Higuera, at the northwestern limits of the reserve. Despite the great inconvenience for travelers, who must make a huge detour to get, for example, from Cádiz to Huelva, Spain is pleased to make this small sacrifice for such a worthy cause.

$\mathcal{V}$ISITING COTO DOÑANA

Coto Doñana exists mainly for conservation and investigation, but in recent years it has been opened to the public. Visits must be made by jeep and arranged through the local cooperative, which oversees this preserve. The jeeps (shared with other passengers) will meet you at the headquarters in Almonte or in Torre de la Higuera. I prefer, however, to follow the route of the El Rocío pilgrimage, crossing the Guadalquivir at Sanlúcar de Barrameda (information on boats is available at Casa Bigote at the waterfront) and having a jeep waiting on the other side. Visits range from three hours to all day, and prices vary accordingly. Early morning or late afternoon is best to see most wildlife, and I suggest staying the night in Sanlúcar de Barrameda in the province of Cádiz or in Mazagón or Ayamonte.

There are constant arrivals and departures of wildlife at Coto Doñana; what you see depends on the time of year (June is ideal) and the hour of the day. Jeep drivers know the Coto like the back of their hand and take you to appropriate areas and point out animals that you might not otherwise see.

For reservations call or write Cooperativa Marismas del Rocío, Almonte, Huelva, or call tel. (955) 43 04 32, about one month in advance.

$\mathcal{V}$ISITING THE PROVINCE OF HUELVA

COTO DOÑANA One of the world's great wildlife preserves (see text).

ALMONTE Near this town, the passionate El Rocío pilgrimage takes place (see box, p. 406).

MAZAGÓN Come to Mazagón for a restful stay at the **PARADOR CRISTÓBAL COLÓN** Carretera Matalascañas tel. (955) 37 60 00, ideally located atop the beautiful beach bluffs. Comfortable motel-style rooms open to the pool. (Moderate–expensive.)

LA RÁBIDA The monastery where Columbus lived while awaiting permission to set sail (see text).

PALOS Most of Columbus's crew was from this small town (see text).

MOGUER Some of Columbus's crew were from here, and the town is the proud birthplace of Nobel Prize–winning poet Juan Ramón Jiménez. His simple home has been conserved as a museum. See also the fourteenth century **CONVENTO DE SANTA CLARA** and its beautiful cloister and tombs. Moguer is famed for its strawberries.

HUELVA Capital of the province, at the juncture of the Tinto and Odiel rivers, this port city has beautiful views of the sea. A monumental statue of Columbus, a work by Gertrude Vanderbilt Whitney, looks toward America and was a gift from the United States government. An eighteenth century earthquake destroyed most of the city's historic buildings.

THE TUMULTUOUS EL ROCÍO FESTIVAL

Although the tradition of worshipping a feminine deity in these deserted lands is thought to date from before Roman times, ever since the thirteenth century this mad celebration has taken place seven weeks after Easter Sunday. Pilgrims come by the hundreds of thousands to the marshlands of Almonte—almost uninhabited the balance of the year—through the sands of Coto Doñana and by barge across the Guadalquivir (see Sanlúcar de Barrameda). They come on horseback, in colorful carriages and carts, or by jeep (cars can't make it through the sand), dressed in flamenco style and already in a partying mood, dancing and drinking the days and nights away.

The culmination comes when the Virgin of the Dew (Rocío) is brought out of her sanctuary on a float and is treated in the most unmannerly fashion by her delirious young male admirers from Almonte, who struggle to keep all other hands away from her. Melees erupt, and the Virgin sways precariously, as everyone strives to at least touch her. It's a madhouse—either watch it on TV or try to rent a jeep for the day (from Sevilla or Sanlúcar de Barrameda, returning that night)—or attend instead the somewhat smaller-scale El Rocío Chico which takes place every seven years, August 18–20 (the last one was in 1991).

LOS GORDOS   Carmen 14 tel. (955) 24 62 66, a classic in this city, is a tavern with a thin veneer of elegance. It is named after its owners, known to all as "The Fat Ones," who yell a lot and like to put on a show for their happy clientele. At Los Gordos everyone eats the same food, and it is all superb: cured ham and pork loin (*lomo*) from Jabugo, enormous grilled or sautéed flounders, and Manchego cheese with candied squash (*cabello de ángel*) for dessert. (Moderate.)

NIEBLA   An unexpected sight on the road from Huelva to Sevilla: an Arab town enclosed by a three-kilometer perimeter of Moorish walls with forty-six watchtowers and a castle. The Santa María de Granada church, built over a mosque, conserves two Mozarabic (see Index) portals from the tenth and eleventh centuries and a lovely Moorish patio.

AYAMONTE   A pleasant, whitewashed village with a waterfront promenade and colorful port and crowned by the parador, which commands panoramic views of the village, the Guadiana river, and Portugal. Along the Calle Real, see the chapel El Socorro and its statue of Christ, primitively sculpted by Peruvian Indians in the sixteenth century. Have tapas (especially shrimp) near the waterfront at one of the tapas bars.

PARADOR COSTA DE LA LUZ   El Castillito   tel. (955) 32 07 00. (Moderate; pool.)

♦ A newly constructed bridge links Ayamonte and Portugal. Spend a pleasant afternoon visiting the nearby Portuguese towns of Tavira and Castro Marín.

♦ The pine-bordered beaches, miles long, of **ISLA CRISTINA** are a short drive from Ayamonte. On the beachfront, **CASA RUFINO**   Carretera de la Playa s/n   tel. (955) 33 08 10, is always popular for seafood (moderate)—or you can eat at one of the *merenderos* set up on the beach.

PEÑA DE ARIAS MONTANO   From this mountain viewpoint, on a clear day, you can see most of the province (take the road shortly before or after Aracena, direction Fuenteheridos).

ARACENA   If you like caves, the one here, **GRUTA DE LAS MARAVIL-LAS**, is exceptional (ignore the banal patter of the guides).
CASA CASAS   Colmenitas 41   tel. (955) 11 00 44, is charmingly cluttered with antiques. It of course serves fine Jabugo ham but also specializes in fresh Jabugo pork loin. I will always remember the outstanding soft-set eggs with reed-thin wild asparagus that I ate here. (Moderate.)

JABUGO   The fabled town around which Iberian pigs are bred and where the ham is cured (see the hams—800,000 of them—hanging in a huge underground room at **SÁNCHEZ ROMERO-CARVAJAL**, San Juan del Puerto s/n (request visit in advance).

Nearby at **LOS ROMEROS**, Barco s/n you can sample exquisite Jabugo ham, cured pork loin (*lomo*), and chorizo.

THE PROVINCE OF CÁDIZ

THE PROVINCE OF CÁDIZ (*cah*-deeth), although eminently maritime, has more variety than any other in Andalucía. It borders the Atlantic Ocean, briefly touches the Mediterranean, has miles of fine beaches and impressive dunes and marshland, and yet it has a mountainous interior of pleasing landscapes and wonderful villages.

The coast of Cádiz is one of the sunniest in Spain, and its people have a disposition to match (the typical flamenco of Cádiz is not sad—indeed, the style is called "Alegrías"). Temperatures are moderate and rainfall minimal; the beach sands are white and fine, and the turquoise ocean water crystalline clear. All this interests today's traveler, but in history it was Cádiz's key location on the Atlantic coast that made it so important.

Phoenicians were already trading here a thousand years before Christ, and for the Greeks and Romans, Cádiz was an essential commercial link to Spain. The Arabs, on the other hand, were more oriented to the land and therefore gave less importance to Cádiz. With the discovery of America, the region's Golden Age began; Cádiz was a logical point from which to depart on transatlantic journeys, and often the first stop when returning. Its ports were busy with the comings and goings of ships, and as long as sea power was vital to Spain's well-being, Cádiz, guarding the Strait of Gibraltar, was crucial and a frequent target for pirate raids and attacks by the navies of France and England. It was at Cape Trafalgar in the province of Cádiz that the British, under the command of Lord Nelson, brought Spanish naval supremacy to an end.

Seafood, quite naturally, is the gastronomic highlight in the province of Cádiz, as well it should be; the selection and quality of the fish and shellfish are extraordinary. Besides the common varieties that are found all along the coast of Andalucía, there are species peculiar to Cádiz: *urta*, a sweet porgy that has spent its life dining on shellfish and is baked under a mound of salt (*a la sal*) or in a sauce of tomatoes and peppers (*a la roteña*); special prawns called *langostinos*, found at the mouth of the Guadalquivir river; tiny flounders (*acedías*); crab claws (*Bocas de la Isla*); the insuperable mackerel, found in the waters around Cádiz; and the esteemed *lenguado de estero*— flounder trapped in salt marshes by the receding tides—which have a firm texture and uncommonly fine flavor.

Moving slightly away from the shore of Cádiz, you are surrounded by another world, and the land is steeped in different traditions. Breeding splendid horses and raising noble fighting bulls are part of an aristocratic heritage, and it is here that you will find another of Cádiz's claims to fame: sherry and its close kin, Manzanilla, unique and quintessentially Andalusian contributions to the great wines of the world.

The surprise of Cádiz province is its extensive interior, with its wonderful White Towns in dramatic settings: on hillsides or in cliff faces. This is well off the tourist track, and we love the beauty and timelessness of travel in this little-known area of Cádiz.

Cádiz is not a province of grand monuments or world-class museums. We like to come here at the end of an active trip, when we are sated with sightseeing and need to clear our minds. We make the city of Cádiz our base and revel in the spirited street life, especially in the evenings. Our days are spent visiting tiny interior villages, exploring towns along the coast, enjoying the beaches, watching exceptional sunsets, and letting the majesty of this ocean environment envelop us.

THE CITY OF CÁDIZ

Cádiz has long been one of the cities that we love the most. Mind you, everyone doesn't respond the same way. Most guidebooks glide over Cádiz with a few cursory words (". . . it is devoid of major interest . . . ," Frommer reports). True, it has no three-star attractions, but we don't come here for that: It's the city's charm, relaxed pace, and small-town qualities, its fine eating, and especially the overwhelming hospitality of its people (called Gaditanos) that bring us here time and time again.

The people of Cádiz have touched us with their warmth, their vitality, and their fun-loving spirit. They will bend over backward to show you the best of the city they so dearly love, and to make you love it too. Gaditanos have showered us with their generosity and affection, and Americans whom we have sent to Cádiz are equally impressed.

The city of Cádiz occupies an unusual site, surrounded by water and built on a peninsula that is attached to Spain by a narrow neck of land just wide enough for a two-lane road and the railroad tracks ("Its purpose," writes the nineteenth century author Benito Pérez Galdós, "is so that the

mainland does not have the misfortune of being separated from Cádiz").
Cádiz, sparkling in the sunlight, is aptly nicknamed Tacita de Plata—Little
Silver Cup, a graphic description of the city's glimmer and its rounded
shape. There is an unreal clarity to the air that characterizes the entire
Atlantic coast of Andalucía, and it is most appropriately called The Coast of
Light.

> Cádiz, like a rotating panorama, came into view, revealing suc-
> cessively the distinct faces of its vast circuit. The sun, firing the
> crystals of thousands of belvederes, sprinkled the city with gold
> dust, and the white breakwater stood out so cleanly and purely
> against the water that it seemed to have been created at that
> moment, or to have emerged from the sea like the mythical city
> of Saint Gennaro.
>
> *Benito Pérez Galdós*

Close your eyes as you approach the chaotically constructed, modern
high-rise extension of the city; open them as you go through Puerta de
Tierra (Land Gate), which protected the city from mainland invasions, and
you'll see a city that has changed very little in the past two centuries.

The streets of Cádiz are hardly the width of one small car, and house
corners are protected from cars maneuvering tight turns by cannons left over
from the 1812 War of Independence. Most Gaditanos, however, choose to
walk, and I join them, relishing the intimacy of the streets and looking
upward at splendid balconies and *miradores* (glassed-in terraces) and at the
towers that peek above flat-roof houses and serve as windows to the sea. In
the early evening, when just about everyone is out for a *paseo*, the streets are
undulating masses of people—and more scampering, jumping, and cycling
children than you could ever imagine. The relatively generous space of the
Calle Ancha—literally, Wide Street, so named because it is a whopping seventeen feet from building to building—is particularly popular for the
evening stroll.

The charming Plaza del Tío de la Tiza is so filled on summer nights
with outdoor tables for tapas or dinner that Gaditanos have to pull in their
chairs and tuck in their stomachs to allow the occasional car to pass by;
waiters authoritatively direct traffic. Residents and cabbies do at times
grumble about difficult circulation through the streets, but they know that
had the streets been any wider, Cádiz could never have reached the 1990s
looking so much like the eighteenth century.

The history of Cádiz is dominated by the sea. Cádiz holds the distinction of being the longest continually inhabited city in the Western world; it
was first colonized by the Phoenicians more than three thousand years ago
and named Gadir (although in legend its founding goes back still further
and is attributed to none other than Hercules). Cádiz became an important
center of Roman Spain because of its outlet to the sea, but languished under
the Arabs and is one of the few places in Andalucía where Moorish influence is less apparent.

Its strategic but vulnerable location made it the object of countless
attacks by the French and the British; Cádiz was attacked by Sir Francis
Drake and sacked by the forces of the Earl of Essex. The massive defensive

walls that ring the city attest to Cádiz's embattled past. The city monopolized trade with the New World, and it was to Cádiz that many ships returned, bringing first word of new lands and fabulous riches. The muddy bottom of the Bay of Cádiz is littered with thousands of treasure ships that completed the perilous journey home, only to end up wrecked on shoals or sunk by enemy ships. In later years the center of operations for New World activity shifted to Sevilla, and Cádiz became a city of past glories.

Cádiz regained the spotlight once more in the nineteenth century when Napoleon overran Spain and the city put up heroic resistance, thus becoming the only Spanish territory not occupied by French forces and the logical seat of the deposed Spanish government. In Cádiz a new liberal constitution was devised, officially abolishing the Inquisition (although it had not functioned for some time) and emphasizing human rights and social reform. It unfortunately did not survive the restoration of Ferdinand VII to the throne.

The sea continues to dominate daily life in Cádiz, and you are never more than a few blocks from the sight of the Atlantic or the Bay of Cádiz. Gaditanos are finely attuned to shifting winds that signal changes in the weather. Salty breezes cause whitewash to flake from buildings, and the ocean wreaks havoc with the golden-domed Baroque cathedral, which has been weakened by the sea's assault (you can hear the thunderous waves that crash against its underground level). There was always a certain charm in the genteel decay of Cádiz, but the city has now entered a new era. A long-overdue face-lift has dressed its houses in fresh coats of paint, monuments are under restoration, palaces and city mansions are being refurbished. Cádiz is more delightful than ever.

Fishing is much more than a sport or a livelihood for Gaditanos; it is a way of life. No matter what the hour, you are sure to find dozens of fishermen on the bridge (which today provides an additional way to reach Cádiz from the mainland) or along the lovely waterfront promenade, casting from thick fishing poles long lines that must reach down some twenty-five feet just to touch the water's surface. Other fishing enthusiasts choose to hunt shellfish off La Caleta, Cádiz's old Phoenician port, where the receding tides leave puddles and gulleys that imprison the luckless creatures. When morning comes, the night's catch is hawked on street corners, and on Mondays, when there is no fish market (the professionals do not go to sea on Sundays), restaurants rely on these amateurs for the freshest fish.

Eating in Cádiz is an experience. I have never heard so much conversation about seafood: how shellfish must never be refrigerated once cooked, how to distinguish the male langoustine from the female (the latter is the tastier, although my uneducated palate loves both), the horror of "drowning" the taste of fresh fish with a sauce or even a squirt of lemon, and how ideally the fish should still be twitching when sent to the kitchen.

Fish is preferred fried, and *freidurías*—stores dedicated to frying fish for take-out—abound in the city ("To eat fried fish in Cádiz is like tasting an anthology of the ocean," writes José María Pemán). But there are, of course, other preparations that Gaditanos love, like shark in saffron sauce (*Cazón en Amarillo*), thin crisp shrimp pancakes (*Tortillitas de Camarones*), and fish baked under a crackling sea-salt crust (*Pescado a la Sal*). During your stay in Cádiz, it is best to forget that you ever heard the word *meat*.

ẞIENMESABE
(IT TASTES GOOD TO ME)

Cut any firm-flesh fish (preferably shark or monkfish) into one-inch cubes, marinate in garlic and lemon juice, and refrigerate overnight. Flour, and fry in hot oil.

There is one image of Cádiz that frequently comes to my mind. It is of a tiny trinket shop, not much bigger than a newsstand, where an elderly man standing behind a counter open to the street is singing in flamenco style to a young child, accompanied by rhythmical clapping. "Long live my child, long live my child," he croons. Then he turns to me and continues, "Long live Cádiz! If everyone in the world were like us, what a wonderful world it would be!"

Hear, hear.

ẞEEING CÁDIZ

CATHEDRAL   Begun in Baroque style in 1718, the cathedral's upper portion was finished much later in nineteenth century neoclassic style. Especially sumptuous are the church treasures: an enormous seventeenth century monstrance laden with silver that is paraded through Cádiz on Corpus Christi, and "El Millón," another monstrance that receives its name from the extraordinary number of jewels encrusted into it.

SAN FELIPE NERI   A seventeenth century church, elliptical in shape and classic in design, where Spain's first liberal constitution was proclaimed in 1812 (see text). The walls are filled with plaques presented by other nations in recognition of this event.

HOSPITAL DE MUJERES   This eighteenth century convent has a grand stairway, a beautiful patio, and an important painting by El Greco, *Ecstasy of San Francisco*.

MUSEO DE CÁDIZ   Among other exhibits, there is an extensive and exceptionally fine collection of Zurbarán paintings, portraying religious figures clothed in luminously white robes.

DRAGO MILENARIO   This remarkable dragon tree, on the patio of the university, is thought to be more than a thousand years old and is like those seen in the Canary Islands.

EL PÓPULO AND SANTA MARÍA   Two of the oldest and most charming neighborhoods of Cádiz.

PLAZA DEL TÍO DE LA TIZA   This intimate square of whitewashed houses, flower-filled balconies, and a well at its center makes you feel as though you have entered a tiny Andalusian village.

WATERFRONT PROMENADES (Alameda Apodaca, Alameda Marqués de Comillas)   One of the great pleasures in Cádiz is strolling these promenades, set over the high seawalls. Sunset is an especially beautiful time.

♦ Avoid travel to and from the city of Cádiz on summer weekends. Everyone is heading for the beaches, and traffic can be horrendous.

♦ A ship leaves each evening from Cádiz for the Canary Islands.

STAYING IN CÁDIZ

HOTEL ATLÁNTICO   Avenida Duque de Nájera 9   tel. (956) 22 69 05   A parador, this hotel is well cared for and on prime property overlooking stunning views of the Bay of Cádiz, the Atlantic Ocean, and crimson sunsets. All rooms have water views, and at night from my terrace I love to watch the liners—ablaze in light—and the solid little fishing boats making their way to the open sea. Best rooms are those with a salon and a large terrace, in the older wing—particularly 2R, 3R, and 4R. (Moderate–expensive; pool.)

EATING IN CÁDIZ

EL FARO   San Félix 15   tel. (956) 21 10 68   Indisputably the best in Cádiz, an impeccable establishment of maritime décor expertly overseen by owner Gonzalo Córdoba. El Faro specializes in the finest fish of Cádiz and luscious Jabugo ham. Besides traditional preparations, chef José Manuel Córdoba, son of Gonzalo, also creates many new dishes with equally delicious results. (Moderate–expensive.)

VENTORILLO DEL CHATO   Carretera N-IV   tel. (956) 25 00 25   An eighteenth century inn at the beachfront on the isthmus of Cádiz and interesting for its colorful history as a place frequented by King Ferdinand VII, when he retreated to Cádiz during the French occupation of Spain (see text). Well-prepared seafood. (Moderate.)

MESÓN EL CANDIL   Javier de Burgos 19   tel. (956) 22 19 71   If you get the urge for meat, this casual *mesón* is the best place in town for garlic chicken and garlicky strips of beef tenderloin (*puntillitas de solomillo*). (Moderate.)

TAPAS BARS

BAR BAHÍA   Avenida Ramón de Carranza 29   An all-time favorite of mine, as much for the homemade *guisos* (tapas in sauce—there's no frying here) as for the delightful company of owner and talented cook Salvador Lucero.

EL ANTEOJO   Alameda Apodaca 22   Outdoor tables over the bay make this an ideal spot for tapas at sunset.

TABERNA LA MANZANILLA   Calle Feduchy 18   The wine barrels in this eighteenth century tavern are a hundred years old and store a variety of *manzanilla* sherries.

BAR MANTECA   Calle San Félix   Joined to a small grocery store, this bar is popular for excellent cured pork loin (*lomo*).

JOSELITO   San Francisco 38   Specializing in a wide variety of shellfish.

SHOPPING

OMNIA   San Francisco 36   Elegant leather goods: snake, turtle, and crocodile handbags, attaché cases, and many other gift items. Be sure to speak to owners Pepe and Paqui Delfín, who will graciously offer their assistance in making your stay in their beloved Cádiz a special occasion.

FIESTAS

CORPUS CHRISTI   Nine weeks after Easter. Elaborate street processions.

CARNAVAL   Approximately forty days before Easter. This is one of the few places in Spain where the pre-Lenten tradition of merrymaking is still fervently observed. Local amateur singing groups called *chirigotas* brilliantly poke fun at politicians, fashion, pornography, or any other hot topic of the preceding year. All Cádiz takes to the streets in costume.

SANLÚCAR DE BARRAMEDA

We especially love to spend evenings in Cádiz, but during the day we choose short trips to the beaches, to the city of Jerez de la Frontera, to delightful towns and villages and to excellent restaurants and beachside *chiringuitos*, all within easy reach of Cádiz.

Spending part of a day in Sanlúcar de Barrameda is at the top of my list because of its exceptionally beautiful location at the mouth of the Río Guadalquivir, its long beachfront and promenade, and the aristocratic demeanor of its houses.

Sanlúcar's Old Quarter stands above the beach on a hill, overlooking the Río Guadalquivir, the Atlantic Ocean, and the incomparable Coto Doñana wildlife preserve and bird sanctuary. Although once at water's edge, river silting has left the original town some distance from

the shore. Along the streets of the old Barrio Alto (Upper Town), elegant wrought-iron work covers windows; patios are lush with plants; and the glaringly white bodegas, where *manzanilla* is made, appear surreal. The sixteenth century palace of the Dukes of Medina Sidonia, once part of the ancient Arab fortress nearby, crowns Sanlúcar; the current Duchess of Medina Sidonia lives here and has put aside three delightful guest rooms.

Sanlúcar now extends over the silted land at sea level, and this is where most of the town's summer activity takes place. I always head for the quaint old fishermen's quarter called Bajo de Guía, where heavy-hulled white fishing boats, accented with bright blues, greens, and reds, swing in the channel breeze or gently keel on the soft sands.

If you can possibly be here about six and a half weeks after Easter, you will witness a wonderful Andalusian tradition: the annual crossing from Sanlúcar to the marshlands, where the Virgen del Rocío (Virgin of the Dew) is worshipped (see box, p. 406). The navy is called in to assist, providing launches to transport hundreds of thousands of people, colorfully dressed in flamenco style, plus horses, carriages, jeeps, and tractors, also dressed up for the occasion.

Although this is a religious event, it is also one big party. While revelers patiently wait their turn to cross the river, there are spontaneous outbursts of song and frequent asides to bars for drinks and tapas. It's an infectious atmosphere, which warmly embraces visitors as well as participants.

Apart from such special occasions (there are also horse races on the beach in August and many other local festivals), another major attraction in Sanlúcar is the shrimp called *langostinos*, and they are really what bring me back here religiously. You must try these sweet, succulent creatures. We are among the many loyal fans who flock to Casa Bigote for the best *langostinos*, more than worthy of their fame, served by cherub-faced Fernando Hermoso and his brother Paco. Follow the *langostinos* with a delectable brochette of monkfish with *alioli* or a local fish fry (including tiny flounders called *acedías*), and you have a meal difficult to surpass.

Sanluqueños pair their *langostinos* with a very dry, nutty fortified wine of a pale golden color that is called *manzanilla* and matured in the manner of sherry. It can only be made in Sanlúcar, for if you take the same grapes and age them just twenty-four kilometers away in Jerez de la Frontera, you get sherry, not *manzanilla*. This phenomenon has yet to be completely explained; some say it is the salty ocean air and a climate slightly different from inland Jerez, the center of sherry production, that are responsible.

Sanlúcar lovers claim that the town and its environs have everything you could ask for: vineyards, olive groves, sea, river, ports, pine forests, agriculture, marshlands. See if you don't agree.

SEEING SANLÚCAR DE BARRAMEDA

SANTA MARÍA DE LA O   The most significant features of this fourteenth century church are its elaborately carved portal, in Mudéjar style, and a beautiful *artesonado* ceiling within.

BONANZA   A ten-minute drive upriver from Sanlúcar takes you to Bonanza, the port from which Columbus set sail on his third voyage and where Magellan began his journey around the world in 1519 with a crew of 265 (just 18 men returned three years later, without their captain, who died during the voyage). Local fishing boats dock here for the daily, very animated fish auction.

◆ The bodegas of Sanlúcar can be visited by previous appointment. I especially like **ANTONIO BARBADILLO**   Luis Eguilaz 11   tel. (956) 36 08 94.

STAYING IN SANLÚCAR DE BARRAMEDA

◆ Boat service up the Guadalquivir river to Sevilla has recently been inaugurated and is a delightful way to travel between the two cities.

PALACIO DE MEDINA SIDONIA   Conde de Niebla 1   tel. (956) 36 01 61 Contiguous to the Santa María de la O church, this private palace of the Duchess of Medina Sidonia has three guest rooms (request the Red Room) and provides a unique travel experience. (Inexpensive; no credit cards.) You can arrange to take a tour of the rest of the palace.

POSADA DEL PALACIO   Caballeros 11   tel. (956) 36 48 40   In a typical Sanlúcar house of noble bearing, well cared for and run by an enthusiastic young couple. (Moderate.)

EATING IN SANLÚCAR DE BARRAMEDA

CASA BIGOTE   Bajo de Guía   tel. (956) 36 26 96   The finest of the local catch of Sanlúcar: prawns, fried fish, monkfish brochette, either at the animated bar or in the restaurant. Reservations suggested. (Moderate.)

◆ **CASA BALBINO**   Plaza del Cabildo, is a busy bar with a large selection of tapas. I liked *Patatas Rellenas*—potatoes filled with tuna.

◆ Cloistered nuns in the Madres de Dios convent, on a street of the same name, sell their homemade sweets, passed to you by way of a revolving shelf (*torno*).

FIESTAS

HORSE RACES   On the beach at the beginning and end of August.

EL ROCÍO   The colorful crossing to El Rocío from Sanlúcar takes place in the spring. (See text.)

Jerez de la Frontera

There is no way to dissociate the city of Jerez de la Frontera, named Xera by the Phoenicians, from sherry; its importance hits you wherever you turn. Bodegas are everywhere. In bars and restaurants everyone is drinking *jerez*, as sherry is called in Spanish, and this special wine is responsible for the town's obvious wealth and aristocracy. Sherry has made the city's name famous worldwide ("sherry" is a corruption of the name *Jerez*).

Real sherry comes only from Jerez, and although some imitations are attempted, only sherry from Jerez has all the subtleties—a complex interplay of climate, terrain, and traditional know-how—that make this one of the world's great wines.

Weather is warm and predictable in Jerez, and the chalky *albariza* soil ideal for trapping precious moisture below the ground's surface to nourish the grape vines. After the harvest, the mystery of sherry begins. For it is only in some of the wine barrels that a yeast called *flor* forms on the wine's surface, producing the dry *fino* sherry. Other barrels containing wine made from the same grapes yield a much sweeter wine. As all of these wines age, they are blended with still older wines (through the *solera* process) and for this reason sherry has no vintages. Finally, the wines are fortified to bring them to a strength of 16 percent to 20 percent alcohol. *Fino* and its close kin *manzanilla*, made in nearby Sanlúcar de Barrameda, are held in highest regard by Andaluces and are the ideal accompaniment to the wonderful tapas of Andalucía.

You can see and sense a British presence in Jerez, for most sherry bodegas have British names. Osborne, Byass, Croft, Terry, Garvey, Harvey, Sandeman, Williams & Humbert, for example, were originally British, but their descendants are thoroughly Andalusian. Nevertheless, an affinity for all things British and close contacts with England continue. The British are still sherry's greatest fans and buy a large percentage of the production. And the passion in Jerez for fine horses and horse-related events and festivals also shows the ties that still bind. The Andalusian School of horses has become synonymous with the fine quality and the elegant performances of the horses bred here.

No one better personifies the aristocratic air of Jerez and its noble lifestyle than José Ignacio Domecq, whose generous-size nose and uncanny ability to judge the taste and bouquet of his Pedro Domecq sherries has earned him the title of "The Nose." One of the most famous stories in the annals of Jerez tells of a visit by Henry Ford to the Domecqs. At the end of his stay, Mr. Ford, impressed with what he had seen, declared that although he might be wealthier than the Domecqs, he certainly couldn't equal their way of life. To which Mr. Domecq reportedly replied, "You are right and you are wrong. Certainly life in Jerez is far superior to what you know, but you are wrong to think that you have more money than I do."

There are many other fascinating sherry tales: the body of Lord Nelson, who lost his life in the battle at Cape Trafalgar down the coast from Cádiz, was kept in a sherry keg to preserve it for the trip back home; the *Mayflower* was a sherry runner between Sanlúcar and Southampton before bringing pilgrims to the New World; much of the monumental construction in Jerez is of English stone, used as ballast on the empty ships coming from England to pick up sherry and dumped to make room for the sherry brought home.

Seeing Jerez de la Frontera

OLD QUARTER   Declared a national monument, it includes the Colegiata, in Renaissance and Baroque style; the churches of San Mateo, sixteenth century Gothic, built over a mosque; San Miguel, with its Baroque facade; fifteenth century San Marcos; Santiago, profusely decorated in Isabelline style (see Index); and the Mudéjar San Dionisio. There is also a Moorish Alcázar from the eleventh century.

LA CARTUJA   Four kilometers from Jerez on the road to Medina Sidonia and Algeciras is this still grand fifteenth century monastery with Baroque additions, one of the foremost monuments of the province.

ESCUELA DE ARTE ECUESTRE   Avenida Duque de Abrantes   The famous "dancing horses" of Jerez rehearse every weekday from 11:00 a.m. to 1:00 p.m. (open to the public), except on Thursdays, when they put on a show at 12:00 noon.

STAYING IN JEREZ DE LA FRONTERA

HOTEL JEREZ   Avenida Álvaro Domecq 35   tel. (956) 30 06 00   Not very exciting for a five-star hotel, except for its pool, in a lush garden setting. (Expensive.)

EATING IN JEREZ DE LA FRONTERA

For fine dining **LA MESA REDONDA**   Manuel de la Quintana 3   tel. (956) 34 00 69, is among the best of the city. (Moderate.) This is a city for tapas: Try **TENDIDO 6**   Circo 10, near the bullring; **LA VENENCIA**   Calle Larga, downtown; and **LA TASCA**   Edificio Jerez 74.
◆ There are two fine roadside stops outside Jerez, in the tradition of the venta: **MESÓN LA CUEVA**   ten kilometers on the road to Arcos   tel. (956) 32 16 20, where the lively bar serves, for example, *Pincho Moruno* (miniature shish kabob), fine Jabugo ham, and shellfish; and **VENTA ANTONIO**   five kilometers on the road to Sanlúcar   tel. (956) 33 05 35, in the style of an Andalusian country house, known for its seafood.

SAMPLING CONVENT SWEETS

A strong tradition of convent-made sweets (see box, p. 398) continues in Jerez. **MADRES DOMINICAS**   Espíritu Santo 9, specialize in cupcakes and sponge cakes; **MADRES AGUSTINAS ERMITAÑAS**   Santa María de Gracia 2, make a variety of cakes.

FIESTAS

WINE HARVEST FESTIVAL   (Vendimia)   An occasion for colorful processions, for bullfights, and for a flamenco fest. September.

FERIA DEL CABALLO   Important and impressive horse fair that goes back to the thirteenth century and features magnificent horses and exciting horsemanship. There are bullfights and a general air of merriment. Second week of May.

VISITING THE BODEGAS

Sherry bodegas can be visited weekday mornings until about noon. Some are by appointment only, while large companies are open to the general public. See, if possible, the impressive Domecq installations, where the bodega stores 40,000 kegs and is made to resemble a Moorish mosque.

VISITING THE PROVINCE OF CÁDIZ

The Coast

ALGECIRAS   The place of departure for boats to Tangier and a city close to Gibraltar. It is undistinguished except for a very good hotel, **REINA CRISTI-NA**   Paseo Conferencias s/n   tel. (956) 60 26 22 (moderate–expensive; pool), which has beautiful grounds and a certain British Old World charm, attributed to its historic connection with Gibraltar. **PEPE MORENO** Murillo s/n   tel. (956) 65 28 03, serves excellent Andalusian fish dishes. (Moderate.)

Just outside **SAN ROQUE**, a steep town of picturesque plazas, is **LOS REMOS**   Villa Victoria, km 2   tel. (956) 76 08 12, in an elegant mansion and specializing in seafood from the Bay of Algeciras. Stick to simple fish preparations. (Expensive.)

SOTOGRANDE   Carretera N-340, km 131   tel. (956) 79 21 00, is a deluxe bungalow-style hotel in a secluded setting. Horseback riding and polo are popular sports. (Expensive; pool.)

♦ From here to Vejer de la Frontera, the road passing through Los Barrios is bucolic, with grazing cows, cork trees, fields of sunflowers, and pine forests.

GIBRALTAR   The famous rock, still a British possession (see box, p. 419).

CASTELLAR DE LA FRONTERA   In a setting of low mountains and scrub bushes and completely contained behind stone walls, this village, entered through an arch in its thirteenth century castle, used to lock its wooden gates after hours. Wonderful views of Gibraltar and a nearby reservoir. There are still a few hippies left over from the sixties living here.

CASA CONVENTO DE LA ALMORAIMA Finca La Almoraima, tel (956) 69 30 50, is nearby in a protected woodland and is the former hunting lodge of the Dukes of Medinaceli. The dukes no longer reign, but a certain nobility remains. Small, friendly, almost like a private house. Guests eat together at a long elegant table. Hunting, fishing, horseback riding, jeep excursions. (Expensive; pool.)

TARIFA Strategically located at the narrowest point of the Strait of Gibraltar and presided over by its one-thousand-year-old Moorish castle, this was the first Spanish town taken by the Moors in 711. It was named after its conqueror, Tariq ben Malik. The chief attraction here is the indescribably beautiful views of the peaks of Africa, just eight miles away, emerging, dreamlike, from the sea-level mist (there are days when they disappear completely in the fog), and a constant parade of ships passing through the strait. Drive a few kilometers east to the overlook for the best views. I could spend all day here just watching this splendid sight in all its changing lights. Sunset is particularly special, as are the evenings, when the lights of Tangier sparkle in the distance. You can take a hydrofoil to Tangier from Tarifa. In recent years Tarifa has become the windsurfing capital of Europe. A good town for tapas.

DOS MARES Carretera Cádiz-Málaga, km 79 tel. (956) 68 40 35, is a simple but cozy hotel along the road. (Moderate; pool.)

♦ The beaches in and around Tarifa are spectacularly beautiful: **PLAYA DE TARIFA**, of fine drifting sands and stunning views of

THE ROCK OF GIBRALTAR

"Call Gibraltar the hill of Tarik or Hercules if you will, but gaze upon it for a moment and you will call it the hill of God," said nineteenth century evangelist George Borrow.

It was the ancient Punics who, legend tells, raised the Columns of Hercules on either side of the Gibraltar Strait after Hercules demolished the mountains that had closed off the Mediterranean, thus creating the strait (more pragmatic accounts attribute this event to earthquakes). The ancient Arabs named this natural fortress in honor of their hero Yebel Tarik (thus Gibraltar), who came here in 710, just before the Arabs entered Spain (Gibraltar is attached to Spain by a narrow isthmus). In the eighteenth century the British took control of The Rock, and it has been a point of contention between Spain and England ever since. During the Franco era, entry from Spain was prohibited. Although the border is once more open, Gibraltar is a mere shadow of its former self, and a place whose raison d'être no longer exists.

Still, the setting is breathtaking: a vertical rise of bare rock looming from the flatlands of Spain to one side and from the sea to the other. It certainly deserves a visit.

The British cling to Gibraltar as a matter of pride and tradition and take extra care of the friendly monkeys that live high up on The Rock. Tradition says that as long as they are there, Gibraltar will be British. A plaque reads, "On this site HM Queen Elizabeth and the Duke of Edinburgh together with their Royal Highnesses Princess Anne and Prince Charles made friends with the apes on the 10th May 1954."

Africa; **PUNTA PALOMAS**, with towering dunes; and **RUINAS DE BOLO-NIA**, enclosed by a cape of dunes and named for the ancient Roman town that is being excavated nearby.

ZAHARA DE LOS ATUNES   Named after the tuna roundups that take place off its shores, the town has a long, curved beach and mountain views.

VEJER DE LA FRONTERA   Not far from the coast, one of the most immaculately kept and appealing of Andalucía's clifftop White Towns, where houses hang at the edge of a precipice. Labyrinthlike streets are strikingly Arab, and women until very recently veiled their faces. Just south of here, fighting bulls, appearing tame and timid behind barbed wire, are raised and can be seen from the road.

HOSPEDERÍA DEL CONVENTO DE SAN FRANCISCO   La Plazuela s/n tel. (956) 45 10 01, is a simple but pleasant hotel that was once a convent. (Moderate–expensive.)

VENTA PINTO   Barca de Vejer   tel. (956) 45 00 69, at the foot of the village, serves quality food (meals or tapas) and excellent cured ham, all at moderate prices.

CAPE TRAFALGAR, not far from here, was the site of the battle in 1792 between the Spanish and the British under the command of Lord Nelson (here he said the famous words "England expects every man to do his duty"). Lord Nelson lost his life, but the British won the battle. Trafalgar Square in London is named after this Spanish cape.

CAÑOS DE MECA is a beautiful beach (popular with nudists) edged by fallen boulders and impressive cliffs, from which water trickles from mountain springs. The turquoise waters of the Atlantic have crystal clarity.

SAN FERNANDO   The elaborately worked grilles that cover windows as tall as doors give a special appearance to the town. San Fernando is surrounded by salt marshes from which the prized *lenguado de estero* is fished; it can be sampled at **VENTA DE VARGAS**   Carretera N-IV, km 637   tel. (956) 88 16 22. (Moderate.)

EL PUERTO DE SANTA MARÍA   A typical Atlantic town at the mouth of the Guadalete river. Good eating (I prefer tapas and simple restaurants to the stylish establishments catering to the well-to-do summer crowd). There is a famous bullring here, known for its fervent aficionados. In the famous words of legendary bullfighter Joselito: "He who hasn't seen a bullfight in El Puerto doesn't know what a bullfight is all about."

Try tapas at **ECHATEPAYÁ**, a minute portside tapas bar (thus its name, "Move Over"), specializing in local fried fish. Dine or have tapas at **CASA FLORES**   Ribero del Río 9   tel. (956) 86 35 12, which features outstanding batter-fried shrimp (*Gambas en Gabardina*), Jabugo ham, and seafood *salpicón*, plus fish from the Bay of Cádiz. (Moderate.)

EL FARO DEL PUERTO   Carretera Rota, km 0.5   tel. (956) 87 09 52, elegantly set in a magnificent villa, belongs to Gonzalo Córdoba of El Faro in Cádiz. It has similarly fine seafood, but prepared in more stylish, creative ways by one of Gonzalo's sons, Fernando Córdoba. (Moderate–expensive.)

VENTA EL CORNETA   Carretera Madrid-Cádiz, km 659   tel. (956) 86 26 15, a modest restaurant along the main road, has top-quality prawns and an excellent *Bienmesabe* (see box, p. 411). (Moderate.)

MONASTERIO SAN MIGUEL   Larga 27   tel. (956) 86 44 40, a former convent, has been elegantly converted into a large hotel. It has a grand stairway, a lovely cloister, and a sixteenth century church.(Moderate–expensive; pool.)

ROTA   A seaside village that feels small, despite the presence of a huge American base nearby. From the old ramparts is a wide-open view of Cádiz beyond the sparkling blue Bay of Cádiz.

PLAYA DE LA BALLENA, a beautiful open stretch of beach, is nearby on the road to Sanlúcar de Barrameda.

The Interior

OLVERA   An Arab stronghold, and not surprisingly so; the Moors were almost invincible in this mountain village of steep streets topped by craggy rocks within which an Arab fortress was constructed. The setting is incomparable.

SETENIL   A singular village, built under cliff overhangs and hollowed from the mountainside. The carefully whitewashed facades are just that; inside, the homes are cozy caves with undulating walls. Little remains of the Arab castle that once stood here.

UBRIQUE   A mountain village where leather items are made for some of the most prestigious stores in Spain and Europe, such as Loewe and Cartier. Shops sell at wholesale prices.

ZAHARA DE LA SIERRA   In a remote landscape of olive groves, this spotless village is in the folds of a rocky mountain and overlooks a beautiful reservoir.
HOSTAL MARQUÉS DE ZAHARA   San Juan 3   tel. (956) 13 72 61, is small and neat and set in a noble home. (Inexpensive.)

ARCOS DE LA FRONTERA   An old Arab outpost in a spectacular setting, perched on the edge of a sheer cliff more than 200 feet above the Río Guadalete ("Poised to fly," as one poet puts it). The din of singing frogs colors the night air. There are delightful winding streets, and starkly whitewashed houses with cheerful patios of Moorish flavor.
     The beautiful **PARADOR CASA DEL CORREGIDOR**   Plaza Cabildo s/n   tel. (956) 70 05 00, is precipitously perched at cliff's edge—its terraces leave you afloat in space. (Moderate–expensive.)
VENTA LOS TRES CAMINOS   tel. (956) 70 10 26, is a pretty restaurant on the road to El Bosque, at the foot of Arcos, and has a traditional Andalusian menu. (Moderate.)
EL CONVENTO   Maldonado 2   tel. (956) 70 23 33, is a simple restaurant set in an old convent that serves well-prepared local dishes. (Inexpensive.) There is also a hotel here by the same name with just four rooms. (Inexpensive.)
CORTIJO FAÍN   Carretera de Algar, km 3   tel. (956) 70 11 67, is as close to staying in a private home as you can get. Señora Soledad Gil has reserved a few rooms for herself and turns the rest over to guests, furnishing the rooms

with her own antiques and memorabilia. Meals are made by the family cook. The house is splendidly set in olive groves, and staying here is a unique experience. (Expensive; pool.)

MEDINA SIDONIA   a remote, unspoiled hilltop town highlighted by the horseshoe Arab arch, Puerta de la Pastora, built into the ancient town walls. Through the arch are beautiful views of the surrounding countryside. Sweets of honey and nuts called *alfajores* are a specialty here.

THE PROVINCE OF SEVILLA

SEVILLA PROVINCE is the largest of Andalucía, yet composed of land that is often underutilized. To the north the Sierra Morena, a mountain range presumedly named for the velvety brown carpet created by acres of scrub bush, is of unspoiled beauty. It is thick with cork and eucalyptus trees and home to innumerable deer and wild boar, making the province celebrated hunting grounds. To the south the vast marshlands create a strange, dreamy landscape that is barely populated by man but teeming with aquatic birds.

The mighty Río Guadalquivir (from the Arabic, meaning Great River) cuts through the province and flows on to the Atlantic. The river attracted ancient peoples to Sevilla, and near its banks arose one of the most important cities of Roman Spain, Itálica. The emperors Trajan and Hadrian both knew Spain as their homeland; Trajan, the first non-Roman ruler of the empire, was probably born in Itálica, and Hadrian's father was from Itálica, his mother a native of Cádiz. Historically the Guadalquivir was a source of commerce for the province (the city of Sevilla, on the banks of the river, was in the seventeenth century the center for administration of the American colonies), and today the river is the umbilical cord that physically and psychologically binds Sevilla to the coasts of Cádiz and Huelva. The broad plain around the Guadalquivir is fertile ground for vegetable and grain crops and ideal for raising the majestic black fighting bulls that arouse passion in this bullfighting province.

Sevilla is a gay land, known for its flamenco song and even more for its world-famous flamenco dances called Sevillanas. Sometimes tragic but more often lighthearted, quick-paced music punctuated with heel taps and rhythmic clapping, Sevillanas are taught and danced today from Madrid to New York. No need for young Sevillanos to be instructed, however. They seem to be born with an intuitive sense of timing, style, and grace.

In Sevilla the weather is generally mild throughout the year, but it can get stunningly hot in summer. I've never minded, however, for the heat necessitates additional stops at small bars to sample tapas—refreshing ones based on salads and vinaigrettes—and to appreciate an icy-cold Spanish beer or chilled *fino* sherry.

Sevilla is tapas country without equal; you can find good tapas just about anywhere, and great ones more often here than anywhere else in Spain. They are based on fish from the Costa de La Luz (see Index)—fried and cooled in vinaigrette or escabeche, or cooked with oil and garlic—marinated and grilled meats and local game; stews in surprisingly light sauces, often with hints of Arab spices like cumin and coriander; cured ham and *chorizo* from the sierra; marinated tart green olives; green and red peppers in vinaigrettes and gazpachos.

Sevilla's villages are typically whitewashed, immaculately clean and neat as a pin, laden with geraniums and cascading bougainvilleas, and of pronounced Arab character. I expect you will visit several, but the city of Sevilla outshines anything else in the province. It is in fact the focal point of all western Andalucía, and it is Sevilla that makes this province one of my very favorites.

THE CITY OF SEVILLA

"¡*Viva Sevilla y Olé!*" exults a Sevillana flamenco song. Indeed, who has not fallen under the spell of Sevilla? The city has charmed the world and captured its heart. It is so alive, so aristocratic, so sophisticated, so filled with great historic monuments, and yet so small-town—and therein lies a great deal of its appeal.

Sevilla is for most purposes the capital of Andalucía, and so much of what we commonly associate with Spain is related to Sevilla: bullfighting, flamenco, the wiles of Don Juan, the fire of *Carmen*, dark-haired women with *peinetas* and black lace mantillas. The color and folkloric character of Sevilla that persist to this day made the city the setting for great literary works and caught the fancy of the opera world. *Carmen*, *The Barber of Seville*, *Don Giovanni*, *La Forza del Destino*, among other operas, are set in Sevilla.

Many of this century's legendary bullfighters were from Sevilla. Juan Belmonte and Joselito fought with the skill, bravery, elegance, and grace associated with the Sevilla school of bullfighting. In literature, the city gave birth to Gustavo Adolfo Bécquer, great lyric voice of the nineteenth century. It was the home of playright and priest Tirso de Molina, who created the literary character of Don Juan. Several of Spain's master painters of the seventeenth century were connected with Sevilla. Murillo was born here and did most of his work for Sevilla convents; Zurbarán, although born in Extremadura, spent most of his professional life here; and Velázquez, who worked at Court in Madrid, was born in Sevilla of nobility, and his art reflects an exquisite elegance that is a product of his upbringing in Sevilla. The paintings of all three have in common a remarkable glow, which I attribute to the extraordinary quality of the light these artists found in Andalucía.

If your vision of Spain has been culled from such colorful and sometimes folkloric sources, you will have a limited picture of the country, to be sure, but an enchanting one nonetheless and one shared by many Spaniards. But legends and past glories do not begin to describe the overwhelming attraction of Sevilla and its people.

Just as the province of Sevilla is dissected by the Guadalquivir, so too is the city, which lies in the Guadalquivir valley. It is in the monumental old quarters of Sevilla that most visitors concentrate their time. The Arab influence lingers. You see Moorish arched underpasses and alleyways everywhere, and streets that come to abrupt halts in delightful culs-de-sac and patios. Exuberantly colored ceramic tiles are the city's characteristic decorative element, and there are whitewashed buildings with doorways and windows outlined in bright yellow. Cool, serenely elegant patios, lush with greenery, are private, yet proudly open to public view through wrought-iron gates. All tell in small ways of the city's Arab past. On a grander scale there are the Alcázar palace, second only to the Alhambra of Granada in its Moorish beauty, and the delicately worked tower, La Giralda, next to the cathedral.

The Giralda is the Sevilla landmark that can be seen from afar and orients you when you are in the city. It is a tower beloved to Sevillanos, and was once the minaret of the Arab mosque from which the devoted were called to prayer. Adjoining the Giralda is the city's immense cathedral, aglitter in the gold and silver brought from the New World and rich in artistic treasures. It is the world's third largest, built in the fervor of the Reconquest and designed to astound the world with its massive size. Church canons, it is said, vowed to produce a cathedral so large that anyone beholding it would think them utterly mad.

The Giralda, the Alcázar, and the cathedral are Sevilla's main sights and are concentrated in the stately, somewhat subdued, and aristocratic central quarters of the city. But be forewarned: Unless you venture beyond this downtown core, you will miss the very essence of Sevilla. That's what happened to me on my first visit many years ago, and my notes from those times read, "A very private city, hard to feel its pulse. Lack of animation . . . little nightlife." How very wrong I was!

Then one hot Sunday afternoon a gregarious taxi driver, Miguel Ruz Abad, offered to show us his neighborhood and take us to his favorite tapas bars. We crossed the Guadalquivir into Triana—the fishermen's quarter when the Guadalquivir was navigable all the way to Sevilla (the river has once more been reopened)—and we were transported into an entirely different Sevilla, hopping with life well into the early morning hours, especially in summertime when everyone prefers the streets to cramped, airless apartments. Sidewalks filled with strollers, cafés overflowed with clients—in short, everyone in Triana was outdoors, engaged in vivacious conversation, eating tapas galore, sipping *fino* sherry or downing prodigious quantities of beer.

Today we still keep our travel headquarters on the other side of the river in the Moorish splendor of the Hotel Alfonso XIII, but our evenings are invariably spent in Triana, immersing ourselves in a life-style so unlike that at home, and eating tapas to our hearts' content. And what tapas they are, glistening fresh and prepared with love! Forget about restaurants (with a few exceptions) while you are in Sevilla, and live on tapas. There is no better way to be a part of Sevilla's life than through the tapas experience. Tapas bring all social classes together and while in other parts of Spain tapas are a pleasant diversion, here they are an integral part of daily activity.

Sevilla, you see, is a fiesta, an endless holiday in which one special occasion flows seamlessly into the next. Mundane matters like working and earning money are somehow squeezed into the schedule by the least painful means possible (this sometimes means losing a night's sleep). During Holy Week, for example, the city virtually closes down for seven days, its streets turned over to masses of strolling pedestrians and religious processions. It is spring, the weather is mild, and the glorious scents of orange blossoms and jasmine are in the air.

Then within two weeks "routine" comes to a halt once more for the world-famous Sevilla Fair (Feria de Sevilla). Then there is Carnaval; after that the paraded floats of Corpus Christi and the Epiphany; El Rocío pilgrimage follows (see box, p. 406), to which Sevillanos throng in horse-drawn carriages; there are special weeks of bullfights; the holiday of the city's patron saint, Virgen de los Reyes; the Cruces de Mayo neighborhood celebrations; and the Triana festivals of Little Corpus and the Velá de Santiago in July.

Almost all of these festivals are religious in nature, and here is where Sevillanos, in particular the men, are unique: They combine devoutness with irreverence and somehow capture the best of both. Their skill in conversation is unequaled, their sense of humor, innate and legendary. Either telling a joke or just describing an event, a Sevillano has the knack of producing in his audience tears of uncontrolled laughter. Coming from anyone but a Sevillano some of the jokes might be considered coarse, but the gentle and understated delivery breaks down even the most prudish.

Sevilla is the city of which the sixteenth century mystic Santa Teresa (who was known for her direct and down-to-earth approach to religion) supposedly remarked, "Anyone who can avoid committing sin in Sevilla would be very lucky indeed." This is the city where helpless women unfailingly succumbed to the charms of Don Juan, although he eventually paid for his escapades with his life (see box, p. 432).

Perhaps the best example of this odd juxtaposition of the sublime and worldly comes during the glorious spectacle of Sevilla's Holy Week, Semana Santa. It is a celebration that dates back to the sixteenth century when a Sevilla nobleman returned from Jerusalem and built his mansion, Casa de Pilatos (see "Seeing Sevilla"), at a distance from the cross on Sevilla's Oriente street that equaled the length of the Via Dolorosa in the Holy Land. This became the first processional route through the city, and the "stations" are marked by ceramic plaques.

Semana Santa lasts a week, as its name suggests, but Thursday night before Easter is the highlight. Procession after procession leaves its parish and follows the same path through Sevilla, winding through Sierpes street, passing the Plaza de San Francisco, continuing on Reyes Católicos street, entering the cathedral, then ending the following afternoon in the churches from which they originated. Each procession consists of one, two, or three floats (pasos—steps—as they are called) depicting a lifelike Christ and a serene Virgin. Forty, fifty, up to one hundred youths, many built like prize-fighters and hidden beneath the float's skirts, support the pasos on their shoulders, "dancing" them to the rhythm of the saeta drumbeats and trumpets. Even in an age when penance has lost its grasp, Sevillanos would not hear of wheel power as a substitute for human sweat.

The lifelike Christ figures are generally works of important sculptors from the seventeenth to nineteenth centuries (Montañés, Juan de Mesa, and Roldán are some well-known names), while the Virgins are doll-like figures richly dressed in gold and silver brocade. The floats sparkle with gold and silver and are bedecked with flowers and awash in candlelight. Preceding and following the *pasos* are the penitents from the *cofradías* (brotherhoods), often several hundred of them, dressed in long robes, their faces covered with conical masks through which only their eyes can be seen (traditionally, this was to protect the identity of one who had sinned).

Although all this may sound quite grim—far from it! The city is awake all night for the show, the streets a throbbing mass of people. There are minutes of awed silence when a float passes (you need not be religious to feel the awe), followed by cries of "¡Guapa!" (You're beautiful!) directed to the Virgin, bursts of applause and cheers, then a short critique ("Wasn't she especially lovely tonight! How well they 'danced' her!") and a discussion of the finer points of the performance, as if it were an affair of state. Sevillanos treat these religious figures—most especially the Cristo del Gran Poder, El Cachorro, La Macarena, and the Cristo del Silencio—as dear friends.

Between *pasos* there is a break for a little partying as everyone makes haste to the nearest tapas bar or buys freshly fried *churros* (see box, p. 35), at street stands. Thus fortified, all stand by to await the next *paso*. "Penitence is much more palatable," a Sevillano told us, "if accompanied by a few fresh shrimp and a glass of *fino*."

Yes, *alegría* is pervasive in Sevilla, and I can think of no greater privilege than to participate in the life of this exceptional city. Sevilla is captivating. "¡Viva Sevilla y Olé!"

SEEING SEVILLA

CATHEDRAL   Begun in the fourteenth century shortly after the expulsion of the Moors, on the site of the Great Mosque, and not finished for more than a century, the cathedral, in Gothic-Renaissance style, guards many great treasures and works of art. Its design is original, for the cathedral lacks a central apse, and instead has a wide hallway that leads to the Capilla Real (Royal Chapel).

The main altarpiece is the world's largest—65 feet high and a dazzling sheet of gold-leafed wood, carved in greatest detail and enclosed behind a splendid gold and wrought-iron Renaissance grille. The sixteenth century Plateresque Capilla Real holds the remains of Alfonso the Wise and Pedro the Cruel (see Index), among other royalty.

To one side of the cathedral are sculptures of four kings of Spain—larger-than-life alabaster figures in bronze robes, bearing the coffin of Columbus (there are those who dispute that his body is here, for it had previously been buried in Valladolid, in Santo Domingo, and in Havana, Cuba), a belated tribute to the great navigator who died in disgrace. See the series of Zurbarán paintings on the life of Saint Peter in the Capilla de San Pedro. See also in the sacristy works by Murillo, Goya, and the locally renowned seventeenth century sculptor Martínez Montañés (responsible for some of the most beautiful *pasos* of Holy Week), and the grand silver monstrance by Juan de Arfe.

The **PATIO DE LOS NARANJOS,** courtyard of the original mosque, is filled with orange trees and singing birds and conducive to quiet contemplation.

LA GIRALDA   Adjoining the cathedral, the Moorish delicacy of this brick minaret, which might also have served as an astronomical observatory, is in sharp contrast to the massive stone bulk of the cathedral. In the sixteenth century it was topped by La Giradilla, a bronze statue that acts as a weather vane (thus the tower's name: *girar* means to turn). Inside is a winding ramp, wide enough to accommodate the horsemen who rode up to announce prayer hour (you can go up—it's a steep climb, but the view of Sevilla is special).

ALCÁZAR   (Reales Alcázares)   The fortress-like stone wall seen from the street gives no hint of the sumptuous interior. The Alcázar was first an Arab palace, then rebuilt by the Christians, who employed Arab craftsmen to re-create the lacy, delicate walls and arches, the *artesonado* ceilings and colorful tiling of the Moors. The palace is enormous and complex, with typical Arab intricacies of winding garden paths, delightful interior patios, and charming suites of private rooms. The facade, as seen from the Montería patio, is a masterpiece of Mudéjar art. The most artistically exciting part of the Alcázar complex is the palace of Pedro El Cruel, the king who brought Sevilla back to Christian rule. Particularly sumptuous are the **PATIO DE LAS DON-CELLAS** and the **SALÓN DE EMBAJADORES** with their minute stucco work (some of it still showing the original polychrome) and ceramic tile of geometric design.

Queen Isabel, who also resided at the Alcázar, met here with Columbus and heard his pleas for aid. She later received him when he returned from his second visit to the New World. The voyages of Magellan and Balboa were both organized here, and in the so-called Admiral's Room a highly unusual painting shows the Virgin of Sailors protecting under her robes the Indians, the Spanish discoverers, their boats, and local Sevilla officials. The Alcázar saw as well the wedding of Emperor Charles V to Isabel of Portugal.

I am particularly taken with the **PATIO DE LAS MUÑECAS**—the Doll Patio, so called because of its diminutive size and the tiny carvings of two faces that can be seen embedded in the plaster. The room is warm and cozy, rising delicately in stucco wedding-cake tiers to a skylight over the central sunken fountain. Queen Isabel's bedroom adjoins this courtyard, and her chapel, of yellow, blue, and green tiles, is anything but sober.

Many modifications were made to the Alcázar over the centuries by subsequent monarchs, but the patios of the Doncellas and the Muñecas, the Salón de Embajadores, and the quarters of Queen Isabel all remain incomparable works of Mudéjar art.

MUSEO DE BELLAS ARTES   Set in a sixteenth century monastery (Don Juan's creator, Tirso de Molina, was a friar here), this is one of Spain's most notable museums, with paintings by Velázquez, many works of Zurbarán, and dozens of Murillo canvases.

MUSEO ARQUEOLÓGICO   Works from the nearby Roman city of Itálica and the ancient Carambolo gold jewelry collection from the sixth or seventh century B.C., perhaps related to the lost civilization of Tartessus (see Index).

FÁBRICA DE TABACOS   Of *Carmen* fame and once employing thousands of women, this immense eighteenth century factory, second in size in Spain only to El Escorial, processed tobacco brought back from the New World. It is today part of Sevilla's university.

PARQUE DE MARÍA LUISA   A thickly shaded park designed in the nineteenth century by Forestier. Within the grounds are a pavilion and the Plaza de España, both left from the 1929 Iberoamerican Fair. An unusual semicircle of colorfully tiled benches in the plaza shows detailed scenes from the history of each of Spain's provinces.

BARRIO DE SANTA CRUZ   Once the ancient Arab, then the Jewish quarter of Sevilla, of narrow and twisting cobbled streets and elegant patios—the only hint that here are many of the town houses of Andalucía's rich and famous. Although much changed from those early times, El Barrio de Santa Cruz retains an uncommon flavor and vitality. It is a place to walk, by day and by night—and to sit outside for tapas in the Plaza de los Venerables.

◆ Under the plaza of the **CRUZ DE LA CERRAJERÍA,** the ashes of painter Murillo are interred (Murillo lived and died in Santa Cruz).

PLAZA DE TOROS   The legendary eighteenth century bullring, "Alma Mater of the Bullfight," in the words of nineteenth century British traveler Richard Ford. Because of the fervor, knowledge, and discernment of Sevilla fans, this is one of the key places to see a bullfight in Spain.

BARRIO DE TRIANA   Popular quarter on the other side of the river, with its own marked personality (see text).

TORRE DEL ORO   Another Sevilla landmark, on the banks of the Guadalquivir, called the "Golden Tower"—some say, because in Moorish times it was covered with gold tiles. More likely it was faced with ceramic tiles, which in the bright Sevilla sunshine sparkled like gold. An identical twelve-sided tower once stood across the river, attached to the Torre de Oro by a massive chain, which closed off the city from sea invaders.

CASA DE PILATOS   A magnificent Renaissance palace of the sixteenth century, combining Plateresque and Moorish styles and profuse with ceramic tile, which most strikingly covers every inch of a four-flight stairway.

ARCHIVO GENERAL DE INDIAS   Here resides most of the prodigious documentation concerning Spain's New World colonies. Open mainly to scholars, it has an exhibit for the public that is insultingly limited. But the building is beautiful, designed by Juan de Herrera, sixteenth century architect of El Escorial, and there are some interesting documents and firsthand drawings related to the new lands on display.

STAYING IN SEVILLA

HOTEL ALFONSO XIII   San Fernando 2   tel. (95) 422 28 50 (very expensive; pool)   In the heart of Sevilla, it is my unqualified favorite. Elegantly done in Moorish style with decorative blue ceramic tiling everywhere and a marble central patio. Despite its downtown location, it has a swimming pool in a tranquil garden setting—a perfect place to spend the siesta hours when the city closes down (you can have a light lunch at the pool; I'm fond of their club sandwich and homemade potato chips). The hotel's bar in the evening attracts the *Who's Who* of Sevilla.

HOTEL MURILLO   Lope de Rueda 9   tel. (95) 421 60 95   This hotel is cherished for its location in the evocative Barrio de Santa Cruz. It's charming, but a bit inconvenient, since cars are forbidden in this area. Ask the hotel to send a cart for luggage. (Moderate.)

DONA MARÍA   Don Remondo 19   tel. (95) 422 49 90   Simple, well cared for, and ideally situated in front of the Giralda. (Expensive; rooftop pool.)

THE JOYS OF TAPAS HOPPING IN SEVILLA

Restaurants are not always up to par in Sevilla, although there has been some recent activity to correct this situation. For elegant dining with a creative touch (and a surprisingly extensive game menu in season), try **EGAÑA-ORIZA**   San Fernando 41   tel. (95) 422 72 54, set in an airy mansion overlooking Murillo park. (Expensive.)

I will forgo tapas hopping in Sevilla for **LA DORADA**   Virgen de Aguas Santas 6   tel. (95) 445 51 00, in Triana. The seafood is superb: Begin with boiled shrimp and prawns and a mixed fry of tiny fish and baby squid. Proceed to fish baked in salt, grilled flounder, or monkfish. (Moderate–expensive.)

SEVILLA-STYLE MARINATED GREEN OLIVES

Drain, rinse, and lightly crush ½ pound large green unpitted olives and place in a jar with ½ teaspoon each of thyme, rosemary, and oregano (or, preferably, 1 tablespoon each of fresh herbs), ½ teaspoon of crushed cumin and of fennel seeds. Add 2 bay leaves, 4 cloves garlic, lightly crushed, and 4 tablespoons vinegar. Cover with water and marinate at room temperature for several days. They will keep, refrigerated, for months.

TRIANA

BAR CASA RUPERTO   Santa Cecilia 2   See Ruperto and his cheerful nephew, José, for outstanding tapas in simple surroundings—marinated grilled quail, *cabrillas* (snails), fried almonds, *Pringá* (a grilled sandwich of meats and sausage), and *Pincho Moruno* (marinated miniature kabobs). This is a required stop for me in Sevilla.

SOL Y SOMBRA   Castilla 151   A delightful bullfight ambiance, featuring cured ham, *Puntillitas* (beef tenderloin in garlic sauce), and *Gambas al Ajillo* (garlic shrimp).

KIOSCO LAS FLORES   Calle Betis 1   Set by the river, most tables are outdoors. Tiny garlicky clams called *coquinas*, *Cazón en Adobo* (marinated fried shark), and *gambas fritas* (fried shrimp) stand out.

LA ALBARIZA   Calle Betis 6   With wine kegs as tables, this looks like an Andalusian bodega, with whitewashed arches and more wine barrels lining the walls. *Serrano* ham, plump green Sevilla olives, and cheese.

LOS CHORRITOS   Calle Betis   Just a stand set up by the river, but famous for its grilled sardines.

LA DORADA   Virgen de Aguas Santas 6   The previously mentioned restaurant of the same name also has a lively tapas bar, serving the same excellent seafood.

RÍO GRANDE   Calle Betis s/n   On a terrace overlooking the Guadalquivir River; clams *a la marinera*, shellfish salad.

CENTRAL SEVILLA

CASA ROMÁN   Plaza de los Venerables 1   In the heart of the Barrio de Santa Cruz, for cured ham, cured pork loin, and *chorizo*.

HOSTERÍA DEL LAUREL   Plaza de los Venerables 5   Next to Casa Román, the Hostería del Laurel, of Don Juan fame (see box, p. 432), has the same cured-meat specialties as Casa Román and a restaurant as well.

BAR MODESTO   Cano y Cueto 5   Near the Plaza de Santa Cruz; the tapas are excellent and varied. Try *Tío Diego*—a stir-fried dish of shrimp, mushrooms, and cured ham—and *coquinas* (sautéed clams).

ENRIQUE BECERRA   Gamazo 2   Try any of the specialties of the day; they are always first rate. A popular restaurant as well.

FIGÓN DEL CABILDO   Plaza Cabildo s/n   Marinated trout and assorted other tapas (also a restaurant).

SHOPPING

ARTESPAÑA   Plaza de la Concordia 2   One of the network of Spanish handicraft centers sponsored by the government.

LOEWE   Plaza Nueva 27   For exquisite leather goods.

CALLE SIERPES   A pedestrian shopping street (referred to by nineteenth century writer Richard Ford as the "Bond Street of Seville"), shaded from the hot sun by awnings stretched from one house across to the next. There are many stores, especially **SEVILLARTE** (#66) and **MARTIAN** (#74) for hand-painted local ceramics; an old-fashioned hat store, **MAQUEDANO** (#44), for Andalusian and other kinds of hats; and **OCHOA** (#45), a great pastry shop.

EL CORTE INGLÉS   Plaza Duque de la Victoria   The city's bustling department store.

CONVENT SWEETS   The age-old custom of making convent sweets (see box, p. 398) remains strong in Sevilla. At the **CONVENTO DE SAN LEANDRO** in the Plaza de San Ildefonso (commonly called Pila del Pato), the celebrated specialty of the cloistered nuns is *yemas*—egg yolk candies—delivered to you from a brass studded eighteenth century revolving shelf. Leftover egg whites go the **CONVENTO DE SANTA INÉS**   Dona María Coronel 5, where they are turned into light-as-air *bollitos* and other simple pastries (ask for a *surtido*, or sampler box). And at the **CONVENTO DE SANTA PAULA**   Santa Paula 11, the nuns gift-package their handiwork and offer a variety of jams, bitter-orange marmalade (from famous Seville oranges), quince paste, and delectable *Tocino de Cielo* that you'll have to eat right away or refrigerate.

NIGHTLIFE

I do not often care for professional flamenco shows (they are generally geared to tourists and much too commercial), but if you would like to see one, Sevilla is one of your best bets.

EL TABLAO DE CURRO VÉLEZ   Rodo 7   for authentic flamenco song and dance.

LOS GALLOS   Plaza de Santa Cruz 11   tel. (95) 421 69 81   An intimate setting in the old quarter, Barrio de Santa Cruz.

EL PATIO SEVILLANO   Paseo Cristóbal Colón, 11 (next to the bullring) tel. (95) 421 41 20   Decorated in the style of an Andalusian patio.

EL ARENAL   Rodó 7   tel. (95) 421 64 92   In a seventeenth century building with a typically Andalusian look.

♦ Take extra care with your belongings in Sevilla, especially in the downtown area frequented by tourists.

♦ A buggy ride is a wonderful way to get a feel of the city, day or night. Price is negotiable.

FIESTAS

HOLY WEEK   The key days to be in Sevilla are Thursday and Friday before Easter. Get yourself a schedule of events in Thursday's *Correo de Andalucía* newspaper, rent a seat along the processional route, and keep it for all of Thursday night. A float will pass about every hour. See especially El Cristo del Silencio, La Macarena, and El Cristo del Gran Poder. There will be little time left over for sleep.

On Friday, go first to see the return of the Macarena to her church at about 1:30 p.m. Then concentrate on Triana, where the crowds will be fewer: Watch the emergence of El Cachorro at 4:00 p.m. and hear the *saetas* sung in its honor. Between midnight and 1:00 a.m. catch Nuestra Senora de la O when it passes narrow Pureza street in front of the Esperanza church. It pauses here to pay homage to that church's Virgin. El Cachorro returns over the San Telmo bridge at about 2:00 a.m.

FERIA DE SEVILLA (SEVILLA FAIR) Two weeks after Easter, originally a fair of livestock and the like, today it is an internationally known festival during which the aristocracy is on parade riding fine horses and in elegant Andalusian dress. They hold court at their private tents or *casetas* (others are open to the public), and there is flamenco dancing, bullfights, nonstop eating and drinking. Although centered on the fair grounds, the fiesta spills over into all of Sevilla, and the city is transformed, taking on added *alegría*. Crowds are everywhere, and there are always spontaneous expressions of joy. The fiesta goes on for a full week.

CORPUS CHRISTI Nine weeks after Easter Sunday. The spectacular silver monstrance from the cathedral passes through Sevilla's streets along with other floats. In the cathedral, Los Seises (six costumed young boys) dance to the sound of castanets.

VELÁ DE SANTIAGO In honor of Spain's patron saint, Santiago, on July 25. Booths and tents are set up in Triana along the Guadalquivir, and it is an occasion for dance, drink, song, and a generally good time.

THE ETERNAL FASCINATION OF DON JUAN

It does not surprise me in the least that the character of Don Juan is a Spanish creation, that the setting is the streets and palaces of Sevilla, and that the seventeenth century author, Tirso de Molina, was a priest (who resided in the monastery that is today the Museo de Bellas Artes). Cold and calculating—hardly a romantic figure at all—Don Juan served as an example of the perils of the carnal world.

Don Juan and his archrival, Don Luis, have made a bet to see who can seduce more women in the space of one year. One year to the day later, they meet at an inn (in the play's nineteenth century version it is the Hostería del Laurel in the Barrio de Santa Cruz) in the midst of carnival festivities. The city is filled with masked and costumed revelers, adding intrigue to this much-awaited reunion. Don Juan, naturally, is the victor, with seventy-two conquests "from a royal princess / to the daughter of a fisherman / oh! my love has traveled / up and down the social scale."

Don Juan declares that not only will he now seduce a nun, but Don Luis's bride-to-be as well. He boasts that six days will suffice: "one day to make them fall in love / one day to seduce them / one day to abandon them / two days to substitute them / and one hour to forget them."

When Don Juan pursues a nun, the beautiful Doña Inés, he incurs the wrath of God and is condemned to hell—in the original Tirso de Molina script, that is. In a nineteenth century play by José Zorrilla, Don Juan falls in love with Doña Inés, is absolved of his sins and sent to heaven. It was this romanticized version that captured the public imagination, and to this day the play is performed in Madrid every year on November 1—All Souls' Day.

$\mathcal{V}$ISITING THE PROVINCE OF SEVILLA

ITÁLICA   Just outside San Isidoro del Campo, the remains of an important Roman city from the third century B.C., named to commemorate Italy. An amphitheater of elliptical shape and grand proportions—the third largest in the world—has been uncovered, as well as stretches of city streets. Digging continues (see Sevilla's Museo Arqueológico for exhibits of Itálica's sculptures and mosaics). Music and dance festivals are held here in summer.

SAN ISIDORO DEL CAMPO   (Santiponce) Fifteenth century monastery with an outstanding altar by Montañés and a lovely Mudéjar cloister.

CASTILLEJA DE LA CUESTA   An old Roman town, where Hernán Cortés lived until his death in a Mudéjar-style palace, still here in the center of town.

LAS MARISMAS   A unique landscape of marshlands outside Sevilla, filled with birds in spring. We stop for tapas at any of the bars in the town of **CORIA DEL RÍO,** then board the primitive car ferry across the calm waters of the Guadalquivir and continue on to Jerez or Cádiz.
♦ Stick to the principal roadways, or you could get hopelessly lost, as we have, in a maze of dead ends and small islands. A few remaining dromedaries are chance sightings—difficult to see unless you stray onto less traveled roads.

EL PALMAR DE TROYA   On the Utrera–Jerez de la Frontera road, fourteen kilometers from Utrera, amid sunflower fields, appears a grandiose cathedral of ten towers and an enormous dome. It is the domain of a self-styled pope, Papa Clemente, who is fond of excommunicating anyone he doesn't like and canonizing those he admires. From the enormity of this project, I assume he has many ardent followers.

MARCHENA   A walled town of noble homes. Just before Marchena, direction Écija, is **LOS FAROLES** for excellent tapas well presented in almost meal-size servings. There is also an inviting dining room. (Inexpensive.)

CARMONA   An immaculately kept walled town thirty-three kilometers from Sevilla, entered, then exited on the other side, through beautiful multiarched Moorish gateways. Noble homes and an exceptional fountain, surrounded by stone lions, that is immortalized in flamenco song ("Carmona has a fountain / with fourteen or fifteen spouts"—my count is fifteen). This was a most important city of Moorish Spain.
The **PARADOR ALCÁZAR DEL REY DON PEDRO**   Alcázar s/n tel. (95) 414 10 10, is built on the grounds of a Moorish fortress that was later the palace of Pedro el Cruel and residence of the Catholic Kings during the Reconquest of Granada. It is done in Mudéjar style and is topnotch. The views are expansive, the pool inviting. A wonderful place to spend a night, but by no means a substitute for staying in Sevilla. (Moderate–expensive; pool.)

A nearby **ROMAN NECROPOLIS** contains some 800 tombs—200 have been excavated—and cremated remains rest in urns in wall niches. Some of the mausoleums are more elaborate than others—one is a complete villa; another had dining rooms and kitchen facilities for banquets.

ÉCIJA   Called the "City of the Towers" because of its eleven ceramic-tiled Moorish belfries that rise above the town. The curved Peñaflor palace on the main street has a continuous wrought-iron balcony across its facade and trompe l'oeil paintings. Écija is unflatteringly known as the Frying Pan of Andalucía, for it usually records the most elevated temperatures in Spain— so hot that they say you can fry an egg on the pavement. Spaniards are generally astonished that anyone would, of their own free will, come here in summer. We have done so many times.

♦ In any local bar or cafeteria, try *bolletes*—bread somewhat like an English muffin, toasted and spread with butter or marmalade or drizzled with olive oil.

OSUNA   First Iberian, then an important Roman town (there are remains of an amphitheater and necropolis), Osuna today has lovely noble homes and palaces. In the Renaissance Colegiata church we were charmed by the two-tiered patio and the chapel of the Dukes of Osuna, where the ancestors of the present duke are buried.

MESÓN DEL DUQUE   Plaza de la Duquesa 2   tel. (95) 481 13 01 has changed hands, but is still fine for tapas and simple foods, and an obligatory cold drink to revive the wilted traveler. (Inexpensive.)

THE PROVINCE OF MÁLAGA

MÁLAGA (*mah*-lah-gah) divides into two very distinct zones of interest. The wonderful interior mountain ranges, like the Serranía de Ronda, with lovely white villages and high peaks, is a peaceful, timeless world. But the mountains are never far from the province's 150 kilometers of coast and often rise abruptly from the shore. One of Spain's most beautiful stretches of coastal road, in fact, winds at cliff's edge from Nerja to Almuñécar near the rugged Mediterranean shore and plunges through tunnels hollowed from the mountains.

Because of its year-round mild dry climate (although in winter an occasional fierce Mediterranean storm does brew), Málaga is a popular vacation area in summer, of course, but also during off-season. Most of the coast is lined with private homes and apartments, mass market high-rise hotels, and deluxe hotels nestled in garden settings by the sea. For good reason Málaga's coast became universally known as the Costa del Sol, the Sun Coast, and although it is much too commercial and overdeveloped for my taste, it continues to attract visitors from all over the globe—those on package tours as well as many of the world's wealthiest people.

Málaga's history is one of invasion and colonization by foreign powers. The Phoenicians came first, giving the region the name Malaka, then the Greeks, Carthaginians, Romans, and Arabs, who made Málaga's harbor an important port of their Al Andalus empire. Málaga's Arab past is present in the castles and the fortresses along the coast that have withstood the centuries, and in the dozens of watchtowers that rise at regular intervals over the Mediterranean. Each was placed in sight of the next to signal—with smoke by day, fire by night—impending danger or invasion from the sea by expelled Moors or pirates (the expression "¡Hay moros en la costa!"—Moors on the coast!—has come to mean "Someone's watching"). In the interior are remains of a far more ancient past; the dolmens of Antequera take us back to the beginnings of civilization. And in the city of Málaga, Roman remains (such as the theater) are reminders of the importance of Málaga to the ancient Romans.

Mediterranean seafood, of course, prevails in Málaga. I am particularly fond of plump, sweet Málaga shrimp, simply boiled in their shells, and fresh sardines that are often grilled on spits over beach fires. But I am also partial to the delectable fish fry, *Fritura Malagueña*, found all along this coast, and most especially I love two of its components: white anchovies (*boquerones*) and tiny *chanquetes*, fish so small that hundreds enter into a single portion. They are light and crisp and as addictive as potato chips. For a few years they had disappeared because of overfishing, but they have happily made a comeback and can now be found in bars and restaurants all along the Málaga coast.

A meal centering on *Fritura Malagueña* and beginning with Málaga's unique white gazpacho, *Ajo Blanco de Málaga*, made with almonds and garnished with grapes (see box, p. 438), will give you two of the dishes most typical of Málaga and most perfectly suited to this dry southern climate. The province also lends its name to a dense, syrupy-sweet dessert wine, *vino de Málaga*, that is made from grapes that have soaked up the intense Málaga sunshine. The same grapes become plump Málaga raisins.

The province also gives its name to the distinctive flamenco songs of melancholy and tragic lament called Malagueñas. They sing of love, death, nostalgia, jealousy, and they "wound like a dagger and burn like fire" (Tomás Andrade de Silva).

THE CITY OF MÁLAGA

Málaga was founded by the Phoenicians, formed part of the Roman Empire, and gained considerable importance under the Moors. After it was reconquered by the Catholic Kings, the city fared poorly until the eighteenth century, when it became an important seaport for the American colonies. Today its life revolves around its harbor and around tourism; Málaga is one of three major international gateways to Spain (Madrid and Barcelona are the others).

I have always liked Málaga, even though for many visitors to Spain it is little more than a place to arrive or to catch a flight out of the country. My reasons are partly sentimental; my first visit to the city was when I was still a college student. I was there to greet Luis, my husband-to-be, who was dressed in Spanish army khakis and heavy boots. I hadn't seen him in a year, and although he was still studying medicine, he had been shipped to Spanish North Africa to serve in the Spanish army. He was in Málaga on leave. And it was in Málaga that years later we befriended Jesús, a young shoeshine boy with a cute face and lots of street savvy, who beguiled us with his innocence and his naïve questions ("Is the United States about the size of Málaga?" "How far away is next year?"). He's grown now, and we hope he has gone on to better things. Although we haven't seen him in a long time, he is, nevertheless, still very much a part of Málaga for us.

And yet despite such bittersweet thoughts, Málaga is far from low-key or sad; it is one of Spain's liveliest cities. I always enjoy spending a night or two here.

You must make your way through New Málaga's maze of typical high-rise apartments to get to the old port city at waterfront, which is the hub of Málaga. Málaga depends on the sea but it has a clean, crisp waterfront with none of the ugliness and grime of bigger ports. The Mediterranean is big and blue here; the old fishermen's quarters still retain their quaintness, undiminished by the seafood restaurants and tapas bars that have sprouted everywhere; and the wide seaside promenade, Paseo del Parque, lushly shaded by palms and jacarandas (tropical trees brought from America), is always cool, even in the crushing heat of August. It is, I think, Spain's most beautiful promenade, inviting huge crowds of strollers and cavorting kids. Everyone munches on coconut wedges and candied almonds (*almendras garrapiñadas*) and carries fragrant stems of jasmine, all sold by a multitude of street vendors. This is also where horse-drawn carriages gather to take you on pleasant jaunts around the old city.

You will want to visit the Arab fortress, La Alcazaba, on your first visit, and probably also the cathedral, but from then on Málaga is a place to thrive on tapas, to savor the stunning views from the parador in the heights of Gibralfaro, and to walk the promenade in early evening. A short ride will take you to the locally popular Pedregalejo beach, where a village of whitewashed houses hugs the water's edge. Sardines grill outdoors, and seafood restaurants provide contented patrons with all the best of Málaga's waters.

We often end our trips to Spain in Málaga, boarding a flight from the Málaga International Airport to New York, and our last impression of Spain is the unforgettable view from our terrace at the parador of the glittering lights of the city and the port, and the soundless entry and departure of ferries and cruise ships. Before we have even left, we are already anticipating our next visit.

SEEING MÁLAGA

LA ALCAZABA   Constructed in the eleventh century, this was the palace and fortress of the Moorish kings, which commanded the harbor. Around it the Arab quarters consisted of the mosque (converted into the cathedral) and a bustling *zoco* (market), which in turn became the Plaza Mayor. La Alcazaba has the tranquil touches the Moors were so fond of—secluded gardens and patios with channeled water, fountains, and profusely flowering plants. Within the confines of La Alcazaba are the remains of the Roman theater, only partially excavated, and an archaeological museum displaying prehistoric and Roman remains and interesting examples of antique ceramic and glass, much of it in Moorish style.

CATHEDRAL   Building began early in the sixteenth century on the site of the ancient mosque by order of the Catholic Kings after Málaga was seized from the Moors in 1487. It is a medley of styles, and its present facade is eighteenth century. One tower is incomplete, thus the cathedral's popular nickname "One-Handed." Note particularly the beautiful choir stalls.

MUSEO DE BELLAS ARTES   Housed in an old Arab palace, the museum has works by Morales "The Divine," Ribera, Zurbarán, and Murillo. It also has a Picasso section (Picasso was born in Málaga at Plaza de la Merced 15).

GIBRALFARO   This mountain towers over the city and overlooks the harbor, and it was a key Moorish stronghold (the ruins of the fourteenth century fortress are still here).
All rooms at the **PARADOR DE GIBRALFARO**   Gibralfaro   tel. (952) 22 19 02 have terraces commanding dazzling views of the harbor, particularly at night. The parador has a very good restaurant, also with a terrace and great views (white gazpacho and Málaga fish fry are two specialties). There are only twelve rooms, and reservations are necessary well in advance. (Moderate–expensive; pool.)
◆ Walk down to the city on the beautiful Puerta Oscura road (but consider a cab for the return uphill).

STAYING IN MÁLAGA

PARADOR DE GIBRALFARO   See above.

MÁLAGA PALACIO   Cortina del Muelle 1   tel. (952) 21 51 85   not a top-notch hotel (although recent renovations have brought improvements), but ideally located overlooking the port. Rooms in the -09 line, eighth floor and up, have great views. (Moderate–expensive; rooftop pool.)

EATING IN MÁLAGA

I have never been thrilled with any of Málaga's restaurants—even though **ANTONIO MARTÍN**   Paseo Marítimo s/n   tel. (952) 22 21 13, is a classic

ℳÁLAGA'S UNIQUE WHITE GAZPACHO, AJO BLANCO DE MÁLAGA

Place in a food processor 4 ounces blanched almonds, 2 peeled garlic cloves, and 1½ teaspoons salt. Beat until the almonds are very finely ground. Soak in cold water 4 slices day-old bread, crusts removed. Squeeze to extract most of the moisture.

With the motor running, gradually add the bread to the almond mixture. Slowly add 6 tablespoons olive oil in a thin stream, then pour in 3 tablespoons vinegar, scraping the bowl occasionally. Beat in 1 cup cold water. Transfer to a bowl, and stir in 3 more cups water. Add more salt and vinegar if desired. Strain, pressing with the back of a wooden spoon to extract as much liquid as possible. Chill. Serve very cold with a garnish of peeled seedless grapes. Serves 6.

and serves good food (moderate)—and I always find tapas bars much more satisfying; their crowded outdoor tables envelop you in the lively atmosphere of Málaga as no restaurant can.

I like to begin in the fishermen's quarters around La Alameda for a sip or two of Málaga wine at the nineteenth century **ANTIGUA CASA GUARDIA** (Alameda 18) and some tapas on any of the terraces of Calle Trinidad Grund. Then I cross La Alameda to the pedestrian-only streets around Marqués de Larios and follow the crowds to the tumultuous **BOQUERÓN DE PLATA**—the Silver Anchovy (Marín García 11)—where everyone drinks mugs of beer accompanied by boiled shrimp that are consumed by patrons with ravenous speed. An *Ensaladilla Rusa* (vegetable and potato salad) and fried white anchovies (*boquerones*), a specialty of the bar, round out this first part of the tapas meal before we continue to a typical Málaga tavern, **BAR LO GÜENO,** which is next door. Thin-sliced cured ham, *Habas con Jamón* (fresh fava beans with ham), *callos* (tripe), *Pincho Moruno* (miniature kabobs), quail, and *Flamenquín* (rolled pork and ham dipped in bechamel and fried) are among my favorites.

Let the crowds direct you to dessert—at the **HELADERÍA CASA MIRA,** Marqués de Larios 5—for outstanding ice cream cones. Any of the spacious outdoor cafés on the Alameda will give you good coffee and good views of the lively passing scene.

◆ In **EL PALO,** the old fishermen's quarters just east of Málaga, **EL TINTERO** Playa del Chanquete tel. (952) 29 00 01, has an ample terrace and grills at large barbecues. When the fish is ready, it is announced, and diners raise their hands to place orders. A plate count determines your bill. (Inexpensive–moderate.)

◆ At Pedregalejo beach (see text), five minutes outside Málaga (take the road to Almería, turning to the right when you see the Cínema Lope de Vega on your left), **BAR MORATA** Copo 21 tel. (952) 29 26 45, at water's edge, serves all kinds of fine seafood. I am partial to their boiled Málaga shrimp, sardines grilled on an open beach fire, *coquinas* (tiny sautéed clams), and fried squid.

FOOD SHOPPING

ULTRAMARINOS LA FAMA   Bolsa 14, carries a good selection of cheese, wine (especially Málaga wine), Málaga raisins, and cured meats.

◆ Málaga is known for a variety of convent sweets—candies of coconut and of quince, cookies, and cupcakes. They can be purchased directly from the nuns at: **CONVENTO DE LAS CLARISAS**   Zumaya 1; **MONASTERIO DE LA ASUNCIÓN**   Plaza Java 25, Puerto de la Torre; and **ABADÍA DE SANTA ANA**   Cister 11.

FIESTAS

HOLY WEEK   The processions are especially beautiful in Málaga, with statues by noteworthy artists carried on floats and the Virgins elaborately dressed.

THE COSTA DEL SOL

Although the name Costa del Sol officially refers to the entire southern coast, from Tarifa in the west to Cabo de Gata in Almería, what most people think of as the Costa del Sol belongs to the coast of Málaga, and it divides into two distinct zones. To the west of the city are the famous enclaves for foreign visitors and retirees, while to the east the crowd tends to be more local, the scenery more beautiful, and the coastline more rugged.

I have never warmed to Spain's sunny international playground, despite its extensive coastline, fine weather, and the magic its name evokes all over the world. Just about every tour to Spain stops here for a few days; it is a center for cheap tourism and at the same time attracts glitzy jet-setters, publicity seekers, and Arab sheiks (who have even built a mosque here). It's the Marbella area that is particularly chic, and you see instantly that it is well tended and less chaotic. Throughout the summer Spain's press—both tabloids and high-brow publications—tells you more than you ever wanted to know about reigning and deposed royalty, and other assorted rich and famous trendmakers, who stay in sprawling homes enveloped in dense greenery. You are not likely to see much of them; their world is very private and completely apart from what most tourists will experience.

Yet for me Costa del Sol represents all that Spain is not. It is too busy, too crowded, too overbuilt. Even its beaches of pebbly gray sand are not the best. This coast has lost its character, becoming a veritable high-rise jungle. Who would know that these tourist towns were once peaceful fishing villages with histories going back millenniums? You might just as well be in Miami Beach.

Of course, when I first visited the Costa del Sol twenty-five years ago, it was just barely awakening to the twentieth century. Torremolinos was in the throes of hotel and apartment construction, but villagers still tried to carry on their traditional ways. One of my most vivid recollections is of a

burro sauntering into my hotel bungalow room to nibble on a box of choco-
lates.

On the Costa del Sol, burros are pretty much a thing of the past.
Hotels, snack bars, pizzerias, discotheques, and boutiques are the norm. But
if you are looking for relaxation at a fine resort hotel with swimming pool,
tennis courts, and golf, there are many five-star hotels and many highly
regarded restaurants as well. I do hope, however, that you will take time to
travel just a few miles north from the coast into the mountains to see a different world—of nature, wildlife, and quiet beauty.

VISITING THE COSTA DEL SOL
AND THE NEARBY HILLS

MARBELLA—despite being a wealthy international enclave, the town's
Old Quarter, paved in red, has been charmingly preserved, although most of
the original houses are now occupied by luxury boutiques and restaurants.

There are several ultra-deluxe hotels, each enclosed in beautiful garden settings with pools, tennis, shops, and elegant restaurants, all on or near
the water: **LOS MONTEROS**   Carretera de Cádiz, km 187   tel. (952) 77 17 00
(Deluxe; pool; with a very fashionable restaurant nearby); **MELIÁ DON
PEPE**   Finca Las Merinas s/n, tel. (952) 77 03 00 (very expensive; pool), set in
acres of gardens; and **PUENTE ROMANO**   Carretera de Cádiz, km 176   tel.
(952) 77 01 00 (Deluxe; pool), designed in typical Andalusian style. **MAR-
BELLA CLUB**   Carretera de Cádiz, km 178   tel. (952) 77 13 00 (Deluxe), is
conceived in a more informal bungalow style and has a lively jet-set restaurant; and **RINCÓN ANDALUZ**   Carretera de Cádiz, km 173   tel. (952) 81 15
17 (expensive; pool), imitates an Andalusian village. **DON CARLOS**
Carretera de Cádiz, km 192   tel. (952) 83 11 40 (Very expensive, pool), is set
among pines and is one of Marbella's most fashionable hotels.

Fine restaurants abound, many dedicated to nouvelle and imaginative
cooking: **LA HACIENDA**   Carretera de Cádiz, km 193   tel. (952) 83 11 16
(very expensive), has long been considered among the best in Spain; **LA
MERIDIANA**   Camino de la Cruz s/n   tel. (952) 77 61 90 (very expensive), in
a garden setting, has fine food and beautiful views; the elegant **LA FONDA**
Santo Cristo 9   tel. (952) 77 25 12 (very expensive), owned by Horcher in
Madrid, is in a nineteenth century mansion with lovely patios and serves
creative cooking; **LA DORADA**   Carretera de Cádiz, km 176   tel. (952) 82 10
34 (moderate–expensive), a branch of the Sevilla restaurant (p. 429), serves
exquisite fried and grilled seafood; **GRAN MARISQUERÍA SANTIAGO**, is
a popular seafood restaurant on the Paseo Marítimo, tel. (952) 77 00 78 (moderate–expensive);

♦ There are tapas bars, pubs, discos and nightclubs everywhere.

♦ I like to view Marbella from afar, in the tranquil mountain village of
OJÉN, in the midst of a wildlife preserve, where the protected long-horned
wild Spanish goat, *Capra Hispanica*, roams in large numbers (but you'll have
to get up pretty early to see one); see box, p. 441. It is a wonderful retreat
from civilization. If you go up to the *mirador*—walking through the thick

woods, marveling at the utter silence—the Costa del Sol appears as if in a dream through a wedge in the pyramid-shaped mountains. The view is fascinating, in ever-changing light and cloud formations.

PARADOR DE JUANAR Sierra Blanca s/n tel. (952) 88 10 00, once a palace used by Alfonso XIII for hunting, is a short distance from town, in absolutely peaceful surroundings. (Moderate; pool.)

♦ Ojén is known all over Spain for an anisette-flavored liqueur by the same name.

FUENGIROLA—a busy summer resort with a very attractive beachside promenade and many outdoor cafés serving excellent seafood tapas. The small-scale fishermen's quarters give an idea of what this village was before the skyscrapers went up.

TORREMOLINOS The first Costa del Sol town to explode with international notoriety, it is nevertheless the poor cousin of Marbella, attracting an abundance of international tourists but lacking Marbella's glamour and fragrance of Big Money. There is a honky-tonk business district, and nondescript high-rises crowd the beachfront.

Around **LA CARIHUELA BEACH** you will find lively and simple seafood restaurants and tapas bars, and all have good fish, especially **EL ROQUEO** Carmen 35 tel. (952) 38 39 46.

MIJAS, in the mountains just north of Torremolinos, is beautifully situated. Although it retains something of its small-town atmosphere, and certainly still has its fans, a preponderance of trinket shops and "burro taxis" give the town a contrived air.

BYBLOS ANDALUZ Mijas Golf tel. (952) 47 30 50 (deluxe; indoor and outdoor pools), is a super-luxurious hotel–health spa near Mijas featuring "healthy" gourmet food, a gym, sauna, Jacuzzi, massage, and a health program under medical supervision.

NERJA I still like the hilly, flower-laden, whitewashed Mediterranean town of Nerja, east of Málaga, despite its popularity and rapid development. Maybe it's because the parador, just on the edge of

THE REBEL GOAT

While trying to catch a glimpse of the *Capra Hispanica* in Ojén we imagined we might uncover the illusive "rebel goat" described by Nobel Prize–winning writer Camilo José Cela in his hilarious *Memorias del Cabrito Smith* (Memoirs of Goat Smith):

My name is Robert Smith Jabalquinto. . . . My role in life should have been one of an honest goat, spending lazy hours stretched out in the shade of a fruit tree, grazing on fresh herbs . . . seeing the spring clouds go by. . . . But life left me no time for contemplation, and today I find myself leader of a gang that fears me and obeys me. I am a goat of action. ¡Vaya por Dios! . . . I am a rebel goat, an insurrectionist, who fled to the mountains because I could not bear to be in bondage. . . . I know through the newspapers that a price has been put on my head and that hunting parties have been organized for my capture. They will never get me.

town, is a sea of tranquillity; or because new town construction blends successfully with local architecture; or because the delightful palm-lined promenade, **BALCÓN DE EUROPA** (Balcony of Europe), so named by King Alfonso XII on a visit to the town, juts out into the Mediterranean and provides extensive views of the coast. In early evening the promenade pulses with activity, as hundreds stroll and peanut and ice cream vendors hawk their wares. There is no more pleasant pastime than to be here on a warm summer evening.

PARADOR DE NERJA   Avenida Rodríguez Acosta s/n   tel. (952) 52 00 50 (moderate–expensive; pool), has a delicious patio and rooms with spacious terraces—ideal for breakfast—overlooking the patio or the pool. The views of the sea, the rocky coastline, and the looming mountain ranges to the north are without equal. An elevator takes you down the cliffside to the ample beach of Burriana.

There are many tapas bars in the town of Nerja and *merenderos* (snack bars) on the beach below the parador. The parador itself has a fine restaurant with a wall of windows looking out to the sea. Most of its food is very good, from the *entremeses* (a selection of sixteen tapas), white gazpacho, and local fish to the grilled steaks and chickens. For a lighter meal, go to the bar or terrace for what was, on last tasting, the best *Pepitos* (sautéed veal or pork on a roll, then grilled and served with mustard), and accompany it by an *ensaladilla* (potato and vegetable salad).

♦ If you like caves, **LA CUEVA DE NERJA,** just outside town, is among the best, because of its great size and the beautiful illumination of its stalactites and chambers. So huge is the cave (discovered accidentally by some curious children some thirty years ago and once a burial chamber for prehistoric man) that during Nerja's summer festivals, the last two weeks in August, it is the setting for summer concerts and ballet performances.

FRIGILIANA is just a short distance into the Tejada mountains, north of Nerja. The town suddenly appears on a hilltop, blindingly white against the deep mountain greens and the bright blue sky. It is not the primitive village it was just a few years ago, but it still evokes Arab times as few other places can. The whitewashed walls of cavelike homes undulate; life is hidden from view in private patios; its streets are a maze of alleys, small squares, and dead ends.

♦ The road from Nerja east to Almuñécar, which runs along the rugged winding coastline, is simply spectacular.

RONDA

The beauty of Ronda! It rises above the deep rocky chasms and overlooks a tranquil valley. Its landscape of dizzying heights and sudden plunges is spectacular, and because of its strategic and seemingly impenetrable situation, Ronda was first a Celtic settlement, called Arunda, then Roman, and an Arab stronghold under the caliphate of Córdoba until captured by the Catholic Kings, thus opening the way to the conquest of Granada. In the nineteenth century Ronda played a vital role in the struggle against

Napoleon, falling to his forces, but was also the object of constant raids by guerrillas, who hid in the hills. In modern times the city, although not mentioned by name, became the setting for the Spanish Civil War massacre of civilians described in Hemingway's *For Whom the Bell Tolls.*

It was not warfare but the poetry of the town and its glorious site that won the hearts of so many writers. Rainer Maria Rilke, who lived for a time in Spain, especially loved Ronda, and described it in a December 17, 1912, letter to Princess Marie von Thurn und Taxis-Hohenlohe:

> The incomparable phenomenon of this city piled up on two steep rock masses divided by the narrow deep river gorge . . . it is indescribable, surrounding the whole a spacious valley . . . mountain behind mountain, forming the stateliest distance. As for the city itself, it cannot but be odd, rising and falling here and there so open toward the abyss that not one window dares look that way.

Ronda is really two towns, the original old town, isolated on its rocky heights, and the new extension, El Mercadillo, in an area that once was grazing land. The fearsome gorge of the Guadalevín river divides the two, and they are linked only by the eighteenth century New Bridge (the Old Bridge, from Arab times, stands nearby). The Old Quarter of Ronda is lovely: seignorial mansions graced with delicate and distinctive wrought-iron balconies are interspersed with humble whitewashed homes. There is no particular monument to highlight in Ronda; it is the town as a whole, coupled with its amazing location, that makes Ronda so special.

Ronda will always be remembered for another significant reason: It was here that the great Pedro Romero, the most illustrious of several generations of Romero bullfighters, was born in the eighteenth century. The influence of the Romero family on the art was crucial and established bullfighting as it is known today. Grandfather Francisco is said to have invented the muleta and been the first to confront the bull face-to-face, rather than on horseback. Pedro fought an unheard-of five thousand bulls in his long career, with nary a scratch. The "Ronda style" came to mean great bravery, sobriety, and a classic, elegant style, personified by Pedro Romero, who remains to this day a godlike figure in bullfight annals.

If you walk through Ronda's legendary bullring (when no fight is in session, of course), you can imagine yourself a revered bullfighter. Pull out a red scarf, strike a bullfighter pose, and hear from the stands the adulation of the fans. ¡Olé!

SEEING RONDA

COLEGIATA DE SANTA MARÍA LA MAYOR   On the site of the Arab mosque (the minaret has become the church belfry, and an iron arch was once the entrance to the mihrab). The church was built by order of the Catholic Kings when they conquered Ronda.

PALACES AND MANSIONS   Among the many noble homes in Ronda's old quarter are **CASA DEL GIGANTE,** a mansion of Arab flavor, so named for an oversize figure represented on one of its walls, and **CASA DE MONDRAGÓN,** an Arab palace used by the Catholic Kings after the conquest of Ronda. From the gardens of the Casa del Moro the remains of 365 steps descend to the river; the Arabs used hundreds of Christian slaves to carry water up from here to the town.

BAÑOS ÁRABES   Elegant and brick-arched, these baths are impressive for their size and refinement (the water was heated).

PLAZA DE TOROS   Once on the outskirts of town, but with the growth of Ronda, now right at its center, this is one of Spain's oldest and most beautiful bullrings, inaugurated at the end of the eighteenth century. It is an elegant neoclassic design with double arches supported by 176 columns. You can visit when a bullfight is not scheduled.

Just outside the bullring, **JUAN PINTEÑO** has a shop where he fashions horse gear of straw, yarn, and leather. One of my prize purchases is a colorful *cabezal*—a festive horse headdress made of straw and brightly colored wool, fringed and hand-stitched into intricate patterns and looped into pompons.

◆ The views from the field below the gorge just under the bridge give a very different and equally impressive perspective of Ronda.

STAYING IN RONDA

◆ Stay the night for the full flavor of Ronda. The gorges are illuminated.

REINA VICTORIA   Doctor Fleming 25   tel. (952) 87 12 40   Just outside Ronda, quite stuffy, as its name might suggest, and badly in need of renovation, this was a British outpost, built to house British engineers working on Spanish railways. Rilke also stayed here (". . . to crown it all the devil prompted the English to build here a really excellent hotel. . . ."). His room is now kept as a museum. Request a room facing the cliffside. (Moderate; pool.)

◆ Near Ronda, in Benaojén, is the **HOTEL MOLINO DEL SANTO** Bajada de la Estación s/n, tel. (952) 16 71 51, in the peaceful setting of the national park of Grazalema. It was once a mill and has just ten rooms. (Moderate; pool.)

EATING IN RONDA

DON MIGUEL   Villanueva 4   tel. (952) 87 10 90   A wonderful setting, in a house hanging at cliff's edge. Partridge and pheasant from the surrounding countryside and desserts from the convent nuns (see p. 445). (Moderate.)

SHOPPING

There are numerous antique shops in Ronda, most of them around the Puente Nuevo.

The cloistered Carmelite nuns, Plaza Merced 2, sell homemade breads, pastries, and marmalades, passed to you by means of a revolving shelf.

FIESTAS

GOYESCAS   During the first two weeks of September. Bullfights performed in eighteenth century costume in honor of bullfight legend Pedro Romero (see text).

✦ The roads to Ronda offer thrilling views, particularly the one from San Pedro de Alcántara.

$\mathcal{V}$ISITING THE PROVINCE OF MÁLAGA

CASARES   Hidden from sight until the last turn in the road, suddenly a mountain blanketed in white houses and set in virgin surroundings appears. The village is given a special look by the boxy houses with slit windows and a castle and church at the top.

✦ Sit at **LA TERRAZA** restaurant, at the entrance to town, for a drink and a wonderful view.

ANTEQUERA   A town whose origins go back to the Bronze Age. See the Old Quarter, which has an Arab air, and in particular the fine Renaissance Colegiata de Santa María La Mayor with its Plateresque facade and *artesonado* ceiling; the Baroque altar of the Iglesia del Carmen; and the Arab castle over the city. You can have an enjoyable lunch on the terrace of the **PARADOR DE ANTEQUERA**   Paseo García del Olmo s/n   tel. (952) 84 02 61   A tortilla, crusty bread, and salad are ideal (moderate). Although the parador is pleasant, I see no reason to spend the night in Antequera.

✦ Near the entrance to Antequera, see the dolmens of the **CUEVA DE MENGA**—funeral chambers constructed with massive monoliths dating back 4,500 years to the Bronze Age.

EL TORCAL, twenty-one kilometers beyond Antequera, is a natural wonder, a maze of odd-shaped boulders that take human and animal shapes. Some teeter atop one another amid an eery landscape of gray rubble. Someone has kindly mapped out two routes—the long and the short—but they are both much too long. See what you can from the entrance; that is more than enough.

ARCHIDONA   A town with a very unusual octagonal plaza called La Ochavada. It is whitewashed, with three red brick-arched entrances and brick framing the windows, in the Mudéjar style.

THE PROVINCE OF CÓRDOBA

CÓRDOBA (*core*-doe-bah) is—both literally and figuratively—one of Spain's most colorful provinces, vibrant with flamenco sounds of fandangos and *alegrías*, flawlessly whitewashed, bursting with cascading scarlet and pink geraniums, white jasmine and carnations, pink fuchsia, purple bougainvilleas, daisies, impatiens, begonias, chrysanthemums. Summers are searingly hot, winters generally mild, and in spring the province is in full glory.

The Guadalquivir river cuts a wide swath through Córdoba from east to west, dividing it into the heavily forested region of the Sierra Morena to the north—a paradise of small and large game—and the fertile Guadalquivir valley, known as La Campiña, gently undulating and filled with fruit orchards and olive groves (some of the country's most celebrated virgin oils have the Baena designation of origin). The fighting bulls of Córdoba are bred in La Campiña, and the province has lent its name to and gained world renown for superstar bullfighter El Cordobés, for the jaunty, wide-brimmed aristocratic Cordobés hat, and for cordovan leather. It was also home to the all-time great torero Manolete, who holds godlike stature in Córdoba, and to a wine known as *montilla*—resembling sherry and ranging similarly from dry to sweet. It's heresy to ask for *jerez* in Córdoba; here, *un montilla* accompanies your tapas.

The Romans, appreciating the metalurgical richness of this land, made Córdoba the capital of what was known as España Ulterior, or Baética, and the province was the site of battles between the forces of Julius Caesar and Pompey. The arrival of the Moors in 711 eventually converted Córdoba into the learning center of the Western world, the capital of Al Andalus, and gave the province the unique and colorful flavor that survives to this day.

Córdoba's cooking is based on olive oil and garlic, both used in Roman times. They are the two essential ingredients for cooling gazpacho and its Cordobés cousin, *salmorejo*, which is of similar ingredients, but somewhere between a very finely chopped salad and a soup. It was the Moorish occupation that gave Córdoba's gastronomy its special characteristics, most notably in Arab-influenced sweets like *alfajores* (made with honey and nuts), *Pastel Cordobés* (puff pastry filled with sweetened squash), and *pestiños*, fried pastries dipped in honey and scented with anise. Today, restaurants such as El Caballo Rojo have dedicated themselves to unearthing and reviving more dishes from Moorish and Sephardic times: *Cordero a la Miel* (lamb with honey) and *Rape Mozárabe* (monkfish with raisins) are two particularly appealing discoveries.

Pledging allegiance to neither Roman nor Arab influence is oxtail stew (*Rabo de Toro*), a Cordobés dish par excellence and not surprising to find in this bull-breeding land. Popular also are large and small game from the Sierra Morena, and a variety of fine-quality cured hams and sausage. Quite prevalent today, although not native to Cordobés gastronomy, are *churrasco*, charcoal-grilled beef, and fried fish (Córdoba has no coastline, but is within easy reach) that is cooked to a turn, of course, in local olive oil.

Artisan crafts of Córdoba are likewise Arab influenced: delicate silver filigree work, for which the province is celebrated; Cordobés embossed polychrome leatherwork; and hammered copper, bronze, and brass.

There is little doubt that Córdoba province owes its greatest splendor to the city of Córdoba and to that city's centuries of distinguished contributions to world culture.

THE CITY OF CÓRDOBA

In Córdoba there are not Jews, Moors or Christians. . . . In Córdoba there are probably not even Spaniards. In Córdoba there are Cordobeses; who are Spaniards, yes—and Jews or Moors or Christians; but who are touched, to their benefit, with that divine virtue of assimilation. . . . A Cordobés is Cordobés besides—and above—being Jew, Moor or Christian, being Roman, Almoravid or Spanish, and what distinguishes him is not his creed, nor his flag nor the color of his skin. . . . And that is why the Roman Seneca, the Moor Ben Darrach el Qastali— delicate poet—and the Jew [Maimonides], were—and continue to be—Cordobeses. . . .   *Camilo José Cela*

It is the fusion of cultures, the joining of past and present, East and West, that was characteristic of Córdoba's history and is immediately apparent in Córdoba today. Compare, for example, Granada's Alhambra, an elite refuge for politically besieged Moorish rulers that perches imposingly above the city, crying out for admiration and respect. In contrast, the great Arab Mosque of Córdoba (La Mezquita) sits squat and unassuming, a building open to the masses and situated in the very heart of what was once an integrated Jewish, Christian, and Arab quarter. In Córdoba there was freedom to practice all faiths, and distinct cultures effortlessly intertwined.

While the rest of Europe languished in the Middle Ages, Córdoba thrived under Abdu'r-Rahman III in the tenth century as an independent caliphate, the grandest city of the Western world. It had paved streets, libraries, dozens of synagogues, hundreds of Arab baths, and as many mosques, and a world-renowned university where some of the greatest minds of the times taught mathematics, philosophy, and theology. The city had a million inhabitants, compared with just 300,000 today. Córdoba was living its golden years.

Its glory, however, was to be relatively short-lived. Subsequent weak rulers divided the empire into feuding factions, which led to political decline and opened the way for the Christian Reconquest in 1236. Nevertheless, cultural activity continued unabated. In the twelfth century Maimonides—rabbi, scholar, and physician—recorded his works on Jewish law, on medicine, and on philosophy, and an Arab contemporary, Averroës, expounded his influential interpretations of Aristotle.

What remains of Córdoba's past today speaks of merging cultures. You will enter the city by way of a multiarched Roman bridge, dating to the times of Julius Caesar; you'll see statues in tribute to great Roman statesmen, to Seneca, a native of Córdoba, to Maimonides, and to Averroës; you will surely visit the synagogue and the Great Mosque (be sure to also see the lovely Moorish summer palace, Medina Azahara, just outside the city) and walk the whitewashed alley-like streets of Old Córdoba, laden with flowers. These are not dark, brooding, and mysterious streets like those of Jewish and Arab quarters elsewhere in Spain. Córdoba's *alegría* brings light, color, and airiness to the streets and cheer to the patios. Andalusian joie de vivre is everywhere. (See box, p. 455.)

For me, the Great Mosque and the city's gay patios define Córdoba, for they represent openness and a spirit of accommodation and sharing. I first experienced these convivial qualities of both the Mosque and of Cordobés patios through Feliciano Delgado, Jesuit priest and professor of fifteenth century literature at Córdoba University. Fiftyish, with a boyish grin, a penchant for blue jeans, and a passionate love for his city, Feliciano became a friend years ago through a chance conversation at the Caballo Rojo restaurant. He lived then and still lives just steps from La Mezquita in the so-called Jewish Quarter, which he quickly pointed out had really been a melting pot of cultures and religions.

We joined him the following day in a walk from his house to the Mosque—a pleasant stroll ever since the Old Quarter was closed to traffic. The Mosque is massive, covering several square acres of land, and except for a few decorative doorways (some of them later Christian additions) it is a relatively plain building, typical of the Moorish philosophy that beauty is an intimate and very personal experience.

But what a spectacle once you have crossed the Patio de los Naranjos, with its orange trees and gurgling fountains (once used for ritual ablutions), and entered into the Mosque's ethereal environment. If you've never seen Córdoba's Mosque, you can't imagine what it is; no picture can capture the appearance nor describe the sensations. Here, wherever you turn, are red- and white-striped double arches on marble columns—hundreds of them, leading you down aisles that branch off in many different directions. The Mosque is like a maze, and it's quite possible to lose your way. Some say the

arches recall oases of palm trees. "Besides their spectacular appearance, the combination of brick and stone in these arches cleverly allows for expansion and contraction in accord with weather conditions," Feliciano tells us. "Strangely enough, they serve no structural purpose and do not support anything; they are purely decorative."

Begun in the eighth century and enlarged over the years, the Mosque was finally completed in the tenth century. "The Moors were open to all influences," explains

Feliciano. "They used Roman-style arches, borrowed marble columns from previous Greek, Roman, and Visigothic structures [experts know which are which by the type of marble] and appropriated the capitals from early Christian churches; some are from San Vicente church, which stood here before the Arab conquest. The Arabs had prodigious decorative skills, but their architectural knowledge was quite limited: They lacked the technology to construct a stone dome, so the Mosque's ceiling is flat and made of wood, although at one time it was beautifully polychromed."

As we walked across the Mosque the decoration became progressively more profuse until we reached the pièce de résistance, the mihrab, or sacred niche, which indicates the direction of Mecca.

"Have you noticed that the most beautiful decorative elements in the Mosque are high up?" asks Feliciano. "That's because so much time was spent prostrated on the floor in prayer, eyes raised to Allah, that it was easier to appreciate the ceiling than the lower walls and floor." The mihrab is the most outstanding example of this philosophy: billowing, multitiered scalloped arches lead up to a striking horseshoe arch of astoundingly intricate crushed colored glass and gold dust mosaic. On the ceiling an octagonal strapped cupola (remember the Arabs did not know how to make a real dome) is done in similar mosaic and gives a Byzantine touch that is not surprising in this once international city. The mihrab is Moorish art at its most brilliant.

Feliciano directs our attention to two rooms flanking the mihrab—the space to the left for bookkeeping, the one to the right for storing money. Prayer was just one function of the Mosque; it was also a tax collection center for Arabs, Christians, and Jews, a learning center for all faiths, and a focus of political activity. "Never, of course, were women allowed into the Mosque nor included in any of the Mosque's activities," Feliciano reminds us.

Suddenly, for the first time, we notice something different in the distance through the sea of striped arches. To our amazement it is a full-blown cathedral, buried, almost lost in the immensity of the Mosque, its steeple (sheathing the original minaret) and Gothic arches piercing the Mosque's flat roof and ascending skyward. Feliciano has deliberately steered us clear of the cathedral until the end. For although mosques all over Spain were wantonly destroyed in a fit of religious fervor after the Reconquest, and churches built on their sites (Sevilla supposedly had a mosque to rival Córdoba's), La Mezquita of Córdoba, in accord with the city's inimitable ecumenical style, was the only one to survive. The cathedral was built within the Mosque in the fifteenth century, apparently much to the dismay and protestation of Cordobeses, who treasured this unique example of Moorish artistry.

Even Charles V, who had approved the construction of the cathedral (without having seen the Mosque), was dismayed when he finally came to Córdoba and saw how the Moorish temple had been compromised by a cathedral of minimal artistic worth. Indeed, the contrast is unfortunate: This dark, austere, and laborious monument of Christendom is in direct conflict with the poetic lightness and grace of the Mosque. Its only redeeming quality, aside from its marvelous choir stalls and some other artistic details, is the unique experience of seeing two cultures and religions side by side and the realization that it is precisely the construction of the cathedral that saved the Mosque from destruction.

Córdoba never regained its grandeur under Christian rule, despite a brief period during which the Catholic Monarchs made Córdoba their center of operation for the Reconquest of Granada. Economically and politically, Córdoba became a small-time provincial capital, but its Mosque endures as living proof of the glory that once was Córdoba.

When we emerged from the coolness of the Mosque to a fiery afternoon sun, seething pavements, whitewashed glare, and wilting temperatures, Feliciano invited us to his seventeenth century home to see his antique-filled patio and sample his mother's fine gazpacho. We were greeted by "*Ésta es su casa*" (My house is yours), a phrase I've heard more often in Córdoba than anywhere else in Spain. We entered through a wrought-iron gate and were immediately enveloped, just as we had been in the Mosque, in its coolness and tranquillity. The gazpacho refreshed our parched throats, and we basked in the beauty of Andalusian life.

REFRESHING GAZPACHO FOR A SIZZLING CÓRDOBA DAY

Combine in a processor 1 pound garden-ripe tomatoes, 1 pound canned plum tomatoes, 1 green pepper, 1 small onion, 1 small cucumber, 2 tablespoons sherry vinegar, 3 tablespoons wine vinegar, 2 tablespoons olive oil, 1½ teaspoons sugar, a garlic clove, 1 cup of cold water, and salt to taste. Blend, in several steps if necessary, until finely puréed. Strain, pressing with the back of a wooden spoon to extract as much liquid as possible. Check the seasoning, adding more salt or vinegar if necessary. Chill several hours or overnight.

Until you have experienced Andalusian summers, you may not realize the considerable comfort and practicality of patios. They are open-air, it is true, but their cool stone walls, awnings that keep the sun at bay, and flowing fountains create a refreshingly airy environment worlds away from the panting city. In Córdoba life revolves around the patio and is inconceivable, in fact, without it.

The patios of Córdoba are not, generally, the serene, lushly green patios of Sevilla that often serve merely as hallways or vestibules. There are patios of that kind in Córdoba, but more often than not Cordobés patios are a collage of color, as bubbly, exuberant, and unpretentious as Cordobeses themselves.

The most delightful and most striking patios in Córdoba are not those of wealthy aristocrats, but communal affairs in which several houses face a common space with a well at its center (once providing the water supply) and where children can safely play. It's impossible, however, to imagine anything in Córdoba being strictly utilitarian; the Cordobés sense of beauty prevails in sumptuous floral displays. Green and red pots hang by the dozens from walls, from balconies, filling the perimeters of the patio, surrounding the fountains, and the flowers grow profusely. So devoted are Cordobeses to their flowers that the Festival de los Patios in May becomes a major event, a friendly contest to see which neighbors can create the most aesthetically pleasing patios with the finest flowers. Prizewinners gain instant notoriety and attract crowds of appreciative Cordobeses (see box, p. 451).

Try to be in Córdoba in spring to see the prizewinning patios in all their glory, but even at the height of summer they are lovely and worth seeking out. Don't hesitate to walk in—you will be welcomed and most likely greeted with "*Ésta es su casa.*" In fact, one of the best ways to strike up a conversation with a Cordobés or a Cordobesa is to compliment his or her flowers.

There are some cities in which you immediately feel at home—protected, warmly received, at ease. Córdoba is one of them.

Seeing córdoba

LA MEZQUITA   Allow plenty of time to see this stupendous Mosque at a relaxed pace (see text).

CATHEDRAL   Begun in 1523 but not completed for more than two hundred years, the cathedral, set within the Mosque, encompasses a range of architectural and artistic styles. Highlights are the eighteenth century mahogany choir stalls, among the most beautiful in Spain, and the Churrigueresque pulpits of wood and marble.
♦ See the Mosque first, then the cathedral, to fully appreciate their contrasting styles and philosophies.

ALCÁZAR   Built in the fourteenth century over a Moorish palace, here the Catholic Kings held court for several years while involved in the Reconquest of Granada. Granada's last ruler, the unfortunate Boabdil (p. 461), was briefly incarcerated in the Alcázar, then released on the condition that he swear loyalty to the kings. It was also here that on two occasions the kings received Columbus and supposedly at that time made the decision to support his venture. There are beautiful formal gardens and a lovely view of Córdoba from the top of the tower. See also the valuable collection of Roman mosaics.

SYNAGOGUE   Far from the magnificence of the Toledo synagogues, this temple is nevertheless an interesting example of Moorish art applied to a Jewish house of worship (the decorative wall writing

The best of córdoba's patios

Check the tourist office in Córdoba (facing the Mosque on Torrijos street) for the latest prizewinners, but the following usually walk off with some awards:

BADANAS 15   Eighteen families share in the care of this delightful patio.

MONTERO 12   Eight neighbors here love to tell you about the beauty and evening coolness of their three adjoining patios.

SAN BASILIO 27   Its patio is attractively framed by wooden balconies, and **SAN BASILIO 50** has a flower-laden well at its center.

MANRIQUE 4   A more formal example of a Cordobés patio, complete with Moorish-style brick arches.

DEANES 3   Charming, with antique copper, brass, and ceramic pieces covering the walls.

done by Moorish craftsmen is in Hebrew rather than Arabic). It is the only remaining synagogue in Andalucía.

CAPILLA DE SAN BARTOLOMÉ   A fascinating glimpse of Moorish craftsmanship used for a Christian structure, and Córdoba's first church after the thirteenth century Reconquest. It is located within the university's school of Philosophy and Letters (ask for the key at the reception desk). The Gothic influence is apparent, but the work was done by Moriscos (Moors converted to Christianity) who had not quite mastered the Christian style. So they used a strapped dome, as they had in the Mosque, rather than one of true Gothic design. Ceramics on the walls also show the Arab touch, for instead of fired multicolored tiles—a technique unknown to the Moors—these colorful designs are made by ceramic inlay.

JEWISH QUARTER   Historic documents show that indeed this area near the Mosque was the ancient Jewish quarter (some of the present street names correspond to those of the fifteenth century). But it was not a segregated community; Jews coexisted here in relative peace with Christians and Arabs. Whitewashed, cobbled, enveloped in flowers, it is today one of Córdoba's most charming and evocative neighborhoods (its only jarring quality is an excess of trinket shops).

MUSEO ARQUEOLÓGICO   Here you will find Iberian stone lions, Roman mosaics, remains of the polychromed ceiling of the Mosque, and a magnificent bronze deer from the Medina Azahara palace (see "Visiting the Province of Córdoba").

PALACIO DE LOS MARQUESES DE VIANA   In this splendid palace there are more than a dozen patios, each carefully orchestrated to evoke a mood of reserved elegance as well as unrestrained vivacity. The palace also has a collection of Cordobés art and a library specializing in books related to hunting.

CÓRDOBA'S DISTINCTIVE PLAZAS AND STREETS

PLAZA DEL POTRO   An austere square faced by the Convento de la Caridad and a former inn, La Posada del Potro (mentioned by Cervantes in *Don Quijote*). There is a sixteenth century fountain at its center featuring a prancing pony, or *potro*.

PLAZA DE LOS CAPUCHINOS   Also called Plaza de los Dolores, this is one of the most typical and well-known squares of Córdoba. Here the convent of the Capuchins and simple whitewashed homes frame a large, highly venerated crucifix, El Cristo de los Faroles (Christ of the Lanterns), which is fenced and surrounded by street lamps on undulating wrought-iron posts.

PLAZA DE LA CORREDERA   An immense, porticoed four-story plaza with heavy brick arches. The houses are uniformly seventeenth century, except for two from the sixteenth century in the southeast corner, one of them formerly a jail. This was once the site of bullfights and is a market-place in the mornings.

CALLEJA DE LAS FLORES   One of the most charming corners of Córdoba. This narrow street is hardly wider than an alley, joyful with flowers. Look up the street and see the steeple of the cathedral, perfectly framed.

STAYING IN CÓRDOBA

There are no ideal accommodations in Córdoba. Some possibilities are:

The **HOTEL MAIMONIDES**   Torrijas 4   tel. (957) 47 15 00 (moderate–expensive), although not a grand hotel by any means, is ideally located just across the street from the Mosque. Other alternatives are the somewhat gaudy **ADARVE**   Magistral González Francis 5   tel. (957) 48 14 11 (expensive), also across from the Mosque; the **PARADOR LA ARRUZAFA** Avenida Arruzafa 33   tel. (957) 27 59 00 (moderate–expensive), inconveniently located just outside town, but with lovely vistas, a pool and gardens; and two very small hotels occupying old homes in the Jewish Quarter: **ALBU-CASÍS**   Buen Pastor 11   tel. (957) 47 86 25 (moderate), and **GONZÁLEZ** Manrique 3   tel. (957) 47 98 19 (moderate).

EATING IN CÓRDOBA

EL CHURRASCO   Romero 16   tel. (957) 29 08 19   In the Old Quarter with a lovely Andalusian patio at its heart, this restaurant specializes, as its name indicates, in grilled meats, but also has fine fish and regional specialties, like white gazpacho. (Moderate.)

EL CABALLO ROJO   Cardenal Herrero 28   tel. (957) 47 53 75   Just steps from the Mosque, a long-standing restaurant that has its ups and downs but deserves praise for its efforts to revive centuries-old dishes of Arab and Jewish origin. *Cordero a la Miel* (lamb with honey), partridge with almonds, and monkfish with raisins are specialties. Of course the classic *Rabo de Toro* (oxtail stew) is always on the menu. (Moderate–expensive.)

ALMUDAINA   Campo Santos Mártires 1   tel. (957) 47 43 42   The menu here strays somewhat from traditional into more creative cooking. The setting in a sixteenth century palace is superb. (Moderate.)

EL BLASÓN   José Zorrilla 11   tel. (957) 48 06 25   Run by the son of El Caballo Rojo's owner, this restaurant, in an elegant tavern setting, strives for more creativity while not neglecting classic Andalusian fare. (Moderate.)

TAPAS BARS

BAR SANTOS   Magistral González Francés   Facing the Mosque, here you will find one of Spain's best tortillas and an outstanding sangria (see box).

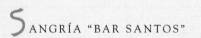

SANGRÍA "BAR SANTOS"

Combine a bottle of hearty Spanish red wine with a cinnamon stick, 1 tablespoon each of brandy, light rum, orange liqueur, and sugar. Add slices of lemon and orange and wedges of peach. Refrigerate several hours or up to several days. To serve, mix with 1 cup seltzer and add ice cubes.

LA MEZQUITA   Cardenal Herrero   Known throughout Spain for its excellent *Boquerones en Vinagre* (marinated white anchovies).

CASA RUBIO   Puerto de Almodóvar 5   An old and ever-popular bar with a good selection of tapas.

CASA SALINAS   Puerto de Almodóvar 2   A variety of tapas and good *montilla* wines.

SHOPPING

The crafts of embossed leathers and silver filigree jewelry are still practiced in Córdoba. Avoid trinket shops and visit authorized jewelers if you're looking for real jewelry, not cheap imitations. Antiques and local pottery can be found in some shops in the Jewish Quarter, and the **ZOCO MUNICIPAL,** Judíos s/n, unites many small shops where local craftsmen are often at work.

On the Calleja de las Flores are two shops specializing in traditional embossed leather: **CARLOS LÓPEZ OBRERO** and **TALLER MERYAN.**

♦ Avoid July and August in Córdoba if at all possible—tourism is overwhelming and robs the city of its unique flavor.
♦ Although Córdoba, in particular the area around the Mosque, is well patrolled by local police, beware of handbag snatchers who whiz by on motor scooters.
♦ A buggy ride is a delightful way to see Córdoba, particularly in the evening. Price is negotiable.

VISITING THE PROVINCE OF CÓRDOBA

LAS ERMITAS   This former hermitage, in isolated mountain surroundings on the outskirts of Córdoba, goes back to earliest Christian times. Today there is a Carmelite religious community here, but one of the tiny, sparse-to-the-extreme quarters of those earlier religious recluses, preserved and furnished as it was then, is a fascinating look at self-imposed duress. Beautiful views of Córdoba and the Guadalquivir valley.

MEDINA AZAHARA   Also on the outskirts of Córdoba, this was the summer palace (really a self-contained city) built by Abdu'r-Rahman III in 936 to satisfy, so legend has it, the whim of a young Arab woman. Nestled in the fold of a mountain to capture the cool breezes of the sierra, it had three terraces perfectly adapted to the lay of the land: the palace, gardens, and orchards are at the upper levels, and the mosque and palace dependencies are below.

Its beauty won world admiration in its time, but Medina Azahara was reduced to rubble by Berber invaders just seventy-four years after its completion. There it sat buried—a legend, a mere memory—until in the last decades this glorious Moorish palace and *mezquita* painstakingly rose again. Today we see a place of inordinate beauty with that special unencumbered charm of a royal summer palace. This is a place that is instilled with human intimacy and makes the Moorish presence in Córdoba come alive. Don't miss it. (Closed Tuesdays.)

FIESTAS: THE BEAUTIFUL MONTH OF MAY

May is an important month on the Cordobés calendar, with one fiesta after another, and hardly leaves a Cordobés time to put in a full day's work or have a decent night's sleep. It is, says writer Enrique Uceta, when "nature brings good temperatures . . . air dense with fragrance, and puts flowers in the hundreds of pots that crowd doorways, patios, windows, walls and balconies. Cordobeses add contagious *alegría* and the deep and simple sentiment of the pleasure of living."

This is the ideal month to visit Córdoba. During the first week the neighborhood festival of Las Cruces de Mayo takes place when beautiful flower-laden crosses are raised in patios and plazas all over the city. The best are awarded prizes, and joyous flamenco dance accompanies the occasion. Hot on its heels comes the Festival de los Patios, May 5–12 (see box, p. 451). There is still time to spare in May: the Feria de Mayo is next on the agenda, with its party atmosphere and tents set up along Paseo de la Victoria. They're public and therefore more accessible than those at the Feria de Sevilla. And as if this were not enough, every three years in mid-May the Concurso Nacional de Arte Flamenco is celebrated—a good chance to hear some authentic flamenco (held every third year, and 1992 is one of those years).

PALMA DEL RÍO   A large well-kept town in typical Andalusian style, birthplace of celebrated bullfighter El Cordobés (see text).
HOSPEDERÍA SAN FRANCISCO   Avenida Pío XII s/n   tel. (957) 71 01 83 (moderate), is set in a monastery built in 1492 that played an important role in the spiritual "colonization" of the New World. It provided lodging for Spanish Franciscan friars, such as Fray Junípero Serra, who were en route to California. America's first oranges were those from Palma del Río. The hotel is monastically simple, the restaurant somewhat pretentious.
♦ From Palma del Río you can drive into the beautiful **SIERRA MORENA**. Take the road San Calixto–Los Morenos, which is surrounded by a veritable forest of cork trees, and picnic en route. See free-range Iberian pigs, deer, pheasant, and white-tailed rabbits.

ALMODÓVAR DEL RÍO   Here is one of Andalucía's most striking castles, emerging from the tip of a rocky spike, as if part of the natural landscape.

MONTILLA   The city in which *montilla* wines, related to sherry, are produced. **BODEGAS ALVEAR**   Avenida María Auxiliadora 1   tel. (957) 65 01 00, are the best-known wineries here. Morning visits by appointment.
LAS CAMACHAS, right outside Montilla on the Córdoba-Málaga road, km 42, tel. (957) 65 00 04 (inexpensive), serves a wide selection of excellent tapas and has a good dining room as well.
♦ *Alfajores* candies from Montilla are, I think, the best in Spain and can be purchased at **PASTELERÍA M. ÁGUILA**   La Corredera 29.

LUCENA   See the San Mateo church and its extraordinary eighteenth century chapel, profusely carved in the flowing Churrigueresque manner. In Lucena, the Moorish king Boabdil (see box, p. 461) was imprisoned for a time in the Torre del Moral (in the Plaza de España).

BAENA   A whitewashed hilly town featuring beautiful wrought-iron window grates. You can visit the eighteenth century *almazara* (oil mill) of **NÚÑEZ DE PRADO**, where first-rate virgin oil (unfiltered) is made from hand-picked olives. Olives are pressed in November, but you can visit anytime.

T̄HE PROVINCE OF GRANADA

WHAT EXTREMES the province of Granada (grah-*nah*-dah) encompasses, from the loftiest peaks of Spain in the Sierra Nevada, snowcapped even in summer, to the blazing Mediterranean coast. In spring you can be skiing in the morning and basking in tropical sun and bathing in the sea by afternoon.
   The mountain scenery is awesome (the Mulhacén towers more than 10,000 feet over the sea), the fertile valley of the Genil river bears fruits and

vegetables, and near the coast sugarcane and such subtropical fruits as *níspero* (medlar fruit, related to the crab apple), *chirimoya,* papaya, and avocado all thrive. Ski resorts and Mediterranean beaches vie for the tourist trade, making this one of Spain's most popular provinces.

The Moors ruled the region until the end of the fifteenth century, and their influence on architecture and on provincial life is still plainly visible so many centuries later. And of course the Alhambra, supreme Moorish achievement, is here in the city of Granada, beloved to the Moors and their last official domain on Spanish soil. But they had to abandon this land that they had made lush and green through intricate irrigation systems and on which they had bestowed their highly developed artistic sensibility and their concept of sensual beauty.

Although Granada is a province dominated by its principal city, it also has wonderful mountain villages of unique architecture in Las Alpujarras, and entire towns of cave dwellings, fitted with all the amenities of the twentieth century. The coastline has been turned over to tourism, and with few exceptions I frankly find it the least exciting part of the province.

Mountain cured ham from the town of Trevélez in Las Alpujarras has its gastronomic admirers in Spain, although in recent years it has been eclipsed by the superb hams of Huelva, but otherwise the cuisine of Granada divides into the fine seafood of the coast and the heartier foods of the interior, based on meat and sausage. Even in the mountains, gazpacho is popular in summer, and *Tortilla Sacromonte*—a tasty omelet of vegetables, calf's brains, and "mountain oysters," named after the hills around the city of Granada—is found throughout the province, as are the liqueur-soaked cakes filled with custard called *piononos*. Heightened interest in the Moorish influence on Granada's cuisine should, I think, soon result in a wealth of unusual and long-forgotten recipes. The Mirador de La Almorayma restaurant in the city of Granada, for example, has begun to feature such dishes.

Granada is also a region of fine handcrafts—not just touristy trinkets but also quality items made by skilled craftsmen in a tradition going back to Moorish times. Marquetry (*taracea*), guitars, copperwork, embossed leather, rugs, delicate glass-and-bronze lanterns, and ceramics of detailed design, often painted with the province's popular pomegranate motif (the word *granada* means pomegranate), are typical of Granada.

And then there is Granada's strong Gypsy heritage and its particular contributions to flamenco song and dance. Nighttime bashes called *zambras* take place in the Gypsy caves of Sacromonte to the music of Granaínas and are performed with instinctive sensuality and abandon. They can be exciting events, even if you must see them within the context of a "show."

And yet Granada is a province that displays greater reserve than the light-hearted western provinces of Andalucía. We see more of Spain's tragic sense of life and less of the *alegría*. A good example is Federico García Lorca, born in the province. His lyricism and his romantic and erotic imagery and his preoccupation with dramatic and sudden death are closely linked to the spirit of his homeland.

THE CITY OF GRANADA

I tread haunted ground and am surrounded by romantic associations. From earliest boyhood when on the banks of the Hudson I first pored over the pages of an old Spanish story about the wars of Granada, that city has ever been a subject of my waking dreams, and often have I trod in fancy the romantic halls of the Alhambra.   *Washington Irving*

Granada is a magical city, and no matter how often I visit nor how crowded it becomes with visitors, I never fail to fall under its spell. Its setting alone makes it sensational: a city of seven hills at the foot of the Sierra Nevada, cut by the deep clefts of the Río Darro, which runs under the modern city, and the Genil, which feeds into the Guadalquivir and converges here with the Darro. The older quarters of the city, where you will see *cármenes*—Moorish-style villas built on hilly streets with beautiful enclosed gardens and orchards—follow the course of the rivers, climbing steeply to one side into the old Moorish Albaicín and then into the Gypsy quarters of Sacromonte.

On the other side of the river, Granada rises to ethereal summits, and the ruddy stone palace of the Moorish kings—the fabled Alhambra (meaning "red one")—seems to float over the city. Within clear view are the snow-covered heights of the Sierra Nevada, which in the words of Washington Irving "shine like silver" and "give Granada that combination of delights so rare in a southern city: the fresh vegetation and the temperate airs of a northern climate, with the vivifying ardour of a tropical sun and the cloudless azure of a southern sky." A poem etched in marble over the entrance to a watchtower of the Alhambra says it all:

> Give him alms, good woman,
> For in life there is nothing
> like the heartache of being blind in Granada.
>   *Francisco de Icaza*

But this is just the beginning, for aside from such breathtaking vistas, the Moorish ambiance of the city and the dreamlike beauty of the Alhambra palace can arouse even the most jaded traveler. My impressions of Granada are colored by my first two visits, one as a student when, alone and with a copy of Washington Irving's *Tales of the Alhambra* under my arm, I climbed from downtown Granada, sweltering in August's heat, into the hills of the Alhambra; there everything was verdant and lush, thanks to the Arabs who had guided the waters of the Sierra Nevada through canals, irrigating the land and creating tranquil pools and gurgling fountains. The air cooled, the sound of rushing water was all around me, and I was transported into another world, unchanged since the times of the Arab caliphs.

I paused every so often to catch my breath and read from Washington Irving, putting myself in the mood for the visit that awaited me.

While the city below pants with the noontide heat and the parched vega trembles to the eye, the delicate airs from the Sierra Nevada play through these lofty halls, bringing with them the sweetness of the surrounding gardens. Everything invites to that indolent repose, the bliss of southern climes, and while the half-shut eye looks out from shaded balconies upon the glittering landscape, the ear is lulled by the rustling of groves and the murmur of running streams.   *Washington Irving*

I leafed through the chapter of "Legend of the Moor's Legacy," which describes Peregil, the water carrier, bringing icy water down from the sierra in jugs wrapped with fig leaves, and I appreciated the thirst for cool water and the passion for fountains that the Moors, coming out of the African desert, must have had.

When I finally reached the Alhambra I was confronted with a solid and powerful mass of stone, every bit the fortress it was meant to be, but certainly not how I imagined the Alhambra to look. But once I entered I was astonished by the splendor that greeted my eyes. Here were two large rectangular courtyards around which the palace rooms were clustered. There was delicate, lacy plasterwork on the walls, and even though the polychrome painting had faded, the floral and geometric patterns were no less compelling. Arab calligraphy, also traced in the plaster, carried the words of the official Alhambra poet, Ibn Zamrak, as well as texts from the Koran, and the repeated words "Allah is Great."

The Patio de los Arrayanes was serene, reflecting the towers of the Alhambra in its elongated pond. In the Hall of the Ambassadors (Salón de Embajadores), next to the courtyard, I saw intricately wood inlaid (*artesonado*) ceilings and walls covered in colorful ceramic tile. In the Patio de los Leones, twelve stylized lions encircled a fountain around which a veritable forest of 144 slender columns arose. Marvelous honeycomb stuccowork in unimaginably complex designs was on the ceiling of the Sala de las Dos Hermanas (Room of the Two Sisters) and the Sala de los Abencerrajes, both entered through the patio. Bubbling fountains created music all around me. I could hardly believe the magic the Moors had wrought, and was particularly struck that something so seemingly fragile had survived the centuries.

The powerful impression the Alhambra made on me that first time did not, however, prepare me for another experience I had there several years later when I returned with my family.

We had toured the Alhambra in the morning, a bit disappointed because the crowds robbed us of the calm needed to fully appreciate the tranquillity that the Alhambra was designed to convey. After dinner we could not resist climbing just once more to the Alhambra to experience its mystery by night. To our surprise it was open, and

we were ushered in, but warned that closing time was in ten minutes and the lights would go out. Our voices dropped, our steps slowed; we were awestruck by the sight before us. Four people were sitting on the stone floor in silence, gazing upon the still green waters of the Patio de los Arrayanes pond, which reflected gracefully carved columns. Everyone was lost in revery, and we immediately succumbed to the mood. It was a religious, almost mystical, experience.

So spellbound were we that we failed to notice that other visitors had disappeared. At precisely midnight, all the lights were extinguished and the Alhambra was enveloped in total darkness. We clutched each other and took tentative steps in the direction from which we had entered. Now I could vividly imagine Washington Irving's terror during his first night alone in the palace:

> A vague and indescribable awe was creeping over me. I would fain have ascribed it to the thoughts of robbers awakened by the evening's conversation, but I felt that it was something more unreal and absurd. . . . Everything began to be affected by the working of my mind.

In the Sala de los Abencerrajes, where an entire family of opponents to Granada's king were beheaded, and whose blood, it is said, can still be seen in the fountain, I could almost hear the clanking chains and the murmurings that legend tells are the spirits of those so ignobly massacred. After what seemed an eternity, we were escorted out. But ever since that unforgettable evening I know that to completely capture the enchantment of the Alhambra, a visit at night, in relative solitude, is absolutely essential.

The Moorish kings lived, it would seem, in idyllic surroundings, but there were bloody battles taking place around them, and the fighting among themselves approached civil war. By the fifteenth century it was obvious that the Moors were losing their foothold in Spain. As the Catholic Kings took control of Moorish Spain, Granada's rulers isolated themselves in the well-defended Alhambra, which became a self-contained fortress and a city in itself. Even when summer's heat sent the kings in search of more temperate climates, they merely transferred their residence to the cooler, higher elevations of the romantic summer palace of the Generalife in the Alhambra complex. But the signs were irrefutable: The Moorish domination of Spain had come to an end.

Boabdil, the last Arab ruler of Granada (see box), en route to exile in the mountains of Las Alpujarras (p. 466), turned around for one last glimpse of his beloved Granada and tearfully exclaimed "*Allah Akbar!*" and with a deep sigh bid farewell to Granada. His hardhearted mother, Aixa, showed nothing but contempt for her son: "You cry like a woman for the kingdom that you could not defend as a man," she reportedly exclaimed. This spot has ever since been known as El Suspiro del Moro—the Sigh of the Moor.

Despite the imposition of Christianity in Granada, the Catholic Kings were obviously charmed by the Alhambra and left it relatively untouched. The impressive central mosque, however, was destroyed and a grand cathedral constructed in its place. Because of the great symbolic significance of the fall of Granada, Fernando and Isabel had special affection for Granada. "I hold this city dearer than my life," said Isabel. They chose to be buried here in a special chapel of the cathedral. Their grandson, Charles V, later built a magnificent Renaissance palace within the Alhambra grounds, and although it is by any standards an exceptional building, it is much too stern to be contemplated in the same breath as the sensual Alhambra. Charles did, however, appreciate the beauty of the Alhambra, reportedly exclaiming when he saw it, "Pity on he who lost it." And echoing the biting words of Boabdil's mother, he added, "She was right to say what she did and the king wrong to do what he did; because if I were he, or if he were I, I would take the Alhambra as my grave rather than live without my kingdom in the Alpujarras."

THE UNFORTUNATE BOABDIL: LAST MOORISH KING OF GRANADA

Poor Boabdil is still maligned after five hundred years as a vacillating weakling, a traitor, and a collaborator, unable to hold on to his beautiful kingdom of Granada.

A gentle man of slight figure, aquiline nose, small mouth, and sensitive eyes, Boabdil had a tumultuous rule. With the support of his mother, Aixa, he unseated his father, Abul (Muley) Hassan, but was subsequently taken prisoner by the Christians and jailed in Córdoba. His father regained control while Aixa negotiated her son's release with the Catholic Kings. They agreed to restore Boabdil's rule in Granada, on the condition that he swear loyalty to them, help them against his father, and give his young son to the Catholic Kings as hostage. The arrangement did not sit well with Boabdil's subjects: He was despised as a vassal of the Catholic Kings, and the combat between rival Moorish factions left him ineffectual.

When Granada finally fell, Boabdil retreated to Las Alpujarras with his supporters, his mother, his wife Moraima, and his son, who was returned to him after seven years in captivity. Moraima died shortly thereafter, and Boabdil's grief knew no bounds. After just one year he was expelled from Spain. Inconsolable, he crossed to Africa and lived in Fez to the age of sixty-three in a castle he built to resemble his beloved Alhambra.

Seeing Granada

LA ALHAMBRA   The name refers to the whole complex on this hill high above Granada, but more specifically to the glorious Moorish palace. In the palace you must see the delightful courtyards and patios with their fountains and ponds, and the detailed decorative designs of plaster tracery, stucco, and ceramic of the walls and ceilings (see text). And you should see all this on your own, at your own pace, and at a time of day when the crowds have thinned: Lunchtime (about 1:30 to 3:30) or before closing (this varies according to the time of year) are best. In any case, plan your visit to Granada around an evening at the Alhambra; it is open Saturday nights all year, 8:00 p.m. to 10:00 p.m. (winter hours), and Tuesday, Thursday, and Saturday nights in summer, 10:00 p.m. to midnight (check posted days and hours for any changes).

◆ If possible, for the evening visit bring a Walkman with you and a recording of "Remembrances of the Alhambra" by Tárrega. The beautiful guitar music blocks distracting noise and enhances the intimacy of the experience.

You will need at least a half-day for the visit to the Alhambra. Remember that besides the palace there are the remains of the Moorish summer palace of the Generalife, overlooking the Albaicín and decorated in the same lavish stucco, tile, and *artesonado* of the palace itself. The gardens are lush and carefully tended, and water coming from the Sierra Nevada constantly flows through them.

If time permits another part of the visit can be the Alcazaba—the original Arab fortress—and its watchtowers (from here the flag of the Catholic Kings flew to proclaim victory). And there is also the austere Renaissance palace of Charles V, adjacent to the Alhambra, incorporating an unusual circular porticoed patio and two museums, one with objects from the Alhambra, the other a fine arts museum.

◆ I suggest buying at the Alhambra a detailed guide with sketches of the layout of the complex; the design, especially of the Alhambra palace, is complex, and you could take a wrong turn and miss something extraordinary.

◆ On your way down from the Alhambra see the **PLAZA CAMPO DEL PRÍNCIPE,** formerly the orchards of the Arab kings and now a spacious square from where the typical houses of Granada (*cármenes*) climb the hillside. There are many tapas bars here (see TAPAS BARS).

CATHEDRAL   Built over the former Great Mosque (which was downtown for the common people), the Catholic Monarchs showered attention on Granada's cathedral, for it represented Spain's complete return to Christianity. Designed by Diego de Siloé, it is a grand work of Renaissance architecture, the first Renaissance church in Spain, and one of the world's largest, with five immense naves.

But of particular artistic importance is the lavishly decorated Capilla Real, separate but attached to the cathedral, where Fernando and Isabel,

their daughter, Juana la Loca (see box, p. 99) and her husband, Felipe el Hermoso, are all interred. The chapel was originally quite simple, according to the kings' wishes, but grandson Charles V embellished it with Carrara marble and gave the kings elaborate sarcophagi. The stupendous wrought-iron and gilt screen enclosing the chapel and representing the unification of Spain is by Master Bartolomé, who left his mark all over eastern Andalucía. At the altar, notice several unusual figures (like the polychromed jester in maroon- and black-striped pants and checkered shirt pouring hot oil over a man cooking in a kettle). To the right is the lovely kneeling statue of Queen Isabel (to the left is the king), and below her, are scenes of the Reconquest of Granada.
◆ In the Sacristy, see Isabel's exceptionally fine personal art collection centering on Flemish masters. There also is the minutely hand-painted prayerbook of the queen and banners of her conquering army.

CORRAL DEL CARBÓN   The oldest Moorish structure in Granada. In keeping with one of its original functions as commercial exchange and hostelry for merchants, today it houses a government Artespaña store that features handcrafts of Granada.

LA ALCAICERÍA   Once the Moorish silk exchange, these alley-like streets have stores that overflow with local crafts, as well as cheap souvenirs, and retain the ambiance of an Arab marketplace.

EL ALBAICÍN   This was the first Arab settlement of Granada, and the kings had their quarters here until in the thirteenth century King Alhamar moved his court to the other side of the Darro river and built the Alhambra. At one time there were more than thirty mosques and today the Moorish flavor is intact in its hilly cobbled streets and its Moorish-style houses, called *cármenes*. This is a delightful and most animated neighborhood.
◆ A visit to Granada is not complete without seeing the spectacular view of the Alhambra and the Sierra Nevada from the Albaicín at the overlook in front of San Nicolás church—by day, at sunset, or at night when the Alhambra is illuminated.

SACROMONTE   The Gypsy quarters of Granada beyond the Albaicín, where homes are dug out of the hills and almost every one has a room set aside for flamenco shows (afternoon and evening performances). It's much too commercial and touristy, but an interesting experience, nevertheless. It's best to sign up with a group rather than go on your own.

LA CARTUJA   See this monastery of Baroque gone wild, a decadent excess of inlaid marble, gold leaf, and elaborately carved stucco that has been called the swan song of Spanish Baroque. In the sacristy, the intricate marquetry of the doors and chests is exceptional.

EL SUSPIRO DEL MORO   Twelve kilometers from Granada on the road to the mountains of Las Alpujarras, with Granada still visible in the distance, this is the historic (or at least traditional) site from where Moorish king Boabdil cried for his lost Granada (see text). Despite the romantic association, the spot is unfortunately marked only by a roadside restaurant.

STAYING IN GRANADA

To capture the spirit of Granada it is essential to choose a hotel in the vicinity of the Alhambra. There are several choices, ranging from the modest and modestly priced **GUADALUPE**   Avenida Alixares s/n   tel. (958) 22 34 23, and the classic **WASHINGTON IRVING**   Paseo Generalife 2   tel. (958) 22 75 50 (he apparently slept here), to more elegant accommodations like:

PARADOR SAN FRANCISCO   Recinto de La Alhambra   tel. (958) 22 14 40—Within the Alhambra grounds, this former convent was founded by the Catholic Kings, and they were buried here until the completion of the Royal Chapel. This is one of the most sought-after accommodations in all of Spain, and reservations are always at a premium. (Expensive.) In summer there is pleasant outdoor dining on the terrace.

ALHAMBRA PALACE   Peña Partida 2   tel. (958) 22 14 68—Recently renovated in grand style and sparing no expense, this hotel pays tribute to the Alhambra in its unrelentingly Moorish décor. High above Granada, the hotel has views that are splendid, if you get a room facing the city. (Moderate–expensive.) Room 707, with salon (more expensive), particularly impressed me with its exquisite décor and expansive vistas. From here the sounds of song, children at play below in the city, and croaking frogs above in the Alhambra drift through our window. A good restaurant and a wonderful terrace from which to contemplate Granada.

EATING IN GRANADA

I'm afraid Granada is not much of a restaurant town. Stick with the classic **SEVILLA**   Oficios 12   tel. (958) 22 12 23 (moderate), for Andalusian cuisine and specialties of Granada; or try **MIRADOR DE MORAYMA** Callejón de las Vacas 2   tel. (958) 22 82 90, a stunning *carmen* in the Albaicín. Food is well prepared; particularly good was a lettuce and tropical fruit salad and hake in a sauce with chopped apple. (Moderate.) Legend says that here Boabdil's beloved wife Moraima was confined while he was in prison, and from here she could see the Alhambra.

TAPAS BARS

There are many tapas bars in the Albaicín area; you can also go tapas hopping in the lovely setting of the Plaza Campo del Príncipe (at **LOS MAR-TINETES** and **BAR CASA CRISTÓBAL,** for example) or in bars around the cathedral, like **SEVILLA** and **EL CONVENTILLO,** which is across from the Royal Chapel and specializes in *serrano* ham, *chorizo*, and smoked fish—try the *surtidos*, or tastings, of *ahumados* (smoked fish) and *embutidos ibéricos* (cured meats). For a novel experience seek out **TASCA JUAN LABELLA,** Avenida de Cervantes 16 (see box, p. 465).

NIGHTLIFE

None of the possibilities for flamenco in Granada is satisfactory. There are *zambra* flamenco fests in the Gypsy quarters of Sacromonte, and at downtown **JARDINES NEPTUNO** a more elaborate spectacle is performed but lacks the intimacy and spontaneity essential to flamenco.

SHOPPING

Despite so much tourism there are still quality handcrafts in Granada. Going up to the Alhambra on Cuesta de Gomeres there are many shops, and in the Alcaicería and the Albaicín you will find more shops for Granada crafts like marquetry, copperwork, pottery, embossed leather, wrought iron, brass and tin lanterns, and guitars.

ARTESPAÑA, a government handcraft shop at Corral del Carbón, is always a trustworthy place.

For marquetry (*taracea*), the specialty of the city, go to Miguel Laguna, Calle Real 30 (across from the parador), or to Francisco González Ramos, on Cuesta de Gomeres, two highly regarded craftsmen who still work in the traditional manner.

"AND I'M NOT CRAZY!!"

Juan Labella may not seem at first glance like much of a businessman, but does his bar attract crowds! The show begins at 1:30 in the afternoon, when Juan emerges from his bar, **TASCA JUAN LABELLA** Avenida de Cervantes 16, for a trumpet call, announcing to the faithful that the paella is ready.

Granadinos come by the hundreds, for not only does Juan give them a tapa of paella with every glass of beer ordered, he also gives away a pound bag of chickpeas, a salami, or perhaps a half-dozen eggs (he gave away more than 3 million eggs in the past six months alone). An order of five beers entitles you to a free bottle of wine, eight beers a watch. Some housewives do their grocery shopping here, although they get a bit tipsy in the process. Juan's motto is "And I'm Not Crazy!!" You may think otherwise.

FIESTAS

HOLY WEEK   The floats incorporate statues created by Andalusian masters from centuries past and parade through the streets against the incomparable backdrop of Granada and the Alhambra. (Wednesday, Thursday, and Friday before Easter Sunday are the key days.)

INTERNATIONAL FESTIVALS OF MUSIC AND DANCE   Held at the palace of Charles V and in the Generalife gardens at the end of June.

LA ALPUJARRA DE GRANADA

Although the Moors and their king, Boabdil, left the city of Granada in 1492, many stayed in Spain in the high mountains of Las Alpujarras (the name in its plural form refers to La Alpujarra de Granada and La Alpujarra de Almería), their last refuge in Spain. They created, just as they had in Granada, irrigation systems that brought water from the sierra and turned the mountain valleys into flourishing orchards. Until recently Las Alpujarras were quite isolated from the rest of Spain, allowing the Moors, in 1568, to plot a rebellion, although it was eventually crushed. They remained, however, until the beginning of the seventeenth century, when Philip III ordered their expulsion.

An area "more frequented by the clouds than by man" (Pedro Antonio de Alarcón), Las Alpujarras today are still a delightful refuge for those seeking beauty and tranquillity. Many Spanish and foreign artists like to spend time here, and there is even a Tibetan Buddhist community. Perhaps it is a certain Arab air and the storybook setting that make this a region that has always attracted me and a place where I love to come for a few peaceful days. Its villages are picturesque (the highest village in Spain, Trevélez, 5,000 feet above the sea, is here) and of a style peculiar to the region, resembling Berber architecture of North Africa: flat roofs and primitive chimneys topped with surrealist "hats."

There are several villages to explore. **LANJARÓN,** at the beginning of the La Alpujarra de Granada is quaint. A popular old-fashioned spa, with shady tree-lined streets and hotels and apartments from the turn of the century, Lanjarón is still popular among elderly vacationers, who carry glasses in straw holders and coupon books that give them access to the "healing" waters. Herbs, displayed in the streets in large sacks, are labeled according to their medical powers (curing gastritis, eliminating kidney stones, lowering cholesterol, even treating insomnia and depression). Ham from nearby Trevélez and potato chips are the principal snacks, guaranteed to increase thirst and water sales.

BUBIÓN, PAMPANEIRA, and **CAPILEIRA** are three exceptionally beautiful whitewashed towns in sublime settings. Within view of one another, they are profuse with geraniums, fuchsia, petunias, flowering cacti, and rhododendrons and heavy with the scent of the honeysuckle that cascades over thick walls. The houses of exposed timber beams cling to the verdant mountainsides, twisting to conform to the irregular terrain.

From Capileira you can drive directly to Granada if you're as crazy as we are, following a dirt road that is the highest in Europe, at more than 11,000 feet above sea level (from there, Trevélez is just a white dot on the landscape). It takes you into a desolate but beautiful scene of lakes and glacier-like snowbanks before reaching the Sierra Nevada ski resorts and descending to Granada. Take food and drink along—you'll not find a bar up here—have your gas tank full, and pick up just-baked bread from the oven of Capileira's old-fashioned village bakery.

Alternatively, there are many outdoor activities that also take you into the highest peaks. Trekking, horseback riding, and hiring a jeep are some of the ways to embark on exhilarating excursions to the awesome Mulhacén, more than 11,000 feet above the sea. The mountain is named for Moorish king Boabdil's father, Muley Hassan, who warred with his son and then asked to be buried here, far from the turmoil and the evils of man. Legend says his body is in the mountain, encased in ice, uncorrupted.

STAYING AND EATING
IN LAS ALPUJARRAS

VILLA TURÍSTICA DE BUBIÓN   Barrio Alto s/n   tel. (958) 76 31 11 (moderate)   A modest complex of bungalows constructed in the style of the region and made to resemble a village. All hotel services are provided, including a very pleasant restaurant that features some mountain specialties. I, for one, am mad for *longaniza* and *morcilla* sausage, so the *Plato Alpujarreño*, a mixed grill including these two items besides other meats, a fried egg, and sautéed potatoes, was just my style.

The terrace of the **PACO LÓPEZ** restaurant in Capileira is a pleasant place to lunch on local sausage, soups, and omelets. (Inexpensive.)

♦ To arrange for jeeps, camping, and horseback riding, contact **NEVADENSIS**   Verónica s/n, Pompaneira   tel. (958) 76 31 27.

◯ISITING THE PROVINCE OF GRANADA

The Interior

LACALAHORRA   Come here to see the town's sixteenth century castle of four rounded towers, reached by car or on foot along a steep, unpaved road. The exterior is solid and unadorned, but inside is an ornate and elegant double-arched patio of golden stone, studded with carved coats of arms. A one-of-a-kind work in Spain, done in Italian Renaissance style (the owner, the Marqués de Zenete, honeymooned in Italy and had an Italian architect design it). Views of an endless plain and the Sierra Nevada in the distance. Visiting hours are on Wednesdays. Otherwise, call ahead to make an appointment, tel. (958) 67 30 98.

GUADIX   An important town since remote times because it was a crossroads between Andalucía and the coast of the Levante and a town the Arabs needed to maintain their power (they called it Wadi Asch; from this came the name Guadix). Once Guadix fell to the Catholic Kings, it was inevitable that Granada would soon follow. There are reminders here of Arab rule (the walls and the Alcazaba), and monuments from the times of the Reconquest—palaces, churches, and the cathedral, which gracefully

THE CAVE DWELLERS OF GUADIX

You can't miss them: In a surrealistic scene of undulating hills, TV antennas and six-foot whitewashed chimneys protrude from the ground, looking for all the world like a family of cartoon ghosts. On a lower level are whitewashed doorways, cut from the soft tufa stone. Yes, these are homes—hundreds of them—and they are inhabited.

Don't expect, however, any club-swinging Cro-Magnons to emerge. These troglodyte dwellings are strictly twentieth century, with several added advantages: constant year-round temperatures; no maintenance, rent, or mortgage; and the possibility of enlarging the quarters for a growing family by just digging another room. Some homes have up to twelve rooms and have been in the same family for centuries. The light is electric, the furniture store-bought, and no one would dream of being without television.

"My grandfather, my father, and myself—we were all born right here," an elderly woman explained as she rocked gently in her chair outside her doorway. "I raised ten children in these rooms." On the bedroom dresser was a yellowed photo of a young bride in a flowing white gown and long trailing veil being carried over the threshold of her cave.

curves in a semicircle around formal gardens. The elegant Plaza Mayor is porticoed.

I come to Guadix principally to see the fascinating troglodyte dwellings, still inhabited as they have been since ancient times (see box).

♦ Near the beginning of the cave quarters, **PEDRO HIDALGO ARANDA** Cañada Ojeda 1, who also makes rush chairs, will show you his cave dwelling for a gratuity.

PURULLENA Pottery shops line the road through town, but most shops are also cave dwellings. Chances are, if you have made a purchase, you can also arrange to visit a home.

MONTEFRÍO The fifteenth century Santa María church-fortress, as if possessing protective coloration, blends right into the browns of the mountains behind it and juts out at the edge of a sharply angled rock formation. The cliff cave dwellings take on a special charm, with whitewashed terraces extending over the precipices.

LOJA Another Andalusian town of Moorish style set in mountainous and isolated surroundings. Its Alcazaba once guarded the pass between Málaga and Granada.

In this unlikely setting is one of Spain's great hotels, **LA BOBADILLA** Finca La Bobadilla   tel. (958) 32 18 61 (deluxe; indoor/outdoor pool). (See box, p. 469.)

SANTAFÉ The campgrounds of the Catholic Kings while they lay siege to Granada, this small town just five kilometers from Granada is entered through one of four gateways. The kings met here with the Moors to arrange a peaceful surrender of Granada and received Christopher Columbus, giving their approval and support for his bold venture.

SIERRA NEVADA

With some of the highest peaks in Spain, the Sierra Nevada offers magnificent scenery, with views of the Alpujarras and south to the sea. There is good skiing.

◆ In the Sierra Nevada are several ski lodges, among them the **PARADOR SIERRA NEVADA** Carretera de Sierra Nevada, km 35 tel. (958) 48 02 00. (Moderate.)

The Coast

SALOBREÑA A rocky hill erupting from flat land, covered with white houses and crowned by a Moorish castle, Salobreña, where jasmine pervades the air, is surrounded by a forest of sugarcane that reaches to the water's edge.

HOTEL SALOBREÑA Carretera Cádiz-Almería, km 341 tel. (958) 61 02 61, just outside town, is modest, but the setting is lovely, near the sea and looking out onto the Salobreña castle. (Moderate; pool.) Stay away from town beaches, and enjoy, as we did, the hotel's private beach in a small cove of clear-as-crystal water and a perfect outdoor lunch of local fish at the beach *merendero*.

MESÓN DURÁN Carretera de Málaga, km 341 tel. (958) 51 01 14, overlooks the sea and Salobreña's illuminated castle. Reserve, or get there early, for an outdoor table. (Moderate.)

LA BOBADILLA: A BRILLIANT CONCEPT IN LUXURY HOTEL DESIGN

In the midst of olive groves and rolling hills near Loja is La Bobadilla, to me the finest hotel in Spain. There are no chic towns anywhere around, and no golf courses, but it attracts a well-to-do international clientele.

La Bobadilla was conceived to enhance the landscape and peacefully coexist with it, and the hotel complex was designed to look like an Andalusian village. Sparrows swoop and chirp through the open hallways of the hotel, building their nests in improbable nooks.

Everything is simply the best, and no expense was spared: The lobby has Moorish-style brick arches, marble columns, and a wall of glass overlooking the countryside; a spectacular pool looks like a lake; the restaurant, in my view, rates among the top three or four of Spain; and guest rooms are individually designed and decorated in exquisite taste. Most are suites with private terraces and sumptuous baths. Service is impeccable and unobtrusive, and there is not a hint of commercialism anywhere. Luxurious, yet deliberately understated, La Bobadilla is a unique and perfectly restful experience that embodies the sensibility and sensitivity of the Moorish spirit of Andalucía.

THE PROVINCE OF JAÉN

OLIVES ARE the very heart and soul of Jaén (ha-*en*). Arriving from another province, you know when you have hit Jaén: Suddenly the landscape is dominated by silvery-leafed olive trees, sparkling in the bright sunlight. You are never likely to see in your life more olive trees, thousands upon thousands, neatly planted at regular intervals, olive trees climbing up and down the mountains in dizzying arrow-straight rows as far as the eye can see, olive trees covering the plains.

> Ancient thirsty olive trees
> under the bright daytime sun,
> dusty olive trees in Andalusian fields!
> Andalusian fields combed by the dog days sun
> from slope to slope striped
> by olive trees and more olive trees!
> The lands are
> sun drenched
> wide slopes, distant hills
> of olive trees embroidered!
>
> *Antonio Machado*

Life in Jaén revolves around olives. It is not only the scenery but also the cuisine, fiestas, and the livelihood of Jienenses that speak of the noble olive tree.

The land is dry and ruddy red—in striking contrast to the dark stubby trunks and green growth of the olive trees—and the climate is sunny and warm, providing ideal conditions for olive trees to reach maturity and bear fruit of the fullest, fruitiest flavor. The Guadalquivir valley is fertile farmland, but otherwise Jaén is a very mountainous, rugged province, where the Sierra Morena rises to the north, the Segura and Cazorla ranges to the east. In these mountains the mighty Guadalquivir river, which flows from here across all Andalucía to empty into the Atlantic, is born. Not surprisingly, Jaén is a hunter's paradise, an international meeting place in the fall for those in quest of partridge and quail, deer, wild boar, and wild goat.

Jaén's cuisine corresponds to what the land produces: olive oil, kid, and game from the sierras (quail and partridge, sometimes stewed with fruit, cooled in escabeche for summer dining, or made into delicious pâtés). Jaén has its very own version of gazpacho: *Pipirrana Jaenera*—really more of a salad than soup—consisting of finely chopped tomato, peppers, onion, tuna and hard-cooked egg, dressed with vinegar and fruity Jaén olive oil.

Some vestiges of leaden medieval cooking are still to be found. Even natives hesitate to eat *Andrajos* (the unappealing name translates as "rags"), a mix of bread, vegetables, tomatoes, salt cod, hare, clams, crabs, and whatever. You need plenty of the province's Torreperogil wine, with its high alcohol content, to wash this down! On the other hand, one of the most delightful meals I ever enjoyed was at the ranch of our friends Carmen and Juan Pablo Jiménez Pasquau, just outside the city of Úbeda. It was *Migas Ubetenses*, a dish of fried eggs with mounds of bread croutons crisped in

SPANISH OLIVE OIL:
LIQUID GOLD FROM THE OLIVE TREE

Olive oil—liquid gold to its many passionate fans—has been essential to mankind for six thousand years. Greek mythology, the Bible, and the Koran all speak of olive oil, and the olive branch is a traditional symbol of peace. Not only was olive oil associated with food and good health, it was also prized as a skin cream, an ingredient in soap, and a means of illumination. Indeed, recent scientific studies show that olive oil is capable of reducing cholesterol and may cure or prevent a variety of human disorders.

It was the Romans who first cultivated the olive tree in Spain and sent its much-admired oil back to Rome (seals of Spanish producers on amphoras found in Italy show this). Today Spain is the world's largest olive oil producer, and Andalucía alone is responsible for 20 percent of world production.

Olive trees are slow to develop (it takes five years before they bear fruit) and lead long and productive lives, surviving for more than one hundred years. They thrive in hot, dry Mediterranean climates and most particularly in Spain; for this reason Spain has dozens of varieties of olives and produces high-quality oils of unique flavor, ranging from mild in northern areas of the country to wonderfully fruity oils from Andalucía.

Harvesting methods have hardly changed in Spain since ancient times because the mountainous terrain prevents the use of machinery, and the fruit is still collected by hand. A first pressing with no chemical intervention and an acidity of less than 1½ percent produces virgin oil and "extra" virgin (a misnomer to be sure).

High-quality Spanish olive oils have at last arrived on our shores, and their recognition and appreciation is certainly long overdue.

olive oil and garnished with grapes, bacon, green peppers, and roasted heads of garlic. We ate it outdoors and within sight of the formidable fighting bulls that they breed.

Appreciated by the Romans for its silver mines, Jaén was throughout history an important crossroads between Andalucía and Castilla; the pass at Despeñaperros in Jaén is for all practical purposes the only way out of Andalucía, and it has historically joined these two regions. Here was the frontier between Christian Spain to the north and the Moorish south, and it was the scene in 1212 of the most famous battle of the Reconquest, Navas de Tolosa, a crucial event in Spanish history. Although almost three centuries more would pass before the Moors were expelled from Spain, this battle marked the turning point for the Christians and the beginning of the end for the Arabs (see box).

The grand works of sixteenth century Renaissance architecture that we see in the province of Jaén are not related to olive wealth but are a result of the titles and monetary rewards given to soldiers of the Reconquest and of the gold and silver brought from the New World that came to Jaén by way of some of its leading citizens. Unfortunately, Jaén's golden years abruptly came to an end, and the province fell into relative oblivion, from which it has never fully recovered.

THE RENAISSANCE TRIANGLE: ÚBEDA, BAEZA, AND JAÉN

I always wondered why so many Renaissance works—some of the most important in Andalucía—were concentrated in the forgotten province of Jaén, and more specifically, in the three cities of Jaén, Úbeda, and Baeza. But our good friend Natalio Rivas, a town historian of Úbeda and proud master of a sixteenth century palace, made it all clear to me. The genesis can be traced to Moorish times and the Reconquest, for this area at one time formed the frontier between Christian and Moorish Spain. As such, Christian warriors and noblemen flocked here to carry out Spain's crusade

THE CRUCIAL BATTLE AT LAS NAVAS DE TOLOSA

It was a monumental battle: El Miramolin Alnasir Mohamen ben Yacub commanded, it is said, a force of 600,000 infantry and 90,000 horsemen. The Christians were represented by several Spanish kingdoms, joined in arms with Frenchmen and aided in their holy crusade by Pope Innocent III.

The bulk of the troops were from Castilla, under the command of King Alfonso VIII. They were a disparate lot of peasants, noblemen, priests, several bishops, and even an archbishop, hastily organized and poorly armed. Their only chance of victory was to catch the Arabs by surprise: Their plan was to attack by way of a treacherous gorge, the Barranco de Losa. The Christian forces fought tenaciously and courageously, but if not for the intervention of a shepherd, who led the army through a secret pass, the outcome of the battle could have been radically different. Chroniclers, obviously representing Christian interests, claimed 200,000 Moslem losses compared with just 25 or 50 Christian deaths.

Although final victory over the Moors was still almost three hundred years away, Navas de Tolosa was the turning point in the centuries-long struggle to expel the Moors from Spain.

Mementoes of the battle of Navas de Tolosa are scattered around Spain. Among them, the beautiful Moslem standard and a Christian cross in Las Huelgas convent in Burgos; the Christian standard in the Santa María church of Castro Urdiales in Cantabria; chains that surrounded the tent of the Arab chieftain in the Colegiata of Roncesvalles in Navarra. Those chains are today symbolized in the coat of arms of Navarra and in the national coat of arms of Spain.

against the "infidels." Once Jaén province returned to Christian control in the thirteenth century, these heroes of the Reconquest, already well established, chose to remain and build grand mansions, graced by family coats of arms, in the Renaissance style of the times. In short, a building boom, unprecedented in the history of Spain, took place.

All three cities became wealthy, each for slightly different reasons: Jaén because it was along the route from Granada to Castile (by way of Despeñaperros), and therefore a major commercial center; Baeza because of its cathedral and university; and Úbeda because of New World gold and silver that poured in through its most powerful citizen, Don Francisco de los Cobos.

Eventually the university and cathedral in Baeza lost their importance and were disbanded. New World activity shifted to Sevilla, thus draining Úbeda of its wealth, and Jaén went down with them. This is why sixteenth century Renaissance architecture predominates in this triangle, while monuments and palaces from the later Baroque period are almost nonexistent (as are earlier Christian styles like Romanesque and Gothic, neither of which existed in Moorish-dominated Spain). The monumental districts of Úbeda and Baeza became museum pieces; only Jaén retained some vitality as a trade route, an episcopate center, and a commercial center for the region. It later became capital of the province.

We can thank the long Arab occupation of these cities, their later prominence (coincidentally, at the height of the Spanish Renaissance), and their precipitous decline for the architectural harmony we see today.

ÚBEDA

Natalio Rivas dedicates whatever time he can to the restoration of his palace, Vela de los Cobos, and the conservation of Úbeda's rich past.

"You can see great works of art all over Spain," he is fond of saying, "but only in Úbeda can you find such a homogeneous assemblage of works from the Renaissance period." Indeed, there are fourteen churches and more than twenty-five mansions and palaces in this small town, and just about all of them are Renaissance.

Úbeda (pronounced *oo*-bay-dah), near the border with Castilla, is an odd mix of noble golden-stone buildings—austere in the Castilian style— and of Andalusian charm reflected in humble luminously whitewashed dwellings and narrow cobbled streets. Purely Renaissance are the buildings surrounding the Plaza de Vázquez de Molina: Eight of Úbeda's most noteworthy structures, all dating from the sixteenth and early seventeen centuries, are here. At the eastern end, the Sacra Capilla del Salvador, an undertaking of the region's favorite and most prolific architect, Andrés de Vandelvira, is a masterpiece of Spanish Renaissance. And adjoining it, the palace of Don Francisco de los Cobos, also by Vandelvira, speaks of the collaboration of two men most responsible for Úbeda's architectural grandeur.

Don Francisco de los Cobos, descendant of a conqueror of Úbeda, had accumulated great wealth and power as secretary and confidant to Emperor

Charles V, and later to King Philip II. He supervised Spain's New World colonies, and in payment, a percentage of all gold and silver coming from America went to him. Although his name in history is obscure, his fabulous wealth made Úbeda a showplace for Spain's new affluence.

As a devoted patron of the arts, Cobos enlisted Vandelvira to build his massive and soberly understated palace (only the facade remains, embellished by the Cobos coat of arms) and the adjoining Sacra Capilla del Salvador, originally a private chapel for the Cobos family. These impressive building ventures inspired other Ubetenses to follow suit, each trying to outdo the other in the splendor of their residences (several were also designed by Vandelvira). Consequently, the civilian architecture in Úbeda is as impressive and interesting, if not more so, than the religious—an unusual situation in Spain, where a community's wealth traditionally revolved around the church.

Seeing Úbeda

Úbeda's monumental heart is concentrated in a small area and can easily be seen on a short walking tour. Inquire at the parador or the tourist office in the Plaza de Vázquez de Molina for detailed maps and historical material. Among my favorite sights:

SACRA CAPILLA DEL SALVADOR   Originally designed by Diego de Siloé but completed by Vandelvira, the sacristy is particularly impressive, glittering with gold leaf and graced by caryatids (Vandelvira's signature detail).

SANTA MARÍA DE LOS REALES ALCÁZARES   Built on the site of a former Arab mosque and noted for two extraordinary wrought-iron chapel grilles, works of Renaissance Master Bartolomé.

CASA DE LAS TORRES   The delicately carved Plateresque facade, flanked by two massive towers, is typical of Reconquest architecture and a magnificent example of a fortified Renaissance house.

PALACIO DE VELA DE LOS COBOS   A seignorial home built by Vandelvira that has been restored with utmost care by Natalio Rivas. One of the few major palaces in Úbeda still privately owned (to visit, just knock, or ask the parador to call ahead).

CASA MUDÉJAR   Today an archaeological museum, this house is a unique example in Úbeda of fourteenth century Mudéjar architecture.

CASA DE LOS SALVAJES   This is a favorite of mine; above the doorway are amusing carvings of savages covered in plumage, as if they were birds. Úbeda's noble residences were built at a time when secondhand reports were arriving in Spain of cannibals, giants, and other strange creatures living in the New World, which inspired artistic fantasy.

PARADOR CONDESTABLE DÁVALOS Plaza Vázquez de Molina 1 tel. (953) 75 03 45 One of Úbeda's Renaissance mansions on the Vázquez de Molina square, with a delightful central patio. (Moderate-expensive.) The parador has an attractive, well-serviced restaurant that is the best place to eat in Úbeda, featuring some excellent regional specialties like *Espinacas Estilo Jaén* (baked eggs and spinach), stewed partridge or partridge salad, and two unusually good desserts that I would travel especially to Úbeda to eat: *Natillas con Borrachuelos* (soft custard with fried pastries) and *Tocinillos del Cielo*, rich candy-like flan for which Úbeda is famous. (Moderate.)

SHOPPING

Since Moorish times, Úbeda has been an important handcraft center for ceramics (they are typically green), esparto, and wrought iron. All are on display and for sale in a large shop under the Palacio Municipal on Vázquez de Molina square. There are several shops along Valencia street, most notably **ALFARERÍA TITO** (number 44), and there are also antique shops around town carrying regional items.

BAEZA

Once capital of an Arab kingdom, Baeza was the first town in Andalucía reconquered by the Christians. Perhaps because the city was important under the Moors and because its capture had symbolic significance for the Christians, construction of an important cathedral began in the thirteenth century on the site of the former mosque. Later a university took shape, and noblemen from the Reconquest built mansions in Baeza. The town reached its most glorious period in the sixteenth century, and therefore its flavor is distinctly Renaissance.

Baeza is just minutes from Úbeda, and in some ways is very much like Úbeda, but on a smaller and simpler scale. It feels like a little village, white, winding, and cobbled, but its impressive monuments and mansions suggest a much grander history. Go directly to the town's centerpiece, the Plaza de los Leones, with its Lions Fountain, brought from the ruins of the Roman town of Castulo, and feel the serenity, austerity, and grandeur of Baeza.

Brochures and maps from the tourist office, located in the square's outstanding building, the Plateresque Casa del Pópulo, will help you plot a walking tour. Be sure to see more of architect Vandelvira's works, like the cathedral (embellished with beautiful wrought-iron work by Master Bartolomé), San Andrés church, and San Francisco church (in ruins, but the main chapel and portal are well preserved).

And take away with you the words of poet Antonio Machado, who taught elementary school here:

Land of Baeza
I will dream of you
when I can no longer see you!

STAYING AND EATING IN BAEZA

Make your base in the parador of Úbeda, but if you happen to be in Baeza at mealtime, there is a simple unpretentious restaurant (overlooking a gas station!) that has a fine reputation all around Jaén province: **JUANITO** Paseo del Arca del Agua s/n   tel. (953) 74 00 40, serves food of the region, particularly stews like *Faisán con Setas* (pheasant with wild mushrooms) and *Cabrito con Habas* (kid with fava beans). (Inexpensive–moderate.) The same **JUANITO** provides simple accommodations. (Inexpensive.)

THE CITY OF JAÉN

From the Arab word *geen*, meaning "caravan route," Jaén was just that, and in many ways remains the same today. It is a crossroad from Granada to Castilla, a place often passed but rarely visited. Jaén is a busy city, capital of the province, and a major commercial center. Like Úbeda and Baeza, it has its share of noble mansions from the golden years of the sixteenth century and an old quarter with a Moorish air. When I come to Jaén it is to see yet another work of Vandelvira—his last and one of his grandest, the cathedral—and to spend a night at the fabulous parador, which soars above the city.

SEEING JAÉN

CATHEDRAL   Like so many others, this cathedral was built upon a mosque. It was Vandelvira's last work (he is buried in Jaén in the Parroquia de San Ildefonso), and although additions continued into the eighteenth century, there is no mistaking the master's hand. Of particular note are the elaborately carved choir stalls. Tradition says that the cloth used by Veronica to wipe Christ's face is here in a bejeweled reliquary.

CAPILLA DE SAN ANDRÉS   Sixteenth century chapel, with Mudéjar influence. See here especially another of Master Bartolomé's exceptionally delicate gilt grilles.

CASTILLO DE SANTA CATALINA   Built by the Arab king Mohammed Ben Nasar who some say was also responsible for the Alhambra in Granada, and wrested from him by King Fernando III on the day of Santa Catalina (thus it was named in her honor). It rises from the edge of a cliff (stick to the pathways and carry a flashlight at night; there are no guardrails). The panorama is spectacular indeed. The parador is next to this castle (see below).

STAYING IN JAÉN

PARADOR CASTILLO DE SANTA CATALINA   tel. (953) 26 44 11   I love this parador, so dramatic in its setting, so theatrically conceived. High above Jaén, the views are vertiginous: olive trees running to infinity and city buildings looking like so many tiny toys. Ingeniously set into the mountaintop, this parador is not a castle, as it appears, but a modern construction designed to blend with the adjacent castle ruins and built within the old castle defensive walls. Inside, the deception is masterly, creating an ambiance as old and austere as it is surrealistic and extravagant. A room with a terrace overlooking the mountains and olive groves is a must. (Moderate–expensive; pool.)

EATING IN JAÉN

Jaén is poor in restaurants—so try tapas along the Calle Nueva or on Consuelo street behind the cathedral. Or better still, dine in the fantasyland that is the parador dining room, featuring regional dishes like *pipirrana* and some of the best marinated green olives you will find anywhere.

ⓥISITING THE PROVINCE OF JAÉN

CAZORLA MOUNTAIN RESERVE   A deep-green oasis of cypresses and pines settled in the midst of Andalucía's arid lands, these serene surroundings, where the air is utterly pure, are a delight. A mecca for butterfly lovers, Cazorla is principally a wildlife preserve: You will find unusual brown squirrels with hairy ears, boar, fox, royal and imperial eagles, *Capra Hispanica*, vultures (there are a few of the rare "bone breaker" variety), even osprey. In fact, more wildlife is concentrated here than anywhere else in Spain except Coto Doñana (in the province of Huelva). There are a turquoise lake where deer roam on an island at its center, a fine fishing river, and a parador. It would be hard to envision anything more relaxing.
PARADOR EL ADELANTADO   in Sacejo (twenty-six kilometers from the town of Cazorla)   tel. (953) 72 10 75, is in a paradisiacal setting, overlooking the forests. (Moderate.)
CAZORLA, a lime-washed village of steeply winding streets, nestles among the peaks of the Cazorla range and is flanked by a castle on either end.
LA IRUELA nearby is a tiny village set against the ruins of its castle, constructed—impossibly, it would seem—on the tip of a needle-like sheer cliff.

At **MANUEL MENDIETA** in **PEAL DE BECERRO**, minutes away, you can find rugs and other esparto crafts.

SEGURA DE LA SIERRA   A delightful village high in the Segura mountains, dominated by an elegant castle. It commands stunning panoramic views of the surrounding countryside and endless vistas of olive trees and is the birthplace of celebrated Renaissance lyric poet Jorge Manrique. Some of Spain's best olive oil (see box, p. 471) comes from the mountains of Segura.

HORNOS   Also in the Segura mountains, in an incomparable setting above an aquamarine reservoir, this tiny village is nestled within a natural rock wall.

IZNATORAF   On an isolated mountaintop, overlooking the olive groves, the village, as its name clearly indicates, is of Arab origin. Streets too narrow for cars are cool and shaded from the blazing sun. You could imagine robed Arabs walking about.

SANTA MARÍA DE LA CABEZA   This sanctuary in the Andújar mountains, where legend says the statue of the Virgin remained hidden from the Moors for five centuries, played an important role in the Spanish Civil War. Surrounded by Republican forces, a handful of Civil Guards and their families barricaded themselves here and held out for eight months against impossible odds and with little food or military supplies. Quite aside from its historical and religious connotations, the sanctuary has an approach that is beautiful, as are the views once you reach there.

BAÑOS DE LA ENCINA   From the road, the town's grand turreted thousand-year-old castle of ruddy stone is a wonderful sight. Close up, it is empty but in excellent condition, and a plaque proclaims: "In the name of God the Merciful, Compassionate, this castle was built by God's servant, Al-Hakan II Almostasir bila Emir Almuminin . . . in the year of the Ramadan 357 (968 A.D.)."

LA CAROLINA   In the heart of partridge country, this town is famous for its excellent partridge pâté. You can purchase or sample it at **LA PERDIZ** on the Andalucía-Castilla route N-IV, km 269   tel. (953) 63 03 00, and also try the well-prepared stewed partridge. (Moderate–expensive.)

LAS NAVAS DE TOLOSA   A monument marks the spot where this famous battle took place in 1212, a date every Spanish schoolchild knows as well as Americans know 1776 (see box, p. 472).

T HE PROVINCE OF ALMERÍA

ALMERÍA (ahl-mer-*ee*-ah), Spain's long-forgotten province, will never win accolades for its cultural attractions, but for its many scenic attributes, I give it top ratings: It is a most spectacular and unique area of Spain that you will never confuse with any other.

It does have its history, of course, and a colorful one at that. Almería was well populated by prehistoric man (cave drawings attest to this), and it was a site of operations for early civilizations, attracted by its gold and silver mines. A popular refrain boasts:

> When Almería was Almería
> Granada was its *alquería* [farmhouse].

Always closely tied to the Mediterranean (Almería in Arabic means "Mirror of the Sea"), Almería in Moorish times was an important center of commerce with the East. Once part of the Córdoba caliphate, it later became independent, but when its Moorish king fled, unable to deal with attacks from other Arab factions, law and order simply disintegrated, and Almería became an outpost for Berber pirates. They grew too bold, sailing out of the Mediterranean into the North Atlantic and attacking Galicia, and King Alfonso VII decided enough was enough; he lay siege to Almería and conquered it. But ten years later it once more reverted to the Moors and remained in their hands until in 1489 its ruler, Zagal, uncle of Boabdil of Granada, ceded Almería to the Catholic Kings. An earthquake in the sixteenth century caused devastation from which the region never recovered, and Almería remained a site of pirate activity long after the rest of Spain was secured.

Aside from the advantages of its Mediterranean coast, Almería could not offer much more to its invaders, for the province presents what must have been for early civilizations the most inhospitable climate and terrain in all of Spain. The scenery is nothing short of astonishing: an almost lunar landscape of bare mountains, deeply gullied by sudden downpours and completely devoid of vegetation, except for a brief period in spring when brightly colored wildflowers manage to eke out enough moisture from the earth to sustain their all too brief lives.

River names reflect the climate: Río Seco (Dry River), Río de Aguas, and Río Aguas (River of Waters) all signal a preoccupation with Almería's most precious commodity, water. Most of the year these so-called rivers are just cracked beds, distant memories of their fleeting spring flows. It's no wonder that Almería was chosen by filmmakers to produce American westerns and their "spaghetti" offshoots (those multilingual productions starring Clint Eastwood, filmed in Spain by Italian directors). Some desert scenes from *Patton* and *Lawrence of Arabia* also take place here.

Certainly if you are a lover of lush green landscapes, Almería will not be to your liking, and although I count myself among this group, I find the parched earth of Almería majestic and awesome. Traveling through the interior is a never-to-be-forgotten experience.

But along with the aridity you do have dazzling sunshine, perhaps more days of sun than anywhere else in Spain; for that reason powerful telescopes were installed here for stellar observations. Warm weather most of the year, beautiful beaches (from wide expanses to intimate rocky coves), and spectacularly clear, aquamarine waters that are the delight of submarine fishermen and seekers of submerged treasure have made Almería in recent years a tourist attraction. This once poverty-stricken land has gained economic well-being through tourism and by taking advantage of year-round sunshine to grow hothouse vegetables, tropical fruits, and flowers. The intensity of the sun makes the quality of Almería grapes and oranges world famous.

But exploitation threatens to damage the unusual natural beauty of Almería, and I can only hope that future growth is handled in an ecologically sound manner. Certainly Almería's distinctive, almost surrealistic architecture continues to dominate new construction, retaining a distinctive Arab-African flavor in both the lava-like flow of some of its villages and the flat-roofed cubism of others.

Almería is relatively poor gastronomically, but the simplest foods are, in any case, the most appealing in such arid climates. Almería supports little livestock and few traditional crops, and looks to the sea for its finest food. One of my strongest memories of Almería, in fact, is of a huge platter of plump, luscious grilled red *carabinero* shrimp, purchased just hours before at the Garrucha fish auction. When you complement such delectable seafood with cooling gazpachos, wonderfully fresh and flavorful vegetables, and sweet tree-ripened fruits, who could ask for anything more?

THE MOORISH CHARMS OF MOJÁCAR

The city of Mojácar covers an entire mountaintop, resembling in its architecture a cubist painting or a stepped pyramid that dwindles in size until it reaches its summit in one single house. Now imagine a bucket of white paint spilling over the mountaintop, and you have some idea of the outstanding setting and unusual appearance of Mojácar. At night it sparkles from afar like a gem, but climb its steep labyrinthine streets that seem to deliberately mislead and misdirect you, and you will feel the great air of mystery that Mojácar's pronounced Arab heritage creates.

When I first visited Mojácar more than fifteen years ago, elderly women still covered their faces in Moslem fashion, securing their head scarves with their teeth; they carried earthenware jugs and huge wash baskets on their heads and descended to the foot of the village to draw water and wash clothes in the communal troughs. The uppermost reaches of the town, once a thriving Jewish quarter, enlarged by Jews fleeing periodic repression in Córdoba and Sevilla, were quiet, dark, and deserted, its buildings crumbling. The town's symbol, the Indalo, a human figure holding an arc (perhaps a rainbow) in his hands and representing an all-powerful and protective god, appeared everywhere, a kind of talis-

MOJÁCAR'S GOOD LUCK CHARM: EL INDALO

The Indalo symbol can be seen in prehistoric cave drawings in Cueva de los Letreros in Vélez Blanco. It was used in pagan times and later adopted by the Christians to serve similar purposes as protection from evil spirits. The figure and the legend became entrenched in Mojácar, and today it is the city's official emblem. So appealing is the Indalo that it appears everywhere in Mojácar, painted on walls, on manhole covers, over doorways, and as jewelry.

"CHRISTIAN: I AM
A SPANIARD LIKE YOU"

In 1488 the Moorish rulers of Almería province, knowing their days were numbered, arranged to meet with the Catholic Kings to swear their loyalty. Representatives arrived from everywhere except Mojácar. The kings, eager to maintain cordial relations with the Moors, sent an emissary, Garcilaso de la Vega, to meet with Mojácar's mayor, Álabez, and the rendezvous took place at Mojácar's fountain. Mayor Álabez offered these touching words:

Christian, tell your kings that they should not take insult from our actions. I am as Spanish as you are. My people have been living in Spain more than seven hundred years and now you say to us, "You are foreigners. Return to the sea." In Africa an inhospitable shore awaits us, where surely they will say as you do, "You are foreigners; cross the sea from whence you came and return to your country."

We are hostages, caught between two shores that deny us bread, friendship, and shelter. Is this human?

I never took up arms against Christians. Allah is my witness.

I believe, then, that we should be treated as brothers, not like enemies, and that you should allow us to continue working our land, the land of our fathers and grandfathers.

If, as it is said, Doña Isabel and Don Fernando unite goodness of heart to their other grand virtues, I trust in Allah that they will listen to our demands. We in turn promise fidelity to the Christian Kings. Otherwise, my people will do what they have to. Before surrendering myself like a coward, I will die like a Spaniard. May Allah protect you!

The queen offered her goodwill, and the Moors of Mojácar, true to their word, supported the monarchs during the subsequent Moorish uprising in the mountains of Las Alpujarras.

For this the Royal House awarded a coat of arms to the "most noble and most loyal city of Mojácar." The Moors lived in peace in Mojácar, and Mayor Álabez was eventually baptized into the Christian faith.

man to ward off harmful spirits (see box, p. 480). It seemed more than appropriate in this bewitching environment.

Mojácar has changed dramatically since then. Today the Indalo appears on T-shirts and trinkets. In the Jewish quarter luxuriously refurbished homes have arisen from the rubble, but are commendably in keeping with Mojácar's traditional appearance. The fountain and wash troughs remain, albeit badly renovated, and you can still read a plaque that records the sorrowful and heartrending words of Mojácar's last Moorish mayor when he surrendered the city to the Catholic Kings. His eloquence made a powerful impression on me and brought to life, as few things can, the Arab presence in Spain (see box, p. 481).

To savor Mojácar as it once was, come in spring and fall, when the weather is warm but vacationers are few. Then you can sense the town's continuing Arab presence, enjoy the lovely parador from whence the town beckons seductively, relax without crowds at the nearby beaches of Carboneras and Algarrobico, and take a short ride to the fishing port of Garrucha to sample succulent giant red shrimp, among other fine seafood. Wander Mojácar's dim, haunting streets, and you will comprehend the grief of the town's Moorish mayor, forced to surrender his beloved city.

STAYING IN MOJÁCAR

PARADOR REYES CATÓLICOS   Playa de Mojácar   tel. (951) 47 82 50 Located at the foot of the town on the beachfront, it is still my favorite place to stay in Mojácar (ask for a room with private entry to the pool esplanade). (Moderate–expensive.) Some like the **INDALO** complex, Carretera de Carboneras s/n   tel. (951) 47 80 01, (moderate), which attempts to evoke a small whitewashed town, but I find it a trifle artificial.

EATING IN MOJÁCAR

EL ALMEJERO   Explanada del Puerto, Garrucha   tel. (951) 46 04 05   Just minutes away from Mojácar, overlooking the fishing boats of Garrucha's port. Exceptional local shrimp (*gambones de Garrucha*) and *Pescado a la Sal* (fish baked in salt). (Moderate–expensive.)

⊤HE CITY OF ALMERÍA

There is not much to detain you in the capital of Almería, for it is not a particularly beautiful nor exciting city. But I would suggest a brief stop to see its Moorish fortress and the unusual neighborhood of La Chanca.

Almería's Alcazaba, among the finest examples in Spain of an Arab fortress, was constructed by the Moors in the eighth century and is situated imposingly on a rise: Its massive dark stone walls sharply contrast in color and scale with the simplicity and whiteness of the houses that adjoin it, and its ramparts descend to the sea. Within the walls a mosque and an Arab palace, both destroyed in a sixteenth century earthquake, have recently been restored.

The folkloric La Chanca neighborhood abuts the mountains on one side and the Alcazaba on another. You can see the area from the heights of the Alcazaba before descending for a walk through its streets. Many of the houses are hollowed out from rock, and others are one-story cubicles that look like toys and follow the undulations of the land. The houses are dead-white, then splashed with vivid reds, yellows, and greens and a blue that matches the brilliant sky.

$\int$ EEING THE CITY OF ALMERÍA

CATHEDRAL   This sixteenth century Gothic cathedral occupies the site of a former mosque and was constructed like a fortress, with a flat roof and four defensive towers, to protect against the pirate attacks by Turks and Berbers that continued well into the sixteenth century. The altar is of marble and jasper, and the choir screen is especially beautiful.

$\mathcal{V}$ ISITING THE PROVINCE OF ALMERÍA

LA ALPUJARRA DE ALMERÍA   This is the extension of La Alpujarra de Granada. Take the Sierra de Gador road through stunning scenery of bleached-white mountains—rounded mounds that are deeply cracked and furrowed and contrast with the deep green valleys where sweet Almería grapes are grown.

CABO DE GATA   This striking cape, with its beautiful stretch of beach and its volcanic surroundings, has been declared a national park zone. Nearby are salt mines and a curious old village, **LAS ALMADRABAS DE MONTEVELA.**

At **BAR JOSÉ MARÍA**, near the Gabo de Gata lighthouse, try a tasty little local fried fish called *caramel* (a member of the perch family).

NÍJAR   A center for the *harapas*, traditional craft of weaving pieces of fabric and rags (*harapos*) to create rugs and wall hangings.

TABERNAS   America's Wild West has been transported to this desolate mountain landscape, and all the mainstays of the genre are here: Main Street, the General Store, a red brick saloon, sheriff's office, dilapidated hotel, and the hanging tree. You can see it from afar—the buildings are just facades—but you will have to pay admission to see the shoot-outs and barroom brawls that are regularly enacted.

◆ Just outside Tabernas on the Murcia-Almería road, **CAFÉ BAR "ALFARO"**   tel. (951) 36 54 04, is plain and utilitarian, but we had a simple and unforgettable lunch: fried eggs with *serrano* ham, mixed salad, and grilled quail (one order of each is plenty for two). (Inexpensive.)

SORBAS   A spectacularly situated village, naturally fortified by rock formations; its houses "hang" over a precipice.

VÉLEZ BLANCO   The beautiful sixteenth century turreted castle of the Marquis of Vélez sits atop a hill, overlooking a whitewashed, meticulously kept village and backed by the barren mountains of Almería. The castle's exquisite patio was transferred to the New York Metropolitan Museum of Art.

◆ In the nearby **CUEVA DE LOS LETREROS,** the prehistoric Indalo (see box, p. 480) is painted on a cave wall.

INTRODUCTION TO SPAIN'S
ISLAND PROVINCES

Las Islas Baleares, in the Mediterranean off the eastern shore of Spain, and Las Islas Canarias, in the Atlantic near Africa's northwest coast, comprise three Spanish provinces and have several things in common: undeniable scenic beauty, perennial sunshine, moderate temperatures year-round (although noticeably cooler in winter, especially in the Baleares), and innumerable beaches and coves. For these reasons the islands have become thriving resorts. Many mainland Spaniards and foreigners own homes on the islands; many others come, usually on package tours, and stay at one of the thousands of hotels from which to chose. But as the popularity of the Canarias and Baleares grows, a part of their beauty and tranquillity diminishes; you have to look harder to find that out-of-the-way town, that idyllic beach, that quiet cove.

If your travel intentions are principally to relax and enjoy good weather, you will find both in the islands. But I warn you: Come only in the off-season or on the fringes of high season, when the weather is best but the crowds are thin. And even if you come as part of a group tour and stay in a large resort hotel, do rent a car and go off on your own. The islands are small, and you'll be surprised how quickly you can leave the high-rise beach-side constructions behind and discover the islands' true colors and extraordinary natural beauty.

Island environments have the ability to make you lose your sense of place. So I suggest visiting the islands in conjunction with a trip to the Spanish mainland, because even though the islands are politically a part of Spain, they are a world unto themselves. To see the islands and think you have seen Spain is a mistake.

[Mallorca] . . . is, of course, Spanish land. . . . But I don't know what subtle suggestion infiltrates in one's spirit, making him think . . . that he is far from all official countries. . . . In the golden island I felt like . . . a citizen of the world . . . of Nature and of peace.

Miguel de Unamuno

Although Unamuno was referring specifically to Mallorca, the same sentiments apply equally well to Las Islas Canarias, to the rest of the Baleares, and to many other islands in the world.

Getting to the islands from the Spanish peninsula, or vice versa, is simple: You can choose either a short flight or a pleasant boat ride on a modern ship or, in the case of the Baleares, sometimes a quick crossing by hydrofoil. You might combine a tour of the Canarias with a visit to western Andalucía, and a trip to the Baleares with travel in Catalunya or the Levante.

13

LAS ISLAS BALEARES: THE LIGHT-HEARTED ISLANDS

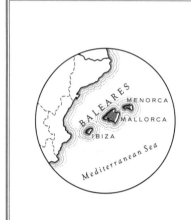

| 0 | 10 | 20 | 30 | Miles |
| 0 | 16 | 32 | 48 | Kilometers |

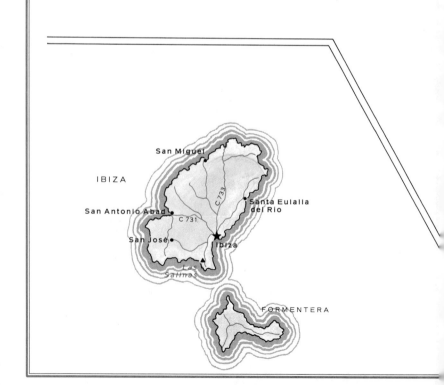

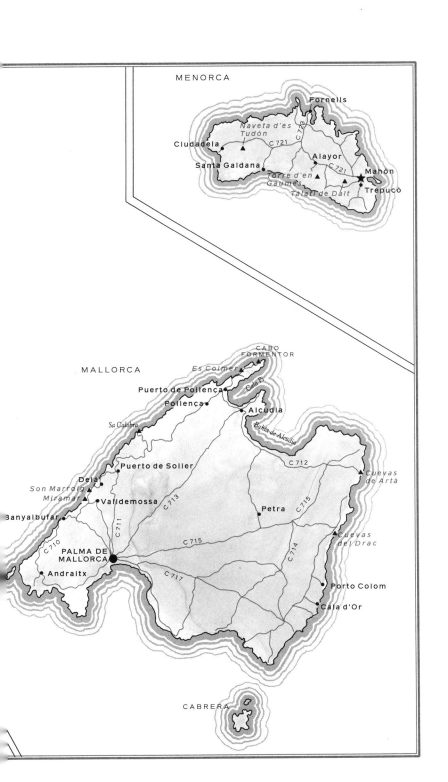

MENORCA

Fornells

Naveta d'es
Tudón

Ciudadela

C 721

Alayor

Santa Galdana

C 721

Mahón

Torre d'en
Gaumes

Trepucó

Talati de Dalt

MALLORCA

CABO
FORMENTOR

Es Colmer

Puerto de Pollença

Cala Pi

Pollença

Alcudia

Sa Calobra

Bahía de Alcudia

Puerto de Soller

C 712

Cuevas
de Artà

Deià

Son Marroig

Miramar

Valldemossa

C 713

Petra

C 715

Cuevas
del Drac

Banyalbufar

C 711

C 715

C 710

PALMA DE
MALLORCA

C 714

Andraitx

C 717

Porto Colom

Cala d'Or

CABRERA

LAS ISLAS BALEARES, in the Mediterranean off the east-central coast of Spain, consist of three main islands: Mallorca, Ibiza, and Menorca. Mallorca is the largest, and its capital, Palma de Mallorca, is also capital of the Balearic region. There are two much smaller islands—Formentera, near Ibiza, and tiny Cabrera, just off the southern coast of Mallorca—that have little importance but make pleasant day excursions.

The Baleares have been inhabited since time immemorial, and ancient indigenous civilizations have left puzzling monoliths, stone dwellings, and tombs for archaeologists to study. These primitive natives tried in vain to keep invaders at bay. Although they developed formidable skills as "slingers," hurling huge rocks at the enemy, they were eventually dominated. For ancient seafaring civilizations, the islands were strategically crucial as a place from which they could watch over the Mediterranean and carry on trade. Beginning with the Phoenicians and continuing with the Greeks, Carthaginians, Romans, Arabs, and Christians, who took permanent control, voyagers from well-established cultures came to the Baleares en route to the Spanish mainland and left evidence of their passing. The Arabs, here for five hundred years, contributed their sophisticated irrigation systems, which still function today.

The Baleares were reconquered in the thirteenth century by Jaime I of Aragón, who also returned Valencia to Christian rule, and except for a relatively brief period when the Baleares formed an independent kingdom, the islands were part of the kingdom of Aragón for most of the Middle Ages. During the early Christian era and even into the eigh-

FOODS AND WINES OF LAS ISLAS BALEARES

GENERAL
Pork, fish and shellfish, cured sausage, sweet and savory pastries

SPECIALTIES
Ensaimada—a sweet bread
Sobrasada—soft sausage seasoned like *chorizo*
Butifarrón—cured sausage with pine nuts and herbs
Tumbet—sautéed potatoes, peppers, eggplant, and zucchini
Caldereta de Langosta—lobster stew
Sofrit Pagès—stew of sausage and meats
Sopas Mallorquinas—thick vegetable soup
Arroz Brut—rice, pork, and vegetable casserole
Escaldums—chicken and meatball stew
Frit—sauté of liver, peppers, and potatoes
Greixonera—bread pudding
Queso de Mahón—semisoft cow's milk cheese

WINES AND LIQUEURS
José Luis Ferrer from Binisalém
Palo—syrupy-sweet herb-scented liqueur
Hierbas de Mallorca—dry anisette with herbs

teenth century, the Baleares were the object of pirate raids and attacks by warring European powers (Menorca, in fact, was a British colony for almost one hundred years); the islands were well fortified with protective walls, some of which remain today.

The rural people of the Baleares, called *payeses*, are clearly no strangers to foreign occupation, nor to celebrated international trysts, like that of Lord Nelson and Lady Hamilton in Menorca and of Chopin and George Sand in Mallorca, and today they take the invasion of tourists in stride. While agriculture and maritime pursuits were once the sustenance of the islands, today it is tourism. The Baleares have become an international playground; Palma's airport is the busiest in Spain, and the islands accommodate more visitors than any other area in Spain. Tourists come for the scenic beauty, the fine weather, the peaceful coves and crystalline waters. But unless you travel away from tourist enclaves and come at the right time of year, you could leave without having experienced the pleasures of the Baleares.

Since the Baleares are separated from one another by distances that were substantial before air and motorized sea travel, and, besides, have distinct topographies, each developed a singular personality. Mallorca, often called "The Island of Tranquillity," is the most exciting scenically; Ibiza is less mountainous than Mallorca but has splendid coves, and its "anything goes" atmosphere has become world famous. Menorca is flatter still and quite sedate (a reflection of its British heritage), and its prehistoric remains are most tantalizing.

When Jaime I initiated the Christian repopulation of the islands, he brought many settlers from Catalunya (he encouraged Jews as well to set up residence in the islands). Thus today the language of the islands (besides Spanish) is a derivation of Catalan with its own peculiarities. For example, the articles *el* and *la* become *es* and *sa*, respectively; *son* is a local term for a neighborhood; *ca'n* means "house of" (as it does in Catalan, without the apostrophe), and, by extension, often forms part of a restaurant's name. Balearic cuisine also shows a marked connection to Catalan cooking, and yet because of the islands' isolation and the limited produce that the soil supports (there are few rivers to irrigate crops), a cooking style unique to the Baleares developed.

If you travel through the islands' interiors you will see what grows on the land, principally vineyards, gnarled olive trees, hundreds of years old, and almond trees. Pigs are the most common domesticated animal, although in Menorca the land is suitable for cows, and of course the sea adds considerable diversity to the diet. In short, you have peasant cooking that is occasionally heavy but is always interesting and at times exceptional.

High on my list of the contributions of the Baleares to Spanish cuisine is its spreadable cured sausage called *sobrasada* and its sweet and savory pastries. The black-hoofed Iberian pigs of the island, from which *sobrasada* is made, are the same strain as those that produce the magnificent cured hams of the mainland, and were apparently responsible for renewed trade activity in the last century after a prolonged decline. But conditions here are less than ideal for curing meat for extended periods, so the pork is chopped and mixed with paprika and spices, stuffed into skins, and briefly cured to produce *sobrasada*. Mixed into an omelet, grilled in a sandwich, or as a filling for turnovers, it is irresistible—unlike any other sausage I know.

People of the Baleares have a considerable knack for making flaky pastry crusts, empanadas, and sweet rolls. The airy *ensaimada* is spiraled like a snail shell and is traditionally served at breakfast time, either plain, custard-filled, or filled with candied squash. Pastry shops cram their display cases with such appetizing creations as *cacarrois* (a turnover filled with greens, raisins, pine nuts, and scented with mint), little meat pies (somewhat like British pork pies), sweetened cheese pastries called *robiols*, and mint-flavored cheese cake called *flao*. *Ensaimadas*, when mixed with egg, milk, sugar, and sometimes walnuts and cheese, become the typical bread pudding *greixonera*. Surprisingly, breads tend to be dry and saltless and not at all appealing.

But the islands' olives, small and bitter, are especially good; I also like a sauté of red peppers, eggplant, and zucchini with potatoes called *Tumbet*; *Escaldums*, a chicken and meatball stew; tasty, rib-sticking *Sopas Mallorquinas*, a thick soup of cabbage, greens, and pork; *Arroz Brut*, a rice, pork, rabbit, and vegetable casserole; and from Ibiza *Sofrit Pagès*, a stew of meat and sausage. The selection of foods from the sea is immense. Two preparations I love are *Caldereta de Langosta*, fresh lobster in a delicious broth of garlic, thyme, onions, peppers, and almonds, and *Mero a la Mallorquina*, grouper baked with raisins, pine nuts, tomatoes, and potatoes. *Burrida de Ratjada*, skate in almond sauce, is popular in Ibiza.

It is said that mayonnaise takes its name from the city of Mahón in Menorca and originated in the Baleares (see box, p. 504). Native cheeses, like *Queso de Mahón* from Menorca, are sold at gourmet shops around Spain; *Queso de Mahón*, in its mass-produced version, becomes Spain's most common processed cheese. The dairy industry flourishes in Menorca, and ice cream under the brand name La Menorquina is sold nationally.

Fine Balearic wines are few but on the increase. Recently two Mallorcan wines of the Binisalém designation, José Luis Ferrer 1984 and 1985 red Reservas, were rated among the best in Spain. And island liqueurs, like Palo, herb-scented and syrupy sweet, and Hierbas de Mallorca, a dry anise, are locally popular.

Native crafts are disappearing, but you can still find some embroidery, native cotton cloth (typically in designs of bleeding colors), basketry, and blown glass. On a more industrial level, Balearic shoes are exported to many countries and sold at the finest stores, and Majorica pearls, although artificial, look so much like the real thing that they have achieved worldwide popularity.

GETTING TO AND STAYING IN
THE BALEARES

Modern cruise ships with moderately priced staterooms can take you from Alicante to Mallorca and Ibiza, and from Barcelona or Valencia to Mallorca, Ibiza, and Menorca. Most crossings are overnight trips. Hydrofoil service from Denia in Alicante to Ibiza is available from the end of June until the last week of September (approximately a two-hour trip).

By air the choices are ample: to Palma de Mallorca from most major cities of the mainland, as well as from many European cities; to Ibiza and Menorca from Madrid and Barcelona; and to Ibiza from Valencia.

◆ If you have rented a car on the mainland, leave it behind; rental prices on the islands are extremely low and much less than the price of transporting a car. If you make short trips without luggage, the open-air mini-jeeps are the fun way to travel.

◆ If at all possible avoid the month of August, and try to stay away in July as well. Come in June and September, when the weather is splendid and tourism is at a reasonable level.

◆ Many hotels and restaurants close in off-season, from November through March or April.

TRAVELING BETWEEN THE BALEARIC ISLANDS

The islands are not very close to one another. By boat it takes about four hours from Palma to Ibiza; Menorca is a six-hour ride from Mallorca. There are hydrofoils in season (June through September) that are much quicker, covering Palma to Ibiza in about two hours, leaving in the morning and returning in early evening. You can travel from Alcudia in northern Mallorca to Ciudadela in Menorca in one hour. Daily service from Ibiza to Formentera takes twenty minutes.

There is air service from Palma de Mallorca to Ibiza and to Mahón (Menorca), and from Menorca to Ibiza.

THE ISLAND OF MALLORCA

If you were to visit only one of the Baleares I would suggest coming to Mallorca (mah-*yor*-cah). Its capital, Palma de Mallorca, has character and cultural interest, and the island's coastal scenery is dazzling. Ever since the last century, Mallorca has been known in Europe as a romantic hideaway. Frédéric Chopin and George Sand came to the island in the nineteenth century, lured by the idyllic picture of the island painted by friends in Paris. So, too, Archduke Ludwig Salvator of Austria was a passionate admirer of the island and made it his home for fifty-three years. Today King Juan Carlos spends his summers in Mallorca.

In this century Mallorca became a typical place for newlyweds to spend their honeymoon, and such writers as British novelist Robert Graves lived here for many years. Today Mallorca is a busy center of tourism. You can come to Mallorca, as many do, with nothing more in mind than swimming, golfing, yachting, and taking it easy. I propose instead one day seeing the city of Palma and two days traveling the rocky coast. If you don't get into the countryside and up to the north, you will have missed the best of Mallorca.

THE CAPITAL CITY OF PALMA DE MALLORCA

The city of Palma has the look you might associate with southern latitudes. Encircling a big beautiful bay, Palma feels open and airy, and its waterfront promenade, Paseo de Sagrera, and broad, shaded boulevards, like La Rambla, filled with flower stalls, and Rey Jaime III and Passeig des Born, both lined with elegant shops, burst with healthy trees and plants that are dense with shiny deep-green foliage. It is a city that invites languor and exudes the Good Life. And yet it is a city with history.

Because of its large and well-protected port, Palma was the focus of several successive cultures that occupied the island. The Romans were apparently the first to build a city here, and they called it Palmaria. The Arab kings, who named the city Medina Mayurka (from this the name Mallorca evolved), made it their headquarters during the centuries they reigned. But it was in the Middle Ages and in subsequent centuries that Palma acquired its veneer of nobility and of wealth, a result of its flourishing Mediterranean trade. The city's aristocratic past can be seen in its cathedral, its churches, and in the mansions that have survived.

As you walk the city's boulevards you will come upon many of these noble homes, from the Gothic through the Baroque periods. Many are built in a style peculiar to Palma: austere, lightly ornamented exteriors and flat roofs that often extend into deep, heavily carved eaves. The houses are entered through broad low arches that lead to a patio of grand proportions, sometimes irregularly shaped and typically highlighted by flattened arches and graceful upper galleries, reached by a regal stairway. Casa Verga and the Ayuntamiento (Town Hall) are fine examples of the style.

The older sections of Mallorca include what was once a substantial and extremely prosperous Jewish quarter, located, as such neighborhoods were wont to be, near the Arab and later the Christian center of the city. In Mallorca this was east of the palace of the Arab kings, La Almudaina, and the cathedral. Both of these buildings today open to the sea, although they were once protected behind thick city walls. The streets are dark and labyrinthine, and the many mansions struggle in these cramped quarters to flaunt their elegance. Besides the neighborhood itself, the Jews left little tangible evidence of their important role in the life of the city, and remaining from the long Arab occupation are a few arches, the patio of La Almudaina palace, and the exceptional Arab baths.

The cathedral, especially when seen from the sea, is immediately striking, standing tall over the city. Its slender, closely spaced Gothic flying buttresses give it a grace and delicacy that are accentuated by the magnificent waterfront setting. This is Palma's jewel, sparkling above the Bahía de Palma in the sunlight and in glorious illumination by night.

Seeing Palma de Mallorca

⬧ Pick up a plan of city streets and monuments at your hotel or at the tourist office, Rey Jaime III 10.

CATHEDRAL   Built between the thirteenth and fourteenth centuries in Gothic style, the cathedral dominates the view of the city. The spaciousness and light in the interior are immediately impressive, a result of the cathedral's immense size, slim pillars, and unusual height, and also, it seems, a consequence of remodeling carried out by master architect Antoni Gaudí (see Index) in this century. He replaced the stained glass, thereby allowing more light to enter; he moved the choir out of the central aisle, where it customarily stands in Spanish churches, and removed the altarpiece from the apse. In its place he left a free-standing wrought-iron sculpture in the wonderfully tortuous Gaudí style. Somehow it blends perfectly with the cathedral's Gothic design.

BAÑOS ÁRABES   Of unusual design, these well-preserved tenth century Arab baths feature an octagonal shape that supports a delicately pierced brick dome, made square by four corner columns.

LA ALMUDAINA   This was once the palace of Mallorca's Arab rulers. What remains—a patio and a balcony over a wide arch that was once a gate in the town walls—is from the Gothic period when the Christian kings resided here. The rest of the building has been restored and is used as military headquarters, but it is open to the public.

MANSIONS AND PALACES   They are everywhere in the city and most display typical Mallorcan detail (see text). Among the most distinguished examples are **CASA BERGA, CASA MORELL,** the **AYUNTAMIENTO** (Town Hall), **CASA OLEZA,** and **CASA BALAGUER** (see a city map for the locations of these and other noble homes).

CASTILLO DE BELLVER   A fourteenth century fortress and palace of the kings of Mallorca, Bellver, surrounded by a moat, has an unusual circular design. Its walls are round, and a cylindrical Tower of Homage rises from the castle. The round double-arched patio is especially beautiful, and the views over Palma and the mountains are panoramic.

LA LONJA   Facing the sea, at what was once the port entrance to the city, this commercial exchange was an extremely busy one. Turreted like a fortress but softened by delicate Gothic windows, it is a finely designed and well-proportioned example of civil Gothic architecture.

SAN FRANCISCO   An exuberantly carved Baroque portal and a spacious Gothic cloister are among the outstanding features of this fourteenth century Franciscan convent.

STAYING IN PALMA DE MALLORCA

In Palma you can either stay on the outskirts of the city at resort-style hotels or choose downtown accommodations, which are adequate, but hardly fancy. We chose the latter, reasoning that we were here to see Palma and be in the city, and would have many opportunities once we headed into the countryside for superior hotels in scenic locations with beaches and pools. In any case, avoid hotels in the beachfront resort called Playa de Mallorca; it is a bad dream, thronged with those on package tours and crowded with German beer parlors and cheap trinket shops. It felt like Coney Island.

SOL JAIME III   Paseo de Mallorca 14   tel. (971) 72 59 43, and **PALLADI-UM**   Paseo de Mallorca 40   tel. (971) 71 39 45, are simple hotels without pretensions and among the few acceptable hotels in the downtown area. (Moderate.)

For more elegance and a water view (but a somewhat less convenient location) there are **VALPARAÍSO PALACE**   Francisco Vidal 23   tel. (917) 40 04 11 (very expensive; pool), and **MELIÁ VICTORIA**   Avenida Joan Miró 21   tel. (971) 23 43 42 (very expensive; pool).

SON VIDA   Castillo Son Vida   tel. (971) 79 00 00, occupies a thirteenth century castle, today elegantly appointed, and is in a wonderfully secluded location in the mountains five kilometers from Palma. Son Vida is a self-contained resort, where many upscale tour groups stay. Transportation is provided into town. (Very expensive; pool.)

EATING IN PALMA DE MALLORCA

Even locals despair of the scant restaurant offerings in Palma, and I suspect many visitors dine in their hotels. The food tends to be international, and it is difficult to find Mallorcan specialties. Tapas are not especially interesting either. Nevertheless, there are several good choices:

PORTIXOL   Sirena 27 (in the fishermen's quarter of Cala Portixol)   tel. (971) 27 18 00   A short ride from downtown, this restaurant has décor that is maritime and a setting around an illuminated pool. The fish is first rate: Try *Caldo Marinero* (fish soup), *Mero a la Mallorquina* (grouper in a tomato, raisin, and pine nut sauce), or any of the other choices from their extensive fish selection. For dessert there are local specialties like almond cake and Mallorcan cheese tart. (Moderate–expensive.)

BAHÍA MEDITERRÁNEO   Paseo Marítimo 33, fifth floor   tel. (971) 45 76 11   Magnificent views of the bay and international cooking. This is a favorite of Spain's King Juan Carlos when he summers in Mallorca. (Expensive.)

RIFIFI   Joan Miró 186   tel. (971) 40 20 35   Classic fish preparations, such as grilled shellfish and *Candereta de Langosta* (lobster stew). (Moderate–expensive.)

PORTO PI   Joan Miró 174   tel. (971) 40 00 87   Set in a stately mansion, this restaurant is a newcomer and currently among the most fashionable places in town. The menu is elegant, with dishes like hake in champagne sauce and lamb with spinach and dates, but you can always find simple fish dishes as well. (Expensive.)

LA LUBINA   Muelle Viejo s/n   tel. (971) 72 33 50   Down by dockside, this restaurant is excellent for simply grilled fish, *Pescado a la Sal* (fish baked under a crust of salt), Mallorcan lobster stew, and a selection of rice dishes. (Moderate.)

CELLER SA PREMSA   Plaza Obispo de Palou 8   tel. (971) 72 35 29   A huge rustic place resembling a wine cellar and very popular for its low prices and its many Mallorcan dishes. Service is no-frills, and while the food is not as good as it could be, the atmosphere is lively and inviting. Closed weekends.

♦ For more casual eating, I enjoy purchasing food from one of the many fine bakeries offering wonderful savory pastries—a specialty of Mallorca—that you can take to the waterfront park and eat as a picnic or munch as you tour the city. For breakfast, a freshly baked *ensaimada* is a must in Mallorca.

Among the best bakeries are **FORN FONDO**   Unió 15; **HORNO SANTO CRISTO**   Pelaires 2; and **FORN DES TEATRE**   Plaza Weyler 9. For outstanding *sobrasada* sausage, another sausage called *butifarrón*, and local cheeses, go to **CA'N TIÁ**   Plaça de Cort 5, a gourmet shop where you can eat in or take out.

GELATERÍA CA'N MIGUEL   Rey Jaime III 6, is always popular for its excellent ice cream in twenty-four flavors, some of them quite unusual, like carrot, garlic, and Roquefort.

SHOPPING

Many elegant shops, often international boutiques and jewelers, abound, especially along Rey Jaime III and Passeig des Born.

ARTESPAÑA   Rey Jaime III 27, a government-sponsored handcraft shop, has high-quality artisan products, many of them from Mallorca.
♦ Typical of Mallorca are *siurells*—painted clay whistles in human and animal shapes that in ancient times were used as votives but today are charming decorative items.

TOURING THE INCOMPARABLE ISLAND OF MALLORCA

It is absolutely essential once you have seen Palma to visit Mallorca's northwestern coast; it is for me what makes this island truly extraordinary. Rent a car, as we always do, and travel at a relaxed pace. Leave Palma in the morning, stay on the northern coast, then continue down the eastern coast and swing into the interior. Although Mallorca is by far the largest of the

Baleares, it is surprisingly easy to see most of it in a short space of time, although I would choose to spend at least one week.

On one such visit to Mallorca, we headed toward **BANYALBUFAR,** just twenty-two kilometers west of Palma, but otherwise a world away. We turned south to the Mirador de Ses Animes for the first of many splendid views of this rocky coastline. You wouldn't think that the panorama could get any better than this, but little did we suspect what was still to come. Banyalbufar is set on a mountain, engulfed by terraced land that slopes down to the sea; tomato plants thrive. A delightful family-operated hotel, Hotel Mar i Vent, captures the tranquillity and has stunning views, and you might be content staying here for several days reading a good book before continuing on.

Traveling north sixteen kilometers on a winding road brought us to **VALLDEMOSSA,** a medieval stone town, exquisitely preserved, where prosperous Mallorcans, mainland Spaniards, and foreigners who have fallen in love with the town like to spend summers. Valldemossa has become a place to pay homage to Frédéric Chopin, because it was here in the abandoned Carthusian monastery that Chopin lived the winter of 1838–39 in the company of George Sand and her children (see box, p. 497).

Beyond Valldemossa, the road turns closer to the coast, and the **SON MARROIG** palace of the vast **MIRAMAR** estate appears high above a cobalt-blue sea and looks down at La Foradada, a rocky mass that snakes its way into the water. The property belonged to Austrian Archduke Ludwig Salvator, who was an ardent admirer of the Mallorcan flora and fauna; he carved trails into the woods and erected belvederes to facilitate nature walks and capture the beauty of the sea from various vantage points.

We could easily have spent an afternoon here, hiking through the estate grounds, but instead we continued north to **DEIÀ** and found another delightfully restored town of dark-stone construction that Miguel de Unamuno describes as so perfect that it looks unreal, as if it were artificially conceived for the tourist. For many years this was the home of British writer Robert Graves, who was instrumental in maintaining the character of the town. In a secluded spot above Deià is a quietly elegant hotel, La Residencia, which I am told is a magnet for the world's rich and famous in search of anonymity. Surely they can find it here in this sixteenth century seignorial mansion, nestled in the mountains, and I have La Residencia in my memory file for many more return visits.

The wonderful cliffside road we were traveling continued for a few kilometers before we descended to **PUERTO DE SÓLLER,** a port town enclosed by mountains on an idyllic bay. It is a busy but well-cared-for tourist center, and a charming tramway can bring you here for the day from Palma.

It is twenty-eight kilometers along a road with overlooks toward the sea and toward the mountain interior before the turnoff for the cove **SA CALOBRA**. The road dives through cliffs and makes stunning hairpin turns; one such curve is called La Corbata (Necktie) because it loops a full 360 degrees before directing you once more toward the sea. From this precious sandy cove, cliffs loom vertically, enclosing you in the amazing setting. There are terraces for drinks and food (a surprising number of people find their way here), and some restaurants have rooms available.

Between Sa Calobra and Puerto de Pollença, the waterfront extension of the interior town of Pollença, the views grow increasingly spectacular and the overlooks more frequent; just beyond Puerto de Pollença there are three successive viewpoints over the sea, known as **ES COLMER.** You might think the first one provides the ultimate in awesome vistas, but wait until you reach the last overlook, where the cliff heights and the staggering sheer drops are a wonderwork of nature. Even George Sand, prolific writer that she was, sensed her lack of vocabulary to express what she saw on this coast:

> . . . word-painting is so inadequate a mode of expression. . . . It takes the artist's pencil and the engraver's burn to reveal Nature's splendours to lovers of foreign travel.

CHOPIN AND GEORGE SAND IN MALLORCA

Frédéric François Chopin and George Sand came to Mallorca lured by reports of the island's idyllic setting and excellent weather, hoping that a change in scenery and climate would reverse the decline in Chopin's health. They took up residence with George Sand's two children in the Carthusian monastery of Valldemossa, abandoned three years earlier as a result of the Disamortization Law (see Index), promulgated by liberal prime minister Mendizábal. He was by chance an acquaintance of George Sand's; she, a free thinker, greatly admired Mendizábal's attempt to diminish the power of the church in Spain.

The municipality of Valldemossa decided to lease the monk's former cells, and although they had few takers, George Sand and Chopin thought it an inspirational setting that would allow her to write and him to compose. In fact, both of them were highly productive during this winter. Chopin composed some of his finest works; most of his *Preludes* are a product of his stay in Mallorca. Supposedly the happier ones reflected the sunny days when he was in good health, the somber ones, rain and gloom and thoughts of the departed monks. He also created the *Polonaises* that recalled his Polish homeland, all this on the worst piano imaginable.

They both marveled at the setting in which they found themselves. Chopin expressed his feeling about Mallorca in his letters to friends, George Sand in her book *Winter in Majorca:*

> It is one of those overwhelming views that leaves nothing to be desired, nothing to the imagination. Whatever poet and painter might dream, Nature has here created . . . everything! . . . For myself, I never felt the emptiness of words more keenly than in my hours of meditation at this monastery.

And yet, these were not happy times. They arrived to an uncharacteristically cool and damp winter and endured, according to George Sand, two months of downpours. Chopin was in very poor health, and George Sand writes that the townsfolk treated them abominably, obviously not looking kindly on their illicit relationship and angry, besides, that they were staying in what had once been a monastery. They made the couple's life difficult, refusing to sell them food or offering it at exorbitant prices. Inexplicably, they chose to stay three months.

Today the quarters of this famous couple have been lovingly conserved and embellished with Chopin memorabilia.

We returned to sea level and stopped for the night at the Hotel Formentor, which stands in isolated splendor facing the pine-covered cove of Cala Pi, and from our terrace appreciated the sight of the bay of Pollença, bathed in moonlight. The following morning we climbed the cliffs once more and passed through rock-strewn pine forests to the very tip of the island, the desolate **CABO FORMENTOR.** This is the northernmost point of Mallorca, and the views are once more extraordinary. Passing the walls of the old Roman town of Alcudia and circling the wide bay of Alcudia, we eventually reached Mallorca's eastern coast. It is much flatter and, I must say, somewhat anticlimatic; its beautiful little coves of aquamarine water and its fishing towns, sadly overconstructed, were much too tame after what we had already seen.

As we headed south to Palma we visited the fantastic grottoes of **ARTÁ,** passed through Porto Cristo, a lovely town on a rock-lined, tightly enclosed port, and saw the **CUEVAS DEL DRAC,** celebrated for their exceptional natural beauty. An inland route through olive and almond groves took us to **PETRA.** Here was born Fray Junípero Serra, who established nine Franciscan missions in California that eventually developed into the cities of Los Angeles, Monterey, San Diego, San Jose, and San Francisco, and his humble house is preserved as a museum. We finally returned to Palma, then to the mainland, but the island's beauty stayed fresh in our minds.

> In Mallorca I finally saw the sea of my dreams, clear and blue as the sky, like a sapphire plain carefully ploughed into gently undulating furrows.   *George Sand*

ᕙISITING THE ISLAND OF MALLORCA

ANDRAITX   A town in one of Mallorca's loveliest locations, in a mountain setting with exceptional views over the Mediterranean. In the port area are wonderful coves. Because it is so easy to get here from Mallorca, this has become a popular resort.

BANYALBUFAR   See text.
HOTEL MAR I VENT   tel. (971) 61 80 00, is a small peaceful hotel, charmingly decorated and ideally set over the sea. (Moderate; pool.)

VALLDEMOSSA   Be sure to walk through this distinguished town, then visit **LA REAL CARTUJA,** the Carthusian monastery. Substantially modified over the years, the monastery is where Chopin stayed when he lived in Mallorca. Among the many mementoes of the composer are some of his letters and musical scores and a simple upright piano at which he created some memorable works (see box, p. 497). The pharmacy, once a part of the monastery, continued to service the village after the monastery was abandoned, and provided the ailing Chopin with medicines. The ceramic jars and glassware of the pharmacy, made in Mallorca, have been preserved.

Adjacent to the monastery is the so-called **PALACIO DEL REY SAN-CHO**, of which, in reality, nothing remains. This is a pleasant country mansion decorated with antiques; chamber concerts are frequently held here.

CA'N PEDRO   Archiduque Luis Salvador s/n   tel. (971) 61 21 70, a rustic village restaurant, made somewhat sophisticated by the impressionistic paintings on the walls and plants hanging from the ceiling, is a pleasant setting to sample Mallorcan cooking. The grilled meats are excellent, and I particularly enjoyed grilled rabbit with *alioli* preceded by a *sobrasada* omelet. (Inexpensive–moderate.)

MIRAMAR   Within this grand estate of the Archduke Ludwig Salvator, which as its name suggests, overlooks the sea, is the archduke's Son Marroig palace, where his varied collection of Mallorcan prehistoric and antique objects is on display.

DEIÀ   See text.

LA RESIDENCIA   Finca Son Canals s/n   tel. (971) 63 90 11   Deluxe accommodations in a country setting. The hotel is quiet, exclusive, and tastefully decorated with antique country furnishings. It has a fine, elegant restaurant, El Olivo, and a lovely beach in a small cove, just a short walk downhill. (Very expensive; pool.)

PUERTO DE SÓLLER   See text.

SA CALOBRA   See text.

PUERTO DE POLLENÇA   The road runs right along the edge of this town's large bay, where people fish from the beach and windsurf offshore.

HOTEL FORMENTOR   Puerto de Pollença   tel. (971) 53 13 00, is a distinguished hotel in a stunning setting. It's a little too formal for my taste (everyone dresses in his best for dinner, jackets required, and there is dancing every evening on the terrace), but you can dine instead in the more informal grill and outdoor garden, where the food is quite good, although somewhat overpriced. The hotel's private beach is studded with pine trees and couldn't be prettier. (Very expensive; pool.)
◆ The Pollença Music Festival in July, August, and September attracts some of the world's great orchestras, soloists, and opera stars.

CUEVAS DE ARTÁ   Near the end of a beautiful cape, facing the sea, this cave is massive, up to 120 feet high with lacy stalactites that look like a fairyland forest of tree trunks. To heighten the sensation of having entered a Dantesque world, the guide sets off flashing lights accompanied by a Bach fugue.

CUEVAS DEL DRAC   These dramatic two-kilometer-long caves near Porto Cristo are another fantasyland, featuring impressive stalactites and stalagmites and the huge, still, and transparent Lago Martel, a lake more than 500 feet across and covered by a myriad of slender stalactites that when illuminated make this look like a stage setting. Visitors cross the lake by boat.
◆ Not far away, in Porto Colom, there is an excellent restaurant, **CELLER SA SINIA**   Calle Pescadores s/n   tel. (971) 57 53 23, serving the best of Mallorcan seafood: sautéed shrimp with garlic and parsley; a fish called *servi-*

ola with sweet red peppers; and an outstanding version of the Mallorcan lobster stew, *Caldereta de Langosta*, all at the hands of an expert in Mallorcan cooking, Toni Ramón. (Moderate.)

Near Cala d'Or in S'Horta, **SA FARINERA**   Sexta Volta 41, Carretera Felanitx–Cala d'Or   tel. (971) 83 72 28, is a charming country house whose owner, once a fisherman, serves well-prepared Mallorcan dishes like *Sopas Mallorquinas*, *Arroz Brut*, *Tumbet*, and *Escaldums de Pollo y Albóndigas*.

PETRA   You can see in this small town the simple whitewashed dwelling where the eighteenth century missionary Fray Junípero Serra was born and the monastery where he was instructed in the priesthood. It is said that he named his California missions after the saints who were represented in Petra's monastery chapels: San Francisco, San Diego, and San José.

THE ISLAND AND CITY OF IBIZA

Ibiza (ee-*bee*-tha), known locally as Eivissa, is the southernmost of the three principal islands of the Baleares and the closest to the mainland. Historically it was the most strategically situated, and especially under the Carthaginians the island carried on a lively Mediterranean trade; Ibiza's salt and its purple dyes were particularly in great demand. The Carthaginians held the island in such high regard that it was to Ibiza that they came to rest and to die; thousands of ancient graves have been uncovered. Perhaps it was the mystery of these primitive civilizations and the artwork they left behind that first attracted artists and writers and a large hippie community to Ibiza.

The Greeks called the island Pitiusas (islanders call themselves Ibicencos), in reference to the pine forests that covered the land. Almond and olive trees also thrive in this dry climate—driest of the Baleares—as do aromatic plants like thyme, fennel, marjoram, and mint. The herbs are used, among other things, to make a liqueur called Frígola.

Although Ibiza lacks the stunning heights of Mallorca, its craggy coast and innumerable coves create sites of great beauty. But Ibiza is only twenty-five miles long, and the island's "no holds barred" atmosphere has made it wildly popular and internationally famous among stylish, trendy crowds and those who merely like to observe the antics of others (a visit to the nightclub KU is the best way to capture the island's mood). Undiscovered secluded beaches are a thing of the past, and building has run rampant; yet if you choose to come off-season, you can find tranquillity and some of the beauty that made Ibiza so popular in the first place. The city of Ibiza without the crowds is still the medieval enclave it has been for centuries.

The ancient city of Ibiza, founded by the Carthaginians in the year 645 B.C., is set high on a hill overlooking a bay that today is filled with pleasure craft. The upper town is called Dalt Vila and looks like a fortress, completely enclosed by stone walls that were rebuilt under Charles V, over previous Moorish walls, to protect against piracy. Four gateways give access to the Old

Quarter, where the noble houses and mansions vie for space with simple lime-washed houses that have a cubist, somewhat North African appearance. The irregular streets climb steeply to the cathedral and castle remains that occupy the crown of the hill. Life can be relatively quiet in this quarter, but in high season it is a spectacle. Crowds funnel into its narrow streets, and vendors (some of them hippies from the 1960s) display their artsy wares.

Make your way down to the waterfront to the area called La Marina and Sa Penya, the old fishermen's quarters, and the scene, day and night, is frenzied. Restaurants, cafés, discotheques, and boutiques, featuring avant-garde fashions, crowd the narrow streets creating a lively multinational atmosphere. The names of some stores and restaurants—the End, Café In, Amnesia—give you an idea of the ambiance.

Seeing Ibiza

The sights in Ibiza center on people watching. Aside from this, you will of course want to explore Dalt Vila and walk up to the thirteenth century **CATHEDRAL.** Its interior was remodeled in Baroque style, but frankly the views from here are more compelling than the cathedral's artistic interest. Near the Plaza de España, also commanding fine views, is the sixteenth century **SANTO DOMINGO** church, noteworthy for its simple whitewash and domes covered in vertical rows of tile, which makes them look like straw hats. It is a good example of the Ibicenco style of architecture.

In the cathedral square you might visit the **MUSEO ARQUEOLÓGICO,** featuring archaeological finds from the various civilizations that populated the island, from indigenous peoples to the Carthaginians, Greeks, and Romans. **MUSEO DEL PUIG DES MOLINS,** a second museum in the southern sector of the city, is at the site of a Carthaginian acropolis, where thousands of tombs have been uncovered. The museum has a fine collection of Carthaginian objects, including two splendid busts of the goddess Tanit and other statues with richly carved detail, decorated ostrich eggs, jugs, amulets, and primitive necklaces.

STAYING IN IBIZA

The city of Ibiza is not the favored place to stay on the island (many of the best restaurants are also outside the city), and most of the city's hotels are at the nearby beaches, like the **TORRE DEL MAR** hotel at Playa den Bossa, tel. (971) 30 30 50. (Moderate–expensive; pool.) **EL CORSARIO** Ponent 5 tel. (971) 30 12 48, however, is right in Dalt Vila and affords beautiful views of the town and the port. The hotel is small, and reservations are hard to come by. (Moderate.) Another possibility in town—much larger and more impersonal—is **ROYAL PLAZA** Pedro Francés 27 tel. (971) 31 00 00. (Moderate–expensive; pool.)

EATING IN AND AROUND IBIZA

MESÓN DE PACO   Bartolomé Roselló 15   tel. (971) 31 42 24   Simple fish dishes and Ibiza specialties like *Sofrit Pagès* (sausage and meat stew) and *greixonera* (bread pudding) bring visitors and residents to this simple restaurant. (Moderate.)

GRILL SAN RAFAEL   Carretera de San Antonio, km 6   (San Rafael)   tel. (971) 31 54 29   In a beautiful setting near the San Rafael church, this stylish restaurant serves "imaginative" cooking. (Moderate–expensive.)

LA MASÍA D'EN SORD   Carretera de San Miguel, km 1   tel. (971) 31 02 28 A magnificently restored and decorated country house, serving regional and international cooking. (Moderate.)

AMA LUR   Carretera de San Miguel, km 3   tel. (971) 31 45 54   Among the island's best restaurants, elegantly set in an Ibicenco house with a patio for outdoor dining. The menu is Basque inspired. (Very expensive.)

IBIZA'S FAMOUS NIGHTLIFE

Spanish tabloids are filled with reports of the frenetic nighttime activities in Ibiza, especially at **KU,** Carretera Ibiza–San Antonio, km 6 (San Rafael), tel. (971) 31 70 66, a cavernous club that centers on an indoor swimming pool and is the ne plus ultra of discos. The star attraction is the clientele, each patron attempting to outdo the other in outrageous dress and behavior. The madness continues throughout the night. Surprisingly, the restaurant is considered one of the best of Ibiza, featuring food of nouvelle Basque influence. (Moderate–expensive.)

♥ISITING THE ISLAND OF IBIZA

♦ Roads in Ibiza do not generally follow the shoreline; the only way to get a comprehensive view of the island's coast is from a boat or plane. All major roads radiate from the city of Ibiza.

LAS SALINAS   In this area of salt pans are fine beaches and many beach-side restaurants and bars, like **KU BEACH** and **CHIRINGUITO MALIBÚ,** among the island's trendiest.

SAN JOSÉ   (Sant Josep)   Off the coast southwest of this town is **VEDRA** island, little more than a rocky peak that looms almost 1,200 feet above the sea.
CA'N JOANA   Carretera Ibiza–San José, km 9   tel. (971) 80 01 58, is a most charming restaurant for outdoor dining and has a stylish menu. (Moderate–expensive.)
ES BULDADO   In the beautiful Cala D'Hort, this beachside restaurant serves fresh fish and some Ibiza specialties. (Moderate.)

S'ESPARTA, located in the Cala Tarida, a family-run restaurant, serves fine fish stews and other seafood dishes. (Moderate.)

SA TASCA   (San Agustín)   tel. (971) 80 00 75, is in a country-style Ibiza house. The specialty is beef, and of course seafood. (Moderate.)

CA'N BERRI VELL   Plaza Mayor 2 (San Agustín)   tel. (971) 34 43 21   In a beautiful seignorial house on the main square of the tiny village of San Agustín, a pleasant restaurant serving regional and Spanish cooking. (Moderate.)

SAN ANTONIO ABAD (San Antoni Abat)   A pretty spot, backed by green-covered mountains and set on a sparkling bay. It has become much too busy and is known for trendy discotheques.

PIKES   Camino Sa Vorera s/n   tel. (971) 34 22 22, is a small, much-sought-after rustic hotel in a quiet setting of lush greenery. (Expensive; pool.)

SA CAPELLA   Carretera Santa Inés, km 0.5   tel. (971) 34 00 57, occupying a very old chapel, is a restaurant that serves Spanish and Balearic cuisine. (Moderate–expensive.)

SAN MIGUEL (Sant Miquel)   A tiny village just eighteen kilometers from Ibiza. The highlight here is the **HACIENDA NA XAMENA**   Puerto de San Miguel   tel. (971) 33 30 46, a hotel sensationally situated on a secluded promontory overlooking the sea. (Very expensive; pool.) This is Ibiza's most exclusive hotel, and it has a very fine restaurant as well.

◆ Continuing east to San Juan Bautista, and then turning north, takes you to Cala de Portinatx, a beautiful cove in a setting of pine-covered cliffs.

SANTA EULALIA DEL RÍO (Santa Eularia d'es Riu)   The only river on the island passes this town and makes the area unusually fertile. The new quarter of Santa Eulalia is very fashionable and most popular with the tourist trade; the old quarter, Puig de Missa, high on a hilltop, is a fine example of traditional Ibiza peasant architecture.

CA NA RIBES   Calle San Jaime 67   tel. (971) 33 00 06, has its dining room in the patio of a rustic house; the food is simple and well prepared. (Moderate.)

CHIRINGUITO DE JOAN FERRER   Cala Mastella (San Carlos), owned by a fisherman, is on the beach, and the menu, naturally, is fish, simply prepared in stews and sometimes cooked with rice. (Moderate.)

◆ Just eighteen kilometers from Ibiza is the small island of Formentera (the name means "wheat" in Latin and was given by the Romans). It is connected to Ibiza by regular boat service and is popular for day trips to its fine beaches, although there are also several hotels here, such as **LA MOLA** Playa de Mitjorn   tel. (971) 32 80 51 (moderate–expensive; pool).

THE ISLAND OF MENORCA

Menorca (may-*nor*-cah), called Minorca in English, is the most eastern of the Baleares and just a little larger than Ibiza. Menorca is filled with beaches and coves and is famous for its abundance of lobster; *Caldereta de Langosta Menorquina*, now prepared all over the Baleares, originated here. Known as the quietest of the Balearic Islands, Menorca is peaceful partly because it is the least scenically spectacular, and therefore attracts fewer visitors, but mostly because its British heritage has encouraged a low-key life-style.

The history of Menorca took a different turn from the other islands when the 1713 Treaty of Utrecht, which ended the War of Spanish Succession (see Index), gave Gibraltar and Menorca to England. Menorca remained British for almost a hundred years; Gibraltar still belongs to England.

British influence is apparent in Menorcan architecture. Many houses are without balconies and have casement windows (rare in Spain) framed by colorfully painted shutters. The island's agriculture also shows ties to England. Since Menorca is a little wetter and more fertile than the other islands, its green rolling hills in the interior have made it a dairy land. An ice cream brand bearing Menorca's name, La Menorquina, sells all over Spain; there is an excellent cow's milk cheese, brushed with oil, butter, and paprika, called Mahón, after the island's capital; and the bulk of Spain's processed cheese, such as El Caserío, is produced here. Also under the influence of the English, Menorca became a producer of gin, which is made from the juniper berries that grow on the island.

The British, who love the island's quiet ways, continue to frequent Menorca, and Menorquinos, protective of their privacy, strive to keep the island the peaceful haven it has traditionally been. Overdevelopment is discouraged, and new constructions must be built in character with the local architecture.

MAYONNAISE, MADE IN MAHÓN

It is practically impossible to pinpoint exactly where mayonnaise—the sauce made from the most common Mediterranean ingredients, oil and egg—had its origin. But its name in Spanish, *mahonesa*, or *mayonesa*, certainly suggests a connection with Mahón, and in fact is the generally accepted derivation of the word. The French, however, claim the word comes from *moyeu*, an old French word for egg yolk. Yet another explanation joins the French and Spanish versions; it tells of the Duke of Richelieu, who led the brief French occupation of the island in the eighteenth century, tasting mayonnaise in Menorca and taking the recipe back to France.

Personally, I am partial to the Mahón explanation if for no other reason than that the island's abundance of lobster mandated the invention of mayonnaise as the ideal accompaniment.

What is truly special about Menorca and gives the landscape a curious appearance is the remains of a Bronze Age civilization thought to have developed between 1500 and 2000 B.C. Little is known about this indigenous culture, which existed well before the island's conquest by other Mediterranean civilizations. Menorca is a veritable outdoor museum, and up to one thousand examples of three characteristic prehistoric structures can be seen in the fields, mostly in the southern sector of the island, where the land is protected from wind and cold.

The **TALAYOT** is an unmortared construction, some examples of which are of impressive size and shaped like a truncated cone. They were built on high ground, dominating the surroundings, and thought to perhaps be "palaces" of tribal chiefs or the foundations upon which such princely houses were built. One at **TREPUCÓ** and those of **TORRE D'EN GAUMÉS,** south of Alayor, are among the best examples (there are about two hundred of them on Menorca).

Unlike anything else in the world is the **TAULA,** a massive stone column wedged into the ground. Over it a huge stone slab sits like a tabletop, suggesting that perhaps these belonged to temples, either functioning as supports for other structures that have disappeared or as mammoth "altars" for religious rites. One of the finest examples is at **TREPUCÓ;** another is at **TALATÍ DE DALT.**

The **NAVETA** is the third kind of structure, a long stone funerary chamber that narrows at the top, resembling the upturned hull of a boat (thus the name). One of them, **NAVETA D'ES TUDONS,** is not far from Ciudadela.

℘ ISITING THE ISLAND OF MENORCA

MAHÓN (Maó)   From a long, narrow, and well-protected port faced with humble dwellings, the whitewashed capital city of Mahón rises steeply to an upper quarter of seignorial homes. Activity centers on the waterfront, where there are many shops and restaurants. Mayonnaise is said to have originated in Mahón (see box, p. 504). Lord Nelson stayed here briefly, reputedly with his mistress, the beautiful Lady Hamilton, wife of the British ambassador to Naples, and his residence, **SAN ANTONIO,** known to the British as the Golden Farm, from which there is a beautiful vista of the port, has been preserved as a museum.

PORT MAHÓN   For de l'Eau s/n   tel. (971) 36 26 00, a hotel with an Old World air, overlooks the sea. (Moderate–expensive; pool.)

HOTEL DEL ALMIRANTE   Carretera Villacarlos–Puerto de Mahón (in Es Castell–Villacarlos)   tel. (971) 36 27 00, is three kilometers from Mahón in an eighteenth century mansion. (Moderate; pool.)

ROCAMAR   Cala Fonduco 32 (in Puerto de Mahón)   tel. (971) 36 56 01, is perhaps the island's finest restaurant, featuring an elegant and creative menu. (Moderate–expensive.)

PILAR   Forn 61   tel. (971) 36 68 17, a charming locale with Menorcan décor; the restaurant concentrates on Menorcan dishes. (Moderate–expensive.)

TREPUCÓ   There are remains of prehistoric talayots and taulas here (see text).

ALAYOR (Alaior)   Although an industrial town, its Old Quarter of starkly whitewashed houses and mansions on narrow, alley-like streets is among the best kept and most beautiful on the island.

CALA'N PORTER, to the south, is an inlet around which cliffs arise vertically. A large cave, **SA COVA D'EN XOROI,** is carved from the cliffs and is a bar by day, disco by night, with wonderful views and a "Stone Age" setting.

FORNELLS   In the area of this harbor are some of the island's most beautiful beaches and coves. Fishermen capture lobster nearby, and the city is known for *Caldereta Menorquina.* Try it at dockside at either **ES PLÁ**   Pasaje d'es Plá   tel. (971) 37 66 55, or **HOSTAL S'ALGARET**   Plaza S'Algaret   tel. (971) 37 66 66.

◆ From the mountain of **MONTE TORO** you can see the entire island of Menorca. At the top there is a sanctuary, where a statue of a Virgin that miraculously appeared here is worshipped.

SANTA GALDANA   The town has a lovely cove and beach, encircled by pine groves and high cliffs.

CIUDADELA (Ciutadella)   Formerly the island's capital and also a port city. Because of its picturesque old streets—some porticoed with whitewashed arches—and its noble demeanor, Ciudadela has been declared a National Historic-Artistic Complex. The local shoe industry is centered here, making footwear for some of Spain's and Europe's finest shops.

CASA MANOLO   Marina 117   tel. (971) 38 00 03, at the port, is a restaurant for island dishes like *Caldereta de Langosta,* fish and rice casseroles, and a variety of simply prepared local fish and shellfish. (Moderate.)

◆ About five kilometers east of the city is **NAVETA D'ES TUDONS,** the most important example of Menorcan prehistoric funerary monuments (see text).

LAS ISLAS CANARIAS:
THE FORTUNATE ISLANDS

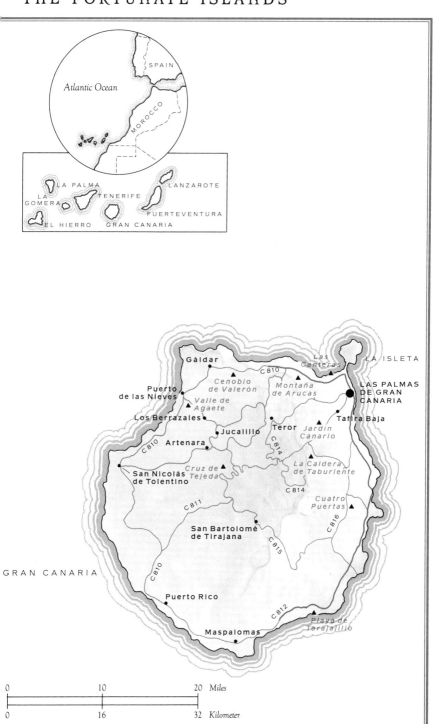

KNOWN BY the ancient Greeks as Las Islas Afortunadas—the Fortunate Islands—Las Islas Canarias are indeed blessed: lushly green, fertile, and temperate all year-round. Off the northwest African shore in the Atlantic Ocean, the Canary Islands (there are seven of them, plus several islets) are some 700 miles from the Spanish mainland. Contrary to what one might suppose, they were not named after the canary songbirds, which are, in fact, native to the islands, but the reverse: The birds take the name of the islands, which in turn were called Canaries in reference to the dogs (*canis* in Latin) that apparently once populated the islands in large numbers.

Las Islas Canarias were created by volcanic upheavals, and most of the islands have a volcanic mountain at their center. They emerged from the ocean (or, according to some theories, are the peaks of the submerged continent of Atlantis; see box, p. 530) millenniums ago. The dramatic mountains and craters that resulted are what make the Canaries visually exciting. But most who travel to the Canary Islands do not come expressly for the scenery. It is the islands' ideal climate that attracts vacationers from all over the world, especially in winter, but increasingly in summer as well. Even though the Canaries are offshore from the Sahara desert, the weather is tempered by cool ocean currents and by the trade winds, creating a perpetual springtime. Air temperatures vary little from one season to another, and water temperatures are similarly constant (the air and sea are usually within a few degrees of each other); the beaches and clear ocean waters are splendid any time of year.

For me, however, it is the variety of terrains that makes the Canaries so remarkable: from volcanic cones and cool high mountains enveloped in thick forestland to craters, carefully terraced and dense with subtropical vegetation that spills down to the edge of the sea, and to genuine deserts, where not a single tree grows and beaches are

FOODS AND WINES OF
LAS ISLAS CANARIAS

GENERAL
Fish, pork, potatoes, tropical fruits, and
vegetables

SPECIALTIES
Patatas arrugadas—"wrinkled" potatoes
Mojo—sauce accompaniment to potatoes and
fish
Potaje de Berros/Zaramago—watercress or
mustard green soup
Puchero Canario—chickpea stew
Sancocho Canario—salt fish, sweet potatoes,
spicy sauce
Gofio—polenta of toasted grains
Quesadilla—cheesecake

WINES
Monje, Viña Flores, Viña Norte from
Tacoronte
El Grifo (Malvasía wine) from La Geria

black volcanic ash. Palms mingle with pines, cactus
with chestnut trees. The indigenous dragon trees,
some of them thousands of years old, their upturned
branches as thick as tree trunks, their clusters of
spindly green leaves reaching skyward, look like prehistoric monsters and lend one more curious note to
an already exotic scene. The land yields impressive
crops of bananas, tobacco (Canary Island cigars are
famous), tomatoes, potatoes, coffee, sugarcane, and
many other continental and subtropical fruits and vegetables, despite a traditional scarcity of water. In the
Canary Islands, European, African, and American plant life all find receptive soil.

Las Islas Canarias are divided into two Spanish provinces: Las Palmas,
which includes the islands of Gran Canaria, Lanzarote, and Fuerteventura,
and Santa Cruz de Tenerife, covering the islands of Tenerife, La Gomera, La
Palma, and El Hierro. For practical purposes, however, you should think of
each island as a separate entity. While all are similarly formed by volcanoes,
each has a character of its own.

The sights in the Canary Islands are more breathtaking than you
could imagine such small islands could provide (in contrast, however, there
is a noticeable deficit of cultural pursuits). You probably will not see all of
the islands on one visit, so choose your islands according to your interests.
If you seek quiet, La Palma, La Gomera, and El Hierro are for you. If beaches and fishing are important, Fuerteventura is a best bet. But if you want to
see what makes the Canary Islands different from anything else in the
world, you must see the interior of Tenerife and Gran Canaria, and for
striking contrast, spend a day or two in the surreal volcanic desert of
Lanzarote.

Before the fifteenth century the Canary Islands were inhabited by an
isolated Stone Age people called Los Guanches, whose origins remain a
mystery (see box, p. 530). Las Islas Canarias came under the influence of
Spain in 1402, when they were explored and conquered by Jean de
Béthencourt, a Frenchman from Normandy in the service of Castilian king
Enrique III. The Catholic Kings made the islands a permanent part of Spain
in 1496, and the Canaries became active ports and a way station on the
route to the New World. For Columbus this was the last stop on familiar soil
before setting out to the west. He was encouraged by reports of a landmass
that natives had often seen on the horizon (". . . many honorable Spanish
men swore . . . that every year they saw land west of Las Canarias . . ."),
wrote Columbus, as reported by Bartolomé de las Casas (the original diary
has never been found). And although many adventurers had proposed
exploring this "eighth" Canary island, none had done so. The island proved
to be a visual trick played by the mists floating over the ocean surface. For
natives, however, this was the magical island they called San Borondón,
which, it was said, appeared and disappeared at one's will, a dreamland in
which all one's wishes would be fulfilled.

Columbus stopped in the Canary Islands on all three of his subsequent
trips to America, some say because of his romantic involvement with the
widow of the governor of La Gomera. Hernán Cortés, Francisco Pizarro,

Hernando de Soto, and many others off to conquer new lands also made port here. In modern times, Santa Cruz de Tenerife and Las Palmas de Gran Canaria continue to be important commercial ports and places where pleasure ships dock. Tourists are particularly attracted to Las Islas Canarias as duty-free ports.

As a crossroads in the Atlantic Ocean, the islands have seen the influences of many cultures. Today international crowds frequent the Canaries, and consequently restaurants are more ethnically oriented than anywhere else in Spain. Chinese, Japanese, Hindu, German, and South American establishments mix with the Galician, Asturian, Basque, Catalan, and Castilian restaurants run by emigrés from the Spanish mainland. Foreign ingredients and culinary influences, especially Cuban, Argentine, and even African, create an interesting local cuisine. Tomatoes and potatoes, native American products today so important to Canary cooking, traveled to Europe by way of Spain, and I wouldn't be at all surprised if they were cultivated here before reaching the European continent.

Unfortunately Canary cuisine sometimes is pushed aside in restaurants where so many cooking styles compete for attention. But it is a cuisine well worth exploring. Based on fish, (especially local varieties like *vieja, cherna,* and *sama*), distinctive *patatas arrugadas* (small local potatoes cooked in heavily salted water that wrinkles the potatoes when it evaporates), and tropical fruits and vegetables, Canary cooking takes typical Spanish dishes and gives them an exotic twist.

Puchero Canario, for example, is similar to the Castilian stew *cocido* (see box, p. 34) but adds sweet potatoes and pears to the stew's chickpeas, meats, and potatoes. To a Spanish bean stew, big bunches of watercress are added. A popular fish and potato dish, *Sancocho Canario,* takes on Canary character with the addition of sweet potatoes and an accompaniment of figs and grapes. Canary dipping sauces for fish and potatoes are made of typically Spanish ingredients and are prepared in three ways: *mojo colorado,* made with paprika, garlic, cumin, oil, and vinegar; *mojo picón,* which is similar but much spicier; and *mojo verde,* a green dip made with cilantro, which is not, however, found in mainland cooking.

Gofio, a kind of polenta of toasted ground wheat, corn, or chickpeas, was inherited from the Guanches (and is similar to something found in African cooking) and typically accompanies meals in the place of bread. The grains are mixed with water or milk at serving time and shaped into balls. *Gofio* is also used to make a breakfast porridge, as a thickener in stews, or sweetened to create desserts like *Raspaduras de Gofio.* Despite the huge amounts of bananas produced on the islands, they rarely appear in cooking, perhaps because they were introduced here at a later time, but they are the principal ingredient in fried pastries called *Tortas de Plátanos. Quesadilla,* a kind of cheesecake, is another popular dessert.

Malvasía wines—also called *malmsey*—are made in the Canaries, although they were first produced on the tiny Greek island of Malvasia in southeast Peloponnesus, where, coincidentally, my grandfather was born. Malvasía from the Canaries was famous centuries ago, especially among the British, and was mentioned by such sixteenth century writers as Shakespeare and Ben Jonson:

But that which most doth take my Muse and me is a pure cup of
rich Canary wine.   *Ben Jonson*

Malvasía is best known as a sweet wine, although today it appears as a
semidry wine as well. It no longer commands celebrity status, but it continues to be produced in Lanzarote from vineyards that grow in volcanic ash
and is a popular accompaniment to island cuisine. The island of Tenerife,
however, is now the largest wine producer of Las Islas Canarias, concentrating on light young red wines that in the last few years have made spectacular
gains in quality; some of them have been rated among the best of Spain's
young wines.

GETTING TO AND STAYING IN
LAS ISLAS CANARIAS

There is frequent air service from Madrid and Barcelona to the provincial capitals of Las Palmas and Santa Cruz de Tenerife. Other provincial mainland capitals also provide service, and there are flights as well from Europe and the United States. A modern cruise ship departs from Cádiz, takes two nights to reach the islands, and stops in Santa Cruz de Tenerife and Arrecife (Lanzarote).

♦ A rented car is a good way to explore the islands.

♦ Hotels tend to be very large and often fully booked by tour groups. For smaller-scale establishments with a local flair, the paradors are your best bet, and there is one on every island except Gran Canaria and Lanzarote. You will not find many small, exclusive, privately operated hotels like those in the Baleares.

♦ Winter (November to March) is high season in the Canary Islands; summers tend to be humid and hazy, but certainly a fine time to come as well.

One of your first tasks in the Canary Islands is to sort out the multitude of place names that include the words *palma* and *cruz*:

Las Palmas—one of the two Canary Island provinces.
Las Palmas de Gran Canaria—capital city of Gran Canaria island and of the province of Las Palmas.
La Palma—island in Santa Cruz de Tenerife province.

Santa Cruz de Tenerife—capital city of the island of Tenerife and of Santa Cruz de Tenerife province.
Puerto de la Cruz—resort town on the island of Tenerife.
Cruz de Tejeda—town on Gran Canaria island.
Santa Cruz de la Palma—capital of the island of La Palma.

TRAVELING BETWEEN
LAS ISLAS CANARIAS

From Santa Cruz de Tenerife and Las Palmas de Gran Canaria there is daily
service to Lanzarote, La Palma, and Fuerteventura.

Ferries and hydrofoils run between Gran Canaria and Tenerife. Ferries also take you from the capitals of these islands to the other islands; some are overnight trips, and others are quite short.

SHOPPING

You can still find some native Canary crafts, in particular openwork embroidery, basketry, and handwoven silk. As duty-free ports, the islands also sell items from all corners of the world.

THE PROVINCE OF SANTA CRUZ DE TENERIFE

THE ISLAND OF TENERIFE

Dominated by Spain's highest peak, Mount Teide, Tenerife (ten-er-*ee*-fay) is the largest Canary island and a thriving resort. Its activity centers on **PUERTO DE LA CRUZ,** a city just north of the island's capital, **SANTA CRUZ DE TENERIFE,** and on the beaches of the southwest coast, such as Los Cristianos and Playa de las Américas. There are dozens of high-rise resort hotels in all of these areas, and most visitors spend their days in the sun at water's edge or around swimming pools. My goal when I come to Tenerife is not to stay long at such locations, but to rent a car and head for the hills. Tenerife is small enough to see in a day or two, either from a base along the coast or, better still, from the mountain parador.

I begin my tour of Tenerife departing from Puerto de la Cruz, and just outside the town I preview the island's stunning variety of trees and flowers at the marvelous Botanical Gardens (Jardín de Aclimatación de La Orotava) established by Carlos III in the eighteenth century. The king's purpose was to acclimatize American and Asian plants to a new environment, thus increasing their chance of survival in the colder latitudes of Madrid and Aranjuez, where he had palaces and extensive royal gardens. The Botanical Gardens are today a fantasyland of native vegetation combined with alien plants, like orchids and rubber trees, that were brought here and adapted beautifully to the Canary climate.

The road to La Orotava climbs through an amazingly lush and fertile valley filled with banana trees, whose broad deep-green leaves create a velvety ground cover as far as the eye can see. From the **MIRADOR HUMBOLDT,** a sublime panorama unfolds, extending over the valley all the way to Puerto de la Cruz and the sea. The overlook was named after the German scientist Alexander von Humboldt, a world traveler who had explored the

Andes and the Amazon, studying their plant life. And yet supposedly he fell
to his knees in awe at the beauty before him.

The nearby town of **LA OROTAVA,** enveloped by banana plantations, is one of Tenerife's loveliest, an old-fashioned place of noble houses
with wood balconies and red tile roofs (San Francisco street is particularly
attractive) and of beautiful flowering gardens. Carlos III also established
Botanical Gardens here, but they pale in comparison to the variety of specimens found in the gardens of Puerto de la Cruz.

The road continues its upward climb, at times slicing right through
lava rock, and the vegetation gradually changes from tropical to continental. **EL PICO DEL TEIDE,** barren and volcanically shaped, looms dreamlike in the distance, more than 11,000 feet high and snow-covered most of
the year.

> The eyes rest on that vision as if on something lacking tangible
> substance, as if on something that had arisen for the pleasure of
> the eyes and at the suggestion of the heart.
>
> *Miguel de Unamuno*

The air is nippy—in fact, downright cold when we came here in winter—and it didn't seem possible that just minutes before we had been basking in subtropical warmth. Mount Teide, Spain's highest peak (only
Granada's El Mulhacén, some 700 feet shorter, can compare), is all the more
striking because its steep ascent is so near to the sea. To ancient mariners, it
was a wonder and a kind of beacon that guided them home.

When we reach the mountain pass of El Portillo, an immense lava
crater fifteen kilometers across called **LAS CAÑADAS** (the word *cañada*
refers to valleys between volcanically formed mountains) comes into view.
From this crater the Teide rose in volcanic eruption eons ago. The steep
ravines, or *barrancos,* that form the south side of the crater, present a palette
of subtle colors created by mineral in the solidified lava. A myriad of streams
trickle down to the sea, watering the valleys along the way. Here in Las
Cañadas, at the foot of Mount Teide amid huge lava rocks, is Tenerife's
parador, a small and peaceful mountain lodge and a perfect place to pause
for lunch, or better still, to spend the night.

A cable car nearby takes us on a spectacular ride to the top, where we
peer into the volcanic cone. Mount Teide has not erupted in three centuries, but when Columbus stopped in the Canary Islands before heading off
on his voyage of discovery, an eruption was in progress. In his diary, as
recorded many years later by Fray Bartolomé de Las Casas, Fray Bartolomé
noted: "They saw a great conflagration coming from the mountains on the
island of Tenerife, which is high in a grand way." From these privileged
heights we can see all the Canary Islands and even as far as Africa. We are
lucky, of course, to have an exceptionally clear day.

From Mount Teide, you can only go down, but the descent can be
made by several different routes. The road that forks to the right at El
Portillo passes along the mountain edge, from where there are wonderful
views of both the northern and southern coasts. It cuts through the thick
pine and eucalyptus forest of **LA ESPERANZA** and finally returns to sea
level and the tropical surroundings of Puerto de la Cruz.

If you stay the night at the parador, the following day you can take the road south, which passes a curious lava formation, **EL ZAPATO DE LA REINA** (the Queen's Shoe), thus named because of its resemblance to an elegant upended shoe, and continue to **VILAFLOR,** highest village in the Canary Islands. A turn to the right a few kilometers down the road at Granadilla de Abona leads us toward the western coast and past another splendid overlook, Mirador de la Centinela. Soon the beachside tourist developments of Playa de las Américas and Los Cristianos come into view. We instinctively bypass them and head north up the coast, detouring to Adeja to see the extremely narrow 1,000-foot gorge, **EL BARRANCO DEL INFIERNO.** The vegetation is bountiful because spring water cascades down this dark ravine, where sunlight never penetrates, and transforms the earth into rich agricultural land. Some twenty kilometers north, a stunning black cliff drops vertically to the sea from a height of some 1,500 feet and is aptly called **LOS GIGANTES** (the Giants).

We reach the north shore and **GARACHICO,** destroyed by a river of lava from an eighteenth century eruption of a nearby volcano. The town today sits at sea level, but behind it mountains of petrified lava still look fluent, and it is not difficult to imagine the catastrophic scene as the volcano boiled over and blanketed Garachico with its deadly magma. The beaches are still black from the volcanic ash, but a sixteenth century seaside castle, San Miguel, somehow survived.

ICOD DE LOS VINOS, a town of noble houses that is named after its vineyards and immersed in dense vegetation, claims the island's most ancient dragon tree, perhaps three thousand years old, a marvel of nature that looks like a vision from Alice's descent into Wonderland. By now we have had our fill of mountains and yearn for the seaside and drive to nearby **SAN MARCOS,** a beautiful black beach in a tightly enclosed cove. It is packed with sun-blistered German tourists enjoying paella, while local musicians delight everyone with their rendition of *"¡Viva España!"*—a catchy song that most visitors to Spain will learn sooner or later. Although the atmosphere is boisterous and not at all what we had in mind, it is at the same time lively and infectious, and we add our voices to the song's last line, *"¡España es la mejor!"* (Spain is the best!).

♡ ISITING THE ISLAND OF TENERIFE

SANTA CRUZ DE TENERIFE   Capital of the island and of Tenerife province, this city, centered on its busy port and surrounded by tall mountains, has retained a certain provincial air (tourism did not evolve here, but in other beachside areas). A colorful city, filled with flowers, gardens, and parks, it was here in the eighteenth century that Lord Nelson (see Index) lost his arm in battle while laying siege to the city from the sea (he lost the battle as well). At the sixteenth century castle, **SAN CRISTÓBAL** (Castillo de Paso Alto), there is a cannon called Tigre (Tiger) that, according to tradition, wounded Lord Nelson.

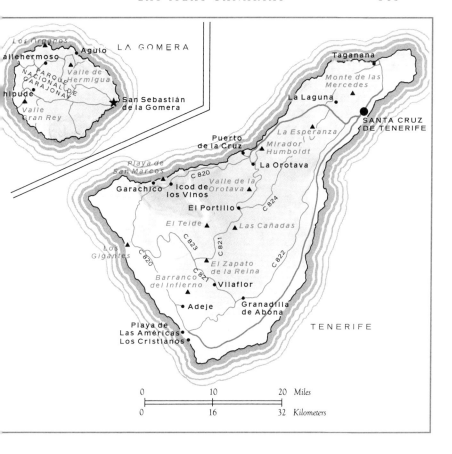

The **MUSEO ARQUEOLÓGICO** (in the Palacio Insular) conserves many interesting prehistoric remains, plus mummies, utensils, and ceramics from the island's Guanche civilization.

◆ In the Plaza de la Candelaria, **MERCADO DE ARTESANÍA** and **LA CASA DE LOS BALCONES** sell Canary crafts, such as fine embroidery work.

MENCEY José Naveiras 38 tel. (922) 27 67 00, is a deluxe hotel centrally located in a lush tropical garden setting not far from the port. (Very expensive; pool.)

CAFÉ DEL PRÍNCIPE Plaza del Príncipe tel. (922) 27 88 10, in an attractive setting, is a popular restaurant for Canary specialties, like *Ensalada de Papa Negra con Langosta* (black potato and lobster salad) and *Vieja al Cilantro* (fish with cilantro). (Moderate.)

LA RIVIERA Rambla General Franco 155 tel. (922) 27 58 12, is elegant and one of the island's best, serving Spanish and international cuisine. (Moderate–expensive.)

LA LAGUNA Surrounded by pine forests and named for a lake that has since disappeared, this was once the island's capital and still is an important inland city and university town. La Laguna's monuments are not especially noteworthy, but nonetheless the city has an air of history, and it is pleasant to walk its old narrow streets. Notice the typical Canary wood-framed, paned windows, the balconies of the houses, and the beautiful Canary-style upper gallery of the **CONVENTO DE SANTA CATALINA** in the Plaza del Adelantado. The **IGLESIA DE LA CONCEPCIÓN** has a fine Mudéjar ceiling.

EL DRAGO   Carretera del Socorro   tel. (922) 54 30 01, a restaurant fifteen kilometers northeast of the city in Tegueste, is in a delightful landmark Canary mansion that centers on a patio where a dragon tree stands; it serves authentic Canary cooking. (Moderate.)

♦ North of the city in the pine and laurel forest of **MONTE DE LAS MER-CEDES** there are two exceptional overlooks with views of the Anaga mountains, its valleys, and the coast. A winding road takes you to the village of **TAGANANA**, in a beautiful setting at the northern edge of Tenerife, where the beaches are black volcanic sand.

BOSQUE DE LA ESPERANZA   See text.

PUERTO DE LA CRUZ   A waterfront tourist center with flower-laden parks and seafront promenades. The Botanical Gardens (see text) are outstanding.

MELIÁ BOTÁNICO   Richard J. Yeoward s/n   tel. (922) 38 14 00, a hotel in a luxuriant garden setting, is just beyond town, next to the Botanical Gardens. (Expensive; pool.) Two centrally located and less expensive alternatives are **CONCORDIA PLAYA**   Avenida Generalísimo 3   tel. (922) 38 55 00, and **ATLANTIS**   Avenida de Venezuela 15   tel. (922) 38 54 11 (moderate; pool).

SEMIRAMIS   Urbanización La Pax   tel. (922) 38 55 51, is a high-rise hotel that descends along the face of a cliff. You enter on the upper floor and go down to your room. (Moderate or expensive, depending on season; pool.)

MI VACA Y YO   Cruz Verde 3, tel. (922) 38 52 47, is a most inviting restaurant, in the style of a rustic Canary house, centering on a large patio and filled with plants and country antiques. Although international cuisine is on the menu, there is traditional cooking as well. (Moderate.)

VALLE DE LA OROTAVA   See text. In the town of La Orotava, in two seventeenth century mansions at San Francisco 5, is the **CASA DE LOS BALCONES**, a center for Canary crafts.

CORPUS CHRISTI (nine weeks after Easter) is especially colorful here. Carpets of flowers are arranged in the streets of the Old Quarter, and different colors of volcanic sand from Mount Teide form interesting patterns. Religious floats, folkloric groups, and townsfolk in colorful costume parade through town.

LAS CAÑADAS DEL TEIDE   This is the crater from which Mount Teide arises (see text).

PARADOR LAS CAÑADAS DEL TEIDE   Las Cañadas del Teide   tel. (922) 33 23 04, couldn't be better located, near the foot of Mount Teide and overlooking the ravines of Las Cañadas. Its swimming pool is said to be the highest in Spain. (Moderate; pool.) In the parador's restaurant, island specialties are served.

EL TEIDE   Spain's highest peak (see text).

LOS CRISTIANOS and **PLAYA DE LAS AMÉRICAS** Tenerife's southern resort centers, both lined with luxury hotels, among them **SIR ANTHONY** Avenida Litoral s/n (Playa de las Américas) tel. (922) 79 71 13 (Very expensive; pool); **LAS PALMERAS** Avenida Marítima (Playa de las Américas) tel. (922) 79 09 91 (moderate–expensive; pool); and **GRAN HOTEL ARONA** Los Cristianos, tel. (922) 75 06 78 (moderate; pool).

You can eat well at **BISTRO** Avenida República de Honduras s/n (Playa de las Américas) tel. (922) 79 07 18, specializing in seafood (moderate), and **L'ESCALA** La Paloma s/n (Los Cristianos) tel. (922) 79 10 51, serving foods of the Spanish mainland. (Inexpensive–moderate.)

BARRANCO DEL INFIERNO See text.

LOS GIGANTES See text.

THE NORTHERN COAST (Icod de los Vinos, Garachico, San Marcos) See text.

ᴛHE ISLAND OF LA GOMERA

La Gomera (lah go-*mer*-ah) is all mountain, just twenty kilometers across, with abrupt drops to the sea through narrow ravines. The high center of the island is kept in its natural state by the creation of the **PARQUE NACIONAL DE GARAJONAY**. Agriculture is the island's principal livelihood, and there are glorious green valleys everywhere, meticulously terraced; **VALLE GRAN REY,** at the foot of a great gorge thick with banana trees and palm groves that slopes down to a beautiful sandy beach; **VALLEHERMOSO** (the name means "Beautiful Valley"), dedicated to banana production and blocked from the sea by the tall columns of lava rock, **LOS ÓRGANOS,** thus named for their resemblance to organ tubes; and **VALLE DE HERMIGUA,** blanketed with banana trees, surrounded by high cliffs, and nourished by water from the beautiful Cedro forest. There are delightful villages like Agulo, nestled near the sea and from where Mount Teide on Tenerife island appears hazily in the distance.

So steep are the ravines in La Gomera that communication and travel were traditionally a problem for islanders, and, as a result, they elevated whistling to an art. They sought variety of sounds by running a gamut of pitches, rhythms, and inflections that in essence made whistling into a language.

La Gomera entered history books as the last place where Columbus stopped before heading off on his mission to find a westerly route to the Indies. He came for provisions and to either replace or repair one of his ships, the *Pinta* (". . . its steering wheel was in bad shape, and she was taking on water, and he wanted to replace [the ship] with another, if he could find one"—*Diary of Columbus*). Columbus heard Mass in the Asunción church in the island's capital, San Sebastián, stayed at a small white house that has been preserved as a museum, and finally set sail on September 6, 1492.

When he left on his next two trips to America, he again paused at La Gomera—as rumor had it, because of his love affair with Beatriz de

Bobadilla, widow of the island's governor. They supposedly rendezvoused at her residence, **TORRE DEL CONDE**. Only a tower now remains, but it was once part of a building complex where treasures from the New World were stored. By the time Columbus set out on his fourth and last voyage to America, Beatriz de Bobadilla had remarried. And that is why, it is said, he anchored at Las Palmas and conspicuously avoided the island of La Gomera.

The island's capital, San Sebastián de la Gomera, enclosed by mountains at the end of a ravine, is not much more than a village, but as such is a pleasure. La Gomera has no airport (although there is a ferry that makes the brief crossing from Los Cristianos in southern Tenerife), and tourism is light. All the better for those of you seeking a place of absolute tranquillity.

STAYING ON LA GOMERA

PARADOR CONDE DE LA GOMERA   La Horca s/n   tel. (922) 87 11 00, in the capital of San Sebastián, is styled like a local seignorial house. It looks over the sea from a hill and is surrounded by lush gardens. (Moderate–expensive; pool.) The restaurant specializes in local cuisine.

Another hotel, **TECINA**   Playa de Santiago   tel. (922) 89 50 50, is south of San Sebastián in a secluded setting over Santiago beach. Accommodations are bungalows, designed in Canary country style. (Moderate; pool.)

SHOPPING

The sculpture in the local church of **CHIPUDE,** near Valle Gran Rey, gives you an idea of the talents of local artisans. The typical red pottery made here, which serves practical and decorative purposes, is shaped without the aid of a potter's wheel. Crafts of this village can also be found in San Sebastián de la Gomera at **ARGODEI,** Medio 69.

THE ISLAND OF EL HIERRO

El Hierro (el *eeyair*-oh) has the abrupt coastline so common to these volcanic islands, with the difference that the mountains rise, then flatten into a meseta. This was the last island to emerge from the sea, and evidence of lava flows is still relatively fresh. At **EL LAJIAL,** near La Restinga, the lava hardened into unique bumps, billows, and protrusions that are a strange sight indeed today. To the ancients, El Hierro was the most westerly patch of known land, and therefore Punta de Orchilla, the western point of the island, was designated longitude 0. That honor was of course later transferred to Greenwich, England. Today a lighthouse stands at this cape to guide ships en route to America; this was the last land Columbus saw after he left La Gomera on his first trip.

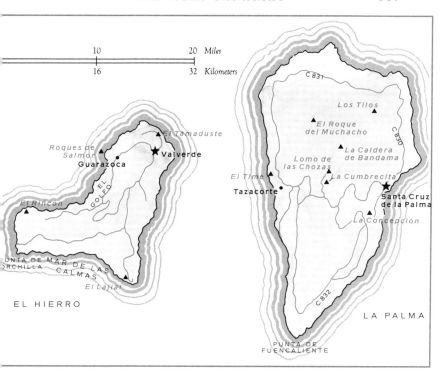

This is the smallest Canary island, pockmarked with volcanic craters and heavily wooded with pines, beech trees, and savins (juniper trees related to the red cedar). Some livestock is raised, and a fresh cheese made from goat's, cow's, or sheep's milk, or a mixture of all three, is produced here and is the main ingredient in the island's famous cheesecakes called *Quesadillas* (they are made in Isora, ten kilometers from the capital). The island is planted with sugarcane, pineapple plants, and banana trees, but the amount of arable land is limited, and El Hierro can only support a small population. That is why many islanders took advantage of the boats passing here on their way to America, and left to seek their fortunes in the New World. El Hierro is today a quiet island, unable to attract significant tourism because it is practically without beaches. In their place, however, are wonderful natural pools, some of them quite large, like **EL TAMADUSTE** in the north, and they are used as swimming holes. The rocky coasts are popular for snorkeling and submarine fishing.

A scenic highlight of El Hierro is **EL GOLFO,** a fertile valley surrounded by wooded cliffs, which produces a bounty of sugarcane and bananas and was once part of an ancient crater. The rest of the crater is submerged in the sea and forms a wide gulf. In the mountains and on the **ROQUES DE SALMOR,** just off the coast, lives the giant prehistoric Salmor lizard, only found in El Hierro. The views of the gulf from the lookout of El Rincón and another near Guarazoca, are simply sensational.

A concentration of venerable savin trees, twisted, thick-limbed, and low to the ground for protection from the winds, creates the most important forest of its kind in Europe. The dry, uninhabited Dehesa pastureland of the meseta drops sharply to an unusually peaceful stretch of Atlantic waters, appropriately named Mar de las Calmas (Sea of Calm).

Just about the entire population of El Hierro lives in the capital, **VALVERDE,** the only island capital that was kept far from the sea as protection from pirate attacks. From its mountain setting it commands wonderful views of the coastal cliffs, the sea, and El Teide, peeking over La Gomera from Tenerife.

STAYING ON EL HIERRO

PARADOR ISLA DE EL HIERRO   Las Playas   tel. (922) 55 80 36, ten kilometers from Valverde, is designed like a traditional Canary country house and is in a secluded plant-filled setting overlooking a black volcanic beach and the sea. (Moderate; pool.) The restaurant features Canary cooking.

CLUB PUNTA GRANDE   Punta Grande, Valle Frontera   tel. (922) 55 90 81, near the southern village of Restinga, is a tiny hotel with just four rooms, and if you can get a reservation you are indeed lucky to stay in this complex, which has been given historic designation. It is in a setting of utter tranquillity. (Moderate.) The restaurant sits at the rocky edge of the sea, and its menu is based on the fish and fruits of the island.

THE ISLAND OF LA PALMA

La Palma (lah *pahl*-mah) has more height in proportion to its size than any other island in the world. It is the greenest of the Canaries, lushly covered with banana plantations, almond and palm trees, and woods of linden and pine trees, and at its center is the world's largest crater, **LA CALDERA DE TABURIENTE.** From there the island descends in profound ravines to the sea, giving birth to natural springs along the way.

A drive around the perimeter of the island is a rewarding excursion. You can head north from Santa Cruz to an area of small fishing villages and to the thick linden-tree woods of **LOS TILOS.** Or you can go south to see the sensational views of the island's capital, Santa Cruz de La Palma, from **LA CONCEPCIÓN** overlook, continue to the black beach of **LOS CANCA-JOS,** circle around **FUENCALIENTE** at the tip of La Palma to see the San Antonio and Teneguia volcanoes (the latter erupted in 1971), and then up the western coast to **EL TIME,** from where once more you are presented with fantastic views, this time of the gorge of Las Angustias and the plains, carpeted with banana trees. The fine beaches of **TAZACORTE** are below.

You will have to cut straight across the island to reach La Palma's most incredible sight, the immense crater of **LA CALDERA DE TABURI-ENTE,** some five miles in diameter and more than 2,000 feet deep. From the overlooks of **LA CUMBRECITA** and the **LOMO DE LAS CHOZAS,** the view of this enormous volcanic depression spreads out before you in spectacular beauty. Tall pine trees line the volcanic bowl, and this is the site of the Parque Nacional de Caldera de Taburiente. From here you can also see **EL ROQUE DEL MUCHACHO,** the island's highest peak, at more than 7,000 feet, where an important international observatory has pointed huge telescopes to the skies.

La Palma's capital, **SANTA CRUZ DE LA PALMA,** is set against the side of a mountain, at the edge of La Caldereta crater, and descends steeply to the sea. From La Concepción *mirador*, south of the city, the sight of Santa Cruz can best be appreciated. Amid the high-rise buildings on the Avenida Marítima, along the waterfront, there are still some whitewashed two-story houses with quaint colorful balconies. Calle Real, the city's main street, takes you to the Plaza de España and El Salvador church, which has wonderful *artesonado* ceilings. The city's port was once one of the busiest debarkation and arrival points for travel to and from the Spanish American colonies, and although relatively calm today, it is still the way you are most likely to arrive in La Palma.

STAYING ON LA PALMA

PARADOR SANTA CRUZ DE LA PALMA   Avenida Marítima 34,   tel. (922) 41 23 40, located in the capital, is a typical Canary house with views of the ocean. (Moderate.)

EATING IN LA PALMA

CHIPI-CHIPI   Carretera de Velhoco s/n   tel. (922) 41 10 24, outside of Santa Cruz, has a charming Canary-style patio and simple local cooking, like marinated rabbit and "wrinkled" potatoes with *mojo* dipping sauce. (Inexpensive–moderate.)

SHOPPING

Handwoven raw silk is the specialty of La Palma. You can see how it is made at, among other places, **BERTILA PÉREZ,** Barrial de Abajo 9, in El Paso, west of the capital, or you can purchase silk fabric by the meter or made into garments at **GERMÁN GONZÁLEZ,** Avenida del Puerto, and other shops in Santa Cruz de la Palma.

THE PROVINCE OF LAS PALMAS

THE ISLAND OF GRAN CANARIA

Gran Canaria (grahn cahn-*ahr*-eeah) is the third largest of the Canary Islands, a round landmass rising to more than 6,000 feet at its highest point, then dropping sharply to the sea in the north and west, with a more gentle decline in the south. The dramatic high-mountain scenery alternates with Gran Canaria's typically lush greenery of palms, coffee and tomato plants, banana trees, and sugarcane. Fruits like pears, mangoes, strawberries, and cherries also grow here.

In contrast, the south of Gran Canaria is a desert landscape, and the vast, gently undulating beaches are magnificent. Naturally, this is the area that has become the focus of tourist development; hotels and apartment complexes have arisen all along the shoreline. To really see Gran Canaria, as is generally the case in the Canary Islands, you will have to travel to its volcanic core—the most exciting part of the island—and then circle around the western and northern coast. The eastern and southern areas are the least interesting.

Gran Canaria's capital, Las Palmas, was the first city founded by the Spanish in the Canary Islands and today is by far the largest. Unlike Santa Cruz de Tenerife, Las Palmas has participated fully in the tourist boom and is well endowed with hotels, mostly dedicated to tour groups, and they ring the beautiful beach of Las Canteras. Because of its busy international port, Puerto de la Luz, the city has acquired a certain cosmopolitan air as well, and become a place where diverse cultures commingle.

The modern city arose on a previously undeveloped neck of land that joins the port and a small protrusion of land called La Isleta, where the fishermen's quarters once were. Unlike most cities that evolve around their ports (where you will find the oldest quarters), in the area around the harbor of Las Palmas there are modern neighborhoods of apartment buildings and private homes in garden settings (La Ciudad Jardín). This neighborhood is in fact packed with parks and gardens, bars and restaurants. Especially lively is the Parque Santa Catalina.

La Vegueta, north of the port, a charming cobbled quarter of old mansions, cool patios, narrow streets, small pretty squares (like Plaza del Espíritu Santo and the Plaza de Santo Domingo), and artistically worked wood balconies made from the local pine called *tea*, dates from the fifteenth and sixteenth centuries. The cathedral is in La Vegueta and is finished in neoclassic style, although clearly Gothic inside. Several bronze dogs stand guard at its entrance in the Plaza de Santa Ana; they represent the dogs that gave the Canaries their name.

Culturally and artistically Las Palmas is quite limited, and you will, I think, be more interested in touring the scenically exceptional interior, seeing the cave dwellings and other evidence of the native Guanche inhabitants, or simply heading for less congested beaches.

SEEING LAS PALMAS

MUSEO CANARIO   There is a fine and comprehensive collection here of items related to the native Guanches (see box, p. 530), including religious figures, mummies, skulls, and ceramics.

CASA DE COLÓN   Today a museum of period pieces from the times of Columbus, this lovely building faces a delightful patio. When Columbus stayed here on several stopovers in Las Palmas, this was the governor's palace. He heard Mass in the nearby **SAN ANTONIO ABAD** church before heading off to sea.

PUEBLO CANARIO   An artificial town (something like the Poble Espanyol in Barcelona) that reproduces typical structures of traditional Canary architecture. Regional dance and song are performed here Thursday afternoons and Sunday mornings and demonstrate how Spanish and native influences interacted to create a typically Canary style.

STAYING IN LAS PALMAS

SANTA CATALINA   León y Castillo 227   tel. (928) 24 30 40   The city's classic hotel, in a quiet setting within the Doramas park, surrounded by lovely gardens. This is one of the most elegant examples of Canary architecture on the island. The city's casino is here. (Expensive; pool.)

SANSOFE   Portugal 68   tel. (928) 22 40 62   On the Las Canteras beach, this recently remodeled hotel has excellent facilities. (Moderate–expensive.)

EATING IN LAS PALMAS

JULIO   La Naval 132   tel. (928) 27 10 39   A restaurant that has been here for years, appreciated for its fine seafood and its Canary cooking. (Moderate.)

EL POTE   Juan María Durán 41   tel. (928) 27 80 58   A place known as much for its restaurant as for its tapas bar, where the portions are ample. The food is principally mainland Spanish. (Moderate.)

LA PARRILLA   Alfredo L. Jones 40   tel. (928) 26 01 00   On the eighth floor of the Hotel Reina Isabel, the views of the port and the beach from this elegant restaurant are exceptional. The menu is international-nouvelle. (Moderate–expensive.)

TENDERETE   León y Castillo 91   tel. (928) 24 63 50   A restaurant noted for the special care it takes with Canary dishes, like "wrinkled" potatoes and *Gofio,* and for its seafood. (Moderate–expensive.)

FIESTAS

CORPUS CHRISTI (nine weeks after Easter) is celebrated here in grand style, and the streets become colorful carpets of artistically arranged flowers.

$\mathcal{V}$ISITING THE ISLAND OF GRAN CANARIA

◆ The best roads circle Gran Canaria; some leading to the volcanic center are dead ends, so to see the main sights, a certain amount of backtracking is inevitable.

Northeastern Gran Canaria

MONTAÑA DE ARUCAS   This volcanic mountain overlooks the white-washed houses of Arucas, which are in an incredibly fertile valley filled with banana trees. From here you can also see the port of Las Palmas.
MESÓN DE LA MONTAÑA   tel. (928) 60 14 75, is high up in the Arucas mountains and serves Canary specialties and grilled meats. (Inexpensive–moderate.)

CENOBIO DE VALERÓN   Under a roof of lava, this network of thousands of lava caves looks like a Swiss cheese. For the Guanches this was apparently some kind of convent, where they sent their daughters, either permanently or until they married.

GÁLDAR   Here was a residence of the Guanche kings. In the **CUEVA PINTADA** are puzzling geometric drawings—squares and triangles in red, white, and black—of unknown significance. Just beyond the town in the lava rock is the **GUANCHE NECROPOLIS.**

PUERTO DE LAS NIEVES   Off the coast of this small fishing village, which sits around a black beach, is a surprisingly elongated rock that points high out of the water. Because of its shape it is poetically named Dedo de Dios (Finger of God).
LAS NASAS   Las Nieves 5   tel. (928) 89 84 25, specializes in seafood and looks out over the sea. (Inexpensive–moderate.)
◆ From here a road toward the interior town of Agaete goes through the narrow **VALLE DE AGAETE** and zigzags through fields of banana, coffee, papaya, and avocado plants.
     Deep in the Valle de Agaete at **LOS BERRAZALES** is **PRINCESA GUAYARMINA**   Valle de Agaete   tel. (928) 89 80 09, a small hotel in an extremely peaceful country setting, surrounded by tropical vegetation. (Inexpensive; pool.)
◆ Another road from Puerto de las Nieves to San Nicolás de Tolentino is exceptional, running along the cliffs at water's edge.
◆ If you choose to visit the beautiful but touristy beaches of Puerto Rico, Maspalomas, Playa del Inglés, and Playa de San Agustín along the desertlike

southern coast, take the curvy road from San Nicolás de Tolentino toward Mogán. You will find many hotels, among them: **IBEROTEL MASPALO- MAS OASIS**   Plaza Las Palmeras (Maspalomas)   tel. (928) 76 01 70, in a peaceful spot on the water, surrounded by gardens (Expensive; prices double to deluxe in high season; pool); **ORQUÍDEA**   Playa del Tarajalillo, km 44 (in Juan Grande)   tel. (928) 76 46 00, well located on the beach (moderate; pool).

     Some of the good restaurants in this area are: **SAN AGUSTÍN BEACH CLUB**   Plaza de los Cocoteros (San Agustín)   tel. (928) 76 04 00, with elegant and haute cuisine, considered one of the finest restaurants of Gran Canaria (moderate–expensive); and **TENDERETE II**   Avenida San Bartolomé de Tirajana (Playa del Inglés)   tel. (928) 76 14 60, serving the best of Canary produce, from fish to lamb, goat, fruits, and vegetables (moderate).
✦ In Maspalomas you can turn to the central mountains for a spectacular drive along the Fataga gorge to **SAN BARTOLOMÉ DE TIRAJANA**, set in an enormous crater, and return to the road by way of Santa Lucía.
✦ As you head back north to Las Palmas, see the mountain of **CUATRO PUERTAS**, filled with caves used by the Guanches as burial sites.

The Interior of Gran Canaria

JARDÍN CANARIO   Near the town of Tafira Baja, southwest of Las Palmas, is this botanical garden, which preserves the enormous variety of plant species indigenous to the island.

CALDERA DE BANDAMA   From a viewpoint over this impressive crater, which is 2,500 feet across, you can look into the volcano, out to Las Palmas, and across the water to Mount Teide in Tenerife.
✦ A short distance from here in Santa Brígida is **LAS GRUTAS DE ARTILES**   Carretera del Valle de la Angostura   tel. (928) 64 05 75, serving typical Canary dishes in a delightful cave setting (moderate). And just beyond here, in San Mateo, **RESTAURANTE-MUSEO CHO-ZACARIAS**   Avenida Tinamar s/n   tel. (928) 64 06 27, is a country restaurant with down-to-earth Canary cooking—watercress soup, fish with cilantro, roast lamb (moderate). Several of the cottages in this village have been arranged into a museum, displaying country utensils, jugs, and the like.

CRUZ DE TEJEDA   From this cross that stands at the mountain pass there are splendid views of a hugh crater and of Roque Nublo, an enormous rock sacred to the Guanches. Miguel de Unamuno described the scene: "It is a tremendous commotion of the entrails of the earth, it looks like a petrified storm." A road to the left goes to **POZO DE LAS NIEVES**, where the island's highest mountain, often snow-covered, is almost 6,000 feet above the sea. From here the panoramic views of the island and the ocean are spectacular.
HOSTERÍA DE LA CRUZ DE TEJEDA   tel. (928) 65 80 50, was a parador, but today just a restaurant belonging to the paradors. Canary dishes are always on the menu. (Inexpensive–moderate.)

JUNCALILLO   Cave dwellings formed by lava that are still inhabited, fixed up and furnished just like conventional homes.

ARTENARA   This is the island's highest village. Here, **MESÓN LA SILLA**   La Silla 9   tel. (928) 65 81 08, in a cave at an overlook, has magnificent views. The food is Canary style (moderate; lunch only). You can continue to the end of the road to see **PINAR DE TAMADABA**, thick pine woods at the edge of a cliff overlooking the sea.

TEROR   A whitewashed town of noble homes with Canary-style wood and wrought-iron balconies and charming patios in a tropical setting. The patron saint of the island, Nuestra Señora del Pino (Our Lady of the Pine), is worshipped here in the church of the same name.

THE ISLAND OF LANZAROTE

The attractions of Lanzarote (lahn-thar-*oh*-tay) are few but sensational. This is the most exotic of the Canaries, utterly unique. The entire island is a desert of black volcanic ash, where the ground still smolders beneath the surface. Lanzarote is virtually treeless—a lunar landscape transferred to earth, starkly surreal, as if created by an artist's brush. And, in fact, a Spanish artist of international fame, César Manrique, native of the Canary Islands, has taken Lanzarote under his wing, protecting it from the onslaught of developers.

Lanzarote and César Manrique feed from each other; the island inspires the artist, who in turn creates works that become part of the landscape, in effect, artistically enhancing nature. His hand can be seen everywhere, in his embellishments of the caves of **LOS JAMEOS DEL AGUA;** in the dramatic **JARDÍN DE CACTUS** (Cactus Garden), in Arrieta; in the modernist overlook **MIRADOR DEL RÍO;** in his unique hotel designs; and in what is perhaps his ultimate creation, his own home, built on various levels into lava caves.

Lanzarote's desolate yet majestic landscape is the result of eighteenth and nineteenth century eruptions that covered most of the small island in lava and ash and left it a desert. You would think that animal and plant life could not possibly survive in such inhospitable surroundings, lacking water and buffeted by desert winds (Lanzarote is just eighty miles from Africa). And yet through this natural disaster the people of Lanzarote created an ingenious system to make life possible once more on the island. They observed how the volcanic ash absorbed the early morning dew. Plowing the earth with the aid of dromedaries (the island's typical beast of burden), they planted crops and covered the ground with a layer of volcanic ash. They dug shallow holes into the bleak earth (adding man-made craters to the already crater-pocked island) and planted grape vines, once more carefully spreading black ash over the earth. Then they built miniature stone walls around each plant to protect against the winds; the crops thrived. The labor, however, is a work of art that admits no mechanical aid and is testimony to man's perseverance in the face of adversity.

Malvasía, or *malmsey*, wines are made here from grapes grown in this manner in an area called **LA GERIA.** Although far from regaining the celebrated status they held in Shakespeare's times, most likely you will be drinking Malvasía, in its semidry or sweet form, during your stay on Lanzarote.

Today the blackened earth of Lanzarote alternates with vineyards and plantings of melons, figs, and tomatoes to create a sea of green. Flat-roofed whitewashed houses, framed in a bright green similar to the color of the crops and to the hulls of the fishing boats, stand out in stark contrast. Brilliantly red geraniums add one more cheerful note of color. César Manrique's fertile imagination could not have created anything more electrifying.

The sights of the island are as startling as the general landscape. In the eighteenth century the **MONTAÑA DE FUEGO** (Mountain of Fire), within what is today the Parque Nacional de Timanfaya, unexpectedly arose from the earth in a tumultuous eruption of molten lava. And although the volcano is now dormant, the searing heat just a foot or so below the surface, especially in an area called **ISLOTE DE HILARIO,** is enough to vaporize water, fry an egg, or light a fire. A restaurant atop the mountain proves this by serving foods grilled with volcanic heat.

The summit of the Montaña de Fuego is reached on camelback (more precisely, on one-humped dromedaries), but you can walk if you dislike camels and their swaying gait. From there you look upon an amazing sight: more than three hundred volcanic cones whose craters glow with iridescent light and glittering, bewitching hues of pastels, ochers, and blues created by the soil's iron particles.

At seaside, below the Timanfaya park, are three more extraordinary sights: **LAS SALINAS DE JANUBIO,** salt pans that contrast strikingly with the blue sea and the blackened hills; **LOS HERVIDEROS,** an area of black rocky coast where the water literally boils; and **EL GOLFO,** a crater sloping into the sea, where a deep green lagoon stands out against the black sand and high undulating reddish cliffs of the shore.

At the northeastern tip of Lanzarote, three more of the island's natural wonders are within a short distance of one another. **LAS CUEVAS DE LOS VERDES,** a tube four miles long, was created by a flow of lava that formed a thick shell and left a vast hollow inside. These extraordinary caves are in some places eighty feet high, and spectacular lighting heightens the grandeur of the scene. **LOS JAMEOS DEL AGUA** is an extension of the caves, and in its underground lagoon, fed by the sea, tiny white crabs, lacking pigment and blinded by their dark world, manage to survive. César Manrique took charge of this badly neglected cave and embellished it, creating an exquisitely tasteful bar, restaurant, and nightclub below the ground at the cave entrance, in a patio where a huge cactus reaches toward the daylight.

The artist's presence is once again felt at the **MIRADOR DEL RÍO,** a dramatic rocky height over the sea at the Punta de Fariones. From here Graciosa island, with its fine white dunes, appears offshore. The edge of this dramatic precipice was inaccessible until César Manrique envisioned a brilliant design of cliffside walkways and whitewashed caves, where he installed an aesthetically pleasing restaurant.

Two castles, San Roque and San José (the latter houses a contemporary art museum—of course including works by César Manrique—and a restaurant), look over the capital city of **ARRECIFE,** named for its reefs. It is a small, pleasant, and brightly whitewashed city, but not likely to be the place where you will stay in Lanzarote. Just about all of the island's hotels—

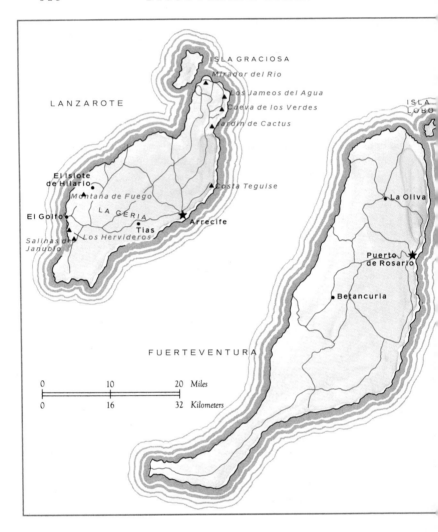

and there are some extraordinary ones—are within a few miles of Arrecife in **TÍAS** and **COSTA TEGUISE** (the coastal extension of the former inland capital of Teguise) on marvelous beaches. Today no buildings over four stories are permitted in Lanzarote, and there is not a billboard in sight. César Manrique has seen to that.

STAYING ON THE ISLAND
OF LANZAROTE

MELIÁ SALINAS   Costa Teguise   tel. (928) 81 30 40   A stunning hotel by the beach, built to blend with the natural landscape; there are cascades, fountains, interior gardens, terraces down to the sea, and a swimming pool that looks like a lagoon. (Deluxe.) The restaurant has many Canary specialties.

LOS FARIONES   Puerto del Carmen (Tías)   tel. (928) 51 01 75   A beautiful and tranquil site on the sea, surrounded by tropical greenery. (Expensive; pool.)

EATING IN LANZAROTE

EL PESCADOR   Centro Comercial Pueblo Marino (Costa Teguise)   A dazzling restaurant of carved woodwork and simple high-quality foods, principally grilled fish and shellfish. (Moderate.)

LA CHIMENEA   Centro Comercial Las Cucharas (Costa Teguise)   tel. (928) 81 47 00   One of the island's best restaurants, serving grilled meats and fish. (Moderate.)

LA ROMÁNTICA II   Centro Comercial Atlántico (Puerto del Carmen)   tel. (928) 82 57 20   A well-appointed restaurant serving Spanish and regional fare. (Moderate.)

CASTILLO DE SAN JOSÉ (Arrecife)   tel. (928) 81 23 21   In the San José castle, this elegant restaurant serves a varied menu of international, Spanish, and Canary foods. (Moderate–expensive.)

EL DIABLO   Islote de Hilario   tel. (928) 84 00 57   On the Montaña de Fuego, this otherwise uninteresting restaurant prepares grilled foods with volcanic heat. (Inexpensive–moderate.)

LOS JAMEOS DEL AGUA   tel. (928) 83 50 10   located in the famous cave of the same name, serves international and Canary dishes. (Inexpensive–moderate; Tuesday, Friday, and Saturday evenings only.)

T HE ISLAND OF FUERTEVENTURA

Fuerteventura (fuer-tay-ven-*tour*-ah) is the driest of the islands, under the influence of the African Sahara, just a hundred kilometers away. Its bare volcanic hills, blowing sands, cactus and palms and searing sun create a desolate scene, occasionally relieved by patches of green, cultivated land. Miguel de Unamuno visited the island during the exile imposed on him by the dictator Primo de Rivera and called Fuerteventura the "skeletal island" because of its bareness and its long skinny shape.

Fuerteventura is a lightly populated island where goats graze on marjoram and are raised to produce the famous cheese of Fuerteventura, *Queso de Majorero*, which takes on a subtle herb flavor (it is named after the primitive early inhabitants of the island). If you are looking for outstanding white sand beaches, impressive dunes, and the chance to snorkel and to engage in submarine and deep-water fishing, this should be your kind of island. But don't expect much more than that.

Traditionally most of Fuerteventura's towns formed a line, like a skeletal spine, through the mountainous interior, the best location from which to

LOS GUANCHES: MYSTERIOUS INDIGENOUS INHABITANTS OF THE CANARIES

When the Canary Islands were conquered by Spain in the fifteenth century, its native inhabitants, Los Guanches, put up a fierce fight but were eventually subdued. Some were deported, others intermixed with the Spaniards, and little trace of them is left today. All that we know is gleaned from archaeological remains and from the written reports of the conquerors of the islands. It is unclear where they came from and why in the fifteenth century they still lived in the Stone Age.

Apparently close to seven feet tall, Los Guanches were light-skinned, blond, and blue-eyed, and lived in caves and huts. Guanche society was well structured, ruled by a king and governed by a council of noblemen. They had a religion and a belief in the afterlife that included mummifying the dead. The use of metal was unknown, and, surprisingly, these island people knew nothing about boat building.

Most theories consider them Berbers from Africa (apparently some Berbers were fair like the Guanches). When the climate of the Sahara changed and the land became desert, the Guanches moved to the Canaries. What cannot be explained is how they arrived by sea without boats. That is why another theory has great appeal: It claims that the Canaries are the peaks that remained above water after the continent of Atlantis sunk. The inhabitants, traditionally mountain people, were stranded in an ocean environment and naturally knew nothing about sea travel.

repel pirate raids. Here also is the island's underground water supply, brought to the surface by windmills that still function, and logically, this was the most propitious place to plant crops. The town of **BETANCURIA,** in the mountains at the center of the island, was the original capital, named after the island's conqueror, Jean de Béthencourt. It still shows traces of grander times (an old cathedral has wonderful *artesonado* ceilings and two interesting choirs). **LA OLIVA,** at another time the island's capital, preserves many noble homes.

Now, of course, Fuerteventura's long coastline is its greatest asset, and a new capital, **PUERTO DEL ROSARIO,** was established by the shore. The small island of Lobos, just three kilometers from the narrow southern tip of Fuerteventura, is sought out by nudists, who like its long, isolated beach, and by sport fishermen, thrilled by the abundance of game fish that pass through the strait between Fuerteventura and Africa.

STAYING ON FUERTEVENTURA

PARADOR DE FUERTEVENTURA   Playa Blanca 45   tel. (928) 85 11 50, is a lovely beachside parador outside of the capital, refreshingly plant-filled, in contrast to the desert-like dryness of the island. (Moderate; pool.) The restaurant serves Canary specialties.

ROBINSON CLUB-HOTEL   Playa Jándia   tel. (928) 54 13 48, is on the coast at the southern end of the island. It's a Club Med–style operation in which meals are included and extra expenses are paid with "chips" rather than cash. (Expensive; pool.)

APPENDIXES:

APPENDIX 1: SUGGESTED ITINERARIES

THE FOLLOWING TRIPS are fairly fast-paced; they cross through several regions of the country (for travel suggestions confined to particular regions, consult individual chapters); they include a variety of scenery, foods, and cultural visits; and they cover most of the places that I love best in Spain. If you have any doubts about setting off on your own, I hope that by plotting a course for you I can put your mind at ease. And I can assure you that any one of these trips will show you aspects of Spain that few visitors ever have the chance to see.

All these trips begin and end in a city with an airport, and they span ten to fifteen days. You can make them shorter (except Itinerary 6) or longer, according to your available time and your personal interests (all except the last two itineraries divide easily into two segments). If I have allowed only one night in a city or town,* it is because I think you can see the principal sights either the day you arrive or the following morning before you leave, but you may prefer to set a more leisurely tempo. You will find more information on all the places mentioned in these itineraries in each chapter.

*Overnight stops appear in *italics*.

ITINERARY 1

MADRID, CASTILLA-LEÓN, CASTILLA-LA MANCHA, EXTREMADURA, ANDALUCÍA

This trip is specifically designed for those of you who have never been to Spain before and would love to see the cities that have become legends, like Segovia, Ávila, Toledo, Sevilla, Córdoba, and Granada. Madrid, the country's lively capital, and El Escorial, the artistically rich palace and monastery of Philip II, are also on the route, as are some lesser-known places that are among Spain's hidden treasures: the delightfully rustic village of Guadalupe and its sumptuous monastery, where Columbus and the conquistadores prayed; the beautifully preserved Roman theater at Mérida; Los Toros de Guisando, lifelike prehistoric stone bulls; Trujillo, hometown of Francisco Pizarro; and the crafts centers of Lagartera, Talavera de la Reina, and El Puente del Arzobispo.

1. *Madrid*
2. *Madrid*
3. Madrid–Valle de Los Caídos–*El Escorial*
4. El Escorial–La Granja (by way of the Navacerrada pass)–*Segovia*
5. Segovia–Riofrío–*Ávila*
6. Ávila–Toros de Guisando–*Toledo* (by way of Escalona and Maqueda)
7. *Toledo*
8. Toledo–Talavera de la Reina–Lagartera–Oropesa–Puente del Arzobispo–*Guadalupe*
9. Guadalupe–Trujillo–*Mérida*
10. Mérida–Zafra–*Sevilla*
11. *Sevilla* (Itálica)
12. Sevilla–Carmona–Écija–*Córdoba*
13. *Córdoba* (Medina Azahara)
14. Córdoba–Jaén–*Granada*
15. *Granada*

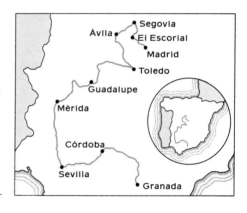

GRANADA

ITINERARY 2

GALICIA, CASTILLA-LEÓN, EXTREMADURA, ANDALUCÍA

Beginning in Galicia, one of the country's most beautiful and least explored regions, which is uniquely Celtic and has wonderful villages, beaches, and craggy coasts, this route stops in towns and cities that have some of the country's most sensational paradors. You will see the extraordinary cathedral of Santiago de Compostela, built around the tomb of the Apostle Saint James, and the cathedral of León, with its resplendent stained-glass windows; the walls of Lugo and the temple of unknown origin in Santa Eulalia de Bóveda; Celtic thatched cottages in the mountains at Cebreiro; and a work by Gaudí in Astorga.

There are stunning polychrome art and Isabelline decorative work in Valladolid; reminders of Juana "The Mad" in Tordesillas; grand Plateresque buildings in Salamanca. The mountain town of La Alberca is a national monument; it was to the Yuste monastery that powerful Emperor Charles V retired to lead an ascetic life; and the world's smallest monastery is at El Palancar. The trip continues to the monumental town of Cáceres and into the mountains of Aracena, where legendary Jabugo hams are made; returns to the sea at Palos, where Columbus recruited his crew, and at La Rábida, the monastery where the navigator lived for a time. This itinerary finishes in Spain's friendly, fun-filled cities of Cádiz and Sevilla, with side trips to Jerez de la Frontera, where sherry is made, and to the wildlife preserve and bird sanctuary in the sand dunes of Coto Doñana. There is exceptionally good eating all along the way.

1. Santiago de Compostela–
   Pontevedra
2. Pontevedra–Combarro–
   La Toja–Armenteira–
   Cambados–Padrón–
   Santiago de Compostela
3. *Santiago de Compostela*
4. Santiago de Compostela–
   Betanzos–*La Coruña*
5. La Coruña–Caaveiro
   monastery–Cedeira–
   San Andrés de Teixido–
   Garita de Herbeira–*Villalba*
   (by way of the coast as far
   as Vivero)
6. Villalba–Lugo–Santa Eulalia
   de Bóveda–Lugo–
   Cebreiro–Ponferrada–
   Astorga–*León*
7. León–San Miguel de la
   Escalada–Medina de
   Rioseco–Valladolid–
   Tordesillas

8. Tordesillas–Toro–Zamora–
   Salamanca
9. *Salamanca*
10. Salamanca–La Alberca–Peña
    de Francia–Miranda del
    Castañar–Hervás–Yuste–
    Cuacos–*Jarandilla de la Vera*
11. Jarandilla de la Vera–
    Plasencia–El Palancar–
    Garrovillas–Alcántara–
    Arroyo de la Luz–*Cáceres*
12. Cáceres–Mérida–Zafra–
    Jabugo–Aracena–*Mazagón*
13. Mazagón–Palos de la
    Frontera–La Rábida–Coto
    Doñana–*Mazagón*
14. Mazagón–Niebla–Itálica–
    Sevilla
15. *Sevilla*
16. Sevilla–Arcos de la Frontera–
    Jerez de la Frontera–
    Sanlúcar de Barrameda–
    Puerto de Santa María–
    Cádiz
17. *Cádiz* (return from Jerez de la
    Frontera airport)

PALOS DE LA FRONTERA

CÁCERES

SANLÚCAR DE BARRAMEDA

ITINERARY 3

MADRID, CASTILLA-LEÓN, ASTURIAS, CANTABRIA, BASQUE COUNTRY, LA RIOJA

There are several spectacular sights on this route, such as the Roman Aqueduct in Segovia and the awesome Picos de Europa, which dominate the landscape in Cervera de Pisuerga and Fuente Dé (fishermen take note: This is trout and salmon country). See the perfectly proportioned Frómista Romanesque church; the artistic gems of the city of Oviedo; Santillana de Mar, one of Spain's most beautiful and untouched villages; the caves of Altamira, a treasure of prehistoric art. The route continues along the coast to San Sebastián, known for its splendid setting and outstanding restaurants.

The scenic road through the Bidasoa valley passes quaint villages. You might want to stay awhile in Pamplona if the bulls are running, but otherwise continue to lush La Rioja. Its fertile valleys produce distinguished wines, and here in San Millán de la Cogolla poet Gonzalo de Berceo first put the Castilian language to paper. As you return to Castile, Burgos and its magnificent Gothic cathedral and the remarkable Cartuja de Miraflores monastery will be on this itinerary. The Santo Domingo de Silos monastery, with its memorable cloister, lies to the south, and there are several small towns that are the epitome of Castilian rural style and where roast lamb is the specialty. The peaceful El Paular monastery-hotel and the royal summer palace in La Granja, with its "dancing fountains," are the last stops before reaching Madrid. This is another uncommonly good gastronomic route.

1. Madrid–Guadarrama–
   Riofrío–*Segovia*
2. Segovia–Turégano–
   Peñafiel–Palencia–Monzón
   de Campos–Frómista–
   Olleros–*Cervera de Pisuerga*
3. Cervera de Pisuerga–Potes–
   Cosgaya–*Fuente Dé*
4. *Fuente Dé* (Picos de Europa,
   Cares gorge, Sotres)
5. Fuente Dé–Potes–Posada de
   Valdeón–Desfiladero de los
   Beyos–Cangas de Onís–
   Covadonga–*Oviedo*
6. *Oviedo* (Santa María de
   Naranco, San Miguel de
   Lillo, Santullano, Santa
   Cristina de Lena)
7. Oviedo–Valdediós–
   Villaviciosa–Tazones–
   Comillas–*Santillana del Mar*
8. Santillana del Mar–Cuevas de
   Altamira–Castro Urdiales–

Portugalete–Guernica (by way of Baquio, Bermeo)–*San Sebastián*

9. *San Sebastián*

10. San Sebastián–Bidasoa valley–Pamplona–Puente La Reina–Estella–Los Arcos–Laguardia–Haro–*Santo Domingo de la Calzada*

11. *Santo Domingo de la Calzada* (bodegas, Haro, San Millán de la Cogolla, Nájera)

12. Santo Domingo de la Calzada–*Burgos*

13. Burgos–Quintanilla de las Viñas–Covarrubias–Santo Domingo de Silos–Peñaranda del Duero–Refugio de Rapaces–Maderuelo–Sepúlveda–Pedraza–*El Paular* (by way of Puerto de Lozoya)

14. El Paular–La Granja–*Madrid*

15. *Madrid*

SEGOVIA

SAN SEBASTIÁN

ITINERARY 4

MADRID, CASTILLA-LA MANCHA, ARAGÓN, LEVANTE, ANDALUCÍA

Passing through Alcalá de Henares, distinguished by the Plateresque facade of its old university, and through beautiful Medinaceli, a Roman town conserving a Roman arch, your first night is spent in the cool oasis of the Piedra monastery. The trip continues to Fuendetodos, birthplace of Francisco de Goya; to the bombed-out town of Belchite; and on to the quiet, picturesque medieval villages of the dramatic Maestrazgo mountains and the Montes Universales of Aragón. The village of Albarracín is exceptional, and fishing opportunities are ample. Spend the following night in either Villarluengo or Morella.

Descending to the Valencia coast at Peñíscola, where fourteenth century Antipope Benedict XIII took refuge in its castle, the route goes south through dense orange groves to Sagunto, site of dramatic events in Roman times, and to El Saler, on the Mediterranean just outside Valencia and engulfed in a green sea of rice paddies. Approaching the Castilian meseta, rivers have carved deep gorges and created natural fortification for the astonishing villages of Alcalá del Júcar, Alarcón, Jorquera, and Cuenca, where its famous Hanging Houses rise from the edge of cliffs. In La Mancha, Don Quijote's country, the famous windmills appear on the plains, and Almagro, known for its lacework, is a town of unusual Castilian-Flemish architecture. Not far from Madrid is Aranjuez, stately summer palace of the Bourbon kings. Before arriving in Madrid, there is a stop in Chinchón, a beautiful village whose circular central plaza still serves as a bullring.

1. Madrid–Alcalá de Henares–
   Guadalajara–Medinaceli–
   Piedra monastery
2. Piedra Monastery–
   Fuendetodos–Belchite–
   Almonacid de la Sierra–
   Daroca–*Albarracín*
3. *Albarracín*
4. Albarracín–Teruel–
   Cantavieja–(*Villarluengo*)–
   Mirambel–*Morella*
5. Morella–Castellfort–Ares de
   Maestre–*Peñíscola*
6. Peñíscola–Castellón de la
   Plana–Sagunto–*El Saler*
7. *El Saler* (Valencia)
8. El Saler–Alcalá del Júcar (by
   way of Requena–
   Casas Ibáñez)–Jorquera–
   Alarcón–Valeria–*Cuenca*
9. Cuenca (Ciudad Encantada,
   Hoz del Júcar, Ventano del
   Diablo)

10. Cuenca–Belmonte–
    El Toboso–Campo de
    Criptana–Almagro
11. Almagro–Las Tablas de
    Daimiel–Consuegra–
    Tembleque–Aranjuez–
    Chinchón or *Madrid*
12. *Madrid*
13. *Madrid*

VALENCIA

LA MANCHA

CUENCA

ITINERARY 5

CATALUNYA, ARAGÓN, CASTILLA–LA MANCHA, MADRID

Here is a tour that includes both Barcelona and Madrid, but concentrates on Catalunya and its three principal areas of interest: gracious Barcelona and its outstanding museums and extraordinary Gaudí creations (with side trips to Penedès wine country, the important Roman city of Tarragona, and Poblet, a jewel of monastic art); the rugged Costa Brava, where there are reminders of an important Jewish past in Gerona and Besalú, a Salvador Dalí museum in Figueres, and remains of Greek and Roman civilizations in Empúries; and the majestic Pyrenees, where villages nestle in narrow verdant valleys against the backdrop of imposing peaks.

The trip continues into Navarra and to two of the country's most unusual and artistically exceptional monasteries, Leyre and San Juan de la Peña. In Aragón there is a visit to the wonderful village of Sos del Rey Católico, where Catholic King Fernando was born; the road passes the distinctly Moorish towns of Tudela and Tarazona; and in Castilla-León you will see the one-of-a-kind cloister of San Juan de Duero in Soria. After a night in Sigüenza, another uncommon village, crowned by one of Spain's finest paradors, the trip comes to a close in Madrid.

1. *Barcelona*
2. *Barcelona*
3. *Barcelona* (Vilafranca del Penedès, Tarragona, Poblet)
4. Barcelona–Girona–*Aiguablava*
5. *Aiguablava* (Empúries, Figueres, Pals)
6. Aiguablava–Girona–Besalú–Sant Joan de les Abadesses–Ripoll–Bellver–*La Seu d'Urgell*
7. La Seu d'Urgell–Sort–Rialb–Espot–Aigües Tortes–Bonaigua–Salardú–*Artiés*
8. *Artiés* (Vielha, Bossost, Taüll)
9. Artiés–Vielha–El Pont de Suert–Ainsa (by way of Castejón de Sos)–Garganta de Añisclo–*Monte Perdido*
10. Monte Perdido–Ainsa–Boltaña–Torla–Biescas–Jaca–San Juan de la Peña–Leyre–Sangüesa–*Sos del Rey Católico*
11. Sos del Rey Católico–Uncastillo–Tudela–Tarazona–Ágreda–Soria–

GAUDÍ (BARCELONA)

ARTIÉS

SAN JUAN DE LA PEÑA

ITINERARY 6:
THE ROUTE TO SANTIAGO

BASQUE COUNTRY, NAVARRA, LA RIOJA, CASTILLA-LEÓN, GALICIA

A fascinating step back in time, this trip follows the medieval pilgrimage route from Spain's northeast border with France to the tomb of Saint James in Santiago de Compostela. Your entry point is in the Basque Country at San Sebastián, and from there the trip follows the course of the beautiful Río Bidasoa, then crosses into France to enter Spain as the pilgrims did at the majestic mountain pass of Roncesvalles. Over the centuries millions have traveled this route, gathering in France and traversing all of northern Spain to Galicia.

Vivid reminders of the pilgrims and of their times are here in the villages: in churches, hospitals, and bridges built to attend to the downtrodden travelers, in great cathedrals (in Burgos, León, and Santiago de Compostela), and in exceptional Romanesque churches and monasteries (in Estella, San Millán de la Cogolla, Frómista, and Nájera). Much of the route passes through areas little changed since medieval days, and when you finally arrive in Santiago de Compostela after the last rugged stretch from Astorga to Cebreiro, you will appreciate the wonder the pilgrims felt when they reached their goal after so many months of travel.

1. *San Sebastián* or *Fuenterrabía*
2. San Sebastián–Irún–
   Bidasoa valley–Vera–
   Cambo-les-Bains (France)–
   St.-Jean-Pied-de-Port
   (France)–Roncesvalles–
   Pamplona
3. Pamplona–Puente La Reina–
   Estella–Los Arcos–Nájera–
   Santo Domingo de la Calzada
4. *Santo Domingo de la Calzada*
   (San Millán de la Cogolla)
5. Santo Domingo de la
   Calzada–San Juan de
   Ortega–*Burgos*
6. *Burgos*
7. Burgos–Castrojeriz–
   Frómista–Carrión de los
   Condes–Sahagún–*León*
8. León–Hospital de Órbigo–
   Astorga–Castrillo de los
   Polvazares–Rabanal del
   Camino–Foncebadón–
   El Acebo–Molinaseca–
   Ponferrada–*Villafranca del
   Bierzo*

9. Villafranca del Bierzo–
   Cebreiro–Monte del Gozo–
   Santiago de Compostela
10. *Santiago de Compostela*
    (Padrón)

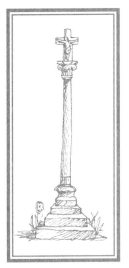

GALICIA

PAMPLONA

LA RIOJA

APPENDIX 2:
NATIONAL PARADORS
OF SPAIN (by region)

Note: I include here the addresses and telephone numbers of only those paradors not discussed in the text. Further information on all the other paradors can be found under the provinces in which they are located. Check the Index.

MADRID

Hostería del Estudiante (restaurant only), Alcalá de Henares (Madrid)
Parador de Chinchón, Chinchón (Madrid)

CASTILLA-LEÓN AND LA RIOJA

Hostería Pintor Zuloaga (restaurant only), Pedraza de la Sierra (Segovia)
Hostal de San Marcos, León (León)
Parador Antonio Machado, Soria (Soria)
Parador Condes de Alba y Aliste, Zamora (Zamora)
Parador Enrique II, Ciudad Rodrigo (Salamanca)
Parador Fernando II de León, Benavente (Zamora)
Parador Fuentes Carrionas, Cervera de Pisuerga (Palencia)
Parador de Gredos (Gredos) (Ávila)
Parador Marco Fabio Quintiliano, Paseo Mercadal s/n, Calahorra (La Rioja), tel. (941) 13 03 58 (moderate–expensive)
Parador de Puebla de Sanabria, Puebla de Sanabria (Zamora)
Parador Raimundo de Borgoña, Ávila (Ávila)
Parador de Salamanca, Salamanca (Salamanca)
Parador Santo Domingo de la Calzada, Santo Domingo de la Calzada (La Rioja)
Parador de Segovia, Segovia (Segovia)
Parador de Tordesillas, Tordesillas (Valladolid)
Parador de Villafranca del Bierzo, Villafranca del Bierzo (León)

CASTILLA-LA MANCHA

Parador de Almagro, Almagro (Ciudad Real)
Parador Castillo de Sigüenza, Sigüenza (Guadalajara)
Parador Conde de Orgaz, Toledo (Toledo)
Parador de La Mancha, Albacete (Albacete)
Parador de Manzanares, Manzanares (Ciudad Real), tel. (926) 61 04 00 (moderate; pool)
Parador Marqués de Villena, Alarcón (Cuenca)
Parador Virrey Toledo, Oropesa (Toledo)

EXTREMADURA

Parador de Cáceres, Cáceres (Cáceres)

Parador Carlos V, Jarandilla de la Vera (Cáceres)
Parador de Guadalupe, Guadalupe (Cáceres)
Parador Hernán Cortés, Zafra (Badajoz)
Parador de Trujillo, Trujillo (Cáceres)
Parador Vía de la Plata, Mérida (Badajoz)

GALICIA

Hostal de los Reyes Católicos, Santiago de Compostela (La Coruña)
Parador del Albariño, Cambados (Pontevedra)
Parador Casa del Barón, Pontevedra (Pontevedra)
Parador Conde de Gondomar, Bayona (Pontevedra)
Parador Condes de Villalba, Villalba (Lugo)
Parador del Ferrol, Ferrol (La Coruña)
Parador de Monterrey, Verín (Orense)
Parador de Ribadeo, Ribadeo (Lugo)
Parador San Telmo, Tuy (Pontevedra)

ASTURIAS AND CANTABRIA

Parador Gil Blas, Santillana del Mar (Cantabria)
Parador Molino Viejo, Gijón (Asturias)
Parador Río Deva, Fuente Dé (Cantabria)

EL PAÍS VASCO

Parador de Argómaniz, Argómaniz (Álava)
Parador El Emperador, Fuenterrabía (Guipúzcoa)

NAVARRA

Parador Príncipe de Viana, Olite (Navarra)

ARAGÓN

Parador La Concordia, Alcañiz (Teruel)
Parador Monte Perdido, Bielsa (Huesca)
Parador Fernando de Aragón, Sos del Rey Católico (Zaragoza)
Parador de Teruel, Teruel (Teruel)

CATALUNYA

Parador Castillo de la Zuda, Tortosa (Tarragona)
Parador Costa Brava, Aiguablava (Girona)
Parador Don Gaspar de Portolà, Artiés (Lleida)
Parador Duques de Cardona, Cardona (Barcelona)
Parador de La Seu d'Urgell, La Seu d'Urgell (Lleida)
Parador del Valle de Arán, Vielha (Lleida)
Parador de Vic, Vic (Barcelona)

EL LEVANTE

Parador Costa del Azahar, Avenida Papa Luna 5, Benicarló (Castellón de la Plana), tel. (964) 47 01 00 (moderate–expensive; pool)

Parador Costa Blanca, Jávea (Alicante)
Parador Luis Vives, El Saler (Valencia)
Parador Puerto Lumbreras, Puerto Lumbreras (Murcia)

ANDALUCÍA

Hotel Atlántico, Cádiz (Cádiz)
Parador El Adelantado, Cazorla (Jaén)
Parador Alcázar del Rey Don Pedro, Carmona (Sevilla)
Parador de Antequera, Antequera (Málaga)
Parador La Arruzafa, Córdoba (Córdoba)
Parador de Bailén, Bailén (Jaén), tel. (953) 67 01 00 (moderate; pool)
Parador Casa del Corregidor, Arcos de la Frontera (Cádiz)
Parador Castillo de Santa Catalina, Jaén (Jaén)
Parador Condestable Dávalos, Úbeda (Jaén)
Parador Costa de la Luz, Ayamonte (Huelva)
Parador Cristóbal Colón, Mazagón (Huelva)
Parador del Gibralfaro, Málaga (Málaga)
Parador del Golf, Torremolinos (Málaga), tel. (952) 38 12 55
   (moderate–expensive; pool)
Parador de Juanar, Ojén (Málaga)
Parador de Nerja, Nerja (Málaga)
Parador Reyes Católicos, Mojácar (Almería)
Parador San Francisco, Granada (Granada)
Parador Sierra Nevada, Sierra Nevada (Granada)

LAS ISLAS CANARIAS

Hostería Cruz de Tejeda (restaurant only), Cruz de Tejeda (Gran Canaria, Las Palmas)
Parador Las Cañadas del Teide, Las Cañadas del Teide (Tenerife, Santa Cruz de Tenerife)
Parador Conde de La Gomera, San Sebastián de la Gomera (La Gomera, Santa Cruz de Tenerife)
Parador de Fuerteventura, Puerto del Rosario (Fuerteventura, Las Palmas)
Parador Isla de El Hierro, Valverde (El Hierro, Santa Cruz de Tenerife)
Parador Santa Cruz de La Palma, Santa Cruz de La Palma (La Palma, Santa Cruz de Tenerife)

SPANISH NORTH AFRICA

Hotel La Muralla, Plaza Nuestra Señora de África, Ceuta, tel. (956) 51 49 40 (moderate–expensive; pool)
Parador Don Pedro de Estopiñán, Avenida Cándido Lobera, Melilla, tel. (952) 68 49 40 (moderate; pool)

HOTELS ASSOCIATED WITH THE PARADORS

Parador Colaborador Arlanza, Covarrubias (Burgos)
Parador Colaborador Conde Jaume de Urgell, Balaguer (Lleida), tel. (973) 44 56 04 (moderate; pool)
Hotel Huerto del Cura, Elche (Alicante)

SELECTED READINGS ON SPAIN

Pío Baroja. Six decades of literary outpouring leave us with an ample taste of the quick wit, intelligence, and literary abilities of this writer of fiction and essay, who so well described Spain and the Spanish character. His works include *The Quest* (La Busca) (1904) and *The Tree of Knowledge* (El Árbol de la Ciencia) (1918).

George Borrow, *The Bible in Spain*, 1842. An account by an Englishman of his efforts to spread the gospel in Spain and his observations on Spanish life.

Gerald Brennan, *South from Granada*, 1957. Reflections of a British writer who carried on a lifelong love affair with Spain.

Camilo José Cela. Cela is a recent Nobel Prize winner, but one of his earliest works, *The Family of Pascual Duarte* (La Familia de Pascual Duarte) (1942), is still his best, presenting a chilling portrayal of life in a Spanish village after the Spanish Civil War.

Miguel de Cervantes Saavedra, *Don Quixote of La Mancha* (Don Quijote de la Mancha), 1615. A classic of world literature, as fresh now as it was when first published.

Richard Ford, *A Hand-book for Travellers in Spain*, 1845. One of the finest and most entertaining descriptions of nineteenth century Spain by a man who traveled throughout the country.

Federico García Lorca. The exquisite lyricism and intense emotions of this Andalusian poet and dramatist (he met an untimely death during the Spanish Civil War), brought him international renown. His most celebrated works include *The House of Bernarda Alba* (La Casa de Bernarda Alba) (1936), *Blood Wedding* (Bodas de Sangre) (1933), and his collections of poetry.

Ernest Hemingway. The writer's passion for Spain led him to set several of his most acclaimed novels, such as *The Sun Also Rises* and *For Whom the Bell Tolls*, on Spanish soil. His diverting and incisive look at bullfighting, *Death in the Afternoon*, is an invaluable introduction to this centuries-old Spanish tradition.

Robert Hughes, *Barcelona*, 1992. An engrossing history of Barcelona from a cultural perspective and a penetrating look into the Catalan psyche.

Victor Hugo, *The Alps and Pyrenees* (Alpes et Pyrénées), Journals 1839–1843. The French writer's sojourn in northern Spain.

Edward Hutton, *The Cities of Spain*, 1906. A fascinating travelogue of Spain at the turn of the century.

Washington Irving, *Tales of the Alhambra*, 1832. A native of Tarrytown, New York, this prolific writer captures the haunting beauty of the Alhambra and the adventure of nineteenth century travel in Spain.

Antonio Machado. His lyric poetry, such as the collection *Solitudes* (Soledades) (1903), beautifully captures his personal sadness, his profound love for his country, and his keen sense of eternity.

James A. Michener, *Iberia*, 1968. The best-selling author, who was introduced to Spain decades ago while still a student, presents a diverting and engrossing look at Spain and the Spanish character.

Jan Morris, *Spain*, 1964. A beautifully written, off-beat analysis of Spain's history, its people, and its traditions.

George Sand, *Winter in Majorca* (Un Hiver à Majorque), 1841. The ill-fated months that the writer spent on the island of Mallorca in the company of Frédéric Chopin.

The Song of El Cid (El Cantar de Mío Cid), an anonymous work of the twelfth century and Spain's most celebrated epic poem.

Hugh Thomas, *The Spanish Civil War*, 1961. Carefully documented and perhaps the best overall study of this tragic conflict that was the focus of world attention.

Miguel de Unamuno, *The Tragic Sense of Life* (El Sentimiento Trágico de la Vida), 1913. A great philosophic work from one of Spain's finest twentieth century writers, who was also a poet of note.

INDEX

Penelope Casas was born in New York City, graduated from Vassar College with a magna cum laude in Spanish literature, studied at the University of Madrid, and for a time taught Spanish literature and language in New York. She has written about Spanish food and travel for the New York Times, Gourmet, Connoisseur, and Condé Nast Traveler. Penelope Casas teaches courses on Spain at New York University, where she is an adjunct professor, and has been awarded by the Spanish government the Spanish National Prize of Gastronomy and the Medal of Touristic Merit, and was named Dame of the Order of Civil Merit. She lived in Spain for several years, and although she now makes her home in New York, she and her husband, a physician who was born in Spain, have spent the past thirty years exploring the country. They also lead tours to Spain.

A NOTE ON THE TYPE

The text of this book has been set in Goudy Old Style, one of the more than one hundred typefaces designed by Frederic William Goudy (1865–1947). Although Goudy began his career as a bookkeeper, he was so inspired by the appearance of several newly published books from the Kelmscott Press that he devoted the remainder of his life to typography and to an attempt to bring a better understanding of the movement led by William Morris to the printers of the United States. Produced in 1914, Goudy Old Style reflects the absorption of a generation of designers with things "ancient." Its smooth, even color, combined with its generous curves and ample cut, marks it as one of Goudy's finest achievements.

Composed by North Market Street Graphics, Lancaster, Pennsylvania
Printed and bound by R.R. Donnelley & Sons, Harrisonburg, Virginia
Maps and illustrations by David Cain
Designed by Iris Weinstein